ADJUSTMENT AND GROWTH: THE CHALLENGES OF LIFE

Spencer A. Rathus

NORTHEASTERN UNIVERSITY

Jeffrey S. Nevid

HOFSTRA UNIVERSITY

NEW YORK   CHICAGO
SAN FRANCISCO   DALLAS
MONTREAL   TORONTO
LONDON   SYDNEY

ADJUSTMENT AND GROWTH: THE CHALLENGES OF LIFE

HOLT,
RINEHART
AND WINSTON

To Sophie Rathus
and the memory of Gustave Rathus

To Eleanor and Marvin Nevid

Library of Congress Cataloging in Publication Data

Rathus, Spencer A
   Adjustment and growth.

   1. Adjustment (Psychology)   I. Nevid, Jeffrey S.,
joint author.   II. Title.
BF335.R28   158′.1   79-25479
ISBN 0-03-055216-8

For permission to use copyrighted materials the authors wish to thank the following:

Cover photograph: Four by Five, Inc.

Chapter 1: p. 6, Walter Genbrugge/Camera Press; p. 7, Ellis Herwig/Stock, Boston; p. 9, Office of Public Affairs, Brandeis University; p. 10, Berndt/Stock, Boston; p. 13, Channel 13—WNET; p. 18, Cary Wolinsky/Stock, Boston; p. 19, Christopher Morrow/Stock, Boston; pp. 20, 21, The Museum of Modern Art/Film Stills Archive.

Chapter 2: p. 29 (both photos), The Museum of Modern Art/Film Stills Archive; p. 31, Mike Mazzaschi/Stock, Boston; p. 32, B.C. by permission of Johnny Hart and Field Enterprises, Inc.; p. 33, © Ylla, Rapho/Photo Researchers, Inc.; p. 34, Roger Lubin/Jeroboam; p. 35, drawing by Dana Fradon, © 1979 The New Yorker Magazine, Inc.; p. 37, "At Seventeen," words and music by Janice Ian, copyright © 1974 by Mine Music Ltd. and used by permission. p. 38 (left), Robert Eckert/EKM—Nepenthe (right), Jeff Albertson/Stock, Boston; p. 39, Wide World Photos; p. 42, Edward Peterson/O.K. Harris; p. 43 (left), Robert Eckert/EKM—Nepenthe (right), John R. Maher, EKM—Nepenthe.

Chapter 3: p. 57, courtesy Dr. Roberts Rugh; p. 59, James Holland/Stock, Boston; p. 60, © Erika Stone/Photo Researchers, Inc.; p. 60; p. 62 (top left), John R. Maher/EKM—Nepenthe (top right), John R. Maher/EKM—Nepenthe (bottom left), © 1978 Ray Ellis/Photo Researchers, Inc. (bottom right), Carey Wolinsky/Stock, Boston; p. 63 (bottom), B.C. by permission of Johnny Hart and Field Enterprises, Inc.; p. 65, Tom Barrett; p. 69, © Eric Kroll 1978/Taurus Photos; p. 70, Stock, Boston; p. 71, Jill Freedman/Magnum; p. 74, drawing by Ed Arno, © 1978 The New Yorker Magazine, Inc.; p. 77, Figure 3.1, reprinted from *Psychology Today* magazine, copyright

© 1975 Ziff-Davis Publishing Company; p. 78, Robert Eckert/EKM—Nepenthe; p. 78 (side), George Cohen/Stock, Boston (bottom), Colin Davey/Photo Trends.

Chapter 4: p. 88, courtesy of the Menninger Foundation; p. 89, Baxter Venable; p. 91, Frederick D. Bodin/Stock, Boston; p. 98, The Bettmann Archive, Inc.; p. 100, Ken Heyman; p. 101, Animal Behavior Enterprises, Inc.; p. 102, Spencer Rathus; p. 103, The Museum of Modern Art/Film Stills Archive; p. 107, from *Non-Being and Somethingness* by Woody Allen, drawn by Stuart Hample, copyright © 1978 by IWA Enterprises, Inc., and Hackenbush Productions, Inc., and reprinted by permission of Random House, Inc.; p. 108, Wide World Photos.

Chapter 5: p. 118, University Museum, Philadelphia; p. 109, Spencer Rathus; pp. 120, 121, The Museum of Modern Art/Film Stills Archive; p. 123 (all photos), Spencer Rathus; p. 128, United Press International; p. 133 (all photos), The Museum of Modern Art/Film Stills Achive; p. 136, from *Non-Being and Somethingness* by Woody Allen, drawn by Stuart Hample, copyright © 1978 by IWA Enterprises, Inc., and Hackenbush Productions, Inc., and reprinted by permission of Random House, Inc.; p. 143, Ken Heyman.

Chapter 6: p. 152, Table 6.1, © 1967 Pergamon Press, Ltd., and reprinted by permission; p. 153, The Museum of Modern Art/Film Stills Archive; p. 155, Anestis Diakopoulos/Stock, Boston; p. 156, Robet Eckert/EKM—Nepenthe; p. 161 (left), Robert Eckert/EKM—Nepenthe (right), California Cooperage; p. 165, Robert Eckert/EKM—Nepenthe; p. 169, Karen Collidge/Taurus Photos; p. 171, from "Birches," from *The Poetry of Robert Frost*, edited by Edward Connery Latham. Copyright 1916, © 1969 by Holt, Rinehart and Winston. Copyright 1944 by Robert Frost. Reprinted by permission of Holt, Rinehart and Winston, Publishers; p. 174, Jeff Albertson/Stock, Boston.

Chapter 7: p. 178, The Museum of Modern Art/Film Stills Archive; p. 179, Jeff Albertson/Stock, Boston; pp. 183, 185 (side), Robert Eckert/EKM—Nepenthe (bottom), The Museum of Modern Art/Film Stills Archive; p. 186, Spencer Rathus; p. 191, B.C. by permission of Johnny Hart and Field Enterprises, Inc.; p. 192, photo by Margaret Suckley, from the Franklin D. Roosevelt Library Collection; p. 196 (both photos), Robert Eckert/EKM—Nepenthe; p. 199, Robert Eckert/EKM—Nepenthe; p. 200, Bonnie Freer.

Chapter 8: p. 210, The Museum of Modern Art/Film Stills Archive; pp. 219, 221, Baxter Venable; p. 224, Frank Siteman/Stock, Boston.

Chapter 9: p. 239, Peter Southwick/Stock, Boston; p. 241, Photo Trends; p. 236, Table 9.2, © 1978 by the American Psychological Association and reprinted by permission; p. 246 (top left and right; bottom left), John Maher/EKM—Nepenthe (bottom right), The Stockmarket and the Burton Holmes Collection; p. 251, Constantine Manos/Magnum; p. 257, © B. Kliewe/Jeroboam.

Chapter 10: pp. 265 (both photos) and 271 (both photos), Scott Wagner; p. 272, Frank Siteman/Stock, Boston; p. 273, Malcolm Perkins/Stock, Boston; p. 275, Peter Menzel/Stock, Boston; p. 278, Robert Eckert/EKM—Nepenthe; p. 283, Spencer Rathus; p. 287, Robert Eckert/EKM—Nepenthe.

Chapter 11: p. 295 (top left), Stock, Boston (top and bottom right), UPI; p. 296 © 1965 by Sanley Milgram, from the film *Obedience*, distributed by the NYU film library; p. 301 (bottom), William Vandivert; p. 304, © Donald Dietz 1976/Stock, Boston; p. 305, CBS Newsphoto; p. 306 (both photos), UPI; p. 308, Spencer Rathus; p. 314, Michael Weisbrot; p. 315, © 1979 Universal Press Syndicate; p. 319, drawing by W. Miller, © 1979 The New Yorker Magazine, Inc.; p. 321, UPI; p. 324, B.C. by permission of Johnny Hart and Field Enterprises, Inc.

Chapter 12: p. 332, John Maher/EKM—Nepenthe; p. 333, B.C. by permission of Johnny Hart and Field Enterprises, Inc.; p. 335 (left), Frank Simon/Stock, Boston (right), photo by Eric Pollitzer/O. K. Harris; p. 338, Wide World Photos; p. 339, Mark Jones, The Stockmarket and the Burton Holmes Collection; pp. 342, 347, 352, Robert Eckert/EKM—Nepenthe; p. 353, B.C. by permission of Johnny Hart and Field Enterprises, Inc.; pp. 354, 356, 357, Robert Eckert/EKM—Nepenthe.

Chapter 13: p. 365, Frank Siteman/Stock, Boston; p. 366, Wide World Photos; p. 368, from *Non-Being and Somethingness* by Woody Allen, drawn by Stuart Hample, copyright © 1978 by IWA Enterprises, Inc., and Hackenbush Productions, Inc., and reprinted by permission of Random House, Inc.; p. 369 (top left), Fung Lam (top right), Robert Eckert/EKM—Nepenthe (bottom left), Robert Maher/EKM—Nepenthe (bottom right), Tim Carlson/Stock, Boston; p. 372, Table 13.5, © 1976 Plenum Publishing Corporation and reprinted by permission. p. 378, Figure 13.1, from Charlotte M. Dienhart, *Basic Human Anatomy and Physiology* (Philadelphia: Saunders, 1967), pp. 213, 217, and reprinted by permission; p. 380, Figure 13.2, from Charlotte M. Dienhart, *Basic Human Anatomy and Physiology* (Philadelphia: Saunders, 1967), p. 207, and reprinted by permission; p. 381, Robert Levine, Black Star; p. 385 (left), Peter Menzel/Stock, Boston (right), Charles Gatewood/Magnum; p. 389 (top left), Peter Southwick/Stock, Boston (top right), Wide World Photos (bottom left) © Joel Gordon 1979 (bottom right), Cary Wolinsky/Stock, Boston; p. 393, Peter Simon, Stock/Boston; p. 395, John Maher.

Chapter 14: p. 405 (top left), Baxter Venable (top right), R. Wohl (center right), Jack Simon (bottom left and right), Baxter Venable; p. 406, Animal Behavior Enterprises, Inc.; p. 408, Baxter Venable; p. 411 (all photos), Baxter Venable; p. 412, Arthur Grace/Stock, Boston; p. 415, Animal Behavior Enterprises, Inc.; p. 416, Baxter Venable.

Chapter 15: p. 429, Andy Sacks/EPA Newsphoto; p. 431, Wide World Photos; p. 433, Eric Jacqueir/Stock, Boston; pp. 440, R. Mohl; p. 447, R. Mohl; p. 452, E. Budd Gray, Jeroboam; p. 453, John Maher/EKM—Nepenthe.

Chapter 16: p. 463, from *Non-Being and Somethingness* by Woody Allen, drawn by Stuart Hample, copyright © 1978 by IWA Enterprises, Inc., and Hackenbush Productions, Inc., and reprinted by permission of Random House, Inc.; pp. 466–467, Table 16.1, © 1978 by the American Psychological Association and reprinted by permission; p. 468 (both photos), Robert Eckert/EKM—Nepenthe; p. 470, drawing by Whitney Darrow © 1979 The New Yorker Magazine, Inc.; pp. 472, 473, Robert Eckert/EKM—Nepenthe; p. 474, Wide World Photos; p. 478, ERDA; p. 479, The Bettmann Archive, Inc.; p. 480 (top), drawing by Charles Addams, © 1979 The New Yorker Magazine, Inc. (bottom), Stock, Boston; p. 481, B.C. by permission of Johnny Hart and Field Enterprises, Inc.; p. 484 (all photos), Spencer Rathus; p. 485, Wide World Photos; p. 487, Stock, Boston; p. 488 (left), Robert Eckert/EKM—Nepenthe (right), John Mather/EKM—Nepenthe; p. 489, Hap Stewart, Jeroboam.

PREFACE

Adjustment and Growth: The Challenges of Life was a challenge to write. The psychology of adjustment is a changing and dynamic field. Our challenge was to show how recent developments in psychological theory and research have dramatically increased psychology's applicability to everyday life. At the same time, we wanted to provide a solid core of traditional topics in the psychology of adjustment.

To meet this challenge, we decided at the outset that this textbook would be streamlined, efficient, and balanced. Balance is the book's theme. We balance:

Information and applications. Psychological theory and research have extended to elements of our daily lives from job hunting to drug abuse, weight control to city life, noise pollution to sexual dysfunctions. We report psychological theory and research findings; and then show how readers can apply many of these findings to their own lives through step-by-step, behavioral exercises. We also point out when it is useful to consult the professional, and suggest how to find the right professional for the problem.

Traditional and innovative areas in adjustment. The book discusses areas found in many adjustment textbooks, like marriage, work, and anxiety, but it also focuses on areas that are of very real concern to readers but found less often or not at all. These areas include alcohol and drug abuse, rape prevention, sexual dysfunctions, aging, job hunting, career decision making, and many others.

Psychoanalytic, social learning, and humanistic personality theories. These three major personality theories provide important insights into human behavior, and we believe that a comprehensive adjustment textbook must include them all. The applications of the psychology of adjustment to our everyday lives are based on all three theoretical frameworks.

Substance and readability. Psychology is a dynamic, exciting, growing field, and a textbook with substance should reflect that excitement. We deliberately allow our writing style to echo our enthusiasm for the subject matter.

LEARNING AIDS

Many who take a psychology of adjustment course are first- and second-year students who have had no introductory course in psychology. Adjustment is often the only psychology course they will take. With this in mind, we have included several learning aids:

"Truth or Fiction?" sections to open each chapter. These chapter openings spur interest by challenging folklore or "common knowledge" at the outset of each chapter. They also serve as advance organizers or learning objectives by outlining the material that is to be covered in the chapter.

Marginal glossary definitions. All technical terms (and occasional other words) are defined in the margins, so that concentration is not interrupted by fumbling to locate glossary items at the back of the book. We repeat marginal definitions in several chapters to avoid the need to look back to earlier chapters for the meanings of terms.

Chapter summaries are organized around the opening "Truth or Fiction?" items. This provides each chapter with a sense of closure and an immediate opportunity for testing new knowledge.

Gradual building of knowledge. Basic terms and theory concerning adjustment, growth and development, personality, adjustment problems and major approaches to helping are outlined in early chapters. Within each chapter we have paid careful attention to the orderly introduction of new terms and concepts, being certain that they build upon earlier learning.

Section on SQ3R and other study hints. In Chapter 1 we describe the SQ3R (survey-question-read-recite-review) method for learning textbook material. We have also used chapter and section headers that may be readily converted into questions to help use this method. We have not written section headers as questions because many prefer to do this for themselves.

Section on text anxiety. Early reading of the section on text anxiety in Chapter 8, which offers step-by-step suggestions for overcoming test anxiety, will help those who are concerned about taking examinations.

ORGANIZATION OF THIS BOOK

Adjustment and Growth: The Challenges of Life is organized into five parts, each of which addresses areas of psychology that are central to adjustment and personal growth.

1. The Challenge and the Self

The first five chapters provide the core of theory for the textbook. They begin with definitions of adjustment and personal growth, explore the nature of the self, follow adjustment and growth as lifelong processes, discuss the three major theories of personality in modern psychology, and explore adjustment problems and major approaches to helping.

2. The Challenges of Stress, Fear, and Depression

These four chapters explore the many faces of stress, and some of our defensive and more active responses to stress. The sources of stress include life changes, pain and discomfort, frustration, conflict, and Type A behavior. We place some emphasis on recent research findings concerning use of cognitive methods (like distraction and fantasy) and relaxation to adjust to pain and discomfort, and we report strategies for turning the hectic Type A pace into a sort of "healthy tension" that promotes personal growth. In our discussions of fear and depression, we outline in detail a number of strategies that social learning theory has brought to bear on these most common problems in living.

3. The Challenge of Human Relationships

Violence, social influences, intimate relationships, sexual involvements—these are some of the challenges faced by young people in the modern world. In these four chapters we explore the nature of various types of social problems and social opportunities, from rape to TV commercials, from social shyness to living together, and from group pressure to group sex. We offer concrete suggestions concerning issues like rape prevention, wife beating, developing assertive behavior, and using small talk and other methods to develop intimate relationships. There is a frank discussion of the sexual revolution and of sexual dysfunctions, each of which is a cause of concern for many college people today.

4. The Challenge of Self-Control

From nail-biting to insomnia, from weight-control to cigarette smoking and drug abuse, self-control is a major issue in life. Shall we take charge of our lives and determine our own behavior, or shall we allow ourselves to be governed by impulse, gratification *now*, habit, and a world supermarket of substances ranging from food to alcohol? Theory and research in the past decade have revolutionized the strategies we can use to assert control over our own behavior, and we present these strategies in detail in these two chapters.

5. Personal Growth and the Quality of Life

In recent years American life has undergone several transformations, and the 1980s and 1990s promise to bring more changes in the quality of the environment, the availability of resources, and the character of city and suburban life. In this final chapter we explore the components of the quality of life in America—elements like family, work, and leisure activities—and we see that Americans are by and large doing well in spite of contemporary challenges to the quality of life. We also see that human beings do not stand still when basic needs have been met, but strive to grow or develop themselves in new directions.

ACKNOWLEDGMENTS

Many people participated in the growth and development of *Adjustment and Growth*, and the book underwent a minor adjustment process of its own. It was developed at W. B. Saunders Company in Philadelphia, and, because corporations like people adjust to changing times, was finally produced by Holt, Rinehart and Winston in New York. Fortunately, the staffs at both publishing houses were a pleasure and a comfort to work with. We truly had the best of both worlds.

We are especially grateful to Baxter Venable, who was psychology editor at Saunders. He was always a gentleman and a scholar—and, more important, a good friend. Teddy Dunbar, also at Saunders, made us all pay attention to details that had to be attended to, and deserves another dinner at Bookbinders for her efforts.

We thank Richard C. Owen, Senior Editor at Holt, Rinehart and Winston, who saw to it that the adjustment process in bringing our manuscript to New York was as smooth as possible. And, also at Holt, our special gratitude goes to Herman Makler, who saw the book through the day-to-day nitty-gritty of production, and who was no doubt born with a telephone in his ear. Others at Saunders and at Holt who deserve credit include Amy Shapiro and Dan Loch.

We are also grateful to our professional colleagues for reading and making helpful suggestions with the manuscript: Bernard Cohen, West Chester State College; Rena Krizmus, Chicago State University; Charles Slem and Linden L. Nelson, California State Polytechnic University; William R. Miller, University of New Mexico; and Lona Whitmarsh, Fisher Junior College.

Finally, the first author wishes to reserve his warmest gratitude for his wife, Lois. Writing this book made her, in effect, an author's widow for many, many months. She also excels as a walking dictionary, grammarian, and coffeemaker. Even when we were together, she often noted the vacant, far-off look in my eyes, and would say, resignedly, "You're thinking about the book again, aren't you?" I pleaded guilty. She adjusted very well: the proof is that we are still married.

S.A.R.
J.S.N.

CONTENTS

Contents

4. PERSONALITY: THREE FORCES IN PSYCHOLOGY   86

5. ADJUSTMENT PROBLEMS AND PSYCHOTHERAPY   116

Contents

II: THE CHALLENGE OF STRESS, FEAR, AND DEPRESSION

Contents

xv

Contents

xvi

Contents

IV: THE CHALLENGE OF SELF-CONTROL

V: PERSONAL GROWTH AND THE QUALITY OF LIFE

16. WORK, LEISURE, FAMILY, AND THE ENVIRONMENT: CHALLENGES OF THE FUTURE   462

I

THE
CHALLENGE
OF
THE
SELF

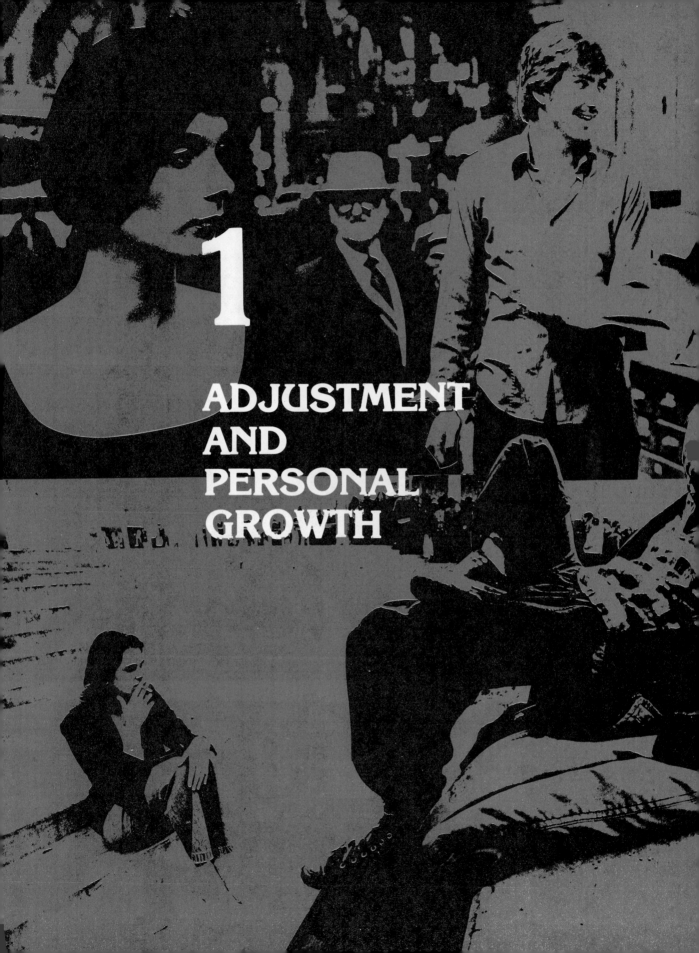

1

ADJUSTMENT
AND
PERSONAL
GROWTH

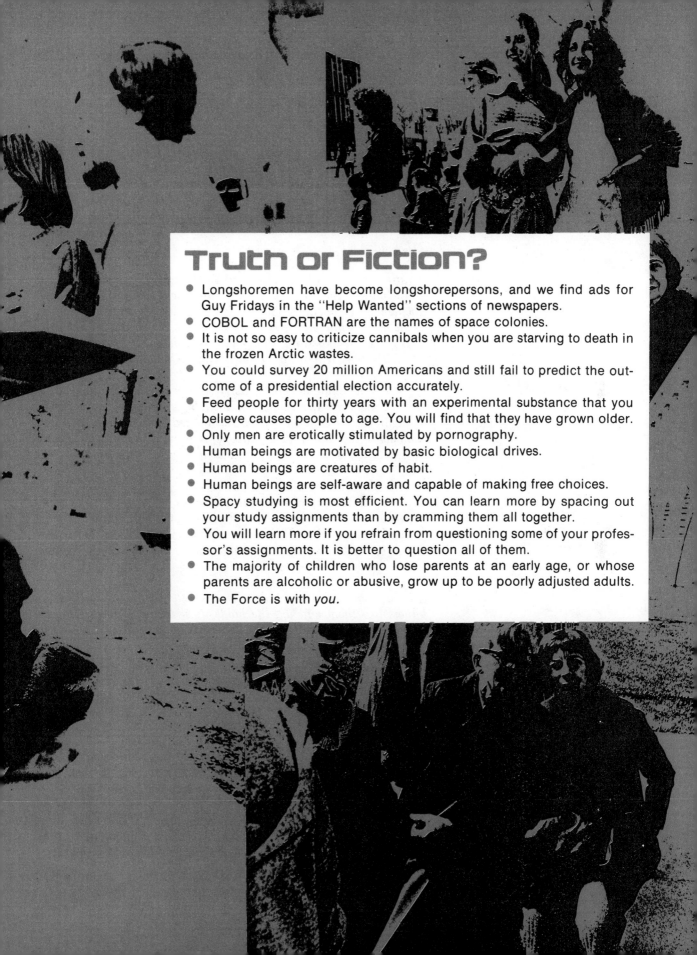

Truth or Fiction?

- Longshoremen have become longshorepersons, and we find ads for Guy Fridays in the "Help Wanted" sections of newspapers.
- COBOL and FORTRAN are the names of space colonies.
- It is not so easy to criticize cannibals when you are starving to death in the frozen Arctic wastes.
- You could survey 20 million Americans and still fail to predict the outcome of a presidential election accurately.
- Feed people for thirty years with an experimental substance that you believe causes people to age. You will find that they have grown older.
- Only men are erotically stimulated by pornography.
- Human beings are motivated by basic biological drives.
- Human beings are creatures of habit.
- Human beings are self-aware and capable of making free choices.
- Spacy studying is most efficient. You can learn more by spacing out your study assignments than by cramming them all together.
- You will learn more if you refrain from questioning some of your professor's assignments. It is better to question all of them.
- The majority of children who lose parents at an early age, or whose parents are alcoholic or abusive, grow up to be poorly adjusted adults.
- The Force is with *you*.

Janice is 20, a good-natured college junior, popular with faculty, dutiful with relatives. She also weighs 225 pounds, trying to dull a secret loneliness with food. While her friends go out on dates, Janice eats, loving herself with food because she feels that there is no one in her life who will love her.

John is 21, a business student who is usually all business. He is dedicated to his books and is willing to invest all his efforts into constructing a solid career for himself. Yet sometimes he wonders why he bothers. He knows he "just can't take tests." He begins to shake two days before a test. His thoughts become jumbled when the papers are distributed. His hand shakes so that he can barely write his name. His grades suffer.

Jennifer, 18, is a college freshman. She has seen the TV shows, gone to the movies. She has read the books and the magazine articles about the new sexual openness. She has been waiting for "the right man" to come along while pressures assault her from all directions. She wonders if there is something wrong with her. She sometimes thinks that she is the only remaining virgin in the freshman class.

Judy, 22, a senior in biochemistry, has been accepted to medical school. She wants to do cancer research, but this means another seven or eight years. Kevin, her fiancé, has landed a fine engineering position across the country. He wants her to come with him, start a family, go to school later. Judy fears that if she gives up school now, she may never return to it.

Dennis, 32, is not sleeping well. He wakes before dawn and cannot return to sleep. His appetite is off, his energy is low. Sometimes he is sexually frustrated, sometimes he wonders if he has any sex drive left. It has been like this since Sue walked out. He wonders if he is going crazy—suicide has crossed his mind.

Janice, John, Jennifer, Judy, Dennis—for them, for millions of others like them and us, life holds its joys and sorrows, ups and downs, victories and defeats. Life has its opportunities. Life has its challenges.

The challenges of life touch all of us at one time or another. Us—you and me. That is what this book is all about. People meeting challenges as they get on with the business of living: growing, learning, making ends meet, finding jobs, building careers. This book brings the knowledge of modern psychology to bear on the common problems that people have in meeting everyday challenges of living, such as anxiety and fears, depression and social shyness, obesity and smoking, marital and sexual frustrations. You will see how psychologists today help people cope with and solve these problems. You will learn how you can often apply this knowledge in your own life. You will also learn about the professional care givers, and when and how to seek their intervention. This knowledge is important: in many ways our lives have become more challenging than they have ever been.

The Challenge
and the Self

4

In this chapter, we first discuss some of the challenges of contemporary life. Then we introduce the concepts of adjustment and personal growth, which are responses to these challenges that permit people to adapt to them and to enhance themselves while doing so. We discuss the science of psychology, an organized way of gaining knowledge about people that combines theory and research to produce ways of helping us to meet the challenges of life more effectively. We explore what psychologists have learned about making studying a more efficient process through a method referred to as "SQ3R." Finally, we discuss "personal power"—something we carry in each of us that we can summon to take charge of our own lives and seek personal fulfillment, or allow to lie dormant and thus lead our lives trying to muddle through to the end of each long day as best we can.

THE CHALLENGES OF LIFE

Long ago and far away our universe began with a "big bang" that sent countless atoms and other particles hurling at fantastic speeds into every corner of space. For 15 to 20 billion years, galaxies and solar systems have been condensing from immense gas clouds, sparkling for some aeons, and then winking out. Human beings have only recently evolved on an unremarkable rock circling an average star in a typical, spiral-shaped galaxy.

Since the beginning of time, the universe has been in flux—changing. Change has led to life and to death, to challenges. Some creatures have adapted successfully to these challenges and continued to evolve. Others have not met the challenges and have become extinct, falling back into the distant mists of time.

At first our survival on planet Earth was far from guaranteed. We had to fight predators like the leopard. We had to forage across parched lands for food. We may have had to go to war with humanlike creatures similar to ourselves in order to compete for what was available. Through all this we prevailed. Only a few hundred years ago a plague known as the Black Death wiped out millions upon millions of us. The human species survived. And prospered. There are still many who go to bed hungry in this world, but those of us who live in the United States and many other nations have prospered to the point where many of us do not worry about having enough to eat or warm clothing to wear through the winter weather. Yet for those of us who have come through, there are still changes and many new challenges.

The Challenge of Changing Roles

Roles in life are constantly changing. Not so long ago women cooked, cleaned, and reared children while men worked with their muscle or sat at a desk computing numbers. Women today are piloting airplanes and shuttle spacecraft, performing surgery, mining coal, and walking the lonely dark beat of the police officer. Longshoremen today are increasingly likely to be longshorepersons. Newspapers today carry "Help Wanted" ads for Gal or Guy Fridays.

Few of us would prefer to return to a time when our life courses were established at birth—a reflection of who our parents were and not who we are. But the sheer numbers of career and job options place tremendous pressures on adolescents, many of whom are encouraged to make tentative commit-

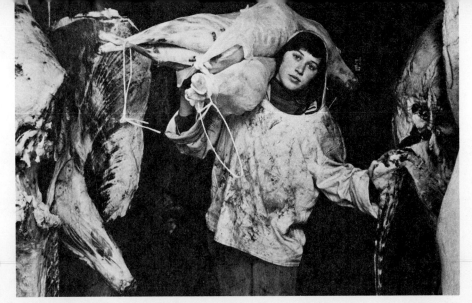

A contemporary woman in a job that might have been closed to her a generation ago.

ments and begin preprofessional training at young ages. Decision anxiety can plague us early in life.

The Challenge of Changing Technology

Yesterday's clerk has often become today's computer programmer, reading and writing several languages, such as COBOL and FORTRAN, that did not exist a generation or two ago. We used to prefer health professionals with some gray at the temple and some creases in the brow. But the technology of today leaps over itself at such a pace that years of experience are sometimes balanced by the freshness of being just out of school. Excellent scientists are hard pressed to keep current with research findings outside their specialities. Technological needs cause us to rely on quite young people to plot the paths of our space-craft, to design efficient distribution and marketing systems for mammoth cor-porations, and literally to hold our hearts in their hands during surgery.

Even as we profit from advances in technology, we may fear that we shall be too slow to keep pace with them. We may wonder if some new procedure or invention will make our skills—our careers—obsolete. New machines replace workers on the assembly line. Audiovisual aids and television sets compete with teachers in the classroom.

The Challenge of Changing Resources

The United States stretches from ocean to ocean. Once its resources seemed infinite. We have constructed an industrial capacity unmatched in the history of civilization. Our Midwest is the food factory for the world. But now some shadows fall across the land of plenty.

Some suggest that our major challenge in the 1980s and the 1990s will be to preserve our enviable life-style in the face of rapidly diminishing resources, such as petroleum, and increased competition from developing industrial cen-ters around the world. Industrial wastes pollute our air and our water. Oil spills and other disasters destroy the very plankton that create the oxygen we breathe. We may be increasingly faced with the need to compromise our standards of living in order simply to survive. Teenagers may do their weekend cruising on bicycles rather than in automobiles as gasoline becomes a rarer, more expensive commodity.

The Challenge of a Changing Society

Though the majority of Americans have a higher standard of living than their parents did, there remain disadvantaged groups and pockets of poverty. During the 1950s and the 1960s we became increasingly aware of the plight of blacks and other ethnic minorities who did not share equally in American prosperity. And during the 1970s we were taught to open our ears and our minds to the pleas of other groups who had been disadvantaged—women and the aging. Women in the work force have demanded equal pay for equal jobs. The aged have struggled to overturn regulations mandating premature retirement. The numbers of the aged grow, and suddenly there are empty spaces in classrooms. The population shifts.

During the 1960s and the 1970s young people experimented increasingly with alternatives to marriage, alternatives to traditional types of work, and—through the explosion in the usage of drugs—alternatives to normal states of consciousness. The late 1970s and early 1980s appear to be witnessing a pendulum swing back toward the popularity of marriage and the so-called Protestant work ethic. A very old drug, alcohol, has reasserted its popularity on the campuses. Values remain in flux.

Changing social roles, growing technology, dwindling resources, social upheavals—all these challenges can tear at the psychological fabric that provides a sense of well-being. Changing roles can confuse our sense of identity. Changing technology can lead us to new riches, but can also lead us to stretch our ability to keep up to the limit—we may fear obsolescence. Diminishing

Behind the scenes in the challenging contemporary world of the computer.

AIRPORT, AIRPORT 1975, AIRPORT, 1977 . . . AIRPORT 1999? SOME RECENT DISASTROUS CHALLENGES OF LIFE

"Some say the world will end in fire," wrote the poet Robert Frost—"Some say in ice." Recent disaster movies have had the world ending in fire, in ice, and in everything in between. *The Poseidon Adventure*, *Earthquake*, *The Towering Inferno*, *When Worlds Collide*, *The War of the Worlds*, *The Beast from 20,000 Fathoms*, *Airport*, *Airport 1975*, *Airport 1977* . . . *Airport 1999?* In these films and in best-selling novels, we have been plagued by bees, comets, floods, blizzards, shipwrecks, monsters, cosmic disasters, international disasters, occult disasters—disasters of every flavor, every size, every conceivable and some not-so-conceivable misfortunes that could possibly befall the human species.

Given that most of us would probably prefer to avoid these disasters, what accounts for their huge success on the screen and in books? Why do we flock in droves to populate the audience of every disaster film from *Jaws* to *Juggernaut?*

We may as well confess that we do not have the ultimate answers. But here are some of the hypotheses that have been advanced by behavioral scientists, religious leaders, politicians, film reviewers, and your friendly neighborhood bartender. Wacky or right on target? What do you think?

- Contemporary life is filled with vague anxieties and ongoing pressures. Disaster films allow us to focus all our apprehensions on one major theme, even if for an hour or two.
- The audience can express their aggressive, destructive impulses through enjoying disasters that afflict other people.
- Disaster films renew our faith in the capacity of human beings to adjust to pressure during a time in human history when life has become incredibly complex, and we feel dehumanized by the advancement of machines and the reliance on numbers rather than names.
- Actually, we are seeking strategies for coping, for adjustment. We wish to see how the heroes and heroines think—what they do and say, the attitudes they assume, how they take charge in the midst of chaos.
- Disaster films increase our awareness of the fragility of life, thus making our own individual lives more meaningful.
- Most of us lead sedentary lives, and our levels of bodily arousal are often too low to afford us feelings of well-being. Disaster films bring our levels of arousal up to the point where we again feel that we are alive.
- Our dates may mistake their feelings of high bodily arousal for sexual attraction to us.
- We are grateful it's not happening to us.
- Charlton Heston is cute.
- They're fun.

resources raise the specter of worldwide panic and international scrambles for what remains. A changing society can provide new freedoms and opportunities, but it can also wipe away that which was comforting and familiar. It can destroy the sense that the world is a predictable, safe, and stable place to be. Change, as we shall see in Chapter 6, is stressful. And stress can lead to psychological problems, to physical illness, and to efforts to avoid, rather than cope effectively with, the challenges of life.

ADJUSTMENT AND PERSONAL GROWTH

The Challenge and the Self

What do people do when they are faced with the challenges of life? We shall have a look at the response of a group of Eskimos, the Netsilik, to the challenges they faced earlier in this century. Then we shall define the concepts of adjustment and personal growth.

> Beneath their nervous laughter lay intense fear of the storms and the blizzards which so often meant starvation. During the winter the caribou were gone and the sealing failed. It is no wonder that the Netsilik Eskimos gorged themselves when the hunting was good. During two bleak winters they had lost 25 of their number to the cold and to the hunger. Perhaps this seems no imposing number, but at their height their population was 259.
>
> During the harshest years, some of the Eskimos are known to turn to cannibalism. Other Eskimos, who have been more fortunate, refrain from criticism. The Netsilik do not eat human flesh with pleasure. They eat human flesh in order to survive.

Here in the frozen Arctic tundra of the 1920s was a recounting (Rasmussen 1931) of the most basic form of human **adjustment** to the challenges of life: raw survival. One definition of adjustment is adaptation—behavior that permits us to meet the demands of the environment.

Sometimes these demands are physical. When we are cold, we adjust by dressing warmly or by turning up the thermostat. Holding down a job to keep the bill collector from the door, drinking to quench our thirst, day-to-day coping with the needs of our children—these, too, are adjustment. Sometimes the demands are more psychological: leaving home for the first time, convincing ourselves to study for a test, preparing for a job interview, coping with the passing of a loved one. Making new friends, exploring the pluses and minuses of studying, rehearsing what we shall say, being with supportive relatives—these, too, are methods of adjusting.

Adjustment (ad-JUST-ment). Behavior that permits people to meet the demands of the environment. Also defined as a response to stress.

Abraham Maslow.

Adjustment is our response to the environment, to stress, to pressures, to unplanned disasters, to the challenges of life. But adjustment goes just so far in explaining human behavior. Adjustment falls short of permitting us to feel fulfilled because it is mainly reactive. We adjust to stresses that confront us. Yet sometimes we behave in ways such that we create our own challenges and pressures.

There is more to life than adjustment, or responding to environmental demands. Humanistic psychologist Abraham Maslow was fond of asking graduate students this question: "How many of you expect to achieve greatness in your careers?" If students were hesitant to signal a personal commitment to significant accomplishment, he would prod them: "Why not?" Maslow was not merely studying modesty or false modesty. He believed that human beings do more than just react to environmental demands. In fact, he believed that what separates human beings from lesser creatures is the capacity for **self-actualization,** or self-initiated striving to become whatever we feel we are capable of being. Through striving to live up to our potentials and to experience what we

Self-actualization (ACK-chew-ul-eye-ZAY-shun). The process of striving to fulfill one's potential. Humanistic psychologists believe that this is an inborn potential.

◢ The Holocaust ▮

ADJUSTMENT OF NAZI CONCENTRATION CAMP SURVIVORS

World War II was one of the bleakest periods of human history. During what was later to become known as the Holocaust, 72 percent of the Jewish population of Europe was killed in Nazi concentration camps. But despite constant fear of impending death, overcrowding, starvation, removal from everything held dear, brutality, and disease, some survived the camps.

Many years later, Joel Dimsdale (1974) of Harvard Medical School interviewed healthy survivors in Jerusalem and in the San Francisco Bay area to find out what adjustment strategies they had used to respond to the demands of the concentration camps. In his interviews, he found ten adjustment strategies that had been used by the survivors. They are very different from one another. Some suggest a high level

A concentration camp used by the Nazis during the Second World War.

can from life we create new demands for adjustment. But by doing so, we can reap great pleasure and experience **personal growth.** Personal growth results from meeting demands to adjust and elevating ourselves beyond mere adjustment.

PSYCHOLOGY AND THE CHALLENGES OF LIFE

Psychology has led to the development of many effective ways for helping to understand and to meet the challenges of contemporary life. Psychology is the science of behavior. Psychology collects, organizes, and seeks to create new knowledge concerning our thoughts, feelings, and behavior through both theory and research. Psychology may study animal behavior as well as human behavior, but usually for the purpose of gaining knowledge that will be applicable to human beings.

Personal growth. Self-initiated efforts to become whatever we believe we are capable of being. Personal growth is seen by humanistic psychologists not as a response to the environment, but rather as the personal taking on of self-imposed challenges.

Psychology (sigh-KOLL-oh-gee). The science of behavior. An organized way of collecting and expanding knowledge about thoughts, feelings, and behavior.

of activity and a "take charge" attitude. Others suggest a lower level of activity and an attitude of surrender. Some may not strike you as effective ways of adjusting at all.

Here are the adjustment strategies Dimsdale reported. Which strategies do you think would fit your personal style of adjusting? Which do you think are most effective? Why?

1. *Differential focus on the good.* Even in the midst of the teeming hells of the camps, some prisoners managed to focus on the beauty of a sunset, or they managed to reflect on the fact that today they had received some crumbs of food and had not been beaten.

2. *Focusing on a purpose.* Some fought to survive for a purpose—perhaps to help a relative, to tell the story of the camps, or even to seek revenge on their tormentors.

3. *Psychological removal.* Some removed themselves from their misery mentally when they could not do so physically. Some told themselves they were not really there, some focused on the thought of immortality, decreasing the impact of the fear of death. Still others psychologically insulated themselves from the camps by withdrawing into apathy or indifference.

4. *Mastery.* Camp inmates had lost control over their own lives, yet some chose to exercise control and mastery in any little way that they could. Perhaps they helped their fellows remain alive, or perhaps they gathered what information they could from others.

5. *Will to live.* For some, only the desire to remain alive managed to blunt the oppression of the camps, yet they did what they could to cling to life.

6. *Hope.* Some managed to find hope in the midst of misery. Some assumed the attitude that the camps were so unnatural and bizarre, so horrendous, that they could not last for long. Others simply thought that so long as they were alive, there was a glimmer of hope.

7. *Group affiliation.* Some found comfort in others. They formed or clung to family groups, friendships, or national groups in order to share feelings, information, advice, and hope.

8. *Regressive behavior.* Regressive behavior is behavior characteristic of earlier periods of life, such as crying or acting helpless. Crying and helpless behavior in children and in adolescents often stimulated a helping response from other inmates.

9. *Fatalism.* Fatalism is the attitude that what happens was meant to be; therefore, nothing can be done about it. A fatalistic attitude decreased the feeling that it was necessary to fight back. This resignation helped some experience the horrors of the camps with a more peaceful outlook. This peace should not be confused with a positive emotion or a good feeling; it is characterized more by an absence of opposition or fighting.

10. *Surrender.* Some were so horrified by what was happening in the camps that they simply could not imagine that it would be taking place if it were evil or wrong. Therefore, they assumed, their tormentors must be in the right and the victims must be in the wrong. In this way, some inmates blunted the feelings of injustice and unfair treatment.

Theory (THEE-oh-ree). A set or group of statements based on certain assumptions that permits us to explain and predict events. In psychology, these events are behavior.

Research. A systematic way of gathering knowledge. In psychology, research includes such behavior as collecting data, performing experiments, and determining whether the predictions of various theories are supported by evidence.

Hypothesis (high-POTH-uh-sis). A prediction about behavior that is derived from theory. Hypotheses are not supported unless they are borne out by evidence.

Case study. A method of research that focuses on an individual in an effort to determine the influences on that individual's behavior.
Survey. A method of research that may focus on large samples of individuals in order to determine the presence or status of characteristics of those samples. We may do attitude surveys and opinion polls, or we may survey the heights and weights of a group of individuals.

A **theory** is a group of statements about behavior that rests on a set of assumptions about behavior and allows us to explain and to predict events. In this century, psychology has seen the growth of new theories concerning the self, human development, personality, behavioral disturbances, and stress. Theory, in turn, has given birth to ideas for helping people to help themselves and each other.

But theory is not enough. Psychology also emphasizes the importance of **research.** Research is an organized way of determining whether the predictions of various theories are supported by the evidence. Only when psychological theory has been supported by sound research evidence should we consider applying it to meet the challenges of life.

The Role of Theory

Atomic theory permitted us to describe and predict the behavior of atoms and subatomic particles at a time when no one had ever seen an atom. Atomic theory also permitted us to harness the atom through atomic power. Psychological theories allow us to describe, explain, and predict human behavior, using concepts like "learning," "adjustment," and "repression." Psychological theories give us frameworks for understanding how certain human problems may develop, and for predicting whether or not certain types of therapy or intervention will be of help.

Predictions that come from psychological theory are called **hypotheses**—educated guesses. Differing theories can lead to different hypotheses. If you are angry with someone, will expressing that anger verbally decrease the probability that you will take aggressive action against that person? Psychoanalytic theory suggests the hypothesis that verbal expression of aggressive impulses may decrease the probability of physical aggression. Behavioral theory suggests that encouragement of one type of aggressive behavior, verbal, may encourage other types of aggressive behavior as well. Theory, then, is not enough.

The Role of Evidence

We raise many questions in this book. Do you imagine that it would be possible to relieve a vicious headache by elevating the temperature in your finger (Chapter 7)? What do you think are the effects of alcohol on aggressive behavior (Chapter 15)? Do you believe that normal people would be willing to deliver severe electric shocks to people who have done them no harm for the sake of a psychological experiment (Chapter 11)? What would you expect the effects of pornography to be on male and female college students (Chapter 13)?

Fighting a headache by raising finger temperature may strike you as a crackpot idea. You may assume that alcohol stimulates aggression. Perhaps you assume that only deranged or very angry people would be willing to shock innocent human beings for the sake of an experiment. What of pornography? Do you assume that pornography leads to deviant sexual behavior? Perhaps that men are sexually stimulated by pornography but that women are revolted?

Perhaps your assumptions, whatever they are, are correct. Perhaps they are wrong. You will find out as you read this book. Assumptions may be right or wrong, and that is why we seek evidence.

We obtain evidence from many different types of research, including case studies, surveys, and experiments. In the **case study,** we interview or we observe the behavior of an individual. From a careful examination of this person's history and current behavior, we may develop tentative explanations of relationships between the person's behavior and past and current influences on behavior. Individual in-depth interviews are also sometimes called the "clinical method" of research. Case studies have many problems, such as problems with the memory of the individual, or purposeful or accidental misrepresentations.

We run **surveys** with several people at a time, possibly thousands. In surveys we may use interviews or written questionnaires to explore attitudes, feelings, and opinions. We may ask people to report their behavior. But we still have problems with the accuracy of self-report. For example, people may not accurately remember the behavior they are reporting. How well can any of us recall events from early childhood? People who choose to respond to questionnaires they receive in the mail may also hold attitudes and opinions different from those who choose not to respond. People who respond to questionnaires concerning their sexual behavior may be more liberal and open about sex than people who do not. If we assume that the responses we receive to mailed questionnaires represent all people, we may be grossly distorting the results.

We use **experiments** to try to overcome problems with the clinical method and the survey. In experiments we try to determine causal relationships by actually introducing factors (called **independent variables**) that we hypothesize will lead to certain results (that we call **dependent variables**). We try to observe and measure results for ourselves. In that way we do not have to worry about the accuracy of self-report. By actually introducing the independent variables for ourselves, we can be more certain that they have the effect that we expect. Careful experiments also have **controls**—ways of showing that it was the independent variable, and not something else, that led to the predicted results.

Experiment. A method of research in which we try out some type of treatment or experimental approach in order to see whether or not it has an influence on behavior. Experiments are considered essential when we wish to determine cause and effect.
Independent variable. A treatment or variable in an experiment. In an experiment we usually wish to determine whether one or more independent variables has an influence on a dependent variable.
Dependent variable. A measure of behavior. In an experiment we usually wish to determine whether a treatment has an influence on one or more dependent variables.
Control. A way of showing that the independent variable alone led to experimental results through holding all other conditions constant.

Figure 1.1. The Roles of Theory and Research

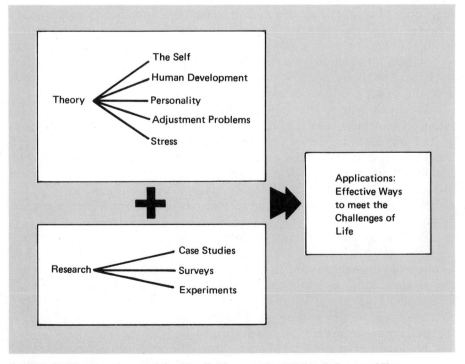

Psychological theory and research lead to effective ways to meet the challenges of life.

Let us hypothesize that a certain chemical will cause people to age. We then administer it to a number of people over a thirty-year period. Lo and behold! We find that these people begin to gray, to lose hair, and to develop some wrinkles. Are we correct in assuming that our independent variable (the chemical) led to signs of aging (dependent variables)? Obviously not. If we had also observed a **control group** for thirty years—a comparable group of people who did *not* receive the independent variable (the chemical)—we would have discovered that they had also aged.

Evidence thus supports, or fails to support, predictions. It is very important to run experiments with techniques of therapy, not only to find out if they are of help, but also to be sure that they do not have harmful side effects. In Chapter 10 we shall see whether aggression decreases or encourages future aggression. Theory is not enough.

PSYCHOLOGY AND ADJUSTMENT

Psychologists attempt to describe and explain the processes of human adjustment and personal growth from the vantage points of psychological theory. However, different psychological theories or **models** explain adjustment and personal growth in differing ways, and not all psychologists subscribe to the same theory.

There are three major psychological theories or models that have been very influential in studying the processes of adjustment and personal growth in the twentieth century: the psychoanalytic model, the behavioral model, and the humanist-existential model. When they originated, these theories were very different from one another, and psychologists adhering to one of them might even have been in conflict with psychologists adhering to other theoretical points of view. Some psychologists still adhere to these theories in close to their original forms. But other psychologists have modified their theoretical viewpoints over the years, so that there are now some psychoanalytic and behavioral psychologists who would also consider themselves to be humanists.

We shall study these three major psychological theories in depth in Chapter 4, but here is a preview of each, and a glimpse at how each theory would account for the processes of adjustment and personal growth.

Psychoanalytic or Freudian theory has emphasized our tendencies to respond to biological **instincts** and desires. According to psychoanalysis, we are basically motivated to seek gratification of these instincts and desires, yet to do so in ways that will permit us to escape condemnation by others and by the self. Our desire to escape self-condemnation may result in our being unaware of many of our motives. From the psychoanalytic perspective, major objectives of helping include fostering insight into the hidden motives that prompt our actions.

Behavioral theory has emphasized our capacities to learn from experience. We can learn that one thing will lead to another and that we can meet our needs by engaging in certain types of behavior. Since much of this learning can occur without our conscious intention, and at very early ages, the behavioral model is somewhat mechanical in nature. From the behaviorist perspective, the major aim of helping is the substitution of adaptive or helpful habits for maladaptive or harmful, self-defeating habits.

Humanist-existential theory recognizes the roles of biological instincts and learning, but stresses our awareness of ourselves. From this perspective,

Control group. A group of subjects in an experiment who do not receive the experimental treatment, but for whom all other conditions are held constant.

Model. A representation of an object. A model is similar to a theory, but need not be so complex. A model can be synonymous with a "perspective" or a "view."
Psychoanalytic theory (SIGH-ko-an-al-IT-ick). The theory of human behavior developed by Sigmund Freud, which emphasizes our motivation to satisfy biological instincts and desires.
Instinct. In psychoanalytic theory, a biological urge, like hunger, which impels a response—in this case, eating. The resultant behavior, eating, gratifies the instinct.
Behavioral theory (bee-HAVE-your-al). The theory of human behavior that has emphasized learning to respond to the environment in a habitual manner.
Humanist-existential theory (eggs-is-TEN-shull). The theory of human behavior that begins with the assumptions of human self-awareness and the ability to exercise free choice.
Sigmund Freud and the early behaviorists saw human behavior as responsive to instincts or the environment. Humanists claim we can initiate our own behavior through our conscious awareness.

our central motivation is to strive toward our visions of what we can become. We are self-aware. Not only do we respond to gut-level instincts and environmental stimulation, we are also self-actualizing: we initiate action to strive toward ideals. From the humanist view, the major aim of helping has been to provide people with an atmosphere of warm acceptance in which they can learn to harness this self-actualizing tendency.

Adjustment and Psychoanalysis

From a psychoanalytic point of view, adjustment implies keeping our drives and instincts at tolerable levels. Adjustment means walking a tightrope—finding outlets for internal pressures that permit us to meet our needs, yet also permit us to avoid social sanctions and self-condemnation. There are prices to pay for adjusting, such as **displacing** our desires onto obtainable objects when our first choices are not available, such as **deluding** ourselves that we have acceptable reasons for unacceptable behavior.

Freud believed that the processes of personal adjustment are mostly unconscious, that people are unaware of the real reasons for much of their behavior. Neo-Freudians, "ego psychologists," have felt that this is too dim a view of human nature. Analysts such as Erik Erikson, Erich Fromm, and Henry Murray have expressed the belief that some human functioning is fully conscious, that human beings can experience prosocial, selfless motives as well as gut-level urgings.

These neo-analysts have been dissatisfied with the Freudian model of man. They stress personal growth in addition to adjustment.

Adjustment and Behaviorism

From a behavioral point of view, adjustment implies learning responses to the environment that will enable us to have reasonable expectations and to attain rewards. Behavior that is repeatedly rewarded becomes habitual. Yet it is possible to develop habits that lead us to avoid challenges rather than to meet them head on.

Behaviorists like John B. Watson and B. F. Skinner have believed that the processes of personal adjustment are not developed by conscious effort, but are shaped automatically by environmental cues and **rewards.** Neo-behaviorists, "cognitive behaviorists," have felt that this is too mechanical a view of human nature. Cognitive behaviorists such as Albert Bandura and Michael Mahoney have expressed the belief that some human functioning is fully conscious, that human thoughts and intentions interact constantly with habitual responses, and that what we tell ourselves about ourselves can be as influential as, or more influential than, external rewards.

Cognitive behaviorists have been dissatisfied with the mechanical model of man. They, too, emphasize personal growth.

Adjustment and Humanistic Psychology

Humanists like Abraham Maslow and Carl Rogers view human beings as more than just the sum total of their gut-level urgings and their mechanical re-

Displacement (dis-PLACE-ment). A psychological means of adjusting to the lack of availability of a desired object by substituting an available object. According to psychoanalytic theory, displacement takes place unconsciously—without awareness.
Delusion (dee-LOO-shun). A false belief or opinion. Some self-delusion is quite common, but persistent delusions that are not supported by sensory evidence can suggest psychological problems (Chapter 5).

Reward. Positive, desired consequence for behavior. The opposite of a reward is a punishment.

Adjustment
and Personal Growth

15

sponses. From a humanist-existential point of view, adjustment implies our conscious efforts to cope with stress. *And more:* When Abraham Maslow asked his students if they intended to achieve greatness, he did not necessarily mean that one student must vow to become another Einstein, or that another student must vow to run a four-minute mile. He meant that each of us is capable of finding self-fulfillment if we strive to achieve distant goals that we have set for ourselves. We shall feel most alive and our actions will seem most proper to us when we strive to achieve goals that are personally meaningful.

Humanists view people as *actors*, not *reactors*. Reactors can do no more than adjust. Actors can enhance themselves, actualize themselves, and grow even when they are not prodded by gut-level urgings or environmental stimulation. Reactors attempt to reduce or remove sources of stress. Actors may consciously take on new sources of stress to achieve meaningful life goals.

Seaweed, Rocks, Waves, and Personal Growth. On a trip to the West Coast, Carl Rogers, a humanistic psychologist, was reminded of the capacity of life to do more than simply adjust to stress. He was caught up in the drama of life's capacity to develop, to grow toward distant goals, to push forward into the most difficult of environments in order to keep on the course established by some inner blueprint:

> During a vacation weekend some months ago I was standing on a headland overlooking one of the rugged coves which dot the coastline of northern California. Several large rock outcroppings were at the mouth of the cove, and these received the full force of the great Pacific combers which, beating upon them, broke into mountains of spray before surging into the cliff-lined shore. As I watched the waves breaking over these large rocks in the distance, I noticed with surprise what appeared to be a tiny palm tree on the rocks, no more than two or three feet high, taking the pounding of the breakers. Through my binoculars I saw that these were some type of seaweed, with a slender "trunk" topped off with a head of leaves. As one examined a specimen in the interval between the waves it seemed clear that this fragile, erect, top-heavy plant would be utterly crushed and broken by the next breaker. When the wave crunched down upon it, the trunk bent almost flat, the leaves were whipped into a straight line by the torrent of the water, yet the moment the wave had passed, here was the plant again, erect, tough, resilient. It seemed incredible that it was able to take this incessant pounding hour after hour, day after night, week after week, perhaps, for all I know, year after year, and all the time nourishing itself, extending its domain, reproducing

Carl R. Rogers.

itself; in short, maintaining and enhancing itself in this process which, in our shorthand, we call growth. Here in this palmlike seaweed was the tenacity of life, the forward thrust of life, the ability to push into an incredibly hostile environment and not only hold its own, but to adapt, develop, become itself [Rogers 1963, pp. 1–2].

Throughout this book we shall see that the three major models—psychoanalytic, behavioral, and humanist-existential—all have something to contribute to our understanding of human nature and to our construction of methods that will promote adjustment and personal growth. Much of our behavior appears driven by instincts or biological urgings, and it does seem that we manage, at times, to fool ourselves about our motives or simply to be unaware of them. We do develop habitual ways of responding to the environment. We are also self-aware and have the ability to use self-awareness to meet the challenges of life effectively and to grow from them. These three models have been growing somewhat closer together in recent years, although they each tend to retain something of their original emphasis. We shall attempt to piece them together as best we can to derive the most useful suggestions for meeting the challenges of life.

Now let us turn our attention to an approach to studying which will allow you to derive the most important information from this book—and from textbooks for your other courses.

SPONGES, PLANS, AND SQ3R— ACTIVE STUDY METHODS

Put some water into a bathtub. Sit in the tub. Wait a few moments. Look around in the tub. You will notice that the water is still there, although you may have displaced it a bit.

You may have been dry when you sat in the tub, but you are not a sponge. You will not simply soak up the water. You would have to take rather active measures to get it inside you—perhaps a straw and a great deal of patience and single-mindedness would be of help. And please: do it bit by bit.

The problems of "soaking up" the knowledge in this and other books are not entirely dissimilar. You will not accomplish much by sitting on it (except, perhaps, looking an inch taller). That you know. But psychological theory and research have also taught us that it is better to have an active approach to studying than a passive approach—to look for the answers to specific questions rather than just to flip through the pages "like a good student." Also, do not try to do it all at once, especially when you have a few bathtubsful of academic material floating around you.

Plan Ahead

Begin your active approach to studying by assessing the amount of material you must master during the academic term and then measuring your rate of learning. How long does it seem to take you to read a chapter, or a book? How many hours per day do you spend studying? Does it add up right? Will you make it?

Once you have determined how much study time you will need for each course for the term, try to space out your study periods evenly. For most of us,

Plan ahead to do some work each weekday, leaving weekends relatively free.

spaced or distributed learning is more efficient than cramming or massed learning. So try to outline a study schedule that will provide an approximately equal amount of time to work each weekday, but leave weekends relatively free so that you can have some time for yourself and extra hours for reviewing notes and working on assignments that may be causing difficulty.

Do not study adjustment Monday, physics Tuesday, and literature Wednesday. Study each for a little while each day, so that you will not become bored or dulled by too lengthy an immersion in the same subject.

If it seems that you cannot push yourself to study enough each day at first, find a more comfortable level and then build gradually toward the amount of daily study time you will need. Find a place to study that is relatively comfortable and free of distractions. Let this place—your room, a study lounge, a spot in the library—come to "mean" studying to you. Try to do nothing but study there—no socializing, no snacking. But after you have met a goal, like finishing half your study period, you may want to reward yourself with a break—like person-watching in a more active section of the library. Reward yourself somehow for meeting daily study goals. Do not try to be a martyr and put off all pleasures until the end of the term. Some people can do this, but if you have never spent that much time in nonstop studying, you may be asking too much of yourself at the beginning.

SQ3R: Survey, Question, Read, Recite, and Review

Don't question some of your professor's assignments. Question all of them. Educational psychologist Francis Robinson (1970) of Ohio State University originated a method of studying—SQ3R—in which you can actively soak up academic material by phrasing questions about it as you go along and then answering them. SQ3R has been successful in helping students study more effectively and raise their grades at a number of colleges (Benecke & Harris 1972). There are five steps to the SQ3R method: survey, question, read, recite, and review.

Some people destroy their pleasure in reading mystery novels by turning to the last pages to find out "whodunit" when their curiosity gets the best of them. While skipping through the pages of a novel may harm the dramatic impact by revealing information without an adequate buildup of suspense, it can be an excellent method of learning textbook material. In fact more and more textbooks are being written in such a way that you are stimulated to *survey* the material before reading it. This book has "Truth or Fiction?" sections at the beginning of each chapter, major and minor headers throughout the chapter, and then a summarizing section at the end that integrates the material in terms of the "Truth or Fiction?" lead-ins. If drama and suspense are your goals, you may wish to read the chapters page by unfolding page. But if learning the facts is first, it may be more effective (sigh) to examine the "Truth or Fiction?" section, turn the pages focusing on the headers, and then read the summary material—all before you get into the meat of each chapter. Familiarity with the skeleton of the chapter will provide you with a framework or "advance organizers" for learning the meat of the chapter as you ingest it page by page.

Phrase *questions* for each of the "Truth or Fiction?" lead-ins and for the headers in each chapter. In books without lead-ins you can only phrase questions for headers. If the books do not have headers, get into the material page by page and phrase relevant questions as you go along. This is a skill that you will develop with practice. The following questions are phrased from the major and minor headers of the first several pages of Chapter 1. Notice that the indenting follows the outline structure of the chapter and gives you an immediate sense of how the material is organized.

What are the challenges of life?
    How have roles been changing?
    How is technology changing?
    How are resources changing?
    How has society been changing?
What are adjustment and personal growth?
Etc.

You may have phrased the questions differently. Your way may have been more efficient for you. You will learn what works well for you with some practice.

Once you have phrased each question, *read* the relevant subject matter with the purpose of answering that question. This will help you attend to the central points of the chapter or the section. If the material is fine literature, you may wish to read it once to appreciate its poetic features fully and then use the SQ3R method the second time through—again, to tease out essential information.

Find a place to study that is relatively comfortable and free from distractions.

Adjustment
and Personal Growth

In *The Wizard of Oz*,
Dorothy and her friends
learn to rely on
themselves.

Put down the book once you have read the section and answer your question as clearly and briefly as possible. Jot down a few key words that will telegraph the answer to you. *Recite* the answer aloud if possible. (This may depend on where you are, who is near you, and how you feel about what you expect they will think of you.) It is efficient to keep notes in two columns—questions on the left, key response words on the right.

Review the material briefly at the conclusion of each study session and then on a reasonable schedule—perhaps weekly. Cover the answers and read your questions like a quiz. Perhaps you can enlist friends to read them. Then recite the answers and check them against the key response terms. Reread the subject matter if you forget the answer to an occasional question. Forgetting too many answers may mean that you are not phrasing the questions in a way that is most efficient for you.

By taking a more active approach to studying—by taking a more active approach to life in general—you will find that you can more efficiently develop your academic powers or abilities. By questioning the meaning of your thoughts, feelings, behavior, and relationships, you may find that you can develop all your personal powers or abilities.

PERSONAL POWER: YOU—YOU'RE THE ONE

Wicked witches, talking trees, the yellow brick road, and, shining in the distance, the Emerald City. Four people with problems—Dorothy, ripped away from her Kansas home by the tornado; the Scarecrow, lacking a brain; the Tin Man, without a heart; the Cowardly Lion—off they go to find the wonderful "Wizard of Oz," who can fix anything.

But wizards, our heroes find, are made of flesh and blood. Their barks can be bigger than their bites. Still, the Wizard of Oz was not without insight, not without compassion. To the Scarecrow he gave a diploma, to the Tin Man a ticking clock, to the Lion a medal—all of these external emblems of that which they already had inside themselves. Dorothy, who wished to return to Kansas, was told she need only click her heels together three times and say, "There's no place like home."

The Wizard, in his wisdom, understood that many of the solutions to personal problems can be found within ourselves. Only we can determine what is of value to us. And once we have made these determinations it is often up to us to apply the things we learn to become personally effective in our own lives. Unfortunately, too many of us are taught to look to others for support and for solutions to our problems. When we fail to look inward, our goals, our *selves* remain mysteries to us "for good reason," as Friedrich Nietzsche wrote— "How can we ever hope to find that which we never sought?"

The Challenge and The Force

Some behavioral scientists believe that people begin life as a **tabula rasa,** or blank stone, which is written upon by experience. Others stress the role of genetics in the gradual unfolding of behavior. Others, including humanists, are impressed by the extent to which self-awareness and self-creation influence the courses both of nature and of nurture.

Self-awareness, this human force, stands between life's challenges and our reactions to them. Self-awareness, this human force, creates new challenges for many of us even after environmental challenges have been swept aside. It reminds us of "The Force" in the film *Star Wars*. During the battle scene that

Tabula rasa (TAB-you-lah RAH-sah). The state of mind before it has received sensory impressions. A "clean slate."

(Right) A dejected Luke Skywalker contemplates the impossible odds against him in the film *Star Wars*.

(Left) Luke and his comrades receive their just rewards after they have learned to use "The Force" to overcome their enemies.

climaxed the film, Luke Skywalker, the young hero, chose to believe in himself rather than an unreliable and inhuman computerized targeting system. With self-confidence he struck home and vanquished the enemy.

Psychoanalyst Alfred Adler noticed something akin to The Force during his early professional years. There were many circus people among his patients who had striven to overcome childhood disabilities and become skilled athletes and performers. The poet Lord Byron had shaped a lame foot into the working tool of a magnificent swimmer. Adler was impressed by the common human tendency to **compensate** for weaknesses and deformities. The weak child becomes a scholar. The cripple becomes a dancer. The child poor of hearing becomes a musician.

Adler would not have been too surprised by what happened some fifty years later at the 1960 Olympics in Rome. A young black woman, Wilma Rudolph, stunned the world by winning three gold medals in track. What was incredible was that Wilma had suffered from polio as a child.

The theme continues in our lives and in our fantasies. Rocky Balboa, the fictional hero of the Oscar-winning film *Rocky*, received his education in the proverbial school of hard knocks. An uneducated fighter and strong arm for underworld figures in Philadelphia, Rocky had put into action the advice he received from his father: "You weren't born with much of a brain, so you'd better develop your body." Rocky had been scraping by—a brawler rather than a boxer, a sad figure in the underworld bars, fight gyms, and tacky flats of the perennial loser. Aging, with no future prospects in sight, Rocky was given the chance of a lifetime as a promotional stunt—a heavyweight title fight with the champion of the world. Obsessed with the single goal of ending the contest standing on his feet, Rocky trained a body past its prime beyond any limits of endurance he had earlier known. And he won—not the championship, but he reached his goal. He was on his feet after fifteen rounds and he had not looked foolish.

Can all frogs become handsome princes? Not necessarily, but our self-awareness, our abilities to compensate, to strive, and to grow can provide us with more opportunities than we might at first have realized. Whether we are driven by our gut-level urgings for a lifetime, whether our behavior simply reacts mechanically to the stresses and strains of the environment, or whether we look deeply into ourselves and make the personal commitment to strive for goals at or beyond the very limits of our capacities—this is largely up to us.

The Invulnerables

Invulnerable is a rather long word, but it is learned by many American children at an early age because one of their favorite comic strip heroes—Superman—is invulnerable, or incapable of being harmed. We are not surprised that Superman is invulnerable. He can fly, he has X-ray vision and immense strength—so long as he keeps a respectable distance from kryptonite and an assortment of talented evildoers. But we were somewhat surprised when psychologist Norman Garmezy and others identified some Americans as "invulnerables" in the late 1970s. These persons had experienced severe hardships and deprivations in childhood, the loss of one or both parents, abusive parents, alcoholic parents. Yet, as adults, they were well adjusted. It was natural that psychologists would claim that we should spend as much time studying "invul-

Compensation (kom-pen-SAY-shun). In psychoanalytic theory, a method of adjusting to a weakness or undesirable trait through building strength or desirable traits.

Invulnerable (in-VULL-nurr-uh-bull). Incapable of being successfully wounded, injured, or attacked.

nerables" as we spent studying life's casualties. In fact, we might have even more to learn from those who had fared well despite hardship.

One study at the University of California Institute of Human Development (Macfarlane 1964) traced the life patterns of individuals from infancy through the age of thirty. With boring predictability, this research team had expected that individuals with happier childhoods would become the happier adults. And vice versa. This was a safe bet, from either an environmentalist or a genetic view. Happy environments would lead to happy children. Whatever genetic influences might foster adjustment or maladjustment would also be passed on from generation to generation.

But the prediction that unhappy children would be unhappy at the age of thirty failed in two of three cases. Many who had suffered as children were now leading productive, satisfying lives. Others who had had "every advantage" were unhappy, unfulfilled. The predictions had failed to account for the sense of *self*.

Bad events can be treated as signs that we need to do something, or as insurmountable catastrophes. Those of us who react rather than act—those of us who do not attempt to take charge of our emotions, our behavior, and our relationships establish ourselves as life's *victims*. When adversity strikes, we shall surely be in its path.

It is possible to learn to feel helpless, to expect that we shall not be able to achieve rewards and fulfillment through our own efforts. In Chapter 9 we see that these feelings of helplessness may lead to many bodily changes, even to biochemical changes in the brain that effectively decrease our activity levels and lead to depression.

But it is also possible to develop the feeling that one is responsible for one's own successes and failures, despite good or bad luck, and that it is possible to have a significant influence upon one's own life course. According to the University of California research team, it may be that the child who is exposed to "controllable" levels of stress at an early age is more fortunate than the child who is overly protected. Children who are given everything do not need to learn to manage stress. As adults, relatively mild frustrations and disappointments may assume major proportions.

To view stress as a sign that there are problems to be solved, to act to attain meaningful goals, to take charge of our feelings, our behavior, and our relationships—these are the skills of the invulnerables. The belief that we can exert a significant influence upon the course of our lives—this is The Force of the invulnerables. Fortunately, the skills of the invulnerables are learnable. Fortunately, The Force of the invulnerables is not mystical or mysterious—it is an attitude toward one's *self* and one's life. The skills, The Force can be a part of you.

Summary

- *Longshoremen have become longshorepersons, and we find ads for Guy Fridays in the "Help Wanted" sections of newspapers.* True. Society changes and individual roles change. Such changes place demands upon us to adjust.
- *COBOL and FORTRAN are the names of space colonies.* They may sound like it, but they are actually the names of computer languages, sys-

tems of symbols that people use to communicate with machines. Young people today are learning these languages and others, and acquiring new skills to adjust to the demands of contemporary technology. Older people fear that their skills may become obsolete.

- *It is not so easy to criticize cannibals when you are starving to death in the frozen Arctic wastes.* It is certainly true that many people have behaved in ways that would be quite disturbing to us when they have had to resort to them in order to survive. Eskimos and people trapped in lifeboats have used cannibalism and sentenced the weak among them to death in order to assure survival of the group. Adjustment is behavior that permits us to adapt to the environment. But people are capable of more than adjustment—they are capable of personal growth, which is the individual challenge to become whatever we are capable of being.

- *You could survey 20 million Americans and still fail to predict the outcome of a presidential election accurately.* True. You must be certain that the people you sample actually represent the population you assume that they represent. In 1948, a survey of 8 million readers of a popular magazine suggested that Thomas Dewey would be elected President. Harry S. Truman laughed at these predictions the morning after the election. Truman was a Democrat, and the magazine was read predominantly by Republicans.

- *Feed people for thirty years with an experimental substance that you believe causes people to age. You will find that they have grown older.* True, but this fact demonstrates the importance of having control subjects in experiments—subjects who do not receive the independent variable (in this case, the aging substance), but for whom all other circumstances are the same (they, too, are observed for thirty years). Only with adequate controls can we assume that our dependent variables (in this case, aging) are the result of manipulating our independent variables.

- *Only men are erotically stimulated by pornography.* Many believe this to be so, but, as we shall see in Chapter 13, it is actually false. In psychology we insist upon evidence as well as opinion and theory.

- *Human beings are motivated by basic biological drives.* True. We are motivated by thirst, hunger, the need for warmth, and so on. Psychoanalytic theory has emphasized our biological motives and our efforts to gratify them, but there is more to the human being than biological motives.

- *Human beings are creatures of habit.* Not quite. We can learn habitual ways of responding to the environment in order to gain rewards and avoid punishments, as the behavioral view of human beings has pointed out. But there is more to people than habit.

- *Human beings are self-aware and capable of making free choices.* Hopefully, most of us are, although when environmental demands are too great, we may find it difficult to make choices. Yet even in concentration camps, inmates have been able to find some strategies for adjustment. Self-awareness and free choice reflect humanist-existential theory, and there are many psychoanalysts and behaviorists today who would also consider themselves to be humanistic.

- *Spacy studying is most efficient. You can learn more by spacing out your study assignments than by cramming them all together.* True, distributed practice is more efficient than massed practice, and it requires planning ahead. It is also useful to plan ahead in order to spend study time in a place free of distractions, to reward yourself for meeting gradually increasing study goals, and to rotate studying from one subject to another.

- *You will learn more if you refrain from questioning some of your professor's assignments. It is better to question all of them.* True. If you follow the SQ3R method, you will question the material and perhaps study more efficiently. First survey the material, formulate questions, read to answer your questions, recite the answers, and review the material regularly.

- *The majority of children who lose parents at an early age, or whose parents are alcoholic or abusive, grow up to be poorly adjusted adults.* False, fortunately. The Berkeley study (Macfarlane 1964) showed that the majority of children who were abused and deprived become well-adjusted adults. We are not simply slaves to our pasts. We have the capacities to carve out our own destinies. The past becomes a stronger trap when we believe that we cannot combat its influences.

- *The Force is with* you. We hope so. "The Force" is the belief that you, as a sovereign and intelligent human being, have the capacity to influence your own life here and now—in spite of impulses, habits, and handicaps. This choice is yours alone.

2

THE SELF

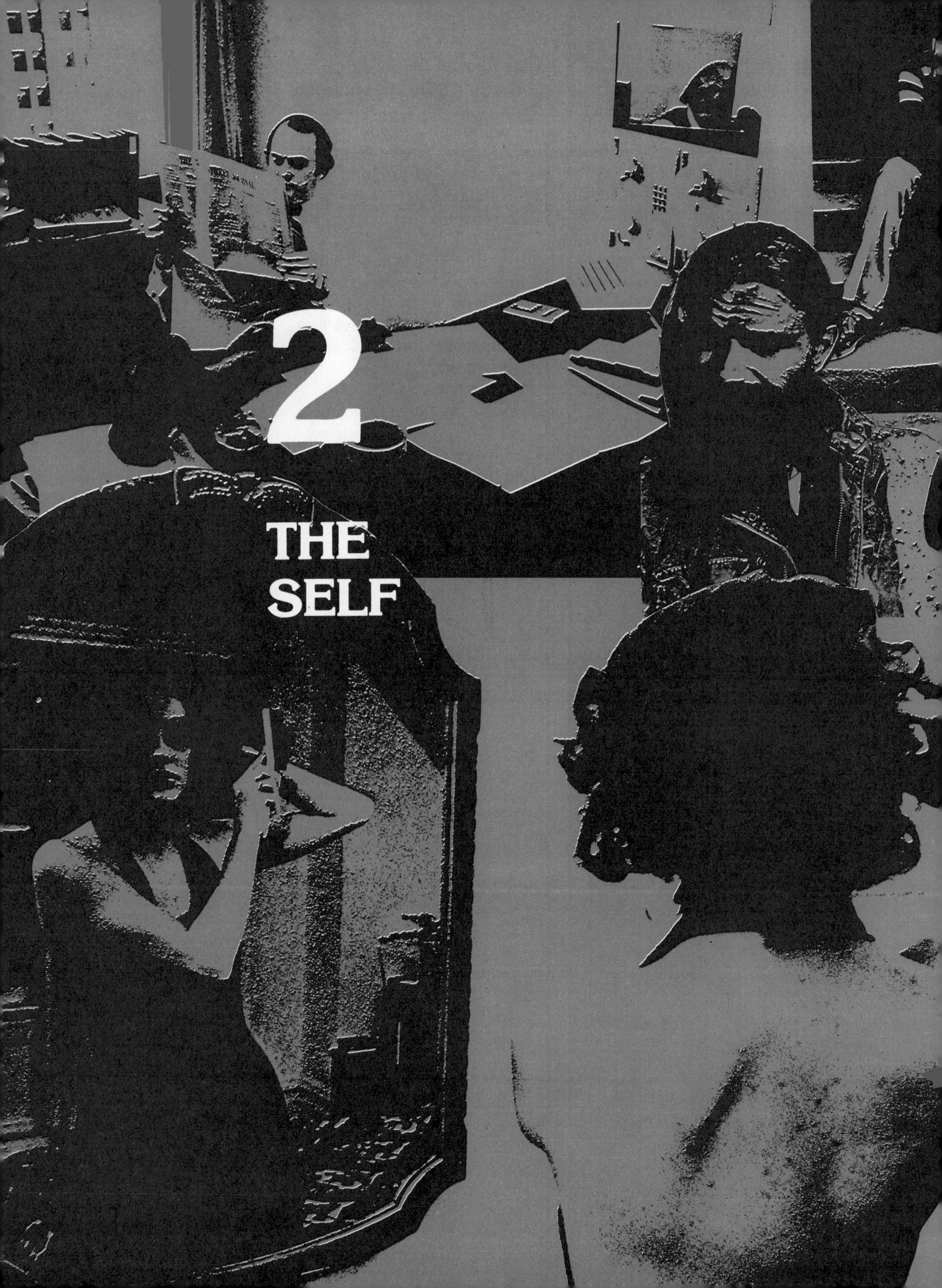

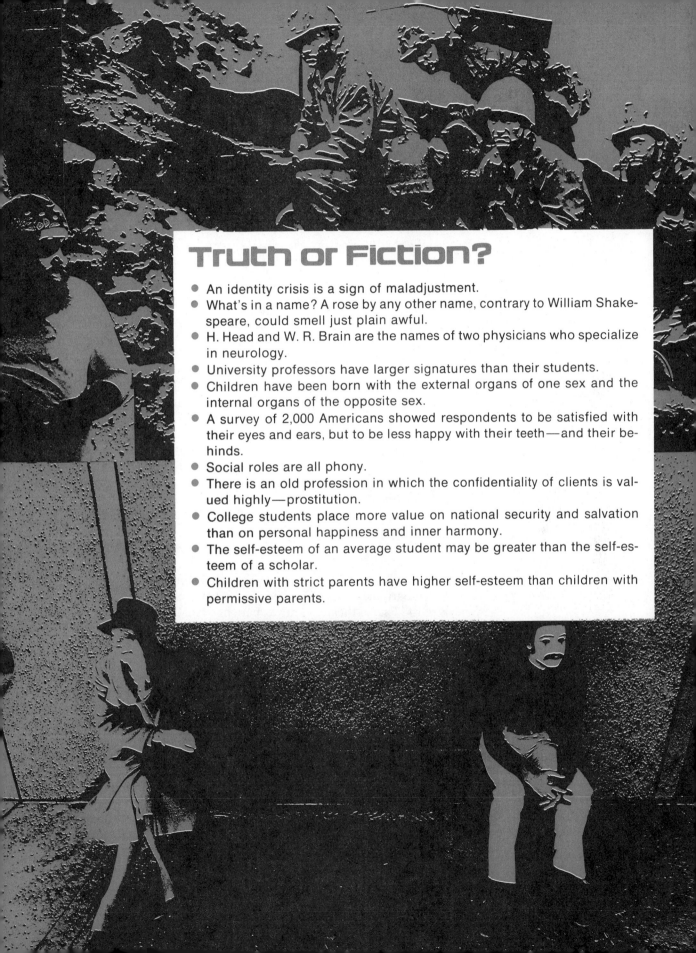

Truth or Fiction?

- An identity crisis is a sign of maladjustment.
- What's in a name? A rose by any other name, contrary to William Shakespeare, could smell just plain awful.
- H. Head and W. R. Brain are the names of two physicians who specialize in neurology.
- University professors have larger signatures than their students.
- Children have been born with the external organs of one sex and the internal organs of the opposite sex.
- A survey of 2,000 Americans showed respondents to be satisfied with their eyes and ears, but to be less happy with their teeth—and their behinds.
- Social roles are all phony.
- There is an old profession in which the confidentiality of clients is valued highly—prostitution.
- College students place more value on national security and salvation than on personal happiness and inner harmony.
- The self-esteem of an average student may be greater than the self-esteem of a scholar.
- Children with strict parents have higher self-esteem than children with permissive parents.

For the United States, the Second World War in the Pacific meant island hopping. Repeatedly, marines landed on hostile beaches, drew enemy fire, and worked their painful way up to gaining footholds on these blasted patches of dirt that protruded through the ocean. And during the Second World War, as during other wars, some participants chose to make their contribution through the medical corps, to follow the bloody battles and try somehow to minimize the human tragedy, rather than contribute to that tragedy themselves.

One young man, strongly opposed to the killing and the bloodshed, was stuck through the night on one such beachhead as the soldiers around him struggled to keep them all from being pushed back into the ocean. Enemy fire raged through the night. Shells burst into light, illuminating the ghastly scene—the corpses and the embattled alike. Bullets whistled in the air, gunpowder cracked, bullets smacked into the sand with dead thuds. Air and naval support had been promised but had not come. Soldiers cursed their commanders, the navy, the island, the human species. Resentments combined with fear, and the level of arousal of the medical corps officer grew such that his perceptions and his memories became clouded and unreal.

Later he remembered that he had been required to unload ammunition, rather than attend to the sick and the wounded. He recalled a superior officer screaming profanities. His last memory of that long night was of someone handing him a machine gun.

When he awoke in the field hospital the next day, he began to be plagued by feelings of "jumpiness," anxiety, and severe headaches. His condition worsened, although no physical ailments could be found. Finally he was removed stateside, and he was referred for treatment at the Mt. Zion Veterans' Rehabilitation Clinic in San Francisco, where he was treated by a psychotherapist named Erik H. Erikson.

Battlefield neurosis (new-ROW-sis). A disorder experienced in wartime that stems from conflicting impulses and results in loss of ability to function adequately. Conflicting impulses might be the desire to avoid killing and the desire to preserve oneself.

Erikson worked with many such young men, soldiers suffering from what became called **battlefield neurosis.** They had all recently returned from the battlefields of the Pacific theater. They experienced intense feelings of anger and anxiety, especially when startled by noises or awakened from recurrent battlefield nightmares.

During therapeutic sessions with the medical corps officer, Erikson (1963) learned the young man's history. His childhood had been wracked by parental outbursts and his mother's drinking. During one episode of drunken rage, his mother threatened him with a gun. He grabbed the weapon from her, broke it in two, and threw it out the window. That day he left home. He vowed never to drink, swear, or carry a gun. He affirmed his sense of who he was as an individual by rejecting those aspects of his mother's behavior. Nonviolence, sobriety, self-control, clean speech—all these became central elements of this young man's **self-identity,** his sense of who and what he was as an individual.

Self-identity (eye-DEN-tuh-tee). An individual's perception of who he or she is.

That terrible night in the Pacific, when he was confronted with the swearing of a respected officer, when a gun was thrust into his hands and he went spinning out of control, his self-identity as a good and honorable person had been shaken.

He and other soldiers developed battlefield problems that had little to do

A marine-landing on a Pacific island during the Second World War, from
the film *The Sands of Iwo Jima.*

John Wayne, American folk hero, in *The Sands of Iwo Jima.*

with fear or cowardice. Erikson sensed that many of these soldiers had done things that were incompatible with their self-identities. It was as if they no longer knew who they were or what their lives were about. Successful adjustment depends on developing and maintaining a stable sense of who we are as individuals—a stable self-identity. When the self-identity is threatened by disease, tragedy, personal crisis, or awareness that our actions are inconsistent with our values, we may experience anxiety, panic, a sense of loss of self, and feelings of being cut adrift from life's purposes and meaning.

ERIK ERIKSON AND THE CHALLENGE OF SELF-IDENTITY

Erikson's evaluation of the problems of the medical corps officer reflected his personal questioning as a child of who he was and what he was to become. In his autobiography, Erikson (1975) told of the identity confusion or crisis he himself had experienced. His natural father had deserted his mother just before his birth, and the young Erikson was raised by his mother and stepfather, Theodor Homburger, a physician. But his mother and stepfather did not want the young boy to feel strange or different, so he was not told of his natural father till many years afterward.

Though both his mother and stepfather were Jewish, Erikson resembled his natural father, a Dane, with his blond hair and blue eyes. In his stepfather's synagogue, he was considered a Gentile. To his classmates he was a Jew. He began to feel different from other children, alienated from his family. He fantasized that he was the offspring of special parents who had abandoned him. "Who am I really?" was a question that permeated his quest for identity.

As he matured, Erikson came to face another identity issue: "What am I to do in life?" His stepfather encouraged him to follow in his footsteps and pursue medical studies. But Erikson sought his own path in life. He studied art and traveled through Europe as a youth, leading the bohemian life of an artist. This was a period of serious questioning and soul-searching—a personal drama that Erikson later came to label an **identity crisis.** He would come to see resolving the question "What am I to do in life?" as the central task of adolescence.

Identity crisis (CRY-sis). A period of serious personal questioning in an effort to determine one's own values and sense of direction.

As a result of his own search for identity, he became oriented toward his life's work: psychotherapy. He left his wanderings and plunged into training in psychoanalysis, the method of Sigmund Freud, under the personal supervision of Freud's daughter, Anna Freud.

From the personal turmoil of his own identity crisis, Erikson had forged a meaningful and personal life pattern or self-identity. He came to view the identity crisis not only as a time of strife and personal upheaval, but also as an opportunity for growth and change. The emotional impact of the identity crisis provides the motivational impetus for growth and decision making. Psychological maladjustment is not indicated by the presence of an identity crisis. Such a crisis is perfectly normal. Maladjustment stems from failure to use the crisis as an opportunity for growth.

Self-identity is one aspect of the self. In this chapter we shall first define what is meant by the self. Then we shall discuss several aspects of the self: the physical self, the social self, and the personal self. Finally we shall explore what is meant by the self-concept and its various components, including self-esteem and the self-ideal. We shall learn various ways in which the self attempts to maintain and enhance self-esteem.

THE SELF: THE CENTER OF AWARENESS

What would you do if you wanted to communicate the fact that you had a stomach cramp, but every time you complained the doctor examined your entire family or everyone with you at work? Or imagine the plight of a gentleman who has been driven wild with desire but has a certain problem in communicating. Every time he professes his love for his girl friend, you see, she runs away, protesting that she is simply not interested in group sex. In *Anthem*, Ayn Rand (1946) described a man with a similar problem in making himself understood to others—and himself.

In *Anthem*, Ayn Rand portrayed a future society in which the words "I" and "Me" had been utterly stricken from the language in order to encourage unselfish, group-oriented behavior. Equality 7-2521, the hero of the story, could refer to himself only as "We" or "Us." But collectivism—Ayn Rand's term for any system of government that places the group ahead of the individual—did not fully control Equality 7-2521. As Equality put it, "We were born with a curse."

Anthem tells of Equality's increasing friction with society, of his eventual break from the group. But not until the climax of the novel, when Equality stumbles across ancient writings in a prehistoric home, does he manage to find the concepts with which finally to talk precisely and think precisely about his center of awareness: his **self. I.**

What was Equality's "curse"? Ayn Rand seems to suggest that there was something inborn in Equality, perhaps inborn in all of us, that strives to develop and to be expressed—something that ultimately defines us as individuals, or as selves. Ayn Rand has not been considered a psychologist, but her assumptions about Equality are similar to those of the humanistic psychologists, like Carl Rogers and Abraham Maslow, who did theorize that we all have selves, a fluid way of experiencing the world and organizing our perceptions of the world that is essentially inborn. The self is certainly influenced by experience, and its growth can be stunted if conditions are harmful to its development. But humanistic psychology begins with the assumption of the self. The

Self. The individual's center of awareness, a fluid way of organizing perceptions of the world. "I."

The questions "Who am I?" and "What do I stand for?" are central to our self-identities.

self is because it is. The limits of self separate that which is you from that which is not you.

In this section we shall further define what is meant by the self. Then we shall see how the self becomes differentiated from the rest of the world, and how we come to use special words called names to refer to ourselves. We shall see that names do much more than label us—they also tend to determine something about what we shall become.

The Quest for the Self

In each of our homes are objects that carry very special meanings. We find them in several rooms. We may carry them about with us. Some of us will not leave home without one. Keys? Good luck charms? Wallets? No—mirrors.

Can you recall one day in your life when you did not look into a mirror? Can you recall ever looking into a mirror without feeling an emotion? Pride, perhaps, if you are fond of the way you look or pleased with something you have done. Concern, perhaps, if you are doubtful about your appearance or your behavior. Mirrors reflect what is most essential to all of us: the sense of self, the center of our experiencing of the world, of our awareness. Mirrors reflect our physical selves, of course, and they also demonstrate how important our physical selves are to the personal selves within that cannot be seen or touched.

The self is an abstraction. It cannot be felt or measured in a physical sense. It is a concept that serves as a shorthand for clusters of perceptions, attitudes, feelings, thoughts, and all those interior parts of ourselves that can be experienced by us alone. We can try to explain to other people what is taking place in our selves, but no one else can directly experience our selves.

Some psychologists are reluctant to talk about the concept of self, because the current trend in the behavioral sciences is to talk about things that can somehow be measured and quantified, preferably things that can be touched directly by some instrument. Yet any discussion of human behavior and experience that excludes the sense of self seems incomplete and dissatisfying. For the self is the essence of being human.

We think of the self as that portion of our experiencing that attempts to organize our own private world and to give us direction. The self asks many questions: "Who am I?" "Where am I headed?" Throughout life we undergo a series of periods of self-questioning, of self-examination: "Should I go to college?" "Should I look for a job or go into business for myself?" "Have I come as far as I thought I would by this age?" "Have I made the right decisions?" "Have I done the right things with my life?"

Teachers do not have the answers to these questions, of course. Nor are they to be found in textbooks. When clients ask them in psychotherapy, psychologists are likely to respond, "What do *you* think?" For each of us, the answers may be very different. But for all our hesitancies and confusions, for all our self-doubts and even our self-delusions, we are in the best positions to know our own selves. Others can make the effort to know our selves by paying close attention to our words and our behavior. But only we can directly experience our selves.

In order to answer questions about who we are and where we are going, we shall see that we must look inward as well as outward. For the answers to whether we have made the proper decisions and invested ourselves in seeking the proper goals ultimately depend on our own personal values. Other people can sometimes be of help when our values have become muddied to us and we cannot differentiate them from the values of others. They can provide an encouraging atmosphere in which we can search for our own values. But ultimately the values we adopt must be our own. Otherwise, our apparent goals will be meaningless to us and our behavior will seem meaningless.

This Is Me, No One Else: The Differentiation of the Self. The process of looking at ourselves begins in childhood. We must learn to distinguish *that which is me* from all *that which is not me*. During the first months of life, children may live in a state of oceanic oneness with the world. Everything is brought to the mouth—lipped, sucked, gummed, perhaps chewed, possibly swallowed. Children soon learn that some things are hard, cold, sharp, or bitter—to be spit out, not to be integrated as part of the self.

Children also learn that mother is not always there when needed, that mother and the self are separate beings. The oneness of the womb is shattered. The challenges of individual life begin prior to the development of language and the clear definition of the self. As children explore the sights, smells, and other sensations of their early environments, they gradually come to distinguish a sound that is often repeated and seems to help separate them from every other living and nonliving thing: a **name**. Names are our first labels for ourselves. They are an intrinsic part of us. Not only do they help us understand who we are; they can also give us feelings about what we are.

Name. A word or phrase by which an individual is known and separated from those persons or things that are not the individual.

Love at first sight? It may be that not only humans have a sense of self.

The Self

33

What's in a Name? A Great Deal.

> *Alice:* Must a name mean something?
> *Humpty-Dumpty:* Of course it must. . . . My name means the shape I am. . . .
> With a name like yours, you might be any shape, almost.
>
> LEWIS CARROLL, *Through the Looking-Glass*

President James Earl Carter? Who? President Jim Carter? Not quite. Names do more than fill the lines on report cards and driver's licenses. They convey something about you as a person. Jimmy Carter wants people to think of him as warm, friendly, down-to-earth. The stuffy formality of James Earl Carter just would not ring true.

The slang for "name" in the Old West was "handle." Names give us one of our first handles on life—a way others react to us, and a way we grow to think about ourselves. Sometimes we adjust to our names. Sometimes we shape our names, like Jimmy Carter, to adjust the expectations of other people.

The "voyages of the Starship Enterprise" were more dynamic with Captain Kirk and Mr. Spock than they might have been with Captain Weinstein and Mr. Garbinski. The Reggie candy bar appears to provide more quick energy than the *Reginald*. Tony Curtis and Marilyn Monroe draw better at the box office than Bernie Schwartz and Norma Jean Baker. "Dr. J" is more a wizard on the basketball court than is Julius Erving. The Fonz has *cool*—Arthur Fonzarelli is just another nice guy. Richard Starkey is a factory worker in Liverpool. Ringo Starr is a—well—star. Alfred Hitchcock, on the other, is no Alfie. Ernest Hemingway is not an Ernie. Walter Cronkite is more dignified than Wally.

Mirrors reflect what is most essential to all of us: the sense of self.

"Sincerely yours, Jim Hartwig. No—make that: Sincerely yours, Dick Mason."

What we call ourselves reflects our attitudes about ourselves. Are you a Bob or a Robert? A Dick or a Richard? A Liz or an Elizabeth? A Pam or a Pamela? Shakespeare wrote that a rose by any other name would smell as sweet, but perhaps a rose by the name of skunkweed would impress us as smelling just plain awful.

Our names form part of our personal identities. Names can help shape our identities. Psychiatrist Eric Berne wrote that the names parents give their children often suggest what they want their children to become:

> Charles and Frederick were kings and emperors. A boy who is steadfastly called Charles or Frederick by his mother, and insists that his associates call him that, lives a different life-style from one who is commonly hailed as Chuck or Fred, while Charlie and Freddie are likely to be horses of still another color. Naming a boy after his father or a girl after her mother is usually a purposeful act on the part of the parents, and puts an obligation on the offspring which they may not care to fulfill, or may even actively rebel against, so that their whole life plan is permeated by a slight bitterness or an active resentment [1976, p. 162].

Berne then refers us to the names of two world-famous neurologists: H. Head and W. R. Brain.

Names are often a clue as to how we view ourselves. Sometimes our names work to our social advantage, sometimes not. Just ask "The Boy Named Sue" in the song by Johnny (not Jonathan) Cash.

Psychologists, too, have found that different names mean different things to people. In a British study (Marcus 1976), "John" received high ratings on kindness and trustworthiness. Tonys were considered sociable. Agneses? Well, Agneses were considered old, and both Agneses and Matildas were rated unattractive. Robins were bright and young. Anns were nonaggressive.

Do unusual names create problems for children but contribute to success in adulthood? In an American study (Marcus 1976), men with names like David, John, Michael, and Robert were considered better, stronger, and more active than men with names like Ivan, Raymond, or Dale. Children with common names also tend to be more popular (McDavid & Harari 1966). Though children with uncommon names may experience social difficulties, and boys named Sue have more than their share of barroom brawls, adults with unusual names seem to fare better. College professors and army officers frequently have unusual names: *Omar* Bradley, *Dwight* Eisenhower. Richard Zweigenhaft (1977) of Guilford College discovered high frequencies of unique, even odd names in *Who's Who*. Zweigenhaft also surveyed the names of eleven thousand North Carolina high school students who had participated in a state-wide talent study, and found that boys and girls with unusual names had more than their fair share of academic achievements. Do some people with unusual first names bear the brunt of social ostracism during childhood and develop the desire to "show them"?

Now we turn our attention to three aspects of the self: the physical self, the social self, and the personal self.

The Physical Self

Physical self. The physical person that is part of the individual. Physical features such as height, weight, complexion, and so on.

It should not be surprising that the physical person you carry around with you plays an enormously influential role in your self-concept. You may tower above others or literally constantly look up to them. Others may look at you and smile, or they may pretend you are not there. You may assume that you will be up to new athletic challenges, or you may have already come to believe that the sporting life does not include you. The book *Our Bodies, Ourselves*, written by the Boston Women's Health Book Collective (1976), emphasizes repeatedly how intertwined the business of having female features and structures is with the identity of women. Men's organs and features are no less important in contributing to their self-concepts.

When the **physical self** is healthy and attractive, we feel secure in meeting the challenges of relating to others. But if we are unattractive, or have suffered

Sign Here

SIGN ON THE DOTTED LINE

Sign your name here: _____

Now sign your name as if you were the President of the United States: _____

What do we reveal about ourselves through our signatures? Were the signatures as yourself and as President of equal size? Psychologist Richard Zweigenhaft (1970) asked students at Wesleyan University to sign both ways, and found that 75 percent signed their names larger as President. The presidential signatures were also often less legible. Status, it seems, is associated with larger signatures and lower legibility. Witness the scratchings of many physicians.

In another study, Zweigenhaft found that professors at Wesleyan signed their names larger than individuals of lesser status, such as students and blue-collar university employees.

YOUR SIGNATURE, PLEASE

Your full name is John David Smith, but you may write it differently at different times: John Smith, John D. Smith, J. D. Smith, J. Smith, and so on. Which form or forms do you prefer? When?

Try this experiment before you sneak a look below. Take the name John David Smith and either sign it in full or use an abbreviated form that appeals to you as though you were signing:

    a job application

    a note to your teacher

    a petition

    a personal letter to a friend

    a check

    a note to your work supervisor

    a love letter

    a letter to the President

    a complaint to the city about collection of refuse

    a Letter-to-the-Editor of your newspaper

What form or forms did you use most often? J. D. Smith? John Smith? J. Smith? J. David Smith? Just John? Johnny?

In a study of New Zealanders (Boshier 1973) on a task similar to the above, J. D. Smith was the most common form, followed by J. Smith and John Smith.

Use of different forms appeared to reflect differences in personality. For instance, John Smiths were more liberal than J. or J. D. Smiths. Are liberals more willing to disclose information about themselves?

Richard Zweigenhaft (1975) replicated this experiment with junior-college students in California. The majority (61 percent) of the students preferred John Smith, 30 percent used J. D. Smith, and the other 9 percent used a variety of other styles most often. Contrary to the New Zealand study, Zweigen-haft found no relationship between signature and personality. High "self-disclosers" did not use John Smith more often. But men and older respondents were more likely to use their middle names. A desire for dignity?

disabling illnesses or accidents, we may develop negative self-appraisals. In "At Seventeen," songwriter Janis Ian expressed her dismay at being a teenage girl with a "ravaged face":

I learned the truth at seventeen
That love was meant for beauty queens
And high school girls with clear-skinned smiles
Who married young, and then retired
The valentines I never knew
The Friday night charades of youth
Were spent on one more beautiful
At seventeen, I learned the truth
  And those of us with ravaged faces
  lacking in the social graces
  desperately remained at home
  inventing lovers on the phone
  who called to say, "Come dance with me"
  and murmured vague obscenities
  It isn't all it seems at seventeen
. . . The world was younger than today
And dreams were all they gave for free
To ugly duckling girls like me. . . .

The Self

Each of us has a rather unique physical self which plays an enormously influential role in our self-concepts.

While some aspects of our physical self such as weight and length of hair may change rapidly (though for weight, sometimes more grudgingly than we'd like), our sex and race are considered permanent aspects of our physical identity. Your sex and race are determined permanently at birth. Or are they?

There are some people who feel trapped in the body of the opposite sex. These people are called **transsexuals,** and they feel that they are really members of the opposite sex who received the wrong genitals through a mistake of nature. As a result of sex-reassignment surgery, many transsexuals are better able to live out the life-styles consistent with their sense of self—as in the case of tennis player, Renée Richards, who was surgically changed from a man to a woman.

There are also some rare instances of children who are born with the external genitals of one sex and the internal structures and genetic code of the opposite sex. John Money (1965, 1976) of Johns Hopkins University studied two children who possessed the female genetic type and internal structures, but what appeared to be male genitals. One of these children was labeled and raised as a boy. By the age of five he displayed traditional masculine behavior and held a firm personal identity as a boy. The other was identified as a girl and raised accordingly. At the age of five she had a firm identity as a girl, and showed sex-typed behavior appropriate to her assigned sex. Researchers believe that gender identity and sex-typed behavior are determined more by our life experiences than by biological factors.

Our racial identity is also considered a fixed measure of our physical selves. But what would it be like to experience life as a member of a different race? One man, John Howard Griffen, sought to understand firsthand the experiences of blacks living in the South in the 1950s by changing his skin color from white to black for a period of several weeks. Through the use of skin-darkening drugs, ultraviolet rays, and skin dyes, Griffen was able to pass as a black man among blacks and whites alike, and he recounted his experiences in his book *Black Like Me* (1960). Within a few days of his conversion, his iden-

Transsexual (trans-SEX-you-ul). An individual who feels trapped in the body of a member of the opposite sex, and who may wish to change sexes through surgery.

The Challenge
and the Self

38

tity as a black man became more than skin deep. He soon learned what it felt like to be called "nigger" and "boy," to experience stares of contempt from white people, to sit in a "sphinxlike," dumbfounded manner on public buses, and to be denied the use of race-restricted rest rooms, lodging, and cafeterias. He felt united with the other blacks with whom he shared meals and lodging, and began to appreciate the humanity and dignity of his "fellow" blacks. When his skin color returned to white, he wrote, "I was once more a first-class citizen, all doors into cafes, rest rooms, libraries, movies, concerts, schools, and churches were suddenly open to me. After so long I could not adjust to it. A sense of exultant liberation flooded through me. I crossed over to a restaurant and entered. I took a seat beside white men at the counter and the waitress smiled at me. It was a miracle. I ordered food and was served and was not molested. No one said, 'What're you doing in here, nigger?'" (p. 130).

For most of us, adjusting to some traits that define the self-concept—such as sex, race, and height—means self-acceptance. But other physical traits can be modified: weight, athletic performance, hair style. These are parts of the physical self where our own determination, decisions, and actions are generally more influential than our heredity.

The Social Self

It's their first date. He's Mr. Debonair. She's Ms. Ever-So-Cool. He projects an urbane, sophisticated elegance; she, a slightly reserved and mysterious allure. By the end of the evening they are entranced with one another. But they have only come to know each other's masks.

The **social self** refers to the various masks or social roles we play in various situations—suitor, student, worker, husband, wife, mother, father, citizen, leader, follower.

Playing social roles and wearing masks is a natural and adaptive response to the social world. In a job interview you may project an image of self-confidence and sincere interest in hard work. You may refrain from expressing self-doubts and ambivalent feelings about the company. On the other hand, you may take a calculated risk and reveal some relatively minor personal shortcomings, balanced with your expressed desire to work hard, in order to impress the interviewer with your honesty and lack of conceit. You will probably have prepared several such "scripts" and approach the interview as if it were a stage performance, picking the particular script that you predict will maximize your chances for employment.

Are these social roles and masks merely lies and deceptions? Usually not. The social roles we enact or the masks we wear do contain elements of our inner selves. Our job hunter is likely to possess both strengths and shortcomings, merely electing to show the former and not the latter. You may also be exceptionally respectful when you are stopped by a highway patrolman. This is not dishonesty. It is your attempt to meet the requirements of the situation.

However, when our entire lives are played behind masks, it may be difficult to discover our real selves. You may have been projecting an image of dainty femininity with your husband or boyfriend for so long that you begin to question whether you have it "in you" to be assertive and strong. When you begin to get in touch with the "real you" and let your true self speak for you rather than through the masks you wear, you are moving in the direction of **authenticity,** of becoming your own person. A mark of a mature and comple-

For many years, Dr. Richard Raskin, like other transsexuals, felt trapped in the body of a member of the opposite sex. After a sex-change operation and hormone treatments, he became Renee Richards, known on the women's professional tennis circuit.

Social self. The self we show to others through playing social roles, such as parent, child, employer, lover, citizen.

Authenticity (aw-then-TISS-uh-tee). Expressing one's own true feelings, being spontaneous and genuine, dropping social roles—when necessary—to express real feelings.

"I'LL TAKE THE RAQUEL WELCH MODEL, PLEASE"

Imagine a futuristic society in which plastic surgery was perfected to such an extent that you could literally have your entire body sculpted to your exact specifications. You would leaf through a "Whole Human Catalog" and select the dimensions of face and form that you would prefer. Zap! Your physical self would come out custom-made. But we wonder if such nonclassic forms as Barbra Streisand's nose or Kirk Douglas's cleft chin would even survive in this mix-n-match society? Would anybody select less than "ideal" features to lend an air of individuality to his physical self, or would there be one perfect body matched to the perfect face?

How satisfied are you with your physical features? Check your responses to the following questionnaire and then compare your attitudes about your body with those of a nationwide sample of 2,000 *Psychology Today* readers (Berscheid, Walster, & Bohrnstedt 1973).

Directions: Checkmark the most appropriate response which describes your feelings about the following parts of your body.

	Quite or Extremely Dissatisfied	Somewhat Dissatisfied	Somewhat Satisfied	Quite or Extremely Satisfied
My overall body appearance	_____	_____		_____
FACE				
overall facial attractiveness	_____	_____	_____	_____
hair	_____	_____	_____	_____
eyes	_____	_____	_____	_____
ears	_____	_____	_____	_____
nose	_____	_____	_____	_____
mouth	_____	_____	_____	_____
teeth	_____	_____	_____	_____
voice	_____	_____	_____	_____
chin	_____	_____	_____	_____
complexion	_____	_____	_____	_____
EXTREMITIES				
shoulders	_____	_____		_____
arms	_____	_____	_____	_____
hands	_____	_____	_____	_____
feet	_____	_____		
MID-TORSO				
size of abdomen	_____	_____	_____	_____
buttocks (seat)	_____	_____	_____	_____
hips (upper thighs)	_____	_____	_____	_____
legs and ankles	_____	_____		_____
HEIGHT, WEIGHT, AND TONE				
height	_____	_____	_____	_____
weight	_____	_____	_____	_____
general muscle tone or development	_____	_____	_____	_____

**Table 2.1 Results of the *Psychology Today* Poll (in percentages)
Satisfaction and Dissatisfaction with Body Parts**

	Quite or Extremely Dissatisfied		Somewhat Dissatisfied		Somewhat Satisfied		Quite or Extremely Satisfied	
	Female	Male	Female	Male	Female	Male	Female	Male
Overall Body Appearance	7	4	16	11	32	30	45	55
FACE								
Overall facial attractiveness	3	2	8	6	28	31	61	61
hair	6	6	13	14	28	22	53	58
eyes	1	1	5	6	14	12	80	81
ears	2	1	5	4	10	13	83	82
nose	5	2	18	14	22	20	55	64
mouth	2	1	5	5	20	19	73	75
teeth	11	10	19	18	20	26	50	46
voice	3	3	15	12	27	27	55	58
chin	4	3	9	8	20	20	67	69
complexion	8	7	20	15	24	20	48	58
EXTREMITIES								
shoulders	2	3	11	8	19	22	68	67
arms	5	2	11	11	22	25	62	62
hands	5	1	14	7	21	17	60	75
feet	6	3	14	8	23	19	57	70
MID-TORSO								
size of abdomen	19	11	31	25	21	22	29	42
buttocks (seat)	17	6	26	14	20	24	37	56
hips (upper thighs)	22	3	27	9	19	24	32	64
legs and ankles	8	4	17	7	23	20	52	69
HEIGHT, WEIGHT, AND TONE								
height	3	3	10	10	15	20	72	67
weight	21	10	27	25	21	22	31	43
general muscle tone or development	9	7	21	18	32	30	38	45

Table 2.1 suggests that most respondents to the *Psychology Today* poll had a positive self-image about their physical selves. It seems that women are generally less satisfied with their bodies than men, perhaps because society places a greater value on female attractiveness. Both sexes, it may be added, were generally approving of their sexual features, with only one woman in four expressing dissatisfaction with her breasts, and an even smaller percentage of men, 15 percent, expressing dissatisfaction with the size of their penises. When the investigators looked at the responses from people of various age groups, they found, unexpectedly, no major decline in body satisfaction with increasing age. In fact, older men were more satisfied with their mid-torso than were younger men, and older respondents of both sexes

(*Continued*)

[*Continued from page 42*]

were more satisfied with their complexion—presumably because adolescent acne problems were no longer a worry. However, older respondents were less satisfied with their teeth, and older women voiced higher levels of dissatisfaction with the objects of so many detergent commercials: their hands.

With the general positive thrust of self-satisfaction we find among these respondents to the poll, would you think that a futuristic clinic specializing in read-to-go body reshaping might suffer for business

after all? It is difficult to say. We must keep in mind that *Psychology Today* readers do not represent the American public at large, and that the who readers responded to the questionnaire might not even be representative of all *Psychology Today* readers. It is possible, for example, that people with very negative body images tend to ignore such questionnaires so that there would be a positive bias in the results. In any survey or experiment, it is very important to attempt to select samples that represent the persons to whom we wish to generalize the results most fully.

Is this *Playboy* "bunny" (a Duane Hanson statue, by the way, not a real person) behaving authentically or playing a social role in order to earn a living?

menting relationship is the degree to which partners can be authentic with one another—to drop the masks that separate them. Without authenticity, life may be the exchange of one cardboard mask for another.

The Personal Self

In Mark Twain's *The Prince and the Pauper*, a young prince is sabotaged by enemies of the throne. He seeks to salvage the kingdom by exchanging places with Tom Canty, a pauper, who looks exactly like him. It is a learning experience for both. The pauper learns how others will flatter you and praise you when you are in a position of power. There are hilarious moments as the pauper adopts princelike ways and hones his rough edges, of which there are many. The prince, on the other hand, must stand or fall on his own for the first time. Merit, not social position, must now support him. But there is compensation: for the first time the common people tell him what they think, not what they believe he wants to hear.

Toward the end of the tale there is a dispute: Who is the prince? Who is Tom Canty? The two lads are identical in appearance, and Tom has acquired the necessary social skills. Why does it matter? Both, perhaps, can lead the realm as well. Yet the court officials seek the one whose personal self—whose *inner identity*—is that of the prince. There is more to life than appearances, they recognize. The ending of the story is happy. The true prince is identified, the palace intrigue is exposed, and the evildoers are punished. Tom earns the permanent protection of the throne.

The personal self is the self seen by you and you alone. It is the day-to-day experience of being you, of experiencing a changing display of sights and sounds and feelings to which you hold the only ticket of admission. It is the inner experience of being you, and you alone.

A most important feature of the personal self is one's own **value system**, one's personal sense of priorities, of what is important.

Values

"What should I do with my life?" "What is right for me?" Janice was concerned about her overeating because she valued slenderness and self-control. Jennifer

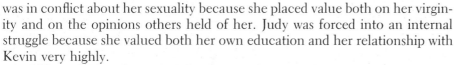

The person at the left plays the role of stockbroker, while the person at the right enacts the role of police officer.

was in conflict about her sexuality because she placed value both on her virginity and on the opinions others held of her. Judy was forced into an internal struggle because she valued both her own education and her relationship with Kevin very highly.

Values, ethics, the personal sense of right and wrong are essential parts of the self. Values are derived from relationships with others as well as from our own logical processes. It is not surprising that our values sometimes reflect the values of our parents, our teachers, and close acquaintances. It is not surprising that our values often differ from those of people close to us—and that when these differences are significant, they can give birth to intense interpersonal conflict.

Different people have different values, yet almost all people think of themselves as having values and as trying to do the right things in life. Values, in fact, sometimes lead us to **rationalize** or explain away acts that are not in keeping with our values. Values form an integral part of our identities. During periods of life when our values are in flux, such as during adolescence, we may experience what Erik Erikson has labeled an identity crisis. Behavior seems purposeless, without meaning, when it does not grow out of personal values.

Values give birth to personal goals and tend to place limits on the means we feel comfortable in using to attain our goals. Determining values is an essential step in the growth of the self. It is a personal step. It requires looking inward. We shall be asking you to take time out from your books and your homework assignments to examine your values as they relate to critical areas in your life—your career, sex roles, the formation of intimate relationships, the expression of your own feelings. Sometimes we shall ask you to challenge your values, to test their logic and the emotions attached to them. But values that are authentic and genuine must fit with the sense of self.

THE SELF-CONCEPT

Your **self-concept** is your impression or your sense of yourself. It includes your concept of the traits or characteristics that you consider important, and your personal evaluation of where you stand in respect to these traits.

You may think of these traits as existing along dimensions such as those

Value system. The individual's sense of what is right and what is wrong, of what is more important than what.
Value. The worth of an object or of behavior, that which is desirable for its own sake, a social principle.
Ethics (ETH-icks). Standards of conduct or behavior, moral judgments.
Rationalization (RASH-un-ul-eye-ZAY-shun). In psychoanalysis, a way of explaining unacceptable behavior so that it becomes acceptable or justified.

Self-concept. The individual's perception of himself or herself, including personal traits and an evaluation of these traits. The self-concept includes the self-identity, self-esteem, and the ideal self or self-ideal.

The Self

43

VALUES, ETHICS, AND PROSTITUTES

Almost all people tend to think of themselves as having values, as being ethical, as trying to do the right things in life. We even hear of "honor among thieves." We may disagree with other people's ways of looking at life, but we would probably be surprised if people with whom we disagreed suddenly confessed, "Yes, you're right and I'm wrong. You have logic and decency on your side. My only aim has been to hurt, to deceive, and to destroy."

Prostitutes have long struggled with self-concepts influenced by the stigma of the labels others have placed on them. Yet prostitutes also have a sense of self and undergo crises in identity. We need not be surprised that *Coyote Howls*, the newsletter of an organization of prostitutes based in San Francisco, printed the following code in a recent issue.

CODE OF ETHICS AMONG PROSTITUTES

- No prostitute who wishes to be viewed as a professional shall contact the employers or families of customers or prospective customers to expose their involvement in prostitution.
- No prostitute may expose the identity of another prostitute to employers, families, or friends.
- No prostitute may encourage or coerce another person into prostitution.
- No prostitute may steal or rob another prostitute's book or list of customers. Violation of this is treated like petty theft or robbery.
- If a customer approaches a prostitute, another prostitute may not approach the customer until she/he sees that the conversation is ended with the first prostitute, unless she/he is asked to approach the customer by the customer or by the first prostitute.
- Every prostitute is expected to report to other prostitutes those customers they know to be dangerous. These reports should be exchanged among working cohorts, reported to the local hooker organization and/or the police.
- When one prostitute asks another to work with her/him on a specific customer, a 50/50 split is reasonable.
- A prostitute may not purposely cause another prostitute harm within the scope of the business.*

Are codes of ethics unique to prostitution? What other professions offering services have codes of ethics that address issues such as the confidentiality of clients, relationships with the clients of other practitioners, and splitting fees? What role do such codes play in solidifying the identity of groups of professionals?

* Reprinted from *Coyote Howls* 5, no. 1 (Spring 1978): 9.

below, which have been used by researchers into the self-concept (e.g., Pervin & Lilly 1967; Schwartz & Tangri 1965; Sherwood 1962; Siegel, Rathus, & Ruppert 1973). To define your own self-concept—that is, the way you think of yourself—with respect to the traits listed below, place a check mark in one of the seven spaces for each dimension according to this example for the first dimension, fair-unfair:

1 = extremely fair
2 = rather fair
3 = somewhat fair
4 = equally fair and unfair, or not sure
5 = somewhat unfair
6 = rather unfair
7 = extremely unfair

The Challenge and the Self

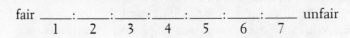

fair ___:___:___:___:___:___:___ unfair
     1   2   3   4   5   6   7

independent	___:___:___:___:___:___:___	dependent
	1 2 3 4 5 6 7	
religious	___:___:___:___:___:___:___	irreligious
	1 2 3 4 5 6 7	
unselfish	___:___:___:___:___:___:___	selfish
	1 2 3 4 5 6 7	
self-confident	___:___:___:___:___:___:___	lacking confidence
	1 2 3 4 5 6 7	
competent	___:___:___:___:___:___:___	incompetent
	1 2 3 4 5 6 7	
important	___:___:___:___:___:___:___	unimportant
	1 2 3 4 5 6 7	
attractive	___:___:___:___:___:___:___	unattractive
	1 2 3 4 5 6 7	
educated	___:___:___:___:___:___:___	uneducated
	1 2 3 4 5 6 7	
sociable	___:___:___:___:___:___:___	unsociable
	1 2 3 4 5 6 7	
kind	___:___:___:___:___:___:___	cruel
	1 2 3 4 5 6 7	
wise	___:___:___:___:___:___:___	foolish
	1 2 3 4 5 6 7	
graceful	___:___:___:___:___:___:___	awkward
	1 2 3 4 5 6 7	
intelligent	___:___:___:___:___:___:___	unintelligent
	1 2 3 4 5 6 7	
artistic	___:___:___:___:___:___:___	inartistic
	1 2 3 4 5 6 7	
tall	___:___:___:___:___:___:___	short
	1 2 3 4 5 6 7	
obese	___:___:___:___:___:___:___	skinny
	1 2 3 4 5 6 7	

The self-concept is multifaceted. It contains your evaluation of your personal worth, or your self-esteem; and your sense of who and what you would like to be, your ideal self. We shall see that self-esteem depends on many factors, including the approval of others, competence, and the discrepancy between the self-concept and the ideal self—the distance between the way you see yourself and the way you think you ought to be.

Self-Esteem

> Oh, that God the gift would give us
> To see ourselves as others see us.
> ROBERT BURNS

Actually, the Scottish poet Robert Burns was being unduly pessimistic. We do tend to see ourselves as others see us. This is where **self-esteem,** or self-approval, begins—with parental love. Children who have been loved and

Self-esteem. Self-approval. One's regard, respect, or favorable opinion of oneself.

RANKING YOUR VALUES.
WHAT IS IMPORTANT TO YOU?

Freedom, recognition, beauty, eternal salvation, a world without war—which is most important to you? Are people who put personal pleasure first likely to behave differently from people who give priority to salvation, wisdom, or personal achievement?

Psychologist Milton Rokeach of Washington State University devised a survey of values that allows people to rank their life goals according to their personal order of importance. How will you rank yours? Eighteen values are listed below in alphabetical order. Select the value that is most important to you and write a 1 next to it in Column I. Then choose your next most important value and write a 2 next to it in the same column. Continue until you have ranked all eighteen values. This should take ten minutes to half an hour.

	I	II	III
A COMFORTABLE LIFE a prosperous life			
AN EXCITING LIFE a stimulating, active life			
A SENSE OF ACCOMPLISHMENT lasting contribution			
A WORLD AT PEACE free of war and conflict			
A WORLD OF BEAUTY beauty of nature and the arts			
EQUALITY brotherhood, equal opportunity for all			
FAMILY SECURITY taking care of loved ones			
FREEDOM independence, free choice			
HAPPINESS contentedness			
INNER HARMONY freedom from inner conflict			

cherished by their parents come to view themselves as being worthy of that love. They become capable of loving and accepting themselves.

While your self-concept is your conception of yourself along a variety of dimensions, your self-esteem rests on your approval or disapproval of your positioning on them. Your self-esteem is a personal judgment of your worthiness, and it is based on your perception of the discrepancy, or distance, between the way you see yourself and the way you think you ought to be—that is, the discrepancy between your self-concept and your ideal self.

Psychologist Stanley Coopersmith (1967) looked at self-esteem patterns among fifth- and sixth-grade boys and found that boys with high self-esteem were more likely to come from homes in which parents were strict but not

The Challenge
and the Self

MATURE LOVE sexual and spiritual intimacy			
NATIONAL SECURITY protection from attack			
PLEASURE an enjoyable, leisurely life			
SALVATION saved, eternal life			
SELF-RESPECT self-esteem			
SOCIAL RECOGNITION respect, admiration			
TRUE FRIENDSHIP close companionship			
WISDOM a mature understanding of life			

Now put yourself in the place of someone with whom you are very close, perhaps a relative, perhaps an old, trusted friend. Rank the eighteen values as you believe that person would in Column II. Now put yourself in the place of someone with whom you have experienced serious disagreements, someone with whom you just have not been able to get along. Rank the eighteen values as you feel this person would in Column III.

Now compare the rankings of the values in the three columns. Are your own values ranked more similarly to those of your close friend or to those of your adversary? Is it possible that you and the individual represented in Column III have had your difficulties because you order your values quite differently?

Now compare the ranking of your own values with those of the Rokeach samples at the end of this chapter (p. 52). Does your own ranking appear to be similar to those of students at these two universities? If not, what are the differences? What do you think these differences might predict about your own behavior as compared to theirs?

Finally, compare your ranking with those of some of the other people in your class. Do you seem to be largely in agreement, or are there major differences? Do you seem to agree with the majority view? How do you feel about your relationships with other people in the class? Is this predictable from comparing your values to theirs?

harsh or cruel in discipline. These parents were also highly involved with their sons' activities. Parents of children with low self-esteem were more permissive, but harsh in disciplining.

Parental involvement with children with high self-esteem may have communicated a sense of worthiness to the children. The setting of strict limits may also be an expression of caring coupled with a demand that children become competent at coping with the challenges of life. Greater permissiveness may be a sign of lack of interest. Placing reasonable demands on children may foster competence, and competence in intellectual tasks (Flippo & Lewinson 1971) and in the mastery of skills, such as swimming (Koocher 1971), has been shown to heighten self-esteem.

The Self

Once self-esteem has been established, it remains a rather enduring characteristic. Coopersmith found a significant relationship between his subjects' self-esteem levels at a three-year interval. We may all have failure experiences now and then, but individuals whose sense of self-worth is initially high will probably retain greater faith in themselves and make more persevering efforts to adjust. Sadly, low self-esteem can become a self-fulfilling prophecy: the individual with a low self-evaluation may carve out little to boast about in life.

The Ideal Self

In addition to our concepts of who and how we are, we also have concepts of what we ought to be or should be. This is the **ideal self.**

How about you? What "oughts" and "shoulds" are you carrying around? You already checked off the places where you thought you fit according to a list of traits on pages 44–45. Now check off places along these dimensions again—but this time according to the ways you think you ought to be. (Don't look back to pages 44–45 until you are done.)

Ideal self. One's perception of what one ought to be or should be. A model of perfection for the self. Also called the self-ideal.

MY IDEAL SELF

	1	2	3	4	5	6	7	
fair	:	:	:	:	:	:		unfair
independent	:	:	:	:	:	:		dependent
religious	:	:	:	:	:	:		irreligious
unselfish	:	:	:	:	:	:		selfish
self-confident	:	:	:	:	:	:		lacking confidence
competent	:	:	:	:	:	:		incompetent
important	:	:	:	:	:	:		unimportant
attractive	:	:	:	:	:	:		unattractive
educated	:	:	:	:	:	:		uneducated
sociable	:	:	:	:	:	:		unsociable
kind	:	:	:	:	:	:		cruel
wise	:	:	:	:	:	:		foolish
graceful	:	:	:	:	:	:		awkward
intelligent	:	:	:	:	:	:		unintelligent

artistic ____:____:____:____:____:____:____ inartistic
　　　　1　　2　　3　　4　　5　　6　　7

tall ____:____:____:____:____:____:____ short
　　　1　　2　　3　　4　　5　　6　　7

obese ____:____:____:____:____:____:____ skinny
　　　　1　　2　　3　　4　　5　　6　　7

STOP! You were just about to turn back to pages 44–45 again, weren't you? Just give us another minute first. Below is a summary list of the seventeen traits listed above. Select a small number of traits that make you feel rather pleased with yourself, and then an equal number of traits that make you feel rather disappointed with yourself. What, you only have one "bad" trait? Then select only one good trait as well.

It should not be too difficult to come up with four or five good traits (or pluses) and another four or five negative traits (or minuses). Go through the list and place a plus sign (+) in front of the good traits you have chosen, and a minus sign (−) in front of the negative traits. Remember: select an equal number of each.

____ fair-unfair　　　　　　　　____ educated-uneducated
____ independent-dependent　　____ sociable-unsociable
____ religious-irreligious　　　____ kind-cruel
____ unselfish-selfish　　　　　____ wise-foolish
____ self-confident–lacking confi-　____ graceful-awkward
　　　 dence　　　　　　　　　　____ intelligent-unintelligent
____ competent-incompetent　　____ artistic-inartistic
____ important-unimportant　　____ tall-short
____ attractive-unattractive　　____ obese-skinny

Now you may go back to pages 44–45 and make some comparisons. Compare your self-concept with your ideal self. Is there a tendency for your ideal self more often to be closer to the positive end of the dimension? Or at least the end of the dimension that is more positive for you? (That is, some wish they were taller, some that they were shorter.)

Now note the **discrepancies** or differences between your self-concept and your ideal self for the dimensions that you assigned pluses and minuses above. For instance, let's say that you are five feet nine but wish you could be a star center in basketball. The discrepancy between your self-concept (S) and your ideal self (I) might look like this:

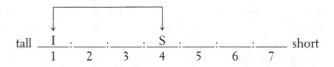

The discrepancy between your self-concept and your ideal self on this dimension is 4 − 1 = 3. Or, more generally,

Discrepancy = Ideal Self − Self-Concept

Discrepancy (dis-KREP-pan-see). A difference or lack of agreement between the self-concept and the ideal self, or between two thoughts, or thoughts and behavior. Discrepancies between the self-concept and the ideal self may motivate striving to become like the ideal.

Figure out the discrepancies for the dimensions that please you and the (equal number of) dimensions that displease you. Add together the discrepancies on each side. For instance,

_+_	fair-unfair	_−_	competent-incompetent
_+_	kind-cruel	_−_	educated-uneducated
_+_	sociable-unsociable	_−_	wise-foolish

if you placed plus signs before fairness, kindness, and sociability, add the discrepancies for these three dimensions together. Then add the discrepancies for the three dimensions (competence, education, and wisdom) about which you are disappointed. Compare the total discrepancies for each side. We shall be pleased to take bets that the total for the dimensions that disappoint you is greater than the total for the dimensions about which you are pleased.

Why are we confident about our bet? Simply because the traits that please you contribute to your self-esteem. And your self-esteem is related to the discrepancies between your self-concept and your ideal self. The closer you are to your ideal self, the higher your self-esteem. The farther away you are, the bleaker your self-evaluation looks to you.

How can we raise our self-esteem? Let us count the ways. First, you can act to improve yourself so that your self-concept will approach your ideal self. Second, you can challenge the realism of your ideal self. Are you shooting too high? If you are five-three and are practicing jump shots as though you were six-eleven, you are indeed shooting too high. Challenge the standards you have set for yourself. Can you hope to meet them? If not, can you adjust them or make them more realistic for you? Psychologist Albert Ellis (1977) points out that our "oughts" and "shoulds" often guarantee that we make ourselves absolutely miserable by constantly shooting too high and neglecting to pat ourselves on the back for our more realistic accomplishments.

There are other ways in which we can raise our self-esteem. We can decide that the dimensions on which we do well are the truly important dimensions in our lives, and that the other dimensions are less important or irrelevant. The short basketball player may shoot for A's in chemistry. The less attractive individual may become more educated and wise. Accentuating the positive is an excellent way to adjust to our self-concepts and raise our self-esteem—unless the dimension we decide to classify as irrelevant is actually so important to us that we cannot ignore it. Then, perhaps, we should again try challenging our self-standard (ideal self) for that dimension or strive harder to achieve our standard. It may be difficult to ignore the fact that you are an atheist if your profession is that of a priest or rabbi.

Where do our self-ideals or self-standards come from? Many of them reflect standards of people and groups who are quite close to us, especially our parents. Our love for our parents and our fear of their disapproval appear to work together to influence us to try to be like them, to **internalize** or incorporate their standards as parts of ourselves. We may also adopt the values and ideals of groups, such as church groups or peer groups, to which we belong. In the case of adolescents who adopt **deviant** standards, it is often the case that inability to compete according to middle-class measuring rods of academic excellence and family status contributes to the displacing of middle-class values with the standards of the gang (Rathus & Siegel 1973; Senna, Rathus, & Siegel 1974; Siegel, Rathus, & Ruppert 1973). Dimensions of toughness and independence may become more important than standards of education and kindness.

Internalization (in-turn-ul-eye-ZAY-shun). The process of making the attitudes, ideas, and standards of other people one's own. *Deviant* (DEEV-ee-ant). Turning aside from the standards and values considered normal or appropriate for one's society.

Self-esteem also develops as a result of increasing competence or ability to take charge of your own life (Flippo & Lewinson 1971; Koocher 1971). The major task of this book is to help foster competence in taking charge of our own emotions, relationships, behavior, and—ultimately—the quality of our own lives.

Summary

- *An identity crisis is a sign of maladjustment.* False. It is quite normal to experience an identity crisis, especially during the adolescent years—to wonder "who" you are and where you are going. Maladjustment may stem from inability to resolve such a conflict, or, as in the case of "battlefield neurosis," from engaging in behavior that is inconsistent with your self-identity.
- *What's in a name? A rose by any other name, contrary to William Shakespeare, could smell just plain awful.* True. Names are early labels for our selves—the centers of our experiencing of the world—and names suggest what we ought to try to become or what we are.
- *H. Head and W. R. Brain are the names of two physicians who specialize in neurology.* It may be just a coincidence, but it is true. It seems that individuals with very unusual names, such as Omar or Dwight or Ophelia, may view themselves as quite separate from the crowd and work hard to try to get ahead. Similarly, a Frederick or a Charles may behave somewhat more formally than a Fred or a Chuck.
- *University professors have larger signatures than their students.* True. It appears that the size of our signatures tends to reflect our relative status in life. We also sign our names in different ways for different purposes—on love notes and on checks. We use our names to communicate something about our selves.
- *Children have been born with the external organs of one sex and the internal organs of the opposite sex.* True. Such children are usually "assigned" to one sex or the other through surgery, but they typically develop firm self-identities as members of the sex to which they have been assigned—as do other children—by a very young age. The physical self is an important aspect of the self, as are the social self and the personal self.
- *A survey of 2,000 Americans showed respondents to be satisfied with their eyes and ears, but to be less happy with their teeth—and their behinds.* True. Your satisfaction with your physical self is an essential ingredient of your self-esteem. Self-esteem is determined, in part, by the discrepancy between your self-concept—that is, your evaluation of yourself as you observe yourself to be—and your ideal self, or your image of what you ought to be like.
- *Social roles are all phony.* False. We learn social roles—complex ways to behave under certain social conditions—in order to meet the requirements of those conditions. Roles help us to adjust. However, if our social behavior is inconsistent with our values, we may feel that it is improper or meaningless, and we may experience lowered self-esteem or challenges to our self-concept.
- *There is an old profession in which the confidentiality of clients is valued highly—prostitution.* Prostitutes differ from one another and are

not tightly organized, as are physicians and lawyers, but the importance of confidentiality is given enough value by many prostitutes to have been published in a newspaper printed by and for prostitutes. Most people view themselves as having values and ethics. Most people try to live their lives in accordance with their values, as far as possible, even though impulses, such as anger, and habits can sometimes make it difficult to do so.

● *College students place more value on national security and salvation than on personal happiness and inner harmony.* False. Students on two campuses rated values such as personal happiness and inner harmony as most important, while rating national security and salvation relatively low. However, it would be wrong to conclude that they are highly selfish; they rated values like self-respect and mature love above values like comfort and excitement.

University Student Responses to the Survey of Values (pp. 46–47)

	Washington State University	Michigan State University
A comfortable life	12	15
An exciting life	13	13
A sense of accomplishment	10	10
A world at peace	9	6
A world of beauty	15	12
Equality	11	9
Family security	8	11
Freedom	4	2
Happiness	1	1
Inner harmony	3	3
Mature love	5	4
National security	18	18
Pleasure	14	14
Salvation	16	17
Self-respect	6	8
Social recognition	17	16
True friendship	2	5
Wisdom	7	7

The survey of values was administered to several hundred students at Washington State University and Michigan State University during the mid-1970s (Rokeach 1978). Above are the average rankings assigned these values by students at these universities.

Both samples placed happiness at the top of the list. However, these university students apparently believed that happiness did not derive from hedonism and physical comforts, since they ranked pleasure, comfort, excitement, and beauty in the teens. They placed more emphasis on inner harmony, freedom, and mature love. Accomplishment and recognition take a back seat to self-respect, friendship, and wisdom.

● *The self-esteem of an average student may be greater than the self-esteem of a scholar.* True. Self-esteem depends in part on the discrepancy between the way we see ourselves, our self-concepts, and the way we think we ought to be, our ideal selves. If the scholar has much higher self-expectations than the average student, academic success may be looked upon as a minimally adequate achievement rather than an accomplishment of which to be proud. When we are too harsh in our self-demands, it is difficult to maintain high self-esteem.

- *Children with strict parents have higher self-esteem than children with permissive parents.* True. Coopersmith found that such parents were not harsh in their discipline, and it may be that children with strict parents believe that their parents love them, and that these children are also stimulated to show competence. Competence has been found to contribute significantly to self-esteem.

3

HUMAN DEVELOPMENT THROUGH THE LIFE CYCLE

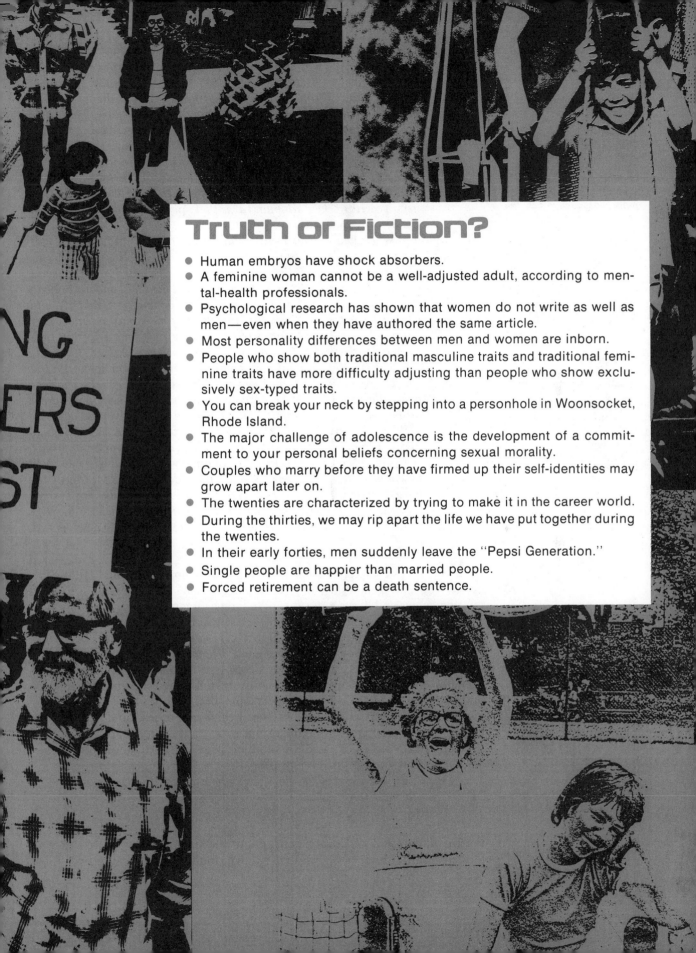

Truth or Fiction?

- Human embryos have shock absorbers.
- A feminine woman cannot be a well-adjusted adult, according to mental-health professionals.
- Psychological research has shown that women do not write as well as men—even when they have authored the same article.
- Most personality differences between men and women are inborn.
- People who show both traditional masculine traits and traditional feminine traits have more difficulty adjusting than people who show exclusively sex-typed traits.
- You can break your neck by stepping into a personhole in Woonsocket, Rhode Island.
- The major challenge of adolescence is the development of a commitment to your personal beliefs concerning sexual morality.
- Couples who marry before they have firmed up their self-identities may grow apart later on.
- The twenties are characterized by trying to make it in the career world.
- During the thirties, we may rip apart the life we have put together during the twenties.
- In their early forties, men suddenly leave the "Pepsi Generation."
- Single people are happier than married people.
- Forced retirement can be a death sentence.

Ovum (OV-um). The female reproductive or egg cell, which develops into a new member of the species following fertilization by a male reproductive cell. Plural: ova.

Ovulation (ov-you-LAY-shun). Releasing an egg cell from an ovary.

Uterus (YOU-turr-us). The hollow organ within females inside of which the fetus develops. Also called the womb.

Sperm. The male reproductive cell, which combines with the female reproductive cell in order to produce a new member of the species. Short for spermatozoon.

Conception (kon-SEPP-shun). Penetration of an ovum by a sperm, resulting in the development of an embryo. Also known as impregnation.

On a summerlike day in October, Elaine and her husband Dennis rush out to their jobs as usual. While Elaine, a buyer for a New York department store, is arranging for dresses from the Chicago manufacturer to arrive in time for the spring line, a different drama is being played out in her body. Hormones in her blood are causing a follicle (egg container) within an ovary to rupture and release an egg cell or **ovum**. The release of the ovum is called **ovulation**. For the next twenty-four hours or so, Elaine will be capable of conceiving. When released, the ovum begins a slow journey down the four-inch long Fallopian tubes that connect the ovaries to the **uterus** or womb. It is usually within the Fallopian tubes that **sperm** and egg cells unite in the act of **conception**.

When Elaine and Dennis make love that evening, Dennis will ejaculate hundreds of millions of sperm that will begin an odyssey upward toward the Fallopian tubes. Only a hundred to a thousand sperm will survive this journey. Several will bombard and attempt to penetrate the egg cell. Only one will succeed and fertilize it. While Elaine is sleeping comfortably, this odyssey may take one and a half hours. The fertilized ovum is but $1/175$ of an inch long—a tiny stage for the drama that will unfold.

The genetic material from Dennis' sperm cell combines with the genetic material in Elaine's egg cell. The combined genetic instructions dictate that the being conceived this night will grow arms rather than wings, a mouth rather than gills, and hair rather than scales. From the moment of conception, your stamp as an individual distinct from all others—with the possible exception of an identical twin—has been assured. It will determine whether you will have yellow or black hair, someday become bald or develop a widow's peak, or have a straight or curved nose. The human sciences have not yet determined exactly what impact these instructions will have on psychological factors such as intellectual functioning or aggressiveness.

In this chapter we explore human growth and development throughout the life cycle. We see that each stage of growth, each season of our lives, holds its various challenges and its opportunities. We largely organize our journey through the life cycle around the developmental theory of Erik Erikson, who suggested that human beings undergo eight major stages of development, and experience a particular challenge or crisis during each. We also focus our attention on a number of issues in addition to those raised by Erikson: the challenges of the **prenatal** environment; the stormy, controversial issues surrounding the acquiring of sex roles; some details of development during adulthood—the "Trying Twenties," the "Catch Thirties," the "Fearsome Forties," and beyond; and finally, we explore many of the important issues of the later years—forced retirement, death and dying, and the ultimate stage of human development, according to Erikson: integrity versus despair.

THE CHALLENGE OF THE PRENATAL WORLD

Prenatal (pree-NATE-ul). Existing prior to birth.

Zygote (ZY-goat). A fertilized ovum, an egg cell that has been penetrated by a sperm to become a single cell that will multiply and eventually grow into a new member of the species.

For the nine months following conception, the single cell or **zygote** that was formed by the union of sperm and egg will multiply—becoming two, then

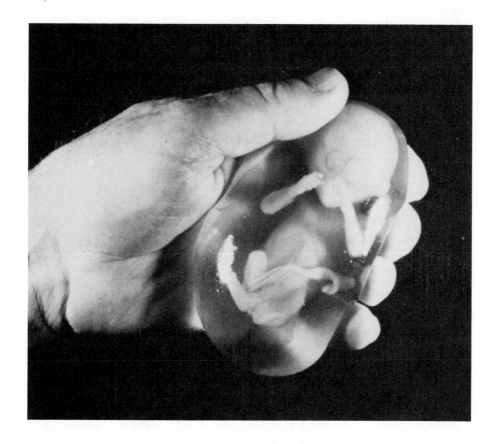

four, then eight, and so on, eventually forming tissues and organs and structures that increasingly resemble those of the human being. In the first week, the zygote will multiply into a ball of cells and become lodged or nested within the uterine wall. At this stage, the organism is called an **embryo,** and it has begun a dependent relationship with its mother that will continue beyond birth and into the early years of childhood. By the third week of development a primitive human heart begins to beat. It will continue to beat every minute of every day without rest for perhaps eighty or ninety years.

Following the eighth or ninth week, the embryo stage passes, and the stage of fetal development begins. The **fetus** is now about one inch long, and human features such as the face, eyes, arms, and legs can be seen. During the next seven months, the fetus will grow twenty times in overall size, so that at the time of birth it will be about twenty inches long and weigh, on the average, seven pounds for girls and seven and one-half pounds for boys.

The embryo and fetus develop within a protective environment in the mother's uterus called the **amniotic sac.** The sac is surrounded by a clear membrane and contains **amniotic fluid,** which suspends the infant and serves as a shock absorber to prevent the mother's movements from jarring the infant.

This private and dark world of creation is temperature-controlled and connected to the mother through a membrane called the **placenta,** a type of relay station between mother and infant. The exchange of oxygen, water, nutrients, and waste products between the mother and the fetus takes place in the placenta. The **umbilical cord,** connecting the child to the placenta, contains blood vessels that carry oxygen, water, and nutrients to the infant and carry waste products away. The mother's and infant's blood do not mix.

Embryo (EM-bree-oh). The name given to developing young in the uterus for the first two months.
Fetus (FEE-tus). The name given to developing young in the uterus from the beginning of the third month until birth.
Amniotic sac (am-nee-AH-tick). A closed sac or bag that surrounds the developing young in the uterus.
Amniotic fluid. Fluid contained in the amniotic sac.
Placenta (pluh-SENT-ah). An organ that connects the unborn child to the uterus, and through which the exchange of oxygen, food, and waste products with the mother takes place.
Umbilical cord (um-BILL-lick-ul). A flexible tube or hollow cord connecting the unborn child to the placenta.

When the mother is healthy, the fetal environment is comfortable and is responsive to all the needs of the fetus. But if the mother is malnourished or has consumed drugs such as tetracycline, streptomycin, thalidomide, narcotics, or even large doses of aspirin, these chemicals may enter the fetus through the placenta and impair its development in various ways. In the 1960s, many children whose mothers had taken thalidomide, a sedative drug, during pregnancy were born with absent or deformed limbs. Aspirin usage has been associated with respiratory and bleeding problems in the infant. The use of just moderate quantities of alcohol or heavy smoking during pregnancy increases risks to the infant's physical and intellectual development. Other common prenatal risk factors include exposure to X-rays, incompatibility of mother and fetal blood types, and maternal illnesses like rubella, mumps, hepatitis, and flu.

A fetus can do little to ward off the risks of an unhealthy prenatal environment. These early challenges of life must be met by the mother in consultation with her physician. The mother must seek out and be willing to apply competent medical advice.

The First Breaths

From the dark and private prenatal world, the baby is thrust into a room of lights, noise, incomprehensible movements, and cold. The first challenge following birth, to begin breathing on its own, is usually eased by the medical staff or a midwife.

Neonate (NEE-oh-nate). A child just after birth.

Mucus and fluid that clog the respiratory tract are wiped away when the **neonate's** head appears. Once birth is accomplished, the baby is turned upside down in order to prevent fluids from entering the respiratory tract. The neonate does not cry at once: first the mucus must be cleared and breathing must begin. Gentle rubbing of the back—not the old-fashioned slap on the behind—induces crying. Crying helps discharge any fluids remaining in the respiratory tract (Turner & Helms 1981).

EIGHT STAGES OF HUMAN DEVELOPMENT

Infancy (IN-fan-see). The first two years of life.

Maturation (mat-your-RAY-shun). The process of the unfolding of the genetic or inherited heritage. Maturation takes place with time and adequate nutrition. Learning is not required.

Erik Erikson, a psychoanalyst who emphasized the importance of our social relationships, taught that there were eight stages of human development that spanned the years from **infancy** to maturity. These stages are identified largely in terms of the types of relationships we are likely to develop during each, but these relationships are also related to processes of physical **maturation**. For instance, the parent-child relationship is essential during the early stages of life because of the infant's general helplessness. Our development of intimate love relationships during late adolescence and early adulthood would not be possible if we had not attained physical maturity.

Erikson identified each stage of human development in terms of the challenge or life crisis characteristic of it. Erikson was not pessimistic about the presence of all these "crises." He did not believe that life is harsh or cruel, unless we make it so. He believed that with proper parental support during the early years, most of us are well on our way toward resolving each crisis in a positive manner. The positive resolution of a life crisis leads to a firmer sense of self-identity, and we grow in self-esteem and in our expectations of success for the future. If we do not respond to the life crises well—or if during the early

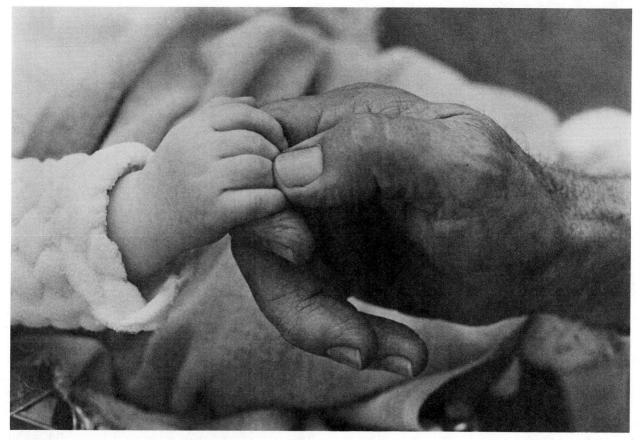

At a very early age we begin to learn that people are trustworthy and dependable—or, perhaps, that they are not.

years our parents are too harsh and negativistic—we may tend to look upon ourselves as foul-ups, unworthy and incompetent, and our self-esteem suffers.

Erikson's eight stages are outlined in Table 3.1, which indicates the time period of each stage and the challenge presented during that stage.

The Stage of Trust vs. Mistrust

In the Richards home down the street, seven-month-old Johnny's self-development is already being shaped in a positive direction. His parents treat him with warmth and affection. When he's hungry or wet, they attend to his needs reliably. He is learning that people are trustworthy and dependable. The world is an okay place to live, and he is made to feel welcome. These lessons are being learned before he speaks his first word.

It's not all roses and Pampers, however. Sometimes Mother isn't there at the very moment she's needed. People aren't perfect—a fact he will need to know later in life so that he will not expect too much. On the whole, though, Johnny's trust in the world outweighs his mistrust. He has a sense of optimism, a belief that his needs will be met.

Across the street, nine-month-old Sally is learning mistrust. Her parents marriage is failing. Sally's conception was her mother's vain attempt to restore

Table 3.1 Erik Erikson's Stages of Human Development

Time Period	The Life Crisis	The Challenge
Infancy	Trust vs. mistrust	Coming to trust the mother and the environment—to associate surroundings with feelings of inner goodness
Early childhood	Autonomy vs. shame and doubt	Developing the wish to make choices and the self-control to exercise choice
Pre-school years	Initiative vs. guilt	Adding planning and "attacking" to choice, to be active and on the move
Grammar-school years	Industry vs. inferiority	Becoming eagerly absorbed in skills, tasks, and productivity; mastering the fundamentals of technology
Adolescence	Identity vs. role diffusion	Connecting skills and social roles to formation of career objectives
Young adulthood	Intimacy vs. isolation	Committing the self to another; sexual love
Middle adulthood	Generativity vs. stagnation	Needing to be needed; to guide and encourage the younger generation; creativity
Later adulthood	Integrity vs. despair	Accepting the timing and placing of your own life cycle; wisdom; dignity

Source: Erikson (1963), pp. 247–69.

Reflex (REE-flecks). A simple, unlearned response to environmental stimulation.

marital harmony. It didn't work, and now she resents Sally since she feels trapped in the home as well as in a deteriorating marriage. Sally, of course, cannot possibly understand this. Yet she feels her mother's anger and coldness when her mother touches her, and she is often left alone for long periods of time. She is learning that people are undependable and that the world is an unwelcome place to be. Sally is developing a basic mistrust toward the world which might later in life color her relationships with others. As an adult she may still find it difficult to give completely of herself in an intimate relationship. The world may still seem to her to be a threatening place, where even lovers cannot be fully trusted.

The newborn infant requires food, water, oxygen, and an even temperature of at least 70° F (21° C). Excretion is a **reflex**—a simple muscular act that responds to environmental (in this case, inner environmental) stimulation. Babies are not concerned with the social proprieties of toileting. Many reflexes —breathing, vomiting, blinking, coughing, sneezing, and sucking—have survival value. Reflexively the infant orients its head toward a food source, such as a nipple, that touches its cheek. Reflexively the infant sucks objects placed in its mouth and swallows the contents.

The newborn infant is limited to simple movements like kicking, lifting and turning the head, and waving the arms. At about two months, it makes clumsy swipes at objects in the environment, but has not yet learned how to grasp. Within eight months the infant will sit without support, stand with someone's help, and begin to crawl. At about a year, the infant walks. At first the infant feeds itself with its hands, perhaps a discomfiting scene to those who are highly refined. Later a spoon is used, but early practice sessions resemble food-throwing exercises.

During the first year, the infant comes to trust that the environment, and people, will meet its needs, or may come to look upon the environment as a harsh and fickle place. Erikson warns that a basic sense of mistrust may close the child off from truly opening itself to experiencing the world further.

The Stage of Autonomy vs. Shame and Doubt

There is hell to pay in the nursery. Eighteen-month-old Bernie has just soiled in his crib. His mother had spent fifteen minutes in the bathroom with him, pleading with him to use the potty. "Do it for Mommy," she had exhorted. "Your grandmother says we all did it when we were only fourteen months old." Bernie doesn't quite follow all this, but Mommy is upset, and he is upset, and somehow he has failed to produce or to control himself. He is riddled with feelings of shame and self-doubt.

Toilet training is only one of the challenges commonly faced during the second year of life, a time when children are mobile and getting into everything in the household. Warmly encouraging parents may teach a child to be proud of the newly developed **autonomy.** Parents who demand too much too soon, or who are too restrictive, can lead a child to feel that self-control is too great a challenge and, perhaps, to begin a lifelong pattern of self-doubt.

Autonomy (aw-TAHN-oh-me). Independence, self-government. In Erikson's theory, a sense of autonomy results from the positive resolution of the crisis of autonomy vs. shame and doubt.

The Stage of Initiative vs. Guilt

Grace is now four. She can walk and "talk up a storm." She uses language and symbols to think and plan. She uses her plans to initiate actions and carry out activities. When she succeeds in her actions and is praised for her accomplishments, she begins to acquire a sense of independence and competence. But Miriam, the child who too frequently makes mistakes and can't seem to get things right, begins to feel guilty over her sense of powerlessness—particularly when she has been ridiculed or scolded harshly for her failures.

The balance in this crisis weighs between **initiative** and a feeling of self-competence on the one hand, and guilt and a sense of incompetence on the other.

Initiative (in-ISH-ee-uh-tiv). Originating new ideas and new behavior, taking the responsibility for new behavior. In Erikson's theory, a sense of initiative results from the positive resolution of the stage of initiative vs. guilt.

The Stage of Industry vs. Inferiority

In virtually every schoolyard there is a kid like Benjie. The girls call him Sad Sack. With the other boys, he's often the object of ridicule. While the other boys choose up sides for softball, Benjie stands on the sideline, looking withdrawn. Or when he does get the chance to play, he usually winds up making the big error of striking out at the worst time. In the classroom, too, Benjie seldom raises his hand to answer a question, and when he does he begins to shake all over. He's only eight and already he's begun to think of himself as a failure.

These are your grammar-school years of six to twelve. This is the stage in which you begin to evaluate your sense of self-competence by comparing yourself to your peers. Probably all of us, like Benjie, have hurt within when our accomplishments did not compare favorably with those of our friends and classmates. If you perform competently in sports, social, and school activities, you're more likely to take part and be industrious and productive. If the scale swings too far in the direction of incompetency and failure, Erikson suggests that this may lead to withdrawal and to a sense of inferiority.

These four stages describe Erikson's concept of self-development through childhood. In the first two years the child has begun to develop a basic positive or negative relationship with the world (trust vs. mistrust) and has come to

Human Development
Through the Life Cycle

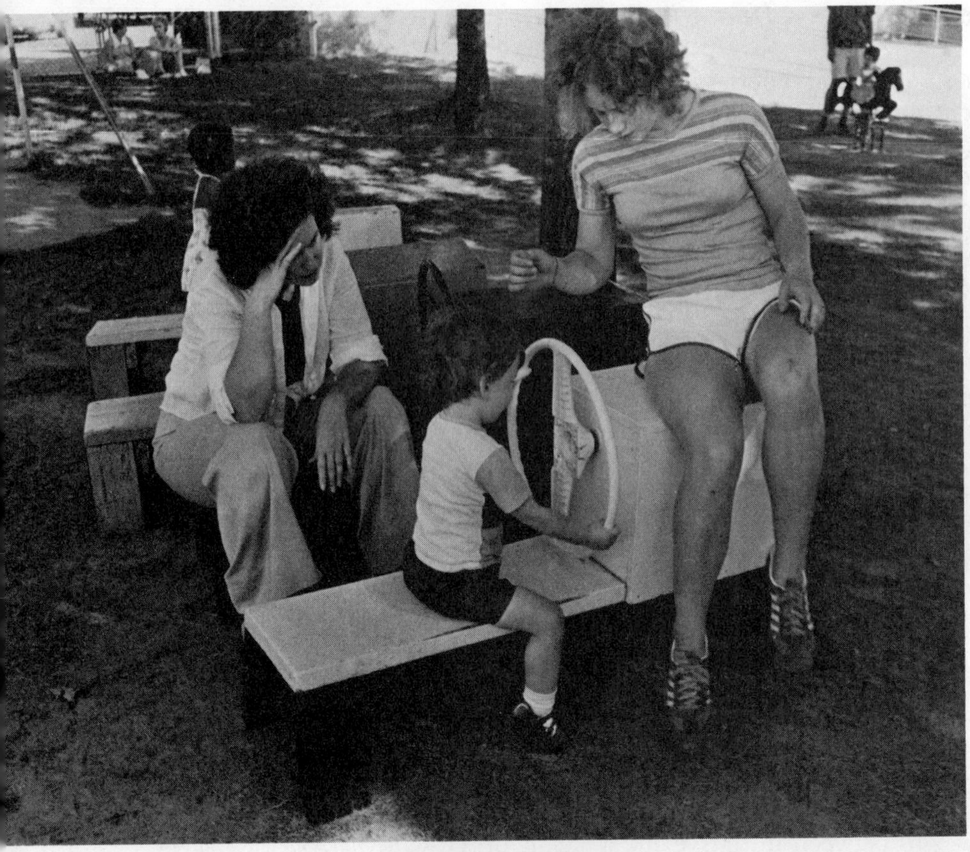
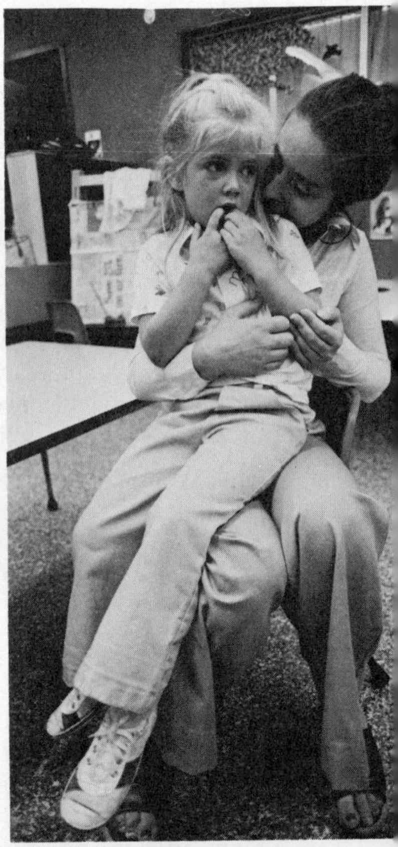
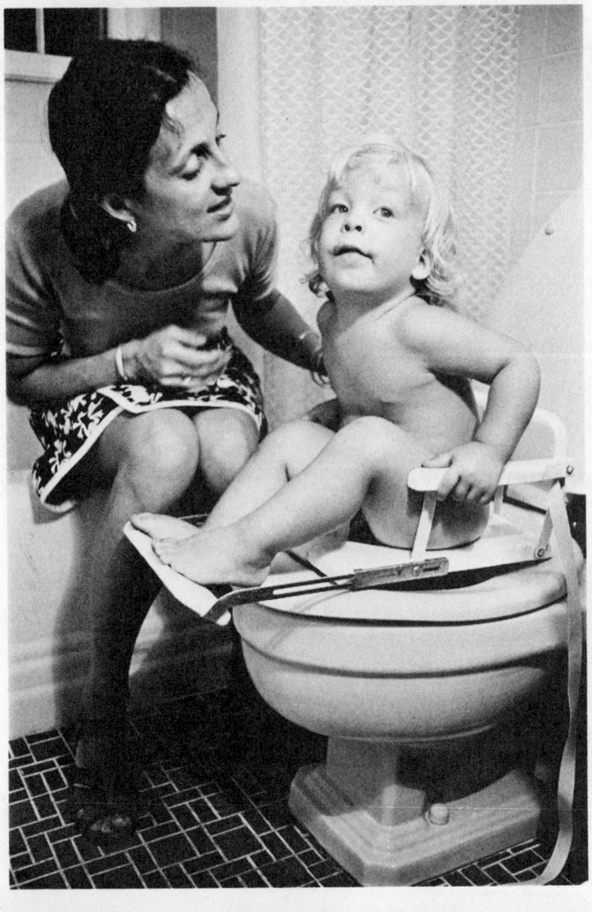
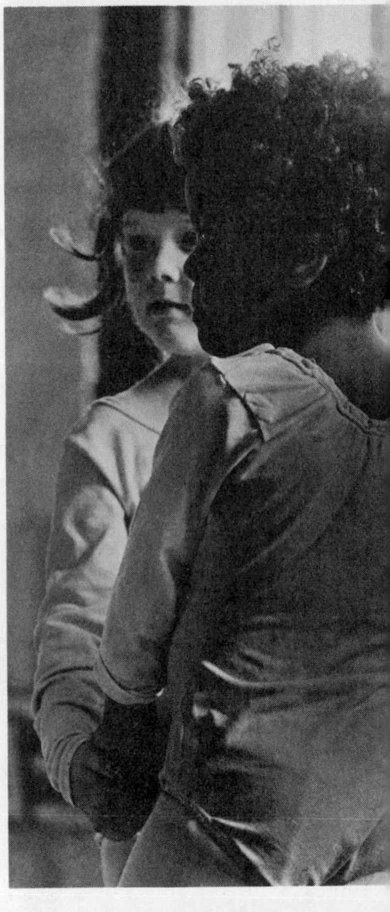

grips with the growing sense of control and independence (autonomy vs. shame and doubt). In the later years of childhood, the child's relative successes or failures in interacting with his environment, first in the home and family (initiative vs. guilt) and then in the social environment among peers (industry vs. inferiority), will further shape the self either toward competence and productivity or toward guilt, inferiority, and withdrawal.

Now we shall turn our attention to an extremely important challenge of the childhood years—the acquiring of sex roles.

The Challenge of Sex Roles

A **sex role** is a complex grouping of ways in which people behave depending on the sex to which they belong. We may be born as males or as females, but sex roles are largely learned and are related to the expectations that other people have of us. Consider the experiences of Garrett, an eighteen-year-old freshman in a junior college, and Lorraine, a twenty-three-year-old student in dental school.

Garrett: "When I was a kid, it was always important to be the toughest kid on the block. We didn't get into many fights, just staring contests mostly. But it was important that everyone think you were tough. You were never supposed to back down, even if you knew you were in the wrong. I remember my father telling me that the world was a rough place and that you had to be tough in order to survive 'out there.' I never felt that I was allowed to be gentle or to express affection. I can't recall hugging my father even once. It's as if there was a voice inside my head that insisted, 'You've got to be strong. Stand up straight like a man!'"

Lorraine: "I was raised with two brothers, one younger and one older. When they were running around or fighting in the backyard, it always looked like they were having so much fun, but Mom always told me that girls would get hurt if they played like that. My parents pushed my brothers to do well in

Sex role. A complex group or cluster of ways in which people belonging to one of the sexes behave. The expectations for the behavior of a person belonging to one of the sexes.

ARE YOU GOING TO BE A SUCCESS?

According to Erik Erikson, individuals who have managed to come through the crises of childhood in a positive way will be generally optimistic about their futures. They will have the trust, the sense of autonomy, the drive of initiative, and the belief in their own competence to face the challenges of work and family with self-confidence.

What about you? Do you believe that you are likely to meet with success in most of your future efforts? Take the expectancy for success scale devised by Bobbi Fibel and W. Daniel Hale (1978) at the

University of Massachusetts, and then compare your score to those of some undergraduates taking psychology courses according to the instructions at the end of this chapter.

THE HALE-FIBEL GENERALIZED EXPECTANCY FOR SUCCESS SCALE

Directions: Please indicate the degree to which you believe each statement would apply to you personally by circling the appropriate number, according to the following key:

1 = highly improbable
2 = improbable
3 = equally improbable and probable, not sure
4 = probable
5 = highly probable

In the future I expect that I will

1. find that people don't seem to understand what I am trying to say _____ 1 2 3 4 5
2. be discouraged about my ability to gain the respect of others _____ 1 2 3 4 5
3. be a good parent _____ 1 2 3 4 5
4. be unable to accomplish my goals _____ 1 2 3 4 5
5. have a stressful marital relationship _____ 1 2 3 4 5
6. deal poorly with emergency situations _____ 1 2 3 4 5
7. find my efforts to change situations I don't like are ineffective _____ 1 2 3 4 5
8. not be very good at learning new skills _____ 1 2 3 4 5
9. carry through my responsibilities successfully _____ 1 2 3 4 5
10. discover that the good in life outweighs the bad _____ 1 2 3 4 5
11. handle unexpected problems successfully _____ 1 2 3 4 5
12. get the promotions I deserve _____ 1 2 3 4 5
13. succeed in the projects I undertake _____ 1 2 3 4 5
14. not make any significant contributions to society _____ 1 2 3 4 5
15. discover that my life is not getting much better _____ 1 2 3 4 5
16. be listened to when I speak _____ 1 2 3 4 5
17. discover that my plans don't work out too well _____ 1 2 3 4 5
18. find that no matter how hard I try, things just don't turn out the way I would like _____ 1 2 3 4 5
19. handle myself well in whatever situation I'm in _____ 1 2 3 4 5
20. be able to solve my own problems _____ 1 2 3 4 5
21. succeed at most things I try _____ 1 2 3 4 5
22. be successful in my endeavors in the long run _____ 1 2 3 4 5
23. be very successful working out my personal life _____ 1 2 3 4 5
24. experience many failures in my life _____ 1 2 3 4 5
25. make a good first impression on people I meet for the first time _____ 1 2 3 4 5
26. attain the career goals I have set for myself _____ 1 2 3 4 5
27. have difficulty dealing with my superiors _____ 1 2 3 4 5
28. have problems working with others _____ 1 2 3 4 5
29. be a good judge of what it takes to get ahead _____ 1 2 3 4 5
30. achieve recognition in my profession _____ 1 2 3 4 5

Source: Reprinted with permission from Fibel and Hale (1978, p. 931).

school and were crushed when they came home with poor grades. I always did well, but grades didn't seem to be very important with me. 'That's nice,' Mom would say, and then she'd sort of drop it.

"In high school I wanted to be popular more than anything else. I got great grades, but would have traded them in if I could have been more the cheerleader type. Now I really love what I'm doing, and my husband understands that my dental school is as important to me as his law school is to him. But do you know that when my folks call up, they always ask how he's doing in law school and they ask me how the apartment's shaping up and what we're thinking this year about having kids. They may ask me about dental school as an afterthought. They can't picture me as a dentist. It's weird, but my own parents are more concerned about their son-in-law's career than they are about mine."

Garrett was raised to be a man's man, crisp and lean. He was told that real men say little but act swiftly. Men must make the tough decisions at work and place logic above sentiment. Lorraine was raised to be a model of femininity and refinement. Now her parents feel that her proper role is to support her husband in law school. To use the adjectives suggested by Sandra Bem of Stanford University, Garrett was raised to be a "chesty" male and Lorraine to be a "fluffy" female.

Yet both Garrett and Lorraine are experiencing problems with their sex roles. Garrett is not comfortable with the role of the "typical" man, and Lorraine is seriously frustrated by her parents' efforts to force her into the role of the "typical" woman. It is sometimes like trying to squeeze a square peg into a round hole. Let us explore how boys and girls acquire sex roles.

One of the earliest and clearest elements of our self-identities is our sex. Children typically have a fixed sense of being a boy or a girl by the age of eighteen months (Money & Ehrhardt 1973). From the days of infancy onward, children have it constantly drummed into them that family and society hold different behavioral expectations for little boys and little girls. Boys are expected to be competitive and independent. But girls are made from "sugar and spice and everything nice." They should be passive, dependent, tender, and gentle.

An illustration of sex-role stereotyping in children's books.

"WHY CAN'T A WOMAN BE MORE LIKE A MAN?"

You may recognize the title of the song from *My Fair Lady*—"Why Can't a Woman Be More Like a Man?" It may be that a woman cannot be more like a man because she will be labeled psychologically unhealthy!

In a study by a team of married psychologists, the Brovermans of the Psychology Department at Worcester State Hospital in Massachusetts, a number of psychologists, psychiatrists, and social workers were asked to identify the traits that typified the "healthy woman" and the "healthy man" (Broverman et al. 1970). The healthy woman was described as submissive, dependent, vain, emotional, and turned off by math and science. But the healthy man was described as competitive, independent, firm, objective, decisive, and skilled in the worlds of business and science. You need not dig too far into these lists

to see that the "healthy man" has a more positive evaluation than the "healthy woman."

Another group of professionals was asked to describe the "healthy adult" (sex unspecified). The adjectives chosen typified the healthy male, not the healthy female. The feminine female is seen as healthy as a woman, but she is not an adult!

Women face a catch-22 concerning their self-concepts: "If I'm to be a well-adjusted adult, I've got to be independent, assertive, and achievement-oriented. I've got to be like a man. But if I act like this, my femininity will be questioned." Perhaps the answer is not for women to be more like men, but for both men and women to begin to value traits that have not been arbitrarily linked to one or the other sex by tradition.

Yet psychologists have found only one trait, aggressiveness, that consistently distinguishes the personalities of boys and girls in research (Maccoby & Jacklin 1974). From the onset of social play at two or two and a half, boys show more physical and verbal aggression—although parents discourage excessive aggression in boys as well as girls. But "feminine" timidity and sociability and "masculine" dominance and self-reliance clearly appear to result from parental expectations. In general, boys and girls are more similar than they are different, but sexual **stereotypes** are so strongly implanted in our culture that even kindergartners attribute traits like aggressiveness and strength to men, and

Stereotype (STAIR-ee-oh-type). A fixed, conventional idea about a group of people that does not allow for individual exceptions or critical evaluation.

Table 3.2   Vive la Différence? Just How Different Are the Two Sexes?

Differences Borne Out by Some Research Studies	Differences about Which There Is Greater Doubt	Assumed Differences Which Research Has Shown to Be False
Males tend to be more aggressive than females.	Females are more timid and anxious than males?	Females are more sociable than males.
Females have greater verbal ability than males.	Males are more active than females?	Females are more suggestible than males.
Males have greater visual-spatial ability than females.	Males are more competitive than females?	Males have higher self-esteem than females.
Males have greater ability in math.	Males are more dominant than females?	Females lack achievement motivation.
		Males are more logical and analytic than females.

It has been commonly assumed that there are great differences between men and women, and that these differences reflect heredity or the natural order of things. Yet psychological research has shown the supposed differences to be much smaller than had been assumed. And those differences that remain, such as greater math ability in males and greater verbal ability in females, may reflect cultural expectations and not heredity. (Based on data from Maccoby & Jacklin 1974.)

Table 3.3 Sexual Stereotypes Among Elementary-School Children

Personality Traits Attributed to Men and Women	Percentage of Children Responding in Agreement with Sexual Stereotypes	
	Kindergarten	Second Grade
Traits Attributed to Men:		
aggressive	94	100
strong	81	98
adventurous	83	85
Traits Attributed to Women:		
appreciative	66	66
emotional	62	96
soft-hearted	60	94

By kindergarten, children have already learned to attribute traits such as aggressiveness to men and emotionality to women. By second grade, these sexual stereotypes are even more strongly ingrained. (Adapted from Williams, Bennett, & Best 1975.)

emotionality and soft-heartedness to women. These stereotypes become more firmly entrenched by the time children are in the second grade (Williams, Bennett, & Best 1975).

These sex-role stereotypes are found everywhere in our society—in films, television shows, books, and especially in women's popular magazines. One investigator (Flora 1971) found that feminine themes of dependency and passivity abound in fictional stories in women's magazines intended for "working-class" readers (*True Story* and *Modern Romance*) and middle-class readers (*Cosmopolitan* and *Redbook*). Overall, 41 percent of the stories endorsed female dependency, while only 20 percent presented this trait in an unfavorable light. However, 51 percent of the stories in the middle-class magazines represented dependency as desirable, as compared to 30 percent in the working-class magazines. Perhaps working-class women are more frequently heads of households than middle-class women, or dependency may be less compatible with working-class aspirations of upward mobility. Working-class women may be more likely to be in the forefront of the **feminist** movement than middle-class women.

On Becoming a Man or a Woman. The taking on of sex roles probably involves at least two factors: identification and socialization.

Identification is the process of internalizing or bringing inward the behavior—and what you believe to be the thoughts and feelings—of other people. In Chapter 4 we discuss Sigmund Freud's belief that little boys begin to act like their fathers and little girls like their mothers through an identification process that tends to peak at about the age of five or six. Sexual identification, to Freud, was motivated both by love for the parent and fear of what would happen if the child failed to become like the parent of the same sex.

Others view identification as a very broad sort of learning by imitation (Bronfenbrenner 1960; Kagan 1958). Not only do babies imitate a certain type of behavior; in identification they become generally like the person imitated.

Whom are they likely to imitate? Probably the people who appear to have efficient control of the resources (food, pets, toys) that are important to them (Bandura, Ross, & Ross 1963). That could lead to identification with both parents, and likely does, up to a point. But they are also likely to learn that they

Feminist (FEM-in-ist). A person who believes that women should have economic, social, and political rights equal to those of men.

Identification (eye-den-tiff-uh-KAY-shun). A process by which an individual attempts to be similar to another individual and acquires values, attitudes, and behavior patterns characteristic of the other individual.

THE INFERIORITY OF THE TALENTED WOMAN

We have probably all been taught not to judge a book by its cover, but there is every reason to believe that we judge a book by its author—especially the sex of the author.

Stanford University psychologists Sandra and Daryl Bem (1973) asked students to rate the quality of articles in several fields, including law and education. When students believed the article was written by a man, it received consistently superior ratings, by students of both sexes.

This sexual prejudice is not restricted to the written word. The Bems then asked female students only to rate the quality of works of art, attributed to either male or female artists. Again, the works received higher ratings when attributed to male artists, with one exception: when told the work had won an art contest, it received higher ratings when attributed to a woman. Perhaps, the Bems reasoned, we are trained to be suspicious of the female hopeful in the man's domain. But if a woman does run far ahead of her competition, other women stand ready to take notice and applaud her worth. She must be something special to compete successfully with men. Sad to say, she probably must—being just as good isn't good enough.

Socialization (so-shul-eye-ZAY-shun). A process by which other people influence us to accept the values, attitudes, and behavior patterns characteristic of their society.
Nurture (NURT-your). To raise or promote the development of an organism through supplying nourishment, love, and support.

Androgynous (ann-DRODGE-in-us). Having the characteristics of both males and females.

The Challenge
and the Self

will be more successful at imitating the behavior of people who are similar to them than people who are different. A little boy, for instance, will understand that he might have some difficulty giving birth to a baby—even before he knows all about the birds and the bees. So it is that most of the time boys tend to identify with men and girls tend to identify with women.

We are also influenced by early **socialization** experiences, or messages and experiences provided for us by other people in order to direct our growth in particular directions. Girls are given dolls before they are old enough to stand, and practice **nurturing** and care-taking roles to prepare them for traditional feminine roles once they are adults. It is not surprising that many females take to the mothering role "naturally" when they have children. If the Pittsburgh Steelers had all been urged into changing diapers and caring for younger siblings in the preteen years and then been given jobs as baby-sitters during adolescence, they, too, would all fit "naturally" into the mothering role.

Boys are given trucks and cars and balls and guns and encouraged to compete aggressively with the other boys. Boys are handled more often than girls, and girls are spoken to more frequently. Is it so surprising that boys take to rough-and-tumble sports and girls show greater verbal ability? Even within the first year, boys' play shows more exploration and independence. Girls are more quiet, dependent, and restrained (Goldberg & Lewis 1969).

Schools also spur the socialization process, perhaps even when school officials are committed to minimizing the ingraining of stereotypical sex-role differences. In a study of a nursery school that proclaimed just such a commitment, many subtle forms of influence were uncovered (Joffee 1971). Little girls were more frequently complimented on their clothing than boys, especially when they wore dresses. The books and songs also contained sex messages, as in these lines from a song about a child who made noise on a bus: "And the daddy went spank, spank, and the mommy went shh-shh." The fact that teachers and aides were female, and that the children rarely saw adult males in this setting, would also have affirmed the expectation that women care for children while men shape careers in the business world.

Sex-stereotypical tracking becomes common in the junior and senior high schools. Girls are tracked into courses in homemaking, secretarial work, and dancing, while boys are guided into courses in shop and preprofessional studies (Naffziger & Naffziger 1974).

Mr. and Ms. Androgyny. Today many people are questioning the concept that psychological adjustment means showing sex-stereotypical behavior. The feminist movement has stimulated people from all walks of life to question traditionalist standards of masculine and feminine conduct. Women in increasing numbers pursue careers in medicine, business, and government. Men are learning that it is not a sign of weakness to be tender and supportive, to nurture children, or to raise houseplants. Consciousness-raising groups help both sexes to swerve from restrictive stereotypes.

Individuals who possess characteristics of both male and female stereotypes are called **androgynous.** The androgynous woman can be tough and decisive in business, and warm and tender in her social life. The androgynous man can be nurturant and gentle as well as rugged and logical, depending on the requirements of the situation. Androgynous people are not ashamed to behave in ways considered stereotypical of the opposite sex.

Sandra Bem (1974) has developed a test that measures androgyny by asking respondents to rate themselves on traditionally masculine attributes (ambitious, self-reliant, assertive, independent) and traditionally feminine attributes (affectionate, gentle, understanding). People who rate themselves to possess comparable numbers of masculine and feminine traits are considered androgynous. Of thousands of students who have taken the Bem test, 50 percent appear to adhere to their own sex-role stereotypes, 15 percent are cross-sextyped (endorsing more characteristics of the opposite sex), and 35 percent are androgynous.

Women in increasing numbers are pursuing careers in areas that have been traditionally labeled masculine. Is this woman masculine, feminine, or androgynous?

He, She, and Them

ONE SMALL STEP FOR A PERSON, ONE GIANT STEP FOR PERSONKIND?

Police*man* or police officer? Television anchor*man* or anchorperson? The movement of women into previously male-dominated occupations has led to the creation of gender-free job titles, which is certainly laudable. But the city council of Woonsocket, Rhode Island, raised some eyebrows when they voted to change the word "manhole" to "personhole" in describing the duties of city "utility persons" (not utility men) as including "building personholes."

But soon there was a storm of controversy over the council action. Council president Gaston Ayotte complained, "We are sick and tired of the adverse publicity we [are] getting. . . . All over the United States people [are] laughing at Woonsocket personholes" (reported in *Newsday*, 9/20/78, p. 9). So the

council reverted to the (sexist?) manhole. Will the New York City Council soon debate changing Manhattan to Personhattan?

Sexism in language has also been troubling for writers. Most of us have been raised to use the pronouns *he* and *him* when referring to a person, as in, "A person does the best *he* can." In an effort to avoid accidentally implying that a person always is or ought to be a *he*, we use the plural whenever we can in this text, as in, "People do the best *they* can." Plural pronouns, like *they* and *them*, are fortunately gender-free. Of course, we can't always do this. As organizational psychologist Bernard Bass points out, "*They* kissed *them*" is no substitute for "*she* kissed *him*" (1979). We agree. If you have doubts, ask *him*.

Androgynous men and women appear to lead fuller lives, engaging in behavior considered characteristic of the opposite sex without belittling themselves or experiencing guilt (Bem 1975; Bem & Lenney 1976). Androgyny does not in and of itself erase our sense of traditional male and female roles, but at least it opens the way for both men and women to respond to the challenges of life with a wider range of behavior and emotions.

Adolescence: The Stage of Identity vs. Role Diffusion

According to psychologist Roger Gould's (1975) research with 524 men and women of various age groups, a predominant concern of sixteen- to eighteen-year-olds is parental domination and the yearning for independence. According to Erik Erikson, the fundamental challenge of adolescence is the creation of one's own adult identity, primarily through choosing and developing a commitment to an occupation or life role.

Adolescents become concerned with "how to connect the roles and skills cultivated earlier with the occupational prototypes of the day" (Erikson 1963, p. 261)—that is, with jobs. It is up to the individual somehow to integrate or piece together parts of the physical self, the social self, and the personal self into a meaningful whole. This is no easy task. Many young people become confused when they do not find roles that fit their interests and their aptitudes,

The fundamental challenge of adolescence is the creation of your own adult identity.

and it may be desirable to visit college counseling and testing centers at such times.

But identity is not limited to occupational choice. It also extends to sexual, political, and religious beliefs and commitments. Studies have found that the majority of lower classmen at the State University of New York at Albany are either in serious personal conflict or have not begun to think seriously about occupational choice (Waterman & Nevid 1977). Yet the percentage of students who find themselves in conflict, or an identity crisis, about occupational choice increases from the fall to the spring semester of the freshman year (Waterman & Waterman 1971), and many of these students have emerged from these identity crises into commitments to career roles at some point during their college careers (Waterman, Geary, & Waterman 1974). Commitments made during the college years seem to be more stable than commitments made during high school. Many adolescents seem to turn their attention to resolving their identities in terms of religious and political beliefs only after they have resolved their occupational roles.

Young Adulthood: The Stage of Intimacy vs. Isolation

A central task of young adulthood is the establishment of **intimate** relationships. According to Erikson, young people who have evolved a firm sense of personal identity are now ready to fuse their identities with others'. Erikson warns that we may not be capable of committing ourselves to other individuals until we have established our life roles. If he is correct, marriages that occur during high school or the earlier college years may be in for some difficulty—and, though there are exceptions, these marriages run higher risks of divorce. Often couples who marry early complain that they are "growing apart."

But let us not forget that couples also complain of growing apart in their forties and their fifties, especially when women have foreclosed their personal identities by adopting traditional feminine roles, and discover only at the time that the children are leaving home that the mother role is not enough. Personal reassessment and personal striving to find new meaning in life create stress in many marriages.

Erikson's view of a proper intimate sexual relationship stems from the highly traditional view of his theoretical forefather, Sigmund Freud, who believed that human normalcy was the capacity to love and to work. Erikson was highly specific about his ideal for intimacy. In order for a sexual relationship to be "of lasting social significance," he wrote, it should include these six characteristics: "(1) mutuality of orgasm, (2) with a loved partner, (3) of the other sex, (4) with whom one is able and willing to share a mutual trust, (5) and with whom one is able and willing to regulate the cycles of a. work b. procreation c. recreation, (6) so as to secure to the offspring, too, all the stages of a satisfactory development" (1963, p. 266).

Erikson has been much criticized for this view, of course. For one thing, it suggests that homosexual relationships, no matter how warm, loving, and stable, cannot be of "lasting social significance." It also devalues recreational sex. But you will not be surprised to learn that people with conservative views toward sex and marriage are very much at home with Erikson.

Erikson believed that if the individual is not prepared for the demands of intimacy, there is the danger of a retreat into isolation. The public self is not enough. The intimate self must also be allowed to grow.

A major task of young adulthood is the establishment of intimate relationships. Erikson writes that we must develop a stable identity during adolescence if we are to be able to fuse our selves with the selves of others during young adulthood.

Intimate (in-timm-mitt). Characterizes a relationship in which there is sharing of inmost feelings. Intimate implies trust and caring.

Human Development Through the Life Cycle

SEXUAL MORALITY AND PERSONAL IDENTITY ON CAMPUS

What are your personal views about premarital sex? Have you arrived at a set of beliefs that guide your personal sexual conduct? For many college students, sexual decision making, and not occupational choice, occupies center stage in the resolution of personal identity. You can postpone your occupational decisions, at least for a while, but sexual decision making is an issue college students are likely to face every week, or every weekend.

In one study (Waterman & Nevid 1977), seventy male and seventy female first- and second-year students at the State University of New York at Albany were surveyed to determine whether they had developed a commitment to a set of personal beliefs about premarital sex, and whether these beliefs had developed during a period of serious examination of alternatives—or, as Erikson labeled it, an identity crisis. The survey also investigated the presence of commitments or crisis in other areas, such as occupational choice and religious and political ideologies. On the basis of their responses, students were assigned to one of four identity statuses based on Erikson's theory—identity achievement, foreclosure, moratorium, or identity diffusion:

Identity Achievement: Describes individuals who have resolved their identity crisis in a particular area in favor of a commitment to a relatively stable set of beliefs or a course of action.

Foreclosure: Represents individuals who have adopted a commitment to a set of beliefs or course of action without undergoing a personal identity crisis. Frequently, they have adopted the views of parents or other models without serious personal questioning.

Moratorium: Represents persons who are presently in the throes of an identity crisis, or moratorium—a period of serious examination of alternatives—in order to arrive at stable commitments. Values, attitudes, feelings, and possibilities are all carefully evaluated.

Identity Diffusion: Describes people who have neither arrived at a commitment nor experienced an identity crisis. They have not fashioned stable beliefs or a commitment to a course of action, nor are they presently searching.

The results suggest the central importance of sexual decision making to Albany State lower classmen. In Table 3.4, you can see that the lowest incidence of identity diffusion was in the area of sexual morality, and the highest in political ideology. College students may be able to postpone occupational, religious, and political commitments, but they gen-

---

Trying twenties. Gail Sheehy's term for the period in young adulthood characterized by striving to get ahead in the career world and, often, by the belief that we have undertaken the one true course in life.

The Challenge of the Twenties. Roger Gould's (1975) sample reported the twenties to be a period during which young adults were fueled with ambition, striving to advance themselves in their careers. In *Passages: Predictable Crises of Adult Life,* Gail Sheehy (1976) labeled the twenties the **Trying Twenties.**

Sheehy based her conclusions on interviews with 115 people who came largely from the middle and upper classes, including many managers, executives, and professionals. While her observations may not generalize to all Americans, the young adults in her sample were usually involved in establishing their pathways in life, finding their places in the world. They were generally responsible for their own support, and were coming to feel increasingly independent of parental influences and free to make their own choices—for better or for worse. It seems that it is in the twenties that we are likely to actualize the occupational identities that we construct for ourselves somewhat earlier.

Sheehy also notes that during the twenties we commonly feel "buoyed by powerful illusions and belief in the power of the will [so that] we commonly insist . . . that what we have chosen to do is the one true course in life" (1976, p. 33). As we shall see, the one true course has many swerves and bends.

The Challenge and the Self

72

Table 3.4 Percentage of Students in Each Identity Status in Each Area

	Occupation	Religion	Politics	Sexual Morality
Females				
Identity Achievement	17	23	9	39
Moratorium	24	17	14	16
Foreclosure	20	20	13	39
Identity Diffusion	39	40	64	7
Males				
Identity Achievement	17	23	20	21
Moratorium	23	13	6	6
Foreclosure	21	36	10	64
Identity Diffusion	39	29	64	9

Source: Waterman & Nevid (1977).

erally adopt a philosophy about sex by the time they enter college or early in their college careers.

Differences in identity status between male and female students concerning sexual morality are revealing. Most men (64 percent) were foreclosers on sex, while women were equally split (39 percent and 39 percent) between identity achievers and foreclosers, with another 16 percent still in moratorium —still seeking identity resolution. Most men expressed the attitude, "There's nothing wrong with premarital sex. If we're getting it on together, fine." But the majority had never seriously examined their beliefs about sexual morality, simply adopting the double standard that permits male sexual experimentation.

Women, too, generally endorsed premarital sex, but more frequently in the context of a loving relationship, consistent with the national survey of sexual attitudes by Morton Hunt (1974). To arrive at their views, the women had more frequently undergone an identity crisis in which they ultimately rejected more restrictive parental values. Adolescent women commonly feel caught between pressure from parents to show restraint and from peers to "get with it." The identity crisis is the time during which many come to determine finally what is right for them.

The Challenge of the Thirties.   Gould (1975) noted that the ages of twenty-nine to thirty-four were characterized by self-questioning: "Where is my life going?" "Why am I doing this?" Gail Sheehy labeled the thirties the **Catch Thirties,** the first major period of reassessment in life, when we often find that the life-styles we have tried on during the twenties do not fit quite as comfortably as we expected they would. There is commonly a major discrepancy between the occupational role and the personal self.

"One common response," Sheehy writes, "is the tearing up of the life we spent most of our twenties putting together. It may mean striking out on a secondary road toward a new vision or converting a dream of 'running for president' into a more realistic goal. The single person feels a push to find a partner. The woman who was previously content at home with children chafes to venture into the world. The childless couple reconsiders children. And almost everyone who is married, especially those married for seven years, feels a discontent" (1976, p. 34).

The second half of the thirties, according to psychologist Daniel Levinson of Yale University, is characterized by "settling down" (Levinson et al. 1978).

Catch thirties. Gail Sheehy's term for the fourth decade in life, during which we are likely to experience a major reassessment of our life to date. Many in their thirties come to feel that the pathways of the twenties have lost their meaning.

Human Development Through the Life Cycle

Sheehy similarly found that members of her sample who had successfully ridden out the storm of reassessments of the Catch Thirties began the process of **rooting** at this time. They began to feel a need to put down roots, to make a financial and emotional investment in their homes. Their concerns became more focused on promotion or tenure, career advancement, and long-term mortgages.

Rooting. Planting of roots that tends to occur during the thirties, characterized by a desire to create a sense of stability or permanence in one's life.

The Middle Years: The Stage of Generativity vs. Stagnation

There is some point during the years between thirty-five and forty-five when most of us recognize that our lives may be more than halfway over, that there may be more to look back upon than forward to. The dreams of youth may never be realized. We shall never become president or chairperson of the board. We shall never play shortstop for the Dodgers or dance in the New York City Ballet. There comes another reassessment, and for many, the haunting lyric from the Peggy Lee song, "Is that all there is?"

The middle-level, middle-aged businessman looking ahead to another ten or twenty years of grinding out accounts in his Wall Street cubbyhole may experience a severe mid-life depression. The housewife with two teenagers, an empty house from eight to three, and a fortieth birthday on the way, may feel she is coming apart at the seams. This is the **mid-life crisis,** a feeling of entrapment and loss of purpose that afflicts many of us, and which may propel many into extramarital affairs just to prove that we are still attractive to others.

Mid-life crisis. A second major period of reassessment that occurs in the forties, when one may suddenly feel that life is more than half over and that the dreams of adolescence and young adulthood are unlikely ever to be achieved.

"*Now, see here, Harley. I was forty once, and I never went through any mid-life crisis!*"

The mid-life crisis can ultimately end with renewed embracing of family values, with a personal commitment to generativity, the Eriksonian ideal of helping to shape the new generation. This may involve rearing our own children, or working to make the world a better place in which to live. For those who weather the crisis, experience combines with strength to heighten productivity.

The Seasons of a Man's Life. In *The Seasons of a Man's Life*, psychologist Daniel Levinson and his colleagues (Levinson et al. 1978) examined the mid-life crisis among forty workers, businessmen, scientists, and novelists. They found the early forties to represent a turning point in which these men began to deal with the loss of youth and the passage to middle age. When men are in their thirties, Levinson writes, they still regard themselves as part of the "Pepsi Generation." They are older siblings to youths in their twenties, not members of the "older generation." But in the early forties, they are viewed more as Dad than Buddy, and are suddenly a full generation apart.

At about forty there is some marker event—a physical illness, the death of a loved one, a change on the job, the obituary of a contemporary—that triggers this mid-life crisis. We mourn our own youth and begin to adjust to the specter of old age and the finality of death.

The Dream—Inspiration or Tyrant? Until mid-life, Levinson writes, men may be under the influence of **the Dream**—the overriding drive of youth to *become*, to be the great novelist or scientist, to leave a mark on history. At mid-life men must come to terms with the discrepancy between the self-concept and this particularly demanding aspect of the ideal self, the Dream.

The Dream, you see, may tell the author that the memorable novel is insufficient—it must be a masterpiece. The Dream may lead all of us, not just men, to belittle our accomplishments. The Dream can shatter self-esteem. Only by freeing ourselves from the tyranny of the Dream can we savor our actual accomplishments in life and begin to take more pleasure in the here and now.

The Dream. Daniel Levinson's term for the overriding determination of youth to become something important, to leave a mark on history.

The Challenge of the Later Years: The Stage of Integrity vs. Despair

"Most people say that as you get old you have to give up things. I think you get old because you give up things."
SENATOR THEODORE FRANCIS GREEN, age 87, Washington *Post*, June 28, 1954

"The idea that society can provide only a limited number of jobs, and that the elderly are the logical ones to be left out, is no longer tenable. There are unlimited goods and services needed and desired in American society. Among the greatest resources that could be channeled toward these ends are the experience, skill, and devotion of America's elderly millions."
MAE RUDOLPH, *Family Health*, March 1970

"How old would you be if you didn't know how old you was?"
SATCHEL PAIGE, ageless baseball pitcher

"The true test of maturity is not how old a person is but how he reacts to awakening in the midtown area in his shorts."
WOODY ALLEN, *Without Feathers*

THE PSYCHOLOGY TODAY POLL

- Are married people happier than single people?
- Are younger people happier than older people?
- Are child-free couples happier than parents?

Angus Campbell (1975) and his colleagues sought to answer these and other questions through a survey of a random sample of 2,164 Americans who were asked to rate their life satisfaction and overall mood. Most viewed their lives as worthwhile, hopeful, interesting, and full—in short, as happy! Yet some interesting differences appear for the married and single, the aged and young, the child-free and parents.

As you can see from Figure 3.1, married people are more satisfied with their lives than any of the unmarried groups—the single, widowed, or divorced. The most satisfied Americans are young married women with no children. When children come along, life satisfaction drops off and stress increases, although couples with older children appear happier. Perhaps the responsibilities of child rearing disturb the carefree days of early married life: many couples now report feeling tied down and express doubts about their marriage. But by the time

children are ready for college, the couple's happiness generally rebounds to a point that almost matches the bliss of the newly wed. The so-called empty nest may provide a comfortable retreat in which couples can rediscover one another. Although middle age may have its share of crises, most Americans still reported it to be a time of personal happiness.

Are older childless couples less happy than those with children? Apparently not. Childless married men over thirty appear happier than most others, except, perhaps, for married men with older children, who are now also free of most child-rearing tasks. The childless married woman is less satisfied than her mate, on the average, but almost as happy as women with children.

We cannot truly draw conclusions about cause and effect from this data. For instance, it may be that more satisfied people get married, not that marriage makes us happier. But by and large it seems that the dream of having children does not provide quite as much joy during the early years of parenting as we might expect. Are couples without children child*less* or child-*free*? The choice is up to them.

Integrity. **A sense of firm identity, wholeness, wisdom, and the ability to let go. In Erikson's theory, integrity is the ultimate characteristic of development of the human personality in the later years. Those who do not develop integrity experience despair.**

The Challenge
and the Self

Erikson teaches that during the later years, the central challenge is to accept the finality of one's life cycle, to recognize your distinct time and place upon the panorama and sweep of the history of the human species. It takes wisdom to accept the coincidence of your own life cycle with one brief moment of human history and, at the same time, to find meaning in your life. Yet Erikson believes that if you have resolved life's earlier life crises in a generally positive direction—trusted in your own initiative, autonomy, and competence, found your place in society and developed intimate relationships, and produced in a way that is meaningful to you—such acceptance will be possible. This acceptance, this wisdom, this continuation of the firm sense of self despite physical infirmity—this is what Erikson labels **integrity.** Integrity means wholeness or oneness, a holding together of the self-concept and self-esteem despite a creeping loss of function.

Without integrity, Erikson writes, we may despair. We may look on life as a dirty trick. It is a lofty ideal, Erikson's integrity.

Integrity may be difficult to maintain during the later years, especially when our gradual losses of functioning may be compounded by society's tossing us into the human wastebasket through forced retirement at sixty-five or seventy. In his book *It Takes a Long Time to Become Young,* sixty-years-young film director and writer Garson Kanin (1975) reports U. S. Bureau of Labor statistics that the mean life span among forced retirees is thirty to forty months.

Figure 3.1 Life Stage and Satisfaction

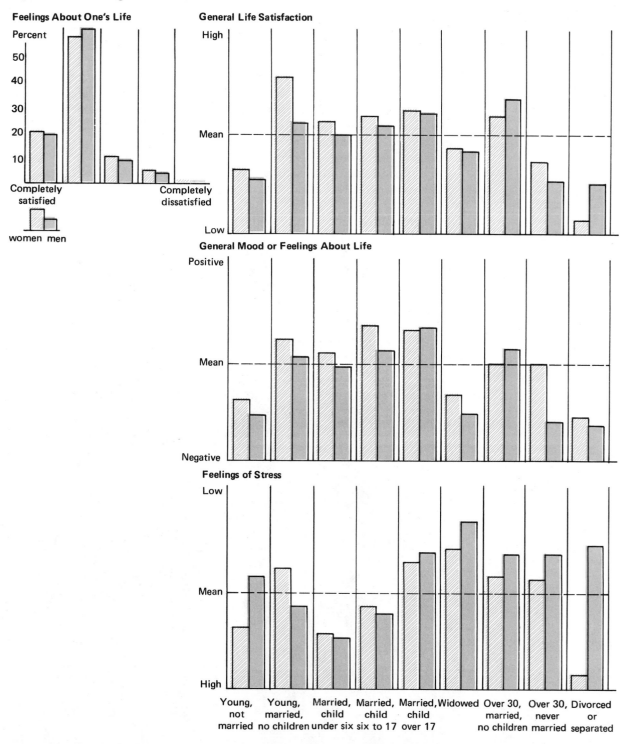

Feelings About One's Life

Percent

General Life Satisfaction

General Mood or Feelings About Life

Feelings of Stress

women men

Young, not married | Young, married, no children | Married, child under six | Married, child six to 17 | Married, child over 17 | Widowed | Over 30, married, no children | Over 30, never married | Divorced or separated

The great majority of Americans are satisfied with their lives; only one percent report being extremely dissatisfied. Dissatisfactions and sex differences show up at various stages of the life cycle, however. Married people are happier than singles, for example, and the childless are happier than couples with young children.

Source: Campbell (1975), p. 40.

One of three marriages breaks up following forced retirement. The suicide rate is twelve times as great as normal for this age group.

Kanin argues that only personal choice or demonstrated inability to perform in one's work should lead to retirement—at eighty-two or forty-two. The older worker's experience often compensates for lowered stamina. He tells a story about a Connecticut town that lost its electrical power. After several days of fruitless poking around, someone sent for the retired electrical engineer who had installed the system many years earlier. The old engineer studied the problem and then tapped his mallet once and threw the switch. The light came on. He sent the town a bill for $1,000.02—two cents for tapping, $1,000 for knowing where to tap. Wisdom does not come cheap.

The opportunity for meaningful work throughout our years is a major aim of the senior rights movement.

On Death and Dying. Death is the last great taboo. Psychiatrist Elisabeth Kübler-Ross (1969) comments on our denial of death in her book *On Death and Dying:* "We use euphemisms, we make the dead look as if they were asleep, we ship the children off to protect them from the anxiety and turmoil around the house if the patient is fortunate enough to die at home, [and] we don't allow children to visit their dying parents in the hospitals, . . ." (p. 8).

During the second half of the thirties, many people settle down and plant roots. Their interests may turn to advancement in a career, long-term home mortgages, and children.

From her work with hundreds of terminally ill patients, Kübler-Ross found some common response patterns to news of impending death and identified five stages that many patients pass through: denial, anger, bargaining, depression, and final acceptance. Those of us who suspect or fear the approach of death in the later years may face similar challenges.

In denial, people feel, "It can't be me. The diagnosis must be wrong." Denial usually gives way to anger and resentment toward the young and healthy and, perhaps, the medical establishment: "It's unfair. Why me? Why should they live while I must die?" Then there may follow a stage of bargaining with God to postpone the inevitable: "What must I do to earn a reprieve of just a month or two?" People would think pure thoughts or do good deeds in exchange for time. Then comes depression, feelings of despair and hopelessness. There are feelings of supreme loss—grief from the specter of parting from loved ones and from life itself. Ultimately, an inner peace may come, a quiet acceptance of the inevitable. But Kübler-Ross points out that this "acceptance should not be mistaken for a happy stage. It is almost void of feelings. It is as if the pain had gone, the struggle is over, and there comes a time for the final rest before the long journey, as one patient has phrased it" (p. 13).

The final hours pose a towering challenge to our integrity. Kübler-Ross believes we might be able to face this challenge more successfully if death and dying were dealt with as facts of life in our culture—and if the dying were helped to die in dignity, preferably in their own home, not in an anonymous hospital.

Lying Down to Pleasant Dreams . . . The American poet William Cullen Bryant lived from 1794 to 1878, yet never in his maturity could he regain the majesty of his poem "Thanatopsis," written at the age of eighteen.

The senior years can be viewed as providing additional opportunities for growth and satisfaction.

Human Development
Through the Life Cycle

"Thanatopsis" expresses Erikson's ideal of maintaining a basic trust throughout life, the belief that it is possible to live the kind of life so that when it is time to "join the innumerable caravan"—the uncountable billions who have died before us—we can leave life with dignity and integrity.

We should live our lives, the poet writes, so that

> . . . when thy summons comes to join
> The innumerable caravan that moves
> To the pale realms of shade, where each shall take
> His chamber in the silent halls of death,
> Thou go not, like the quarry-slave at night,
> Scourged to his dungeon, but, sustained and soothed
> By an unfaltering trust, approach thy grave
> Like one who wraps the drapery of his couch
> About him, and lies down to pleasant dreams.

Bryant, of course, wrote "Thanatopsis" at eighteen, not eighty-five. At that advanced age, his feelings might have differed. But literature and poetry need not perfectly reflect reality. They can serve to inspire and to warm us. The fact that some have looked at death with beauty may help us to ward off despair, to maintain integrity of the self in the face of the inevitable.

summary

- *Human embryos have shock absorbers.* Yes, the embryo develops in the amniotic sac. Amniotic fluid suspends it and cushions it from the mother's movements or even injuries to the mother. All the infant's needs are instantly gratified in the womb, but during the first year of life it learns that there can be a delay between a need and its gratification. This delay leads to the infant's understanding that it is separate from the rest of the world. This sense of separateness is the beginning of the sense of self.
- *A feminine woman cannot be a well-adjusted adult, according to mental-health professionals.* False, of course. But in one study, these professionals attributed traditionally masculine traits, such as competitiveness and logic, to the concept of the "healthy adult," while the "healthy woman" was expected to be tender, passive, and dependent. Such sex-role stereotypes are ingrained in children at young ages through processes of identification and socialization.
- *Psychological research has shown that women do not write as well as men—even when they have authored the same article.* False, but both men and women apparently place less value on the products of women, according to several experiments. There is an exception: the woman who has "made it" earns the full approval of her peers.
- *Most personality differences between men and women are inborn.* False. Even the one trait which consistently distinguishes little boys from little girls, aggressiveness, seems at least in part culturally induced. Other culturally fostered differences that seem to hold up include relatively superior verbal ability in girls and math ability in boys.
- *People who show both traditional masculine traits and traditional feminine traits have more difficulty adjusting than people who show exclusively sex-typed traits.* False. People who show both types of traits are

called psychologically androgynous. Androgynous people have a broader range of responses that they can use to meet the requirements of their situations.

- *You can break your neck by stepping into a personhole in Woonsocket, Rhode Island.* Not anymore. The city council voted to change the word back to manhole, after a brief flirtation with making all job descriptions and related descriptions in Woonsocket nonsexist. Women entering jobs previously dominated by men have made us more aware of sexist job titles, like policeman rather than police officer. Authors are also now beginning to pay attention to sexism in the language, as exemplified in the use of the personal pronouns *he* and *him* to apply to everyone.

- *The major challenge of adolescence is development of a commitment to your personal beliefs concerning sexual morality.* False. Sexual philosophy is an important element in the self-identity of the adolescent, but choosing an occupational role is more central. By adolescence, individuals have been challenged by the stages of trust vs. mistrust, autonomy vs. shame and doubt, initiative vs. guilt, and industry vs. inferiority. During adolescence we develop identity or role diffusion. Development of identity may involve a crisis or moratorium, a period of hard self-questioning. People who avoid this crisis by adopting the views of others foreclose the opportunity to achieve their own identity.

- *Couples who marry before they have firmed up their self-identities may grow apart later on.* True. This appears to happen often enough in our culture, even when women, because of cultural stereotyping, do not feel pressed to develop their own identity until children are about to leave the nest. Erikson wrote that we are only ready to fuse our identities with others', to develop intimacy, when our own identities are firm.

- *The twenties are characterized by trying to make it in the career world.* True, according to the observations of Roger Gould and Gail Sheehy. During the twenties we grow increasingly independent of parents and set out on courses that seem at the time to be the one true course.

- *During the thirties, we may rip apart the life we have put together during the twenties.* True, the thirties often represent a time of major self-evaluation or reassessment. We may begin to find our earlier courses meaningless and set off in new directions. People who weather this reassessment period tend then to settle down or plant roots.

- *In their early forties, men suddenly leave the "Pepsi Generation."* True. According to Daniel Levinson, some marker event causes men who had seen themselves as buddies to men in their twenties to recognize that they are a full generation apart. A new sense of mortality brings on a second major reassessment and, sometimes, a mid-life crisis that includes severe depression. Men who weather the crisis often pour themselves into generativity—shaping the new generation and the world. The observations of Gould and Sheehy suggest that women undergo similar experiences. All must come to grips with the Dream—our appraisal of whether we have met our youthful expectations or self-ideal.

- *Single people are happier than married people.* False, according to the findings of Angus Campbell. The married people are generally more satisfied, and newly married women are especially radiant. Marriages seem to experience stress when there are young children on the scene, but once the children have grown, life satisfaction reasserts itself.

- *Forced retirement can be a death sentence.* True. Bureau of Labor statistics show that people forced to retire have shortened life expectancies. They are more likely than others to commit suicide and run into marital difficulties as well. Senior citizens are demanding that they be allowed to work as long as their capacities to function on the job are intact. Meaningful work is one way to maintain a sense of control over our own lives.

GENERALIZED EXPECTANCY FOR SUCCESS SCALE—SCORING KEY

In order to compute your total score on the expectancy for success scale, first *reverse* the scores for the following thirteen items (change a 1 to a 5, a 2 to a 4, leave a 3 alone, change a 4 to a 2, and a 5 to a 1): items 1, 2, 4, 6, 7, 8, 14, 15, 17, 18, 24, 27, and 28.

Note that the possible range of test scores varies from 30 to 150. The higher your score, the greater your expectancy for success in the future.

Bobbi Fibel and W. Daniel Hale administered their test to undergraduate students in psychology courses and found that the women's scores ranged from 65 to 143, and the men's scores ranged from 81 to 138. The average score for both men and women was 112 (112.32 for women and 112.15 for men).

4

PERSONALITY: THREE FORCES IN PSYCHOLOGY

Truth or Fiction?

- The human mind is like a vast, submerged iceberg, only the tip of which rises above the surface into our awareness.
- There is a watchdog or censor that screens our basic impulses and decides which will become conscious and which must be kept hidden.
- People who are perfectionistic and excessively neat and people who are sloppy and disorganized both experienced severe conflicts with their parents during the second year of life.
- Women who compete with men in the business world are suffering from penis envy.
- Psychologically mature adults prefer to attain sexual gratification through sexual intercourse with an adult of the opposite sex.
- When your team wins, it's "*We*'re number one!" But when your team loses, it's "*They* lost—the bums!"
- You can train a dog to salivate when it hears a bell.
- You can teach a pigeon to peck at a button in the wall when it has the green light, but to stop when the light goes off.
- You can keep a suitor dangling indefinitely through applying the same principle that "addicts" some people to slot machines.
- We may feel that we have freedom of choice, but our preferences and our "choices" are actually forced on us by our environment.
- People who actualize themselves are always future-oriented.
- Children may learn to view their own feelings as selfish, wrong, and even evil.
- Capricorns and Scorpios are more feminine than Geminis.

There is an ancient Islamic tale about several blind men who encountered an elephant for the first time. Each touched a different part of the elephant and claimed that he alone had grasped the true nature of the beast. One grabbed it by the legs and then described the elephant as firm, strong, and upright—like a pillar. But the blind man who had touched the ear of the elephant objected. The elephant, from his perspective, was broad and rough, like a rug. The third man had made the acquaintance of the animal's trunk. He was astounded at the insensitivity of the others. The elephant was narrow and long, he declared—like a hollow pipe. Each of the three had come to know the elephant from a different perspective. Each was blind to the beliefs of his fellows, not only because of his physical incapacity, but also because of his initial encounter with the elephant.

So it is that different ways of encountering human beings have led behavioral scientists to view people in different ways. A way of viewing things is a model. Our Islamic friends held three different models of the nature of the elephant: a pillar model, a rug model, and a pipe model. We who have eyes have a very different "model" of the elephant, seeing it as a large, heavy creature with floppy ears and a long trunk.

Behavioral scientists have tried to build models to describe us— models not of our external appearances, but of our **personalities** *or selves, the ways in which we think, feel, and behave, and the causes or reasons for our thoughts, feelings, and behavior. This is an important piece of business. If we can develop an accurate enough model of personality, we should be able not only to explain human behavior, but also to find excellent ways of helping when things go wrong. Yet when we do construct models of human personality, our problems are similar to those of the three blind men: we cannot directly see or even touch a personality. We must try to construct models of personality on the basis of the behavior that we can see and the thoughts and feelings people tell us about. And because we cannot directly see personalities, it will not surprise you that the impressions of personality that are constructed by different people can be very different from one another.*

Personality. Thoughts, feelings, and behavior that characterize a person's ways of adjusting to the challenges of life. We each have distinct personalities, or styles of adjusting.

In this chapter we explore three models of personality that are held by many psychologists today: the psychodynamic or psychoanalytic model, which emphasizes the importance of dynamic forces hidden deep within us; the behavioral model, which emphasizes the importance of learning to respond to environmental stimulation; and the humanistic model, which emphasizes the importance of self-awareness and the ability to shape our own lives through choice. Although these different models have had different histories and emphases, they have also been growing together.

THE PSYCHODYNAMIC MODEL

What if our three blind men were not blind, but simply held three differing views of the basic personality of an elephant—a psychodynamic view, a behavioral view, and a humanistic (or, in this case, elephantistic) view? What would the man with the psychodynamic view say about the elephant?

He might walk around the elephant a few times, scratching his chin in annoyance. "What we have here," he would finally say, "is the mere surface of the elephant, although a pretty big surface, I must admit. But you can't understand the elephant on the basis of those cute, floppy ears, or that hideous trunk." The elephant snorts. "The essential parts of the elephant are hidden beneath its gray head," he continues, "beneath all that flab." The elephant taps the ground impatiently.

"You see, there are forces at work deep inside the elephant, so deep that even the elephant is not aware of them. Yet they influence most of his behavior. To understand this elephant, we shall have to find a very large couch, have him lie down on it, and start him talking. It may take years, but this is one way for us to learn about the forces the elephant is not aware of, the forces that reside deep within his unconscious mind."

"My what?" asks the elephant.

"Your unconscious mind, flop ears."

"But I'm not aware of any unconscious mind," protests the elephant.

"Aha!" exclaims the gentleman. "I rest my case."

Sigmund Freud and Psychoanalysis

He was born with a schlock of black hair—according to Jewish tradition, a sign of the coming of a prophet. In a Czechoslovakian village in 1856, an old woman told his mother that she had given birth to a great man. The child was raised with great expectations. But when the child grew into a man, he, Sigmund Freud, looked back upon this notion with skepticism. He noted that

Sigmund Freud.

Conscious (KON-shuss). Self-aware.
Preconscious (PREE-kon-shuss). Presently out of awareness but capable of being brought into awareness at any time by simply focusing on it. For instance, what's your phone number?
Unconscious (un-KON-shuss). Out of awareness. Unconscious processes are not readily available to awareness, and even after years of insight-oriented treatment, we would not be able to become aware of many impulses, motives, and memories.
Repression (ree-PRESH-shun). A form of forgetting in which we are motivated to remain unaware of certain impulses or events in order to avoid anxiety. Repression is the most basic of the defense mechanisms.

The Challenge
and the Self

these prophecies were far from rare; "there are so many happy and expectant mothers" (in Jones 1961, p. 6). He added that old peasant women who could no longer bear children could do well as the bearers of such prophecies. After all, you won't make a good living as a bringer of bad news. But this may be one prophecy that was realized. Few individuals have influenced our thinking about human nature so significantly as this man we picture as the bearded Viennese physician.

Freud taught that human personality is characterized by a dynamic struggle, a clashing of opposing inner forces as basic biological drives such as hunger, thirst, and sex come into conflict with social pressures to behave according to laws, rules, and moral codes. His view of personality is psychodynamic or psychoanalytic: the social rules, which clash with our basic drives, also become incorporated as parts of us so that the major struggles are *within*. The outcome of these clashes determines our adjustment to the world.

The Geography of the Mind: Warming Up to the Human Iceberg. Freud was astounded as a young physician to learn that some people experienced problems such as loss of feeling in a hand or paralysis of the legs when there was nothing medically wrong. These strange symptoms often disappeared once patients had recalled psychologically painful events—like feelings of guilt—that had preceded them. But for a long time, these events and feelings had been hidden beneath the surface of awareness. Still they had influenced the behavior of these patients.

From this sort of evidence, Freud came to believe that the human mind is like an iceberg of which only the tip rises above the surface of the water into our awareness or consciousness. The greater mass of the mind remains below, where little light or knowledge can illuminate our deepest urges, thoughts, and fears. The region that pokes into the sunlight above the water Freud labeled the conscious part of the mind. Those regions that lie below he called the preconscious and the unconscious.

The **conscious** mind is another name for the conscious self, or the center of awareness. The content of the conscious mind shifts, depending on where we focus our attention. What are you aware or conscious of right now? The words on this page? The room temperature? Hunger? Plans for this evening? If you are engrossed in concern over whether your car battery will turn over later, you may not be able to give this page a fair shake.

The **preconscious** mind contains elements of your experience that are presently out of awareness but can be brought into consciousness at any time. What is your name? Your phone number? Your birthday? What is your favorite activity? When is the last time you engaged in your favorite activity? If you are still with us, you see how easy it is to bring these thoughts above the surface.

The **unconscious** mind is shrouded in mystery. Little of the light of awareness filters down to it. The unconscious mind contains biological drives and urges that you only partially experience as hunger, thirst, and sexual appetite. Some of these urges simply cannot be experienced fully as thoughts. Our mental pictures and words are not adequate. But other urges, some of which are sexual and some of which are hostile, may be kept below the surface by a process called **repression**. Repression is a kind of forgetting in which we are protected from recognizing the existence of unacceptable sexual or hostile impulses within us.

The unconscious is the largest part of the mind, and it is here that the struggle between biological drives and social rules is most fierce. Since we cannot view the unconscious mind directly, Freud developed a technique of mental detective work called **psychoanalysis.** In psychoanalysis people are prompted to talk about anything that "pops" into their minds while they are comfortable and relaxed. We may gain self-insight by pursuing some of the thoughts that pop into consciousness. But we may also be motivated to avoid talking about certain subjects. The same force of repression that has led us to make unacceptable feelings and thoughts unconscious may lead to resistance to talking or even thinking about them.

The mental detective work of psychoanalysis is slow and tedious. It may literally take years of psychoanalysis in the clinic to learn about the unconscious forces in someone's mind. Yet this painstaking clinical method is what Freud used to arrive at his conclusions about the geography of the human mind.

The Structure of Personality: Id, Ego, and Superego. When is a structure not a structure? When it is a mental or **psychic structure.** Freud considered the opposing, clashing forces in the personality to be psychic structures—structures that cannot be touched or seen, but whose presence is known through people's expressed thoughts and feelings and observable behavior. The outcome of the clashing between these psychodynamic forces or psychic structures determines whether an individual is well-adjusted or disturbed by psychological problems. Freud named these clashing forces the id, the ego, and the superego.

The **id** is the only mental structure present at birth. It represents biological drives and is fully unconscious. Freud described the id as "a chaos, a cauldron of seething excitations" (1964, p. 73). The id demands instant gratification of primitive impulses such as hunger and sex. It cares nothing for social custom or law. It follows what Freud termed the **pleasure principle:** it seeks instant satisfaction without consideration of decency or the needs of other people. If Freud had lived to watch the television show *Sesame Street*, he might have thought that the Cookie Monster made a pretty good id.

The **ego** begins to develop during the first year of life, when an infant learns that there must sometimes be delays before it is gratified. It blossoms more fully as children learn ways to obtain gratifications for themselves, without crying and screaming. Ego is the Latin word for "I," the sense of self. Human beings differ from lower animals because of the ego, the sense of self. The ego places curbs on the appetites of the id, and makes plans that are in keeping with social convention in order to achieve gratification and yet avoid disapproval of others. The id lets you know you are starving for a snack. The ego creates the idea of walking to the refrigerator, making a peanut butter sandwich, and pouring a glass of milk.

Freud wrote that the ego stands "for reason and good sense while the id stands for the untamed passions" (1964, p. 76). Thus the ego is guided by the **reality principle**—taking into account what is practical and possible as well as what is urged. Most of the ego is conscious, but some of its business can be carried out unconsciously. For instance, the ego also acts as a watchdog or censor that screens the urges of the id. When it senses impulses rising that are socially unacceptable so that people themselves would prefer to be able to avoid admitting that they have them—such as some sexual and some hostile impulses—the ego uses psychological defenses to prevent these impulses from surfacing into awareness. Repression is one psychological defense or **defense mechanism.** There are many others, as we discuss in Chapter 6. Freud sus-

The Cookie Monster from the television show *Sesame Street.* Freud might have thought that the Cookie Monster was all id.

Ego (EE-go). In psychoanalysis, the rational portion of the personality that attempts to find means that will gratify the instincts of the id, yet, at the same time, avoid running afoul of social custom or the demands of the superego. A rather neat tightrope act? *Reality principle.* Patterns of behavior that are in accordance with social custom, morals, and the realities of the physical world. The ego operates according to the reality principle. *Defense mechanism.* A method used by the ego to protect itself from experiencing anxiety that could result either from recognizing unconscious impulses or accepting blame for immoral acts. Thus the ego may deny or distort reality. Ego defense mechanisms are generally practiced unconsciously. *Superego* (SOUP-per-EE-go). The sense of right and wrong, the conscience. In psychoanalysis, the superego is the third psychic structure to develop, and typically includes the moral standards of the parents and others who had a hand in raising the child. *Intrapsychic conflict* (IN-truh-SIGH-kick). In psychoanalysis, clashes between the psychic structures, such as the superego punishing the ego for immoral behavior, or the id attempting to force a socially unacceptable impulse into consciousness while the ego struggles to keep it repressed. *Eros* (AIR-rose; rhymes with "BEAR close"). In psychoanalysis, the life instinct. From the Greek word for the god of love. *Libido* (lib-BEE-doe). In psychoanalysis, the instincts of the id. Sometimes used to refer to the sex drive. The energy of the instincts is sometimes called libidinal energy.

The Challenge
and the Self

90

pected that continued feelings of nervousness might actually represent unconscious, repressed feelings of hostility—possibly toward loved ones.

The **superego** develops throughout middle childhood and is often thought of as the conscience or the "voice within." The superego usually incorporates the moral standards and values of the parents and, later on, the standards of other significant individuals and the community. The superego acts like an internal moral guardian throughout life, judging the intentions of the ego and passing out judgments of right or wrong.

The ego doesn't have an easy time of it. Like a referee in a boxing ring, it stands between the id and superego, attempting to play the role of the great compromiser. It attempts at once to gratify id demands, yet to stay within moral limits. Concerning sexual matters, the id urges the ego, "You are aroused!" Perhaps the superego then warns, "But you're not married." The ego than gets stuck in the middle. In a healthy personality, the ego has found ways to gratify most of the demands of the id without seriously offending the superego. You can see that if the ego hasn't found pathways to gratification, or if the superego is rather strict, the ego will be in some hot water. Trying to moderate between clashing forces is never easy—especially when the opposing forces are within the same person. This is the nature of **intrapsychic conflict** —clashes between the different structures of the personality.

Psychosexual Development: On Childhood Sexuality. Freud got himself into a good deal of hot water with the medical establishment of his day by arguing that sexual impulses and the gratification of these impulses are central factors in the development of children's personalities. Freud was not suggesting that children wish to engage in sexual intercourse, but that their most basic ways of relating to the world, and to their parents, involve sexual feelings from the time an infant first suckles its mother's breast.

Freud believed that one of the major instincts of the id is **Eros,** or the instinct to preserve and perpetuate life. Eros contains a certain amount of energy, which Freud called **libido** or libidinal energy. This energy is psychological and related to sexual impulses, or psychosexual. Freud wrote that during the developmental years—from birth through adolescence—this libidinal or psychosexual energy is expressed in different ways. The various expressions of psychosexual energy contribute to **psychosexual development**—the orderly expression of libidinal energy through different parts of the body, or different **erogenous zones,** at several different stages of growth. There are five stages or periods of psychosexual development: oral, anal, phallic, latency, and genital.

The Oral Stage: If It Exists, It Should Be in My Mouth. During the first year of life, the mouth provides a major way in which children experience the world. If it fits, into the mouth it goes. Freud believed that the mouth is the first erogenous zone, and that during the **oral stage** of life, the first year, children seek sexually related gratification primarily through the mouth, through pleasurable activities such as sucking and biting.

Freud also believed that children encounter certain problems or conflicts during each stage of development. During the oral stage, this conflict is likely to center around whether or not an infant receives adequate oral gratification. Early weaning can lead to frustration, but excessive gratification can lead to expectation that the infant will be given everything in life with no effort of its own. Too little or too much gratification in any stage can lead to **fixation** in that stage, or development of personality traits characteristic of that stage.

Freud shocked the medical establishment of his day by portraying children as sexual creatures.

Some oral traits include dependency, gullibility, and optimism or pessimism.

Freud believed that adults with oral fixations can experience an exaggerated desire for oral activities, including smoking, overeating, alcohol or drug abuse, nail biting, and—like the infant whose only means to satisfaction and survival are sucking at the breast and the mercy of the mother—clinging, dependent interpersonal relationships. Freud's own "oral fixation," his habitual cigar smoking, may have led to the development of cancer of the mouth and jaw, which required several operations. Still, he would not forgo this source of "oral gratification." He died from cancer in 1939.

The Anal Stage: "Do It for Mommy?" During the second or third year of life, or **anal stage** of psychosexual development, a child may get the idea that its products of elimination are extremely valuable. After all, it is likely to be during

Personality:
Three Forces in Psychology

91

these years of life that the parents place the child on a "potty" and beg the child to be "good" and do it now—not later, in the crib. It is also during this period that the child tends to learn that waste products are "dirty." If the baby is play-ing with its waste products in its crib and a parent walks in and shouts "Yuck!" the child's ego is likely to get the message that such behavior is unacceptable.

When one feels the urge to eliminate, certainly one would like to do so. Yet parents urge delay of gratification during the toilet-training process, and the value of self-control can become a powerful issue for the developing superego. If the issue of self-control is one of great conflict, the child may ac-quire anal personality traits. These are of two major kinds: **anal retentive** traits, such as perfectionism, order, and cleanliness: and **anal expulsive** traits, such as carelessness and messiness.

The Phallic Stage: Of Greek Kings and Children. During the third year of life, children enter the **phallic stage.** They now shift the focus of sexual gratifi-cation from the anal region to the genital organs. Freud believed that strong conflicts concerning masturbation can develop during the phallic stage, since the child's self-exploration and finding of self-pleasure may lead to a strong, negative parental reaction, punishments, and threats.

During the phallic stage children may develop strong sexual attachments to the parent of the opposite sex, and even begin to view the same-sex parent as a rival for the other parent's affections. Little boys may have fantasies about marrying mommy, and little girls may have fantasies about marrying daddy.

These feelings of lust and jealousy are not easy for little children to live with. They would make home life a constant source of tension. So they remain largely unconscious, although their influence is felt through marriage fantasies and vague hostilities toward the parent of the opposite sex. Freud labeled this conflict the **Oedipus conflict** or **complex** in boys, after the legendary Greek king who killed his father and married his mother. Similar feelings in girls are called the **Electra complex.** Electra was the daughter of the Greek king Aga-memnon. She longed for her father after his death and felt vengeance toward her mother, Clytemnestra, who was involved in his death. We discuss the Oed-ipus conflict further in Chapter 8.

The Latency Period: When Enough Is Enough. Put yourself in the place of the typical five- or six-year-old boy or girl. Your life has been one long sexual struggle. You started life with an effort to attain oral gratification. After a year, the focus of your sexual interests shifted to the anus and you probably experi-enced conflict with your parents concerning gaining control over the process of elimination. You wanted to eliminate where and when you felt the urge. Your parents said, "Not yet" and "Please do it here." Another year passed, and during the third year of life your focus of sexual interest again shifted, this time to the genital region. During the next three or four years you probably encoun-tered additional problems with your parents—this time over masturbation and over rivalries with the parent of the same sex as you sought somehow to possess the parent of the opposite sex. It's been a busy five or six years.

Freud believed that now, at the age of five or six, children are strongly mo-tivated to place all these sexual pressures and parental conflicts behind them. In order to accomplish this they renounce or give up the parent of the opposite sex as a sex object. They reaffirm their closeness to the same-sex parent by identifying or becoming more similar to him or her. This process of identifica-tion has implications for assuming both sex roles and the moral codes and

DO WOMEN WHO COMPETE WITH MEN SUFFER FROM PENIS ENVY?

Sigmund Freud's model of personality has generally been a liberating force in modern history, allowing people to admit to the importance of sexuality in their lives. But it has also been claimed that Freud's views have been repressive of women—suggesting that women who wish to compete with men in the business world are suffering from penis envy.

Freud theorized that penis envy was central in the Electra conflict, that from very early childhood little girls envied little boys because they had penises. Freud went so far as to write that the entire developmental process of girls "may be said to take place under the colours of envy for the penis" in *New Introductory Lectures on Psychoanalysis* (1964).

Freud wrote that if little girls attempted to achieve sexual gratification during the phallic stage by masturbation, they were not likely to find adequate satisfaction, because, Freud believed, the clitoris was not as sensitive to sexual stimulation as the penis. Little girls would soon give up masturbation on their own since they would not want to be reminded of the "superiority" of their brothers and playmates.

Little girls would resent their mothers for bringing them into the world without penises, and would develop the wish to marry their fathers as a substitution for not having penises of their own. Eventually, however, girls would cope with the desire for the father through marriage to a man more their own age, and then make the ultimate adjustment of having a baby. A baby, especially a male child, would unconsciously represent something "growing" from her genital region, and bring some satisfaction. In an ideal marriage, a woman would accept the authority of her husband. This would indicate that she had surrendered the wish to have a penis of her own.

Freud warned that if women retained their first wish, to have a penis, they would become maladjusted. They would probably become competitive and self-assertive. At worst, they might become homosexual. They would show masculine traits as a result of their continued jealousy, and their masculinity could even extend to preferences for sex partners.

Are Freud's assumptions accurate? First, do little girls envy little boys their penises? Karen Horney (1967), a female psychoanalyst, took issue with Freud on this point, noting that he was not most qualified to report on the fantasies and wishes of little girls. Nor did little girls consider themselves inferior to boys.

Second, do little girls stop masturbating because they cannot find sexual gratification through self-stimulation? It may be that fewer women than men masturbate (Hunt 1974), but laboratory studies by William Masters and Virginia Johnson (1966) suggest that perfectly normal women experience intense orgasms through masturbation. In fact, these orgasms may be more intense than the orgasms experienced through sexual intercourse with men.

Psychologist Phyllis Chesler (1972) notes that there is a historic prejudice against self-assertive, competitive women, even among mental-health professionals. Many people still prefer women who are passive and submissive, emotional, and dependent on men. In Freud's time, these prejudices were even more extreme, and his theory reflected the belief that motherhood was the only acceptable avenue by which women could achieve psychological maturity.

A major problem with Freudian theory is that "unconscious" processes such as the Oedipus complex and penis envy cannot be studied directly with scientific methods. Thus they must remain untested opinion.

---

values of the parents, especially the parent of the same sex. Taking on parental values causes the superego to grow rapidly at this time.

At about the age of six children repress their sexual urgings and enter the **latency period** or stage. This is fortunate. According to psychoanalysts, it permits attention to be diverted from sexual pursuits and to be focused in on schoolwork. For a period of several years, it is not uncommon for boys to prefer to play with boys and girls to prefer to play with girls. The latency period, according to Freud, permits the child to rest and recuperate from the stress

Phallic stage (FAL-lick; rhymes with "PAL sick"). In psychoanalysis, the third stage of psychosexual development, in which the child remains till the fifth or sixth year of life. Time for castration anxiety and penis envy, in theory.

Oedipus complex (ED-uh-puss). In psychoanalysis, a conflict experienced by boys during the phallic stage in which they long to possess their mothers sexually and are hostile toward their fathers—their rivals in love.

Electra complex (ee-LECK-truh). In psychoanalysis, a conflict experienced by girls during the phallic stage in which they long to have penises, like their fathers and brothers, and resent their mothers for bringing them into the world so "ill-equipped." All quite controversial, as you might well imagine.

Latency period (LATE-ten-see). In psychoanalysis, the fourth stage of psychosexual development, lasting from six or so until puberty. By six, children have experienced enough sexual conflict, so they repress the libido (keeping it latent or hidden) for a number of years. Fortunate—now they can focus on learning to read in first grade?

Genital stage (JEN-it-ull). In psychoanalysis, the fifth or final stage of psychosexual development, in which adolescents channel their reborn sexual urgings into interests in persons their own age of the opposite sex.

Puberty (PEW-burr-tee). The stage at which boys and girls acquire the physical ability to reproduce and develop secondary sex characteristics such as voice change, bodily hair, and development of breasts. Puberty is the beginning of adolescence.

Inferiority complex. Feelings of inferiority or inadequacy which may be based on a physical problem but, more often, simply result from the perception of smallness and helplessness we experience as children.

and strain of the Oedipus or Electra conflict. Latent means hidden, and Freud believed that during the latency period sexual urges are effectively hidden or kept unconscious.

The Genital Stage: Becoming Followers of Eros.   Freud was an Orthodox Jew, a very religious man. As such, he believed that the primary purpose of human sexual behavior was to follow the command in the Old Testament that people are to "go forth and multiply." The whole thrust of Eros, the life instinct, was aimed toward eventual reproduction and perpetuation of the species. This could be accomplished only through genital intercourse between the sexes. So it is not surprising that this traditionally oriented man believed that mature, appropriate sexual behavior was to be limited to sexual intercourse within an intimate relationship.

Freud wrote that we enter the **genital stage** of psychosexual development with **puberty,** a series of bodily changes that set the stage for the reproduction of the species. With boys, the testicles develop and produce sperm. The voice deepens and hair grows in several areas of the body. With girls, the hips become rounded and ova mature and become capable of being fertilized. The breasts grow, as does bodily hair. The chemical changes of puberty also serve to stimulate the sexual appetite.

With puberty adolescent males may again experience sexual urges toward their mother and adolescent females may again experience sexual urges toward their father. But in our culture we have a strong incest taboo—a strong belief that it is wrong to have sexual feelings toward members of the family. So these sexual urges remain unacceptable and there is still ample motivation to try to repress them. But repression is not enough. Freud believed that these sexual urges toward parents are also displaced, or transferred, onto other people of the opposite sex. Yet boys may be expected to want to find girls "just like the girl who married dear old Dad." Girls are also attracted to males who resemble their fathers in certain ways.

The genital stage represents adult sexuality. From a psychosexual point of view, we remain in the genital stage for the remainder of our lives. People in the genital stage by definition prefer to find sexual satisfaction through intercourse with a member of the opposite sex. Finding pleasure through oral or anal stimulation or through masturbation or through sexual activity with someone of the same sex all represented signs of sexual immaturity to Freud. They represented fixations in pregenital stages of development. They were not in keeping with the life instinct, Eros. They did not lead to perpetuation of the human species.

Other Directions: Descendants of Freud

Freud's great emphasis on the role of sex in human adjustment led to early divisions within the psychodynamic or psychoanalytic school of thought. The first of Freud's followers to break away was Alfred Adler (1870–1937), who believed that people are basically motivated not by sexual or psychosexual urgings, but by an **inferiority complex.** An inferiority complex can be based on actual physical problems, like a weak or diseased organ, but he believed that we would all experience some feelings of inferiority even if there were no physical problems.

Feelings of inferiority lead us, Adler believed, to a **drive for superiority** or

ON BASKING IN REFLECTED GLORY

Every fall several campuses are swept by football mania. At campuses like Purdue, Arizona State, Ohio State, and Notre Dame, "Fans of championship teams gloat over their team's accomplishments and proclaim their affiliation with buttons on their clothes, bumper stickers on their cars, and banners on their public buildings. Despite the fact that they have never caught a ball or thrown a block in support of their team's success, the tendency of such fans is to claim for themselves part of their team's glory; it is perhaps informative that the shout is always, 'We're number one,' never, 'They're number one!'"

Why does this happen? Is it an expression of an unswerving loyalty to the home team, or do fans "bask in the reflected glory" of successful teams but dissociate themselves from unsuccessful teams?

In a recent study (Cialdini et al. 1976), psychologists on several prominent football campuses surreptitiously observed their students on the Mondays after football games. They found that on the Mondays following victories, significantly higher percentages of the students observed wore clothing with their school's insignia or mascot than on Mondays following defeats. But this could mean that students simply liked their schools more on Mondays following victories. Did they actually tend to identify more with their schools on the Mondays following victories?

In a second part of the experiment, these investigators gave their students attitude surveys, part of which asked them to describe the outcome of the past weekend's game. When the home team was victorious, students were likely to write, "We won!" But when the home team lost, they were significantly more likely to refer to the team as "They." In other words, "We won," but "They lost."

These findings fit in with the Freudian concept of identification. We may attempt to identify or associate ourselves with people who are powerful, successful, and admired, but likely to dissociate ourselves from losers. Since we identify with winners, their success becomes our success, giving us a boost in self-esteem. As children we also tend to identify with our parents, who seem so capable of manipulating the environment to cough up the rewards that we may have difficulty obtaining for ourselves. But identifying with a loser will only be an exercise in boosting the agony of defeat.

---

perfection. The drive for superiority is fueled also by compensation, the attempt to overcome actual or imagined inferiorities through individual striving. People who believe they are weak or deformed may seek to excel in athletics or in academic endeavors.

Adler also had a strong humanistic bent. He spoke of a **creative self**—an aspect of the human personality which strives in full self-awareness and consciousness to overcome obstacles to become whatever it is capable of being. Adler called the ideals that we will strive for **fictional finalisms:** images of life and of ourselves as they can be, not as they are. No matter how hard we strive or how far we travel, our fictional finalisms will also probably change to stay a step ahead. Human fulfillment lies in the striving toward ideals, not in believing that we have attained them.

The second major defector from Freud's circle of followers was Carl Jung (1875–1961), a Swiss psychiatrist who had been a favorite of Freud's. Like Freud but unlike Adler, Jung emphasized unconscious biological forces as the major influences on personality. But Jung did not believe that these forces were mostly sexual. He saw them as inherited racial predispositions or tendencies that were contained in a part of the unconscious mind that he termed the **collective unconscious.** The collective unconscious represents the accumulated experience of the human species and is passed down genetically from generation to generation.

Drive for superiority. According to Alfred Adler, this drive may be quite conscious and may impel us to initiate our own strivings toward personal growth. Adler was a humanistic psychoanalyst.
Creative self. Alfred Adler's term for the self-aware, self-organizing tendency that takes charge of our abilities in order to overcome imagined or real inferiorities.
Fictional finalisms. Alfred Adler's term for the goals we seek in life. They are equivalent to the ideal self —what we are capable of becoming. The image of fictional finalisms motivates us to strive toward them.

Personality:
Three Forces in Psychology

Jung characterized the common human belief in a God or gods as an example of such an inherited tendency. He felt that we also have animal, masculine, and feminine tendencies with us, to name a few. Yet Jung also believed in the concept of a self: We all have a unique self within us that is capable of piecing together all the parts of the collective unconscious, and our experiences, into an organized, self-aware whole.

Others who were trained in the psychoanalytic tradition but who broke with Freud over the issue of the importance of sexual influences on the personality include Erich Fromm, Karen Horney, Harry Stack Sullivan, and Erik Erikson. These behavioral scientists place more emphasis on the importance of social influence and social relationships, and also believe that the conscious functions of the personality are more important in fostering adjustment than Freud allowed. For this reason, they are known as **ego analysts.**

THE BEHAVIORAL MODEL

Our behaviorist encountering the elephant might take issue with the psychoanalyst. "What's all this stuff about ids, egos, and superegos?" he might ask with a disapproving shake of the head. "You can't touch or measure ids, egos, and superegos. This isn't science, it's a witch hunt for imaginary 'structures' inside an imaginary mind. If you want to be scientific about this, you have to pull out the camera and the tape measure. Stick to the things you can see and record directly—the weight and color of the elephant, the sound of its trumpet call, the speed at which it runs, its heartbeat, and the chemical constitution of its blood."

"Is that all?" the elephant butts in. "What about my speech? My opinions? My feelings? My dreams? My fantasies? The unconscious forces at work deep within me?"

The behaviorist sighs. "Look, gray buddy, let's strike a compromise. We can use your speech because this is observable behavior. We can also use the *report* of your opinions and feelings, because that is some more speech that we can observe directly. But we'll agree that we can't talk about unconscious processes, because none of us can see them—not even you, long nose."

Behavior Is Elementary, According to Dr. Watson

The psychodynamic model views the self as caught in the midst of a dynamic struggle between the opposing forces of biological drives and social customs. Behaviorists would prefer to view us in terms of concepts that we can all clearly see, measure, and agree upon: environmental forces acting on us, and our observable responses to these forces. If we have minds, conscious or unconscious, behaviorists would prefer to avoid calling on them in explaining and predicting our behavior. This is because the mind is private, a black box to the world, something that cannot be measured by scientific instruments.

While Freud was developing and polishing his psychodynamic theory from his clinical contacts with patients in Vienna, a psychologist at Johns Hopkins University by the name of John B. Watson was laying the foundation for the second major model of man—behaviorism. In 1913 Watson published an article, "Psychology as the Behaviorist Views It." He argued that psychology should concern itself with our outward behavior rather than internal states such as feelings and unconscious dynamics. Watson objected to the common method of investigation of his day, in which people would be asked to describe their personal or subjective emotions and sensations. Watson claimed that a person's inner experiences could not be verified by outside observers or measured by objective yardsticks. If psychology was to advance as a science, psychologists would have to rely on observable behavior that could be objectively measured and recorded. Let us scientists study behavior, Watson said, and leave concepts like "mind" and "self" to poets and philosophers. Many psychologists in the behavioral mold do just that today, while others, as we shall see, have included the concept of "mind" in their theories.

Watson then got to work, attempting to describe how learning is the major factor in the formation of behavior. He was heartened to find that, halfway around the world, a Russian scientist by the name of Ivan Pavlov had already experimented with a basic factor in learning, the conditioned reflex.

Classical Conditioning: Turning On a Dog to a Bell

We have a notable preference for having papers returned by teachers with A's on them rather than F's. We are also (usually) more likely to stop our automobiles when we see red traffic lights than when we see green traffic lights. Yet we are not born knowing that A's are good and F's are bad. We are not born knowing that red means stop and green means go. We learn the meanings of these symbols or these stimuli through **association**: we come to understand their meanings through words of explanation that are connected to them. Yet learning through association can also occur automatically, as Ivan Pavlov (1927) demonstrated when he turned some laboratory dogs on to bells.

A dog is constructed so that if you place meat powder on its tongue, it will salivate. Salivation in response to meat powder is a reflex—a simple form of behavior that need not be learned. Human beings have knee-jerk reflexes: a tap below the knee will cause you to kick. If someone blows in your eye, you will blink. This is another reflex. If someone blows in your ear, you may then follow that person anywhere. But that is not a reflex.

An environmental event or change, like dropping meat powder on a tongue, or tapping you below the knee, or blowing in your eye, or a changing stoplight is a **stimulus.** A reflex is one kind of response, or reaction to a stimulus. Reflexes are unlearned, but they can also be *conditioned* or connected to many different kinds of stimuli through association or learning.

Pavlov demonstrated this convincingly by strapping a dog into a harness. He placed some meat powder on the dog's tongue and the animal salivated. Then he repeated the process several times, with just one difference. Each time, he preceded the meat powder by half a second or so with the ringing of a bell. After several pairings of the bell and meat powder, Pavlov rang the bell and did not follow it with the meat powder. What do you think happened? The dog salivated anyway. It had learned to salivate in response to the bell because the bell had been associated several times with the meat powder.

In this experiment, meat powder is an **unconditioned stimulus** (US) and salivation in response to the meat powder is an **unconditioned response** (UR). Unconditioned means unlearned. The dog salivated in response to the bell after several pairings. The bell was originally a meaningless or **neutral stimulus.** But through association it became a **conditioned stimulus** (CS), or learned stimulus, for bringing about the salivation response. Salivation in re-

Association (ass-so-see-AY-shun). The pairing of one event or stimulus with another. We learn to expect that one thing will follow another, like winter follows fall, when they are associated with one another. *Stimulus* (STIM-you-luss). An environmental event or change. In the language of conditioning, a response may be a reaction to a stimulus. Some learning theorists consider all behavior to be responses. *Unconditioned stimulus* (UN-kon-DISH-shunned). An event or change in the environment that brings about a particular response because of the way an organism is constructed. You blink when someone blows in your eye because of the way you are put together, not as a result of learning. A stream of air in your eye is an unconditioned stimulus (US) for the blinking response. *Unconditioned response.* A reaction to a stimulus that is unlearned. Blinking is the unconditioned response (UR) to having someone blow in your eye. Saying "That's a dumb thing to do" is learned, and therefore not an unconditioned response. *Neutral stimulus* (NEW-trall). An event or change in the environment that does not bring about the particular response prior to learning. *Conditioned stimulus* (kon-DISH-shunned). A previously neutral stimulus that acquires the ability to bring about a response through being paired with an unconditioned stimulus.

Personality:
Three Forces in Psychology

Ivan Pavlov and his assistants at the Russian Academy.

Conditioned response. The reaction to a conditioned stimulus (CS). A conditioned response takes place as a result of learning through association.

Extinction (eggs-STINK-shun). An experimental procedure in which the conditioned stimulus (CS) is presented repeatedly without being associated with the unconditioned stimulus (US). Eventually, the conditioned response (CR) should discontinue, or become "extinguished."

sponse to the bell is now called a **conditioned response** (CR): it is like the UR, but it has been learned.

Extinction, Spontaneous Recovery, Generalization, and Discrimination. You may get a dog turned on to a bell through classical conditioning, but just how long do you think a self-respecting dog is going to continue to salivate in response to a bell if the meat supply is turned off? It will salivate several times, especially if there were many pairings of the meat and bell over several days, but it will eventually stop.

Presenting the bell (CS) several times without the meat (US) is an example of **extinction.** The bell loses its meaning as a signal for salivation. Let's look at several examples of extinction. Suppose that your local movie theater specialized in horror films, and that every time you attended you were scared to your wit's end. Soon enough, we would expect from the laws of classical conditioning, you would begin to experience fear by just entering the darkened theater before the movie begins. The same process applies when you experience fear when taking a seat in the waiting room of your dentist's office. In these cases, can you identify the conditioned and unconditioned stimuli, and the conditioned response? You're correct if you labeled the movie theater and dentist's office as conditioned stimuli, the fear experienced watching the movie and the pain during a visit to the dentist as the unconditioned stimuli, and fear as the conditioned response. Now, what if the movie theater stopped showing horror films, or every time you went to the dentist for a checkup you required no painful dental work? Would your conditioned response, fear, continue indefinitely if the CS were no longer associated with the US? Probably not. The CR would eventually extinguish, although it might take considerably longer to extinguish your fear response to a visit to a dentist than to a movie theater. But as we shall see next, conditioned responses have a tendency to reappear spontaneously.

Let us assume that we have gone to the trouble of conditioning a dog to salivate in response to a bell, and then we have also gone to the trouble of extinguishing this conditioned response by continually presenting the CS (bell) without the US (meat). Our week's work done, we make sure that the dog is comfortable, shut off the laboratory lights, don our coats, and go home for the weekend. On Monday morning the dog is again placed in its harness and the CS (bell) is presented once more. What do you think the dog will do?

If you guessed that the dog would again show the CR (salivate), you are perfectly right. It seems that after a vacation from an extinction procedure, conditioned responses have a tendency to show **spontaneous recovery.** They recur as a function of elapsed time. If you were to try to extinguish the CR again, the procedure would go more rapidly the second time around. But a few months later, the dog might salivate when the neighborhood church bells rang some Sunday.

Pavlov showed that a laboratory dog would salivate in response not only to the bell to which salivation had been conditioned, but also in response to the ringing of bells similar in tone. This is **generalization,** showing the CR in response to stimuli similar to the CS. It is fortunate that learning can generalize. Otherwise we might have to learn that a smile is a sign of friendship and a frown a sign of displeasure for each individual we met. It would also be difficult for us to read if we perceived a large WORD to be something different from a small WORD.

Adjustment to this world requires that we also make appropriate **discriminations.** Pavlov could teach a laboratory dog to salivate in response to a tone of very limited range by pairing presentation of that tone only with the US (meat). Eventually the animal would learn to discriminate that tone from others so long as it was capable physiologically of perceiving the difference between them. If you do not learn to discriminate between your parents and other people, you may experience poor treatment at the hands of strangers when you are young. As adults it is important for us to learn to discriminate signs of social receptiveness from signs that people are not interested in us. Otherwise we may not realize that our behavior is ineffective and that we should either change our approach or approach somebody else.

Operant Conditioning: Turning a Pigeon On to a Button

Just what is so exciting about a button sticking out of the wall? Why will a pigeon peck this button whenever it is hungry? Just what is so thrilling about a tiny lever at one end of a cage? Why will a laboratory rat press this lever for several hours, until it is just plain exhausted?

B. F. Skinner of Harvard University showed that buttons could become very exciting to pigeons if you dropped a food pellet into the birds' cages every time they pecked them (Skinner 1938). Rats will press levers continually for food pellets when hungry, or for a burst of electrical stimulation in the so-called pleasure centers of their brains. As you will see in Chapter 7, rats will even learn to increase or decrease the rate of their heartbeats for a good shot of electricity in these brain centers.

Skinner demonstrated that animals would learn to do things that led to **reinforcements,** such as food pellets, water, the opportunity to mate, or the sound of a bell that had been previously associated with feeding. Reinforcements increase the probability that a certain sort of behavior will be repeated. **Positive reinforcers** increase behavior when they are applied. **Negative reinforcers** increase behavior when they are removed. Food and approval are usually found to be positive reinforcers. But we may also learn to plan ahead in order to reduce fear of things going wrong. Removal of fear is negatively reinforcing and increases the frequency of planning behavior. With sufficient reinforcement, behavior will become a **habit,** showing a high probability of repetition under certain circumstances.

Spontaneous recovery. The tendency for an extinguished response to recur in reaction to the conditioned stimulus (CS) when some time has elapsed following the extinction procedure.

Generalization (jen-ur-al-eye-ZAY-shun). The tendency for a response to occur in the presence of stimuli that are similar to the original stimulus to which the response was conditioned.

Discrimination (dis-krim-uh-NAY-shun). The tendency to display a response only in the presence of a particular range of stimuli, following extinction of responses to a wider range of stimuli. If you are wise, you will learn to salivate in response only to those hamburgers that do not have Uncle Ferdinand's secret sauce.

Reinforcement (ree-in-FORCE-ment). An event that makes some behavior more likely to be repeated.

Positive reinforcer. An event that makes some behavior more likely to be repeated when it is applied. Good food, money, approval, and sleek cars that guzzle little gas are positive reinforcers for most of us.

Negative reinforcer. An event that makes some behavior more likely to be repeated when it is removed. You are more likely to repeat the behavior of leaving for school on time if leaving on time removes fear of being rapped across the knuckles for being late. No, we make no recommendations.

Habit. A type of behavior that has a high probability of being repeated in a given situation. Reinforcement can make behavior habitual.

B. F. Skinner and a friend.

Operant (OP-purr-ant). Skinner's term for a type of behavior that results in reinforcement. Here you thought you were working for grades when you were actually engaging in operants for reinforcers.
Primary reinforcer (PRY-mare-ee). A reinforcer that has its reinforcement value because of the way you are constructed—for instance, food when hungry, warmth when cold, water when thirsty.
Secondary reinforcer (SECK-un-dare-ee). A reinforcer that has its reinforcement value because of learning —for instance, money, gold stars, a pat on the back.
Reward. A pleasant consequence of behavior that is likely to increase the frequency of that behavior. Note that the definition of reinforcement, by contrast, makes no assumptions about what is pleasant or unpleasant.

Skinner called the behavior that leads to reinforcement an **operant,** since the individual or animal is "operating" on the environment so that reinforcement can be attained. In classical conditioning, by contrast, a person or animal learning to associate two stimuli with one another need not "do" anything in order to learn that one is being regularly followed by the other.

Reinforcers can be primary or secondary. **Primary reinforcers** have their reinforcement value because of the way you are constructed. Food when hungry, water when thirsty, warmth when cold, escape from physical pain—all these have their value because of the way you are put together and are primary reinforcers. **Secondary reinforcers** acquire their value through learning. We seek money because we learn it can be exchanged for other desired objects. We all come from unique backgrounds, and what is secondarily reinforcing to you may not be secondarily reinforcing to your neighbor. You may both eat when hungry, but you may prefer vanilla and your neighbor may think that chocolate ice cream is cool. You may like poetry and your neighbor prefer sculpture. You may love Beethoven, but your neighbor may get off on that new punk rock group, the Star-Spangled Yogurt Trip. Gold stars, A's on tests, a pat on the back—all these acquire their reinforcement value through learning.

Reinforcers vs. Rewards and Punishments. **Rewards,** like reinforcers, are stimuli that increase the frequency of occurrence of behavior. But rewards also generally carry the meaning of being pleasant events. Skinner preferred the concept of reinforcement to the concept of reward because it did not suggest that we are trying to "get inside the head" of an animal or another human being to guess what is found to be pleasant. All we had to do was to observe the frequency of behavior to determine what is reinforcing. Still, many confuse the concepts of reinforcement and reward, and, for most practical purposes, we shall find that there is no significant difference.

Punishments are painful events that decrease the frequency of the behavior that they are associated with. Punishments, like rewards, can influence behavior, but there are a number of reasons that punishment is undesirable, especially in raising children. First, punishment does not suggest an alternate, more effective type of behavior. Second, punishment tends to suppress undesirable behavior only in the circumstances in which punishment is guaranteed. It does not take the average child long to learn that it is possible to "get away with murder" with one parent, or with one teacher, but not with another. Third, punishment can create anger and hostility. Sufficient punishment will almost always suppress unwanted behavior. But at what cost? A hostile child may displace anger onto other children. And children of child beaters are more likely to beat their own children.

Most learning theorists would agree that it is more productive to reinforce or reward children for desired behavior than to punish them for bad behavior. This means paying attention to them when they are good as well as when they are bad, of course! And it means carefully teaching the child how to make the desired response, when necessary, and then using reinforcement. If we were simply to wait until a young child showed good table manners while we held a half-gallon of ice cream behind our back as a reward, we would probably have a wet dining room floor before we had a child with good table manners.

Skinner believes that practically all behavior, including most human behavior, can be explained through classical and operant conditioning. Behavior, from the behavioristic perspective, is controlled by environmental stimulation. Through classical conditioning, we develop expectations that one thing will be

Through operant conditioning we may learn to do many things for the sake of a bit of reinforcement. Reinforcement has made this hamster something of a swinger.

associated with another. We may learn to experience hope when we see a smile and fear when we see a frown. Through operant conditioning, we learn to behave in ways that will be reinforcing. From the Skinnerian perspective, reinforcers control operant behavior.

Why are you reading this book? (Be kind.) One purpose would be to obtain a decent grade for your course. Or you may have developed the idea that it will give you hints that may make your life somewhat more pleasant—another source of reinforcement. Or have you shown the exquisite judgment to come to enjoy the writing style "for its own sake"? If so, that too is reinforcement—in this case: entertainment. According to Skinner, all these reinforcements are controlling and shaping your behavior. Whether Skinner is right or wrong in believing that reinforcements *control* behavior, we all have to admit that they have an influence on our behavior. In Chapters 14 and 15, we show you how to manage the reinforcements in your own life to make it easier for you to gain self-control over problem habits.

Discriminative Stimuli and Schedules of Reinforcement. There may be some problems in teaching animals how to drive cars, but there is little difficulty in teaching them the meaning of traffic lights, so long as they can discriminate between red and green.

Find a pigeon. Just sit on a park bench and close your eyes—it will find you. Grab it and put it in a cage. Teach it to peck a button on the wall by dropping a food pellet into the cage every time it happens to peck near the button; then tighten up and reward the pigeon for pecking the button only. (You can buy the food pellets from Purina and other companies. There is not only Dog Chow and Cat Chow, but also Rat Chow and Monkey Chow—and more.) Now put a small green light bulb in the cage. Reward the bird for pecking the button any time the green light is on, but never when the light is off. It will not take long for the clever city pigeon to learn that it will gain as much by picking at its feathers or squawking and flapping around as it will by pecking the button when the light is off. The green light will have become a **discriminative stimu-**

Punishment. An unpleasant consequence of behavior that generally decreases the frequency of the behavior it follows. Can you explain the differences among punishment, extinction, and negative reinforcement?

Discriminative stimulus. An event that informs an organism when an operant will lead to a reinforcement. A parent's smile may inform a child that a request for $40 to buy a candy bar may lead to reinforcement. (Inflation.)

Personality:
Three Forces in Psychology

Intermittent reinforcement has made many people into constant companions of slot machines.

Intermittent reinforcement (in-turr-MITT-tent). A pattern of reinforcement in which only some responses are reinforced.
Continuous reinforcement (kon-TIN-you-us). Reinforcement of each response.
Ratio schedule (RAY-she-oh). Reinforcement of a certain percentage of responses, such as reinforcement of every fourth or every tenth response.
Interval schedule (IN-turr-vull). Reinforcement of a response only after a certain amount of time has elapsed, such as reinforcement for a response every thirty seconds or every ten minutes.
Fixed ratio schedule. A ratio schedule of reinforcement in which the percentage of reinforced responses is held steady.

lus. A discriminative stimulus acts as a cue that indicates when an operant (in this case, pecking a button) will be effective (in this case, cause a food pellet to drop into the cage).

In how many ways do discriminative stimuli influence your behavior? Would you rather ask your boss for a raise when she is smiling or when she is frowning? Is it more productive to pick up the telephone receiver and say "Hello" *after* it has rung? Do you think it is wise to try to become smoochy when your date blows smoke in your face? From the behavioral point of view, much human maladjustment stems from lack of ability to read discriminative stimuli correctly, especially the social intentions of others (Ullmann & Krasner 1975).

Discriminative stimuli may signal us when operants will be effective, but how frequently must they be reinforced? Is it necessary that each operant response meet with reinforcement in order to maintain that operant or type of behavior, or can reinforcement be **intermittent**? To explore this question, let us have a look at Arnold and Priscilla.

Arnold is courting Priscilla and phones her to ask her out frequently. How may she date him? Let us count the ways. First, she could accept each invitation. Assuming that Arnold finds Priscilla desirable, this would be a schedule of **continuous reinforcement.** Each operant (each invitation) would be reinforced. If she accepted every fourth or fifth invitation, this would provide a **ratio schedule** of reinforcement, in which only a certain proportion or number of Arnold's operants would meet with reinforcement. What if Priscilla accepted an invitation on only the second and fourth Fridays of the month? This would provide an **interval schedule** of reinforcement—one every two weeks. Ratio and interval schedules are intermittent or noncontinuous schedules of reinforcement.

If you were Priscilla and wanted to get Arnold "hooked" and keep him hooked, how do you think you could encourage him to become attached to you and then "keep him dangling" so that you could share your time with other suitors? What diabolical advice could the behaviorist provide?

At first, Priscilla ought to date (reinforce) Arnold frequently. Frequent reinforcement provides an operant with great habit strength or likelihood of occurrence. That is, Arnold will call her repeatedly if Priscilla always accepts and if he always has a good time. Then Priscilla should begin gradually to taper off her acceptance of Arnold's invitations. At first she should decline the invitation rarely, but then she should gradually increase her "No's."

Priscilla will be very clever if she never lets Arnold catch on to her strategy. If she takes to accepting every third date, Arnold will quickly figure out this **fixed ratio schedule** of reinforcement and simply accuse her of game playing, or else simply come to expect a refusal for two of three invitations. Then he might plan to ask others out for the first two dates he would have scheduled with Priscilla, or simply call three times as often as he would have if she were still providing continuous reinforcement. What if Priscilla accepts an invitation on a precise twice-monthly schedule? Then Arnold will quickly learn to call Priscilla only two times a month and plan to fill his other evenings with other dates. A **fixed interval schedule** will also fail.

Ideally, for Priscilla, she should use **variable ratio** or **variable interval schedules,** so that Arnold cannot discern any pattern. So long as the attraction lasts, he ought to continue to call often, and Priscilla ought to be able to "count on him" even though she continues to date others.

Variable ratio and interval schedules can maintain habits for long periods of time. You can eventually keep a pigeon pecking at a button even though you drop a food pellet into the cage only every several hundred pecks. But gradually taper off—otherwise the pecking will be extinguished before the pigeon learns to expect the austerity budget.

Has your behavior been maintained by variable schedules of reinforcement? Probably. After all, you wouldn't continue to root for the home team if they lost every game. The variable schedule maintains interest. You would not be so engrossed in slot machines if you could predict their exact payoff schedules, and the fact that no matter how long you remained at them, you would lose more money than you won. You may become hooked on a new restaurant that serves excellent food, and only gradually diminish your expectations as the quality of the food becomes unpredictable and slowly declines. It may take a long time to give up on the place. In the long run, good adjustment may mean knowing when to quit.

Other Directions: Descendants of Watson and Skinner

Many psychologists within the behavioral school depart in their thinking from the classical behaviorism of Watson and Skinner and believe that it is important to study our inner processes—our thoughts, attitudes, and feelings—in order to understand our behavior more fully. They believe that the control of behavior is not the environment's alone, but is shared between the environment and the person. This approach is called **social-learning theory** or **cognitive learning theory,** and one representative within this school of thought is the psychologist Walter Mischel (1973).

In Mischel's view, behavior is a function of the relationship between aspects of the person, or **person variables,** and aspects of the environment, or **situational variables.** An example of a person variable is the tendency to for-

Do radical behaviorists view people as similar to R2D2 and C3PO from the film *Star Wars*? Charming and entertaining, but rather mechanical when all is said and done?

Fixed interval schedule. An interval schedule of reinforcement in which the time that must elapse between reinforced responses is held steady.
Variable ratio schedule (VAIR-ee-uh-bull). A ratio schedule of reinforcement in which the percentage of reinforced responses is varied. Have variable ratios of reinforcement encouraged a "bad habit" of yours, even when you have told yourself you are a sucker or a loser?
Variable interval schedule. An interval schedule of reinforcement in which the time that must elapse between reinforced responses is varied.
Social learning theory. A contemporary theory in the behavioral tradition that acknowledges the importance of learning to respond to the environment, but also suggests that people can make free choices.
Cognitive learning theory (COG-nuh-tiv). A contemporary theory that grows out of the behavioral and humanistic traditions and emphasizes learning to respond to the environment and "cognitions"—thoughts, values, fantasies, feelings, and choices. Also called cognitive behavior theory.

BEYOND FREEDOM AND DIGNITY

Is your own behavior a result of your free, conscious choices, or is this only an illusion? The radical behavioral approach of Watson to understanding human behavior largely discards notions of free will, choice, or self-direction. Even your telling yourself that you are an individual and a free person is as surely determined by your environment as is your startling at a sudden loud noise.

In 1924 John Watson sounded the battle cry of the behaviorist movement: "Give me a dozen healthy infants, well-formed, and my own specified world to bring them up in and I'll guarantee to take any one at random and train him to become any type of specialist I might suggest—doctor, lawyer, artist, merchant-chief and, yes, even beggar-man and thief, regardless of his talents, penchants, tendencies, abilities, vocations, and the race of his ancestors" (p. 82).

Watson did not expect that we would actually turn over our children to him for his grand experiment, but he expressed the confidence early behaviorists placed in the capacity of the environment to shape tastes, inclinations, and behavior in spite of the influences of heredity or of "self-direction."

Freedom may be the right to do what we want to do, but some behaviorists have suggested that environmental influences, such as parental approval and social custom, shape us into *wanting* to do certain things. In *Walden Two*, B. F. Skinner described a utopian society in which individuals were happy and content because they had been shaped into behaving in ways that were consistent with social needs (Skinner 1948). They wanted to behave prosocially and felt that they were free, but they had been trained to possess prosocial attitudes and to engage in prosocial behavior by the principles of classical and operant conditioning.

Skinner elaborated his beliefs in *Beyond Freedom and Dignity* (1972): "In the scientific picture a person is a member of a species shaped by evolutionary contingencies of survival, displaying behavioral processes which bring him under the control of the environment in which he lives, and largely under the control of a social environment which he and millions of others like him have constructed and maintained during the evolution of a culture. The direction of the controlling relation is reversed: a person does not act upon the world, the world acts upon him" (p. 211).

It becomes complicated. Skinner is claiming that our process of adjustment to the environment involves our acceptance of behavior patterns that ensure survival. People may respond to the world around them by constructing social rules and laws that will aid the cause of harmony and survival. Other people then respond to the social rules set down. None are really free, although we may think of ourselves as following the directions of others or ourselves.

Some object to radical behaviorist notions by arguing that individuals have rebelled against the so-called necessity of survival by choosing pain over pleasure, or by choosing death over life. For instance, in Aldous Huxley's novel *Brave New World* (1939), a "savage" rebels against a mechanistic society by committing suicide.

Behaviorists like Watson and Skinner may answer that the apparently individual choice of pain or death is forced upon the so-called rebel just as strongly and undeniably as conformity is forced upon others. It's just that the immediate environment of the rebel held different forces—the rebel was shaped by differing outside influences, but the influences remained largely outside.

Is there a way to resolve this issue? It is not clear. Certainly the environment influences us. But social learning theorists note that we also influence the environment. It is an interaction, an ongoing give and take. The question as to which comes first may be as difficult as the question, "Which came first, the chicken or the egg?"

Person variables. In social learning theory, factors within an individual that lead to behavior, such as motives and hypotheses about the future.

The Challenge
and the Self

mulate **"if-then" statements** or predictions about which behavior is likely to lead to which reinforcements. If-then statements are behavioral expectancies, as in the statement, "If I study three hours a night this week, then I should be able to do well on my accounting test next week." Whether the studying will actually be performed will also depend on such other person variables as whether the individual possesses the behavioral competencies to perform the behavior (such as an understanding of the assigned material and an ability to concentrate), and whether the **subjective value** or incentive of achieving a good grade is sufficiently motivating. Situational variables are also important: studying becomes more probable as we come nearer to exam time, and studying would be quickly extinguished if it did not produce positive benefits or rewards. Mischel and the other social learning theorists argue that our understanding and prediction of human behavior will be on firmer ground if we study how person and situational variables interact in determining behavior.

THE HUMANISTIC MODEL

"Gentlemen, gentlemen," the humanist reproves, shaking his head. "What you say may have some truth in it, but our elephant friend here doesn't feel that you've really gotten to the core of his being. For instance, neither one of you has asked him about himself. He must feel very left out of all this."

"That's true," the elephant says, nodding.

"Certainly it is possible that his behavior is influenced by dynamic forces clashing within him. His early childhood experiences may even have led to some of the traits you see in him as an adult, such as the way he sucks in peanuts, popcorn, and candy without any self-control."

The elephant furrows his brows.

"It may also be that the environment plays a powerful influence on his behavior," the humanist continues. "We cannot deny that he goes to lie in the shade or wade in his pool when it is hot out. Certainly he was not born knowing how to fling Crackerjack boxes over fences. This is something he learned from experience."

"All true," the elephant says.

"He was not even born with fear of a mouse—" The elephant trumpets and stands on his back legs. "He had to learn that within our culture it is expected that elephants will fear mice."

"You got me," the elephant says.

"All these things are true," says the humanist, "but they are not the essence of the elephant. They are not the core of his being, they are not his self."

"*His* self?" mocks the behaviorist. "Bad grammar."

"Cool it!" says the elephant, waving his trunk menacingly.

"That's what I said," continues the humanist. "They are not the essence of *his* self, not the center of *his* being. Self-awareness is the most important influence on his behavior and his personality. He can use self-awareness to control or act out on biological urges, and to shape the environment that also shapes him. Self-awareness and the ability to make choices free him from absolute slavery to biological drives and environmental stimulation. He is no steam engine and no robot. He is an . . . elephant."

"Right on!" says the elephant.

"You"—the humanist addresses the psychoanalyst—"insulted his powers of reason when you said that most of his mind was unconscious. You"—he addresses the behaviorist—"would have kept his mental abilities and his feelings locked up in a black box—"

"Yeah," says the elephant.

"Only I recognize the importance of the self, of this creature's self-awareness."

The psychoanalyst shakes his head. "Sounds very pretty," he says, "but your view of the elephant is very superficial."

Situational variables. In social learning theory, factors in the environment that influence behavior in the individual, such as the temperature or the time of day.
If-then statements. An individual's predictions about the consequences of behavior. If-then statements thus influence the occurrence of behavior.
Subjective value. In social learning theory, the experienced value of a goal. The greater the subjective value of a goal, the more likely we shall attempt to achieve it.

The behaviorist shakes his head. "That's about it. Sounds good, but it's all just opinion. It's not science."

The elephant shakes his head. "That may be, fellas, but there's just one of you guys I'm not going to step on. Want to take bets on who it is?"

The psychoanalytic and behavioral traditions paint us as being largely driven by biological urgings or being largely conditioned by environmental stimulation. A third force has risen in psychology, however, that depicts us as essentially self-directed, responsible for our own actions, and motivated to extend ourselves to our highest potentials. This third force is called the humanistic movement, and it holds that the central factor in understanding us involves recognizing our conscious experience of being human in the world.

This humanistic movement owes much of its development to the school of European philosophy called **existentialism.**

The Existentialist Tradition: Authentic Living

According to existentialists like Martin Heidegger and Jean-Paul Sartre, the main task of human life is for us to come to grips with the experience of being mortal and capable of making choices. Life is short, and this fact may lead us to despair. But human beings, unlike animals, have the unique capacity to make their own lives meaningful through exercising their free choice and seeking values that will lead to individual fulfillment.

Our planet is beset by social problems and people may be at the mercy of illness and death. It may be easy for some to despair, to surrender hope of achieving personal fulfillment. Some may surrender the opportunity to make their own choices by adopting the paths set out by others, or even by commit-

Existentialism (eggs-sis-TEN-shull-lism). A philosophy that states that human beings are free to make choices, and that human nature is what we believe it to be. Existentialists emphasize the human experience of being mortal and existing in the world.

ting suicide—although suicide is also a type of choice. By surrendering free choice we default the chance to come to know and develop ourselves—we may feel alienated from ourselves. By making choices and attempting to live our lives meaningfully, no matter how short our time span on planet Earth, we live authentically.

Authentic living is living that is true to oneself—resisting pressures to follow others blindly, showing our true or authentic feelings and values to other people in our lives. We may not be perfectly authentic all the time, but authentic individuals make the effort to come to know themselves and to be whatever they are capable of being. Authentic living is not necessarily always happy living, but there is self-satisfaction in being true to ourselves.

The themes of self-knowledge and becoming whatever we are capable of being find expression in the thinking of two major American theorists within the humanistic school, psychologists Abraham Maslow and Carl Rogers.

Abraham Maslow and the Challenge of Self-Actualization

Maslow challenges us to take a hard look at our lives. Are they meaningful and enriching, or drab and routine? If they are the latter, it may be because we are frustrating the need for self-actualization—the tendency to develop and fulfill our unique potentials. We may be settling, taking the easy way out.

Maslow (1963) recalls the case of a woman who complained of problems such as insomnia, menstrual distress, boredom, and an inability to enjoy life. She had been a brilliant psychology student who had not been able to pursue graduate work because of the Depression of the 1930s. She took, instead, a position as a personnel officer in a chewing gum factory. Maslow writes:

> Half-consciously then she saw a whole lifetime of greyness stretching out ahead of her. I suggested that she might be feeling profoundly frustrated and angry simply because she was not being her own very intelligent self, that she was not using her intelligence and her talent for psychology and that this might well be a major reason for her boredom with life and her body's boredom with the normal pleasures of life. Any talent, any capacity, I thought, was also a motivation, a need, an impulse. With this she agreed, and I suggested that she could continue her graduate studies at night after her work. In brief, she was able to arrange this and it worked well. She became more alive, more happy and zestful, and most of her physical symptoms had disappeared at my last contact with her [1963, pp. 43–44].

Personality:
Three Forces in Psychology

Self-expression or monkey business? The zoo actually sells the artistic productions of this chimp. Do you think the chimp would dabble with the paint brush if it needed to make a living foraging for food and hiding from leopards?

Peak experience. Abraham Maslow's term for a moment of self-actualization that is experienced as fulfillment, rapture, and joy.

Hierarchy (HIGH-ur-are-key). An ordering, a logical sequence. Maslow's hierarchy of needs begins with biological needs and ends with self-actualization.

Maslow believed that we all have the capacity for self-actualization, though we may not all fully realize our potentials. Self-actualizing people are continually growing and developing, achieving some goals and striving to achieve others. Life is motion, and the self-actualizer does not stand still.

Are you a self-actualizer? Maslow (1971) attributes eight characteristics to the self-actualizing personality:

1. Fully experiencing life in the present—the here and now. Not focusing excessively on the past or wishing away your days as you stride down the path toward future goals.
2. Making growth choices rather than fear choices. Self-actualizing individuals take reasonable risks to develop their potentials, rather than basking in the dull light of the status quo.
3. Getting to know yourself. Self-actualizers look inward, searching for values, talents, and meaningfulness.
4. Striving toward honesty in interpersonal relationships. Self-actualizers seek authenticity in their interpersonal relationships. They strip away game playing and social facades that stand in the way of self-disclosure and intimacy.
5. Becoming self-assertive and expressing yourself, even at the risk of occasional disapproval. Maslow writes that the self-actualizer "dares to listen to himself, his own self, at each moment in life, and to say calmly, 'No, I don't like such and such'" (1971, p. 47).
6. Striving toward new goals and seeking to become the best that you can be in your chosen life role. Self-actualizers do not live by the memory of past accomplishments or give a second-rate effort.
7. Involving yourself in meaningful and rewarding life activities so that you may experience brief moments of heightened self-actualization or **peak experiences.** Peak experiences are brief moments of joy or rapture that are filled with personal meaning—completing a work of art, the inspiration to redesign a machine, falling in love.
8. Being open to new experiences. Not holding back for fear that novel events may shatter the way you experience the world; being willing to revise your expectations and your opinions.

The Hierarchy of Needs: What Do You Do When You're No Longer Hungry? Humanists may accuse Freud of getting stuck in the basement of the human condition by focusing so heavily on primitive drives such as sex, hunger, and aggression. Maslow recognized basic needs, but believed that there is an ordering, or **hierarchy,** of needs which ranges from the basement of biological impulse to the attic of self-actualization. Once lower-order needs are met, we are motivated to fulfill higher-order or growth needs—we do not simply snooze away our hours till the lower-order drives prompt us to act again.

Maslow's needs hierarchy includes many levels, from the basement to the attic and, possibly, through the roof:

1. Biological needs—water, food, elimination, warmth, rest, avoidance of pain, sexual release, etc.
2. Safety needs—protection from the environment through clothing and housing, security from crime and financial hardship.
3. Love and belongingness needs—love and acceptance through intimate relationships, social groups, and friends. In our society, generally well

fed and well housed, Maslow believed a principal source of maladjustment lies in frustration of needs at this level.

4. Esteem needs—achievement, competence, approval, recognition, prestige, status.
5. Cognitive understanding—novelty, understanding, exploration, knowledge.
6. Aesthetic needs—music, art, poetry, beauty, order.
7. Self-actualization—personal growth, development of our unique potentials.

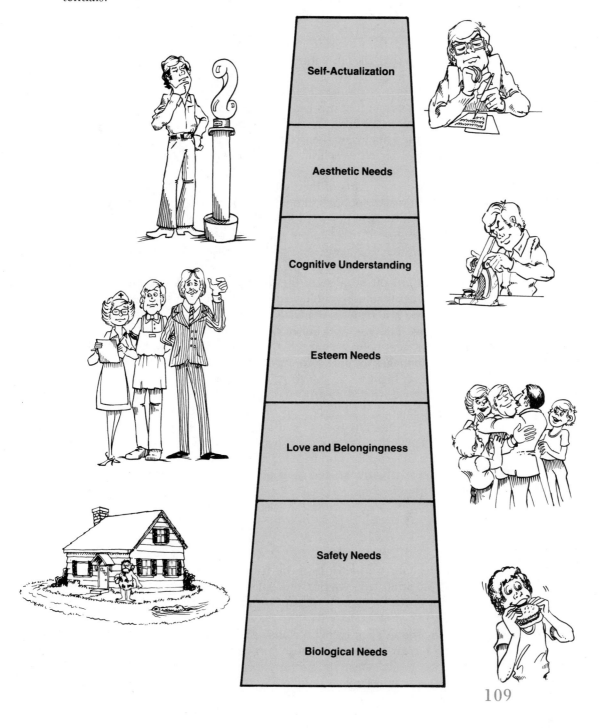

How far has your personal development proceeded up through Maslow's needs hierarchy? Where do you feel you have adequately met your needs? What areas are you focusing on now?

Carl Rogers and the Integrity of the Self

The progress of the self toward self-actualization is also a central theme of Carl Rogers (1951). Rogers' theory is sometimes called self theory because of the importance he places on learning about oneself as a basis for personal growth and feelings of well-being.

Rogers defines the self, or self-concept, as our conscious view of ourself. He believes that human nature is basically good and growth-oriented, but that people can learn to turn a deaf ear to parts of themselves that others have disapproved of, thus forming a distorted self-concept. Children in some families may have learned that it is bad to have ideas of their own about sexual, political, or religious matters. When they find that they do not fully agree with their parents, they may view themselves as rebels and characterize their authentic feelings and beliefs as selfish, wrong, or even evil. In order to keep their distorted self-concepts intact, they may distort or deny their authentic feelings—they may disown parts of themselves.

When we accept our feelings as our own, we experience psychological harmony or unity. Another word for unity is integrity. This is also **psychological congruence**—a fit between our self-concepts and our feelings and beliefs.

According to Rogers, the path to self-actualization includes getting in touch with our authentic feelings, learning what parts of the self we have disowned or cut off because of the disapproval of others. Self-actualization requires integrity and psychological congruence—in short, self-acceptance.

Rogers also believes that we have mental images of what we are capable of becoming. These images are our self-ideals, and we are motivated to reduce the differences between our self-concepts and our self-ideals. But the self-ideal usually manages to remain somewhat in front of the self-concept, like a carrot dangling in front of the burro from a stick that is attached to its head. The burro believes that the carrot is somehow mysteriously fixed ahead and does not recognize that its own forward movement causes the carrot to dangle so invitingly, remaining forever just ahead. According to the humanistic model, we are happiest when our goals seem possible, when they are in reach, and we continue to strive forward to achieve them. We may never quite get there, but the process of striving, the good struggle, gives our lives their meaning and their purpose.

ON ELEPHANTS AND MODELS

Our elephant warmed up to the humanist. Not surprising since humanists stress the importance of our awareness of our selves. They usually "feel" right to us. But feeling right is not sufficient grounds for accepting one model over another.

In Chapter 5 we shall see that each model suggests different origins for psychological problems, or problems in adjustment. We shall also learn that the three models suggest differing approaches to helping people adjust to problems. Yet many people who help others adjust to problems are **eclectic;** that is,

Psychological congruence (kon-GREW-ents). A harmonious fit between our self-concepts and our feelings and beliefs such that we are comfortable with our views and can fully accept them as our own.

Eclectic (eck-LECK-tick). Drawing from different theories in an effort to describe behavior or events fully.

ASTROLOGY—A FOURTH MODEL OF PERSONALITY?

Some people are convinced that all this talk of inner forces, learning, and the self is nonsense. To them personalities are decided by the astrological signs under which people are born, and their day-to-day fortunes are the result of the relationships of the stars and the planets. Their own efforts, they believe, play a lesser role.

What about it? Are different personality types associated with the various signs of the zodiac? Are Leos proud? Are Tauruses stubborn?

To date there have been few attempts to relate astrology to personality. In one study, psychologist Robert Pellegrini (1973, 1975) of California State University at San Jose used the California Psychological Inventory to measure personality characteristics of twelve male and twelve female students born under each sign. Of eighteen personality traits assessed by the inventory, only one was associated with signs of the zodiac: femininity. Men and women born under the signs of Capricorn, Sagittarius, Libra, Leo, Scorpio, and Virgo scored significantly higher on the femininity scale than men and women born under the signs of Gemini, Taurus, Pisces, Aquarius, Aries, and Cancer. High femininity scorers on this test are usually described as patient, gentle, appreciative, moderate, persevering, sincere, accepting of others, conscientious, and sympathetic. Low-feminine scorers are described as outgoing, hardheaded, ambitious, masculine, active, robust, restless, manipulative, opportunistic, and impatient.

The astrologically knowledgeable will recognize that the six signs associated with high femininity scores run consecutively from July 24 through January 20, with the low femininity scores covering the rest of the calendar. Why should the date of birth be related to later personality development? What is so meaningful about these two different halves of the calendar?

Put simply, we do not know. Astrologers might suggest that there is a different set of cosmic forces at work during these halves of the calendar, but there is no evidence to back up this belief. Of course it is also possible that Pellegrini's findings were a statistical fluke or accident. One replication of the Pellegrini study, in Australia (Illingworth & Syme 1977), failed to turn up any relationship between personality and those mysterious signs of the zodiac.

---

they use approaches suggested by each model. Many psychoanalysts now "give more credit" to conscious ego functioning than Sigmund Freud did. Many behaviorists pay attention to the thoughts, feelings, and even fantasies of people they help adjust to the challenges of life. And humanists are aware of both inner, dynamic forces and environmental influences on the behavior of people they work with.

Summary

- *The human mind is like a vast, submerged iceberg, only the tip of which rises above the surface into our awareness.* True, according to the psychoanalytic model of Sigmund Freud, but not necessarily borne out by scientific evidence. Freud separated the mind into the conscious, the preconscious, and the unconscious. We can easily become aware of preconscious material, such as what we ate for dinner last evening, but unconscious material tends to swim in the murk beneath the light perpetually.

- *There is a watchdog or censor that screens our basic impulses and decides which will become conscious and which must be kept hidden.*

Personality:
Three Forces in Psychology

True, again according to Freud's model. Freud wrote that the ego, which plans and makes decisions, may also act to keep hidden or repress unacceptable impulses that threaten to emerge from the id. Repression is one type of defense mechanism, or unconscious method of distorting or hiding unacceptable impulses. Freud also theorized that the superego develops from identifying with the morals and values of our parents and others, and serves as a conscience through life.

- *People who are perfectionistic and excessively neat and people who are sloppy and disorganized both experienced severe conflicts with their parents during the second year of life.* True, according to Freud. Freud wrote that adult personality traits have their origins in childhood experiences. As we go through the oral, anal, and phallic stages of psychosexual development, insufficient or excessive gratification may lead to fixations and the development of traits characteristic of these stages. The overly neat are anal-retentive and the messy are anal-expulsive—these characters represent two styles of adjusting to parents who demand rigid self-control during the anal period, a problem that usually centers around the issue of toilet training.

- *Women who compete with men in the business world are suffering from penis envy.* This is an accurate conclusion from Freudian theory, but it is a source of much controversy, and one female psychoanalyst, Karen Horney, even labeled this view as sexist. Freud believed that boys and girls each identify with the parent of the same sex in order to resolve the Oedipal and Electra conflicts. Boys assume assertive masculine roles and girls take on passive, supportive, mothering roles. Girls, Freud felt, envy boys their physical abilities and, specifically, the pleasure they can achieve from self-stimulation during the phallic period. The well-adjusted girl eventually surrenders the wish to have a penis and substitutes the wish to marry and have children. Women who are assertive and who place career ahead of or on an equal footing with home life have not made adequate substitutions. Freud's theory reflects the societal prejudice of his time that women who work primarily outside the home have not reached full psychological maturity.

- *Psychologically mature adults prefer to attain sexual gratification through sexual intercourse with an adult of the opposite sex.* True, according to Freud. This is adult, genital sexuality. Freud's belief in this ideal appears to stem from his religious orthodoxy, his belief that we have within us a life instinct, Eros, which somehow embodies the biblical command to be fruitful and multiply.

- *When your team wins, it's "We're number one!" But when your team loses, it's "They lost—the bums!"* True, according to an experiment on some prominent football campuses. Apparently we identify with winners because it gives us a boost in self-esteem, but identifying with losers is painful. According to Freud, we tend to identify with our parents because of their power and their ability to take charge of the environment —all this, of course, from the perspectives we hold when we are young children.

- *You can train a dog to salivate when it hears a bell.* True. This is classical conditioning. Simply pair a bell (conditioned stimulus) with meat powder (unconditioned stimulus) several times. The dog will eventually salivate (conditioned response) to the bell alone. The CR will generalize to bells with similar sounds, or you can teach the dog that it will receive meat powder only when it hears bells or certain tones. Then it will learn to discriminate. Present the CS (bell) without the US (meat) repeatedly, and eventually the CR (salivation) will extinguish. But wait a while and ring the bell again. The CR may show spontaneous recovery.

- *You can teach a pigeon to peck at a button in the wall when it has the green light, but to stop when the light goes off.* True. This is operant conditioning. You can teach the pigeon to peck the button by reinforcing this response with a food pellet. If pecking is reinforced only when the green light is on, the green light will become a discriminative stimulus. Use continuous reinforcement at first, but then move to intermittent reinforcement to maintain the new habit.

- *You can keep a suitor dangling indefinitely through applying the same principle that "addicts" some people to slot machines.* Highly probable. Vary the proportion of the time that you go out with your suitor (use a variable ratio schedule) or vary the interval between dates (a variable interval schedule). This keeps him guessing. Fixed ratio or interval schedules are not as effective. Slot machines are intriguing because we (usually) cannot figure out how frequently they are programmed to pay off.

- *We may feel that we have freedom of choice, but our preferences and our "choices" are actually forced on us by our environment.* Perhaps, perhaps not—this is life as the radical behaviorist views it. Whereas psychoanalysts see us as driven by unconscious urges, behaviorists see us as responding mechanically to environmental stimuli. Even the belief "I have free will" is absolutely determined by environmental forces.

- *People who actualize themselves are always future-oriented.* Not quite. Self-actualizers strive to achieve their self-ideals, but they are also capable of living in the here and now and fully experiencing the pleasures of life. According to Maslow, people who have met the more basic needs of life respond to the need to self-actualize.

- *Children may learn to view their own feelings as selfish, wrong, and even evil.* True, and according to Carl Rogers, such children will often come to disown parts of themselves. Adjustment, to Rogers, requires psychological congruence—a fit between our feelings and beliefs, and our self-concepts. Congruence allows authentic behavior, behavior that is consistent with our self-concepts. Congruence and authenticity are essential elements of self-actualization, according to the humanistic self theory of Rogers.

- *Capricorns and Scorpios are more feminine than Geminis.* Perhaps—at least they had higher femininity scores on one psychological test in a recent study in California. But this study was not successfuly replicated. We tend to have differing beliefs about why we are what we are and why we do what we do. Some of us are psychoanalysts, some behaviorists, and some humanists. Some of us adhere to other psychological theories. Some of us, of course, are astrologists. Perhaps there are almost as many models as there are people. What do you believe?

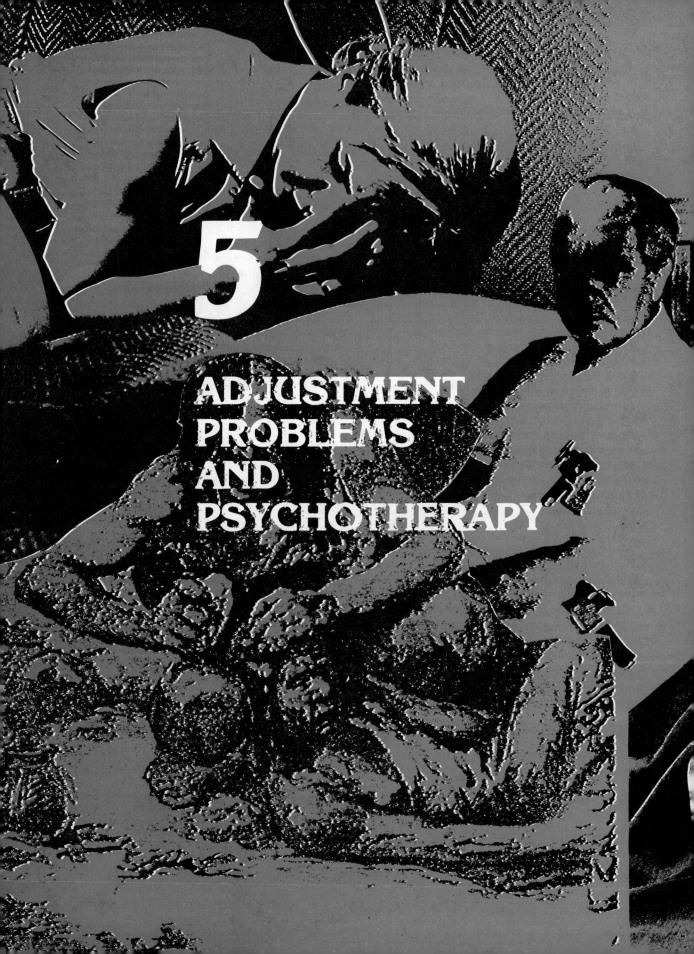

5

ADJUSTMENT PROBLEMS AND PSYCHOTHERAPY

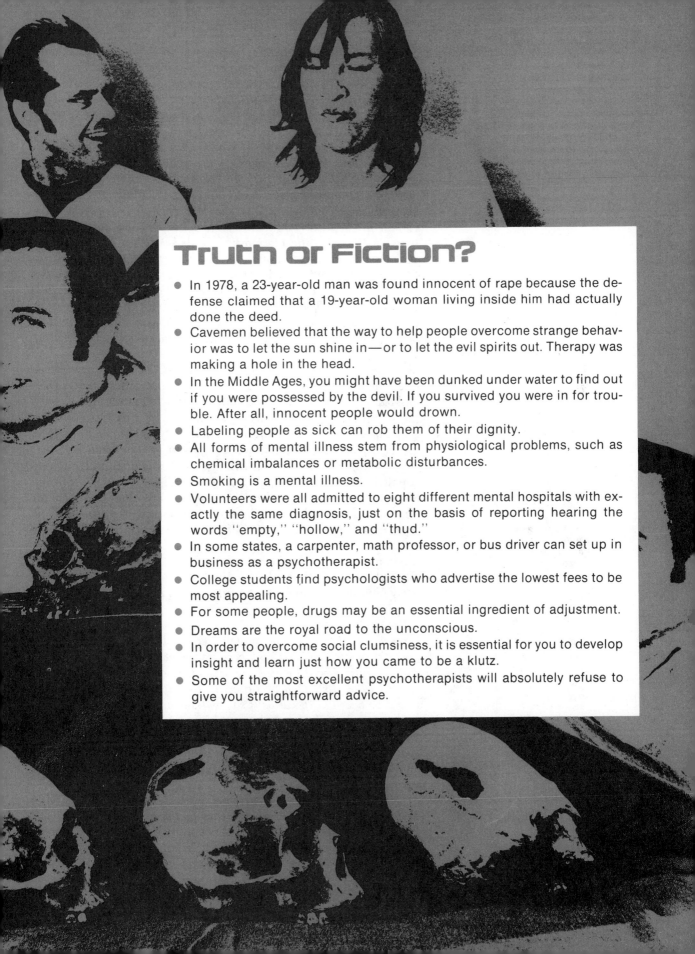

Truth or Fiction?

- In 1978, a 23-year-old man was found innocent of rape because the defense claimed that a 19-year-old woman living inside him had actually done the deed.
- Cavemen believed that the way to help people overcome strange behavior was to let the sun shine in—or to let the evil spirits out. Therapy was making a hole in the head.
- In the Middle Ages, you might have been dunked under water to find out if you were possessed by the devil. If you survived you were in for trouble. After all, innocent people would drown.
- Labeling people as sick can rob them of their dignity.
- All forms of mental illness stem from physiological problems, such as chemical imbalances or metabolic disturbances.
- Smoking is a mental illness.
- Volunteers were all admitted to eight different mental hospitals with exactly the same diagnosis, just on the basis of reporting hearing the words "empty," "hollow," and "thud."
- In some states, a carpenter, math professor, or bus driver can set up in business as a psychotherapist.
- College students find psychologists who advertise the lowest fees to be most appealing.
- For some people, drugs may be an essential ingredient of adjustment.
- Dreams are the royal road to the unconscious.
- In order to overcome social clumsiness, it is essential for you to develop insight and learn just how you came to be a klutz.
- Some of the most excellent psychotherapists will absolutely refuse to give you straightforward advice.

The Ohio State University campus lived in terror between August and October of 1977. Four college women were abducted, forced to cash checks or use their banks' instant cash cards to obtain money, and then driven to an unpopulated area and raped. As told in Time magazine (October 23, 1978, p. 102), a mysterious phone call led to the arrest of a 23-year-old man who had been dismissed from the navy and drifted from job to job. He was not the typical young man.

Interviews led psychologists and psychiatrists to conclude that he actually had ten very different personalities living within him, eight male and two female, as a result of a particularly abusive childhood which, according to the article, had "fractured his psyche." The various personalities had their own facial expressions and voice patterns. Arthur, 22, the most rational, spoke with a British accent. There were a couple of normal, quiet adolescents, Danny and Christopher; a 3-year-old girl, Christene; and 16-year-old Tommy, the personality that had enlisted in the navy. One personality, Allen, was 18 and smoked. The personality that had committed the rapes belonged to Adelena, a 19-year-old lesbian. Who had made the mysterious phone call? Probably David, aged 9, an anxious child personality.

The core personality, Billy, was allegedly "asleep" during the abductions and the rapes. According to psychiatric testimony, Billy had learned to go to sleep as a child in order to protect himself from the physical and sexual abuse of his father. In early October 1978, the examining psychiatrist reported that Billy had pulled himself together to the point where he was competent to stand trial.

The defense claimed that Billy was suffering from **multiple personalities.** He had several distinct personalities living within him. Some were aware of the others, but some believed that they were the only ones. Each had a distinct set of memories, scored differently on intelligence tests, and created distinct artistic products. Billy, the core personality, had been in a "psychological coma" during the commission of the crimes and was innocent by reason of insanity. On December 4, 1978, the verdict was in: Not guilty. But he did not walk away from the trial. He was committed to an institution for the mentally ill.

Joyce was 19. Her boyfriend brought her into the emergency room of a hospital in upstate New York because she had slit her wrists. When she was interviewed by a psychiatrist, her attention wandered. She seemed to be distracted by things in the air or something that she might be hearing. It was as if she had an invisible earphone.

She explained that she had cut her wrists because the "hellsmen" had told her to. Then she became very frightened. Later she explained that the "hellsmen" had warned her about revealing their existence, and that she had been afraid they would punish her for talking about them.

Her boyfriend told the psychiatrist that Joyce had been living with him for a year now. At first they had been together in a small apartment in town. But Joyce did not want to be near other people and had convinced him to rent a small bungalow in the country. There she would make fantastic drawings of goblins and monsters *during the days. Now and then she would become agitated and begin to act as if invisible things were talking to her, giving her instructions.*

"I'm bad," Joyce would say, "I'm bad." She would begin to jumble her words together so that she was hard to understand. At those times Ron, the boyfriend, would try to convince Joyce to come with him to a hospital to get medicine. Joyce would refuse and would shortly try to cut herself. Ron thought he had made the cottage safe by removing all knives and razor blades. But Joyce would always find something.

She would cut herself because the voices told her she was bad and ought to die. She would go to the hospital, have stitches put in, and then be kept under observation and medicated for a few days. Her agitation would decrease and she would stop acting as if she heard the "hellsmen." But then she would insist on leaving, and she could not be kept in the hospital against her will.

Ron always took her back to the cottage in the country. The pattern continued.

If Billy and Joyce had lived in Salem, Massachusetts, in 1692, they might have been hanged as witches. Nineteen people lost their lives in that colonial town that year for allegedly practicing the arts of Satan.

People like Billy and Joyce have been noticed and written about for thousands of years. Yet each age has viewed them differently and suggested differing approaches to dealing with their disturbing behavior and their problems in adjustment.

In this chapter, we explore different ways of explaining the behavior of people like Billy and Joyce. Then we examine the classification system currently used by the American Psychiatric Association to categorize and understand these abnormal behavior patterns. We look at some of the professions and professionals who interact with disturbed individuals in order to help them adjust to the challenges of life. Finally, we learn about the different types of help that are available, from chemotherapy, or use of drugs, to psychotherapy. Each of the models you learned about in Chapter 4 has given birth to ways of helping. We shall discuss the methods spawned by each.

EXPLAINING PSYCHOLOGICAL MALADJUSTMENT

As anyone who has read Homer's *Iliad* or *Odyssey* knows, the ancient Greek gods were a capricious lot, interfering in the lives of people and taking sides in human conflicts. It was also believed that the gods designated the personalities and temperaments of people, including severe problems in adjustment such as those shown by Billy and Joyce.

Hippocrates, the physician of Greece's Golden Age of art and literature (the fourth century B.C.), made the radical suggestion that such problems were caused by something wrong in the brain—that bodily problems can influence thinking and behavior. This incredible notion was destined to lie dormant for approximately two thousand years.

Adjustment Problems and Psychotherapy

A FEW WORDS ON AN ANCIENT ENERGY-SAVING AIR-CONDITIONING TECHNIQUE

Archaeologists make a living at digging into human history. They have uncovered a number of human skeletons, dating back to the Stone Age, that have holes in the skull about the size of an eye socket. This was no primitive effort at air conditioning.

Apparently some of our ancestors developed the notion that strange, disturbed behavior was the result of evil spirits. A model of personality may suggest ways to deal with problems in adjustment. The message of this model was clear: let those irascible spirits out. This was done through the brutal method of breaking a pathway through the skull—called trephining.

Was trephining successful? We think you will agree that threat of trephining is bound to convince you to try to conform. It is likely that trephining most often led to a discontinuation of whatever type of behavior was disturbing to our forebears in those days prior to the dawn of civilization.

Our ancestors may have used "airconditioning" as an effort to deal with bizarre behavior. Threat of trephining could certainly encourage conformity.

On Demons, Exorcists, and Tarantulas

Possession. Control of an individual's body and behavior by an agent of evil or the devil. Possession can result from a punishment for misbehavior or from making a deal with the devil to gain profit.

During the Middle Ages in Europe, and during the early days of American civilization along the coast of Massachusetts, it was believed that disordered behavior was generally a sign of **possession** by some evil spirit or agent of the devil. Such possession could have a couple of origins. First, God might have decided to punish you for your sinfulness by arranging for the devil to take possession of your soul. In this instance we would expect you to be wildly agitated and confused. But it was also possible that you might have decided to gain some earthly power by making a deal with the devil. Power for your eternal soul. In this instance you would be considered a witch, and you might be held responsible for your neighbor's infertility or a poor crop of beans or peas.

In either case you were in for trouble. An **exorcist,** whose function was to persuade these spirits that they would be better off elsewhere, would say some prayers at your side, perhaps wave a cross at you. If the spirits did not have enough, you might then be beaten or flogged. If your behavior was still undesirable, there were other remedies, such as the rack, that have powerful influences on human behavior.

In 1484, Pope Innocent VIII ordered that witches were to be put to death. Something of a craze hit Europe, because at least a couple of hundred thousand so-called witches were put to death in the next couple of hundred years. Europe was no place in which to practice strange ways. The goings-on at Salem were insignificant by contrast.

If you were around in the Middle Ages and the devil did not get you, you would also have been well advised to be on the lookout for tarantulas—spider-like animals with poisonous bites that earn a living menacing people in James Bond movies and horror stories. It was believed that agitated madness, or **tarantism,** could also result from the bite of the tarantula, causing people to cavort and run amok during the scorching days of summer. It was safer to be bitten by a tarantula than to be found to be possessed, since the cures for possession were so lethal. Who could blame you for being bitten by a tarantula?

What did the authorities do to determine whether you were possessed? Do not despair of the human species' uncanny ability to develop means for cutting to the quick of such matters. For instance, one test of possession involved dunking people under water. Failure to drown would prove that you were being supported by the devil—in short, possessed. Then you were in real trouble.

Exorcist (EGGS-or-sist). A person who attempts to cause demons to depart from the body of a possessed individual. *Tarantism* (TAR-ant-tism). A form of "summer madness" that was thought to be caused by the bite of the tarantula. A whole lot of shaking going on. What do you think is the connection between tarantism and the name of that lively Italian dance, the Tarantella?

Summer Madness

FOOD POISONING OR THE WORK OF THE DEVIL?

The year was 1374. The Black Death—bubonic plague—had killed hundreds of thousands in Europe just a generation earlier. And now there were mass epidemics of wild, crazed dancing—the dancing mania. The dancers were called the devilish sect because their sexually provocative and frenetic movements were thought to result from possession. Many dancers were brought to churches for exorcism. "Get thee hence, unclean spirit!" a priest might exhort, holding down the agitated dancer. Some dancers danced till they dropped, some died from exhaustion.

Some scholars (Backman 1952) believe that the children of the village of Hamelin, who followed the Pied Piper out of town and, according to legend, disappeared, had been afflicted by the dancing mania. Backman suggests that the dancing mania was ac-

tually caused by food poisoning of grains (rye, oats, wheat, etc.) which often follows periods of famine and drought, the very conditions that followed the Black Death. This poisoning would have lowered the blood pressure, leading to feelings of suffocation and intense nervousness. The frenetic activity of the dance could have increased the blood pressure and brought temporary relief. It would also have produced stomach and chest pains which would be eased by tight binding of the abdomen—a common practice of the dancing sect.

Some died, either from the continuous dancing or from food poisoning, but for most, the "mania" lasted about ten days and then passed. The people believed that the devil had done his work and then looked for purer pastures. What do you think?

FLYING OVER THE CUCKOO'S NEST

Randle McMurphy is hard to tame. He is a cursing, swaggering misfit who chooses to act crazy to avoid imprisonment, believing that life will be easier in a mental institution. But he does not fit into hospital life any more than he fitted into life on the outside. The well-adjusted patient in the hospital is quiet and passive. The well-adjusted patient takes his medicine and attends his therapy sessions. He doesn't make waves.

Randle makes waves. From the onset he challenges the authority of Big Nurse, who has held unquestioned reign. Big Nurse and the doctors assume that he would not make trouble if he weren't sick. Therefore, he needs medical treatment: chemotherapy and, when that fails, electric shock therapy. But still Randle makes trouble. Finally, he is given the ultimate "medical" treatment—a brain operation that turns him into a vegetable.

In the novel *One Flew Over the Cuckoo's Nest*, Ken Kesey (1962) shows us how we have come to label people we don't like as sick within the framework of the medical model. Soviet psychiatry has often been criticized for labeling dissidents as sick—then warehousing them in psychiatric institutions. It is not very different from the medieval practice of labeling people who were different and resistant to social norms as possessed.

Controversial psychiatrist Thomas Szasz (1960,

1974) claims that the label of sick is often abused, that mental patients are not sick at all. It is just that their behavior deviates from the norm.

Szasz claims that we degrade people when we label them sick because they are different, or because we cannot understand their behavior. He believes that the most degrading aspect of being labeled sick is that it removes responsibility for your own behavior. When you are sick, you are expected to miss school or work, to perform poorly, or to be cranky and irritable. And you are not blamed—after all, the illness is at fault.

Szasz feels that we must all be responsible for our own behavior, especially our criminal behavior. The criminal who is found not guilty by reason of insanity is degraded.

Szasz takes an extreme position. Many are in partial agreement with him, willing to admit that the medical model has been overextended. Still, they point out, some people become confused for medical or other reasons and simply cannot take charge of their own lives—at least for a while.

What do you think? Should Billy have been found guilty of rape even if he had lost control of his own behavior? And if Randle was a social deviant, should he have been punished by the law or been turned over to the mercy of Big Nurse?

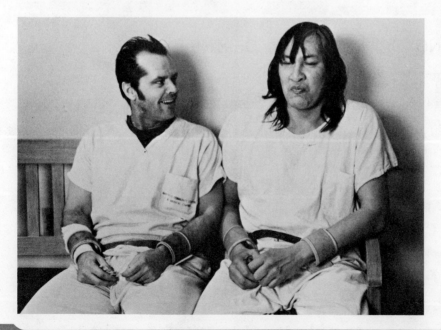

Jack Nicholson as Randle McMurphy in the film *One Flew Over the Cuckoo's Nest.* Here Randle contemplates some mischief with "The Chief."

The Medical Model

Johann Weyer, a German physician, stood alone in the sixteenth century against the doctrine of possession. Disorders of behavior and thinking stemmed from disorders of the body or mind, he argued.

In 1883 Emil Kraepelin published a textbook of psychiatry in which he reinforced Weyer's theme. There were different types of mental disorders, he wrote, each of which was characterized by its own **syndrome** or cluster of symptoms. Each syndrome reflected a physiological problem. Mental diseases, like physical diseases, had specific origins, syndromes, and outcomes.

Kraepelin specified two major groupings of mental diseases: schizophrenia and manic-depression. **Schizophrenia** is a compound of Greek words meaning split (*schizo*) brain (*phren*). In schizophrenia, the emotions are "split off" from thoughts or perceptions, so that schizophrenic behavior may include flat or blunted emotions, or inappropriate emotions such as giddiness in the face of tragedy. In **manic-depression** there are mood swings between elation (manic behavior) and depression.

Kraepelin believed that dementia praecox or schizophrenia was due to chemical imbalances and that manic-depressive illness stemmed from a metabolic disturbance. Today the origins of these problems appear less clear, but they still exist as syndromes, and large segments of the psychiatric community remain convinced that their origins are indeed physiological, or medical.

If a problem is medical, then it makes sense that it should be treated by physicians and that the means of treatment ought to be medical. It is true that many disorders respond to medical treatments, such as **chemotherapy,** or drugs. But medical causes have not been established for the great majority of problems in adjustment, and chemotherapy or other medical forms of treatment are not always applicable or advisable.

Inability to decide whether or not to apply to graduate school, inability to find meaning in life, stress induced by a rush-rush job, clumsiness in social situations—all these are problems in adjustment, though none is likely to give rise to the extremes of behavior we find with schizophrenia or manic-depression. And none of these problems fits the medical model or needs to be "treated" within the medical framework.

Psychological Models of Adjustment and Maladjustment

Poets and playwrights have been aware through the centuries that psychological problems, such as guilt, can lead to the most severe forms of maladjustment. In Shakespeare's tragedy, Macbeth, a nobleman of Scotland, plots to kill his king and seize the throne. Yet Macbeth knows that Duncan, the king, has been a good king, and his mixed feelings lead him to **hallucinate,** or perceive an object which is not really present:

> Is this a dagger which I see before me,
> The handle toward my hand? Come, let me clutch thee.
> I have thee not, and yet I see thee still.
> Art thou not, fatal vision, **sensible**
> To feeling as to sight? Or art thou but
> A dagger of the mind, a false creation,
> Proceeding from the heat-oppressed brain?
> —*Macbeth*, Act II, scene 1

Syndrome (SIN-drome; rhymes with "BEEN home"). A cluster or grouping of symptoms that characterizes a disease.

Schizophrenia (skits-zoh-FREE-knee-uh). A severe adjustment disorder in which the individual's emotions have become "split off" from events or perceptions. Schizophrenia may also be characterized by hallucinations and delusions.

Manic-depression (MAN-ick dee-PRESH-un). A severe adjustment disorder in which there is a profound disturbance of mood, characterized by swings between elation and depression. Manic-depression is an affective disorder.

Chemotherapy (KEY-moh-THER-ap-pee). Use of drugs or chemicals to treat an adjustment problem.

Hallucination (hal-LOOSE-in-nay-shun). A sensory perception that occurs without environmental stimulation. Hallucinations may be visual, auditory, tactile (touch), olfactory (smell), etc.

Sensible. Capable of being felt or touched. (Obsolete usage of the word.)

Orson Welles as the brooding, guilt-ridden Macbeth, in the film of this Shakespearean play.

Yet it was not until Sigmund Freud began to make known his psychodynamic model of personality that a psychological approach to maladjustment began to take hold. The psychological view of maladjustment holds that problems in adjustment can result from our experiences, our patterns of learning, or from our own views of the world. Thoughts, feelings, and behavior itself may all be instrumental in fostering maladjustment. The three psychological models of maladjustment that we shall consider are the psychoanalytic model, the behavioral model, and the humanistic model.

The Psychoanalytic Model of Adjustment and Maladjustment. Freud likened the relationship between the id and the ego to that between a horse and rider. The id is the horse, supplying animal energy through its motivational urgings. The rider, the ego, provides direction. The horse, you see, has blinders. It knows nothing of navigating in the real world. The ego serves as its eyes and ears. It steers a course for the horse between the stumbling blocks of practicality and social decency.

The adjusted individual is able to satisfy the basic demands of the id in ways that are socially acceptable. The id flashes its desires into consciousness. The ego finds the right time and place. If you experience lustful strivings on the train to work, the ego has you keep your shirt on—and the rest of your clothing. If you have passed through the stages of psychosexual development successfully, you will tend to find an appropriate outlet for sexual tensions through intercourse in marriage. You should be able to let off excess energy through sports, play, and work.

In *Civilization and Its Discontents*, Freud (1961) speculated that we channel basic sexual and aggressive impulses into socially applauded behavior patterns. This is the process of **sublimation,** which Freud believed responsible for the great works and achievements of human culture. Buildings, works of art, machines are substitutes for unconscious, or partly conscious, objects of our desires.

When id, ego, and superego have not worked in harmony to help us through the conflicts of childhood, psychological problems in adjustment may arise later on. If we have found no outlets for Oedipal wishes, for example, we may continue to attempt to repress sexual longings and hostilities toward parents. This repressed cluster of unacceptable impulses will clamor for expression, and the watchdog of the ego may have to expend most of its energy to keep them repressed. That may leave little energy for planning and coping, and we may feel constantly drained and subjected to continual feelings of uneasiness—all for reasons we cannot fathom. Yet anxiety represents the threat of impulses about to break loose. Or anxiety may be converted into bodily complaints, as we shall see later.

Adults with great repressed conflicts are like houses divided against themselves. They may not stand for long. So many psychological resources, so much ego strength, is channeled to the task of repression that such people may not be able to lead productive lives. Too strict a superego may narrow the paths the ego can use to gratify basic needs. Id impulses breaking loose into consciousness may create confusion, disorganization, and whirlwinds of emotion. The fantasies of the id may be difficult to discriminate from reality and may be experienced as hallucinations.

It is possible to develop different levels of maladjustment: neurosis and psychosis. A **neurosis** is a form of maladjustment in which individuals attempt to avoid sources of anxiety through defenses like repression and avoidance of

Sublimation (sub-blim-MAY-shun). The channeling of libidinal energy into constructive activities. Sublimation is a partly conscious defense mechanism.

Neurosis (new-ROW-sis). An adjustment problem chiefly characterized by the presence of anxiety. The category of neurosis is no longer used in the current edition of the *Diagnostic and Statistical Manual* of the American Psychiatric Association. It used to apply to a wide range of disorders that were felt to stem from neurotic anxiety.

Are these great works merely substitutes for unconscious objects of our desires, as suggested by the Freudian concept of sublimation?

situations that may bring unacceptable impulses to the surface. There are differing types of neurotic behavior, but they are all chiefly characterized by anxiety or attempts to cope with anxiety. In **psychosis,** maladjustment is so severe that individuals have difficulty maintaining contact with reality and may lose control over their impulses. Hallucinations and delusions are common and, in Freudian theory, reflect the unleashing of the forces of the id.

Freud's method of helping, psychoanalysis, is designed to unravel hidden conflicts and encourage self-acceptance of basic impulses. The repressed dilemmas of childhood may take on a less disturbing character in the light of adult reason.

The Behavioral Model of Adjustment and Maladjustment. Patterns of both adjustment and maladjustment are learned or acquired through experience, according to the behaviorist. Our early learning experiences may condition us to hold realistic or unrealistic expectations. Sex, for some, may hold a promise of beauty and marital happiness. For others, slapped and punished for stimulating themselves at ages too early to remember, sex may be associated with fear. Children with supportive, loving parents may learn to expect that people can be trusted, kind, and good. Children with harsh, punitive parents may learn that people are not to be trusted.

Adjusted behavior also includes knowledge of responses to the challenges of life that will meet with reinforcement—responses that will permit us to earn the rewards of life and to escape from its hardships. If you have not acquired the operants that will help you to succeed in our society, such as positive attitudes toward education and the capacities to read and write well, you may find that much of your behavior will be ineffective.

We learn from our experiences. When we are successful at a young age, we expect to be successful in the future. When we do not acquire the basic skills or operants that are important in our culture, we are likely to learn to expect failure. We may learn that it is more rewarding to escape from academic and social situations than to endure. In this direction lies maladjustment.

Although we learn from experience, it may be difficult to discontinue maladaptive behavior that meets with intermittent reinforcement. We may remain glued to a slot machine for hours, though it only intermittently returns money. We may pursue a love relationship in which we are only intermittently treated decently. In these directions, too, lies maladjustment.

Behavioral psychologists Leonard Ullmann and Leonard Krasner (1975) express the view that when individuals have not found their relationships with others to be rewarding, they may begin to withdraw from others and pay less attention to social cues (social discriminative stimuli) than most people do. As a result, their behavior may take on an odd appearance, or be labeled inappropriate. Schizophrenia is characterized in part by inappropriate social responses. In addition, when the real world loses its reinforcement value, people may become fully absorbed in their own fantasies and lose interest in distinguishing fantasy from what the rest of us consider real—external stimulation. Behaviorists often feel that such an approach explains hallucinations and other behavior characteristic of schizophrenia.

The Humanistic Model of Adjustment and Maladjustment. Abraham Maslow and Carl Rogers assert that we possess natural tendencies to actualize ourselves when our basic needs in life are met and when we need not distort our self-concepts to placate harsh, demanding parents or other powerful figures in our lives. Human beings are basically good and should be nourished fully with love when children. Then our own capacities to love will blossom fully and our behavior will be prosocial.

When we are not able to accept ourselves because of the negative evaluation of others, we tend to develop defenses that encourage us to distort reality and close us off from openly experiencing other people and novel life situations. Rather than allowing ourselves to experience the joy that can be a part of life in the "here and now," we may struggle to try to become things that we are not. We may accept the "oughts" and "shoulds" of others as our own, even if they are not congruent with what we feel we should be, and judge ourselves as being "bad" because we do not fit this distorted self-concept.

If we deny our authentic feelings, we disown important parts of ourselves and may develop the sense that life is unreal. Yet it is not life that is unreal—it is our view of ourselves that is "unreal," or unauthentic.

Carl Rogers (1951) points out that people who are maladjusted commonly express a number of concerns about their behavior, because it does not seem consistent with their concept of their self: "'I don't know why I do it. I don't want to do it, but yet I do,' is a common enough type of statement. Also, the notion, 'I'm just not myself when I do those things,' 'I didn't know what I was doing,' 'I have no control over those reactions'" (p. 510).

Rogers goes on to define psychological maladjustment as existing when people attempt to keep certain experiences out of awareness—both perceptions of ideas and emotional experiences. Then it is not possible to organize these experiences and integrate them as parts of the self. Rather than being integrated and whole, the self thus becomes scattered. Lack of self-acceptance serves as the basis for psychological tension and distress.

The humanistic approach to helping people adjust begins with warm acceptance by the therapist. If people are accepted by others as valuable and interesting for their own sakes, they may come to be able to accept themselves and begin the long journey to discover who and what they are—to get in touch with the thoughts and feelings that were submerged in the effort to earn approval from others.

The humanistic model also takes us far beyond the concept of adjustment, into the realm of personal growth. After we have "adjusted" to the challenges of life and learned to cope with the sources of stress acting upon us, then what? Do we curl up into a ball and fall asleep? Not according to humanistic theory. Maslow and Rogers believe that we use the firm base of self-acceptance to undertake the personal quest for values and meaningfulness in life—the pursuits that provide more than food when hungry and sex when aroused. Once basic needs are met, we seek to actualize ourselves in our own unique ways.

TYPES OF ADJUSTMENT PROBLEMS

Throw some people, some chimpanzees, a few fish, several sponges, and some seaweed into a large room—preferably a well-ventilated room. Stir slightly. What do you have? It depends on how you classify or categorize these creatures.

Categorize them into animals or plants and you lump the people, chimps, fish, and, yes, sponges together. Classify them as life that carries on business on land or under water, and you throw in our lots with the chimps only. How about creatures that can use language and those that can't? Since chimps can be taught to use sign language, it's still the chimps and us. How about creatures that swim and those that can't? Then you lump some of us together with the chimps and, it stands to reason, the fish.

There's a point to all this. The way you lump things together has an effect on what you do, on how you treat them. If you look at this motley group of creatures with an eye to sorting out those that are good to eat, you will decide on a collection that differs from those that you would allow to marry your children—probably.

Classification systems have also been constructed for talking about mild and more serious problems in adjustment. Yet it is sometimes not as easy to tell problems apart as it is to distinguish between people and fish (although if you were a fish, people and chimps might look pretty much the same to you). For instance, Kraepelin distinguished between schizophrenia and manic-depressive psychosis. Yet there is another psychological problem that seems to have elements of confusion, like schizophrenia, and a mood disturbance, like manic-depressive psychosis. It is labeled a schizoaffective problem. Is there really such an animal, or do some people have both problems at once, or is it just that sometimes we can't tell which is which? Good question.

Sometimes mental-health professionals also cannot distinguish reliably between one sort of problem and another. For instance, in one study psychiatric residents agreed with the chief psychiatrist's diagnosis of schizophrenia only 51 percent of the time (Schmidt & Fonda 1956). This was not a fluke. In a second study psychiatrists agreed on the label of schizophrenia only 53 percent of the time (Beck et al. 1962).

All right: different people may desire to categorize problems in adjustment in different ways, and even the problems themselves may not always be as distinguishable as chimpanzees and fish. Yet the classification system that is most often used by mental health professionals is found in the *Diagnostic and Statistical Manual* (DSM) of the American Psychiatric Association. The DSM is updated periodically, and some of the major categories of adjustment problems that are found in the latest version of the DSM, the DSM-III (American Psychiatric Association 1977), are listed in Table 5.1. Table 5.1 also indicates where the problem is discussed in this book. Some problems, such as mental retardation, are altogether beyond the scope of this textbook. In this chapter we acquaint you with the "symptoms" of some of these problems. Others are explored in other chapters.

Schizophrenic Disorders: When Inner Living Blends with Reality

When the psychiatrist examined Joyce's slit wrists and learned that she had been following the orders of "hellsmen," whom she alone could hear, he began to think that she might be schizophrenic. The schizophrenic disorders are typified by disturbances of thinking, emotional response or mood, and behavior. Thinking may become confused and illogical, and there may be difficulty in differentiating fantasies or inner living from reality. Joyce was experiencing both hallucinations and delusions, perceiving things that were present in her mind only—as Macbeth had perceived the dagger—and harboring an inaccurate idea that men from hell were somehow controlling her behavior.

Joyce's words became jumbled, as her thoughts might have been.

Table 5.1   Major Diagnostic Headings of the DSM-III of the American Psychiatric Association Draft Version (1977)

Heading	Examples of Disorders	Discussed in Chapter
Organic Mental Disorders	Alcohol Intoxication	15
Drug Use Disorders	Alcohol Dependence and Abuse	15
	Barbiturate Dependence and Abuse	15
	Opioid Dependence and Abuse	15
	Cocaine Dependence and Abuse	15
	Amphetamine Dependence and Abuse	15
	Hallucinogenic Abuse	15
	Cannabis Dependence and Abuse	15
	Tobacco Use Disorder	15
Schizophrenic Disorders	Hebephrenic Schizophrenia	5
	Catatonic Schizophrenia	5
	Paranoid Schizophrenia	5
Paranoid Disorders	Paranoia	5
Affective Disorders	Manic Disorder	5
	Depressive Disorder	5
	Manic-Depressive Disorder	5
Anxiety Disorders	Phobic Disorder	5, 8
	Panic Disorder	5, 6
	Obsessive-Compulsive Disorder	4, 5
	General Anxiety Disorder	5, 6, 7
Somatoform Disorder	Conversion Disorder	5
Dissociative Disorders	Amnesia	5
	Fugue	5
	Multiple Personalities	5
	Depersonalization	5
Personality Disorders	Paranoid Personality	5
	Asocial Personality	5
	Histrionic Personality	5
	Antisocial Personality	5
Psychosexual Disorders	Transsexualism	2, 13
	Transvestitism	13
	Fetishism	13
	Pedophilia	13
	Exhibitionism	13
	Voyeurism	13
	Sexual Masochism	13
	Sexual Sadism	13
	Sexual Dysfunctions	
	Impotence	13
	Inhibited Female Orgasm	13
	Inhibited Male Orgasm	13
	Premature Ejaculation	13
	Vaginismus	13
Disorders Usually Arising in Childhood or Adolescence	Mental Retardation	
	Bed-Wetting	
	Conduct Disorders	
Reactive Disorders	Post-Traumatic Disorder (such as death of a spouse)	6, 9
	Adjustive Disorders:	
	With Depressive Mood	9
	With Anxious Mood	6, 7
Disorders in Impulse Control	Explosive Disorder	10
Sleep Disorders	Insomnia	14
	Nightmares	14
		(Continued)

and Psychotherapy

127

Table 5.1 *(Continued)*

Physical Conditions in	Obesity	15
Which Psychological	Headache	6, 7
Factors Often Play a	Migraine	6, 7
Prominent Role	Painful Menstruation	6, 7, 13
	Asthma	6
	Hypertension	6, 7
	Ulcers	6

Throughout the interview, her emotions seemed strangely flat or blunted. Her emotional responsiveness was certainly inappropriate to the terrifying beliefs that she appeared to hold. Yet even though her emotions were flattened, she seemed physically agitated and seemed to find it difficult to remain seated.

Joyce was treated with major tranquilizers, chemicals that reduce agitation and are also considered "antipsychotic"—that is, they often seem to help individuals regain control over disturbed thought patterns and perceptions. Schizophrenic disorders are best brought to the attention of a physician, since they are most often treated with drugs that can be prescribed by physicians only.

There are different types of schizophrenics. **Hebephrenic** schizophrenics show silly, incoherent speech and immature behavior. They may throw things, laugh and giggle, or lose bowel or bladder control. They seem engrossed in private worlds of fantasy and hallucinations. The **catatonic** type seem to become detached from the environment, slowing down and becoming immobile or fixed for hours at a time, often in very unusual postures. Although catatonics do not respond to questions, later on they seem to recall everything that went on around them. The **paranoid** type are most common. Paranoid schizophrenics may have delusions of **grandeur** (believing they are Christ or Napoleon, or involved in a mission to save the world) or delusions of persecution (believing that someone or some group, like the Mafia, CIA, or the Communists, are out to "get" them).

Hebephrenic schizophrenia (hee-bee-FREN-ick). A schizophrenic disorder characterized by immature behavior, giddiness, and, often, hallucinations.
Catatonic schizophrenia (kat-tah-TAHN-ick). A schizophrenic disorder characterized by slowing down, holding unusual positions for long periods of time, and, sometimes, excited outbursts.

David Berkowitz, the "Son of Sam" Killer, smiles benignly upon his arrest in 1977. Does his response to his arrest seem appropriate? Because of his inappropriate emotional responses and his claim that a dog had urged him to commit his crimes, many mental-health professionals considered him to be schizophrenic.

An example of a frightening hallucination, which may be experienced in schizophrenia.

Some schizophrenics, called **simple schizophrenics,** may become drifters or lead marginal life-styles. Others, like Joyce, are usually hospitalized when they are agitated or otherwise incapable of continuing to function in the community. But use of chemotherapy has allowed large numbers of schizophrenics to return from hospitals to their communities. Yet chemotherapy often is not enough. Unfortunately, once in the community, many schizophrenics do not receive adequate guidance or psychotherapy, or find little to do with their time, so that adjustment outside the hospital can be very difficult. Some prefer to return to the protected world of the mental institution, and others have become trapped in a "revolving door" between the hospital and the community (Kohen & Paul 1976). Still, chemotherapy and efforts to help schizophrenics to adjust to the community cut the population of mental hospitals by 50 percent in the period from 1963 to 1973 (Jones 1975).

Paranoia

Paranoia is characterized by delusional thinking, such as delusions of grandeur or delusions of persecution, but paranoid individuals are not so disorganized in their thinking as are paranoid schizophrenics. "Pure" paranoia, paranoia without schizophrenic symptoms, is rare, and some question whether it exists as a category separate from schizophrenia at all.

Paranoid schizophrenia (PAIR-uh-noid). A schizophrenic disorder characterized by delusions of grandeur or delusions of persecution.
Grandeur (GRAND-your). Exaggerated belief in one's own importance or specialness. Also called grandiosity.
Simple schizophrenia. A schizophrenic disorder characterized by loss of interest in other people, flattened emotions, and, often, a marginal life-style.

Adjustment Problems and Psychotherapy

ON BEING SANE IN INSANE PLACES

What is it like to be a patient in a mental hospital? In a study by psychologist David Rosenhan of Stanford University (1973), eight volunteers showed up at a number of different hospitals, each claiming that they heard inner voices saying "hollow," "empty," and "thud." The eight included three psychologists, a psychology student, a psychiatrist, a pediatrician, a painter, and a housewife. They claimed no other problems: just "hollow," "empty," "thud."

Each of the eight was admitted with a diagnosis of schizophrenia. Following admission they no longer claimed to hear the voices and behaved absolutely normally. Yet because they made no serious efforts to be discharged, they remained hospitalized for an average stay of nineteen days. During this time no hospital staff members became suspicious of the eight, but other patients later reported that they wondered if some of the eight were journalists or professors "checking up on the hospital." Despite the fact that the eight reported no hallucinations during their stays, they were invariably discharged with the diagnosis of schizophrenia sticking like glue. Apparently once a schizophrenic is always a schizophrenic, in the eyes of many.

Rosenhan's eight subjects were not mistreated on their wards, although other patients were, sometimes for minor things like initiating verbal interaction. The movements, liberties, and privacy of the eight were restricted, as with other patients. They might be observed in their baths and in the toilet. Staff often avoided eye contact with them and shepherded them like reluctant schoolchildren from place to place and activity to activity.

Studies such as this show how some people can be warehoused rather than treated once admitted to the mental hospital, and how insensitive staff can be to individual needs. Yet the effort to maintain patients in the community also shows that many mental-health workers understand how important social interaction with our fellows is to our well-being and our adjustment.

Affective Disorders: Up, Down, and Around

Vince said that as a teenager he became suspicious of his good moods because they were always followed by "the dumps." In his middle twenties, his "highs" were euphoric. He would talk rapidly and nonstop. He would walk up to anyone and begin a long-winded conversation. He was brimming with great plans and self-confidence and would not take no for an answer. When "up," he made huge contributions to charities and once gave his car to a stranger. When he felt that he was about to "crash," or head for the dumps again, he would become terrified. He remembered how low he could feel and could not tolerate the thought of going through it again. Once he attempted suicide because of fear that he was on the way down.

Vince's highs and lows have now been evened out a good deal by a drug that is a salt of the metal **lithium.** He and thousands of others who have a bipolar, or manic-depressive, disorder are now being "maintained" on lithium therapy. These mood swings appear unrelated to environmental events in many people, and many researchers believe that Emil Kraepelin's observations were well taken—that manic-depressive behavior may reflect biochemical imbalances (Becker 1974; Akiskal & McKinney 1975). Some celebrities have publicly admitted to manic-depression and maintained that they learned to stop blaming themselves for their ups and downs since the problem is chemical: Tony Orlando, for instance, made such a pronouncement on the *Mike Douglas Show* in 1978.

Lithium (LITH-ee-um). A metal that is used in a chemical compound (lithium carbonate) to treat manic-depression. *Psychotic depression* (sigh-COT-tick). A severe form of depression characterized by impaired daily functioning, extreme loss of energy, and, occasionally, delusions. Psychotic depression should be brought to the attention of a professional.

The Challenge and the Self

Some individuals become manic at times, but do not share the lows described by Tony Orlando, Vince, and others. They appear to have inexhaustible energy. It has been hypothesized that some individuals who do not appear to have problems in adjustment but who are extremely productive and active may have "mild cases" of manic behavior.

Depressive disorders may be characterized by frequent crying, loss of appetite, feeling drained of energy, loss of sleep, and feelings of hopelessness. In the most severe form of depression, **psychotic depression,** daily functioning is severely impaired and there may be loss of contact with reality. Psychotic depression may be characterized by incessant moaning, feelings of being evil, delusions of having done great harm to others, and even delusions of physical illness.

Today many individuals with extreme depression seem to respond to **antidepressant drugs.** When antidepressant drugs fail, some psychiatrists choose to rely on **electric shock therapy.** It seems that convulsions induced by electric shock can lead to elevation in mood, although no one knows for certain why this may be so. Perhaps shock has some influence on brain activity. Electric shock therapy remains a controversial treatment. We explore the role of brain activity in depression in Chapter 9.

Anxiety Disorders

Anxiety disorders are characterized by nervousness, fears, feelings of misgiving, perspiration, rapid heartbeat, and muscle tension and shakiness. Yet anxiety disorders are frequently treated with psychotherapy, and, as we shall see in Chapters 6 and 7, we can learn to reduce sensations of anxiety through techniques that we can practice on our own—such as relaxation and meditation.

There are several types of anxiety problems. In a **phobic disorder,** there is an excessive fear reaction to an object or situation (see Chapter 8). In a state of **panic,** the individual, overwhelmed by anxiety, feels the need to do something at once, perhaps escape (Chapter 6). **Generalized anxiety** refers to a continuing state of anxiety that does not seem connected to environmental stimulation. Often it is, and some detective work can determine the causes; but even if it cannot, the distress can still be removed (Chapters 6 and 7). In an **obsessive-compulsive disorder,** there may be persistent, recurrent thoughts (obsessions) and urges to engage in repetitive behavior (compulsions), such as repeated handwashing or repeated checking that doors and windows have been locked.

Conversion Disorders: Don't Blame Me, I'm Handicapped

If you lost the ability to see at night, or if your legs became paralyzed, you would undoubtedly be highly concerned. Yet when cases of night blindness or paralysis are **conversion disorders,** victims can be indifferent to their problems.

During World War II, a number of airplane pilots developed night blindness. Although no damage was found in the optic nerve, they could not carry out their nighttime missions. There are rare cases of women with large families who have become paralyzed in the legs.

Conversion disorders seem to have a purpose. The wartime pilots recovered with rest, and their blindness may have afforded them some relief from

Antidepressant drugs (ANT-eye-dee-PRESS-ant). A form of chemotherapy used to treat severe depression. Use of these drugs would be totally inappropriate for the mild forms of depression that most of us experience from time to time.
Electric shock therapy. A "last resort" therapy for psychotic depression. Also known as electroconvulsive shock therapy, and abbreviated EST or ECT. A controversial treatment.
Phobic disorder (FOE-bick). Excessive, irrational fear reaction to a stimulus. We know that our fear is out of proportion to the actual danger but may allow the fear to interfere with our lives. Also called phobia.
Panic (PAN-ick). Overwhelming anxiety which usually leads to immobilization or disorganized flight, but may also lead to disorganized outbursts of aggressive behavior.
Generalized anxiety (ang-ZY-uh-tee). A prevailing state of anxiety that seems unrelated to environmental events. Also called free-floating anxiety.
Obsessive-compulsive disorder (ob-SESS-siv come-PULSE-siv). Disturbance by the intrusion of persistent, recurrent thoughts (obsessions) and urges to engage in repetitive behavior (compulsions), such as compulsive handwashing because of obsessive thoughts that the hands are dirty. Sometimes the obsessions do not lead to compulsive behavior.
Conversion disorder (kon-VURR-shun). Loss of motor or sensory function without a biological basis for the disorder. For example, paralysis of the legs or night blindness that is caused by anxiety rather than damage to the nervous system.

Adjustment Problems and Psychotherapy

FUNNY HAPPENINGS ON THE WAY TO THE FORUM

In the play *A Funny Thing Happened on the Way to the Forum*, a highly excitable character is named Hysterium, presumably the masculine version of the word "hysteria." Conversion disorders were previously called hysterical conversion reactions. It was thought that hysterical or highly volatile, irrational people were likely to develop physical complaints as a result of stress. In a burst of ancient sexism, it was also apparently believed that such problems lay within the province of women alone!

"Hysterical," you see, derives from the Greek word *hystera*, meaning uterus or womb. The ancient Greeks viewed irritability and tension as female characteristics and attributed them to a wandering uterus! As the uterus roamed through the body, they concluded, it would cause pains and odd sensations here and there. Men would never complain of such nonsense. Of course, the Greeks had not met pilots suffering from night blindness during World War II.

their stressful missions or permitted them to avoid guilt they might experience at bombing civilian populations. The paralyzed woman gains a rest from housework and also cannot engage in sexual intercourse, which might lead to another pregnancy. Yet she accomplishes all this without guilt.

Conversion disorders "convert" a psychological source of stress into a physical complaint or problem. They are rare, but their existence helped convince the young Sigmund Freud that "unconscious" processes were at work in people.

Dissociative Disorders: If It's Bad, It Can't Be Me

Dissociative disorder (dis-so-she-uh-tiv). Separation of mental processes such that we may lose awareness of our behavior, we may form multiple personalities, or we may feel that our experiences are not genuine. Dissociative disorders include amnesia, fugue, multiple personalities, and depersonalization.
Amnesia (am-KNEE-she-uh). Loss of memory.
Fugue (like "few" with a "g" on the end). Sudden discontinuation of one's role in life and the assuming of another life role in another location. A person in a fugue state cannot recall the earlier life role.
Depersonalization (dee-PURSE-un-al-eye-ZAY-shun). Feelings that the world or the self is not real.

The Challenge
and the Self

132

Have you ever conveniently forgotten about an episode in your life that reflected your acting out on basic impulses and not being your "best self"? Have you ever felt like simply putting an end to your life-style or your job or schoolwork, moving to another town and beginning a totally new life? These types of behavior are **dissociative**—they represent breaks in the flow of consciousness or the stream of life. Dissociative disorders apparently occur now and then when people cannot accept certain aspects of their behavior or feelings—when there is psychological incongruence between the self-concept and actual thoughts, feelings, or behavior.

Amnesia is motivated forgetting or repression of experiences or activities. The assumption is that the amnesiac would disapprove of or be shocked by the experiences that are forgotten or disowned. **Fugue** is the sudden disruption of significant roles in life—professional and interpersonal—and the taking up of a different set of roles and a new self-identity. Presumably, such individuals have amnesia for their earlier life roles. Billy, who abducted and raped four Ohio State women, was a case of multiple personalities. In multiple personalities, different identities play different life roles and usually have different names, ages, and personality traits. It is again theorized that the victim of multiple personalities may experience a shattering of the self when parts of the self are strongly incongruent. Identity disintegrates into many identities. **Depersonalization** describes the feeling that the world is unreal, perhaps that the self is also not real. Depersonalization is a logic consequence of inability to accept the self: "What is unacceptable can't be me."

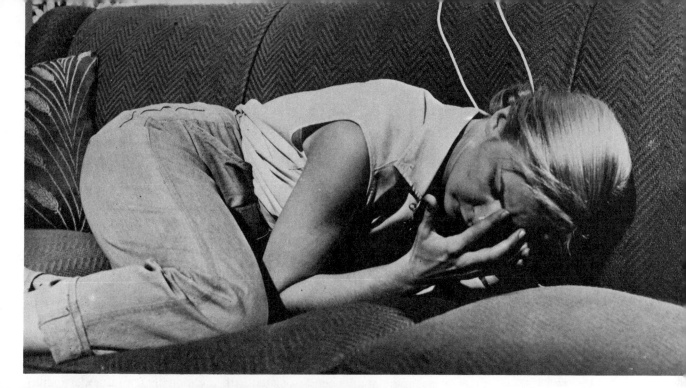

In the film *The Three Faces of Eve,* Joanne Woodward played three personalities in the same woman: the shy, inhibited Eve White (above) the flirtatious and promiscuous Eve Black (left), and a third personality (below) which was healthy enough to accept her sexual and aggressive impulses and still maintain her sense of self-identity.

Feelings of depersonalization and instances of amnesia are found often enough, but fugue and multiple personalities are very rare. When they are found, psychotherapy that fosters acceptance of conflicting impulses may meet with success in reintegrating the personality.

Personality Disorders

Personality disorders are relatively stable maladaptive patterns of behavior or styles of life that are marked by difficulties in interpersonal relationships.

The **paranoid personality** is not disorganized like the paranoid schizophrenic, or blatantly delusional like the individual who becomes labeled paranoid; but people with paranoid personalities generally expect the worst from others, are filled with mistrust, and view people as basically out for themselves. These views serve as a barrier to the development of intimate relationships.

Asocial personalities are seclusive, shy, and avoidant of intimate relationships. Asocial people are often found on the fringes of society, for instance, as prostitutes or hobos—individuals who do not pour themselves into productive activity.

The **histrionic personality** is theatrical, emotional, and dramatic. The category has generally been associated with traditionally feminine personality traits such as coyness and seductivity to generate attention and manipulate others into doing one's bidding. Histrionic personalities are considered highly emotional, immature, vain, demanding, and dependent. In a sexist society that has limited women's power to exercise control, it may be that histrionic behavior is acquired as a subtle way to gain control. Whereas men are usually taught to be direct and self-assertive, women may learn to get their way by appearing helpless, by pouting, by becoming angry, or by crying (Johnson 1976). Yet more than a few men also acquire the label histrionic.

Antisocial personalities often possess deviant moral values, are indifferent to commitments to others and to society, are frequently in trouble with the law, and are not deterred by punishment. They experience little or no guilt about mistreatment of others, and often have difficulty maintaining steady jobs or family lives. They may be characterized as impulsive, uncaring, selfish, troublesome, undependable, and irresponsible. This category includes many habitual criminals, and perhaps some politicians or businesspeople who might step over anyone or break the law to get to the top.

Personality disorder. Deeply ingrained maladaptive life-styles that do not reflect high levels of anxiety or breaks with reality. *Paranoid personality.* A personality marked by suspiciousness and the general belief that people are out for themselves, for what they can get. While some people undoubtedly are, the paranoid personality always suspects the worst.
Asocial personality (ay-SO-shull). A personality marked by seclusiveness, shyness, and avoidance of intimate relationships. *Histrionic personality* (hiss-tree-ON-nick). A personality marked by vanity, selfishness, seductiveness, and highly dramatic complaints about the behavior of others.

Antisocial personality (ant-eye-SO-shull). A personality marked by conflict with society; absence of guilt or notable levels of anxiety; irresponsibility; impulsiveness; but average intelligence and, often, superficial charm.

HELPING PROFESSIONALS: PEOPLE WHO HELP OTHER PEOPLE TO ADJUST

Throughout history various people in many roles have helped others to adjust to the challenges of life. These people have included priests, ministers, and rabbis, grandparents, witch doctors, palm readers, wise men and women, and, more recently, professionals such as psychologists, psychiatrists, counselors, and social workers.

Today there are any number of people who advertise themselves as "therapists," and people who are seeking help in adjusting should know that the claim of being a therapist is no guarantee of professional training or competence. Various professionals, however, have undertaken training and, very often, licensing examinations that do tend to guarantee at least that these professionals have had a common core of educational experiences in accredited institutions of higher learning. Here are some of the types of people who are helping professionals.

Psychologists

In order to call yourself a **psychologist,** you need to have a doctoral degree in most states—a Ph.D., an Ed.D. (Doctor in Education), or a Psy.D. (Doctor in Psychology). Your doctoral level course work must have been predominantly in psychology. In addition, clinical and counseling psychologists should have had internships or their equivalents in supervised experience in clinical work. Psychologists in most states must pass licensing examinations before they engage in private independent work.

Psychologists may use psychological tests to help determine the nature of personality problems or personal assets and liabilities. Psychologists also practice **psychotherapy,** an intense interaction between a client and a helping professional that usually involves the disclosure and discussion of intimate experiences and feelings, and the systematic attempt to foster adjustive behavior.

Most psychologists also receive extensive training in research methods and are taught to be skeptical in matters of psychological theory.

Psychologist (sigh-KOLL-oh-jist). A person with graduate training in psychology who may do psychotherapy.

Psychotherapy (SIGH-ko-THER-ap-pee). An intense interaction between a client and a helping professional that usually involves disclosure of intimate facts and the systematic encouragement of adjustive behavior.

Psychiatrists

Psychiatrists earn the M.D. (Doctor of Medicine) or D.O. (Doctor of Osteopathy) and then have three-year residency programs in which they learn to apply medical skills to problems in adjustment. A practicing psychiatrist must be a licensed physician.

Psychiatrists may prescribe drugs and other medical treatments. Tranquilizing drugs, antidepressant drugs, lithium therapy, and electric shock therapy can be offered by any physician, but most physicians will be reluctant to prescribe psychiatric drugs and therapies other than minor tranquilizers (see Chapter 6) and will refer patients with severe problems in adjustment to psychiatrists. Psychiatrists, like psychologists, may offer psychotherapy. Most psychiatrists do not use psychological tests; they rely on clinical interviews to learn about their patients, or may sometimes refer them to psychologists for personality testing.

Psychiatrist (sigh-KIGH-uh-trist or sick-EYE-uh-trist). A person with a medical degree who may do psychotherapy and prescribe medicine.

Psychiatric Social Workers

Psychiatric social workers usually have the M.S.W. (Master of Social Work) and supervised experience in helping people with problems in adjustment. Like psychologists and psychiatrists, they must usually be licensed by their states to establish private practices.

Social workers can offer psychotherapy, but they cannot prescribe drugs or engage in psychological testing. They commonly engage in marital counseling and may also act as go-betweens for individuals who are attempting to avail themselves of social services.

Psychiatric social worker (sigh-key-AT-trick). A social worker with training in psychotherapy.

Adjustment Problems
and Psychotherapy

135

Psychotherapists

Be very careful if the word "psychotherapy" is not defined, in your state, as limited to professionals such as psychologists, psychiatrists, social workers, and nurses. If the term is not "protected" in your state, anyone can hang out a shingle as a **psychotherapist.** However, if the term is protected in your state, do not be surprised if psychologists and other helping professionals occasionally refer to themselves as psychotherapists or, in brief, as therapists.

Sex Therapists

In recent years many helping professionals have begun to become labeled **sex therapists,** or people who help others overcome sexual dysfunctions like pre-

Psychotherapist (SIGH-KO-THER-ap-pist). A person who practices psychotherapy. *Sex therapist.* A person who helps others overcome sexual dysfunctions, like premature ejaculation or orgasmic dysfunction.

The Challenge and the Self

136

mature ejaculation or difficulty achieving orgasm. As we shall see in Chapter 13, these problems are almost always the results of psychological maladjustment, and not medical problems. For that reason, professionals without medical training, like psychologists and social workers, will be found among the ranks of the sex therapists, just as surely as you will find psychiatrists and psychiatric nurses.

However, too often the term "sex therapist" is not controlled by law, and thus anyone can hang out a shingle as a sex therapist. Newspaper ads may even list "sex therapists" who are willing to have sexual intercourse with people with sexual dysfunctions. But actual sex therapists do not go to bed with their clients.

Psychoanalysts

Psychoanalysts have received extensive graduate-level training in psychoanalysis, the method originated by Sigmund Freud. In the cases of psychiatrists and psychologists, this training will be postdoctoral. Social workers are also admitted to psychoanalytic training in some states.

Psychoanalyst (SIGH-ko-AN-al-list). A person who has received graduate training in psychoanalysis, the therapy originated by Sigmund Freud, and who can practice psychoanalytic psychotherapy.

Pastoral Counselors

Pastoral counselors are priests, ministers, or rabbis who have received training in counseling or helping people to adjust. Adjustment is defined within the framework of the particular religion.

Pastoral counselor (PAST-or-ul). A member of the clergy who has received training in helping people with adjustment problems.

Counselors

The term **counselor** is often unprotected, but it should suggest that an individual has a graduate degree in education and supervised counseling experience. Counselors may work in rehabilitation settings, school or college settings, and others.

Counselor. A person with graduate training in education who may advise individuals with adjustment problems.

Others

Many other people are also engaged in helping. These include occupational therapists; vocational therapists; music, art, and dance therapists; and paraprofessionals. Check into the qualifications of anyone you consider consulting. As a rule of thumb, when in doubt check first with a psychologist, psychiatrist, social worker, nurse, or college or university counseling center.

WAYS OF HELPING PEOPLE TO ADJUST

There are many ways of helping people to adjust to life's challenges, and the helper's beliefs about the genesis of adjustment problems will exert a powerful influence on the methods of helping employed.

Adjustment Problems
and Psychotherapy

137

PSST, HOW ABOUT SOME PSYCHOTHERAPY—CHEAP?

What do you do when you feel the need for help? Do you ask friends for the name of a reliable helping professional, let your fingers do the walking through the yellow pages, or leaf through the classified ads in your newspaper?

In recent years, psychologists and other helping professionals have begun to advertise their wares in newspapers. But so have an assortment of "therapists" and helpers that run the gamut from respected professionals to massage experts, "sex surrogates," and even "energy artists."

What kind of ad would you respond to if you were in need of help? Psychologist Patricia Keith-Spiegel (Schaar 1978) of the California State University at Northridge showed hundreds of college students mock newspaper ads in an effort to assess their effectiveness. Some of these ads featured teasers like "My name is Lane, anxiety and depression relief is my game," or "Relieving personal hang-ups is my business." But these ads were "too clever" and received poor ratings for effectiveness. Money-back guarantees were also found ineffective. The students understood that there are no guaranteed results in psychotherapy, and this claim hurt the credibility of the advertisers.

Students preferred ads that indicated that the therapist was highly available, competent, and affordable but not cheap. Cheapest fees did not draw the crowds, just as the cheapest brand at the supermarket often loses out to the familiar and trusted brand when products are equally unknown.

Because of this movement toward advertising, the American Psychological Association has established guidelines for its members. Psychologists may *not*

- mislead by presenting selected, favorable information.
- use endorsements by former clients.
- exaggerate the probability of a successful outcome.
- promise unique, special abilities.
- use an emotional appeal.
- make claims about the quality of their services.

What if these standards were applied to all advertising in the public media? Commercials could not then claim that their products were special or the best. Ball players and actors could not endorse them. We would have to live with straightforward explanations of the features of these products. Commercials would be duller, but they might actually give us some useful information.

Imagine that your car will not start. (For most of us, that will not be difficult.) Your beliefs about why it is so uncooperative will suggest what you should do about it. You might assume that it has been invaded by evil spirits. If so, you might torch a hole through the hood, say a few prayers, and wave a clove of garlic in front of the radiator to get those spirits gone. You might assume that it is catatonic. If so, you might inject major tranquilizing medication into the fuel line. Of course, you might also assume that it has been paralyzed by intense psychological conflict, or that it has not been sufficiently reinforced for starting in the past, or that it has such a low self-concept that it is afraid to get started and continue its shameful ways. You might then call in a psychoanalyst, a behavior therapist, or a humanistic therapist, depending on your view. Of course, if you simply conclude the car is dead, you can call for the undertaker—that is, junk dealer.

In this section we explore four current views of helping: the medical approach, the psychoanalytic approach, the behavioral approach, and the humanistic approach.

The Medical Approach: If I Have a Problem, I Must Be Ill

The medical approach views people with adjustment problems as ill and the problem behavior as symptomatic of the patient's illness. Usually the patient is urged to remove any sources of stress and to enter the hospital, if necessary, in order to rest.

Drugs may be prescribed, either to provide symptom relief or to get at the assumed underlying disease process. In schizophrenia, for example, major tranquilizers provide symptom relief by reducing agitation and tackle the underlying thought disorder through "antipsychotic" activity.

Since the patient is ill, it is seen as the doctor's responsibility to take charge of the patient's life and problems during the recovery process. The good patient follows orders.

There are some instances in which chemotherapy may be more harmful than useful. Nowhere is this clearer than in mild cases of anxiety or depressive disorders. It is a simple matter for maladjusted individuals to become dependent on tanquilizing or antidepressant pills rather than to make those life changes that will result in the experiencing of less anxiety or in an elevated mood. They can attribute feeling better only to the pills rather than to themselves and have done nothing to improve their coping skills.

The Psychoanalytic Approach: If I Can Find Out Why, I Shall Feel Better

You lie down on a couch. Your therapist sits just behind you, out of sight, while you talk about anything that pops into your mind, no matter how seemingly trivial, no matter how personal. In order to avoid interfering with your self-exploration, your therapist may say very little or, perhaps, nothing for session after session. But that is all right, because there are years of therapy ahead. . . .

This form of therapy is called psychoanalysis or psychoanalytic therapy. Psychoanalysis is the name of Freud's model of personality and also of the type of psychotherapy he devised to help people adjust. Its purposes are to reveal the unconscious conflicts that are presumed to be at the root of the problem and to allow the client to express verbally or through socially acceptable behavior the emotions or impulses that have been pent up. This process of gaining personal knowledge is called **insight,** or **self-insight.** Allowing psychic energy to spill forth so that the ego can spend its energy as something other than a watchdog is called **abreaction,** or **catharsis.**

Insight. Knowledge concerning one's motives for behavior or one's history. Also called self-insight.
Abreaction (ab-ree-ACK-shun). The discharge of pent-up emotions. Also called catharsis.

In this way a man with a phobia for knives may eventually come to understand that he has been repressing the urge to kill someone and taste his anger. A woman with a conversion disorder, paralyzed legs, may come to understand how her "physical problem" allows her to escape stress without feeling guilty. She may also taste her resentments at her traditional sex role and, perhaps, decide that she will begin to assert herself.

Psychoanalysis attempts to break through the walls of defense that have prevented the conscious self from gaining insight in several ways. The process is slow and tedious and requires an expert. Too much insight too soon, too much energy released too soon could be devastating. These ways include free association, dream analysis, and transference.

Adjustment Problems and Psychotherapy

Free association. Uncensored discussion of any topic that comes to mind. The central method of psychoanalytic psychotherapy.

In **free association,** the client is asked to discuss freely and pursue any topic that comes to mind. No thought is to be censored. Psychoanalysts do not really believe that free association is free. Damned-up impulses will seek release. When you relax and do not censor your thoughts, you are likely to begin to encounter repressed impulses and memories.

Manifest content (MAN-ee-fest). The subject matter of a dream.
Latent content (LATE-ent). The hidden content of a dream. That which is symbolized by the manifest content.

Freud believed that dreams are the "royal road to the unconscious." He asked clients to write down their dreams on waking so that they could be recalled and then analyzed. Freud believed that dreams have not only a **manifest content** (the subject matter of the dream), but also a **latent content** (or hidden content) that symbolizes repressed conflicts. A frightening dream that your spouse has been hit by a truck can symbolize feelings of resentment toward your spouse that you have been afraid to recognize and express.

Transference (trans-FURR-ents). Process in psychoanalytic psychotherapy in which the client behaves toward the psychoanalyst as toward other people in the past.

Clients are assumed to "transfer" feelings toward others onto the therapist. A young man may see a mature male therapist as a father figure. A woman may see him as a husband or lover. The therapist is to remain neutral though vaguely warm throughout analysis, so that any **transference** results from the client's needs and not the therapist's encouragement. Emerging feelings toward the therapist are then instructive of the ways in which the client relates to others. If a client hates the therapist one week but attempts seduction the week following, this may reflect conflicting emotions toward someone in the client's own background.

A successful psychoanalysis is thought to depend largely on understanding and modifying the feelings that transfer into the therapeutic relationship. Because it may take years for transference to develop fully and be resolved, psychoanalysis tends to be a lengthy and expensive procedure.

Ego analysis. A psychoanalytic psychotherapy in which the psychoanalyst does more face-to-face talking with the client and direct encouraging of adjustive behavior.

Modifications of psychoanalytic therapy have been developed by analysts like Alfred Adler, Karen Horney, and Harry Stack Sullivan. Their forms of therapy are briefer, involve more face-to-face contact between analyst and client, more attention to fostering behavior that is adjustive, and less concentration on the role of transference. These therapists are called **ego analysts** because there is more emphasis on the importance of dealing directly with the client's ego, or conscious self.

The Behavioral Approach: Adjustment Is What You Do

The behavioral approach to helping is to change problem behavior and problem habits directly. Discussion of the possible origins of problems like anxiety, depression, or social clumsiness is permissible, but takes a backseat to the formulation of strategies for acquiring responses that will meet with reinforcement, or for eliminating inappropriate fear responses or habits like overeating or overspending.

Behavior therapy. Application of principles of learning to solving adjustment problems. Also called behavior modification.

The behavioral approach to fostering adjustment is called **behavior therapy** or **behavior modification,** in contrast to psychotherapy. Behavior therapy may be practiced by psychologists, psychiatrists, or other professionals who have received training in behavior therapy techniques and have had supervised experience.

Behavior therapy is the systematic application of the principles of learning to help people adjust to the challenges of life. As such, behavior therapists draw heavily on knowledge of classical and operant conditioning. Some examples of applications of these principles to everyday human adjustment problems follow.

Acquiring Operants. Rather than exploring reasons for lack of assertiveness or for social klutziness, behavior therapists carefully outline the types of behavior that will help their clients attain social rewards. They carefully instruct clients in social responses or skills, have clients practice them, and provide clients with continued feedback until the response appears likely to succeed.

Behavior therapists may help clients acquire operants that they can use to stand up to a demanding boss, ask someone out on a date, make successful small talk, or perform well in a job interview.

Extinction-Based Approaches. When anxiety or fear responses are exaggerated, as in the case of phobias, or inhibit performance in sexual relationships or test-taking behavior, behavior therapists use strategies based on the principle of extinction. It is presumed that the phobic object or situation, or the sexual relationship or the test, has become a conditioned stimulus (CS) for the conditioned fear or anxiety response (CR). If the client can be exposed repeatedly to the phobic object, sexual activity, or test (CS) without experiencing pain or personal tragedy (US), then the conditioned fear response (CR) ought to extinguish. So behavior therapists may encourage clients to approach the dreaded situation gradually, allowing fear to extinguish at each step along the way.

Reinforcement-Based Approaches. We can learn to overcome unwanted habits like smoking or nail biting by being certain that the reinforcements in these situations are redesigned so that stopping the unwanted habit becomes more reinforcing than continuing it. We can learn to pat ourselves on the back for exercising self-control. We can make rewards like films or records dependent on achieving behavioral goals.

We can also become more influential in the lives of others by reinforcing behavior that we wish to maintain, and allowing unwanted behavior to extinguish. For instance, a child may misbehave because your screaming and jumping up and down is perceived as reinforcing. By ignoring (failing to reinforce) the bad behavior and looking for and reinforcing desirable behavior, the "bad child" may become a "good child."

The Humanistic Approach: Liberation of the Self

Humanistic psychologists believe that problems in adjustment stem from roadblocks in the path of self-actualization. Humanistically oriented psychotherapy is an opportunity to learn about ourselves without self-condemnation for having feelings, attitudes, and values that differ from the expectations others have of us. Self-acceptance frees us to make choices and decisions that lead to authentic and personally meaningful behavior.

Therapists like Carl Rogers and Abraham Maslow emphasize the importance of creating a warm, supportive therapeutic atmosphere, one that nourishes self-exploration and self-expression. The most widely adopted method of humanistic psychotherapy is Carl Rogers' client-centered therapy (1951).

Client-Centered Therapy. In **client-centered therapy,** the client takes the lead—listing problems and exploring their meanings. The therapist focuses on reflecting the client's feelings, to help the client get in touch with them. Thus

Client-centered therapy. The therapy originated by Carl Rogers in which the client takes the lead and the therapist reflects the client's feelings.

Adjustment Problems and Psychotherapy

the client begins to gain insight into whether the feelings are genuine and authentic, or reflect the attitudes of other people.

Client-centered therapy can be frustrating for some people because client-centered therapists do not offer concrete advice. They believe that decisions must be arrived at by the clients themselves if they are to be authentic. There is an old joke about a client who says, "If you don't give me a direct answer to my question, I'm going to jump out this window!" The therapist answers, "You feel you will jump out of the window." That ends the session. This kind of answer would be very poor client-centered therapy, but illustrates the importance client-centered therapists attach to clients' falling back on their own resources.

The effective client-centered therapist shows unconditional positive regard, empathetic understanding, genuineness, and congruence.

Unconditional positive regard means placing no demands or restrictions on the client's values or behavior. Thus a warmly accepting atmosphere is created in which clients are given the security and comfort they need in order to follow their own feelings.

Empathetic understanding is the therapist's ability to reflect accurately the client's personal experiences and feelings. It is like seeing the world through the client's eyes, not one's own. The therapist must learn the client's frame of reference for making judgments and decisions, and not assume that it will be similar to the therapist's own.

Genuineness is the therapist's own authenticity in therapist-client relationships. Therapists must be honest and genuine about their own feelings, but not allow their feelings to color acceptance of the client. Only therapists who have personally overcome the need to have others agree with them can at once show genuineness and unconditional positive regard. Therapists must be able to tolerate people with different views. After all, if important people in the client's life had been able to tolerate the client's uniqueness, the client would probably not need therapy.

Successful therapists are thus also congruent—in touch with their own feelings and self-accepting. Congruent therapists serve as models for clients.

Other outgrowths of the humanistic movement include encounter groups, Gestalt therapy, and transactional analysis (TA).

Encounter Groups: Seeing Through the Social Masks. Encounter groups seek to go beyond adjustment or meeting the challenges of life. Also called T-groups or sensitivity-training groups, they are intended to help people who are not experiencing serious psychological problems to become more aware of their own feelings and sensitive to the needs and feelings of others. This goal is achieved through intense encounters, or confrontations, between strangers who, like ships in the night, come together out of the darkness and then sink back into the shadows of each other's lives. But something is gained from the coming together.

Encounter groups stress the interactions between the people in the group "here and now." Discussion of the past may be outlawed. Expression of genuine feelings toward one another is urged. When group members suspect that an individual's social self is vastly different from the personal self, they may descend to rip away the mask.

Since encounter groups can be brief, there may be "opening up" exercises like milling about the room and touching each other with the eyes closed. But some encounter groups are **marathon groups,** continuing without sleep for twenty-four hours or a weekend. The drain of energy helps strip away defenses.

Unconditional positive regard. Total acceptance of the client as a valuable human being. A method of client-centered therapy.

Empathetic understanding (em-puh-THET-tick). Accurate reflection of the client's feelings. A method of client-centered therapy.

Genuineness (JEN-you-in-ness). Honesty in the expression of feelings. A goal of life in humanist-existential theory, and a method in client-centered therapy.

Encounter groups. Group experiences designed to heighten our sensitivity to the feelings of others through a series of intense encounters, or confrontations. Also called T-groups (for "training") or sensitivity training groups.

Marathon groups. Prolonged group experiences designed to help break down group members' defenses and social masks.

Nude therapy groups are related, although many humanists point out that their method does not require physical nakedness. Nude therapy literally strips away much of our social masking. Clothes, you see, may not "make" the person; they may effectively hide the person.

Professionals recognize that encounter groups can be harmful when they urge an overly rapid disclosure of intimate, personal details, or when several members in unison violently attack the facade and defenses of a reluctant group member. Responsible leaders watch for such abuses and attempt to keep groups moving in growth-enhancing directions.

Gestalt Therapy: Getting It Together. The German word **Gestalt** means form. The **Gestalt therapy** of Fritz Perls (1971) urges making contact with all the parts of the self to provide a cohesive wholeness to our personal experience.

In order to seek such wholeness, Gestaltists may use a technique called dialogue, in which clients undertake a verbal confrontation between two conflicting parts of their personalities. These clashing parts of the self may be "topdog" and "underdog," or "masculine" and "feminine." Clients take the part of each, alternatively, to seek some resolution of the inner conflict.

Your "topdog" may conservatively suggest, "Never take chances. Stay with what you have or you might lose everything."

Your exasperated "underdog" may rise up and assert, "You never try anything new. How will you ever get out of this rut if you don't try to take on new challenges?"

Such encounters within the self can promote heightened awareness of the details of opposing feelings and suggest directions toward the integration, or making whole, of one's endeavors. Clients in Gestalt therapy may also be encouraged to express ideas and feelings that they believe to be in direct opposition to their own views, or to role play (act out) the behavior of other people in their lives. Viewing life situations here and now is believed to help clients get in touch more fully with their genuine feelings and the outlooks of others. It shatters distorted views of the world.

Gestalt therapy aims at insight, as do psychoanalysis and client-centered therapy. Unlike psychoanalysis, the focus is on the here and now, on becoming more conscious of current feelings and behavior patterns, rather than exploring the past. Unlike client-centered therapy, Gestalt therapy is highly directive; the therapist carefully leads the client through growth experiences.

Transactional Analysis: I'm OK—You're OK— We're All OK

Transactional analysis (TA) is a popular current therapy rooted in both the psychoanalytic and the humanistic traditions. According to psychiatrist Thomas Harris (1967), who wrote *I'm OK—You're OK*, many of us suffer inferiority feelings, as suggested by psychoanalyst Alfred Adler. We may see ourselves as helpless and dependent, like children. Thus we feel that we are not OK but that other people are OK. The purpose of TA is to help people feel that they and other people are all right: I'm OK—you're OK.

Psychiatrist Eric Berne, who wrote *Games People Play* (1976a) and originated TA, theorized that each of our personalities has three ego states: a parental ego state, an adult ego state, and a child ego state, or, more simply, a

Nude therapy groups. Group experiences in which nudity is intended to help strip away social masks. Not for cold climates.

Gestalt therapy (guess-TALT or gesh-TALT). A humanistic therapy originated by Fritz Perls that is designed to increase awareness of all aspects of the self, all conflicting points of view, hidden motives and fears.

Adjustment Problems
and Psychotherapy

143

Parent, an Adult, and a Child. But note that these are not comparable to the superego, the ego, and the id. They are all "ego states," meaning that they can all be self-aware ways of attempting to adjust to reality.

A **transaction** is an exchange between two people. When two people interact as adults, they feel each of them is OK. But very often we relate to others adults like parents or like children, and the relationships suffer through, crossed exchanges like this, and our relationships become strained:

Bill (adult to adult): Nan, did you see the checkboard?

Nan (parent to child): A place for everything and everything in its place.

When TA is carried out with couples, it focuses on transactions such as these and aims to encourage adult-to-adult relationships. Berne (1976a) wrote that the most commonly played marital game is "If It Weren't for You." In IWFY, people typically marry domineering spouses who will prevent them from doing certain things (such as moving to a new city or taking a more challenging but less secure job) that they are really afraid to do. But now the spouse can be blamed for it.

Other games noted by Berne include "See What You Made Me Do," "Now I've Got You, You Son of a Bitch," "Kick Me," "Look How Hard I've Tried," and "I'm Only Trying to Help You." In all these games, our relationships with others are deceitful. We fail to express our genuine feelings and needs. We are not OK.

Transactional analysis (trans-ACT-shun-ul). A humanistic form of therapy and method for analyzing human relationships in terms of ways in which we relate to each other—as parents, adults, or children. *Transaction.* An exchange between two people.

Figure 5.1 An Unfortunate Transaction

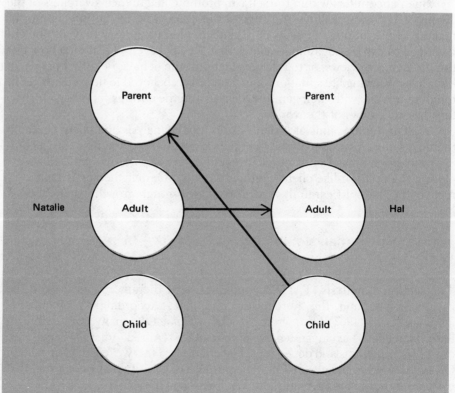

Natalie asks Hal (adult to adult), "Did you have a good time tonight?"
Hal replies (child to parent), "I don't wanna talk about it!"

A major method of TA is to have clients in group sessions describe their blueprints for the future, or "life scripts." Bad scripts involve the games people play, and people are again encouraged to relate to one another as adults. People who are OK and who want others to be OK do not need to resort to games.

Summary

- *In 1978, a 23-year-old man was found innocent of rape because the defense claimed that a 19-year-old woman living inside him had actually done the deed.* True. Billy was found not guilty by reason of insanity. His diagnosis was multiple personalities, one of the many types of problems in adjustment. When problems are severe enough, we may not be held responsible for our own behavior.
- *Cavemen believed that the way to help people overcome strange behavior was to let the sun shine in—or to let the evil spirits out. Therapy was making a hole in the head.* True. This practice is called trephining. Belief in evil spirits was a forerunner of the demonology that has dominated human belief about mental illness or abnormal behavior for the past two thousand years or more.
- *In the Middle Ages, you might have been dunked under water to find out if you were possessed by the devil. If you survived you were in for trouble. After all, innocent people would drown.* True. This was a "catch-22" of the Middle Ages. People whose behavior was disturbed were believed to be possessed either as punishment for their sins or from having made a pact with the devil (witches). Witches were commonly put to death. Exorcism was also a common practice.
- *Labeling people as sick can rob them of their dignity.* True, because when we are considered ill we are not viewed as competent adults. Nor are we held responsible for our imperfections. For such reasons, controversial psychiatrist Thomas Szasz recommends doing away with the concept of mental illness.
- *All forms of mental illness stem from physiological problems, such as chemical imbalances or metabolic disturbances.* This has *not* been found to be the case, but the medical model of mental illness is, in part, based on this conviction. Some disorders, like schizophrenia or manic-depression, may be found to reflect medical problems, but most problems in adjustment are just that—problems in adjustment and not medical problems.
- *Smoking is a mental illness.* False, but "Tobacco Use Disorder" is a diagnostic category in the DSM-III of the American Psychiatric Association, when and if smoking causes distress. The DSM-III is highly inclusive, listing serious and minor problems. It is the most commonly used system of classifying problems in adjustment.
- *Volunteers were all admitted to eight different mental hospitals with exactly the same diagnosis, just on the basis of reporting hearing the words "empty," "hollow," and "thud."* True. The mere reporting of these phony symptoms led consistently to the erroneous diagnosis of schizophrenia, a disorder characterized by disturbances of thought, mood, and behavior, and, often, hallucinations and delusions. Affective

disorders, like manic-depression, show greater disturbance of mood and less disorganization and confusion. The Rosenhan study showed that we are treated according to our labels, and that once we are labeled it is extremely difficult to prompt others to reconceptualize us.

- *In some states, a carpenter, math professor, or bus driver can set up in business as a psychotherapist.* True. Though professionals like psychologists and psychiatrists do psychotherapy, the term "psychotherapist" may not be legally restricted to qualified professionals in your state.

- *College students find psychologists who advertise the lowest fees to be most appealing.* False. A reasonable fee plus indications of competence are rated most favorably.

- *For some people, drugs may be an essential ingredient of adjustment.* True. Major tranquilizers are highly effective with many schizophrenics and have enabled mental hospitals to reduce their populations. Lithium therapy seems to be effective for many people with severe affective disorders. Antidepressants help many who are extremely depressed, although most cases of depression are not severely impairing and may be tackled effectively through self-help or psychotherapy.

- *Dreams are the royal road to the unconscious.* True from the Freudian perspective. Freud believed that dreams had manifest and latent, or symbolic, contents. Dream analysis, free association, and transference are important elements of psychoanalysis, the Freudian method of psychotherapy, which stresses gaining self-insight into the clashing forces of the personality.

- *In order to overcome social clumsiness, it is essential for you to develop insight and learn just how you came to be a klutz.* False, according to the behavioral approach to problems in adjustment, which involves directly shaping desirable behavior and directly eliminating unwanted, problematic behavior. Behavior therapy or behavior modification is the systematic application of the principles of learning—as found in classical and operant conditioning—to solving adjustment problems. Techniques can be employed with or without self-insight.

- *Some of the most excellent psychotherapists will absolutely refuse to give you straightforward advice.* True, client-centered therapists believe that any decisions must be your own if they are to be psychologically congruent or authentic for you. They focus on providing a warm, supportive atmosphere in which you will feel free to explore your own feelings in order to develop self-insight and hence your own potential through self-actualization. Humanistic psychotherapy—whether it be client-centered therapy, the encounter group, Gestalt therapy, or another type of treatment—goes beyond adjustment. It seeks to nourish human potential to its fullest blossoming.

Different types of problems or different interests may suggest different types of therapy. A journey for insight may involve psychoanalysis or humanistic therapy. The wish to eliminate problem habits or to foster social or sexual skills may call for behavior therapy.

II

THE CHALLENGE OF STRESS

6
STRESS
AND
DEFENSIVE
COPING

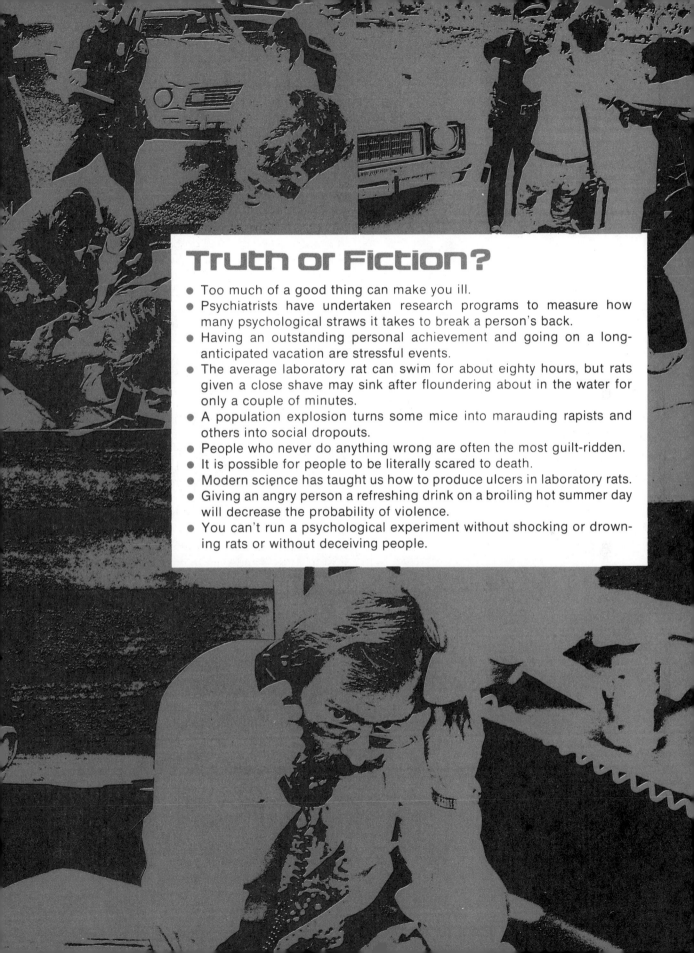

Truth or Fiction?

- Too much of a good thing can make you ill.
- Psychiatrists have undertaken research programs to measure how many psychological straws it takes to break a person's back.
- Having an outstanding personal achievement and going on a long-anticipated vacation are stressful events.
- The average laboratory rat can swim for about eighty hours, but rats given a close shave may sink after floundering about in the water for only a couple of minutes.
- A population explosion turns some mice into marauding rapists and others into social dropouts.
- People who never do anything wrong are often the most guilt-ridden.
- It is possible for people to be literally scared to death.
- Modern science has taught us how to produce ulcers in laboratory rats.
- Giving an angry person a refreshing drink on a broiling hot summer day will decrease the probability of violence.
- You can't run a psychological experiment without shocking or drowning rats or without deceiving people.

THE CHALLENGE OF STRESS

Too much of a good thing can make you ill. You may think that marrying Mr. or Ms. Right, finding a prestigious and well-paying job, moving into a new home, gaining professional recognition, meeting new people, quitting smoking, and winning the state lottery—all in the same year—would put you in a state of unparalleled bliss. Perhaps it would. But it could also lead to hives, headaches, bronchial asthma, or nausea. As pleasant as these events may be, they all involve significant life changes. According to psychiatrists Thomas Holmes and Richard Rahe (1967) of the University of Washington School of Medicine, life changes cause **stress.**

Stress. **The demand made on an organism to adjust.**

Stress is a concept that has been borrowed from the science of physics. In physics, stresses are forces that place pressures on bodies—the weight of tons of rock pressing down against the earth, one car impacting against another on a highway, hands pulling apart an elastic band. The implications? Tons of rock may leave deep impressions in the earth, or even sink below the surface if the earth is soft. Cars destroy one another on the highways all too frequently. The elastic band eventually will snap. Similarly, the many forces or stresses in our lives can press or push or pull on us. Even when they are quite pleasant, we can sometimes feel that "great weights are pressing down" on us. We can feel "smashed." We may think of ourselves as "stretched tight" and being at the point of "snapping."

In psychology, then, stress is the demand made on an organism or person to adapt, to cope, to adjust. Too much stress can tax our adjustive capacities.

In this chapter we explore many sources of stress: life changes, pain and discomfort, anxiety, frustration, conflict, and Type A behavior. We find that stress can lead to a variety of bodily problems, which one Canadian researcher, Hans Selye, has referred to as "diseases of adaptation." Finally, we discuss defensive methods of coping with stress. Defensive coping involves our efforts to minimize the impact that stressful circumstances have upon us. While they may have temporary protective value, allowing us to marshal our resources, they do little to take charge of the circumstances that distress us. We explore more active ways to adjust to stress—and even to grow from the experience of stress—in Chapter 7.

Although stress can create problems and stimulate us to act defensively, do not think that we are going to come out in favor of hiding from stress in our closets for the rest of our lives. Boredom, stagnation, lack of novel stimulation —these can give rise to other sorts of stresses. We must encounter some stress if we are to grow as individuals, and it may very well be that we thrive when we find a level of stress that is suitable to our tastes and to our endeavors.

When we strive to become independent as adolescents, when we enter college, when we enter the work force, when we undertake the responsibilities of establishing intimate relationships with other people—when we do all these things, we encounter stress. Yet we do not consider these experiences destructive. We may find them essential for personal growth. As we proceed throughout the remaining chapters in this book, it becomes clear that our methods of approaching these challenges determine whether we succeed and find a healthy level of stress to accompany us on the path to personal growth, or whether we focus all of our attention on narrowing our experiences in order to defend ourselves from stress.

Now we turn our attention to some of the many sources of stress.

The Challenges of Stress, Fear, and Depression

Stress and Life Changes: "Going through Changes"

We all know that the "last straw" is the one that will break the camel's back. But it would be absurd to try to actually compute the weight that would constitute the "last straw," right? Wrong. In an article in *New York* magazine, Randy Cohen (1978) reported the results of an old treatise on one-humped camels. They were reported to carry from 240 to 1,200 pounds, although one Australian workhorse (or workcamel) had managed 1,904 pounds. There you have it: 1,904 pounds plus one straw and the camel's back would be broken—perhaps. Two-humped camels remain a mystery.

Holmes and Rahe set out to discover how many psychological straws, or stresses, would be required to significantly impair people's ability to adjust to them. Their research involved thousands of interviews with people from varying locations and socioeconomic statuses. They assigned marriage the arbitrary figure of 50 "life-change units" and asked their interviewees to assign numbers of life-change units to other life changes, using the 50 points as a baseline. Most events, as seen in Table 6.1, were rated as being less stressful than marriage, but several were found to be more stressful, including death of one's

Table 6.1 Life-Change Units Scale

Life Event	Value	Life Event	Value
Death of spouse	100	Foreclosure of mortgage or loan	30
Divorce	73	Change in responsibilities at work	29
Marital separation	65	Son or daughter leaving home	29
Jail term	63	Trouble with in-laws	29
Death of a close family member	63	Outstanding personal achievement	28
Personal injury or illness	53	Wife beginning or stopping work	26
Marriage	50	Beginning or ending school	26
Fired at work	47	Revision of personal habits	24
Marital reconciliation	45	Trouble with boss	23
Retirement	45	Change in work hours or conditions	20
Change in health of family member	44	Change in residence	20
Pregnancy	40	Change in school	20
Sex difficulties	39	Change in recreation	19
Gain of new family member	39	Change in social activities	18
Change in financial state	38	Mortgage or loan less than $10,000	17
Death of close friend	37	Change in sleeping habits	16
Change to different line of work	36	Change in number of family get-togethers	15
Change in number of arguments with spouse	35	Change in eating habits	15
Mortgage over $10,000	31	Vacation	13
		Minor violations of the law	11

Source: T. H. Holmes and R. H. Rahe. The social readjustment rating scale. *Journal of Psychosomatic Research,* 1967, *11,* 213–218.

spouse (100 units) and divorce (73 units). On the average, these people felt that the death of one's spouse required approximately twice the adjustment effort of marriage, and that divorce was close to three-quarters (73%) as stressful as loss of one's mate through death. Positive events such as outstanding personal achievement (28 units) and going on vacation (13 units) were also seen to require personal adjustment. They, too, made the list.

So, how many psychological straws do the damage? To find out, Holmes and Rahe explored the recent life events of thousands of individuals, assigning each recorded change the number of units compiled in their Life-Change Units Scale. They found that people with high life-change scores were at astonishingly higher risk for major medical illnesses. Of subjects "earning" above 300 life-change units in the past year, eight of ten had developed serious medical problems. Only one of three individuals with scores below 150 was given to such ailments.

Other researchers have corroborated the psychological and medical impacts of the death of one's spouse. Rees and Lutkins (1967) studied the residents of a small town in Wales, and found that the death rate among 903 people who had lost close relatives during the past year was seven times as great as that for 878 residents of similar age and health who had not been bereaved. Parkes (1972) reports research at Harvard University comparing sixty-eight widows and widowers under the age of forty-five with sixty-eight married people of similar age, social class, and ethnic background. The widows and widowers had greater difficulty sleeping, used more alcohol and tranquilizers, smoked more, and had been hospitalized three times as often during the previous year as the nonbereaved group.

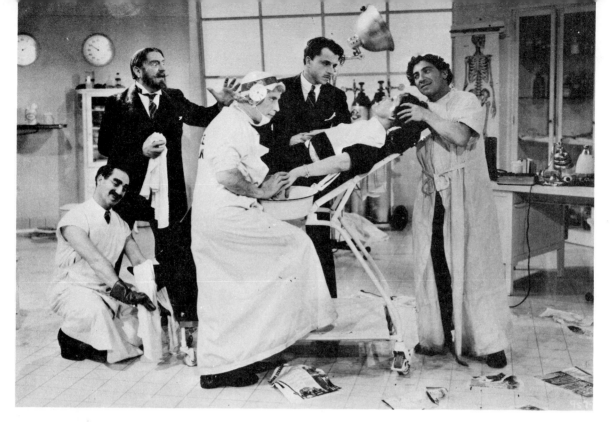

An outing to the dentist's office is usually more stressful than suggested in this Marx Brothers film, *A Day at the Races*. Pain and discomfort tax our abilities to adjust.

Pain and Discomfort

We have to confess that behavioral scientists have done many questionable things to other people and to animals for the sake of gaining new knowledge. In one series of experiments, psychiatrist Curt Richter (1957) studied the effects of painful experiences on the adjustment capacities of laboratory rats.

His approach was to drop rats into a tub of water and measure the amount of time they would be able to swim in order to avoid sinking and drowning. When the water is at room temperature it turns out that most laboratory rats are marathon swimmers, capable of keeping their noses above the surface for about eighty hours. But if Richter blew a noxious stream of air into the animals' faces, or if they were dropped into water that was uncomfortably cold or hot, they would become exhausted after only about twenty to forty hours and then sink to the bottom of the tub.

Rats, like people, are not all alike. Richter noticed that some of them swam consistently in a clockwise direction in the tub, others consistently in a counterclockwise direction. Wondering if the length of their whiskers determined which way his rats would circle, Richter had his laboratory assistants shave the whiskers on one side of a rat's face and then drop it into the tub. The rat thrashed about in the water for only about two minutes and then sank. No, rats do not swim with their whiskers. Richter discovered that the rat had been **traumatized** by the process of having its whiskers shaved. The assistants had

Trauma (rhymes with "DRAW-muh"). A severe instance of stress which can be physical or psychological and results in injury. Verb: to traumatize.

Stress and Defensive Coping

153

STRESS AND CROWDING

Sometimes you do everything you can for mice. You give them all the food they need, handsome and lovely mice of the opposite sex, a comfortable and constant temperature, and protection from such predators as cats and owls, and what do they do? They act like, well, animals.

John Calhoun (1962) studied the effects of crowding with mice so that we might learn how living too closely together affects at least one mammalian species. He simply allowed mice to reproduce without any controls except for the limited space of their laboratory environment. At first they flourished. The males scurried about exploring and gathering females into harems. They reproduced and defended the portions of the laboratory environment that they perceived to be their own territory. They did not covet their neighbors' wives. They fought rarely. The females, unliberated, built their nests and nursed their young. They resisted the occasional advances of strange males.

Unrestricted population growth was the snake in mouse paradise. Beyond a critical point, the tone of the community changed dramatically. The mortality rate rose to 50 percent in less crowded sections, and up to 96 percent in the most dense areas. The family structure broke down, with packs of delinquent males roaming and assaulting females who had been previously sheltered in harems. Only the strongest, most dominant males escaped aggression. Other males were homosexual or bisexual. Some were cannibalistic. Others shunned all social contact, male or female. Many females dropped their feminine ways, huddling together with the males and shunning sexual activity. Upon dissection, many mice in experiments such as these have shown unhealthful changes in body organs and glandular malfunctioning.

What of people in the big city? Are their lives headed toward destinies as foul as those experienced by the mice in Calhoun's laboratory? Social and environmental psychologists have run studies to come up with a scattering of answers.

You may have had the unfortunate experience of being shoehorned with two other people into a dormitory room originally intended for only two people. One group of researchers surveyed such crowded students and found that they were less satisfied with their roommates and saw them as being less "cooperative" than did students who had only one roommate (Baron et al. 1976). Do men and women react to crowding in the same way? Women, it seems, find being crowded in with other women less noxious than men find being crowded in with other men. It is interesting to speculate about the reasons for this sex difference. Are men socialized to develop more competitive feelings about other men in close proximity with them? One group of researchers speculated that women felt that it was appropriate to share their feelings with one another in such situations, a factor that could lead to interpersonal liking, feelings of emotional as well as physical closeness. Men, on the other hand, are often socialized to keep a "stiff upper lip" and refrain from expressing feelings. Sure enough, it

placed the animal in a black bag, allowed only its head to stick out so that they could have full control over the animal, and then shaved it with noisy, grating clippers that must have appeared huge to the small animal. The procedure was repeated with other rats: black bag, chop-chop, splash! None swam for more than a few minutes. The compounded stresses of the whisker clipping and then the splashing into the tub were too much for the animals. Rats allowed several minutes to recover from the clipping before being dropped into the tub swam for the typical eighty hours.

Being dropped into cold water in a tub or jumping into an icy pool, falling into hot water or being burnt, a stream of noxious air or a brisk wind, noisy clippers or a blaring stereo, bright lights, pungent odors, hard physical blows—all these painful experiences are sources of stress that can tax our ability to adjust.

The Challenges of Stress, Fear, and Depression

was found that crowded women who were prevented from talking to one another about their feelings found high density less desirable than women who were permitted to interact (Karlin et al. 1976). Crowding has also been shown to lead to illness, withdrawal, and aggression (Bell et al. 1978).

Most college students will have little difficulty recalling the stress of those crowded registration lines.

Anxiety

"Up-tight," "shaken up," "jumpy," "butterflies in the stomach," feeling as if "the top of my head is about to come off"—these are some of the colorful expressions associated with the unpleasant sensations of **anxiety.** Anxiety may be thought of as a general response to stress, a way of emotionally experiencing stressful situations. Many changes occur in the body when we experience anxiety, but the experience itself is of a sense of dread and foreboding. All of us at one time or another have had the feeling that something terrible is about to happen, or that there is something important that we must take care of immediately. We have had nagging and troublesome thoughts. We have wondered if we would be able to cope.

Anxiety is a central concept in the personality theory of Sigmund Freud.

Anxiety (ang-zy-uh-tee). Feelings of fear and dread. A psychological state characterized by tension and apprehension. A generalized response to stress.

Stress and Defensive Coping

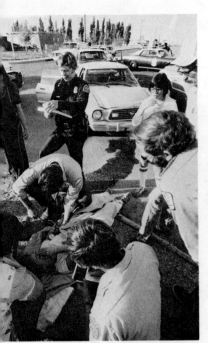

Fear of automobile accidents is an example of reality anxiety that motivates us to drive carefully. Reality anxiety helps us avoid harm.

Reality anxiety. In psychoanalysis, anxiety that stems from perception of a real danger in the environment. Also called objective anxiety or fear.
Neurotic anxiety. In psychoanalysis, anxiety that stems from attempts to control unacceptable impulses. Neurotic anxiety is the chief characteristic of the neuroses.

Freud practiced psychoanalysis with hundreds of anxious patients in turn-of-the-century Vienna, and he came to believe that the sources of anxiety could be conscious or unconscious. He wrote of three major types of anxiety: reality anxiety, neurotic anxiety, and moral anxiety.

Reality Anxiety. **Reality anxiety** is the equivalent of objective fear. It is called "reality" anxiety because it is based on an accurate assessment of our environment: we experience reality anxiety when there is danger. Reality anxiety includes fear of touching a hot stove, fear of social rejection if we behave in a nasty manner, and fear of flunking a test if we haven't studied.

Reality anxiety is considered *rational* anxiety—fears shared by most people. Reality anxiety is the normal and appropriate emotional response to a harmful stressor. John Wayne played a tough marine sergeant in *The Sands of Iwo Jima*, about the taking of that Pacific island in World War II. A private about to enter his first battle asked the sergeant if he was scared. In a fatherly tone John Wayne explained that he was always scared before a battle, even if experience had allowed him to appear composed. It would be foolish not to experience reality anxiety or fear when we perceive danger.

We shall see that fear does not in and of itself remove harmful stressors. It motivates us to do so, however.

Neurotic Anxiety. Imagine that you have been seriously insulted by a family member whom you respect and adore. Imagine that you have also been taught, from a very early age, that it is horrible and disgusting for people to experience anger toward loved ones and family members. You could be a perfect candidate for **neurotic anxiety.** Freud suggested that many times we fail to experience emotions fully—especially strong emotions like anger and sexual attraction—because we have been raised to feel that such emotions are improper or indecent.

Freud wrote that we could be motivated to keep such emotions unconscious, out of our awareness. Yet it is something like trying to keep a tight lid on a full pot of boiling water. The steam has to go somewhere. Most of the time it fizzes out just a bit at a time. Rather than recognize the feeling for what it is, we experience it as neurotic anxiety. He described three types of neurotic anxiety: free-floating anxiety, phobias, and panic.

People with free-floating anxiety are chronically fearful and nervous, though they cannot pinpoint the source of their fears. They may fear being alone, yet fear crowds. They may feel that the world is closing in on them, that something horrible will happen. They may be quite irritable, being constantly upset by "little things."

Phobias are overwhelming, irrational fears. They are shared by a small minority of people, and are out of proportion to the actual amount of pain or harm that would be experienced from contact with the dreaded object. People who cannot bring themselves to take elevators, though they must walk several flights, or to receive injections, though they are quite ill, are said to be suffering from phobias. As we shall see in Chapter 8, Freud felt that the phobia *symbolized* some unconscious fear or concern.

A state of panic is like the lid being blown off the boiling pot. A person in a state of panic suddenly engages in unusual behavioral excesses, such as acts of violence, without visible provocation. To Freud, panic represented a direct discharge of a forbidden impulse—such as sex or aggression—that was pent up too long. You can see why Freud thought that his method of therapy, psychoanalysis, ought to offer his patients a sort of "safety valve." Awareness of some of the sources of emotions like anger could permit at least some steam to escape through fantasized retaliation or talking about resentments.

Moral Anxiety. It may seem very odd that the people who are least likely to injure others can be precisely the people most riddled with guilt. Yet Freud explained this strange occurrence through the concept of **moral anxiety.**

Moral anxiety is experienced when your thoughts, feelings, or actions are inconsistent with the moral standards you have developed. As an emotion, it is equivalent to feelings of guilt and shame. Your thoughts may suggest that you are a rotten, low-down person. Freud noted with irony that many of his most guilt-ridden patients had never insulted or hurt anybody, although they might have been much better off if they had been more self-assertive. People with little moral anxiety, he explained, would be likely to show behavioral excesses and to experience little guilt. But strong moral anxiety would act both to inhibit such excesses and to produce powerful feelings of guilt and shame at the very experiencing of temptation. Most unfair.

Moral anxiety. In psychoanalysis, anxiety that stems from wrongdoing or the thought of wrongdoing. Guilt.

Frustration

You may wish to be a defensive lineman on the varsity football team, but weigh only 120 pounds or be the wrong sex. Your desire for a college diploma may be somewhat attenuated by the need to attend classes and study. You may have been denied a job or an educational opportunity because of your ethnic background. Now and then your wish to gratify an impulse or two may be frustrated by your moral code.

We all experience **frustration**—the thwarting of a motive to attain a goal. And frustration is another source of stress.

In Figure 6.1, a person (S) is strongly motivated (M) to attain a goal (G), but is thwarted by a barrier (B). You (S) may desire (M) to go out for a drink (G), but be a year too young (B). You could cope with the B by waiting patiently for a year or by borrowing someone else's "proof." Or you could try to convince yourself that you didn't really want the drink anyway—thus diminishing the importance of the unattainable G and decreasing the strength of the M.

Many sources of frustration are obvious. Adolescents are used to being too young to wear makeup, to drive, to go out, to spend money, to get married, to drink, or to work. Time is the constant barrier that causes them to delay gratification. No wonder G. Stanley Hall, the first president of the American Psychological Association, characterized adolescence as a time of storm and stress. Lack of social skills may act as a barrier to making new friends. Lack of knowledge of a foreign language may make it impossible to ask for directions abroad.

Other sources of frustration, such as loneliness and social isolation, can be less obvious. People appear to have a need for novel stimulation, so that boredom and lack of stimulation can be frustratingly stressful experiences. In sensory deprivation experiments, people are, in effect, removed from planet Earth. Their eyes are covered so that there is no light. Their hands and arms are padded so that they feel nothing. They are placed in soundproof rooms where the temperature is perfectly comfortable and constant. They are often paid handsomely for doing nothing—just to stay in isolation and do nothing. Few can tolerate such **deprivation stress** for long. Some (Galdston 1954) begin to hallucinate—to sense things that are not really there—as if bogus internal

Frustration (fruss-TRAY-shun). The thwarting of a motive. Ever wait in line for tickets and then learn that no more seats were left? That's frustration.

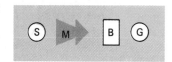

Figure 6.1 A Model for Frustration. A motivated (M) person (S) is prevented from reaching a goal (G) by a barrier (B).

Deprivation stress. Stress that stems from lack of sensory stimulation or input.

Stress and Defensive Coping

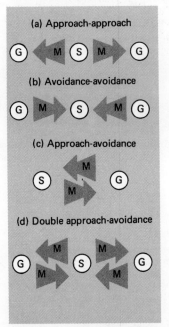

Figure 6.2 Models of Four Types of Conflict.

stimulation were required to compensate for the thwarted need for external stimulation.

We differ in our **tolerance for frustration.** Stress heaped upon stress can lower our tolerance, just as Richter's rats, already unnerved from their close shaves, sank quickly to the bottom of the tub. We may laugh off a flat tire on a good day, but when we are tired and hungry, have just had a fight with the spouse, and the rain is pouring down, a flat tire may seem like the last straw.

Conflict

How common is the experience of feeling "damned if you do and damned if you don't"? Of feeling that anything that you did would be wrong? Of regretting that you couldn't do two things, or be in two places at the same time? We have all wanted to go to a movie but had to study for an exam. At some time or other we have possibly said or done something that we did not fully believe in to get the approval of another. We may have had difficulty deciding which college to attend, whom to ask out. This is **conflict**—being torn in two or more directions at the same time by opposing motives. Conflict can be a major source of stress in our daily lives.

There are several types of conflict. Figure 6.2(a) shows an **approach-approach conflict,** often the least stressful type of conflict. Here there are two goals, each of which is positive and attainable. You may be having difficulty deciding between pizza and tacos, Tom and Dick, medicine and teaching, Nassau and Hawaii. In such cases you may **vacillate** or go back and forth for quite a while before making a decision. If you do make a choice, there may be eventual regrets—especially if your choice falls short of your expectations. You may get nauseous from the pizza, Tom may grind his teeth, medicine requires twenty-four-hour periods on call, it may rain in Nassau. Still, if you do make a choice and approach a goal, you are likely to become more active in reaching it or working for it. If it is satisfying, you are less likely to be concerned about "The Road Not Taken" (see p. 171). Approach-approach conflicts are less stressful than other types of conflicts since each goal is desirable.

An **avoidance-avoidance conflict** (Figure 6.2[b]) is a more stressful situation. You may be frightened to go to the dentist, but you are afraid of your teeth decaying farther if you don't. You don't want to make a contribution to the Association for Advancement of Lost Causes, but you don't want your friends to feel you are cheap or uncommitted either. In Chapter 11 we take a look at the plight of people who were the subjects in a psychological experiment on obedience: they were placed in severe avoidance-avoidance conflicts when the experimenter asked them to do something they found morally objectionable. If they refused, however, they thought they would be standing in the way of scientific progress. When an avoidance-avoidance conflict is especially aversive and no possible resolution is in sight, some people stop behaving altogether or simply leave the situation. Many "missing persons" were simply not able to resolve avoidance-avoidance conflicts at home. In *How to Save Your Own Life*, novelist Erica Jong (1977) wrote about a woman who suffered in an unfulfilling marriage in part because of fears of loneliness and failure if she were to attempt to "make it" again in the social world. She got to the point where she could not get out of bed in the morning to begin the day. At that point she resolved to end the union.

It is possible for the same goal to produce approach and avoidance motives—an **approach-avoidance conflict** (Figure 6.2[c]). Here, too, we may vacillate. People and things have their good and bad qualities, their pluses and their minuses. Cream cheese pie may be delicious, but oh the calories! There is the familiar lament, "Why is everything I like either immoral, illegal, or fattening?" Commonly, the closer we get to the object of our conflicted desires, the more we are impressed by its negative features; yet it may appear most attractive from a distance. Many couples repeatedly break up and then reunite. When they are apart, and perhaps frustrated, they recall each other fondly and swear that if they were to get back together, *this time* they would make it work. Perhaps they cannot even recall how they disturbed each other. But after spending some time together they find themselves confronting the same old aggravations. They think, "How could I have kidded myself into believing that this ingrate would ever change?"

Approach-avoidance conflict. A form of conflict in which the same goal is perceived to possess both desirable and undesirable attributes.

Figure 6.3 The Sources of Stress

The most complex form of conflict is the **double approach-avoidance conflict,** in which each of two or more goals (Figure 6.2[d]) has its positive and negative aspects. Should you study on the evening of an exam or go to the movies? "Studying's a drag but I won't have to worry about flunking; I'd love to see that movie, but then what'll happen tomorrow?" Should you take a job when you graduate from high school or attend college first? If you take the job you will have cash jingling in your pockets very shortly, but you may later feel that you have not lived up to your potential. If you attend college, you may have to delay the independence and gratification that come with earning a living, but you may find a more fulfilling occupation later on.

Conflicts, as we shall see in Chapter 7, can be resolved through making decisions. When conflicts are resolved, they no longer serve as sources of stress.

Type A Behavior

Cardiologists Meyer Friedman and Ray H. Rosenman carried on research into the origins of heart disease for many years at Mount Zion Hospital and Medical Center in San Francisco, and in a book called *Type A Behavior and Your Heart* (1974), they proposed that millions of us seem improbably dedicated to the continual creation of our own sources of stress. **Type A behavior** is stress-producing behavior. Friedman and Rosenman suggest that Type A behavior is a stronger predictor of heart disease than smoking, lack of exercise, poor diet, or obesity.

Type A people are highly competitive and impatient. They order their lives as though one eye were glued firmly to the clock. Type A people find it very difficult to go out on the tennis court and just bat the ball back and forth a few times—they watch their form, perfect their strokes, and demand continuing self-improvement. In the film *A Thousand Clowns*, Jason Robards played a television executive who decided that he was tired of being a "list maker." He quit a prestigious and profitable position so that he could take the time to enjoy things like playing the banjo and visiting the Statue of Liberty. Type A people are list makers; they always have things to do.

When you designate some people as Type A, you are practically obligated to designate others as **Type B.** Friedman and Rosenman are no slackers—they present Type Bs as people who can relax more easily, who are less ambitious and impatient. Type Bs tend to pace themselves and to focus more on the quality of life. Type Bs smoke less and have lower serum cholesterol levels than Type As. Type As often earn higher grades and more money than Type Bs of equal intelligence (Glass 1977). But Type As have more heart attacks than Type Bs, even when we consider the effects of cigarette smoking (Friedman & Rosenman 1974).

THE BODY AND THE CHALLENGE

How is it that too much of a good thing can make you ill? Why is it that recent widows and widowers have a dramatically higher mortality rate than their married agemates? Why do Type A people run the risk of a higher incidence of heart problems than Type Bs? Is it true, for that matter, that you can be "scared to death"?

This Type A business executive is probably sending his blood pressure through the ceiling, but this Type B executive is capable of focusing on the quality of life and allowing himself to relax.

Just how is it that thoughts, feelings, pressures and tensions, and the many passages through life become translated into *bodily* changes that can have a profound effect upon one's health and general sense of well-being? We do not yet have all the answers, but what we do know suggests that the human body, during a time of stress, is very much like a clock with an alarm system that will not shut off until its energy is dangerously depleted.

Arousal

You have a physiological alarm system that goes into operation immediately upon the impact of a stressor—whether that stressor is a change of life, a painful experience, anxiety, frustration, conflict, or your own unrelenting Type A behavior. Your alarm system serves to mobilize or arouse your body in preparation for defensive action.

Early in this century, physiologist Walter Cannon (1929) termed this alarm system the "fight-or-flight **arousal**" reaction. We have inherited this arousal reaction from times when many stressors were life-threatening—a predator at the edge of a thicket, a sudden noise from the undergrowth. The various components of this arousal reaction help prepare our bodies to do physical battle with an aggressor or to flee: our respiration increases and takes in more oxygen; our heart rate and blood pressure increase as the oxygen is distributed through the body; our muscles tense in preparation for harsh activity; blood shifts away from the skin (minimizing bleeding from wounds) and the digestive system and flows toward the heart, the central nervous system, and the muscles; digestive processes slow or stop; sugar reserves are released from the liver to increase available energy; **adrenalin** is secreted from the adrenal medulla, abolishing muscular fatigue, increasing the coagulability of the blood, releasing additional sugar from the liver, and, in circular fashion, further stimulating heartbeat and other bodily functions (Figure 6.4).

Arousal. **A state of alertness.**

Adrenalin (uh-DREN-uh-lin). **A hormone that activates bodily functions. Adrenalin leads to arousal.**

Stress and Defensive Coping

Are You Type A?

DO YOU CREATE YOUR OWN STRESS EACH DAY?

You may have had it with being classified. You probably began your life with a pink or blue baby blanket, according to sex. As you grew you discovered that you belonged to a certain racial group, did (or didn't) practice a certain religion, may have been tall or short, slender or heavy, and so on.

Still, behavioral researchers do not rest easily unless they can do some classifying, so we have hundreds of personality tests. Below is a sort of checklist that will help you reach a personal conclusion as to whether or not you are a Type A person—ambitious and achievement-oriented to the point where you may be your own worst source of stress and tension. The items are developed from discussion by Friedman and Rosenman (1974, pp. 82–85).

Yes answers suggest the Type A behavior pattern, a sense of "time urgency" and constant struggle. In appraising whether you are Type A, you need not be concerned with the number of yes answers. We have no normative data for you. As Friedman and Rosenman write, you will have little difficulty spotting yourself as "hard core" or "moderately afflicted" (p. 85) if you are honest with yourself.

Do you: Yes   No

1. Strongly accent key words in your everyday speech?   ____   ____
2. Eat and walk quickly?   ____   ____
3. Try to hurry other people to get on with what they're trying to say?   ____   ____
4. Find it highly aggravating to be stuck in slow traffic or waiting to be seated at a restaurant?   ____   ____
5. Continue to think about problems and your own business even while listening to someone who is talking to you?   ____   ____
6. Try to eat and shave at once, or drive and jot down notes at the same time?   ____   ____
7. Catch up on work on your vacations?   ____   ____
8. Tend to bring conversations around to topics that are of concern to you?   ____   ____
9. Feel guilty when you spend time just relaxing?   ____   ____
10. Find that you are so wrapped up in your work that you no longer notice scenery on the way to work or decorations or colors in the office?   ____   ____
11. Find yourself concerned with getting more *things* rather than developing yourself as a creative and concerned individual?   ____   ____
12. Try to schedule more and more activities into less time?   ____   ____
13. Feel challenged to compete with other Type A people?   ____   ____
14. Clench your fists, pound them on the table, or engage in other gestures to emphasize your views?   ____   ____
15. Credit your accomplishments to your ability to work rapidly?   ____   ____
16. Feel that things must be done *now* and quickly?   ____   ____
17. Constantly try to find more efficient ways to get things done?   ____   ____
18. Think of your activities and the activities of others in terms of *numbers* of times something has been done?   ____   ____

Autonomic nervous system (aw-toe-NAHM-mick). A branch of the nervous system that controls the activity of internal organs and glands, such as heart rate and secretion of adrenalin. **ANS.** Abbreviation for the autonomic nervous system.

These changes noted by Cannon are largely prompted by the **autonomic nervous system** (often abbreviated ANS). Autonomic means automatic. Without some form of training, we cannot consciously will or direct many of these changes to occur.

The ANS has two divisions or parts: the **sympathetic ANS** and the **parasympathetic ANS.** When you are alarmed or aroused, anxious or fearful, the sympathetic division of the ANS is most active, resulting in the changes shown

Figure 6.4 The Physiology of Arousal. When you are aroused or alarmed, the sympathetic division of the autonomic nervous system is stimulated. You experience many of the bodily changes illustrated here: muscles tense, blood pressure increases, hair may stand on end, pupils dilate, respiration rate increases, and so on.

in Figure 6.4. When you are relaxed, exhausted, or depressed, the parasympathetic division is most active. Parasympathetic activity causes the heartbeat to slow down, the blood pressure and respiration rate to decrease, and digestive processes to become more active.

Our ancestors lived in situations in which the body's alarm system would be deactivated quickly: you fought or ran successfully or, to put it bluntly, you were dead. Sensitive alarm systems would have been strong survival factors. But in modern living, highly sensitive autonomic reactivity may no longer be a blessing. Social structures and sophisticated weapons protect us from previously threatening creatures and provide us with food. No longer are our dreams punctuated by the silent roars of the skulking leopard. Fighting and running are both usually condemned as inappropriate responses to stress.

Nor did our ancestors carry thirty-year mortgages or engage in Type A behavior in the corporate structure. Contemporary pressures and behavior patterns may keep our alarm systems *on*, though not at maximum strength, for hours, days, or months at a time. We may then go through the stages of the **general adaptation syndrome (GAS)**.

General Adaptation Syndrome

Canadian psychiatrist Hans Selye (1976) made the study of stress in people and animals the major portion of his life's work. After many years of observation he noted that people and animals responded somewhat similarly to stressors, whether the source of stress was bacterial invasion, perceived danger, a significant life change, inner conflict, or a wound. He labeled this response the general adaptation syndrome (GAS) because (1) it was similar regardless of the specific stressor, (2) it appeared to help the individual to adapt or adjust to the stressor, and (3) various parts of the organism appeared to work together to handle the stressor. The GAS consists of three stages: the alarm reaction, the resistance stage, and the exhaustion stage.

The **alarm reaction** corresponds to Walter Cannon's "fight-or-flight" arousal reaction. The alarm reaction mobilizes the body to respond effectively

Sympathetic ANS (sim-puh-THET-tick). The division of the autonomic nervous system (ANS) that arouses the body in preparation for vigorous physical activity—for example, accelerating the heart rate, raising the blood pressure, and releasing sugar into the blood.

Parasympathetic ANS (PAIR-uh-sim-puh-THET-tick). The division of the autonomic nervous system (ANS) that operates to slow down bodily processes so that the body's resources can be restored and regenerated—for instance, slowing down the heart rate, lowering the blood pressure, and diverting blood away from the muscles. *General adaptation syndrome.* Hans Selye's term for the stages people go through in response to stress.

GAS. Abbreviation for general adaptation syndrome.

Alarm reaction. The first stage of the GAS: a state of arousal, characterized by activity of the sympathetic division of the ANS.

Stress and Defensive Coping

to stress. Once the threat is removed, the body returns to a lower, more optimum level of arousal. Cannon (1929) termed the body's tendency to return to its pre-alarm status **homeostasis.** It is like a thermostat that turns on the furnace when the temperature is too low and the air conditioning when it is too hot. We all seem to have optimum levels of arousal—neither too high nor too low. We seek to reduce overarousal and to increase deficient levels of arousal: we turn down the radio when it blares and we go to an adventure film or a disco when we are bored.

What if the body is mobilized but the stress is *not* removed? Our bodies may not return to their pre-alarm states. Instead they may enter the **resistance** or adaptation **stage** of the GAS. The level of arousal will not be quite as high as during the alarm reaction, but it is still higher than normal. Thus activated, the body attempts to restore lost energy and to repair whatever damage has been done. Unfortunately, uncomfortably high, prolonged levels of arousal may be disorganizing. We may lose the ability to concentrate and make logical choices.

If the source of stress is still not adequately resisted, we may enter the third stage of the GAS—the **exhaustion stage.** Richter's rats were marathon swimmers, keeping their noses dry for eighty hours, but then they became exhausted. Our individual ability to resist stress varies, but we all eventually deplete our bodily resources if stress is prolonged, and our resistance weakens and then comes to a halt. Continued stress at this time may lead to deterioration, to what Selye called **diseases of adaptation** (from allergies and hives to ulcers and heart disease), and, ultimately, to death.

Sudden Death

You live on a West Indian island. Your family is considered Christian, but everyone knows that dark forces and spirits rule people's lives to a larger degree than the church will admit. In fact, certain people have strange powers and know magical formulas that can bring bad fortune, even death, to their enemies. These people must not be crossed. Then you learn that you have unintentionally insulted one of these magicians and that a curse has been placed on you. No matter what you do you will be doomed. The church cannot help. You watch your hand begin to shake and feel your heart begin to pound. You know it is happening. You sweat, you gasp for air. Your mouth is dry, your throat is tight. You cry for mercy but know that nothing will help. Your shoulders tighten and your last memory is of shooting pains to the head. Such is the power of voodoo.

No less a scientist than Walter Cannon (1957) became fascinated by voodoo magic. He pored over records of apparently healthy individuals who had died within hours or a few days of learning that "voodoo curses" had been placed upon them. No, Cannon did not believe in magic. But these cases of voodoo death reinforced his strong belief in our ability to prolong overarousal when we perceive a threat—even if the threat is only imagined—and in how overarousal can devastatingly diminish our ability to resist stress.

Sudden death is not limited to primitive cultures. Rahe and Lind (1971) interviewed the families of thirty-nine men who had died suddenly from heart disease. Victims with and without histories of heart problems had experienced significant increases in life-change unit scores during the six months preceding death.

Chronic Stress

Not only has stress literally scared people to death. Dr. Herbert Benson (1975) of Harvard Medical School has shown that chronic stress is related to high blood pressure or **hypertension,** and hypertension can lead to arteriosclerosis, strokes, and kidney malfunctions. Experiments carried out in the 1950s showed that stress can lead to **ulcers.**

Psychologist William Sawrey of California State University and his colleagues (Sawrey et al. 1956; Sawrey & Weisz 1956) also turned to the unfortunate laboratory rat in order to study stress. Unlike Curt Richter, they kept their animals on dry land, but they placed them in a severe approach-avoidance conflict. They deprived the animals of food and water, and then placed them in a cage where food and water were supplied. But to the rats' frustration, they received painful electric shock each time they approached these supplies. Eventually they developed ulcers. Starvation and thirst alone do not produce ulcers in rats. Control rats, equally deprived of food and water but not exposed to the electric shock, did not develop ulcers.

Hans Selye (1976) shows how chronic stress may play a significant role in inflammatory diseases, such as arthritis; allergies; premenstrual syndrome; digestive diseases, such as colitis; and metabolic diseases, such as diabetes and hypoglycemia. Selye also cautiously discusses a possible link between stress and cancer. He feels that current observations concerning this relationship warrant further research, but, for the time being, no conclusions.

Why, under stress, do some of us develop ulcers, others develop hypertension, and still others develop no bodily problems that we detect at all? It may be that there is an interaction between stressful experiences and predisposing factors, such as biological or learned differences.

For example, those who develop ulcers under stress appear to have higher **pepsinogen** levels than those who do not (Weiner et al. 1957). Pepsinogen is a substance that helps the body to digest proteins. Infants with high pepsinogen levels tend to come from families with high pepsinogen levels (Mirsky 1958), and Weiner et al. (1957) found that nine cases of ulcers developed among sixty-three army draftees with high pepsinogen levels during basic training, but that no cases of ulcers developed among fifty-seven draftees with low pepsinogen levels during the same period. Levels of blood pressure tend to be higher among blacks than among whites, and among blacks and whites who tend to hold in feelings of anger rather than express them (Harburg et al. 1973). **Asthma** is a disease characterized by narrowing of the airways and consequent difficulty in breathing. It has been estimated that some 37 percent of cases of asthma are predominantly related to psychological causes—that is, stress (Rees 1964). But 86 percent of the asthmatic patients studied by Rees had a history of respiratory infection, strongly suggestive of an interaction between the psychological and the physiological.

A Pain in the Neck: A Note on Headaches. Despite TV commercial cartoons, headaches are probably not the result of little hammers pounding away inside the skull. Most headaches, according to Barbara Brown (1977) of the UCLA Medical School, result from muscle tension. During the first two stages of the GAS, the alarm reaction and the resistance stage, we are likely to contract the muscles in the shoulders, neck, forehead, and scalp. Chronic stress can be associated with chronic muscle tension. Other headaches tend to be vascular in nature, stemming from changes in the supply of blood to the head.

Some jobs expose people to chronic stress. Police officers are particularly vulnerable.

Hypertension (high-purr-TEN-shun). High blood pressure.

Ulcer (ULL-sir). An open sore in the lining of the stomach.

Pepsinogen (pep-SIN-oh-jen). A substance that helps the body digest proteins, and which is thought to play a role in the development of ulcers.

Asthma (AS-mah). A respiratory illness characterized by narrowing of the airways.

Stress and Defensive Coping

Some vascular headaches occur for unknown reasons, but others can result from specific drugs, pollen, certain food chemicals, or changes in barometric pressure.

Brown notes that regardless of the original source of the headache—stress, injury, or chemical agents—we can unwittingly propel ourselves into vicious cycles. Headache pain acts as a stressor that can lead to muscle tension, thereby increasing headache pain. In Chapter 7 you will learn how to break such cycles. You will see that some people have learned to change the blood supply to their heads more directly.

DEFENSIVE COPING: ENCOUNTERS OF THE DEFENSIVE KIND

Pain, anxiety, frustration, conflict, pressure, tension—it is not surprising that a major part of the business of being human involves development of ways to adjust to these and other sources of stress. While we may seek out a "healthy tension" in our lives, enough stimulation to keep us interested, too much tension, too much stress triggers off our alarm reactions.

What will you do once the alarm has been set off? Will you ignore it? Will you scurry around like mad? Will you insist that you take a moment out to stop and think before you act? What will you do?

◢ A Hot Day in July

HEAT AND AGGRESSION

Is keeping your cool more difficult when the midsummer sun begins to bake the sidewalks? As campus and city riots broke out with greater constancy during the broiling summers of the 1960s, politicians, police, and news commentators alike began to anticipate the hot weather with a mixture of excitement and dread, wondering if each year was going to bring another "long, hot summer." The United States Riot Commission (1968) reported that all but one of the riots of 1967, for which they had records, began on a day with temperatures at least in the eighties.

Psychologist Robert Baron of Purdue University and his colleagues (Baron & Lawton 1972; Bell & Baron 1976) undertook a series of experiments to try to determine whether this relationship between heat and aggression was coincidental or actually meant that uncomfortably high temperatures played some causal role in the instigation of aggression. Lest you should feel that researchers are single-mindedly dedicated to the exposure of laboratory animals to stress, these experiments involved people. But there can be problems in running experiments with people. For instance, if you tell a recruit that you are going to raise the temperature and see whether he or she be-

comes violent, the recruit may give you violence simply because it is expected. Thus human subjects are often deceived about the true nature of psychological experiments.

In one experiment, Baron and Bell (1976) asked subjects to participate in a study that involved doing jigsaw puzzles and rating other subjects on personality tests. Some subjects were placed in a room in which they never thought about the temperature—it was in the comfortable low seventies. Another group of subjects was moderately uncomfortable, in a room in the eighties. A third group sweltered in a room in the nineties. Actually some of the subjects in each group were "plants" or confederates of the experimenter; unknown to the "real" experimental subjects, they were working in league with the experimenter. The confederates rated the subjects on several personality traits following the puzzle task. Some subjects were rated as pleasant, modest, and friendly. Others were rated as nasty, conceited, and hostile regardless of their actual behavior. The sole purpose of the rating was to provoke the subject to aggression.

Then the experimenter led the subject and the confederate into another room, ostensibly to study

Throughout the remainder of this chapter, we explore a number of responses to stress that are basically defensive: they serve to reduce the immediate impact of a stressor. They may allow escape or temporary avoidance, but often at the cost of behaving in a socially inappropriate manner (like fighting or running away or "acting like a child"), or of distorting reality (as in the case of rationalization). There are many encounters of the defensive kind. *Aggression* and *withdrawal* are two primitive ways of encountering stressors that appear to be consistent with the mobilizing functions of the "fight-or-flight" or alarm reaction—but not necessarily consistent with the values of intellectually and emotionally developed human beings. They have survival value in a state of nature, but possibly not in a state between Maine and Hawaii. *Fantasy* and *regression* allow us to retreat from stressful situations by using behavior patterns from earlier periods in our own development. *Repression*, *rationalization*, *projection*, *reaction formation*, and *sublimation* protect us from the stress of frustration, guilt, and shame by permitting us to hide or disguise our own motives and failures so that we cannot perceive them.

Aggression.   Some animals are born knowing when it is time to fight. Illinois psychologist Nathan Azrin and his coworkers (1965) planned an experiment to train rats to act more sociably toward one another. But do not think for one moment that here at last we have an experiment in which it sounds as if our

the effects of temperature and humidity on physiological reactions to electric shock. (No, psychologists do not use electric shock in every experiment, although sometimes it seems that way.) The confederate was hooked up to the ominous-looking machinery, and the subject was asked to deliver shocks by pressing any of a set of buttons. The subjects believed they could control the intensity and duration of the shocks, although the confederate actually received no shock at all.

Finally, some subjects were allowed to have a cooling drink prior to delivering the shocks. Others were not. So there you have it. Some subjects were comfortable, some warm, some hot. Some were angered by the confederate's provocation, others were not. Some were refreshed by a cooling drink, others were not. Which subjects were most aggressive, as measured by intensity and duration of the (supposed) shock?

Let us look at subjects in the cool room first. Here, as you have probably guessed, the provoked subjects were more aggressive than those who had been rated favorably (complimented) by the confederates. In the hot conditions it actually turned out that the complimented subjects were *more* aggressive than the provoked subjects. Why? First of all, in-

creasing the temperature to uncomfortable levels apparently *does* foster aggression, since nonprovoked subjects were more aggressive when the heat was on. But the combination of heat *and* provocation was apparently *too much stress* for most subjects to bear at one time. Since they could do nothing about the stressful hot temperatures, they "cooled down" the level of stress by cooling down their own anger. The cool drinks? Provoked subjects in the hot rooms were refreshed to the point where they could maintain their anger: they were more aggressive than provoked subjects in hot rooms who went without refreshment.

Up to a point, then, heat, as other forms of discomfort, provokes aggression. But the experiencing of anger is apparently also aversive, and when the temperature goes too high one may be motivated to defend by letting go of the negative emotion. Thus we would expect that the heat could conceivably be *too* high for a riot. Sure enough, the United States Riot Commission (1968) found that while the temperatures preceding riots were high for the cities in which they occurred, they rarely exceeded 100° F. Violence appears to peak in the eighties, and to fall off above or below that critical level (Baron & Ransberger 1979). When the heat is on, people cool it by themselves.

whiskered friends may escape without pain. Two rats were placed in a box and given electric shock through a floor grid. The experimenters intended to shut off the shock when the rats moved close to one another, thus rewarding them for togetherness. They didn't get the chance. When the electricity was turned on, the rats attempted to escape. When they could not, they attacked one another. There was little chance for Azrin to promote good will. More frequent or intense shocks led to more intense **aggression**.

Aggression (uh-GRESH-shun). Physical or verbal attack.

When you think about it, quick and violent responses are useful for the survival of rats and other animals. In nature a good bite has its shock value, and rats that bite back quickly are more likely to have children than rats who do not. With human beings, violence can also remove threats and, sometimes, other sources of stress. But much of the time the relief experienced is short-lived: punching a professor who gives you a low grade or a policeman who gives you a traffic ticket is likely to create new interpersonal conflicts rather than resolve them. Aggressive behavior may be offensive to others, but most of the time it is an inferior method for handling stress, with only temporary benefits.

Displaced Aggression. You could think of Azrin's rats as picking on the wrong guy. True, they had been exposed to a shocking set of circumstances; but the rat sharing the cage just happened to be in the wrong place at the right time. Dr. Azrin, after all, was responsible for the shock. The rats picked on a victim that was available. This is **displaced aggression**.

Displaced aggression. Aggression that has been provoked by one source but which is directed against an innocent party. Displacement is a defense mechanism.

Through displacement, a stressful impulse like aggression can be partially relieved through changing the object of the impulse to a safer or more available target.

Withdrawal. When you are intensely frightened or feel helpless or believe that any choice you make will be futile, you may feel pressed to withdraw from the situation. During the 1960s and early 1970s many thousands of young people were drawn to communal life-styles or other alternatives as part of the protest movement against middle-class standards—standards that some then saw as narrow, aggressive, and detrimental to the underprivileged. For some, "dropping out" was the logical result of a personal value system, consistent

◗ Dropping Out

WHEN "LIFE IS TOO MUCH LIKE A PATHLESS WOOD"

Poets, too, at times can feel like withdrawing or dropping out. The following lines are from Robert Frost's "Birches":

> It's when I'm weary of considerations,
> And life is too much like a pathless wood
> Where your face burns and tickles with the cobwebs
> Broken across it, and one eye is weeping
> From a twig's having lashed across it open.
> I'd like to get away from earth awhile
> And then come back to it and begin over.

with self-identity. But many others who were highly stressed by the work ethic and the need for personal achievement seized upon this movement as an excuse to drop out, or **withdraw.** Dropping out is ordinarily equated with quitting and is condemned by society. But if you can join a subculture that views dropping out as a positive value when you quit society, you are less likely to experience strong conflict about leaving the mainstream.

Temporary withdrawal can be healthy and productive. If you take a moment to stop and think when you are stressed, you will often derive a more effective method of coping. But continued withdrawal can lead to psychological problems, particularly if a personal world of fantasy begins to replace what the rest of us label as reality. Psychologists Leonard Ullmann and Leonard Krasner (1975) point out that schizophrenic withdrawal and complaint of hallucinating are more likely to occur when efforts to meet one's needs have gone unrewarded.

Fantasy. In the film *The Captain's Paradise*, Alec Guinness portrayed a ship's captain who commuted endlessly back and forth between Gibraltar and North Africa. On Gibraltar, he had a prim and proper English wife who maintained a prim and proper home. In North Africa he was wedded to a sultry siren who was filled with life and gaiety, but who had immense difficulty boiling water. Complications set in, as they always do in comedies, and eventually the captain's real-life fantasy world came apart. But the appeal of the film lay in its portrayal of a common fantasy—in this case, the common desire of men to be both mothered and seduced by the women in their lives.

Fantasy serves many functions in our lives. We may daydream of the many paths we can take in our lives, attempting to focus in on the roads that will be right for us. We can fantasize to escape boredom and deprivation. Fantasy is probably healthy unless it becomes a substitute for effective action. And fantasy is often employed in the therapies of today to help people become more effective in handling stress and personal problems.

Regression. You may have been attempting to explain a fine point in quantum mechanics to your roommate for two hours. Then your roommate asks a question that proves that nothing you have said has been assimilated. You slam your book on the desk, shout "You jerk!" and bang the door on the way out. Then, perhaps, you burst into tears. If you are six years old, this is normal. If you are in college, this is **regression**—returning to an earlier, in this case childish, way of coping under stress. Ah, the disadvantages of maturity.

There are few cases more distressing to a therapist than those of young women in their late teens or early twenties who have developed an overwhelming fear of putting on weight and who consequently seem all bones and hair. A five-foot-five woman so afflicted may weigh sixty-seven pounds. The condition is called **anorexia nervosa**—an abhorrence of eating due to emotional rather than physiological causes. Anorexia usually afflicts teenaged women. While their parents worry and experience enormous guilt, they often devote their energies to arts and crafts in the home—sometimes, ironically, perfecting the art of cooking. Many psychologists feel that anorexia stems from the attempt to avoid sexual and social maturity. By remaining precariously thin, young women can maintain the appearance of little girls. Another example of regression?

You may know people who have quit smoking or stopped biting their nails who return to these habits before an important exam or after a fight with a

Withdrawal. Physical or psychological removal from stress.

Fantasy (FAN-tuh-see). Creation of mental imagery.
Regression (ree-GRESH-shun). Return to a form of behavior characteristic of an earlier stage of development.
Anorexia nervosa (an-or-EGGS-ee-uh nurr-VO-suh). An adjustment problem characterized by a severe aversion to eating.

Sometimes stress can lead us to regress, or to adopt behavior characteristic of younger people or children. Under severe stress, this woman is crawling up into a ball, putting her hand to her mouth, and clutching her stuffed animal.

steady date. These resumptions, also, may be considered regression. A psychoanalyst, in fact, might label the habits themselves regression all the way back to the oral stage of psychosexual development.

Repression. **Repression** is motivated forgetting. We can automatically or unconsciously put things out of our minds in order to protect ourselves from anxiety. Repression of unacceptable sexual and aggressive impulses protects us from neurotic and moral anxiety. Freud theorized that repression is a normal and necessary part of personality development, allowing us to place certain conflicts behind us so that we can function more efficiently in the present. But if we repress the facts that a dreaded paper is due in less than two weeks and that we must begin to make decisions about graduate school or careers, we may find ourselves unprepared to meet the challenges of life.

Repression can also lead us to look at the past through "rose-colored glasses." We recall many pleasant events, but tend to repress the painful events. This is nostalgia—why the old days are often felt to have been so much better.

Suppression. **Suppression** is the conscious, purposeful placing of stressful events out of our minds. Suppression can permit us to function in spite of conflict and fear.

Albert Camus was a French existentialist who wrote that our lives are hopeless because they eventually end, without exception, in death. He was obsessed with this fact. A critic of Camus wrote that it is true that we shall all die; but, he added, only Camus thought about this twenty-four hours a day. The rest of us, the critic implied, are able to do a better job of suppressing this eventuality.

Suppression permits us to minimize the stress that ensues from conflicting values. Many young adults have acquired certain sexual, religious, and philosophical values in the home. Yet social pressures at college and the need to separate from parental values often act in concert to prompt behavior that would have been condemned at home. Suppression of the conflict between old values and behavior now often permits us to get on with the daily business of living. When suppression fails, or when we are anxious about conflicting values, it is wise to talk out conflicts with patient friends, empathic relatives, or helping professionals.

Rationalization. Juvenile delinquents may claim that a mugging was justified because the victim was well dressed and could afford the loss. Violence was necessary because the victim had it coming to him. Prostitutes often point out that they would not be in business if there were no demand for their services. When John Dean participated in the Watergate cover-up, he told himself that his actions were justified because he was protecting the presidency of the United States. When students do poorly on a test, they have been heard to say "It was a dumb test, anyway," or "It was the professor's fault for _____."

Rationalizations are ways of explaining away unacceptable behavior, including immoral behavior and failures. By so doing, we escape self-condemnation. Or we rationalize to cut our losses: "So what if I flunked political science? It wasn't a graduation requirement anyhow." "So the date didn't work out. We're too different to develop a relationship anyhow." "I suppose it's a good thing the cake came out so awful. I couldn't afford the calories anyway."

There is often a kernel of truth in rationalizations. In fact, there may be a

ON MAKING CHOICES, REGRETS, AND NOSTALGIA

Nostalgia, regrets, lost opportunities—every time we choose to do something, we choose not to do all the other things we could have done. When things go wrong, or when we become bored, it is natural to look back and wonder what would have happened if we had taken another path.

Robert Frost looks back upon an approach-approach conflict that occurred at a meaningful time in his life and, in "The Road Not Taken," expresses regret that he had not been able to do two things at once:

Two roads diverged in a yellow wood,
And sorry I could not travel both
And be one traveler, long I stood
And looked down one as far as I could
To where it bent in the undergrowth;

Then took the other, as just as fair,
And having perhaps the better claim,
Because it was grassy and wanted wear;
Though as for that the passing there
Had worn them really about the same,

And both that morning equally lay
In leaves no step had trodden black.
Oh, I kept the first for another day!
Yet knowing how way leads on to way,
I doubted if I should ever come back.

I shall be telling this with a sigh
Somewhere ages and ages hence:
Two roads diverged in a wood, and I—
I took the one less traveled by,
And that has made all the difference.

Why does Frost say that one path had "the better claim" on him? Is the reason he gives accurate, or does he contradict himself later on in the poem? In the last stanza, Frost seems to be laughing at himself as he recognizes that he will probably misrepresent the reasons he made his choice when he tells others about it in the future. How does he plan to *rationalize* his decision? Frost writes that he told himself he would try the other path on another day. Does he really believe he will have this opportunity? Why or why not?

thin line between rationalizing and rational thinking. Perhaps it is for the best when dates do not work out. Perhaps it is better not to have eaten the cake. Purposeful focusing on the positive side of unfortunate events or undesirable behavior may be preferable to blowing it out of proportion. One of the aims of psychotherapy is to help people learn to attach *appropriate* regrets to mistakes and shortcomings—neither to deny losses or guilt nor to exaggerate them.

Projection. A motion picture projector thrusts an image outward onto a screen. A person who never saw a projector before could possibly have the idea that the image comes from the screen itself.

Projection. **Thrusting of one's own unacceptable impulses out onto others so that the impulses appear to be originating within others.**

Stress and Defensive Coping

Sometimes we deal with our own unacceptable impulses by **projecting** them outward onto other people. That way we do not have to recognize them as a part of ourselves, but we fool ourselves when we attribute the impulses to others. A person who is filled with anger may perceive the world as a hostile place in which to be. A sexually frustrated person who feels that sex is evil may continually interpret the innocent gestures of others as sexual advances.

Reaction Formation. Have you ever had the feeling that someone who was sickly sweet and overly polite might actually be sitting on a hotbed of hostility? Perhaps so. Has anyone ever denied feelings so strongly that you suspected they were actually there? In Shakespeare's *Hamlet*, the prince devises a play within the play to reenact the murder of his father so that the guilty parties, in the audience, will appear uncomfortable and give themselves away. A player acting the part of a queen within the play claims that she could never, come what may, even consider remarrying, now that the king is dead. Hamlet's mother, the actual queen of Denmark, remarks that "the lady," in the play within the play, "doth protest too much." By so strongly denying interest in anyone else, she appears to be vulnerable to such advances.

Reaction formation. Behavior that is in direct opposition to an unacceptable impulse.

One way of dealing with an unacceptable impulse is through **reaction formation**—taking an exaggerated position in opposition to one's own feelings. It is possible that some people who go on holy crusades against erotic films have some sexual impulses of their own that they are trying to keep under control. Or it could be that some people who appear to have an infinite capacity for accepting abuse from an aging, insensitive relative may show unending concern for that relative in order to keep aggressive urges repressed.

Sublimation. Why do people build cities, create works of art, and dedicate themselves to poetry and literature? Are their motives noble, or do these activities reflect less artistic motives?

As we saw in Chapter 4, psychoanalytic theory suggests that all these human undertakings—all this majesty and grandeur—represent our efforts to cope defensively with basic aggressive and sexual impulses through channeling them into constructive works. This is **sublimation**.

Sublimation (sub-blee-MAY-shun). The channeling of primitive impulses into the positive, constructive efforts involved in bettering the self or building civilization.

This is a rather dim view of human nature, of course. It takes the nobility out of being noble. Some psychoanalysts disagree with Freud and believe that we can become engrossed with these activities for their own sake. These are the ego analysts, who believe that some human motives are fully conscious and come from the ego—the sense of self. This view is also humanistic.

Compensation. Self-esteem often rests on competence. We may strive to avoid the stress of damaged self-esteem by excelling in one area to compensate for weakness in another. The poor student becomes an athlete. The plain youth becomes a scholar. Adolescents who fail at all school-related activities may feel tempted to gain recognition by excelling within a delinquent subculture.

Defensive Reactions to Career Conflict

What is likely to happen if you are presented with a challenge that leads to the need to change your career? According to Yale University psychologist Irving Janis and Dan Wheeler (1978), the chance for financial gain, the threat that your company may be going under, the departure of a trusted supervisor, and similar pieces of challenging information place you in stressful career conflict. Personally effective individuals use such information to undertake systematic decision making, as we shall see in Chapter 7. Less effective people show a variety of defensive styles in attempting to minimize the impact of challenges.

Complacency. People who are **complacent** ignore challenges, acting as if threats won't really affect *them*. Complacent individuals typically drift along and may accept new positions if they become available without seeking adequate information about the future of the position.

Defensive Avoidance. Some people are fully aware of the threats or opportunities that face them, but they employ defensive thought patterns that deny the magnitude of the challenges. They provide themselves with excuses for not taking decisive action.

Janis and Wheeler note that avoiders use rationalization, **procrastination,** and **buck passing.** Rationalizations often include protestations of helplessness: "Why should I get upset? There's nothing I can do about it." Procrastinators put things off for the future: "Why get bent out of shape now? I'll take care of it when I have to." Buck passers deny personal responsibility: "It's not my fault. Let the bosses take care of it."

Hypervigilance. People who have put off career decisions until they reach the day of reckoning and people who must make an immediate decision may show **hypervigilance**—a highly aroused, near-panic state in which they scurry about frantically seeking ways out of their dilemmas. Hypervigilance makes logical thought difficult, and many people take any way out—make rapid and careless decisions—simply to avert the stress produced by the challenge.

Some of us lead predominantly defensive life-styles. We try to muddle through each day, avoiding as much stress as we can. Sometimes, as a result, our behavior is socially inappropriate. At other times we narrow our perceptions of the world so that we need not look reality in the face.

Of course, our defenses can be very valuable. It is possible that we cannot deal with all the sources of stress that impinge upon us at once. If we need to prepare a homework assignment, it is useful to be able to suppress a conflict with a parent or a friend. But if our defenses continually lead us to avoid stresses we ought to be facing—such as the need to be examined by a doctor for some nagging complaint or the need to make hard decisions about a love relationship or a career—then we need more effective and active strategies for meeting stress. These strategies are the subject matter of Chapter 7.

Complacency (come-PLAY-sent-see). Contentment, self-satisfaction.

Procrastination (pro-krass-tin-NAY-shun). Putting things off, delaying.
Buck passing. Avoiding personal responsibility by arranging for others to handle chores you should have taken care of by yourself.

Hypervigilance (high-purr-VIDGE-ul-ents). A highly aroused state of alertness that is marked by inefficient, hectic efforts to adjust.

Summary

- *Too much of a good thing can make you ill.* Possibly. It appears that too many significant changes, even positive changes, within a short period of time can lead to stress-related problems.
- *Psychiatrists have undertaken research programs to measure how many psychological straws it takes to break a person's back.* True. Thomas Holmes and Richard Rahe constructed a life-change units scale. They anchored the life change of marriage at 50 units, and then

asked people from differing walks of life to assign numbers of units to events ranging from death of a spouse (100 units) to divorce (73 units) and trouble with the boss (23 units). Earning 300 units in one year appears to place one in serious risk of contracting illness.

- *Having an outstanding personal achievement and going on a long-anticipated vacation are stressful events.* True. Achievements and life changes require that adjustments be made and are consequently stressful. Not all stress is bad. In fact, without stress there is no life.

- *The average laboratory rat can swim for about eighty hours, but rats given a close shave may sink after floundering about in the water for only a couple of minutes.* True. One stress compounded by another dramatically decreases coping ability, whether you have whiskers, a beard, or a smooth chin. Pain, conflict, frustration are all sources of stress. Avoidance-avoidance conflicts (like drowning vs. prolonged, fatiguing swimming) are especially stressful.

- *A population explosion turns some mice into marauding rapists and others into social dropouts.* True. Crowding—extremely high population density—appears to collapse social structures, promoting social deviance and sexual abnormalities. Among humans, women appear to have more tolerance of crowding than men.

- *People who never do anything wrong are often the most guilt-ridden.* It seems so. In any event, psychopaths, who continually offend others, are known for their lack of anxiety or guilt. Anxiety is a source of stress, and Freud described three major types of anxiety: reality anxiety, or objective fear; neurotic anxiety, or near breakthrough of unacceptable impulses into consciousness; and moral anxiety, or guilt and shame for felt wrongdoing.

- *It is possible for people to be literally scared to death.* Cannon's study of "voodoo death" suggests that people who believe that a lethal curse has been placed on them can experience such high arousal that they eventually become exhausted and die. This is consistent with Selye's general adaptation syndrome (GAS) to stress: First you experience an alarm reaction, mobilizing the body to fight off an invader or other source of stress. Then you enter the resistance or adaptation stage, in which your level of arousal is somewhat lower but still above normal as you marshal bodily resources in defense. Finally, resources depleted, you enter the exhaustion stage, in which bodily processes are slowed down, providing the opportunity to recover. But if the stressor has not been eliminated or ameliorated, exhaustion can lead to severe illness or death. In voodoo death, the stressor—an imagined lethal curse—remains constant.

- *Modern science has taught us how to produce ulcers in laboratory rats.* Yes. If we deprive them of food and water, then offer them sustenance—but pair it with strong electric shock—they will develop ulcers. People with high pepsinogen levels who are placed under prolonged stress also tend to develop ulcers. With people, psychological stress and predisposing factors appear to combine to produce illnesses such as ulcers, hypertension, and asthma.

- *Giving an angry person a refreshing drink on a broiling hot summer day will decrease the probability of violence.* Actually not. Increasing the heat promotes aggression (at least up to the point where you can barely move, above 90° F), and instigating anger promotes aggression. But the

Because rhesus monkeys such as these have been exposed to pain and discomfort in laboratory experiments, India will no longer export them to the United States. The values of seeking new knowledge which may help people cope better with stress and of avoiding mistreatment of animals are often in conflict in the laboratory, creating moral dilemmas.

two in combination can be so punishing that hot and angry people may decide just to let the anger slide. But give them a cooling drink and you may refresh them to the point where they do become violent!

- *You can't run a psychological experiment without shocking or drowning rats or without deceiving people.* Granted, it sometimes looks that way, but this has been a chapter on the effects of stress and defensive coping with stress. In order to study reactions to stress, you need to create stress in the laboratory as an independent variable. It is true that subjects are often deceived in experiments. This is because if they knew what you were looking for, it might influence their behavior.

However, the types of studies reported in this chapter have given rise to ethical discussions of the price we should be willing to pay to gain new knowledge. In the 1970s and 1980s we have tried to find alternate ways to find knowledge. But often we must expose laboratory animals to stress so that human beings will better learn how to deal with it. In experiments where people are still deceived, we now "debrief" them after the experiment most of the time—explaining the real purpose of the experiment and just why the truth could not be told at the outset.

7

MEETING THE CHALLENGE OF STRESS

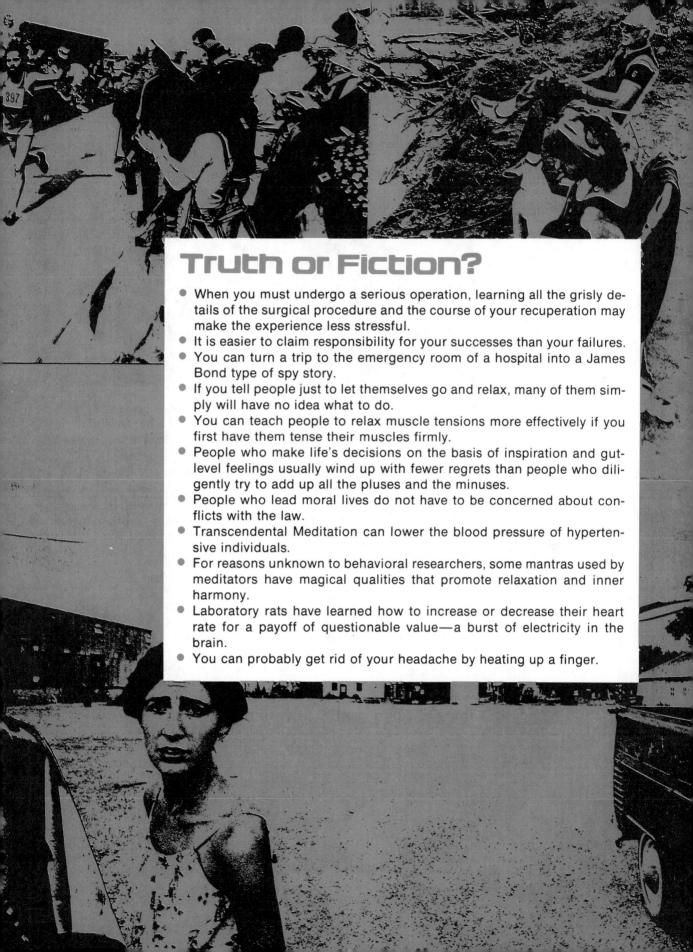

Truth or Fiction?

- When you must undergo a serious operation, learning all the grisly details of the surgical procedure and the course of your recuperation may make the experience less stressful.
- It is easier to claim responsibility for your successes than your failures.
- You can turn a trip to the emergency room of a hospital into a James Bond type of spy story.
- If you tell people just to let themselves go and relax, many of them simply will have no idea what to do.
- You can teach people to relax muscle tensions more effectively if you first have them tense their muscles firmly.
- People who make life's decisions on the basis of inspiration and gut-level feelings usually wind up with fewer regrets than people who diligently try to add up all the pluses and the minuses.
- People who lead moral lives do not have to be concerned about conflicts with the law.
- Transcendental Meditation can lower the blood pressure of hypertensive individuals.
- For reasons unknown to behavioral researchers, some mantras used by meditators have magical qualities that promote relaxation and inner harmony.
- Laboratory rats have learned how to increase or decrease their heart rate for a payoff of questionable value—a burst of electricity in the brain.
- You can probably get rid of your headache by heating up a finger.

Fate, chance, luck, destiny—how many of us allow ourselves to be blown about by the wind, permit our futures to be controlled by the whims and desires of others? How many of us are frustrated, yet, as Thoreau wrote, "live lives of quiet desperation"? At the beginning of Shakespeare's *Julius Caesar*, Cassius and Brutus listen as crowds are heaping honor after honor upon great Caesar. Caesar was made of flesh and blood. In fact, Cassius had once saved him from drowning. So why was it now that Caesar stood upon the "narrow world" like the great bronze statue called the Colossus of Rhodes, while all others were "petty men" who fretted about beneath his legs? Was it fate? Destiny? Where lay the fault? Cassius says to Brutus:

> Men at some time are masters of their fates.
> The fault, dear Brutus, is not in our stars,
> But in ourselves, that we are underlings.

We cannot blame the heavens. We cannot fault astrology. If we are unhappy with our lot in life, it is up to us to take charge and do something about it. It is up to us to take charge of the changes, pains, anxieties, frustrations, conflicts, and Type A behavior that we meet in life. It is up to us to face our desires, measure our limits, and to manage these sources of stress so that we grow from them rather than merely cope defensively with them.

In this chapter we first discuss what it means to take responsibility for our own behavior, for our own successes and failures. Then we explore how we take responsibility for ourselves to help us meet effectively the challenges of pain and discomfort, anxiety, frustration, conflict, and Type A behavior.

ACCEPTING RESPONSIBILITY

We have a museum where we keep rationalizations we have heard people use to avoid accepting personal responsibility for taking charge of their own lives.

Among the warnings against cancer and emphysema in the cigarette smokers' exhibit are: "Why try to quit? I could be hit by a truck tomorrow." In the exhibit of lost weight losers: "I've tried to keep away from fattening foods, but chocolate and potatoes with butter are just stronger than I am." There is an entire floor for people who complain about inflation and rising taxes: "I just haven't gotten around to writing a letter to my congressional representative yet," and "Why bother voting? What does one vote mean?" and "So what can one person do?"

It is not that our museum pieces are entirely wrong. There is an element of chance in life, and there are limits to what we can do. For reasons that we haven't yet learned, but are most unfair, some people smoke two packs of cigarettes a day yet run a six-minute mile at the age of sixty. The drunkard sometimes outlives the teetotaler. The health-food enthusiast and the jogger occasionally die from heart attacks in their forties. The careful worker is passed over for promotion because of favoritism, and the happy-go-lucky fellow down the block may win the lottery. But most of the time life is not so fickle and we exert a significant influence on our lives and our feelings of well-being. Farrah Fawcett and Suzanne Somers did not become superstars by neglecting their appearance and opportunities. Long-distance runners do not build stamina by eating whipped cream sandwiches, watching twelve hours of television a day, and thinking about training at some time in the future. We better our chances to reach distant goals by testing our personal limits and creating plans that enable us to grow.

Internalizers and Externalizers

University of Connecticut psychologist Julian Rotter (1966) describes people who believe they can exert a significant influence over the challenges of life as **internalizers**—they see control over their lives as internal to themselves. Those who see fate as outside their hands are **externalizers**. It should not be too surprising that internalizers are more effective than externalizers in meeting challenge (Rotter 1975).

You may have noticed that human beings are not always consistent in their behavior. Sometimes it is easier to be an internalizer—to accept the responsibility for your own behavior—than others. If you carry the ball seventy yards for a touchdown, it was your clear thinking, monumental strength, and catlike agility that did the deed. If you fumble a punt and the opposition recovers the ball, it was bad luck. When your side wins, it reflects talent and execution. When your side loses, it reflects your team's goofing—not the opponent's supremacy. People tend to credit themselves for their successes and blame luck for their shortcomings (Fitch 1970).

Yet internalizers face reality better than externalizers when they need to. You have probably known someone who was going to have an operation or take an important test. You tried to talk about it. Maybe the response was: "Ooh, yuck! Let's drop the subject! I don't even want to think about it!" Yet when stress is unavoidable, people who have a fuller understanding of what is about to take place, as during a surgical procedure, often appear less anxious than people who do not acquire understanding of the situation (Staub et al. 1971; Shipley et al. 1978). Internalizers tend to seek information even about painful events. Accurate information probably permits internalizers to brace themselves more effectively for the inevitable—also to realize that the stress will not be endless.

Internalizer (in-TURN-uh-lie-zer). In Julian Rotter's view, an individual taking responsibility for attaining reinforcement.
Externalizer (eggs-TURN-uh-lie-zer). In Julian Rotter's view, an individual leaving the responsibility for granting reinforcement to others.

The dilemma: to try to withdraw from conflicts and other sources of stress, to try to deny that they exist? Or to face your conflicts and to grow from them?

ARE YOU AN INTERNALIZER OR AN EXTERNALIZER?

Do you believe that you are in charge of your own life? That you can exert a significant influence on other people and the environment in order to reach your goals? Or do you believe that your fate is in the "stars"? That you are ruled by luck, chance, and other people? Or are you somewhere in between, sometimes internalizing, sometimes externalizing?

Learn more about yourself by answering the following questionnaire, which was constructed by Julian Rotter (1971). Carefully read each pair of statements. For each pair, place a checkmark before the statement that seems more accurate to you.

I more strongly believe that:

or

1. _____ Promotions are earned through hard work and persistence.

_____ Making a lot of money is largely a matter of getting the right breaks.

2. _____ In my experience I have noticed that there is usually a direct connection between how hard I study and the grades I get.

_____ Many times the reactions of teachers seem haphazard to me.

3. _____ The number of divorces indicates that more and more people are not trying to make marriage work.

_____ Marriage is largely a gamble.

4. _____ When I am right, I can convince others.

_____ It is silly to think that one can really change another person's basic attitudes.

5. _____ In our society a man's future earning power is dependent upon his ability.

_____ Getting promoted is really a matter of being a little luckier than the next guy.

6. _____ If one knows how to deal with people, they are really quite easily led.

_____ I have little influence over the way other people behave.

7. _____ In my case the grades I make are the results of my own efforts; luck has little or nothing to do with it.

_____ Sometimes I feel that I have little to do with the grades I get.

8. _____ People like me can change the course of world affairs if we make ourselves heard.

_____ It is only wishful thinking to believe that one can really influence what happens in society at large.

9. _____ I am the master of my fate.

_____ A great deal that happens to me is probably a matter of chance.

10. _____ Getting along with people is a skill that must be practiced.

_____ It is almost impossible to figure out how to please some people.

Source: Rotter (1971).

How did you do? Simply add up the choices you made on each side. Choices on the left side indicate a belief in internal control. Choices on the right side indicate a belief in external control. Did you get 10 points toward internalizing, 10 points toward externalizing, or were you somewhere in between? How did your score compare with your classmates' scores?

Even if you have been an "Ooh, yucker" all your life, you can decide to become an internalizer *now*. In the long run, internalizers may be exposed to less stress than externalizers because their desire for information will permit them to solve problems and make decisions more effectively—even the painful decisions.

MEETING THE CHALLENGE OF CHANGE

Variety is the spice of life, but too much spice can sour the stomach. When we actualize ourselves and grow, we make changes, but at our own pace. Too many changes can overload our adaptive abilities.

It is a terrifying truth known to mental-health workers that elderly people who are placed in nursing homes, or who are moved from home to home, often die within a year. This is not necessarily because they are mistreated or because the staff is unconcerned about them. Nor is it merely the influence of age—persons of similar age who remain with their families fare better. Moving to a new home is the visible change, but there are also many hidden changes: loss of family members, change in number of arguments with relatives, revision of personal habits, changes in recreation and social activities, and on and on. Too much too soon. If you take a look at Table 6.1, you will see that this change in residence (20 life-change units) may actually entail hundreds of *hidden* life-change units.

Become aware of the compounding effect of too many changes in your own life. Do not attempt to quit smoking and lose weight at the same time. If there is a dramatic increase in your income, do not feel an obligation to move immediately and take on a larger mortgage. If you suffer a tragic personal loss, it may be foolhardy to think that moving to a new city and taking on a new job will help you escape from your adjustment problems.

If you are uncertain of the degree of change in your life, keep a daily log of your activities, hour by hour, for a week. At the end of this time, reflect: how many activities, people, and places differ from those of a few months ago? Are there significant changes from day to day in your sleeping or eating habits, in your exercise routine? Are you a weekend runner or tennis player—leading a sedentary life for five days and then trying to "make up" for your unhealthful ways in two? Variety may be the spice of life, but weekend athletes experience significant changes in their recreational habits twice a week up to fifty-two times a year. How about your social life? Forcing yourself out of bed at six-thirty every morning during the week and trying to stay up till three in the morning Fridays and Saturdays will give you chronic "jet lag."

Look for the hidden changes. Become aware of the changes in your life and you will become motivated to meet the challenge of change more efficiently. You will be less likely to sit around wondering why you feel so tense and fatigued.

MEETING THE CHALLENGES OF PAIN AND DISCOMFORT

Your molar is killing you. It pains you right down to the toes. It is unbelievable that the human body is so constructed that it can provide you with this much pain. You have made an appointment with your dentist, and with your history

To Choose One's Own Way

THE LAST OF THE HUMAN FREEDOMS

Austrian psychiatrist Viktor Frankl survived three years in Auschwitz and other Nazi concentration camps during the Second World War, while nine of ten of his fellows died in the first several hours. Everything familiar was snatched away. Undernourished, scantily clad in winter, men slept back to back on narrow boards, sharing overcrowded huts with typhus and lice. In retrospect Frankl wrote, "We who lived in concentration camps can remember the men who walked through the huts comforting others, giving away their last piece of bread. They may have been few in number, but they offer sufficient proof that everything can be taken from a man but one thing: the last of the human freedoms—to choose one's attitude in any given set of circumstances, to choose one's own way." (1963).

Catastrophizing (kuh-TAST-row-fize-ing). Blowing up unfortunate events or minor problems into major disasters.

of cavities, you wouldn't be surprised if it has to be pulled. Let's take a look at some **catastrophizing** things you could be saying to yourself:

"I can't take this pain anymore. It's going to drive me crazy. My God, I'm shaking all over. I'm sweating like a pig. Dr. Yank is such a damn brute. He comes at you with those hairy arms and those needles. I think he likes to see me squirm. The sound of that drill! My heart's going to leap out of my chest! I know it's going to get worse, and there's nothing I can do about it. Those aspirins didn't help a bit. If I can only get through the next two hours!"

Or you could be taking charge of your tendency to catastrophize and be saying things to yourself like this:

"This pain is bad, but I'll survive. Even though it's hard to imagine, tonight I'll be looking back on this and wondering if the pain was really there. You can't remember pain exactly when you look back on it. I'm not crazy about Dr. Yank, but he seems to know his business. Maybe the aspirins will start to work. Maybe the pain will decrease. At least I know it's time limited; it'll be over in a couple of hours. Breathe slowly and deeply. Maybe I can find something to distract myself. . . ."

There is a circular relationship between a stressor and your reaction to it. If you blow it out of proportion, focusing all your attention on it and on your bodily arousal, you may increase its impact. The Greek philosopher Epictetus wrote, "Our minds are moved not by events, but by our judgments thereupon." When you let your judgments run away with you, you set yourself up for heightened suffering and loss of control over the situation.

Getting Control of Catastrophizing Thoughts

Psychologist Donald Meichenbaum has been most impressed with our uncanny abilities to make bad situations worse. We all know people who look upon stressors like pain and discomfort as opportunities to create catastrophes. Yet they are absolutely certain that it is the stress itself, and not their reaction to it, that is responsible:

- You have difficulty with the first item on a test and become absolutely convinced you will flunk.
- You have a misunderstanding with your new roommate and become absolutely convinced the year will be one long battle.

The Challenges of Stress, Fear, and Depression

182

What this woman is telling herself about her pain and discomfort may well be compounding the stress she experiences. She may not be able to totally eliminate her problems, but she can certainly influence what she tells herself about them.

- You haven't been able to get to sleep for five minutes and become absolutely convinced you will lie awake the whole night and be "wrecked" the following day.

Some of us are fully unaware of the things we say to ourselves to make bad situations worse.

Meichenbaum (1976) suggests a three-step procedure for getting in touch with and taking charge of catastrophizing thoughts: (1) Develop an awareness of your catastrophizing thoughts by careful self-observation. You can imagine yourself to be in a stressful situation and then try to picture the thoughts that usually run through your mind and jot them down. Studying the examples below will give you insight into your own thought patterns. (2) Prepare thoughts and images that are **incompatible** with the catastrophizing thoughts. Practice saying these things to yourself. Repeat them firmly. (3) Credit yourself for effective changes in thought patterns. Note what a marvelous job you have done in making things easier for yourself. Heightened awareness of your successes will make it easier for you to repeat them.

Imagine that you are waiting in a hospital emergency room for the doctor. You have a gash in your leg from a fall, and you will most likely need stitches. The leg hurts a great deal, and the sight of blood and the thought of stitches make you dizzy and nauseous. You find yourself catastrophizing, then catch yourself and begin to think adjustive alternatives or incompatible thoughts:

"Oh God, I can't stand this! I wish I were dead. I'll never get through this. They're going to rip this apart cleaning it. It may be infected. Those doctors don't give a damn about your fears—they just think you're being a child. My heart is in my mouth. This is never going to end. Hey, stop and think! Stop and

Incompatible (in-come-PAT-uh-bull). Impeding the progress or activity of another. Not fitting. Incompatible thoughts interfere with one another.

Meeting the Challenge of Stress

Sample Catastrophizing Thoughts	Sample Adjustive Alternatives (Incompatible Thoughts)
"Oh my God, I'm going to lose all control!"	"This is painful and upsetting, but I don't have to go to pieces."
"This will never end!"	"This *will* come to an end, even if I can't see it right now."
"I can't stand this pain! I simply can't stand it! I'm going to go crazy!"	"I'm tolerating this pain right now. It's really bad, but I'm surviving. It *will* end."
"Everything is over! This is it! Nothing will ever be the same!"	"It's hard to imagine right now, but I may be laughing at how upset I was later on."
"I'm an awful person—this must be punishment for horrible things I've done!"	"It's a bad break, but don't take it personally. These things happen."
"My heart's going to leap out of my chest! How much can I stand?"	"Easy—hearts rarely leap out of chests. Breathe slowly, in and out."
"What can I do? There's just nothing I can do!"	"Stop and think! There may be something I can do. Breathe slowly. Take a second and think."
"It's so awful—I just can't get it out of my head for a second!"	"Hold it! Maybe I can distract myself. Count slowly and breathe in and out. Find something to read: read the words out loud, one after another."

think! This may be bad but you're making it a hell of a lot worse! Hold it. To-night you'll be laughing about how upset you were. Just stop and think. Breathe slowly, in and out. Just think about your breathing. Easy, easy. You *are* going to survive. Take it easy: look around you and describe what you see [distraction]. A big, round clock. 4:36 P.M. Concrete block walls, orange blocks, about six inches by twelve inches, two nurses at the desk—hmm, plenty to de-scribe there. . . ."

Pain and discomfort may be severe, but that does not mean that you are failing to live up to your personal standards for integrity when you refuse to focus all your attention on the pain and discomfort. You can defend yourself through distraction and fantasy.

Distraction and Fantasy

During the Spanish Inquisition, some torturers complained because their pris-oners seemed to be indifferent to pain (Bernheim 1964). A good stretching on the rack had little effect on them. These tormentors noted that the prisoners seemed to mutter repeated phrases under their breath, and wondered if they possessed magic charms.

Perhaps they did, but more likely they had practiced ways of diverting their attention from their pain. Some of us repeat comforting, familiar prayers during times of stress. Others may repeat favorite lines of poetry. It is also possible to distract yourself by focusing on details of the environment (Kanfer & Goldfoot 1966)—counting ceiling tiles, hairs on a finger, describing the clothing of people passing by in the hall.

You can also try converting your discomfort into a part of a prolonged fan-tasy (Beers & Karoly 1979; Knox 1972). Perhaps your gash in the leg was the outcome of an Alpine ski chase in which you swerved away from rocks and trees and jumped gullies at thrilling speeds. You can picture all the details of the chase in your mind as you await the attentions of the doctor. Too bad the doctor will be going about his mechanical chores with so little appreciation of the import and the color of the adventure you have just had. A colorless lot, doctors.

Lowering Your Level of Arousal: Turning Down the Alarm

One of the reasons a squash does not become as disturbed as a human when it is assaulted is that it does not catastrophize. Another reason is that it does not have an autonomic nervous system (ANS).

Once you are awake, you no longer need an alarm. Once you have been alerted to pain and discomfort and have taken appropriate action, you no longer need the sympathetic branch of your ANS pounding your blood so fiercely through your arteries.

In Chapter 6 we saw that overarousal involves many bodily activities, including heavy perspiration, rapid heartbeat, muscle tension, and rapid respiration rate or breathing. For most of us, these functions are largely automatic (or "autonomic"), and we would require a great deal of training to gain direct control over them to slow them down. Fortunately this is not the case with breathing.

Diaphragmatic Breathing. Lie down on your back. Place your hands lightly on your stomach. Breathe so that you can feel your stomach rising each time you inhale and falling each time you exhale. This is breathing through the **diaphragm**—a large sheetlike muscle that separates the chest and abdominal regions. Now use these methods to maintain slow and regular breathing: (1) Breathe through your nose only. (2) Take the same amount of time to exhale that you use to inhale. Make both actions continuous and leisurely. If you are

Weary and drained, this runner is nevertheless triumphant. Do you think he finished first by focusing on his pain and discomfort? Or do you think he controlled catastrophizing tendencies and found other things to think about?

Some people control pain and discomfort by making them part of a fantasy, such as a James Bond type of adventure. Doesn't the minor pain in your leg pale when you fantasize that it is but a detail of an intense and thrilling chase?

not sure you are doing it properly, simply count while you take air steadily in ("one thousand one, one thousand two, one thousand three") and then let air steadily out ("one thousand one, one thousand two, one thousand three"). After a few moments, you may count up to four or five.

You can also use diaphragmatic breathing while sitting in a chair. Until you get the knack of it, keep one hand on your chest to see that it remains still, and the other on your stomach to see that it rises and falls as you breathe in and out. Remember to go slowly and steadily, and to keep your mouth shut (but do not press your lips together tightly).

According to John R. Harvey (1978) of the University of Wisconsin, other types of breathing, through the chest and shoulder muscles, are efficient ways to gulp down air for running and other vigorous activities. But they seem linked to increases in sympathetic ANS arousal. Rapid breathing in and of itself can lead to anxiety, tension, fatigue, and even light-headedness. But diaphragmatic breathing can actually directly calm you down by activating the *parasympathetic* branch of the ANS, which can counteract sympathetic overarousal. Research suggests that you cannot relax fully without breathing diaphragmatically (Ballentine 1976; Brena 1971; Hirai 1975). During a period of severe pain or discomfort, diaphragmatic breathing will also help distract you—it will give you something to do with your hands, and you can engage in mental arithmetic to help monitor your breathing.

Muscle Relaxation. Pick a muscle. Any muscle. Contract it hard, without hurting yourself; then, after a few moments, let it go. How hard can you tighten the muscle? We may not have words to describe our feelings, but we perceive limits to the tightening process; a point beyond which we cannot go. But then: How slack or loose can you allow the muscle to go? What would happen to it? What would it feel like? Ah, mystery.

Dr. Edmund Jacobson of the University of Chicago became intrigued by these mysteries. He noted that when people were tense they contracted their muscles, even if they were unaware of it. He developed the notion that if people could learn to do the opposite of muscle tightening, they could probably learn how to relax more effectively. Yet people are often unaware of tightness in the muscles even if they look to you as if they are wearing a suit of armor. And if you tell them just to relax their muscles, just to let go, much of the time, frankly, they simply do not know exactly what to do.

So Edmund Jacobson hit upon the fantastic concept of taking people on a trip through their bodies—having them purposefully tighten and then relax different muscle groups, one after the other, so that they could develop a frame of reference for muscle relaxation (Jacobson 1938). By first tensing, then relaxing muscle groups, you learn to differentiate between the two sensations. This method of learning to relax is called **progressive relaxation:** as you progress from one area of the body to another, you become more and more relaxed.

In research report after report (e.g., Paul 1969b), progressive relaxation has been found to decrease the sympathetic ANS overarousal that accompanies stress and has been found useful with what Selye termed "diseases of adaptation," from headaches (Tasto & Hinkle 1973) to high blood pressure (Taylor et al. 1977).

You can learn how to relax progressively by practicing the instructions given on pages 188–90. Knowing how to relax yourself will give you something more to do if you experience pain or discomfort. The muscle relaxa-

When our muscles are tight, we feel tense. Jacobson experimented with progressive muscle relaxation as a method for reducing tension and anxiety.

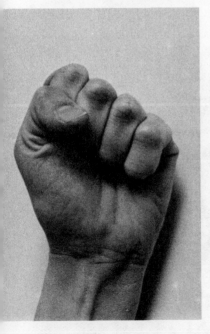

tion along with gentle diaphragmatic breathing will act to counter sympathetic ANS overarousal. And perhaps some physician will someday complain about you in a book. There you were in the emergency room with a gash in your leg. Many people would have been extremely upset. But you remained relatively in control all the time you were being attended—and you muttered all these strange magic words or formulas under your breath ("one thousand one, one thousand two, easy, will be laughing tonight, . . .").

MEETING THE CHALLENGE OF ANXIETY

It might seem strange to you to read that reality anxiety—or objective fear—is not a psychological problem. Yes, we know that fear is not one of your favorite emotions, but when fear reflects real danger, it is appropriate either to remove to yourself from the danger or to change your environment so that you have removed the danger. That is, if a truck is rumbling at you, get out of the street. If you have a wheel shimmy in your car, have the tires balanced. Be grateful for your reality anxiety: it gives you a nice push.

Free-floating anxiety, however, is a juicy psychological problem. You can understand being upset by academic or social problems, but it is mystifying to comprehend why some people feel uptight practically all the time, even when everything seems to be going right. Sigmund Freud, as we pointed out in Chapter 6, felt that much free-floating anxiety represented repressed impulses: the anxious and timid fellow is unconsciously not afraid of being attacked, but of the possibility of attacking *others*. Perhaps.

But some free-floating anxiety is like the magician's assistant floating on the stage during the magic act. If you know the trick, you can find the strings or the supports. The trick is you have to know the trick. Most anxieties, like most people, do not float in the air for very long.

A Detective Story: Functional Analysis

You would probably like nothing more than to be able to think less about your anxieties. It must seem terribly unfair that one excellent way to help you come to grips with free-floating anxieties is to think about them even more, and then to write all about them. But our assumption is that many times increased personal awareness of seemingly "uncaused" events leads to an understanding of just why they occur.

So begin to pay close attention to your anxiety:

- Learn to rate your anxiety on a scale from 0 to 100. About 10 would mean extremely light anxiety; 50, moderate anxiety; 80 would earn you a major role in Mel Brooks's movie *High Anxiety*; and 100 would mean that your anxiety is as bad as it can get.
- Whenever you experience anxiety, jot down (a) the amount of anxiety, from 0 to 100, (b) what you are doing, (c) where you are, (d) the time of day, (e) whom you are with, (f) what or whom you are thinking about.
- Look for recurring patterns, especially when you experience high anxiety. Does your anxiety hit you at a certain time of day, on your way to school or work? When you think about a particular person? In a couple of weeks you should see the things that tend to be associated with your anxiety.

Progressive relaxation. Edmund Jacobson's method of achieving relaxation by tensing and relaxing a muscle group, and then moving on to repeat the process with different muscle groups in the body.

Meeting the Challenge of Stress

HANGING LOOSE THROUGH PROGRESSIVE RELAXATION

If you are tired of being uptight, you can learn to hang loose through progressive relaxation—the system originated by Edmund Jacobson in which you quiet down that internal alarm by alternately tensing and relaxing muscle groups throughout your body. After you have practiced alternate tensing and relaxing for a couple of weeks, you can switch to relaxing muscles only.

Before you relax, create a conducive setting. Settle down on a reclining chair, a couch, or a bed with a pillow. Pick a time and place where you are unlikely to be interrupted. Be sure that the room is warm and comfortable. Dim the lights. Loosen any tight clothing.

Use the instructions below (Wolpe & Lazarus 1966) to relax. Each time you tense a muscle group, tighten it about two-thirds as hard as you could if you were using maximum strength. The feeling that a muscle may go into a spasm is a signal that you are tensing it too hard. When you let go of your tensions, do so completely.

The instructions can be memorized, tape-recorded, or read aloud by a friend or relative. An advantage to having them read rather than taping them is that the reader can always slow down or speed up according to some prearranged signal—such as lifting one finger to indicate slowing down and two fingers to indicate speeding up.

RELAXATION INSTRUCTIONS

RELAXATION OF ARMS (time: 4–5 min)

Settle back as comfortably as you can. Let yourself relax to the best of your ability. . . . Now, as you relax like that, clench your right fist, just clench your fist tighter and tighter, and study the tension as you do so. Keep it clenched and feel the tension in your right fist, hand, forearm . . . and now relax. Let the fingers of your right hand become loose, and observe the contrast in your feelings. . . . Now, let yourself go and try to become more relaxed all over. . . . Once more, clench your right fist really tight . . . hold it, and notice the tension again. . . . Now let go, relax; your fingers straighten out, and you notice the difference once more. . . . Now repeat that with your left fist. Clench your left fist while the rest of your body relaxes; clench that fist tighter and feel the tension . . . and now relax. Again enjoy the contrast. . . . Repeat that once more, clench the left

fist, tight and tense. . . . Now do the opposite of tension—relax and feel the difference. Continue relaxing like that for a while. . . . Clench both fists tighter and tighter, both fists tense, forearms tense, study the sensations . . . and relax; straighten out your fingers and feel that relaxation. Continue relaxing your hands and forearms more and more. . . . Now bend your elbows and tense your biceps, tense them harder and study the tension feelings . . . all right, straighten out your arms, let them relax and feel that difference again. Let the relaxation develop. . . . Once more, tense your biceps; hold the tension and observe it carefully. . . . Straighten the arms and relax; relax to the best of your ability. . . . Each time, pay close attention to your feelings when you tense up and when you relax. Now straighten your arms, straighten them so that you feel most tension in the triceps muscles along the back of your arms; stretch your arms and feel that tension. . . . And now relax. Get your arms back into a comfortable position. Let the relaxation proceed on its own. The arms should feel comfortably heavy as you allow them to relax. . . . Straighten the arms once more so that you feel the tension in the triceps muscles; straighten them. Feel that tension . . . and relax. Now let's concentrate on pure relaxation in the arms without any tension. Get your arms comfortable and let them relax further and further. Continue relaxing your arms ever further. Even when your arms seem fully relaxed, try to go that extra bit further; try to achieve deeper and deeper levels of relaxation.

RELAXATION OF FACIAL AREA WITH NECK, SHOULDERS AND UPPER BACK (time: 4–5 min)

Let all your muscles go loose and heavy. Just settle back quietly and comfortably. Wrinkle up your forehead now; wrinkle it tighter. . . . And now stop wrinkling your forehead, relax and smooth it out. Picture the entire forehead and scalp becoming smoother as the relaxation increases. . . . Now frown and crease your brows and study the tension. . . . Let go of the tension again. Smooth out the forehead once more. . . . Now, close your eyes tighter and tighter . . . feel the tension . . . and relax your eyes. Keep your eyes closed, gently, comfortably, and notice the relaxation. . . . Now clench your jaws, bite your teeth together; study the tension throughout the jaws. . . . Relax your jaws now. Let your lips part slightly. . . . Appreciate the relaxation. . . . Now press your tongue hard against the roof of your mouth. Look for the tension. . . . All right, let your tongue return to a comfortable and relaxed position. . . . Now purse your lips, press your lips together tighter and tighter. . . . Relax the lips. Note the contrast between tension and relaxation. Feel the relaxation all over your face, all over your forehead and scalp, eyes, jaws, lips, tongue and throat. The relaxation progresses further and further. . . . Now attend to your neck muscles. Press your head back as far as it can go and feel the tension in the neck; roll it to the right and feel the tension shift; now roll it to the left. Straighten your head and bring it forward, press your chin against your chest. Let your head return to a comfortable position, and study the relaxation. Let the relaxation develop. . . . Shrug your shoulders, right up. Hold the tension. . . . Drop your shoulders and feel the relaxation. Neck and shoulders relaxed. . . . Shrug your shoulders again and move them around. Bring your shoulders up and forward and back. Feel the tension in your shoulders and in your upper back. . . . Drop your shoulders once more and relax. Let the relaxation spread deep into the shoulders, right into your back muscles; relax your neck and throat, and your jaws and other facial areas as the pure relaxation takes over and grows deeper . . . deeper . . . ever deeper.

RELAXATION OF CHEST, STOMACH AND LOWER BACK (time: 4–5 min)

Relax your entire body to the best of your ability. Feel that comfortable heaviness that accompanies relaxation. Breathe easily and freely in and out. Notice how the relaxation increases as you exhale . . . as you breathe out just feel that relaxation. . . . Now breathe right in and fill your lungs; inhale deeply and hold your breath. Study the tension. . . . Now exhale, let the walls of your chest grow loose and push the air out automatically. Continue relaxing and breathe freely and gently. Feel the relaxation and enjoy it. . . . With the rest of your body as relaxed as possible, fill your lungs again. Breathe in deeply and hold it again. . . . That's fine, breathe out and appreciate the relief. Just breathe normally. Continue relaxing your chest and let the relaxation spread to your back, shoulders, neck and arms. Merely let go . . . and enjoy the relaxation. Now let's pay attention to your abdominal muscles, your stomach area. Tighten your stomach muscles, make your abdomen hard. Notice the tension. . . . And relax. Let the muscles loosen and notice the contrast. . . . Once more, press and tighten your stomach muscles. Hold the tension and study it. . . .

And relax. Notice the general well-being that comes with relaxing your stomach. . . . Now draw your stomach in, pull the muscles right in and feel the tension this way. . . . Now relax again. Let your stomach out. Continue breathing normally and easily and feel the gentle massaging action all over your chest and stomach. . . . Now pull your stomach in again and hold the tension. . . . Now push out and tense like that; hold the tension . . . once more pull in and feel the tension . . . now relax your stomach fully. Let the tension dissolve as the relaxation grows deeper. Each time you breathe out, notice the rhythmic relaxation both in your lungs and in your stomach. Notice thereby how your chest and your stomach relax more and more. . . . Try and let go of all contractions anywhere in your body. . . . Now direct your attention to your lower back. Arch up your back, make your lower back quite hollow, and feel the tension along your spine . . . and settle down comfortably again relaxing the lower back. . . . Just arch your back up and feel the tensions as you do so. Try to keep the rest of your body as relaxed as possible. Try to localize the tension throughout your lower back area. . . . Relax once more, relaxing further and further. Relax your lower back, relax your upper back, spread the relaxation to your stomach, chest, shoulders, arms and facial area. These parts relaxing further and further and further and ever deeper.

RELAXATION OF HIPS, THIGHS AND CALVES FOLLOWED BY COMPLETE BODY RELAXATION

Let go of all tensions and relax. . . . Now flex your buttocks and thighs. Flex your thighs by pressing down your heels as hard as you can. . . . Relax and note the difference. . . . Straighten your knees and flex your thigh muscles again. Hold the tension. . . . Relax your hips and thighs. Allow the relaxation to proceed on its own. . . . Press your feet and toes downwards, away from your face, so that your calf muscles become tense. Study that tension. . . . Relax your feet and calves. . . . This time, bend your feet towards your face so that you feel tension along your shins. Bring your toes right up. . . . Relax again. Keep relaxing for a while. . . . Now let yourself relax further all over. Relax your feet, ankles, calves and shins, knees, thighs, buttocks and hips. Feel the heaviness of your lower body as you relax still further. . . . Now spread the relaxation to your stomach, waist, lower back. Let go more and more. Feel that relaxation all over. Let it proceed to your upper back, chest, shoulders and arms and right to the tips of your fingers. Keep relaxing more and more deeply. Make sure that no tension has crept into your

Continued from page 189

throat; relax your neck and your jaws and all your facial muscles. Keep relaxing your whole body like that for a while. Let yourself relax.

Now you can become twice as relaxed as you are merely by taking in a really deep breath and slowly exhaling. With your eyes closed so that you become less aware of objects and movements around you and thus prevent any surface tensions from developing, breathe in deeply and feel yourself becoming heavier. Take in a long, deep breath and let it out very slowly. . . . Feel how heavy and relaxed you have become.

In a state of perfect relaxation you should feel unwilling to move a single muscle in your body. Think about the effort that would be required to raise your right arm. As you *think* about raising your right arm, see if you can notice any tensions that might have crept into your shoulder and your arm. . . . Now you decide not to lift the arm but to continue relaxing. Observe the relief and the disappearance of the tension. . . .

Just carry on relaxing like that. When you wish to get up, count backwards from four to one. You should then feel fine and refreshed, wide awake and calm.

LETTING GO ONLY

Once you have practiced progressive relaxation through alternate tensing and letting go, you will probably find that you can relax completely through letting go only. Simply focus on the muscle groups in your arms and allow them to relax. Just keep letting go. Allow the sensations of relaxation, warmth, and heaviness to develop on their own. Repeat for your facial area with your neck, shoulders, and upper back; for your chest, stomach, and lower back; and for your hips, thighs, and calves.

You will find that you can skip over many of the instructions. Relaxation in one area can be allowed to "flow" into relaxation in another. Give yourself instructions that feel right for you.

You can probably achieve deep relaxation through letting go in only about five minutes. Then simply continue to relax and enjoy the sensations fully for another ten to twenty minutes. Now and then you can go on a "mind trip" through your body to seek out pockets of residual tension and let them go. We recommend that you return to the full-length Wolpe and Lazarus instructions once every couple of months to renew your awareness of the sensations of bodily tensions. This will keep relaxation skills "sharp."

Once you have learned how to relax, you can *call on your skills as needed, letting go of bodily tensions when you want that alarm turned down. You can also relax once or twice daily to reduce high blood pressure and cut down on Type A behavior.*

One may also be instructed in methods of muscle relaxation and breathing control in preparation for childbirth. They are essential ingredients of the Lamaze method of natural childbirth.

Source: Relaxation instructions reprinted from Wolpe and Lazarus (1966), pp. 177–180.

Functional analysis. A systematic method for determining the environmental context of behavior.

This detective story is known as a **functional analysis** of anxiety. Through systematic self-observation, you come to learn what things tend to precede your anxiety. If thinking about a shaky financial investment turns out to precede your anxiety, and if you do not become anxious at any other time, it is possible that concern about this investment causes your anxiety. In real life, anxiety that seems to be free-floating often has multiple causes—a number of problems we might be better off tackling squarely. If fears are identified, you may find appropriate methods for dealing with them in Chapter 8.

Your functional analysis might reveal that you are particularly anxious when you think about some of the important people in your life. It is just possible that you are somewhat angry with these people and that you have not discovered appropriate ways of expressing your feelings. Or perhaps these individuals are associated with frustrations or conflicts in your life. Someone may be a barrier to your meeting your needs. You may have conflicting feelings about someone. You may be putting off making a decision about how to cope

The Challenges of Stress, Fear, and Depression

with someone else. You may discover that catastrophizing thinking compounds or is even at the heart of your anxiety.

If you have made a conscientious functional analysis of your anxiety and are still totally perplexed as to the origins of your distress, it may be time to talk with a helping professional. Sometimes when we can't see the forest because of the trees, someone else can stand back a bit and pick out groves, leaves, and squirrels. You may also go after some emotional relief by learning to relax, as in the instructions above. To some it seems like a cop-out to try to feel better without unrooting the problems, but we have never been convinced that suffering for the sake of suffering is more virtuous. You should also be aware that some medical conditions, like **hypoglycemia** (low blood sugar), can lead to symptoms like anxiety. Consult a physician if you suspect that your tension and irritability have medical origins.

We deal with phobias in Chapter 8 and discuss panic in Chapter 10. Moral anxiety, feelings of guilt and shame, usually represent conflicts between your value system and your behavior, or behavior that you are actively considering. We noted in Chapter 6 that people who feel most guilty are usually the ones who are least likely to do wrong, so it is not surprising that one of the major thrusts of modern psychotherapy has been to help anxious individuals overcome excessive guilt.

When impulses conflict with values, it is time to make decisions. But values are a matter of individual conscience, and you must determine for yourself those things that are most important to you. If you find it extremely difficult to clarify your own values, it may again be time to talk with someone else.

Hypoglycemia (high-poe-gly-SEEM-ee-uh). A medical disorder in which there is an abnormally low level of sugar in the blood. Symptoms include shakiness, cold sweat, and, sometimes, confusion, hallucinations, and coma.

MEETING THE CHALLENGE OF FRUSTRATION

We heard a short story: It is often wet and raw in Boston in the fall, when the wind comes off the Atlantic. During one such dark and rainy afternoon, a dozen people were huddled at a covered bus stop. They drew scarves in at the neck. They winced when cold water from the gray sky intermittently pricked their cheeks. They had been standing for several minutes when a lone figure ascended from where the street dropped off in the distance and strode toward them. As he neared it was apparent he wore only sneakers, shorts, and a zippered sweatshirt that was open down to the waist. With rhythmic strides he was soon upon them. His face was up to the sky and the wet. His eyes did not squint, he did not frown. Then he was past them. Long before the bus came he was gone.

Perhaps this story has no moral. Perhaps it suggests that one person's barrier is another person's challenge and source of refreshment. A dozen people huddled in a shelter against the rain. The water and the wind off the ocean stood between them and comfort, perhaps between them and health. To the lone runner, the water and the wind were nourishment and renewal. Human flesh, perhaps, is human flesh; but some accept challenges and grow from them while others huddle against the elements.

Frustration arises when barriers lie between people and their goals. How do you react when you are frustrated? Do you rant and rave, kick and scream? Or do you analyze the situation to determine what you can do to pull down those barriers or surmount those obstacles, and, if necessary, to seek acceptable substitute goals? If raving and kicking are your style, turn to Chapter 10 to learn how to control anger.

Challenging Barriers

What of the barriers in your life? There is no doubt that women still experience sexism in their jobs and that blacks and other minorities still suffer from racism, but many women and minorities head corporations and pay taxes in the hundreds of thousands per year. Many adolescents are smaller than the average athlete in the sport of their choosing, but shortstop Freddie Patek is five feet four, some defensive backs weigh 170, and some pro basketball players have been under six feet.

It is essential to plan, to clarify the types of behavior you will have to engage in to surmount obstacles that stand between you and your goals. In academic endeavors, this requires planning a program of study that places courses in proper sequence, being certain that the final courses teach skills that are used in the field you have chosen, and determining that you have all the prerequisites to undertake the program. Professors in your field of interest, academic advisers, and academic counselors at the college counseling center are resources to help provide the information you need.

What barriers frustrate you? What do you need to do to overcome them? What resources do you have? What do you need to know? How do you find out?

Franklin Delano Roosevelt did not allow the obstacle of physical impairment to prevent him from functioning as president. Sometimes we can directly overcome the obstacles that lie in our paths. At other times, we can change unreachable goals to ones that are more likely to be satisfied.

Clarifying Goals

If you cannot overcome barriers in your life, analyze your goals. What about them was alluring or attractive? What needs did you expect these goals to satisfy? Is it possible that other goals could also satisfy these needs, at least in part? Would these goals be more readily attainable? How do you know? How can you find out?

To select goals that may be satisfying, you need information concerning your psychological needs. Psychologists at the college counseling center are one excellent resource for helping you to learn more about yourself.

MEETING THE CHALLENGE OF CONFLICT

There is an old saying: When you sit on the fence too long, a certain part of your anatomy begins to hurt. Conflicts that are difficult to resolve place us up on those fences. Making decisions can resolve conflicts and get us down from them.

Making Decisions: How the Tough Get Going

Making decisions to resolve conflicts involves choosing among various goals or courses of action to attain goals. In order to make profitable decisions, we need to be able to make a bunch of predictions—the relative values of the different goals, whether we can surmount the obstacles lying in our paths, and the costs of surmounting goals. We should also make contingency plans: What will we do if our decisions do not work out? If predictions are to be accurate, we must take steps to ensure that we have adequate information.

The Balance Sheet. People who feel that we should run our lives according to brilliant intermittent flashes of inspiration may think that adding up all the pluses and minuses for any course of action is simply too mechanical and computerlike to lead to human satisfaction. According to Irving Janis and Leon Mann (1977), they are wrong.

In their book *Decision-Making*, Janis and Mann suggested the use of balance sheets to help weigh the pluses and minuses concerning important decisions. For each alternative choice, you use the balance sheet to jot down: (1) projected tangible gains and losses for yourself, (2) projected tangible gains and losses for others, (3) projected self-approval or disapproval, and (4) the projected approval or disapproval of others.

Experiments with the balance sheets have shown that it can be highly effective in a variety of situations, including for high school seniors trying to choose a college and for adults trying to decide whether they should go on diets and attend exercise classes for reasons of personal health (Janis & Wheeler 1978). In these studies, people using balance sheets reported fewer regrets about "the road not taken" and were more likely to stick to their choices than people not using balance sheets.

Janis and Wheeler also report that using a balance sheet increases the probability that individuals will respond to conflict with appropriate **vigilance.** Vigilant people are motivated to obtain necessary information and think logically, but not so highly motivated (or hypervigilant) that logical consideration of alternatives is impossible. The balance sheet also tends to decrease the likelihood of complacency or defensive avoidance.

Meg was a thirty-four-year-old woman who was married to a physically abusive husband. She had married Bob at twenty-seven, and for two years things had gone relatively smoothly, but for the past five years she had been

Vigilance. An alert, watchful attitude that prepares the individual to adjust to stress. What is the difference between vigilance and hypervigilance?

BALANCE SHEET A: Meg's Conflict About Divorcing Bob

Alternative 1: Going Through with a Divorce

	POSITIVE ANTICIPATIONS	NEGATIVE ANTICIPATIONS
Tangible gains and losses for Meg	1. Elimination of fear of being beaten or killed 2. Elimination of Bob's continual insulting and belittling	1. Loneliness 2. Fear of starting a new social life 3. Fear of never having children because of age 4. Financial struggle 5. Fear of personal emotional instability
Tangible gains and losses for others	1. Meg's mother will be relieved	1. Bob might harm himself or others (he has threatened suicide if Meg leaves)
Self-approval or self-disapproval		1. Considering herself a failure because she could not help Bob and save the marriage
Social approval or disapproval		1. Some people will complain marriage is sacred and blame Meg for "quitting" 2. Some men may consider Meg "that kind of woman" —an easy mark

bruised and battered, occasionally fearing for her life. Meg finally sought psychotherapy to help her cope with Bob, her fears, and her disappointments. Her therapist asked if Bob would also come in for treatment, but he refused. Nor could Meg find any ways to please Bob so that she need no longer fear abuse. Finally, she considered divorce—though divorce was as ugly a prospect to her as was remaining with Bob. She vacillated for some time, and then was urged to fill out balance sheets to help consider each alternative. Here is the balance sheet Meg filled out for the alternative of getting a divorce.

Meg's balance sheet concerning the possibility of divorce provided two immediate purposes. It gave Meg and her therapist a clear agenda of concerns to discuss and work out. It also showed that Meg's anticipations were incomplete: Was it really possible that she would have no positive thoughts about herself if she divorced Bob, or that no one other than her mother might approve of her decision? Meg's list of negative anticipations pointed to the need for her to develop financial independence through acquiring job skills, and to realization that her fears about undertaking a new social life were somewhat exaggerated. Yes, making new acquaintances might not be easy—but it was also not impossible. In fact, it was up to Meg.

What of Meg's feelings about herself? Wouldn't she be pleased with herself

The Moral Dilemma

WHEN NOTHING YOU CAN DO IS RIGHT

Sometimes we find ourselves in "impossible" situations, in which we feel we must do something that is morally wrong. Lawrence Kohlberg (1963) points out that in such situations a legal-social rule is often in opposition to a human need. Here are some "impossible" situations in which human needs are or appear to be in conflict with legal or social rules. What would you recommend in each case? Can you use a balance sheet to help add up the pluses and the minuses?

1. Recently in Massachusetts, parents of a child with leukemia, Chad Green, were forced into taking their child for painful chemotherapy by the courts. They had wished to treat him with the experimental drug Laetrile and high doses of vitamins. Later it turned out that they were also treating Chad with Laetrile and vitamins, even though the court ordered them to stop because of possible poisoning from these chemicals. Rather than discontinue a treatment they considered essential, Chad's parents took him to Tijuana, Mexico, where he continued to receive Laetrile and vitamins, along with chemotherapy. Chad's parents acted in direct opposition to a court order that prevented them from leaving Massachusetts or directing their son's medical treatment. Legally, they could have been prosecuted for kidnapping. Do you believe they acted morally? Why or why not?

2. A woman in a Nazi concentration camp during World War II was able to save her family from execution and starvation by having sexual intercourse with the German officers who ran the camp. Do you believe she acted morally? Why or why not?

3. A moral problem from Kohlberg (1963, pp. 18–19): "In Europe, a woman was near death. . . . There was one drug that the doctors thought might save her. . . . [It] was expensive to make, but the druggist was charging ten times what the drug cost him to make. . . . The sick woman's husband . . . went to everyone he knew to borrow the money, but he could only get together about . . . half of what it cost. . . . So [the husband] got desperate and broke into the [drugstore] to steal the drug for his wife." Do you believe he acted morally? Why or why not?

You can see that these are serious problems. For instance, many who believe that Chad Green's parents were foolish to use Laetrile and vitamins to treat his leukemia nevertheless believe that they acted morally because they were attempting to "save" their son from what they thought to be harmful treatment, even though it meant "kidnapping" him. What do you think?

for doing what she thought was necessary, even if divorce also entailed certain problems? And could she be so certain that no one who understood the situation would approve of her choice?

In this particular case, Meg came to the conclusion that many of her negative anticipations were, in fact, exaggerated. Many of her fears could be collapsed into one umbrella fear: fear of change. Fear of change had also led her to play down the importance of self-respect. Meg did obtain a divorce, and at first she was depressed, lonely, and fearful. After a year she was working and dating regularly—not blissful, perhaps, but she had regained a sense of forward motion, had the pride of being self-supporting, and no longer lived in fear.

Making Career Decisions

> . . . if one advances confidently in the direction of his dreams, and endeavors to live the life which he has imagined, he will meet with a success unexpected in common hours.
>
> THOREAU, *Walden*

"Any child can grow up to be president." "My child, the doctor." "You can do anything if you set your mind to it." America—land of opportunity. America—land of decision anxiety. In societies with caste systems, such as India or Old England, children generally grew up to do what their parents did. From their youngest years, they would normally assume that they would follow in their parents' footsteps. Such a system limited opportunities and wasted special talents, but it also saved young people the necessity of deciding what they wanted to "do" with their lives. And what they do can be most important. "*What* do you do?" is a more important question at social gatherings than "*How* do you do?" It is typically the first question asked. Occupational prestige is a major factor in social standing. People tend to identify their own worth with the value society places on what they "do."

Some young people still grow up to do what their parents do, but often because their parents are proud of what they do. In a study on occupational choice among more than 76,000 college freshmen, Werts (1968) found that many sons of prestigious parents leaned toward their parents' professions. This was especially true of sons of physicians, scientists, and teachers. Family traditions can develop even in an open society such as ours. Such traditions may also spare young people decision anxieties, at least when the young people have talents and personality traits that are consistent with that tradition.

Stages in Choosing a Career. Some people just drift along, accepting any relatively attractive position that comes along, according to economist Eli Ginzberg (1966). They never make a personal commitment to any particular occupation. The pattern develops early: such people often drop out of school or take the first job that comes along after graduation.

But middle-class children often undergo a three-stage developmental process in choosing a career (Ginzberg 1966): a **fantasy period**, a **tentative period**, and a **realistic choice period**. Fantasy dominates many children from early childhood until about the age of eleven. Children engage in wish fulfillment and center on the glamour vocations—acting, medicine, sports, law enforce-

Fantasy period. Eli Ginzberg's stage of career choice characterized by wish fulfillment rather than realistic thinking.
Tentative period (TEN-tuh-tiv). Eli Ginzberg's stage of career choice characterized by initial choices that reflect abilities as well as fantasies.
Realistic choice period. Eli Ginzberg's stage of career choice characterized by realistic assessment of one's own interests and abilities and the state of the job market.

We are more likely to choose careers that will lead to a high degree of satisfaction if we accurately anticipate the tangible and intangible gains and losses to be made. We need to determine whether the career is compatible with our abilities and needs, and whether the investment we would have to make is likely to pay off.

ment—with little regard for practical considerations. From eleven through the high school years, children come to know their limitations and make tentative choices that are based on interests and ability as much as glamour. The average learner surrenders the fantasy of brain surgery. Beyond the age of seventeen or so, choices become narrowed and still more realistic. Students carefully consider job requirements, job rewards, and even the future of the occupation. They appraise their own interests, abilities, and personal values more accurately, trying to mesh them with a job.

The Balance Sheet in Career Decision Making. Seniors at Yale found that using the balance sheet in making career decisions made them more aware of gaps in the information they required to make intelligent choices (Janis & Wheeler 1978). The balance sheet helps you to weigh your goals, to pinpoint possible sources of frustration, and to plan action to gather more information or to surmount obstacles.

Gloria, a college freshman majoring in liberal arts, had always wondered if she should work to become a doctor. There were no doctors in her family with whom she could share ideas. To figure out the sort of additional information she would require, she filled out this balance sheet:

Gloria went over her balance sheet with a counselor in her college counseling center, and she saw that she needed dozens of pieces of information to make her decision. For example, how would she react to the intense and protracted studying? Would she be accepted into medical school? How did the daily work of the physician fit with her psychological needs? How would she respond to occasional taunts from people who still thought medicine should be

BALANCE SHEET B: Gloria's Career Decision About Medicine

Alternative 1: Gloria Takes Premedical Studies

	POSITIVE ANTICIPATIONS	NEGATIVE ANTICIPATIONS
Tangible gains and losses for Gloria	1. Solid income	1. Long hours studying 2. Worry about acceptance into medical school 3. Great financial debt
Tangible gains and losses for others	1. Solid income for family	1. Little time for family life
Self-approval or self-disapproval	1. Pride in being a physician	
Social approval or disapproval	1. Other people admire physicians	1. Some people frown on women doctors

a sanctuary for men? Gloria's need for information was not peculiar to the field of medicine, of course. The types of questions that should be answered in considering any career are shown in Table 7.1.

Gloria was given a Wechsler Adult Intelligence Scale (WAIS) at the counseling and testing center, and learned that her level of intellectual development was on a par with persons who performed well in medicine. Thus, academic problems would most likely be the result of lack of prerequisites for a specific subject, or of motivational problems. But her counselor told her that "the best predictor of future behavior is past behavior." Premedical curricula were dominated by chemistry. The fact that Gloria had excelled in high school chemistry was promising.

The balance sheet drew attention to the fact that Gloria had very little information as to how she would feel about herself as a physician. She had only noted the stereotype—that others admire physicians and thus she would probably have pride. But what of her psychological needs? Would they be met? Her counselor provided the needed information by administering a Strong/Campbell Interest Inventory (SCII) and the Edwards Personal Preference Schedule (EPPS). The SCII suggested that Gloria shared interests with people who held careers in the sciences, and the EPPS showed relatively strong needs for achievement, order, dominance, and endurance. These needs fit well with premedical studies—the long hours, the willingness to delay gratification, the desire to make things fit together and work properly. But Gloria had a low need for **nurturance**—the need to care for and promote the development of others.

Nurturance (NURT-your-ents). **The quality of encouraging growth through nourishing, supporting, and, perhaps, loving.**

Contingency Plans. What will you do if your rowboat sinks? What will you do if you get a flat tire? Life preservers and spare tires are proof that the human species has learned that it can make mistakes and that things do not last forever.

When we make decisions and choices, it is useful to have contingency plans—to try to figure out in advance what we shall do if our plans do not work out. Gloria decided to enter premedical studies, more for their own sake than because of a desire to help other people. But she also decided that if her plans did not work out—if she failed to develop any particular desire to help others, or if she failed to be admitted to medical school—she could pursue her studies in chemistry and possibly enter chemical or medical research. These contingency plans significantly reduced the pressure Gloria felt upon her as she undertook premedical work.

Table 7.1 Types of Information Needed for Intelligent Career Decisions

1. Is your intended career compatible with your own intellectual and educational abilities and background?

Have you taken any courses that lead to the career? Have you done well in these courses? What kinds of intellectual development are shown by people already in the field? Is your level of intellectual development comparable? Precisely what intellectual skills are required for this career? How are they obtained? Are there any psychological or educational tests that can identify exactly where you stand in your development of appropriate skills? Would you find this field continually intellectually demanding and challenging? Would you find the field intellectually sterile and boring?

Information resources: College or university counseling and testing center, college placement center, people working in the field, professors in or allied to the field.

2. Is your intended career compatible with your psychological needs and interests?

Is the work repetitious or varied? Do you have a marked need for change or for order? Would you be working primarily with machinery, paper, or other people? How do you feel about socializing? Is the work indoors or outdoors? Are you an indoors or outdoors person? Would you be following instructions or directing others? How strong are your needs for **autonomy** and **dominance?** Is the work artistic or technical? Do you have strong needs for artistic creativity or for perfection in detail? What kinds of stresses and pressures are found in this field? Do they seem attractive to you? How would you tolerate these stresses?

Information resources: Successful people in the field. Do you feel similar to these people? Do you have common interests? Do you like them and enjoy their company? Psychological tests of personality and interests.

3. What is the balance between the investment you would have to make in the career and the probable payoff?

How much time, work, and money would you have to invest in your educational and professional development to enter this career? Do you have the financial resources? The endurance? The patience? What will the market for your skills be like when you are ready to enter the career? In twenty years? Will the financial rewards adequately compensate you for your investment?

Information resources: College financial aid office, family, people in the field, college placement office.

Autonomy (aw-TAHN-oh-me). Self-direction.
Dominance. Exercising authority or influence over other people. What is the difference between autonomy and dominance?

MEETING THE CHALLENGE OF TYPE A BEHAVIOR

Stop driving yourself crazy. Get out and walk. Students and workers too often jump out of bed to an alarm, wash and dress quickly, fight traffic in automobiles or crowds in trains or buses, and then arrive at class or work with no time to spare. Then they first begin work or school, and the rest of the day also may have its compounded stresses.

The first step in coping with Type A behavior is to challenge the value system that usually encourages it. Then you will be ready to take charge of your environment, slow down, and learn how to relax, three techniques suggested by Richard Suinn (1976).

Confronting Your Type A Values and Attitudes

Do you believe in competition or cooperation? Achieving or appreciating? Are you always concentrating in an effort to do your best, or are you selective about your efforts?

Most people tend to fit in somewhere along these continuums, and it may be that by challenging the attitude that one must always or almost always excel that it begins to become possible to adopt a more leisurely, appreciative attitude toward life. Challenge the irrational idea that "something awful" will happen if you are not perfect in all your undertakings.

Taking Charge of Your Environment

Don't clip your whiskers and then jump immediately into a cold bath. Recall that Richter's (1957) rats swam more effectively when they had a respite between stressors. Try some of the following:

- Set your alarm clock as low as possible or buy an alarm with a pleasant sound.
- Get up at least a half hour earlier so that you can sit and relax while you watch the morning news with a cup of coffee, or perhaps meditate. This may mean going to bed earlier.
- Leave home earlier and take a more attractive, less crowded route to work or school.
- If you have been car-pooling with last-minute rushers, drive with a group that leaves earlier or use public transportation.
- Get to school or work early to have a snack or relax before the day begins.
- Don't do two things at once. Try not to schedule too many classes or appointments back to back.
- Use breaks to read, walk, exercise, or meditate. Limit intake of stimulants such as caffeine.
- Space chores out: don't have your car and typewriter repaired, go to work, shop, and drive a friend to the airport all in one day.
- Allow unessential work to go undone till the next day if there is too little time.
- Devote time to yourself. Do things you enjoy. Listen to music, take a hot bath, or exercise regularly. If your life will not permit you to do things like this, get a new life.

This couple has found one way of meeting the challenge of Type A behavior.

Slowing Down

Jogging and running may be excellent for you, but jogging out of a sound sleep and at the dinner table is not.

- Move about slowly when you first get up in the morning.
- Drive more slowly. Driving rapidly not only uses more gasoline, causes parts to wear out more quickly, earns the attention of police officers, and may get you killed—it is also more stressful than driving slowly (Selye 1976).
- Don't rush lunch—get out, make it an occasion, eat slowly, and enjoy yourself.
- Stop tumbling your words out, one over the other. Speak more slowly, and listen with fewer interruptions.

Learning How to Relax

Japanese business executives commonly pamper themselves by lengthy sojourns in hot baths. The goal is not cleanliness, though baths have a way of making you cleaner. It is tension reduction. Leisurely submersion of most of the body in hot water lowers ANS overarousal. Almost certainly, taking time out for oneself also has the effect of placing the day's stresses in perspective.

Increasing numbers of Americans are taking to meditation in order to break patterns of Type A behavior.

Tranquilizers. (TRANK-will-eye-zers). Drugs that lead to a feeling of calmness.
Attribute. To assign, to think of as belonging to or resulting from. Also a noun: trait or characteristic.
Meditation (med-uh-TAY-shun). Dictionaries define meditation as continued thought or reflection. It is interesting that in psychology meditation refers to a narrowing of awareness to a repeated stimulus (word, sight, smell, sound), and a state of relaxation that may be characterized by the *absence* of thought.
Mantra (MAN-trah). A repeated word or phrase used in meditation.

The Challenges of Stress, Fear, and Depression

In the West, we also have ways of relaxing—exercise, vacations, naps, and, sadly, an incredible growing stockpile of central nervous system depressants we call **tranquilizers.** Tranquilizers are prescribed more often than any other drugs. They usually work, at least for a while, but they can lead to problems with dependence that we explore in Chapter 15.

There is another problem with tranquilizers. When tranquilizers lead us to relax, we **attribute** our improvement to the drugs. We have not learned how to relax. We have learned how to pop a pill when we are uptight. We remain externally controlled—by anonymous chemicals. We don't even have the prerogative of getting these drugs on our own. We have to abase ourselves by convincing a physician that we need them, or else seek them illicitly.

But in recent years helping professionals have developed a number of methods that permit us to learn to take direct charge of autonomic overarousal by systematically reducing muscle tension, other bodily functions, or mental hypervigilance. Since we learn to influence our own bodily processes, we remain internally controlled. We are not dependent on outside help. We not only relax, we retain the pride that comes from being in control of our own lives. Three major methods for relaxing that have received increasing attention are progressive relaxation (pp. 188–90), meditation, and biofeedback.

Meditation: Eastern Gods and Western Technology

It is a well-known fact of life that the few individuals who have achieved the highest spiritual truths have long beards, wear flowing robes, and usually set up near some distant mountaintop. It is also fitting if you have to wait for precisely the right season to make the journey, must find one of the rare guides who is knowledgeable about the route, and so on.

So it is not surprising that psychologist Robert Ornstein (1972) recounted the experiences of a group of American travelers scrambling and stumbling through the Himalayas for the secret to inner peace and harmony. Their trip was long and arduous. Many would have turned back. But these hardy travelers expected great rewards at the feet of the venerable Indian guru. Finally, our travelers did reach their goal. At great length they told the guru of their difficult journey, of all the perils and pitfalls, and of the high importance they attached to this fateful meeting. They implored the guru to share his wisdom, to open to them the inner pathways to peace and harmony. Finally the guru said, "Sit, facing the wall, and count your breaths."

That was it? The secret that had been preserved through the centuries? The prize for which our intrepid seekers had traveled round the world?

Yes, for counting your breaths is one type of **meditation**—one way of narrowing your consciousness so that the stresses of the outside world can fade away. Other learned people in other cultures have devised similar methods. The Yogis stare intently at a pattern on a vase or mandala. The ancient Egyptians stared at an oil-burning lamp—the basis of the fable of Aladdin's magic lamp. Islamic mystics of Turkey whirled round and round and round. In the United States hundreds of thousands meditate by repeating "**mantras.**"

All this had been going on in one way or another for centuries. But why, Dr. Herbert Benson wanted to know, would a serious scientist waste his time on anything so far out as meditation? Since 1959, when the Maharishi Mahesh Yogi brought **Transcendental Meditation** (a simplified form of meditation) to the United States, the movement had captured the imagination and allegiance of hundreds of thousands, perhaps millions of practitioners. And there were all sorts of fantastic claims, from the liberating of inner energy to the lowering of blood pressure. It sounded like a wacky new religion. So you can understand

◢ Meditation ▮▮▮

HOW TO MEDITATE

In meditation what you don't do is more important than what you do. There are many types of meditation, but most limit your attention to a repeated stimulus—a phrase or mantra, your breathing, a pleasant sight or odor. You also adopt a passive "what happens, happens" attitude. You take charge of your environment to make it quiet and predictable. You assume a comfortable position. You usually begin by meditating *once or twice a day for ten to twenty minutes.*

Patricia Carrington (1977) of Princeton University suggests additional ways of setting the stage for meditation. Don't eat for at least an hour before meditating and avoid drinks with caffeine for at least two. Seat yourself before a pleasant natural object—perhaps a green plant or incense. Avoid facing direct light. Change your position as necessary; it's kosher to scratch or yawn. Play for time if you're interrupted; yawn and stretch, move slowly. You can check your watch through half-closed eyes if you're limiting yourself.

Above all, "take whatever you get." You cannot will or force meditation. You can only set the stage and allow it to happen. Your experiences will vary, and sometimes you will find little relaxation, especially at first. Just make yourself comfortable, focus your attention on the repeated stimulus, and allow yourself to relax. If troubling thoughts come in, just allow them to "pass through." You don't have to squelch them.

MANTRA MEDITATION: MAGIC WORDS?

"Om," "Shalom," "Holy," "Easy," "Calm," "Relax," "One"—people have used many words to help them distract themselves from stressors and lower ANS overarousal. Some are everyday words, and some are more exotic. In fact, some have wondered if "special" words have magical qualities about them. In TM there are sixteen mantras, including "Ieng" and "Om." TM instructors assign novices their own mantra, supposedly on the basis of individual personality traits and needs. But TM initiating interviews are brief and the insight of the instructors is variable. Still, many TM initiates believe in the specialness of their "own" mantra, and adhere to a pledge of secrecy about it. Of course it may be that sincere belief that your mantra is magical or special is all that is required for you to act, feel, and think as though it truly were. This is called a placebo effect. A sugar pill is also a placebo, and sometimes the placebo gets just about the same effects as the real pill.

TM mantras are euphonious, with open vowels and soft consonants like *r*'s, *m*'s, and *ng*'s. They sound foreign and mysterious. Any mantra, TM or not, can help focus your attention and minimize distraction from intruding thoughts. Benson (1975) suggests the word "One," stating that it is meaningless, soft, easy to say, and as effective as any other word.

Choice of a mantra is a personal matter, and there is no reason why that you cannot try one out for a while and then switch if it does not work for you, but consistent use can give any mantra more potency as a cue to bring about feelings of relaxation. Carrington (1977) suggests mantras like "Ah-nam," "Shi-rim," or "Ra-mah." Or try "One" or "Om." Don't use words like "klutz" and "rats."

Once you have chosen a mantra, prepare for meditation and say the mantra aloud several times, enjoying it. Then say it softer and softer, close your eyes, and only think the mantra. Then think it so passively that it is more like "perceiving" the mantra. Adopt a passive attitude, continue to perceive the mantra. It may grow louder or softer, discontinue for a while and then return. Allow yourself to drift. If intruding "worldly" thoughts flow in, allow them to pass through as you continue perceiving the mantra. Allow it to fluctuate. What happens, happens.

BREATH MEDITATION

There are several types of breath meditation. Some focus on their breath alone, perceiving it flowing in and out through their nostrils. Others coordinate their mantra with their breathing. Benson (1975) suggests perceiving "One" on every outbreath. Carrington (1977) notes one simple method: simply perceive "In" while you are inhaling, and "Out" while you are exhaling.

TM. The abbreviation for Transcendental Meditation. Is TM "transcendental"? Is TM "meditation"? Check your dictionary.

Hypometabolism (high-po-met-TAB-oh-lism). A state in which the processes of life are slowed down.

Alpha waves (AL-fuh). Slow brain waves that are associated with a state of relaxation. We may say a person is "emitting" alpha waves or other brain waves.

Blood lactate (LACK-tate). A substance in the blood whose presence has been linked with anxiety.

why Dr. Benson (1975) was skeptical when the Maharishi's disciples showed up at his laboratory at Harvard Medical School in 1968, requesting that he scientifically verify their ability to lower their own blood pressure through **TM**. Skeptical yet curious, Benson chose to look into TM.

And when Benson chose to look into TM, he did so with a vengeance. He studied practitioners ranging in age from seventeen to forty-one. Business people, students, artists. People who had practiced TM for more than nine years, people who had practiced only a few weeks. His findings made him do an about-face. TM lowered the body's rate of oxygen consumption, the body's metabolism. This lowered rate of metabolism—or **hypometabolism**—differed from sleep. The drop-off was steeper, taking minutes rather than hours, and oxygen consumption was decreased by 10–20 percent, as contrasted to about 8 percent during sleep. The blood pressure of people with hypertension decreased (Benson et al. 1973). In fact, people who meditated twice daily tended to show normalized blood pressure throughout the entire day. Meditators also produce more frequent and intense **alpha waves**—slow brain waves that are associated with relaxation, but infrequent during sleep. Benson's subjects also showed lower heart and respiration rates and a decrease in **blood lactate**—a substance whose presence has been linked with anxiety (Pitts & McClure 1967).

Whether there is anything about meditating that propels its practitioners into any special state of consciousness or heightens creativity or grants self-insight is open to question, but there is little doubt that meditators react less severely to stress. Benson proposes that meditation reduces stress by counteracting the sympathetic ANS arousal of the fight-or-flight reaction. In one interesting experiment, psychologist David Orne-Johnson (1973) exposed meditators and nonmeditators to intermittent loud noises. He measured his subjects' stress reactions by an instrument that was sensitive to the amount of sweat in the palms of their hands. The meditators stopped showing a stress reaction to the noise sooner than the nonmeditators.

If meditation simply blunted your alertness to stressors, it could be a dangerous thing. Yet psychologists Daniel Goleman and Gary Schwartz showed that meditators were at least as alert as nonmeditators. Goleman and Schwartz (1976) took heart rate and sweat as their measures of reactivity to a stress-producing film about accidents and death. The meditators in their study showed a *greater alarm reaction* than nonmeditators when the film was announced, but they *recovered normal levels of arousal more rapidly* during the actual showing of the film. Meditators showed appropriate vigilance, but also had greater adjustive ability.

Biofeedback: Getting in Touch with the Untouchable

There are few things you can take for granted. But two decades ago behavioral scientists were at least certain that some human functions, like lifting an arm or leg, could be directly willed, but others, like heartbeat and blood pressure, were involuntary or autonomic. We could no more control blood pressure directly than we could purposefully cause more blood to flow into our hands.

Once in a while we would hear reports about strange Yoga experts or other exotic individuals who could literally make their hair stand on end or cause themselves to stop bleeding when they put a nail through their cheeks. But these tales were received as horror stories or dismissed as stage tricks, and we went back about our business.

But in the 1960s reports came out from psychologist Neal Miller's laboratory at Rockefeller University that rats had been trained to increase or decrease their heart rates (Miller 1969). Miller's procedure had been quite simple. There is a pleasure center in the brain of the rat. When you send a burst of electricity through this center, the rat feels good—or at least we assume the rat feels good because it will do what it can to get this strange reward. So Miller implanted electrodes in the rats' pleasure centers. Some rats were given electric shock when they increased their heart rates. Others were given electric shock when they decreased their heart rates. After a single ninety-minute training session, rats changed their heart rates by as much as 20 percent—in the directions for which they had been rewarded.

Since that time, many people have been trained to control their heart rates and thus increase their capacities to adjust to stress. Alan Sirota of Penn State and his colleagues (1976) trained twenty women between the ages of twenty-one and twenty-seven to slow down their heart rates voluntarily through **biofeedback training** (BFT). Consequently these women perceived painful electric shock to be less stressful. They had learned to turn down the alarm after it had delivered its message. In the same year, Robert Gatchel and Janet D. Proctor (1976) of the University of Texas showed that college students who had learned to slow their heart rates through biofeedback training reduced speech anxiety.

There have now been hundreds of reports of people gaining voluntary control over many of the components of that dreaded alarm ANS overarousal: blood pressure, flow of blood in the hands and fingers, sweating, muscle tension, on and on.

Biofeedback training. A procedure in which an organism learns to gain control of a biological function through biofeedback.
BFT. Abbreviation for biofeedback training.

Meeting the Challenge of Stress

CURING A HEADACHE WITH A FINGER WARMER?

Stretch your imagination and think of the body's blood supply as flowing between the head and the hands. Most headaches, even muscle-tension headaches, are linked to too much blood in the extracranial arteries—that is, in the head. In Chapter 6 we saw that anxiety results in blood flowing away from peripheral areas of the body, such as the hands, to the central nervous system, including the head. Anxious people and migraine sufferers often complain of cold hands. Psychologist Gordon Derner (1977) of Adelphi University notes that hand temperatures in the sixties Fahrenheit do accompany marked anxiety. Temperatures in the seventies reflect slight anxiety. Temperatures in the high eighties reflect a shift toward a state of relaxation, and, above 92°F, an individual usually feels deeply relaxed.

Many headache sufferers have learned to reduce pain and eliminate headaches altogether by raising the temperature in a finger. Warm hands reflect increased blood flow, and blood flowing into the hands decreases the supply to the head. The biofeedback instrument used is a thermister—a temperature-monitoring device, usually attached to the middle finger, which is highly sensitive to even minor changes in skin temperature. You can set the thermister to give off a higher-pitched sound or a faster "bleep" as skin temperature rises. Then you just learn to raise the pitch of the tone or quicken the bleeps. It takes a bit of time, but it's straightforward enough. So how do you get rid of a headache? Heat up a finger. Simple.

Biofeedback (by-oh-FEED-back). Information about a biological process. Listening to your own heartbeat, or feeling your own pulse, is a sort of biofeedback. *Electromyograph* (ee-LECK-tro-MY-oh-graf). An instrument that measures muscle tension. *EMG.* Abbreviation for electromyograph. *Electroencephalograph* (ee-LECK-tro-en-SEFF-uh-lo-graf). An instrument that measures brain waves. *EEG.* Abbreviation for an electroencephalograph.

So what is **biofeedback?** Nothing more than *some system that feeds information back to an organism about a bodily function*. Neal Miller gave his laboratory rats information as to when they had raised or lowered their heart rates through a burst of electricity. Many instruments have been developed to provide information about bodily functions. For example, an **electromyograph (EMG)** detects muscle tension and an **electroencephalograph (EEG)** measures brain waves. The EMG is a useful aid in progressive relaxation training—providing people with accurate information as to how tense and relaxed muscle groups are at any given time.

As biofeedback instruments become refined and more therapists are trained in using them, we shall undoubtedly hear more about them and their applications to stress-related problems. Fortunately, they also help people maintain internal control. Once they have learned somehow to perceive signs of various functions in their bodies, it is they, and not the machine, who learn to take charge of these functions.

Progressive Relaxation, Meditation, and Biofeedback. Three ways to turn down that internal alarm, three ways to help us adjust to stress. These three methods all have their supporters, but they all have a good deal in common. Each of them, for example, redirects our attention from possible catastrophizing thoughts and feelings of helplessness into a strategy for reducing the bodily sensations that accompany stress. We must also note that many of us simply do not take the time to sit quietly and pay attention to ourselves, rather than the demands of the environment, unless we are undertaking some task as we do so. While the bodily effects of progressive relaxation, meditation, and biofeedback training have received much documentation, it may well be that the cognitive component in all these forms of relaxation training—the focus on the task to allow ourselves to take time out from stressful experiences—is what most strongly unites them.

The Challenges of Stress, Fear, and Depression

We do not believe that there are any mysterious cognitive effects from these forms of relaxation. If they are beneficial, it is probably because we have taken time out to reexamine our lives under more relaxed, unhurried circumstances. Taking time out probably has a very important influence on our values and our attitudes. Perhaps the most important influence is simply the development of the attitude that it is all right to take time out.

Summary

- *When you must undergo a serious operation, learning all the grisly details of the surgical procedure and the expected course of your recuperation may make the experience less stressful.* Yes, people with fuller understandings of stressful procedures seem to be more capable of bracing themselves for the inevitable. "Internalizers" seek more information even about painful events than "externalizers."

- *It is easier to claim responsibility for your successes than your failures.* True enough, but people who accept responsibility for their own behavior are more successful at meeting challenges. When we control for the effects of education, for example, internalizers achieve higher grades and go farther in careers than externalizers.

- *You can turn a trip to the emergency room of a hospital into a James Bond type of spy story.* Yes, fantasy has helped distract many people from severe pain. Incorporation of pain into a fanciful drama permits you to focus on the conflict and intrigue of your fantasy, and thereby also helps you to control catastrophizing thoughts.

- *If you tell people just to let themselves go and relax, many of them simply will have no idea what to do.* So Dr. Edmund Jacobson of the University of Chicago found out. For this reason he invented progressive relaxation as a method to help people adjust to stress, tension, and pressure.

- *You can teach people to relax muscle tensions more effectively if you first have them tense their muscles firmly.* Yes. Dr. Jacobson found that purposeful muscle tension helped his patients get in touch with exactly what tension feels like. They could then more easily do the "opposite of tension"—that is, relax. Some current methods of relaxation use letting go of muscle tensions only, but progressive relaxation is a reliable standby for people who do have difficulty perceiving tension and relaxation in muscle groups in their bodies.

- *People who make life's decisions on the basis of inspiration and gut-level feelings usually wind up with fewer regrets than people who diligently try to add up all the pluses and the minuses.* Not at all. Studies with the balance sheet at Yale University and elsewhere showed that people who carefully weigh the alternatives through listing their advantages and disadvantages are less likely to have regrets and more likely to stick to their decisions. Using the balance sheet also promotes the seeking of the information necessary to make wise choices.

- *People who lead moral lives do not have to be concerned about conflicts with the law.* Unfortunately, this is not always the case, as Thoreau pointed out in *Civil Disobedience* in 1849. One of his concerns at that time was the need for moral men to oppose slavery. Many chose to move to Canada rather than enter the armed forces during the recent Vietnamese conflict for moral reasons. According to Lawrence Kohlberg, adherence to your own moral standards is a higher form of morality than is blind obedience to legal-social rules.

- *Transcendental Meditation can lower the blood pressure of hypertensive individuals.* So Dr. Herbert Benson of Harvard Medical School found out when he investigated the physiological responses of meditators. A host of studies have followed, showing that meditation can help people adjust to stress by reducing ANS overarousal without loss of awareness or vigilance.

- *For reasons unknown to behavioral researchers, some mantras used by meditators have magical qualities that promote relaxation and inner harmony.* No. We have no reason to suspect magic, but mantras that have a foreign and mysterious ring to them may intrigue practitioners and give them the belief that they can help for intrinsic reasons. This is the placebo effect. Any euphonious syllables or word or words without distracting associations may be useful mantras.

- *Laboratory rats have learned how to increase or decrease their heart rate for a payoff of questionable value—a burst of electricity in the brain.* Absolutely. A burst in a rat's pleasure center is highly rewarding. Experiments like these have led to a variety of instruments that allow us to gain control over bodily functions we had previously considered totally involuntary or autonomic. They work by providing us with a continuous flow of information about our bodily functions, from blood pressure to heart rate. This is biofeedback.

- *You can probably get rid of your headache by heating up a finger.* If your headache has anything to do with excessive blood supply to the head, there's a very good chance this will work. When you learn to make a finger warmer, through biofeedback, you shift blood from your head to your hand. This decreases blood supply to the head and reduces or eliminates many headaches. Simple?

8

FEARS, PHOBIAS, AND TEST ANXIETY

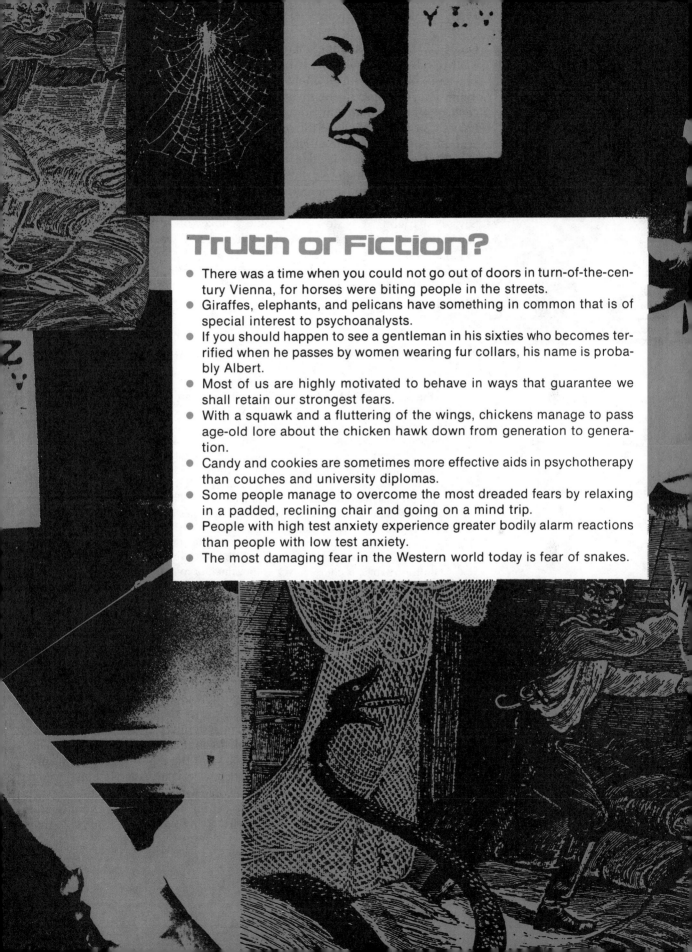

Truth or Fiction?

- There was a time when you could not go out of doors in turn-of-the-century Vienna, for horses were biting people in the streets.
- Giraffes, elephants, and pelicans have something in common that is of special interest to psychoanalysts.
- If you should happen to see a gentleman in his sixties who becomes terrified when he passes by women wearing fur collars, his name is probably Albert.
- Most of us are highly motivated to behave in ways that guarantee we shall retain our strongest fears.
- With a squawk and a fluttering of the wings, chickens manage to pass age-old lore about the chicken hawk down from generation to generation.
- Candy and cookies are sometimes more effective aids in psychotherapy than couches and university diplomas.
- Some people manage to overcome the most dreaded fears by relaxing in a padded, reclining chair and going on a mind trip.
- People with high test anxiety experience greater bodily alarm reactions than people with low test anxiety.
- The most damaging fear in the Western world today is fear of snakes.

Do you want to talk about conflict? Do you want to talk about drama? Do you want to talk about raw, unnerving fear? Well, my friends, forget about Frankenstein's monster. Forget about King Kong. Forget about income taxes and things that go bump in the night. Because there in the heart of turn-of-the-century Vienna, that flourishing European capital of music and the arts, horses were biting people in the streets. Or so was convinced one petrified five-year-old boy by the name of Hans.

Why are some people so fearful of elevators and heights that they refuse high-paying jobs in high-rise office buildings? Why would some people practically prefer to die from an infection than to receive an injection of antibiotics? Why did Hans feel that even the glue factory was too good a fate for the cowboy's best friend? Why do some people "choke" on tests? And, what can be done about these fears? For answers to these questions, and more, stay tuned to Chapter 8.

FEARS AND PHOBIAS

More than a hundred years ago, Charles Darwin, who is known for his theory of evolution, described the emotion of fear quite accurately:

> Fear is often preceded by astonishment, and is so far akin to it, that both lead to the senses of sight and hearing being instantly aroused. In both cases the eyes and mouth are widely opened and the eyebrows raised. The frightened man at first stands like a statue motionless and breathless, or crouches down as if instinctively to escape observation.
>
> The heart beats quickly and violently, so that it palpitates or knocks against the ribs; but it is very doubtful whether it then works more efficiently than usual, so as to send a greater supply of blood to all parts of the body; for the skin instantly becomes pale, as during incipient faintness. . . . [The] breathing is hurried. The salivary glands act imperfectly; the mouth becomes dry and is often opened and shut. I have also noticed that under slight fear there is a strong tendency to yawn. One of the best-marked symptoms is the trembling of all the muscles of the body; and this is often first seen in the lips. From this cause, and from dryness of the mouth, the voice becomes husky or indistinct, or may altogether fail. . . . (1873, pp. 290–291).

It is clear why fear is unlikely to be one of our more favored emotions.

Still, as we noted in Chapter 6, fear is the appropriate emotional response to the perception of danger. It motivates us to do something, possibly to fight or to flee. Such fear should be interpreted as a signal to take action. We would not wish to diminish it, or to avoid it, unpleasant as it can be.

But then some fears are out of proportion to the actual danger. Some people will not enter elevators, for instance. Sure, the cable could break and the elevator could fall. Sure, the ventilation system could fail and it could become stuffy. Sure, the system could break down temporarily and a passenger could be stuck in midair waiting for repairs.* But these problems are unlikely, and it would be foolhardy to walk forty flights twice a day to avoid them, even if the exercise could be a good thing. Some people will not have injections. Sure, injections sometimes are painful. Sure, injections to some very minor degree could be said to impair your "bodily integrity"—in other words, you get a small

* After going through this list of potential elevator problems, we almost convinced ourselves that fear of elevators may not be so irrational at all.

hole put into you (which then fills in). But the fear experienced by people with this **phobia** is totally out of proportion to the pain and damage done by needles. They would more than likely tolerate a painful and damaging pinch to demonstrate that they are not simply "babies" who are afraid of the pain.

Phobias, then, are fears that are out of proportion to the actual danger. They may severely interfere with one's life, prevent the sufferers from working in high-rise office buildings or from taking tests, even though they are fully aware that the fears are irrational. Awareness alone is not enough to counteract the overarousal we experience when we are afraid.

Though they are irrational, phobias are quite common. Agras, Sylvester, and Oliveau (1969) found seventy-seven out of a thousand people in New England to be suffering from some sort of phobia in a recent survey. When we add to our estimates phobias concerning sexual interaction and asking someone out on a date, we must conclude that millions of Americans are suffering from at least one minor phobia, and that many find their lives significantly impaired by their fears.

You are probably familiar with many phobias, such as **claustrophobia,** or fear of tight places; **acrophobia,** or fear of heights; fear of mice, snakes, and other creepy-crawlies; fear of injections; stage fright and speech anxiety; school phobia; test anxiety; and **agoraphobia,** or fear of open spaces, which prevents some people from leaving their homes. But in Table 8.1, we have listed some phobias that you are less likely to have happened across. In the instructor's manual we recommended that students who memorize all these phobias be given A's for the course.

Let us now turn our attention to psychoanalytic and behavioral views of the origins of phobias, as they are suggested by the stories of Little Hans and Little Albert.

Phobia (FOE-bee-uh). An intense fear reaction that is out of proportion to the danger involved, and which is recognized by the fearful individual as being irrational or excessive. Phobias typically motivate escape behavior that may interfere with our capacity to adjust.

Claustrophobia (claws-troe-FOE-bee-uh). Fear of tight places, enclosed places. *Acrophobia* (ack-row-FOE-bee-uh). Fear of heights. *Agoraphobia* (AG-or-uh-FOE-bee-uh). Fear of open places, crowds, perhaps of leaving home. In Greek, agora means marketplace.

Table 8.1 Some Exotic Species from the Museum of Phobias

ailurophobia	fear of cats
belonophobia	fear of needles
ergasiophobia	fear of writing
erythrophobia	fear of blushing
pnigophobia	fear of choking
siderodromophobia	fear of railways
taphephobia	fear of being buried alive
triskedekaphobia	fear of the number thirteen
pantaphobia	fear of everything

A Mystery in Vienna: The Case of Little Hans

In 1908 a distraught physician wrote to Sigmund Freud for advice. His five-year-old son, Hans, feared that he would be bitten by a horse if he left the house. He was most afraid of white horses with black about the mouth and blinders about the eyes. At one point, his fear was so severe that he expected horses would attack him right in his home.

Freud wrote back that the father should make an effort to study Hans's behavior and talk with the boy, drawing him out about his fears. Perhaps some clues would provide Freud and the father with insight into the child's concerns. A year later, Freud would set down a 140-page case history about Hans, one of the more celebrated cases in the literature on psychoanalysis. Freud called the case "Analysis of a Phobia in a Five-Year-Old Boy," and it is in Volume III of his *Collected Papers* (1909).

Let us take a look at some facts of the case and then try to put the pieces together.

Fact 1: From the age of three, Hans showed a growing interest in his "**weewee-maker.**" "When he was three and a half his mother found him with his hand to his penis. She threatened him in these words: 'If you do that, I shall send for Dr. A. to cut off your weewee-maker. And then what'll you weewee with?'" (p. 151).

Fact 2: Hans's father records details of Hans's sexual curiosity. At three and three-quarters years of age, Hans asked his father if he also had a weewee-maker. His father replied, "Of course." Another time he stared intently at his mother as she was undressing for bed. "What are you staring like that for?" she asked. "I was only looking to see if you'd got a weewee-maker too." His mother said that she had one, of course. Didn't Hans know that? "No," said Hans, "I thought you were so big you'd have a weewee-maker like a horse" (p. 153).

Fact 3: Freud wrote that the birth of his sister, Hanna, when Hans was three and a half, was the "great event of Hans's life." Hans woke at seven in the morning to hear his mother groaning in labor. He asked why and was told that the "stork" was coming. After Hanna's birth, Hans noted basins and bowls in his mother's bedroom, filled with blood and water. With surprise, Hans declared, "But blood doesn't come out of *my* weewee-maker" (p. 154).

Fact 4: Hans then grew quite jealous of Hanna as the new arrival gained so much of his parents' attention. Later on he admitted to his father, "I'd rather she weren't alive" (p. 214). After some further conversation his father said, "And then you'd be alone with Mummy. A good boy doesn't wish that sort of thing, though." "But," replied Hans, "he may think it" (p. 215).

"Weewee-maker." The German word was *"wiwi-macher,"* pronounced *vee-vee-mahcher,* with a throaty *ch.* James Strachey, Freud's translator, chose "widdler." We feel "weewee-maker" is closer to the original.

Fact 5: At a zoo, Hans showed fear of animals that had not disturbed him in the past, particularly giraffes, elephants, and pelicans. He appeared afraid of the mammals' large weewee-makers, and he had just recently been struggling with information given him by his father that girls do not have weewee-makers of the same sort as his (pp. 174–178).

Fact 6: One night Hans crawled into bed with his parents, complaining that he had been frightened by a fantasy: "In the night there was a big giraffe in the room and a crumpled one; and the big one called out because I took the crumpled one away from it. Then it stopped calling out; and then I sat down on the top of the crumpled one" (p. 179).

Fact 7: Hans's father described how Hans enjoyed coming into bed with his mother: "Hans always comes in to us in the early morning, and my wife cannot resist taking him into bed with her for a few minutes. Thereupon I always begin to warn her not to take him in bed with her . . . ; and she answers now and then, rather irritated, no doubt, that it's all nonsense, that one minute is after all of no importance, and so on. Then Hans stays with her a little while" (p. 182).

Fact 8: Later Hans's father noted that Hans sometimes came into bed with him in the morning. He asked Hans why, and the child replied, "When I'm not frightened I shan't come anymore. . . . When you're away, I'm afraid you're not coming home" (pp. 186–187). Hans's mother, it turned out, had threatened the child that his father would not come home when he misbehaved. After breakfast one morning, Hans's father rose from the table, and Hans cried out, "Daddy, don't *trot* away from me!" (p. 187).

Fact 9: Freud had one interview with Hans and his father, during which he noted that the father wore a black mustache and spectacles. The rest of the analysis took place by mail.

There is more, much more. But from these isolated facts we should be able to begin to make sense of Hans's phobia and, perhaps, of the fantasy he reported to his parents in Fact 6.

Sigmund Freud, you will recall from Chapter 4, believed that many of our motives, our yearnings, and our impulses were unconscious. We are particularly motivated to repress impulses that would be socially unacceptable. Then we do not have to admit to their existence, and we need not fear punishment or self-condemnation for having them. Yet these impulses seek expression, and often they are expressed, Freud believed, as **symbols.** Underneath it all, it was not horses and giraffes and pelicans that Hans feared—it was what horses and giraffes and pelicans represented to him. In his fantasy, Hans sat down on a crumpled giraffe. Sigmund Freud believed that this was an expression of an unconscious wish to "sit down on" what the giraffe represented. Freud also believed that the "sitting down" represented something else.

The interest the three-year-old Hans displayed in his penis was perfectly normal, and, sad to say, his mother's threat that it would be removed if he played with it is also not unknown. Yet this sort of threat, coupled with the boy's growing knowledge that not all people have "weewee-makers" such as his, could give rise to **castration anxiety.** And who would be the likely castrator? Not his mother, though she made the threat. She, perhaps, had lost a weewee-maker of her own—witness the awful bedroom scene following the birth of Hanna. There was blood in all the basins. Perhaps the one to be feared was Hans's father, mustached and bespectacled. Hans's fear of horses and giraffes and elephants could be symbolic fear of animals with large phallic parts—like his father. Certainly, no intelligent adult could ever jump to conclusions of this

Little Hans had an intense, irrational fear of horses. According to Freud, such irrational fears, or phobias, have symbolic meaning.

Symbol. An object or idea or word that represents something else. Psychoanalysts have suggested that stimuli we fear excessively, as in phobias, actually represent unconscious conflicts.

Castration anxiety (kass-TRAY-shun). Fear that the penis will be removed. In psychoanalysis, unconscious castration anxiety is felt to motivate the boy to resolve the Oedipus conflict toward the end of the phallic stage.

Fears, Phobias, and Test Anxiety

sort. But Freud would have you remember that we are not dealing with an intelligent adult—we are dealing with the unconscious processes of a preschool child.

Let us assume, then, that we know whom Hans feared. But why? If the potential crime is castration, and the feared castrator is the father, what can possibly be the motive? There are several facts that suggest that Hans would like to possess his mother: his jealousy of Hanna and, more important, his crawling into bed with her. Hans admitted that he would prefer it if Hanna were not alive since she competes for his mother's attention. Who else competes? The father, of course! Then what do we make of the fact that Hans showed fear at his father's morning departures? Very simply, Hans fears that his hostility toward his father, his main competitor, will destroy his father or drive him away permanently. Yes, Hans may wish his father gone; but Hans also loves his father and fears his leaving. Such is the nature of unconscious conflict: conflicting impulses may make for erratic behavior, but Freud believed they could quite comfortably inhabit houses next door to one another in the id.

The horse, then, is Hans's father. Fear of being bitten is fear of being castrated. Hans is hostile toward his father—his competitor. Unconsciously he projects his hostility onto his father, and he experiences hostility from his father directed toward him. It is all too frightening and, perhaps, too absurd for the boy to recognize consciously. Thus the drama is enacted through symbols. The conflict has a special name, the **Oedipal conflict**—what Freud believed was an almost universal wish of boys to possess their mothers and destroy their competitors.

It would be too distressing, too overwhelming for Hans to recognize consciously his intense fear of being castrated by his father. *But he can perceive this drama symbolically: he can perceive his irrational fear of being bitten by a horse, his phobia.*

And what of the giraffe fantasy? The big giraffe and the sitting on the crumpled giraffe? Hans's father wrote Freud about his own interpretation of this fantasy: "The big giraffe is myself, or rather my big penis (the long neck), and the crumpled giraffe is my wife, or rather her genital organ. . . . [Hans] was seized in the night with a longing for his mother, for her caresses, for her genital organ, and came into our bedroom for that reason" (pp. 181–182). Freud characterizes the father's interpretation as "penetrating" (p. 182) and then adds, "The '*sitting* down on top of' was probably Hans's representation of taking *possession*," a way of saying, "Call out as much as you like! but Mummy takes me into bed all the same, and Mummy belongs to me!" (p. 182).

But it is also possible that the giraffe fantasy represents **sibling rivalry,** Hans's feelings of resentment toward Hanna for claiming the attention of his mother. Hans's father tested this possibility by saying "Good-by, big giraffe!" to his wife as he left home for the day. "Why giraffe?" asked Hans. But then Hans said, "Hanna's the crumpled giraffe, isn't she?" In this case, the act of sitting on the crumpled giraffe would represent destruction.

According to psychoanalytic theory, must the fantasy have one interpretation or could it have more? Why not? Two or more symbol systems just make it a more "efficient" fantasy; it permits the disguised expression of additional impulses.

Now let us examine a behavioral view of phobias that rests on **classical conditioning.**

Oedipal conflict or complex (ED-ee-pull). A conflict Freud believed was universally experienced by boys during the phallic stage, in which the boy wishes to possess his mother and feels hostility toward his rival—his father.

Sibling rivalry. Competition with siblings—brothers and sisters—first for the attention of the parents, then, perhaps, in school and in later years as well. *Classical conditioning.* A process of learning in which a neutral stimulus is paired with an unconditioned stimulus, and eventually brings forth a learned (conditioned) response that is similar to the unconditioned response. (See Chapter 4 for a full explanation.)

Bad Associations: The Case of Little Albert

Doberman pinschers get a bad rap. In a 1978 *Colombo* television show, a vengeful psychologist trained his two Dobermans to kill an employee who had had an affair with his wife. This psychologist was a movie buff, and he was especially fond of the Orson Welles film *Citizen Kane*. In *Citizen Kane* there was a sled with the word "rosebud" on it. For some dark reason that you will have to try to ferret out for yourself, the psychologist trained the Dobermans to attack and kill when they heard the spoken stimulus "rosebud." It took Peter Falk more than an hour to figure out what had triggered the attack in the dogs. This is fortunate. Otherwise, the show would have ended too early.

What is there about the stimulus "rosebud," whispered, enunciated crisply, or even shrieked that might **elicit** deadly aggression from a couple of rather large pets? Nothing, really. Doberman pinschers are not known for their gardening. We could rightly assume that "rosebud" is a neutral—in fact, meaningless—stimulus to them. However, neutral stimuli can take on meaning for us through learning.

John B. Watson is credited as the father of behaviorism. He took it as his life's work to demonstrate that practically all stimuli get their meanings through being associated with something else. In one small but very significant experiment (Watson & Rayner 1920), Watson and his future wife, Rosalie Rayner, used classical conditioning with an eleven-month-old boy by the name of Albert, a fellow who has had such an impact on behaviorists that he has been referred to as "Little Albert" for decades. Now, Little Albert was a rather **phlegmatic** fellow—not given to ready displays of emotion. However, he did enjoy playing with a laboratory rat. (Such are the toys to be found in psychologists' laboratories.)

Watson set out to show that fear is learned by association. While Little Albert played with the rat, Watson had steel bars clanged loudly behind the infant's head. This was repeated seven times, resulting in overarousal—the fight-or-flight alarm reaction—each time. Then an interesting thing happened. Little Albert showed fear of the rat the next time he saw it, even though there was no more clanging. The rat had been pleasurable to Little Albert. Now, through no fault of its own, it was fearsome. Through association, it had taken on the meaning of the jangling, noxious steel bars.

Nor did his newfound fear stop with the innocent rat. It spread or **generalized** to objects similar in appearance to the rat, including a rabbit and the fur collar of his mother's coat.

Somewhere out there we most likely have a gentleman in his sixties who cringes at the sight of little girls wearing fluffy muffs or fur-collared coats in winter, at small dogs, and, of course, at rats. Why, you might wonder, would he continue to fear rats? After all, now Little Albert is presumably Big Albert. The infant might have been duped into believing that there was something noxious or painful about the laboratory animal. But surely the adult would be able to say to himself: "I seem to have an irrational fear of furry objects. It is pointless, and thus I shall rid myself of it."

That certainly is logical. But these irrational fears are, well, irrational. In theory, repeated exposure to a fear-inducing stimulus, whether it be a white rat or an elevator or an airplane ride, without painful results will result in **extinction** of that fear. At first you may have heavy perspiration, and fear and trembling, but after a number of repetitions, you will get the message that the alarm reaction need not be triggered off.

Elicit (ee-LISS-it). Bring forth a response in reaction to a stimulus. What is the difference between "elicit" and "illicit"? (Watch out for "illicit responses"!)

Phlegmatic (fleg-MAT-tick). Unemotional, slow to respond. The ancient Greeks considered phlegm to be one of the body's four basic "humors" or fluids, and responsible for certain personality traits.

Generalization. The "spreading" of a response to stimuli similar to the original stimulus that elicited the response.

Extinction (eggs-STINK-shun). Discontinuation of a response for lack of reinforcement, or for lack of pairing the unconditioned stimulus with the conditioned stimulus.

Fears, Phobias, and Test Anxiety

This bird silhouette, moving to the right, gets quite a squawk out of ducks and geese.

Avoidance learning. A form of operant conditioning in which an organism learns to avoid an unpleasant stimulus through escape behavior. Escape is negatively reinforced; that is, the reinforcement is removal of fear.

Modeling. Learning that occurs through observation of others, rather than through personal reinforcement.

And that is Catch-22 for the phobic person—the need for repeated contact with the harmless but fear-inducing stimulus. Pain and fear stimulate **avoidance learning.** Put another way, we learn to avoid objects that evoke pain, fear, or other troublesome sensations. When you approach an object that evokes fear, you feel increasingly uncomfortable. When you move away from it, your fear diminishes. Fear reduction is pleasant and rewarding. Thus avoidance behavior is negatively reinforced, and people can acquire tendencies continually to avoid the objects they fear—even when they chide themselves and tell themselves that they are being silly.

Similarly, people who fear injections are not likely voluntarily to undertake a series of desensitizing injections in order to overcome their excessive fear. Knife phobics will not volunteer to carve the turkey. Airplane phobics will not choose to fly rather than to drive. Negative reinforcement of avoidance behavior due to reduction of fear makes it unlikely that we will purposefully act to extinguish our excessive fears.

The behavioral perspective also suggests that some fears may be acquired through observational learning, or modeling.

On Chicken Hawks and Chicken Squawks. Chickens may not be quite so dumb after all. At least they manage to pass on some chickenlore about chicken hawks from generation to generation. As O. Hobart Mowrer (1960) tells the story, newborn chicks are totally indifferent to chicken hawks. But when their elders see the shadow of a chicken hawk swooping along the ground, they get worked up into a chicken frenzy and go flapping and clattering and squawking it up around the whole yard. After a few repetitions, the young chicks start squawking it up on their own if such an ominous shadow should happen to catch their sight. This, of course, is **modeling:** the chicks acquire fear of the chicken hawk's shadow through observing the behavior of other chickens. It is not necessary for them to have had a personal run-in with a hawk. You can see that there is a certain economy to this—otherwise most smart chickens would also be dead chickens.

Human beings are as susceptible to catching the attitudes of others as are chickens. Children are notorious for propensities toward playing with their waste products and running out into the street without concern for traffic. Yet a few parental shrieks of disgust and alarm are usually sufficient to get them to reconsider their uncivilized ways. When people we trust delineate the horrors that may befall us if we, for example, walk alone at night or befriend all strangers, it is not surprising that we may learn to share their fears. Much of the time we are learning common sense, but we can also swallow irrational, excessive fears—especially if we are quite young and illogical ourselves at the time the learning takes place. For instance, if parents squirm, grimace, shudder, and squeal whenever they see mice or dogs or dirt on the kitchen floor, two-year-old observers may acquire some tendency to squirm and grimace as adults when they see mice, dogs, or dirt on the kitchen floor.

In an experiment to determine whether we can learn to experience overarousal through observing the reactions of others, Bandura and Rosenthal (1966) hooked up a confederate to a frightening display of electrical equipment. A buzzer was sounded, and the confederate's arm shot up from the chair arm where it had been resting. It appeared that the confederate had received intense shock, and the confederate yowled and grimaced convincingly—although no shock was actually administered. The real subjects in this experiment merely watched the experimenters' confederate while they were hooked up to apparatus that monitored their physiological responses. After a few repetitions, these subjects began to show high **autonomic** reactivity when the buzzer was sounded—even though they themselves were not in any danger of receiving a shock. An autonomic response can be conditioned to a neutral stimulus even when we know that we are not in danger ourselves.

Of course we do not learn to acquire all the reactions we observe. Sometimes we recognize others' fears to be quite foolish and we simply shrug off what we see. But when we are young or inexperienced and cannot discriminate adequately for ourselves between what we ought to fear and what is just coincidence, we may acquire some strong and lingering fears.

Autonomic (aw-toe-NAHM-mick). Automatic, a response characteristic of the autonomic nervous system. Heart rate, sweating, blood pressure are all examples of autonomic activity.

The Spring of '22—and Beyond

Let us search for ways to overcome excessive fears, for happy endings to the dramas of little Hans and Little Albert. In Vienna in the spring of 1922, Sigmund Freud happened to meet little Hans. But now, at nineteen, he was no longer little. Freud describes him as "strapping." What of his phobia, and what of the traumatic events that had transpired some fourteen years earlier? Freud writes that Hans suffered from no "inhibitions" and that the events surrounding the early inner conflict involving his father and mother and sister, Hanna, had been lost to "amnesia" (1922).

Little Hans had overcome his horse phobia naturally, through a process of maturation in which he made adjustments to his earlier yearnings. His parents had divorced during the intervening years, and each had remarried. Hans now regretted living apart from Hanna, whom he cherished, but he was quite self-sufficient at this point in his life. The ancient inner conflict had faded or somehow resolved with time and maturity. Thus the inner urgings no longer required disguised expression through symbolism. It remains the position of those who walk in the Freudian tradition that successful elimination of phobias requires the resolution of the inner conflicts they are felt to represent.

The Joneses helped Peter overcome fear of rabbits by loading him down with candy and cookies as they brought a rabbit gradually closer.

We have no happy ending for Little Albert. Watson made no attempt to extinguish or otherwise remove the fear of rats he had instilled in Little Albert. Such was not the focus of his experiment. But this logical next step was carried out at the University of California Institute of Human Development at Berkeley with a two-year-old boy named Peter. Professors Harold Jones and Mary Cover Jones (Jones 1924; Jones & Jones 1928) reasoned like this: If fear can be conditioned by painful experiences, why can't it be **counterconditioned** by pleasant experiences?

Peter had an intense fear of white rabbits. The Joneses decided to bring Peter into contact with a rabbit while he was engaging in one of his favorite activities—munching away on candy and cookies. They knew they couldn't do it all at once. If they plopped the rabbit onto his lap while he was eating, very likely the cookies in his hands—and the cookies already eaten—would be decorating the walls. So at first, while Peter munched away in a high chair, they merely introduced the rabbit at the opposite corner of the room. Peter, to be sure, cast a wary eye, but he continued to eat and relax. Gradually the rabbit was brought closer and closer, until Peter was eventually eating while he touched the furry animal. The Joneses theorized that the pleasure gained from eating counterconditioned his fear.

Since the early days of Peter and the rabbit, learning theorists have had marked success with helping people overcome excessive fears through varia-

Counterconditioning. Associating a conditioned stimulus with a stimulus that elicits an incompatible response. For example, a snake may elicit fear and ice cream may elicit pleasure. Combining a snake with ice cream could reduce fear of the snake. But it doesn't sound very tasty, does it? Behavior therapists might actually bring a snake gradually nearer while a child is eating ice cream.

Fears, Phobias, and Test Anxiety

tions on the Joneses' theme. But psychoanalysts have often argued that the gradual-approach method is superficial. Since a phobia is only a symptom of an unconscious conflict, removal of the phobia may lead to **symptom substitution**—the appearance of another phobia, perhaps some sort of conversion reaction, perhaps something else. But research has not demonstrated that people who eliminate fears through learning-theory methods will experience symptom substitution. It must also be noted that Sigmund Freud himself found that psychoanalytic therapy alone did not appear helpful in eliminating phobias. Freud, too, developed the belief that phobics would at some time have to be encouraged to face the object of their fears if they were, indeed, to overcome fear. This is the basis of approaches to the reduction of fears that have been developed by contemporary psychology. In the following sections, we discuss these methods in detail.

An Evaluation of the Psychoanalytic and Behavioral Views of Phobias

The cases of Little Hans and Little Albert are quite elaborate. What are we to believe about them as explanations for the acquisition of irrational fears?

Behaviorists Joseph Wolpe and Stanley Rachman (1960) have criticized Sigmund Freud's interpretation of the events concerning Little Hans by noting that it is quite difficult to piece together a convincing story about something that occurred in the past, especially when the analysis is undertaken from a distance. Wolpe and Rachman also note that (a) there is very flimsy evidence for believing that Hans's quite natural desire to be close to his mother meant that he wished to possess her sexually, (b) Hans never actually expressed feelings of fear or hatred toward his father, (c) there is very flimsy evidence that Hans's fear of horses symbolized fear of his father (it is actually rather common for white horses to have black muzzles, so this combination of features need not suggest that Hans had in any way personalized his perception of the horse to make it consistent with his father), and (d) there is no evidence that fear of the horse disappeared as a result of the resolution of an Oedipal complex—particularly when there was no solid evidence of an Oedipal complex in the first place.

Wolpe and Rachman are certainly correct in pointing out that much of the evidence concerning Hans seems "circumstantial"—a sort of convenient piecing together of facts and interpretation. You will, of course, have to decide for yourself whether or not the Freudian explanation and interpretation of the events in the life of Little Hans seems to reflect an Oedipal complex.

The behavioral view of phobias is also not without its problems. For example, other attempts to associate previously neutral stimuli (such as a rat) with a noxious stimulus (such as a loud noise) have failed (English 1929). Second, even if some phobias have been acquired through classical conditioning, it cannot be assumed that all phobias are learned in this manner.

It may be that phobias come about from a combination of circumstances that provide (1) the opportunity to develop the idea that a neutral stimulus is **noxious,** either through pairing, observational learning, or even through stories or fantasy, (2) the experiencing of overarousal, (3) a tendency to avoid the feared stimulus, and (4) the belief that the neutral stimulus is an awful thing. The phobia then includes arousal in the presence of the stimulus as well as attitudes that interfere with extinction of fear.

As we turn our attention to adjusting to phobias, it will not be surprising that the techniques suggested include ways to reduce arousal in the presence of the stimulus, ways to cope with the desire to place as many miles as possible between the stimulus and oneself, and ways to begin to challenge the idea that the stimulus is truly dreadful and must be avoided at all costs.

MEETING THE CHALLENGE OF FEARS AND PHOBIAS

There's just no way around it. The psychoanalysts and the learning theorists have put their heads together on this one and come to the conclusion that the best way to cope with strong fears is to face them head-on—despite avoidance learning, despite overarousal.

But this is not to say that there are no tricks in the black bag. In fact, the black bag is so brimming over with useful approaches that it might just be possible to overcome fears with very little discomfort, if you are patient enough. These methods include gradual approach, systematic desensitization, modeling, and rethinking or reevaluating the situation. Following discussion of these techniques, there is a separate section on that specter that stalks the campus at least once in the fall and once in the spring: test anxiety.

Gradual Approach

Little Peter came to tolerate his white rabbit because it was brought closer to him gradually. He was also buried with goodies—candy, cookies, and so on. Perhaps the pleasure of these goodies counterconditioned his fear. Perhaps they just convinced him to remain in the situation so that he would gradually learn that the rabbit was not so fearful after all. In any event, numerous studies (e.g., Goldstein 1969; Kimble & Kendall 1953) have shown that gradual approach works.

In using gradual approach, first define the feared object or situation as the **target.** Then write down a **hierarchy** of approaches to the target. You can use these guidelines in constructing hierarchies: If the target is a thing you can touch, you can gradually move closer to it, like Peter and the rabbit. You may first approach the target with a fearless companion, then later by yourself. You can gradually prolong the amount of time you remain with the target. Use index cards to write down some number of steps, perhaps near ten to twenty. Then order the index cards, checking that each step seems easier than the one that follows. If there seems to be too much of a jump between steps, perhaps you need another step or two in between.

Kathy experienced fear of driving, making her extremely dependent on family and friends for commuting back and forth to work, shopping, and recreational activities. Driving thirty miles back and forth to work was identified as her target. She constructed this hierarchy of steps:

1. Sitting behind the wheel of her car with an "understanding" friend who would keep her company
2. Sitting alone behind the wheel of her car
3. Driving around the block with her friend in the car
4. Driving around the block alone in the car

Target. A goal that one wishes to approach.
Hierarchy. A logical sequence of steps, in which each successive step is higher (or lower) than the next.

5. Driving a few miles back and forth with her friend for company
6. Driving a few miles back and forth alone
7. Driving the route to work and back with her friend on a nonworking day
8. Driving the route to work and back alone on a nonworking day
9. Driving the route to work and back with her friend on a working day
10. Driving the route to work and back alone on a working day (Rathus & Nevid 1977)

Kathy stayed with each step until she experienced no discomfort at all before moving on to the next. However, she was not a mechanical doll, and her thoughts during this period were an important part of her experience: she constantly evaluated her own behavior.

Kathy almost quit the first day, in fact, because of her thoughts. After she explained her situation to a close friend who agreed to help her overcome her fears, she had the following thoughts during her first try at step 1: "What a baby I am! Marian is being so understanding, and here I am ruining her day with my stupidity. As if she doesn't have better things to do than baby-sit with me. I've really become a burden to my whole family. I'm such a fool. Everybody would be better off without me." Kathy was not her own best fan.

Of course, her feelings of guilt and inadequacy are understandable. But even if they are understandable, they're also disastrous. They convert an unfortunate situation into a catastrophe. After discussing her attitudes with a helping professional, Kathy practiced more helpful thoughts: "I don't like my fears, but I didn't get them on purpose and I'm working to overcome them. I appreciate people helping me through this, and I would do the same for them. Now, this isn't so bad—you're sitting here without going bananas, so give yourself a pat on the back for that and stop condemning yourself. You'll get there, just give yourself some time. You're gradually gaining control of the situation. You're taking charge and mastering it, bit by bit." Note the themes of Kathy's reevaluation: *self-forgiveness*, *reasonable* gratitude, recognition of progress and *growing personal mastery*, and a good pat on the back.

Systematic Desensitization

Why *wait* until arousal decreases when you are gradually approaching targets? Why not go farther and turn down that alarm by yourself as you get closer? These were ideas that occurred to psychiatrist Joseph Wolpe back in the early 1950s, when he decided to connect gradual approach with progressive relaxation (Wolpe 1958). Wolpe, like Edmund Jacobson, reasoned that you could not feel relaxed and fearful or anxious at the same time. So if you could learn to associate a state of deep muscle relaxation with fear-evoking targets, you could remove their sting. He called this method **systematic desensitization**.

Picture a man fearful of receiving injections reclining in a comfortable, padded chair. He is in a state of deep muscular relaxation. All he does is watch slides projected onto a screen. He has just watched a slide of a nurse holding a needle three times without experiencing any discomfort at all. So now a slide *one step higher* in the hierarchy is presented—the nurse aiming the needle toward the arm of someone about to receive an injection. After fifteen seconds, our armchair adventurer notices a slight twinge of discomfort and raises a finger. He doesn't even bother to speak; speaking might interfere with his state of

Systematic desensitization (sis-tem-MAT-tick de-SENSE-ee-tie-ZAY-shun). Joseph Wolpe's method for eliminating phobias, which pairs muscular relaxation with a hierarchy of fear-evoking stimuli. These stimuli are encountered through imagination, photos, or descriptions, rather than in "real life."

relaxation. The projector operator immediately removes that slide. For a couple of minutes the man in the chair imagines himself lying on a beach under the warm sun. Then the slide is shown again. This time he watches it for twenty-five seconds before experiencing any discomfort. Again the slide is withdrawn, and the man relaxes by visualizing the pleasant scene. When the slide is next presented, he experiences no discomfort for a full thirty seconds of exposure. Twice more the slide is presented but no anxiety is experienced. Now the next slide in the hierarchy is presented—the needle is about to enter the arm. And so it goes. . . .

Psychologist Gordon Paul (1969) of the University of Illinois echoed the enthusiasm many behavioral scientists felt for this new technique, noting that nearly 90 percent of the individuals who had been treated for phobias with systematic desensitization had overcome their fears. Never in the history of psychotherapy had controlled research shown a treatment to be so effective. And Paul added that while critics had speculated that such results would be only temporary, and that "symptom substitution" might occur, these speculations had not been borne out by the evidence.

If you are going to try systematic desensitization, first develop facility with progressive relaxation, as described on pages 188–90. You should be able to relax yourself through brief instructions, or through letting go only, within a few minutes. Otherwise, you will spend two hours a day at it—an hour to get relaxed, 15–20 minutes exposing yourself to hierarchy items, and 30–45 minutes regaining relaxation between items. It's possible, but you could become bored, cranky, and fatigued. But you should know that it is possible to undergo systematic desensitization completely on your own if you take it step by step, as experiments with acrophobia (Baker et al. 1973) and treatment of other fears (Dawley et al. 1973; Rosen et al. 1976) have amply demonstrated. It just takes some care and patience.

Construct a hierarchy of items leading to a target, as with the gradual-approach method. The first item should evoke only the slightest discomfort. If you cannot readily counteract it through relaxation, find a "weaker" first item. If you have trouble progressing from one item to another, try putting one or two items in between.

Progressively relax yourself. Seat yourself or lie down comfortably. You may want to construct some kind of "safe scene" that you can bring in quickly if an item is overly disturbing, or if you have difficulty regaining complete relaxation. Practice the scene a few times: focus on the details vividly.

Make some arrangements so that you can confront the hierarchy item as you wish. This may mean simply imagining items vividly in proper sequence. Or it may mean setting up a slide projector with photos you have prepared. It could mean having a friend help. Focus on each item until it feels slightly disturbing. Then regain complete relaxation. Focus on the item again. When you can focus on an item for thirty seconds or so without discomfort, three times, go on to the next item.

Once you have gained some confidence in your eventual ability to master your emotional reaction to the target, it may be beneficial to try some actual gradual approach to the target as well as to continue with your systematic-desensitization program. Tackling the target "where it lives" is more efficient than systematic desensitization alone (Sherman 1972).

The following case is taken from Rathus and Nevid (1977): Marie, a twenty-one-year-old college junior, was attracted to men but "scared to death" of them. Her personal history showed some plausible reasons for her fears, but

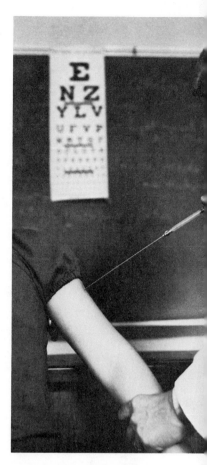

To someone with a fear of injections, all hypodermic syringes may look this big.

was not particularly unusual. Her religious background had emphasized that sex prior to marriage was sinful. Her mother had implied that when she married she would have to do her "duty" for her husband. She had run into an exhibitionist who pretended to be interested in directions from his car when she was in her teens. She did not clearly recall the incident, but the thought of further male nudity was frightful. She had shuddered when college friends had shown her photographs of nude men in popular magazines like *Playgirl*. She would not attend an R-rated film unless a trusted friend had informed her that there was no male nudity. She had done some dating but had been quite nervous. She enjoyed dancing with young men, but recently a partner had achieved erection while they were dancing closely. Marie had been overwhelmed by sensations of fear and threw up in a nearby bathroom.

When Marie decided she must try to overcome her fear, she had been dating a "nice boy" for two months. She thought she might love him. He was not pressuring her into petting, but Marie believed that petting and intercourse were activities she ought to be able to tolerate and enjoy if she felt the desire. She did not believe that the institution of marriage would provide an instant cure. But her thoughts and her autonomic nervous system viewed the prospect differently.

Marie's hierarchy included photographs as well as imagined scenes:

1. Imagining being at the beach and observing men in swimsuits
2. Imagining necking with her boyfriend fully clothed but with bodily contact
3. Looking at slides of men in swimsuits
4. She and her boyfriend, both in swimsuits, are imagined lying next to one another at the beach
5. Imagining that her boyfriend kisses her at the beach, both dressed in swimsuits
6. Looking at slides of nude men in the distance, back view
7. Looking at slides of nude men in the foreground, back view
8. Looking at slides of nude men in the distance, front view
9. Looking at slides of nude men in the foreground, front view
10. Looking at slides of male sex organs
11. Imagining that her boyfriend achieves an erection while they are dancing, fully clothed
12. Imagining that her boyfriend achieves an erection while they are kissing on the beach, dressed in swimsuits
13. Looking at slides of nude couples kissing
14. Looking at slides of nude couples petting
15. Looking at slides of nude couples having intercourse

Marie wanted more than to be able to tolerate her boyfriend's nudity. She wanted to change her attitudes, to rethink and reevaluate her feelings. So Marie read sections of books on anatomy and human sexuality, to give her an understanding of the complexity and fragility of the male organ, which had previously seemed quite simple and overpowering to her. She also studied works of art which involved male nudity, to gain an appreciation of how the male sexual organ was an integral part of half the humans who shared her planet, rather than an arbitrary and unattractive appendage.

The entire systematic-desensitization program required sixteen hour-long sessions in the privacy of Marie's own room. She allowed herself ten minutes at the outset of each session to become completely relaxed, and another five to ten minutes at the end of each session just to enjoy the bodily sensations of deep muscular relaxation.

Marie became less anxious about her boyfriend and engaged in graduated petting with him. She made sure to proceed at her own pace, so that at each stage her pleasure would help counteract any remaining fears. She decided to delay intercourse, but was pleased that she made this decision on the basis of her personal value system and not because of fear.

Participant Modeling: Phobic See, Phobic Do

Psychologists have no special love for snakes. It just seems that way when you take a look at the literature on fear reduction. This is because so many people have a hard time warming up to snakes.

Albert Bandura and his colleagues (1969) compared the effectiveness of three types of approaches toward reducing fear of snakes. One group of subjects received straightforward systematic desensitization from a therapist. A second group relaxed while they ran films showing adults and children approaching and handling snakes. A third group received **participant modeling** —watching a model behave successfully in a phobic situation, then imitating the model's behavior. First they watched a model approach and handle a live snake. Then they were encouraged to stroke the snake as it was held by the model and, after a while, to handle it on their own. For 92 percent of the subjects, the scene soon resembled a snake lovers' convention. By the end of the treatment session, they allowed the animals to crawl all over their bodies. The participant modeling subjects showed greater improvement than people undergoing systematic desensitization or just watching films of other people handling snakes.

Participant modeling would appear especially effective in situations where personal competence in dealing with the target is useful or required. Thus it has been effective in showing children how to play with dogs and adults how to handle snakes. But if fear of the target is so great that participant modeling or gradual approach is not possible, systematic desensitization may be useful first.

Participant modeling (par-TISS-ee-pant). Albert Bandura's term for eliminating fears by observing a model interact with the feared object and then imitating the model.

TEST ANXIETY

"I just know I'm going to flunk." "I don't know what's wrong with me—I just can't take tests." "I study hard and memorize everything, but when I get in there my mind goes blank." "The way I do on standardized tests, I'll never get into graduate school." Few experiences are more frustrating than test anxiety. Especially when students study diligently, test anxiety seems a particularly cruel handicap.

Tests are practically inescapable. From achievement tests in elementary school to SATs, GREs, and civil service examinations, they seem built into every area of our society. It's not unusual for graduate students to introduce themselves to one another by test scores: "How did you do on the Miller Analogies Test?" "Oh, a 74." "I'm a 79." Much can depend on one specific performance on one specific day.

Is It All in Your Mind?

Why do some people become so upset by tests? Is it pure conditioning? That is, do a few bad test experiences mechanically condition a fear response?

Psychologist Kenneth Holroyd of Ohio University and his associates (1978) recruited seventy-two women taking introductory psychology courses into an experiment on test anxiety. Thirty-six of these women showed high test anxiety, as measured by Irwin Sarason's (1972) Test Anxiety Scale, and thirty-six showed low test anxiety. All women were then given anagrams to solve as rapidly as possible. Anagrams are jumbled words. ATSR, for instance, is an anagram for RATS,* STAR, and ARTS. High test anxiety tends to interfere with ability to solve anagrams (Sarason 1973).

The high-test-anxious women did not perform as well on the anagrams as the low-test-anxious women. They took longer to solve the anagrams, experienced more anxiety during the task, and spent a greater percentage of the time they were working worrying about their performance. High-test-anxious women evaluated their performance to be poorer than that of the low-test-anxious women, and it was. But *high-test-anxious women were highly critical of their performance regardless of how long it took them to accomplish their tasks*, whereas the self-evaluations of low-test-anxious women were significantly related to how well they actually did. In other words, high-test-anxious women were down on themselves, period, regardless of how well they actually did. High-test-anxious and low-test-anxious women both showed increases in arousal (including heart rate and sweat in the palm of the hand) as a result of the stress of the testing situation. But a highly critical self-evaluation appears to distract high-test-anxious people from the tasks at hand (Bandura 1977; Sarason 1978).

Holroyd and his colleagues (1978) write that allowing one's anxiety to interfere with the test-taking task is the central difference between high-test-anxious and low-test-anxious people—that their levels of arousal in the test-taking situation are essentially the same. Yet there is other evidence (Doerr & Hokansron 1965) that suggests that high-test-anxious people (as measured by levels of autonomic arousal) do worse than people who function at intermediate levels of arousal during tests.

The most accurate conclusions based on the data available would be that high-test-anxious individuals do not do as well as those who are less anxious on tests, they are more self-critical, they allow themselves to be distracted from their test taking by their concerns, and there is some interaction between a self-critical attitude and arousal. An effective technique for adjusting to test anxiety will thus be directed at challenging self-critical attitudes, avoiding becoming distracted, and, perhaps, also toward the reduction of arousal.

R & R: Rational Restructuring of Test Taking

You can always count on psychologists for a fancy name, but **rational restructuring** simply means taking a more logical and useful view of test taking. In an experiment by Marvin Goldfried of the State University of New York at Stony Brook and his associates (1978), college men and women at Stony Brook and Catholic University were able to reduce their test anxiety significantly through rational restructuring.

Some students allow test anxiety to distract them from studying and concentrating on test items. More skillful students acknowledge their anxiety, but then return their attention to the task at hand.

Rational restructuring (ree-STRUCK-chore-ing). A method of psychotherapy in which an individual is encouraged to challenge self-defeating ways of looking at life, and to construct and practice using more rational thoughts.

The Challenge of Stress, Fear, and Depression

* No, there's simply no way to shake the rats out of a psychology textbook.

THE SUINN TEST ANXIETY BEHAVIOR SCALE

What about you? Do you manage to drive yourself bananas during tests by being overly critical of your performance and expecting the worst? How does your level of test anxiety compare to others? Take the Suinn Test Anxiety Behavior Scale (STABS) items below. Then compare your results with the key at the end of the chapter.

ITEMS FROM THE SUINN TEST ANXIETY BEHAVIOR SCALE

The items in the questionnaire refer to experiences that may cause fear or apprehension. For each item, place a check (√) under the column that describes how much you are frightened by it nowadays. Work quickly but be sure to consider each item individually.

	Not at all	A little	A fair amount	Much	Very much
1. Rereading the answers I gave on the test before turning it in.	___	___	___	___	___
2. Sitting down to study before a regularly scheduled class.	___	___	___	___	___
3. Turning in my completed test paper.	___	___	___	___	___
4. Hearing the announcement of a coming test.	___	___	___	___	___
5. Having a test returned.	___	___	___	___	___
6. Reading the first question on a final exam.	___	___	___	___	___
7. Being in class waiting for my corrected test to be returned.	___	___	___	___	___
8. Seeing a test question and not being sure of the answer.	___	___	___	___	___
9. Studying for a test the night before.	___	___	___	___	___
10. Waiting to enter the room where a test is to be given.	___	___	___	___	___
11. Waiting for a test to be handed out.	___	___	___	___	___
12. Waiting for the day my corrected test will be returned.	___	___	___	___	___
13. Discussing with the instructor an answer I believed to be right but which was marked wrong.	___	___	___	___	___
14. Seeing my standing on the exam relative to other people's standing.	___	___	___	___	___
15. Waiting to see my letter grade on the test.	___	___	___	___	___
16. Studying for a quiz.	___	___	___	___	___
17. Studying for a midterm.	___	___	___	___	___
18. Studying for a final.	___	___	___	___	___
19. Discussing my approaching test with friends a few weeks before the test is due.	___	___	___	___	___
20. After the test, listening to the answers my friends selected.	___	___	___	___	___

Source: © 1971 by Richard M. Suinn. The Suinn Test Anxiety Behavior Scale is available from Rocky Mountain Behavioral Science Institute, Inc., P.O. Box 1066, Ft. Collins, CO 80522.

Participants receiving rational restructuring were given a hierarchy of fifteen anxiety-evoking items from the Suinn Test Anxiety Behavior Scale (STABS). During each of five sessions, three of the items were presented for four one-minute trials. Participants were asked to note what they told themselves as they imagined each of the fifteen situations—their self-defeating, catastrophizing thoughts, and their efforts to restructure the situation more rationally. Self-defeating thoughts included, "I'm going to fail this test, and then everyone's going to think I'm stupid." Rational reevaluation of this

Fears, Phobias, and Test Anxiety

thought might be, "Chances are I probably won't fail. And even if I do, people probably won't think I'm stupid. And even if they do, that doesn't mean I *am* stupid" (Goldfried et al. 1978, p. 34). Participants noted their anxiety levels before and after restructuring, and discussed problems and progress with other participants.

You can use the following steps to undergo rational restructuring of test-taking situations:

- Pinpointing your self-defeating thoughts
- Constructing rational, adjustive alternative thoughts
- Practicing the adjustive alternatives
- Self-reward

Pinpointing Self-Defeating Thoughts. Take the STABS (p. 285). Select about ten items that cause from a little to very much concern in a variety of situations. Sit back, relax, and vividly imagine yourself in that situation. Portray the details, sights, smells, sounds, and so on as completely as you can. Search your mind for thoughts that cause concern. Write them down after a minute or so.

Constructing Rational Alternatives. Carefully examine each of these self-defeating thoughts. Note how it might distract you from focusing on the test itself, and construct rational alternatives, as in the following examples:

Self-Defeating Thoughts	*Rational Alternatives*
"I'm the only one who's going so bananas over this thing."	"Nonsense, lots of people have test anxiety. Just don't let it take your mind off the test itself."
"I'm running out of time!"	"Time is passing, but just take it item by item and answer what you can. Getting bent out of shape won't help."
"This is impossible! Are all the items going to be like this?"	"Just take it item by item. They're all different. Don't assume the worst."
"I just can't remember a thing!"	"Just slow down and remember what this is about. Take a couple of moments and it may come back to you. If not, just go on to the next item."
"Everybody else is smarter than I am!"	"Probably not, but maybe they aren't distracting themselves. Just do the best you can do and then take it easy."
"I've got to get out of here. I can't take it any longer."	"Even if I feel that way now and then, I don't have to act on it. Just focus on the items, one by one."
"I just can't do well on tests."	"That's only true if you believe it's true. Back to the items, one by one."
"There are a million items left!"	"Quite a few, but probably not a million. Just take it one by one and answer as many as you can."
"Everyone else is leaving. They're all finished before me."	"Fast work is no guarantee of correct work. Just take it item by item and do what you can."
"If I flunk, everything is ruined!"	"You won't be happy if you fail, but it's not the end of your life either. All you can do is take it item by item."

Practicing Rational Test Taking. Arrange practice tests for yourself that are as close to actual testing conditions as possible. Time yourself. If the tests are GREs, civil service exams, or specialized graduate school adminssions tests, obtain practice tests and make the testing conditions as realistic as you can.

Pay close attention to the thoughts you experience as you take the practice test. For each self-defeating thought, think a rational alternative firmly. Repeat the rational alternative, again firmly, and then return to taking the test, item by item.

At a prearranged time, go through the list of self-defeating thoughts you had isolated and see if you have left out any. If so, purposefully think them, and then think the rational alternatives. Again, return to the test. Work on it item by item.

Self-Reward. When you think a rational alternative to a self-defeating thought, say to yourself: "That's better, now I can return to the test." When you are finished, think, "Well, I did it. What's done is done, but I certainly got through that feeling much better, and I may have done better as well."

Additional Hints. If you wish, you may focus on your breathing during parts of a troublesome test. Slow down your breathing. Perhaps try **diaphragmatic breathing.** Allow sensations of relaxation to sort of drift in, especially into your shoulders and the back of your neck. But remember that *high arousal is unlikely to do you in*—what you tell yourself about your anxiety is more likely to be the villain. Most people experience anxiety during important tests, but efficient test takers do not allow themselves to be distracted by their fears.

You may wish to try **overlearning** the material you are studying for a test. That is, after you know it fully, study it again. Overlearning aids retention and will give you increased confidence.

When a test is over, let it be over. Check answers only to master material, not to guess your score. Do something you find enjoyable.

Diaphragmatic breathing (die-uh-fram-MAT-tick). Breathing that involves movement of the diaphragm. (See instructions in Chapter 7.)

Overlearning. Practice or continued learning of material *after* it can be practiced without error.

Summary

- *There was a time when you could not go out of doors in turn-of-the-century Vienna, for horses were biting people in the streets.* Not actually, but so it seemed to Hans, a five-year-old psychoanalyzed indirectly by Sigmund Freud through the mails. Freud came to the conclusion that Hans's phobia for horses represented castration anxiety—a fear that is an integral part of the Oedipal conflict, in which little boys are theorized to compete with their fathers for possession of the mother.
- *Giraffes, elephants, and pelicans have something in common that is of special interest to psychoanalysts.* According to Freudian theory, our phobias or excessive fears symbolize unconscious concerns. Giraffes have long necks, elephants have long trunks, and pelicans have extended beaks—all of which Freud believed were symbolic of the male sex organ to little Hans.
- *If you should happen to see a gentleman in his sixties who becomes terrified when he passes by women wearing fur collars, his name is probably Albert.* Could be. In a report published in 1920, John B. Watson and a colleague demonstrated with his celebrated youngster that some fears can be acquired by association. A rat was associated with noxious

clanging of steel bars, and the boy, Albert, learned to respond to the rat with fear. This aversion then generalized to furry objects, like the white collar of his mother's fur coat.

- *Most of us are highly motivated to behave in ways that guarantee we shall retain our strongest fears.* Unfortunately, yes. Even though we recognize phobias to be irrational, our fear motivates us to avoid phobic objects. Thus we may never extinguish our fear of such objects in the natural course of things.

- *With a squawk and a fluttering of the wings, chickens manage to pass down age-old lore about the chicken hawk from generation to generation.* It's not exactly planned, but as Mowrer describes it, older chickens go into a frenzy when a hawklike shadow passes overhead. Their arousal is contagious to the young ones, who then associate this frenzy with the hawklike shadow. The chicks are said to model their fear of chicken hawks after their elders.

- *Candy and cookies are sometimes more effective aids in psychotherapy than couches and university diplomas.* It certainly seemed so with Peter, the two-year-old that the Joneses helped overcome fear of a rabbit by feeding goodies while the rabbit was brought very gradually closer. The joy of eating kept Peter in the situation long enough for fear to be extinguished—or long enough to determine for himself that it was not necessary to fear the rabbit.

- *Some people manage to overcome the most dreaded fears by relaxing in a padded, reclining chair and going on a mind trip.* True, the method called systematic desensitization combines progressive relaxation with gradual *imaginal* approach of phobic objects. It can be a lengthy procedure, but phobic people experience only the slightest discomfort at any given time.

- *People with high test anxiety experience greater bodily alarm reactions than people with low test anxiety.* Not necessarily, according to a recent study by Holroyd and his colleagues, but evidence is conflicting on this issue. But there is solid evidence that people with high test anxiety spend more time in critical self-evaluation and worry in the testing situation, and that they allow their worrying to interfere with their task-mindedness by distracting them. Rational restructuring for test anxiety is aimed at challenging overly critical self-evaluations.

- *The most damaging fear in the Western world today is fear of snakes.* Not so, although there are a great number of experiments in coping with snake phobias. This is largely because so many people are not endeared to our footless friends. Phobias like agoraphobia, acrophobia, and claustrophobia are more damaging, because more people live life-styles in which these fears are actual impairments. We rarely run into snakes crossing metropolitan streets.

NORMATIVE DATA FOR THE SUINN TEST ANXIETY BEHAVIOR SCALE

To attain your total STABS score, assign points to checkmarks in the five columns as follows:

$$
\begin{aligned}
\text{Not at all} &\underline{\quad} 1 \\
\text{A little} &\underline{\quad} 2 \\
\text{A fair amount} &\underline{\quad} 3 \\
\text{Much} &\underline{\quad} 4 \\
\text{Very much} &\underline{\quad} 5
\end{aligned}
$$

You may want to include items on which you scored 4 or 5 in a rational restructuring program (pp. 226–27). Then add all the numbers to arrive at a total score.

Richard Suinn (1969) attained a mean score of 122.00 for a longer, fifty-item version of this questionnaire. This was from a sample of 158 students enrolled in a Colorado state university. If the shorter, twenty-item version of the test had been given, the mean score would probably have been near 49.

We administered the twenty-item questionnaire to a sample of 248 male and female undergraduate students at Northeastern University in 1979. The majority of the sample was white, but there were 28 blacks, 3 Orientals, and 14 Hispanic Americans. Our norms were as follows:

Raw STABS Score	Percentile
68	95
61	80
57	75
52	60
49	50
45	35
41	25
38	20
32	10

9

DEPRESSION, GRIEF, AND SUICIDE

Truth or Fiction?

- HDP is the wrestler's edge.
- Rats that are helpless to terminate a prolonged electric shock develop hormone deficiencies.
- Depressed rats drive their neighbors to drink.
- Depressed people are more likely than nondepressed people to blame themselves for failures and shortcomings—even when they are not at fault.
- During the 1960s, college students all over the United States were struck down by an epidemic of a brand-new neurosis.
- Psychologists have scientifically derived lists of turn-ons that can help you elevate your mood without popping pills.
- Dogs at a University of Pennsylvania laboratory took out permanent moping licenses after being exposed to inescapable electric shock.
- Many churches now hold ceremonies for people undergoing divorce.
- People who threaten suicide are usually just seeking attention. People who actually commit suicide do so without warning.
- Suicide is a sign of insanity.

6-Hydroxydopamine (high-drock-see-DOPE-uh-mean). A chemical substance that appears to be associated with mood.
6-HDP. Our abbreviation for 6-hydroxydopamine.

Depression (dee-PRESH-shun). An emotional state characterized by sadness, lack of enjoyment, social isolation, and a variety of factors that vary with the individual. In this chapter we are primarily concerned with common, mild depression. More severe forms of depression are discussed in Chapter 5 and require professional consultation.

Be of good cheer. In the instructor's manual we urged your professor not to hold you responsible for the spelling of a chemical monster with a name like **6-hydroxydopamine.** Anyhow, this 6-hydroxydo . . . this **6-HDP** stuff was part of some strange goings-on in Gaylord Ellison's psychology lab at UCLA. Within a stone's throw from the movie stars' homes in Bel Air, Sunset Boulevard, and the cliffs of Pacific Palisades, Ellison was having his rats injected with small amounts of 6-HDP for three days in a row. Then nothing would be done for two weeks. Then the rats would receive another series of injections. What was going on was this: Ellison was fixing fights by making these rats *depressed*.

What does **depression** have to do with fight fixing on the West Coast, you wonder? Depression—feeling down, in the pits, in the dumps, in the weeds, at a low ebb—is characterized by indifference and inactivity. A complex and intriguing emotion, it has had poets and scientists looking for the words to describe it for centuries:

> It goes so heavily with my disposition that this goodly frame, the earth, seems to me a sterile promontory.

Hamlet, from the Shakespearean play

> Whenever I find myself growing grim about the mouth, whenever it is a damp, drizzly November in my soul; whenever I find myself involuntarily pausing before coffin warehouses, and bringing up the rear of every funeral I meet; . . . then, I account it high time to get to sea as soon as I can.

Ishmael, from the beginning of Melville's *Moby Dick* (1851)

> I was seized with an unspeakable physical weariness. . . . My nights were sleepless. I lay with dry, staring eyes into space. . . . The most trivial duty became a formidable task. . . . Life seemed utterly futile.

E. C. Reid (1910, pp. 612–613)

> Normally particular about food, he now ate Silvercup bread from the paper package, beans from the can, and American cheese. . . . As for sleep, he slept on a mattress without sheets . . . or in the hammock, covered by his coat. . . . A rat chewed into a package of bread, leaving the shape of its body in the layers of slices. Herzog ate the other half of the loaf spread with jam. He could share with rats too.

From the novel *Herzog*, by Saul Bellow (1961)

Depression is the most common psychological problem we face, the "common cold" of psychological problems, according to psychologist Martin Seligman (1973) of the University of Pennsylvania, yet it often goes unrecognized.

We do not have to call ourselves depressed in order to act depressed. As Hamlet complained, when we are depressed the world looks gray and sterile. Things do not delight us. We seldom laugh or smile. Herman Melville noted Ishmael's grimness, his sullen expression, a growing inner coldness, and a preoccupation with death. E. C. Reid noted a severe disturbance in his sleeping, and endless fatigue. He could not get going. And Saul Bellow poetically painted Herzog's apathy and withdrawal after his wife left him. He cared little about food or sleep. His cozying up to the rat population of his country kitchen was not the expression of an unconscious wish to become a psychologist. It reflected his indifference to his previous standards of sanitation.

Many of the signs of depression are shown in Table 9.1. Depression affects our behavior, bodies, and thoughts as well as our mood.

Table 9.1   Signs of Depression

Mood	Behavioral Deficits	Behavioral Excesses	Physical Signs	Attitudes
Feelings dominated by sadness and blueness	Minimal social participation—"I do not like being with people."	Complaints about: Material problems —money, job, housing	Headaches	Low self-evaluation, feelings of failure, inadequacy, helplessness, and powerlessness
Loss of gratification— "I no longer enjoy the things I used to."	Sits alone quietly, stays in bed much of time, does not communicate with others, does not enter into activities with others	Material loss— money, property The demands of others Noise Memory, inability to concentrate, confusion	Sleep disturbances: restless sleep, waking during night, complete wakefulness, early morning awakening	Negative expectation—"Things will always be bad for me."
Professes to have little or no feeling			Fatigue—"I get tired for no reason."	
Feels constantly fatigued—"Everything is an effort."	Inability to do ordinary work	Lack of affection from others— "No one cares about me."	Gastrointestinal indigestion, constipation, weight loss	Self-blame and self-criticism—"People would despise me if they knew me."
Loss of interest in food, drink, sex, etc.	Decreased sexual activity	Being lonely	Dizzy spells	Suicidal thoughts— "I wish I were dead." "I want to kill myself."
Feelings of apathy and boredom	Slowed speech and gait; monotone speech	Expresses feelings of guilt and concern about: Making up wrongs to others	Tachycardia	
	Does not attend to grooming; neglect of personal appearance	Suffering caused to others Not assuming responsibilities	Chest sensations Generalized pain Urinary disturbances	
	Lack of joy, humor, delight	Welfare of family and friends Indecisiveness— "I can't make up my mind anymore."		
		Crying, weepy, screaming		
		Suicidal behavior— gestures, attempts		

Source: Adapted from P. M. Lewinsohn, Table 1 (p. 23) in M. Hersen, R. M. Eisler, & P. M. Miller (Eds.), *Progress in Behavior Modification*, vol. 1. New York: Academic Press, 1975.

In this chapter we discuss feelings of depression that affect many of us in our day-to-day living. Manic-depression and psychotic depression were discussed in Chapter 5, and these disorders respond best to professional attention. They are recognized by their extremes of despair, extremes of behavior deficiencies (such as almost total inability to "get going"), and behavioral excesses (such as incessant crying and screeching). But these problems are relatively rare. Here we discuss the mild, garden variety sort of depression that is associated most often with stressful events and self-defeating attitudes.

First we explore differing views concerning the origins of such depression, including the roles of prolonged stress, unpleasant events, norepinephrine, reinforcement, learned helplessness, excessive self-blame and other self-defeating attitudes, and loss of meaningfulness in life. Then we explore a number of ways to meet the challenge of depression. We discuss grief, the normal response to a serious loss, and the stages that we typically go through in recovering from losses. Finally we discuss suicide. We place suicide in this chapter because most suicides have been related to depression, but suicides occur for other reasons that we also explore. Suicide is not a cheerful topic, but it is extremely important and must be discussed.

ORIGINS OF DEPRESSION

Humor (YOU-more). A fluid, in the old use of the word.

Melancholia (mell-ann-COAL-ya). An older word for depression, stemming from Greek words meaning "black bile."

Humor is not always funny. Hippocrates, the physician of Greece's Golden Age, believed that many physical and emotional problems were related to imbalances in the body's **humors** or liquids. Depression, he taught, derived from an excess of black bile, a fluid involved in the digestive processes. In fact, another name for depression is **melancholia.** *Melan* is Greek for black, *choler* means bile.

Prolonged stress, losses, feelings of helplessness, self-criticism, loss of purpose and meaningfulness, and, yes, chemical changes in the body—all are capable of bringing on feelings of depression. Once initiated, hormone imbalances and what we tell ourselves about ourselves—our self-defeating expectations—can propel us into a vicious cycle that maintains depression.

"I'm Exhausted!": Depression and Prolonged Stress

"I can't get started." "I just can't seem to get going." "I can't get up for anything these days." Too many times we hear depressed people complaining of being constantly tired, of being drained of energy.

How does a rat that has been swimming for eighty hours finally feel when it lets go and sinks to the bottom of the tub? How does a student who has been unsuccessful in premedical or prelegal studies feel after four long, hard years? Probably as though they are stuck forever in the exhaustion stage of the **general adaptation syndrome** (GAS).

General adaptation syndrome. Hans Selye's term for the stages an organism undergoes in reacting to stress. (See Chapter 6.)

Prolonged stress leads to parasympathetic dominance of the ANS, propelling us into a state of exhaustion, in which heart rate and respiration rate slow down. If the stressor is removed, parasympathetic functioning can help us return to a state of relative calmness, with feelings of relaxation and security. But if the stressor persists, we can sort of "overshoot" this state of calmness and enter the exhaustion stage of the GAS. The psychological counterparts of exhaustion are depression and withdrawal.

The Challenges of Stress, Fear, and Depression

Figure 9.1 The Incredible Balancing Act of the ANS

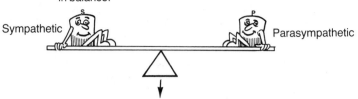

9.1a *No Stress*: Sympathetic and parasympathetic divisions in balance.

Sympathetic   Parasympathetic

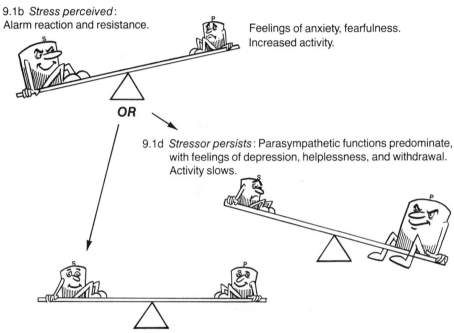

9.1b *Stress perceived*:
Alarm reaction and resistance.

Feelings of anxiety, fearfulness.
Increased activity.

OR

9.1d *Stressor persists*: Parasympathetic functions predominate, with feelings of depression, helplessness, and withdrawal. Activity slows.

9.1c *Stressor is removed*: ANS balance is restored, with feelings of relaxation and security.

When we experience stress, the sympathetic division of the autonomic nervous system (ANS) is activated (1b). Sympathetic activity predominates as we undergo alarm reactions, and, if necessary, resistance. If the stressor is removed, we return to a state of relative calmness (1c), with the sympathetic and parasympathetic divisions of the ANS in balance once more. But if the stressor persists (1d), the parasympathetic division of the ANS predominates, and we become exhausted and, perhaps, depressed.

Depression and Unpleasant Events

The type of stressful experience to which you are exposed may also influence your mood. Psychologist Peter Lewinsohn of the University of Oregon and a colleague (Lewinsohn & Amenson 1978) distributed a checklist of 320 unpleasant events to depressed and nondepressed individuals, and found five factors or groupings of items that were significantly associated with a depressive mood: marital discord, physical discomfort, incompetence, work failure, and work pressure. Items or events that constituted these factors are shown in Table 9.2.

Don't assume that you will be free of a major contributor to depression if you are unmarried. You don't have to have a license to earn the disapproval of

Depression, Grief,
and Suicide

Table 9.2   Unpleasant Events Related to Depression

FACTOR I: Marital discord	Having my spouse dissatisfied with me
	Realizing that someone I love and I are growing apart
	Arguments with spouse
	Being dissatisfied with my spouse
FACTOR II: Physical discomfort	Being physically uncomfortable
	Having a minor illness or injury
	Eating food I don't enjoy
	Bad weather
FACTOR III: Incompetence	Doing a job poorly
	Realizing I can't do something I thought I could
	Having something break or run poorly
FACTOR IV: Work failure	Leaving a task uncompleted, procrastinating
	Having a project or assignment overdue
	Failing at something
FACTOR V: Work pressure	Having too much to do
	Having someone evaluate or criticize me
	Working under pressure

Source: Lewinsohn & Amenson (1978).

someone you care about or to be in the company of unpleasant people. And, as you may recall from Chapter 3, married people, as a group, report greater happiness than unmarried individuals.

Depression and Norepinephrine

Dr. Trueheart Herman, the biochemistry professor, was renowned for his uncanny ability to fill blackboard after blackboard with illegible designs. Just before he was involuntarily relieved of duty, he was seized by a penetrating realization. "Think of it!" he implored his snickering classes. "If we neutralized the **norepinephrine** in your brains, we could create a fearless army! More: fearless basketball players!"

Happily, Herman didn't have the opportunity to neutralize the norepinephrine in anyone's brains. Norepinephrine, you see, is a hormone that works as a **neurotransmitter**—that is, it helps send messages in the brain. In fact, it is needed to help send messages in the brain that lead to sympathetic arousal, as during an alarm reaction to stress. No message, no alarm reaction. No norepinephrine, no message, and no fear. And now, sadly, no Herman—till he recovers. But you can sort of see where he was coming from.

Actually, Herman was probably only partially correct, anyhow. Low norepinephrine levels may decrease sympathetic arousal, but they also seem to permit parasympathetic dominance and thus, perhaps, lead to feelings of depression. Depressed people are probably pretty useless in armies and on basketball courts.

Gaylord Ellison of UCLA suggests that people who are exposed to prolonged stress, and helpless to do anything about it, may actually develop deficiencies of norepinephrine (1977). He refers to experiments with (you guessed it!) rats who are exposed to electric shock. Rats who are exposed to prolonged shock and who are helpless to do anything about it develop deficient levels of norepinephrine in the brain, but rats who can act to terminate the shock do

Norepinephrine (nor-epp-pee-NEFF-rin). A hormone that acts as a neurotransmitter.

Neurotransmitter (new-row-trans-MITT-ter). A substance that facilitates the process of communicating between brain cells.

The Challenges of Stress, Fear, and Depression

236

"ELLISON'S RATS FLAT ON MATS"

They didn't sell popcorn. They didn't sell beer. Hatpin Hannah, ever ready pointedly to display her disaffection for the bad guy, was not at ringside. But there in the straw-floored arena, Gaylord Ellison's (1977) rats held match after match to determine who was the greatest wrestler of all—*numero uno*. Such is the way of rats.

Ellison and his assistants referred to these matches as "'puppy-dog fights." One after another, rats in his experimental colonies would wrestle for dominance. First a pair of rats would "stand and box." Then they would wrestle on the straw floor of the colony, until one rat would pin the other to the ground. The winner was the "top dog." The loser, "bottom dog."

This may all sound normal and healthy, but we have to tell you that these fights were *fixed*. Ellison had injected some of the animals with 6-hydroxy-dopamine, a chemical that depleted the norepineph-rine available to their brains. Results? The 6-HDP-injected rats lost every contest. They also showed kinds of behavior that are characteristic of *depression* in people. They seemed to be apathetic and withdrawn. They lay around in their burrows. Their appetites diminished and they lost weight.

Somehow, these rats were also socially disruptive. In one of Ellison's rat colonies, the animals were raised with free access to water and to alcohol solutions. Here the norepinephrine-depleted rats showed less interest in the alcohol, but they managed to drive their colony mates to drink three times their normal amount! It may not be much easier for humans to spend their time with depressed people. We often allow others to express feelings of rejection, guilt, apathy, and sadness for a while—then we begin to avoid them (Coyne 1976).

not (Weiss et al. 1974). Thus people and rats who have prolonged problems may find themselves doubly handicapped: norepinephrine deficiency may make it harder for them to bounce back. In fact, some drugs that have been developed to help people cope with severe depression appear to act by increasing the available amount of norepinephrine in the brain.

Where Have All the Reinforcers Gone?—Social Learning Factors

The troublemaker in the grammar-school class may sit quietly when he is all by himself. The weight lifters and belly flatteners who parade up and down the beach all afternoon may lie quietly on their blankets and let their bellies plop out when no one else is around. Social learning theorists, like psychoanalysts, point to a relationship between depression and dependence. But social learning theorists do not talk about intrapsychic conflict. Instead, they note that we often depend on other people for reinforcements, and begin to act depressed when the usual level of reinforcement drops off.

Psychologist Charles Ferster (1973) of American University suggests that

Depression, Grief, and Suicide

when we lose people who are close to us, we also lose major sources of social reinforcement. Other people, you see, respond to us when we do and say things. Learning theorists believe that this kind of social responding is as meaningful to human beings as food pellets are to rats and pigeons. We depend on it. When someone close to us dies or leaves, we slow down in our behavior. Slowing down can lead to a vicious cycle: we become less likely to do things that will meet with social response or reinforcement from others.

Peter Lewinsohn adds that depression is compounded by lack of skills (1975). If we do not have the skills it takes to make the environment cough up the reinforcements we need, we are in a plight similar to animals in laboratory boxes who can't find the key to obtaining food pellets. Lewinsohn ties depression to a low rate of behavior that is capable of being reinforced. But depression can lead to alternate reinforcements that are desirable at first, but eventually may serve actually to maintain depression—the supportive interest and sympathy of family and friends. In fact, sometimes the flow of sympathy must end before a depressed individual will become motivated to develop skillful behavior.

Sitting Still for Quite a Shock: Learned Helplessness

Normally, a dog will not sit still for some things, especially for electric shock. If you were to place a dog in a cage with two compartments, and then shock it while it was sitting in one of them, it would be right up and scampering around. If it were safe from shock in the other compartment, you can bet it would make a living by sitting there from then on. This is simple avoidance learning.

Martin Seligman (1975) ran an experiment to see if he could teach dogs that they could *not* escape from electric shock, even when the royal road to the safe compartment was staring them in the face. He simply set up a barrier between the compartments while the dogs received shock. After a few repetitions the barrier was removed. Did the dogs test out the safe compartment the next time they were shocked? No, they sat still for it. Seligman suggests that the dogs learned to be helpless, when in fact they were perfectly capable of reaching safety by themselves.

Their **learned helplessness** led the dogs to show behavior that was reminiscent of depression in people: lack of movement, loss of appetite and weight, and a decrease in the norepinephrine available to the brain. Seligman's work suggests the existence of a particularly cruel vicious cycle that may operate with many depressed people. A few failures, perhaps unavoidable, may lead to feelings of helplessness and the continued expectation of failure. This negative expectation makes continued striving appear futile. Perhaps you know people who have had failure experiences with mathematics. They may come to believe that they were "born without math neurons." Consequently they may feel studying for the quantitative section of the Graduate Record Exam would be useless. Then they may do poorly, confirming their expectation.

"It's All My Fault": Attribution of Failure

What do you tell yourself when you have a date that doesn't work out? That these things happen, that life involves trial and error, that the next time you go out things may work out better? Or that you loused it up, that you'll never change, so you may as well quit before you screw things up again?

Learned helplessness. Martin Seligman's term for feelings of inability to adjust that are acquired through experience.

This football player has done poorly on the last play. Now he is rehashing it. If he tells himself he's just no good and there's nothing he can do, he may be of little use the next time he's on the field. But if he believes his failure was the type of error anyone can make and that he can correct his performance, he may do better on his next opportunity.

Attribution (at-trib-YOU-shun). Assignment; thinking of as belonging to or being produced by.
Internal attribution. Assuming the self to be responsible for outcomes. Adjustive when accurate, but maladjustive when inaccurate.
External attribution. Assuming factors outside the self to be responsible for outcomes.
Stable attribution. An unchangeable attribution.
Unstable attribution. A changeable attribution.
Global attribution. An attribution that assumes an outcome is determined by broad factors, such as one's "basic personality structure" or "the way people or the world are."
Specific attribution. Seeing an outcome as determined by a narrow factor, such as one mistake.

Depression, Grief, and Suicide

Seligman and his colleagues (Abramson et al. 1978; Seligman et al. 1979) note that some people tend to maintain depressive moods by **attributing** their shortcomings to causes that would be practically impossible to change. They point out that the reasons for something going wrong may be thought of as **internal** or **external, stable** or **unstable, global** or **specific.** For instance, when your date does not work out, you may attribute the failure to internal causes ("I loused it up") or to external causes, things outside yourself: "Some couples just don't take to each other," or "If the weather had been better, we could have

Table 9.3   Why I Smashed Up the Car: Attributions of Blame

Attribution Type	Samples
Internal	"It's my lousy driving." "I was careless."
External	"You can't see straight in this smog." "The other car was coming at me like a bat out of hell."
Stable	"They just don't build cars safe anymore." "These roads are poorly marked."
Unstable	"I was pretty tired." "The brakes just happened to fail."
Global	"People are just no damned good." "I'm a horrible person."
Specific	"I should have been more careful at that intersection; it's pretty poorly marked." "This type of car has a poor safety record."

had a better time." Depressed people, unfortunately, are more likely to attribute blame to internal causes—themselves—even when they are actually not at fault (Rizley 1978). Self-blame lowers self-esteem. External attribution helps maintain self-esteem. In fact, people may be motivated to find external causes even when they are at fault ("I only did it because they had it coming to them"); this is rationalization.

Table 9.3 shows some of the attributions you might make about involvement in an automobile accident. Note that internal, stable, and global attributions are most depressing: you blame yourself, even unfairly, and doubt that you will ever change since the fault is so all-pervasive (global). There are two attributions in Table 9.3 that are guaranteed to make you miserable by combining internal, stable, and global causes. Can you find them?

Minimizing and Catastrophizing

Minimizing. A cognitive error in which an event is interpreted as being less important than it actually is or having less significance or impact than it actually has.

Aaron Beck (1976) notes that depressed people make certain cognitive or judgmental errors, such as **minimizing** accomplishments. If a depressed individual should happen to study hard and do very well on an exam, you may not be terribly surprised to hear, "Oh, it's nothing," or "It turned out to be an easy test," or even, "So what difference is it going to make? We'll all be dead in another hundred years anyhow."

Depressed people are also highly sensitive to stress and tend to catastrophize unfortunate events, to blow them out of proportion: "Oh my god, this shirt isn't clean. What am I going to do?" or "How can I go to the concert? I have to get the car inspected before next week."

Few things in life exceed our incredible capacity to make ourselves miserable.

"Where Was I Going?" A Humanist-Existential View

During the 1960s an epidemic swept colleges and universities across the United States. It afflicted students on the West Coast and in the Northeast; no region escaped. Yet this epidemic was largely unrecognized until a report by Hirsch and Keniston (1970) focused on a mild but lingering depression that was dog-

During the 1960s an epidemic of "existential neurosis" swept the college campuses. Many students experienced a crisis in their values and lost their sense of direction.

ging a group of thirty-one men who had dropped out of Yale. These were not academic dropouts. They had proved that they could do the work. Nevertheless, they had lost interest in their classes. They felt they were just going through the motions. This apathy eventually extended to extracurricular activities and their social lives.

This was, indeed, a mystery. The dropouts had not suffered visible losses. They had not been exposed to unusual stresses. The strange clue that rose to the surface in case after case was loss of respect for their fathers—a model whom they had once wished to emulate. For many different reasons, these students who had once idolized their fathers came to feel that their fathers' values could no longer serve as their own. For some, money and the club were no longer relevant. For others, middle-class security was a bore. The dropouts felt cast adrift on gray and meaningless waters. The problem they shared was loss of the vision of what they were to become. Their identities, their sense of self had been shaken. Striving behavior becomes meaningless when our goals dissolve into the background.

Depression, Grief, and Suicide

241

Existential Neurosis. Confused, uncertain, attempting to reintegrate their lives when former values and plans had failed them, these dropouts were depressed and uneasy. They appeared to be experiencing what psychologist Salvatore Maddi of the University of Chicago labeled an **existential neurosis** (1967). Their crisis in the maintenance of their personal identities had made the academic and social competition at Yale meaningless. A struggle without purpose is an empty struggle.

Many other students during the 1960s and early 1970s coped with crises in personal identity by experimenting with alternate life-styles. Some expressed their distaste for the secure middle-class job by joining **communes,** farming, and pouring their creative energies into arts and crafts. Some sought meaning through religious movements that had their origins in the Far East. Others came to terms with apathy and **ennui** by vigorously protesting American involvement in Southeast Asia and racism at home. Still others sought to dull their reactions to mainstream pressures by joining the drug subculture.

Many of the students who joined communes or who experimented with other alternative life-styles during the late 1960s and the 1970s have now adopted mainstream life-styles of one sort or another. A handful have become wealthy by writing popular books about their experiences. Some remain ensnared in the grip of their personal identity crises. They have still not arrived at a commitment to a cohesive set of personal beliefs and actions.

The sources of depression are thus varied, yet once we feel depressed we may find ourselves in vicious cycles in which self-defeating attitudes maintain feelings of helplessness and prolong stress, and vice versa. Now let's turn our attention to breaking free from such vicious cycles.

MEETING THE CHALLENGE OF DEPRESSION

Herman Melville, the great American novelist, used Ishmael to tell the tale of Captain Ahab's relentless pursuit of the great white whale by the name of Moby Dick. When Melville published *Moby Dick*, in 1851, whales were not in danger of extinction. These august mammals dominated the oceans.

Ishmael went to sea "whenever I find myself growing grim about the mouth, whenever it is a damp, drizzly November in my soul; . . ." When he felt depressed, Ishmael took charge of his life and changed his environment. He placed himself aboard ship, where a myriad of chores must be carried out, where he could not allow his moods to isolate him from his shipmates. No retreat from action was possible on a whaling vessel. Ishmael engaged his world head on.

In *Moby Dick*, the sea symbolizes the universe—abundant yet deadly, a constant source of pleasure and danger, beauty and bleak desolation. The contrasts within the sea also symbolize the conflicts within the characters. Ishmael was witness to the unfolding of an existential drama fueled by Captain Ahab's obsession to kill the great white whale. Ahab was a confused man attempting to come to grips with the forces of good and evil inside him. What kept him and Ishmael vital and alive was the active pursuit. Their assertion of the self in an infinite and noncaring universe fended off the pangs of self-doubt and depression.

To meet the challenge of depression, we, too, must choose action over inaction. When we come face to face with that "damp, drizzly November" within us, it is up to us to make the decision to do something about it. When we

---

Existential neurosis (eggs-sis-TEN-shull new-ROW-sis). Salvatore Maddi's term for an adjustment problem characterized by experiencing one's life to be without meaning or purpose.
Commune (KOM-yoon). A group-owned and operated farm, or other commonly shared means of production.
Ennui (en-WE). Fatigue and dissatisfaction that stems from inactivity, boredom, or lack of interest.

In *Moby Dick,* Ishmael took charge of his life and changed his environment by going to sea in order to meet the challenge of depression.

feel least like action, as is so often true when we are depressed, we can choose action. We can learn to recognize depression and take the very apathy within us as our cue to do new things—to reengage ourselves in the struggle for self. It seems a great gamble, yet by meeting the challenge head on, by taking on the struggle we find the potential for meaningful experience and personal growth.

It is never easy to cope with depression, but contemporary psychology has taught us more about the workings of depression than we have ever known. We can recognize it for what it is, analyze it piece by piece, come to understand the attitudes and attributions that help maintain it, and construct personalized plans to overcome it.

Coping with Prolonged Stress

There is no way around it. We usually know what produces prolonged stress in our lives. It is up to us to take charge of environments to remove these sources of stress.

That doesn't mean it's easy. Prolonged stresses may involve unrewarding academic careers, ungratifying jobs, or unhappy interpersonal relationships. We often try to avoid coping with them because they place us in severe avoidance-avoidance conflicts. Changing careers may mean financial sacrifice and insecurity. Ending nonworking relationships may injure innocent people. Try using the balance sheet (Chapter 7) to add up the pluses and minuses. If that is not enough, it may be time to talk things over with a helping professional.

Coping with Inactivity and Low Mood

Believe it or not, some people act as though they must remain faithful to depression. Becky's romance had recently disintegrated, and she was at a low ebb, weepy and withdrawn. Finally two friends prevailed on her to go to a rock concert with them despite her protestations. It took her a while to focus on the music and the excitement of the crowd, but eventually Becky was clapping and shouting along with her friends. Depressive feelings did not return until the following morning. Did Becky focus on the fact that she had found several hours of enjoyment? If she had, we would need another example. She told herself, instead, "Well, what could I expect? I was really depressed *underneath it all*." With that attitude, she set out to remain faithful to her depression for several more days.

We're not unsympathetic. Becky had a right to feel sad that her relationship with her boyfriend had come to an end. This is an appropriate reaction. Becky's feelings were real and authentic. But Becky's assumption that the *only* feelings to which she was entitled were sad feelings acted to maintain her depression. The rock concert, for Becky, was **incompatible** with depression. It was practically impossible for her to listen to that new group, "The Naked and the Dead," and remain miserable.

Incompatible (in-come-PAT-uh-bull). Inconsistent, counteracting.

Table 9.4 Activities Linked with Positive Mood in the Lewinsohn and Graf Study

ACTIVITIES PRODUCING INCOMPATIBLE AFFECT

Thinking about something good in the future
Breathing clean air
Sitting in the sun
Listening to music
Watching wild animals
Being relaxed
Seeing beautiful scenery
Wearing clean clothes

SOCIAL INTERACTIONS

Being with happy people
Being with friends
Having a frank and open conversation
Smiling at people
Expressing my love to someone
Having coffee, tea, a Coke, etc., with friends
Having a lively talk
Kissing
Watching people
Having sexual relations with a partner of the opposite sex
Being told I am loved
Complimenting or praising someone
Meeting someone new of the same sex

EGO-SUPPORTIVE ACTIVITIES OR EVENTS

Doing a project in my own way
Planning or organizing something
Planning trips or vacations
Doing a job well
Reading stories, novels, poems, or plays
Learning to do something new

Peter Lewinsohn (Lewinsohn & Graf 1973; Lewinsohn & Libet 1972) and Lynn Rehm (1978) have undertaken research with both depressed and nondepressed people and found that there is a significant relationship between your mood and the number and types of pleasant events you get involved in. Participants in the Lewinsohn studies were given 320-item versions of the Pleasant Events Schedule shown on pages 248–49. They checked the activities that they would personally find most appealing, and were then each given personalized lists of 160 pleasant events from the 320. At the end of each day, for thirty consecutive days, participants checked the pleasant activities they had engaged in. They were also provided with checklists measuring the extent of depression through many of the signs in Table 9.1, and filled these out daily at about the same time they filled out the Pleasant Events Schedule. Both lists were mailed into the researchers daily.

Substantial relationships were found between mood and pleasant activities engaged in for both studies. Lewinsohn and Graf (1973) found some forty-nine items that contributed to a positive mood in at least 10 percent of the participants. Several of these are listed in Table 9.4. The authors categorize them into three groups: **incompatible affect,** that is, activities that counteract depression by producing incompatible emotional responses; social interactions; and ego-supportive activities or events. We're all different, so don't get the idea that you're somehow lacking if many of these would not work for you. Remember: they may have been effective for only 10 percent of the Lewinsohn and Graf sample.

Incompatible affect (AFF-feckt). A mood that counteracts another mood.

Using Pleasant Events to Lift Your Mood

You don't have to be depressed to use the Pleasant Events Schedule shown on pages 248–49 to enrich the quality of your own life. Just use the following steps:

- Read the Pleasant Events Schedule.
- Select three pleasant events to engage in each day. This is a minimum —not an upper limit.
- Keep a diary and record the pleasant events you engaged in. Add other pleasant experiences that were not preplanned.
- At about the same time toward the end of each day, rate how each event or activity made you feel according to this scale:

> + 3 incredibly super
> + 2 very nice indeed
> + 1 slightly good
>   0 blah, nothing, zilchville, a big zero
> − 1 slightly down
> − 2 pretty poor
> − 3 the pits!

Jot down the rating in your diary.

- At the end of a week, check through your diary for events that received positive—especially very nice and super—ratings.
- For the next week repeat some of the highly successful activities, experiment with a few new ones, and continue to record your reactions.

**Pleasant events
are incompatible
with depression.**

- At the end of the second week, buy yourself some sort of reward. Not too expensive since we're avoiding the excessive-guilt trip.
- You're on your own now with a solid list of activities that you have learned to enjoy regularly.

Achieving Competence

The way to eat an elephant is one bite at a time.

Beverly Johnson on the *NBC Nightly News*, October 27, 1978, the first woman to scale the face of the vertical rock known as El Capitan in Yosemite Park. It took five days.

People do not often attend to the thought processes of dogs, which is a shame. It could certainly simplify housebreaking. Perhaps one of the problems is that dogs do not necessarily think in the languages spoken by their owners. Nevertheless, let's return to Martin Seligman's laboratory at the University of Pennsylvania and have a listen to the thoughts of one of his dogs who has learned to be helpless in the face of electric shock.

Several times the dog has received painful shock and has not been able to escape the experimental compartment. Now the barrier between this compartment and a safe compartment is lifted, and the dog is shocked again. *Thoughts of the dog who has learned to be helpless:* "Ah, what I won't do for the sake of psychological research! There it goes again, markedly unpleasant. What to do? What to do? I have scurried all about this compartment and found my efforts to escape to be futile. Now one wall seems to have vanished, but there is little point to seeing if safety lies in that direction. I'm just a flop, a no-good mangy cur. I'm powerless, helpless, all my past efforts have been in vain. It must be me. Nothing will ever change. I may just resign myself to the facts and seek my permanent moping license."

Perhaps some of you are skeptical and feel that such a line of thought is a bit too formal or stilted for a dog. If you insist on this point, we shall let you win and simply say that the dogs in the Seligman study sort of behaved *as if* their views of the situation might be something like this. Anything to satisfy a scientific purist. But perhaps we can all agree that our furry friend might have been a bit more effective if it had thought along these lines:

"Good grief, shocked again. Science is science, but perhaps I should go on strike. Is there a point to trying to escape again? My past efforts have been futile. True enough, but times change and nothing will be gained by just sitting here and pretending nothing is happening. Perhaps if I carefully scrutinize my environment, I'll be able to find a way out this time. Hmm, that area of the cage seems to have changed, as if a wall had been removed. Is it possible that I shall escape this silliness by scrambling over there? I do believe I'll give it a try. Geronimo!"

Of course the dogs did have the capacity to escape the electric shock once the barrier to the safe compartment was removed. But their recent experience of finding their endeavors to be futile led to failure to continue to struggle. In the same way, people who find themselves in painfully depressing situations often have the capacity to struggle successfully to improve their lives, but do not make the effort because past attempts have been futile. In such situations, it may be productive to:

- Stop assuming that all future efforts will be futile just because past efforts have not been successful.
- Adopt reasonable goals that are consistent with your abilities and your psychological needs.
- Carefully specify the skills or behaviors that are necessary to meet your goals.
- Carefully assess your current level of skillfulness, using a testing and counseling center, if necessary.
- Plan a program to build your skills toward your goals, step by step.
- Reward yourself for successful small steps in building skills. Remember that building skills takes time. You cannot become a skilled carpenter, baseball player, editor, mathematician, date seeker, or job applicant overnight.

Depression, Grief, and Suicide

247

THE PLEASANT EVENTS SCHEDULE

What turns you on? Here is a list of 114 activities and events enjoyed by many people. Rate them according to how pleasant you think you would find them by using the scale given below. Then you may want to enrich the quality of your daily life by making sure to fit in some of them.

2 very pleasant
1 pleasant
0 not pleasant

___ 1. Being in the country
___ 2. Wearing expensive or formal clothes
___ 3. Making contributions to religious, charitable, or political groups.
___ 4. Talking about sports
___ 5. Meeting someone new
___ 6. Going to a rock concert
___ 7. Playing baseball, softball, football, or basketball
___ 8. Planning trips or vacations
___ 9. Buying things for yourself
___ 10. Being at the beach
___ 11. Doing art work (painting, sculpture, drawing, moviemaking, etc.)
___ 12. Rock climbing or mountaineering
___ 13. Reading the Scriptures
___ 14. Playing golf
___ 15. Rearranging or redecorating your room or house
___ 16. Going naked
___ 17. Going to a sports event
___ 18. Going to the races
___ 19. Reading stories, novels, poems, plays, magazines, newspapers
___ 20. Going to a bar, tavern, club
___ 21. Going to lectures or talks
___ 22. Creating or arranging songs or music
___ 23. Boating

___ 24. Restoring antiques, refinishing furniture
___ 25. Watching TV or listening to the radio
___ 26. Camping
___ 27. Working in politics
___ 28. Working on machines (cars, bikes, radios, TVs)
___ 29. Playing cards or board games
___ 30. Doing puzzles or math games
___ 31. Having lunch with friends or associates
___ 32. Playing tennis
___ 33. Driving long distances
___ 34. Woodworking, carpentry
___ 35. Writing stories, novels, poems, plays, articles
___ 36. Being with animals
___ 37. Riding in an airplane
___ 38. Exploring (hiking away from known routes, spelunking, etc.)
___ 39. Singing
___ 40. Going to a party
___ 41. Going to church functions
___ 42. Playing a musical instrument
___ 43. Snow skiing, ice skating
___ 44. Wearing informal clothes, "dressing down"
___ 45. Acting
___ 46. Being in the city, downtown
___ 47. Taking a long, hot bath
___ 48. Playing pool or billiards

Challenging Mental Downers: Bad Self-Talk

Public opinion is a weak tyrant compared with our own private opinion. What a man thinks of himself, that it is which determines, or rather indicates his fate.

Thoreau, *Walden*

Stop having it in for yourself. Learn to recognize and challenge the attitudes that often stand in the way of people who might otherwise overcome feelings of helplessness and develop their instrumental and social skills.

___ 49. Bowling	___ 84. Meditating or doing yoga
___ 50. Watching wild animals	___ 85. Doing heavy outdoor work
___ 51. Gardening, landscaping	___ 86. Snowmobiling, dune buggying
___ 52. Wearing new clothes	___ 87. Being in a body-awareness, encounter, or "rap" group
___ 53. Dancing	
___ 54. Sitting or lying in the sun	___ 88. Swimming
___ 55. Riding a motorcycle	___ 89. Running, jogging
___ 56. Just sitting and thinking	___ 90. Walking barefoot
___ 57. Going to a fair, carnival, circus, zoo, amusement park	___ 91. Playing Frisbee or catch
	___ 92. Doing housework or laundry, cleaning things
___ 58. Talking about philosophy or religion	
___ 59. Gambling	___ 93. Listening to music
___ 60. Listening to sounds of nature	___ 94. Knitting, crocheting
___ 61. Dating, courting	___ 95. Making love
___ 62. Having friends come to visit	___ 96. Petting, necking
___ 63. Going out to visit friends	___ 97. Going to a barber or beautician
___ 64. Giving gifts	___ 98. Being with someone you love
___ 65. Getting massages or backrubs	___ 99. Going to the library
___ 66. Photography	___ 100. Shopping
___ 67. Collecting stamps, coins, rocks, etc.	___ 101. Preparing a new or special dish
___ 68. Seeing beautiful scenery	___ 102. Watching people
___ 69. Eating good meals	___ 103. Bicycling
___ 70. Improving your health (having teeth fixed, changing diet, having a checkup, etc.)	___ 104. Writing letters, cards, or notes
	___ 105. Talking about politics or public affairs
___ 71. Wrestling or boxing	___ 106. Watching attractive women or men
___ 72. Fishing	___ 107. Caring for houseplants
___ 73. Going to a health club, sauna	___ 108. Having coffee, tea, or Coke, etc., with friends
___ 74. Horseback riding	
___ 75. Protesting social, political, or environmental conditions	___ 109. Beachcombing
	___ 110. Going to auctions, garage sales, etc.
___ 76. Going to the movies	___ 111. Water skiing, surfing, diving
___ 77. Cooking meals	___ 112. Traveling
___ 78. Washing your hair	___ 113. Attending the opera, ballet, or a play
___ 79. Going to a restaurant	___ 114. Looking at the stars or the moon
___ 80. Using cologne, perfume	
___ 81. Getting up early in the morning	
___ 82. Writing in a diary	
___ 83. Giving massages or backrubs	

Source: Adapted from MacPhillamy, D. J., & Lewinsohn, P. M. *Pleasant Events Schedule, Form III-S.* University of Oregon, Mimeograph, 1971.

Table 9.5 illustrates several self-defeating thoughts or attitudes. They exemplify several errors in thinking that may serve to depress us: *catastrophizing* problems, *minimizing* accomplishments, overly *internalizing* blame, *stabilizing* problems, and *globalizing* problems. Adjustive alternatives are provided for each self-defeating thought.

You can come to grips with your own self-defeating thoughts by writing them down as they occur in a diary. If you can't pick up on them at first, become sensistive to mood changes. Learn to pay attention to fleeting self-defeating thoughts that so often trigger these changes. Challenge the accuracy of these thoughts. It is possible that you characterize difficult situations as impossible and hopeless? Do you expect too much from yourself? Do you internalize too much

Depression, Grief, and Suicide

Table 9.5 Self-Defeating Thoughts and Adjustive Alternatives

Thought	Types	Adjustive Alternative
1. There's nothing I can do.	Catastrophizing, minimizing, stabilizing	"I can't think of anything to do right now, but if I work at it I may."
2. I'm no good.	Internalizing, globalizing, stabilizing	"I did something I regret, but that doesn't make me evil or less valuable."
3. This is absolutely awful!	Catastrophizing	"This is pretty bad, but it's not the end of the world."
4. I just don't have the brains for college.	Stabilizing, globalizing, catastrophizing	"I guess I really need to go back over the basics in that course."
5. I just can't believe I did something so disgusting!	Catastrophizing	"That was a bad experience. Well, I won't be likely to try that again."
6. I can't imagine ever feeling right again.	Stabilizing, catastrophizing	"This is painful, but if I try to work it through step by step, I'll probably eventually see my way through it."
7. It's all my fault.	Internalizing	"I'm not blameless, but I wasn't the only one involved."
8. I can't do anything right.	Globalizing, stabilizing, catastrophizing, minimizing	"I sure goofed this up, but I've done a lot of things well."
9. I hurt everybody who gets close to me.	Internalizing, globalizing, stabilizing	"I'm not totally blameless, but I'm not responsible for the whole world. Adults can be responsible for themselves."
10. If people knew the real me, they would hate me.	Globalizing, minimizing the positive	"I'm not perfect, but nobody's perfect. I have positive features as well as negative features. Most people do."

blame for shortcomings and failures? Write down accurate, adjustive alternatives for these self-defeating thoughts. Review the diary at your leisure; increase your awareness of your self-defeating thoughts and your more accurate alternatives. When you are alone, you may want to repeat adjustive alternatives aloud firmly. This will increase the probability that your automatic thought patterns will change.

GRIEF

Sometimes it is appropriate to be miserable. When a loved one dies, intense **grief** is expected and fitting.

When a spouse dies, there is likely to be an interplay of many feelings: agitation, anger, guilt, depression (Parkes 1972). It is common to feel that you might have been able to do something to prevent the death if you had been more alert, more caring, more forceful, or more intelligent. It is common to be obsessed with vivid images of the deceased. If death followed an illness or

Grief. Intense feelings of suffering and depression brought about by a loss.

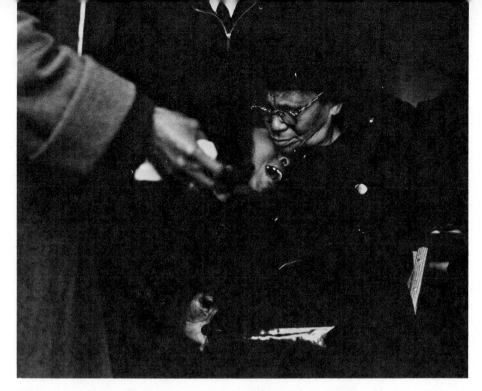

When a loved one dies, intense grief is expected and fitting.

occurred in a hospital, it is common to feel that the doctors might have made some error or been negligent, even if all possible care was given. We would expect you to cry, to lose your appetite, to have difficulty sleeping. If you use tobacco or alcohol, you may at least temporarily use more than usual. We would not be surprised if you were to wish for death at times.

Shock sometimes delays expressions of grief, but they usually closely follow the loss and are intense for at least two to three months. There may be resurgences at anniversaries—birthdays, wedding anniversaries, holidays. Death not only represents great loss, it also requires many stressful life changes: change of marital status, sex life, responsibilities for meeting financial obligations, social activities, sleeping and eating habits.

There are commonly four definable stages to a grief reaction: shock, protest, depression and withdrawal, and recovery. There is little purpose to attempting to rush through these stages, or to encouraging others to rush through them. Two or three months of intense grieving is not uncommon, and people usually go through them in sequence with or without outside intervention.

During a grieving process it is helpful to recognize that a range of intense emotions is normally experienced. It is helpful to have family and friends who show caring and allow you to express your feelings. It is helpful to recognize that extreme feelings of guilt are understandable but probably unwarranted. After several days or a couple of weeks of mourning it can be useful to prod yourself to return to some familiar routines, including working. Return to the familiarity of a supporting social system provides the perspective that life and the business of the world go on despite personal losses. The day-to-day activity of a productive routine seems to be incompatible with the experiencing of excessive, self-punishing grief.

A COMPARISON OF LOSS-OF-LOVE CEREMONIES

April was escorted to the grave by her minister, her children, and her brothers. Close by were her friends, her neighbors, her coworkers. Flowers shone white in the sunlight. Poetry, prayers, and soft music moved the ceremonies along. The funeral appropriately caused those close to April to put their own undertakings aside. No one questioned April's right to sympathy and support. She did not have to ask for them.

Hamilton attended a brief ceremony with a lawyer. He lost not only his wife, but his children, his home, his financial stability. No one sent flowers. No one read poetry. No one sent a card or brought in food. No one even drove him back to his studio apartment. Hamilton had just been divorced.

Nearly one million men and women walk through divorce ceremonies each year in the United States, unaided by the network that assists the adjustment of widows and widowers. Families, churches, neighbors, friends, employers, greeting card manufacturers, and the Social Security Administration make provisions when one experiences the death of a spouse. After a death there is a wake, a funeral, a memorial week, a period of mourning. One "gets" a divorce or "goes to court." There are no labels to make the periods surrounding court appearances meaningful.

Following a divorce there is a new identity crisis, especially for women. Are you Miss, Mrs., or Ms.? Do you return to your maiden name? Do you retain the last name of your children? Divorced men and women are seen as not still married, yet not quite single. Divorce, in the minds of many, connotes failure and lingering attachments: trouble.

Which is more stressful—death or divorce? In Table 6.1 (p. 152) we saw that loss of a spouse by death was rated at 100 life-change units, divorce at 73. But is a death more taxing of our abilities to adjust? Take another look at Table 6.1. A funeral does not signal the loss of children. It may not necessitate the loss of a home or of familiar neighbors.

Consider:

- In death ceremonies, the legalistics are minimal. Divorces may seem to require endless documents and waiting periods.
- Death ceremonies serve to keep families intact. Divorces can splinter a family's fragile remains, with children and other relatives taking sides.
- For the spouse who is not given custody of the children, divorce signals major changes in the parental role as well as the marital role.
- Businesses expect the bereaved to be absent for several days and less-than-usually productive for a lengthier period. But the divorced must usually

SUICIDE

- Each year, according to government estimates, one out of ten thousand Americans commits **suicide** (Barraclough 1973).
- In a study of more than two thousand residents in Los Angeles, 4 percent of the sample had attempted suicide at one or more times in their lives (Mintz 1970).
- Three times as many women as men attempt suicide, but almost twice as many men as women succeed.
- Women prefer to use drugs; men prefer to use guns.
- The suicide rate is two to six times as high among the elderly as among the general population.
- For young people between the ages of fifteen and twenty-four, suicide may be the second most frequent cause of death—ranked only behind accidents (Nemy 1973).
- There is no way of knowing how many deaths associated with automobile accidents, drunken driving, drug overdose, and other violent or careless causes actually stem from suicidal or ambivalently suicidal wishes.

The Challenges of Stress, Fear, and Depression

take time off from personal time, sick leave, or vacation days.

- No one hides a death in the family, but people obtaining divorces may fear the stigma that still prevails and go through the process essentially alone.
- Death is final, but people who are divorcing and divorced may nourish fantasies of reversibility. The antagonisms and other pressures divorce may bring on can stimulate vacillation. "If only . . ." fantasies are common. Short-lasting reconciliations may be brought about by the need to avoid social, religious, or financial pressures.

Briscoe and Smith (1975) compared two groups of depressed people, the bereaved and the divorced, on a number of variables suggestive of the depth and extent of depression: loss of ability to concentrate, irritability, slowing down of thoughts, wishes for death, and contemplation of suicide. The divorced showed greater distress in all areas. Forty-two percent experienced thoughts of suicide.

Then how do divorced people cope with their feelings? With only minimal support from family, friends, coworkers, neighbors, and religious institutions, many divorced people find only one alternative: psychotherapy. Briscoe and Smith also compared the two groups concerning the seeking of professional help. Thirty-one percent of the divorced sample had seen a therapist on an outpatient basis, had been hospitalized for depression, or had experienced both. None of the bereaved individuals in this sample had resorted to professional help.

Following a divorce, depressed individuals may turn to therapy so that they will not be alone, to attempt to work through feelings of personal failure, to gain assurance that their depression will eventually pass. Many need to talk about feelings of helplessness and low self-worth. Those who have been excessively dependent on their mates may need help in redefining themselves as people—as individuals who can develop the capacity to meet the challenges of life through their own resources.

The need for professional help may be minimized if scenes like the following become common:

Betsy and Joe meet at their church for a convivial service. Friends and relatives are in attendance. Betsy wears a new dress, Joe sports a new suit. Prayers are said for them and for their children. They vow to remain friends and to avoid bestowing guilt on each other or on the children. They vow to care for and support the children mutually, to hold precious their good experiences and memories. The minister then pronounces what had been already decreed by a judge: Betsy and Joe are now divorced. The ceremony is followed by a sensitive and low-key reception in which the parties are wished well in their new lifestyles.

Farfetched? Perhaps. But it is being done in a few enlightened communities.

Source: Brown & Rathus (1980).

Suicide on Campus

College, for many the opportunity of a lifetime, can also be the most stressful experience of a lifetime. Life changes tumble over one another within a collapsed time frame. Overnight, college arrivals are plucked away from the homes to which they have been accustomed and faced with changes in sleeping and eating habits, new acquaintances, and different academic demands.

New social pressures may heighten the conflict over the expression of sexual impulses. Some collegians undergo a gradual process of increasing experimentation. Others may feel thrown into a swinging whirlpool in which promiscuity is the norm and also the key to the approval of their peers.

New feelings of independence may be accompanied by major responsibilities as well as by a myriad of nagging chores—underwear that must be washed, toiletries that must be continually replenished. Many must begin to learn to manage money. College may be their first major financial investment. The scramble for grades can be crushing, for grades not only represent achievement in specific courses: they reflect the management of a great emotional and financial investment. Poor grades are equated with squandering of fortunes, a collapsing self-identity, guilt and shame.

Depression, Grief, and Suicide

Often the academic standards of high school no longer apply. Students may have to work for grades for the first time in their lives. Above-average high school students may now be average or below, and undergo a punishing self-reevaluation. For those who have not developed adequate social skills, for those who are highly anxious in social situations, being surrounded by a swarming campus of twenty thousand age-mates will not sweeten the bitter experience of intense and endless loneliness.

Stir into this boiling pot the adolescent quest for identity, the inner challenge to create a cohesive personality structure in the midst of shifting values and intensified conflicts. It is little wonder that these prolonged stresses plague college students with depression and many physical ailments—little wonder that some college students who have their whole lives ahead of them choose to take their lives.

Types of Suicidal Thinking

Different personality theories suggest various explanations of suicide. Psychoanalytic theory usually describes suicide as aggression turned inward, an unconscious effort to punish the persons we have incorporated as parts of the self. Behavior theorists like Ullmann and Krasner (1975) view suicide as one possible outcome of the expectation that life will not provide adequate reinforcements and that death may bring the attention that one has failed to gain through living efforts. Humanists and existentialists view suicide as a response to a life that is without meaning, a life of pain and despair. Victor Frankl (1963) described how many died early in the Nazi concentration camps by running purposefully into the electrified fences.

Others have been more impressed with the variety of reasons for which people take their own lives. Shneidman and Farberow (1970) focused on four types of thinking that may lead to suicide attempts.

Catalogical thinking is characterized by depression and despair, by loss of hope that you can make decisions or take actions that will have the effect of improving your life. Catalogical thinking tends to be associated with intense feelings of loneliness and alienation. From 80 to 94 percent of suicides have been estimated to be associated with intense depression (Barraclough et al. 1969; Robins et al. 1959; Leonard 1977).

But depression does not imply that people who commit suicide are exaggerating their problems. Shneidman and Farberow write that some suicides result from **logical thinking**, particularly among individuals who bear great pain due to irreversible medical illness. A combination of losses such as death of a spouse, financial deprivation, failing health, and old age may be perceived to comprise insurmountable burdens for some individuals.

Those who take their lives in the belief that they will be reborn into a better life, or who engage in ceremonial deaths to gain honor or to avoid disgrace, are showing **contaminated thinking**, according to Shneidman and Farberow. Japanese Samurai warriors who chose to commit suicide when their masters had died, or when they had fought with dishonor, were engaging in contaminated thinking. But this is not an exclusively Oriental passion. Many of those who died at Jonestown, Guyana, in November 1978 may have engaged in contaminated thinking, believing that their "noble" act might earn them eternal life. Viking warriors believed that by dying during battle they would enter Valhalla and attain eternal glory. Now if these individuals were actually

Catalogical thinking (cat-uh-LODGE-ick-kull). Thinking that is characterized by exaggerated feelings of despair and hopelessness.

Logical thinking. Thinking that is characterized by accurate perceptions of reality and the drawing of reasonable conclusions.

Contaminated thinking. Thinking that is characterized by a premise that most people would find to be foolhardy, or even delusional.

The Challenges of Stress, Fear, and Depression

254

correct, it would turn out that Shneidman and Farberow were engaging in contaminated thinking. We can think of no experiment to settle the issue.

Some who commit suicide have experienced **paleological reasoning,** thinking involving hallucinations and delusional ideas, perhaps resulting from a schizophrenic process or a "bad trip" induced by drugs. A paranoid schizophrenic may commit suicide in order to escape an imagined death sentence by the Mafia or from the clutches of evil. Others may hallucinate voices condemning them for imagined evils, and demanding suicide as the only acceptable means of atonement. Or they may believe that they are no longer in control of their actions—that psychics or the devil are actually wielding the death-inflicting instruments. In such cases, the approach to dealing with the suicidal behavior clearly involves physical restraint and treatment of the thought disorder. This requires medical involvement.

Preventing Suicide

When people tell you that they are thinking about suicide, you will probably be frightened and flustered. You may feel that they have unfairly placed an enormous burden on you. It would even be understandable if this made you angry. Make no mistake: your objectives should be to encourage the suicidal individual to consult a professional mental health worker, or to talk yourself to a professional for advice as soon as you possibly can. But if the suicidal person refuses to talk to anyone else, and if you are also afraid that it would be a major mistake to leave him or her alone, there are a number of things you can do (Freedman et al. 1975; Martin 1977; Shneidman & Mandelkorn 1970; Speer 1972):

- Draw the person out. Perhaps ask, "Why do you feel that way?" Verbally expressing even negative feelings can elevate the mood. It also gives you a chance to assess the immediacy of the danger and to think.
- Be empathic: show that you can understand the seriousness of the problem and the negative feelings. Try to view it from the other person's perspective, even if the same stresses would not be as troublesome for you.
- Suggest that steps other than suicide might solve problems and relieve stresses. Say that even if a solution can't be found now, one might be found given some time—or the intensity of the despair might lessen.
- Ask how the person plans to commit suicide. Specific, rational plans are signs of danger. If a specific weapon or a bottle of pills is to be used, ask if the person would feel better if you held on to the weapon, or potential weapon, for a while. Sometimes they will say yes.
- Suggest that the potential suicide go *with you* to obtain professional help—to the emergency room of a general hospital, the campus counseling center or infirmary, or, if necessary, to the campus or local police. Some cities have Suicide Prevention Centers. Some campuses have "hot lines" that you can call for advice or to talk.
- Extract a promise that the person will not commit suicide before talking to you again. Arrange a specific time to talk to the person again, not just "sometime soon." Make it in three hours, or tomorrow morning for breakfast. Be a bit pushy. Show sincere concern.
- If you have not been able to convince the person to go with you for help, obtain professional advice as soon as you are apart.

Paleological reasoning (PAIL-ee-oh-LODGE-ick-kull). Thinking that is characterized by faulty perceptions and ideas, such as hallucinations and delusions.

Depression, Grief, and Suicide

SOME MISTAKEN BELIEFS ABOUT SUICIDE

We have built up many beliefs about suicide in our society. Some of them are correct and some of them are inaccurate. How many of the following myths have you believed?

THE MYTH	THE REALITY
Those who threaten suicide are just seeking attention. Suicides actually occur without warning.	Actually, 70–80 percent of suicides gave verbal warnings within three months prior to the act (Stengel 1964; Leonard 1977). Forty percent of attempters visited a mental health worker during the previous week (Yessler et al. 1961).
Only people making gestures fail at suicide attempts. The serious always succeed.	Actually, 75 percent of successful suicides have made prior attempts (Cohen et al. 1966). Twelve percent of attempters will succeed within the subsequent two years (Shocket 1970).
Discussion of suicide with depressed people may prompt suicide.	Few commit suicide because others have mentioned the topic. Professionals report that it can be helpful to extract a promise that the depressed individual will phone or visit if feelings of desperation arise.
Suicide is a sign of insanity.	Only a minority of suicides show thought disorders. Most who leave notes show hopelessness and despair, but have not lost touch with reality (Leonard 1974).
Suicide occurs at the very pit of depression.	Many take their lives within three months following the greatest depths of depression. Some depressed people show new vitality just before suicide—as if their decision had lifted a burden from them.
Poor people are particularly prone to suicide.	Suicide occurs at all socioeconomic levels, although the sources of stress tend to differ.
People about to commit suicide lose all interest in the details of life.	Many take great pains to leave their finances and other matters in order for their families. Suicide notes often leave instructions for survivors.
If you experience suicidal impulses, you are likely to act out on them.	Suicidal thoughts are actually quite common during times of prolonged stress and depression. But even the majority of suicide attempters find self-destructive urges pass within a couple of years.
Suicide is the coward's way out.	Suicide may be seen as an escape from ongoing despair, but some people confront important personal values and religious beliefs when they consider taking their lives. Some elderly people wish to relieve their families of the burden of caring for them.

The Challenges of Stress,
Fear, and Depression

At suicide-prevention centers all across the country, trained staff man "hot lines" on a 24-hour basis. If someone you know threatens suicide, consult a professional as soon as possible, perhaps by using a hot line.

There are also a number of *don'ts* in suicide prevention:

- Do not tell potential suicides they are crazy.
- Do not minimize their problems or act contemptuously.
- Do not insist on contact with specific people, especially parents. Conflict with parents may have been an important factor in the instigation of the suicidal thoughts.

Despite our best intentions, we may fail. Many professional people have failed at preventing suicides. It is normal to experience regret and grief when we fail. It is also normal to experience anger that we were so heavily burdened with responsibility.

As time passes, feelings of excessive personal guilt are generally placed in perspective. After all, adult people are essentially responsible for their own actions.

Summary

- *HDP is the wrestler's edge.* Just the opposite. HDP (or 6-hydroxydopamine) depletes the quantity of the hormone norepinephrine that is available to the brain. Norepinephrine stimulates sympathetic activity. Deficiency in norepinephrine allows parasympathetic dominance. Parasympathetic activity in some ways counteracts sympathetic activity. For example, heart rate and respiration rate slow down. You may feel exhausted, lethargic, apathetic, withdrawn, indifferent—in short, psychologically depressed. Knowing that you've taken HDP would cause Jimmy the Greek to raise the odds against you.

- *Rats that are helpless to terminate a prolonged electric shock develop hormone deficiencies.* True. Experiments have shown that rats put in this undesirable situation develop deficiencies in norepinephrine. As if the prolonged stress of the shock were not enough to depress them! Norepinephrine deficiency may make it all the more difficult to "bounce back" when you're feeling low.

- *Depressed rats drive their neighbors to drink.* Don't ask us how, but Gaylord Ellison's research at UCLA bears this out. Depressed people can be highly demanding on others, according to James Coyne, so demanding that after a while we try to turn them off. Somehow the presence of rats with norepinephrine deficiencies leads neighboring rats to increase their alcohol intake, as if they were attempting to adjust to some increased stress that the company of depressed rats placed on them.

- *Depressed people are more likely than nondepressed people to blame themselves for failures and shortcomings—even when they are not at fault.* True. If norepinephrine deficiencies are chemical problems associated with depression, then this tendency to be overly self-critical is one of the major psychological problems associated with depression. Depressed people tend to internalize blame, to view their problems as stable and global, to minimize their accomplishments, and to catastrophize sources of stress. These are the so-called cognitive or judgmental errors associated with depression.

- *During the 1960s, college students all over the United States were struck down by an epidemic of a brand-new neurosis.* Perhaps the students' problems were not so unique, but it was in 1967 that Salvatore Maddi characterized a sort of ongoing depression associated with a loss of meaningfulness to life as an "existential neurosis." The students' conflicts concerned crises in their values and their self-identities. Suddenly they found themselves at odds with parental and societal values and could no longer envision themselves as fulfilled in the roles they had earlier planned for themselves. Many young Americans "dropped out" during the 1960s and early 1970s, and experimented with a variety of alternate life-styles.

- *Psychologists have scientifically derived lists of turn-ons that can help you elevate your mood without popping pills.* True enough: it is difficult to remain in an ugly, depressed mood when doing things that we typically enjoy. The "trick" is to push oneself into pleasant activities even when feeling least like doing so. Unfortunately, many people act as if they must remain "loyal" to their depressed feelings. Depression can be an appropriate response when we have suffered loss or been exposed to prolonged stress, but we compound our problems when we remain faithful to depression.

- *Dogs at a University of Pennsylvania laboratory took out permanent moping licenses after being exposed to inescapable electric shock.* True, if you allow us poetic license. Martin Seligman's experimental animals learned to be helpless. Even when their environments changed, they made no effort to escape future shocks. The lesson may be that when we believe that we are helpless to challenge our environment and our low moods, our belief may become a self-fulfilling prophecy. Psychologists therefore urge depressed people to challenge the ways they look at the environment and at themselves.

- *Many churches now hold ceremonies for people undergoing divorce.* Here and there liberal ministers are doing so. They recognize that divorce can be as stressful as bereavement for some individuals, and that a divorce ceremony can provide institutional and social supports that are typically lacking in divorce.
- *People who threaten suicide are usually just seeking attention. People who actually commit suicide do so without warning.* No, this is one of the many myths about suicide. People who take their lives have often warned others frequently, and most have made earlier unsuccessful attempts. On the other hand, experiencing suicidal impulses is quite common and does not mean that you are doomed to act out on them.
- *Suicide is a sign of insanity.* Only in a minority of cases. Shneidman and Farberow described four kinds of suicidal thinking: catalogical, characterized by despair and hopelessness; logical, or prompted by an accurate assessment of one's future possibilities; contaminated, as in the case of ceremonial suicides; and paleological, or prompted by delusions and hallucinations. Paleological reasoning is clearly out of touch with reality.

III

THE CHALLENGE OF HUMAN RELATIONSHIPS

10

VIOLENCE IN CONTEMPORARY LIFE

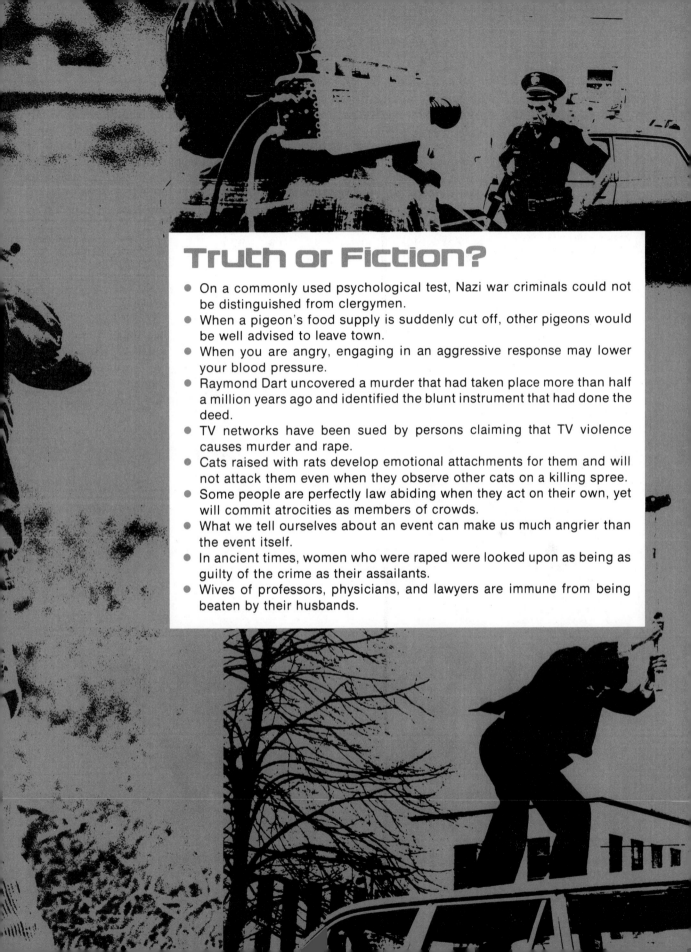

Truth or Fiction?

- On a commonly used psychological test, Nazi war criminals could not be distinguished from clergymen.
- When a pigeon's food supply is suddenly cut off, other pigeons would be well advised to leave town.
- When you are angry, engaging in an aggressive response may lower your blood pressure.
- Raymond Dart uncovered a murder that had taken place more than half a million years ago and identified the blunt instrument that had done the deed.
- TV networks have been sued by persons claiming that TV violence causes murder and rape.
- Cats raised with rats develop emotional attachments for them and will not attack them even when they observe other cats on a killing spree.
- Some people are perfectly law abiding when they act on their own, yet will commit atrocities as members of crowds.
- What we tell ourselves about an event can make us much angrier than the event itself.
- In ancient times, women who were raped were looked upon as being as guilty of the crime as their assailants.
- Wives of professors, physicians, and lawyers are immune from being beaten by their husbands.

VIOLENCE AND THE MYSTERIOUS STRANGER

"What a piece of work is man!" wrote Shakespeare. "How noble in reason! How infinite in faculty! In form, in moving, how express and admirable! In action how like an angel! In apprehension how like a god! The beauty of the world! The paragon of animals!"

We are unique in the history of the Earth. Our species alone is capable of art and poetry, of philosophy and theology, of science and technology. Yet there is a darker side to human nature. The same species that is capable of such intellectual and artistic heights also engages in individual acts of cruelty and destruction that we label torture and crime, in warfare, in mass murder, in **genocide**.

We think of these acts as "brutal." But are they? Mark Twain, the American humorist and teller of tall tales, wrote a vastly uncharacteristic story near the time of his death, "The Mysterious Stranger." He had grown bitter and cynical in his advancing years. This is what he had to say when a boy in the story labeled the destructive actions of a human being as *brutal:* "No brute ever does a cruel thing. . . . When a brute inflicts pain he does it innocently; it is not wrong; for him there is no such thing as wrong. And he does not inflict pain for the pleasure of inflicting it—only man does that" (1916, pp. 192–193).

We may like to think of atrocities like genocide as the work of a deranged, insane minority. But are they? Molly Harrower (1976), now living in Florida, examined the personalities of Nazi war criminals through their responses on

Genocide (JEN-oh-side). The systematic killing of an entire ethnic, racial, or national group of people.

What Do You See?

CLOUDS, INKBLOTS, AND PERSONALITY

Here are a couple of inkblots similar to the Roscharch inkblots. What do you see in them? What do you imagine this might say about your personality?

As far back as the early 1500s the Renaissance inventor and artist Leonardo da Vinci suggested that individual differences in human personality could be studied through interpretations of cloud formations.

About one hundred years later, Hamlet, prince of Denmark, toyed with Polonius in the Shakespeare play by alternately suggesting that a cloud looked like a camel, a hunched weasel, or a whale. Polonius was more interested in ingratiating himself with the prince than in being true to himself, so he agreed with each suggestion.

the Rorschach inkblot test. She had fully expected to find that the personality makeup of mass murderers and war criminals would differ significantly from that of other people. But the Rorschach tests of the war criminals showed a range of personalities. Of eight tests examined by Rorschach experts who were unaware of the identities of the test takers, two suggested "superior" capabilities, two were simply considered "normal," and four showed various adjustment problems. The eight records, as a group, could not be distinguished from those of clergymen and other upright citizens. Harrower concluded reluctantly that a severely disturbed personality is not a prerequisite for cruelty or great crime.

Who is the "mysterious stranger"? The mysterious stranger is the dark side of all of us.

In this chapter we first define the concepts of anger, rage, hostility, and aggression. Then we explore differing views of aggression that stem from biological, psychoanalytic, and social learning perspectives. We see how contemporary psychology has led to the development of a number of techniques for coping with feelings of anger so that aggression can be avoided. Finally, we explore a couple of particularly troubling aspects of human aggression in a section on the war against women: rape and wife beating.

Even our most beautiful works of art often involve themes of violence and brutality.

Anger, Rage, Hostility, and Aggression

Anger is a common emotional response to frustration, especially if we feel that other people have taken advantage of us or purposefully placed obstacles in our paths. Anger is not always a problem. It can be a normal and functional emotional response that motivates us to take action to overcome obstacles. Anger can help mobilize us to confront an aggressor—and, when necessary, to attack.

Anger, like fear and other emotions, involves arousal, But in fear the arousal is predominantly sympathetic—our hearts pound and our muscles are jumpy. These bodily sensations may lead us to feel that we cannot cope and ought to flee. In anger there is also parasympathetic arousal, which tends to counteract overly rapid heartbeat and respiration rate. When we are very angry, it is actually possible to be at once highly aroused and yet experience a "deadly calm." Our muscles are more controlled, and we would be more personally effective if it became necessary to defend ourselves.

Sometimes our anger is so extreme that we lose some of our self-control and may be said to be in a **rage** or a panic. We may shout or scream, insult and threaten. We may attack physically. **Hostility** is similar to anger, but is a more enduring characteristic of a person. Anger is a response to a particular situation, but we speak of some people as having hostile personalities.

Aggression is the attacking of an individual or a group. Aggression may be verbal—as with insults, the threat of physical destruction, sarcasm, and, sometimes, even wit. Aggression may also be physical, or verbal and physical. Aggression can follow from strong emotions, such as anger, hostility, or fear. It

Anger is a common response to frustration, especially if we feel that others have purposefully placed obstacles in our paths.

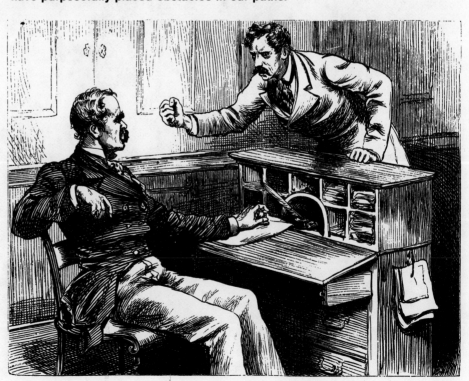

can sometimes be elicited by a powerful stressor. But it is also possible to engage in aggressive behavior in a calculated, "cold," and emotionless manner—as can sometimes be the case in contact sports, military actions, or executions. Moderate to high anger may motivate and contribute to the effectiveness of aggressive behavior. Extremes of anger may overarouse and confuse people.

Aggression as a Natural Response: Biological Perspectives

You have to watch your step when you are around rats and pigeons. That is not news. But only recently have we discovered that aggression may be an **instinctive** or inborn reaction to stress in these species.

Nathan Azrin and his colleagues (1965) found that when a rat was shocked severely and could not escape the shock, it would attack another rat, even though the other animal was guilty of nothing more than sharing the same cage. Was this aggression learned or instinctive? To find out, Azrin used the time-honored tradition of raising some rats in isolation so that no critic could argue that his rats had learned to aggress from watching other rats aggress in similar circumstances. Rats raised in isolation also struck out at their cagemates when shocked.

Did only rats carry this inborn chip on the shoulder? The Azrin group turned their attention to pigeons. First they reinforced some of the birds with food pellets for pecking at buttons. Once the pigeons had learned that all they need do to cause manna to fall from heaven was to peck at a button, the experimenters cut off the food supply. The pigeons pecked harder at the buttons—and also pecked at any fellow pigeons who happened to be in the neighborhood. It is difficult and not very scientific to try to imagine what goes on in the mind of a pigeon, but it does not seem too absurd to conclude that perhaps pigeons are so constructed that frustration can lead to aggressive behavior.

Of course we do not know whether we can generalize the results of these experiments to human beings. To do so, we would have to raise people in isolation—never allowing them to interact with one other human being until the time of the experiment. Since it would be highly unethical to treat children in this manner, we shall have to be content with speculation.

Aggression, Steam Engines, and Safety Valves: Psychoanalytic Perspectives

Sigmund Freud viewed the savagery of the Great War (at the time it was not labeled the First World War; a second war was inconceivable) from the relative sanctuary of his consulting room in Vienna. All around him millions marched to their death for love of country—or was it? Did patriotism and high ideals spur men into battle? Or was it something more basic? Something darker in the human character?

Freud viewed hostile impulses as instinctive and inevitable. He believed that people were basically antisocial and showed concern for the welfare of others only to avoid condemnation by others or by the self. In his later writings, Freud had become so overwhelmed by our capacity to hurt our fellows that he postulated the existence of a death instinct—**Thanatos.**

Freud theorized that we view even the people we love most with both posi-

Instinctive. Unlearned, inborn. What type of research do psychologists do in order to determine whether certain behavior is instinctive?

Thanatos (THAN-uh-toes) In psychoanalysis, the instinct for death.

Violence in
Contemporary Life

tive and negative feelings—with **ambivalence**. He believed that we would take defensive action to *repress* and *suppress* many hostile impulses. Keeping them out of mind would save us from feelings of guilt or moral anxiety. Other hostile impulses might be *displaced*, perhaps *sublimated*. Civilization, Freud thought, might be founded on the sublimation of primitive instincts. Rarely would we have so few outlets for aggressive impulses that an explosion or a panic would occur, blowing us about on the winds of unrelenting emotion, thrusting us into bizarre acts of destruction until enough energy had been discharged. Even then he expected that there would be warning signs of anxiety, a sort of leakage of aggressive impulses; or depression, the outcome of aggression turned inward.

Sandy was a thirty-two-year-old mother of three who sought psychotherapy for frightening fantasies in which her children were struck by cars on their way home from school, fantasies in which her husband died from a heart attack. The fantasies seemed to come from nowhere; she disowned them. But Sandy was the type of person who never expressed anger. She had been raised to believe that decent women placed the needs of their husbands and children ahead of their own. Sandy had wanted to take graduate courses in the evening, but when her husband asked her not to, fearing it might interfere with her chores at home, she had stifled her desires. Though frustrated, she denied any anger. Her children, as other children, could be demanding and troublesome at times. They also symbolized lack of freedom for Sandy. But she had also felt the need to deny that she ever found them burdensome. Were her fantasies a "leakage" of aggressive impulses? Perhaps. Sandy was not in touch with her angry feelings. She used denial so that she could maintain her self-image. Her parents had led her to confuse passivity with decency. Her therapist had to reassure her that it was all right to experience anger toward loved ones. Then Sandy was taught how to express her true feelings assertively, not aggressively, as we shall see later in this chapter. When she experienced and expressed her authentic feelings, the fantasies came to an end.

Freud also believed that much of the violence we witness is not actually intended toward the victim, but is displaced onto the victim. Many male adolescents undergo a rebellious stage—a stage in which they frown upon authority figures. They may poke fun at teachers, pull pranks, have some scrapes with policemen. Many psychoanalysts have suggested that rebellious adolescent boys may be displacing hostile impulses they experience toward their own fathers. Wife beating and child battering may also reflect redirected hostility toward one's boss or one's spouse.

Table 10.1 Some Violence Statistics

1. A violent crime is committed in the United States every thirty-two seconds.
2. Nearly 50 percent of all those arrested for violent crime are teenagers, and the age with the greatest number of arrests is fifteen.
3. Of all violent street crimes, 75 percent are committed by persons 25 years old or younger. This same age group accounts for 44 percent of the murders.
4. Only about half the violent crimes committed are reported to police.
5. In Philadelphia, three of four black adults surveyed will not venture out alone after dark to visit friends or go to the movies.
6. In New York State, the court system can proceed to trial on only 5,000 of the 75,000 felony indictments handed down each year.
7. In 1975, 51 of every 100,000 females in the United States were rape victims.
8. An estimated one in fifteen rape victims reports the assault to police.
9. Each year, more than ten thousand women become pregnant as a result of rape.
10. One rapist in 20 is ever arrested; one in 30 is prosecuted; one in 60 is convicted.
11. More than half of reported rapes take place in the home; 47 percent are committed by an assailant known to the victim.
12. Two-thirds of convicted rapists are married and have sexual relations regularly.

Source: APA *Monitor,* February 1978, *9,* 4.

Authoritarianism. Psychoanalysts at the University of California at Berkeley also suggested that racial and religious prejudices could represent the displacement of hostility toward the father. In the case of Nazi anti-Semitism, German children had been raised in an **authoritarian** tradition that suppressed independence in thought and action, thus generating strong hostilities toward parents and the state, and "weak egos"—little ability to cope as individuals. Jews served as the **scapegoats,** the objects of national hostility. In *The Authoritarian Personality*, the authors (Adorno et al. 1950) suggest that blacks, Jews, and other minority groups have served similar scapegoating functions among segments of American society.

Authoritarian (aw-thar-ee-TARE-ee-an). Characterized by obedience rather than individual, free judgment. *Scapegoat.* A person to whom sinful or wrongful behavior is attributed.

Catharsis. Psychoanalytic theory makes the paradoxical suggestion that one way to prevent aggression is to encourage aggression—on a smaller scale. Controlled aggression is seen as discharging excess steam from the overloaded human steam engine. It can take many forms: aggressive fantasies, humor, sarcasm, complaints, contact sports. This is **catharsis.** Drama critics have hypothesized that plays achieve their power by serving as outlets for human emotions. Television and film dramas, novels with violence, spectator sports—all can have their cathartic effect.

Catharsis may also be expensive. In his book *On Aggression* (1966), Austrian zoologist Konrad Lorenz warned that isolated groups of people invariably built up aggressive impulses since there were no outsiders against whom to direct their hostilities. He recommended smashing a vase as a substitute for hurting people.

There are problems with these psychoanalytic concepts. There is inadequate evidence that hostile impulses are found in everyone. People do displace aggression, but again there is little evidence that such behavior is universal. Evidence for the effectiveness of catharsis is mixed. Some studies (Doob & Wood 1972; Hokanson & Burgess 1962; Hokanson et al. 1963; Konečni 1975) suggest that people who have the opportunity to act aggressively toward people who insult them are less likely to behave aggressively in the future and experience a pleasant decline in arousal. Others, including a recent experiment by Russell Geen and his colleagues (1975) at the University of Missouri, found

Catharsis (kuh-THAR-sis). The expression of emotions. In psychoanalysis, the discharge of psychosexual energy through the expression of repressed impulses.

Violence in
Contemporary Life

that aggression can lead to increased rather than decreased aggression. College students were given electric shock by others working with the experimenter. Then they had the opportunity to retaliate with shock, once or twice. Students who had the opportunity to retaliate twice increased the shock level they used the second time.

DO PEOPLE HAVE A KILLER INSTINCT?

A murder trial took place in the library of anthropologist Raymond Dart. Robert Ardrey held the evidence in his hand—the smashed jawbone of an adolescent. By careful deduction, Raymond Dart had concluded that the adolescent had been struck in the head with the humerus bone of an antelope—a weapon derived from the animal's leg. The angle of the blow, its intensity—these and other pieces of evidence swept aside the possibility that death had been by accident.

What was stunning to Robert Ardrey, dramatist and philosopher, was that this murder had taken place more than 500,000 years ago. The victim was an *australopithecine*, an ape who had grown to something over four feet and weighed ninety pounds, once believed to be an ancestor of man. The murderer would also have been an australopithecine. And here in a flash, to Ardrey, was an explanation of human folly: murder and warfare were not products of modern society and the state. Here in the dawn of time, on the hot African plains, the forebears of the human species had stalked antelopes, baboons, and each other with weapons.

Liberal politicians had argued for centuries that social deprivation is the root of all human evil. Remove poverty, inequality, and social injustice, and there would be an end to crime, aggression, and war. Ardrey labeled this belief a romantic fallacy, founded in part by Jean-Jacques Rousseau, who had said we were noble savages corrupted by twin inventions: private property and the state. Private property created envy. The state provided the social structure to maintain private property. Yet Ardrey knew that on that prehistoric African plain there was no state. *Australopithecus africanus*, he wrote in *African Genesis* (1961), was savage but was not noble. *Australopithecus* carried weapons and killed other australopithecines.

Robert Ardrey had a great impact on American social thought in the 1960s and 1970s. He denied that it was the state that corrupted, that society was "sick." We had inherited a killer instinct and the use of weapons. The state was not the problem. We had intelligently constructed states to protect ourselves from our inner selves. Social controls were our last bulwark against the forces of savagery.

Thus, wrote Ardrey, we could understand the tremendous appeal of the musical *West Side Story*. Something in the audience resonated in empathy with the delinquents who sang out that their violence was not a sign that they were "sick" or had a "social disease." They ridiculed the loving intervention of the social worker because they knew they were not crazy or deprived. They were just being themselves, protecting their "turf." Protecting turf was a theme Ardrey elaborated in *The Territorial Imperative* (1966). Not only were we born with the instinct to use weapons to dominate others, we also had the instinct to create and defend territories.

Along with the Ardrey thesis we found the popular Sam Pekinpah movies in the late 1960s and the 1970s. In *The Wild Bunch*, children burn a scorpion to death. Not because of poverty or frustration, but for pleasure. Outlaws protest the socialization and mechanization of the Old West by attacking the railroad, whose metal structures will be followed by social structures. In *Straw Dogs* a mild-mannered scholar is transformed into a methodical killer when his wife and his territory are attacked. The antihero of *The Getaway* is also an outlaw—a rugged individual doing battle with mankind's encroaching machines. Many in the audience applaud his killing, his ultimate triumph over other outlaws. There is no complaint when he evades the law. Is the film cathartic? Does it permit the mysterious stranger within us a chance to express violent impulses?

Then what do we make of Ardrey's thesis, of his poetic writing? What do we make of Pekinpah's gut-wrenching films? Since the time Raymond Dart handed Robert Ardrey that incriminating skull, we have come to believe it likely that creatures other than australopithecines were our ancestors. Still, Dart's evidence, though highly suggestive of a killing, cannot take us into the inner workings of the killer. Yes, ancient apes used weapons. This does not mean that such usage was instinctive. Apes, like people, can learn to kill.

These university students have paid 25 cents for the privilege of taking a whack at an old automobile. Does smashing the car provide a healthy outlet for aggressive impulses, or does it encourage further aggressive behavior?

Each of these conflicting studies may be more or less accurate. They each involve slightly different experimental situations and suggest that the relationship between an experience we believe is cathartic and further aggression is at the least more complex than Freud suggested. For example, if the "cathartic" experience actually produces guilt and anxiety in the aggressor, future aggression may decrease. But as Geen points out, aggressive behavior may lead some people to feel they must justify their behavior. They may be able to do so by convincing themselves that the victim deserved punishment, and thus increase the probability of future aggression. People make very complex steam engines indeed. We cannot be explained by simple laws of mechanics.

Copycats, Models, TV, and Rewards: Social Learning Perspectives

You have seen it many times. A woman, alone in her apartment, is preparing to go to bed. But outside a sliding glass door, half hidden in the shadows of the terrace, someone is watching and waiting—a hulking, menacing figure. You feel an urge to try to stop the inevitable, to cry out and warn her of his presence. But then you feel silly. After all, this is only a TV drama. No one will *really* get hurt. Or will they?

American children spend more hours per week watching TV than they spend in school. American children watch between ten and twenty thousand people being murdered on TV by the time they are in their late teens. They watch people being killed for money, for love, for kicks, for justice, for country, and by mistake.

How powerful is the influence of TV? Can we be expected to control aggressive and other impulses when we have been exposed continually to shows with bloody violence and uninhibited sex? Recently there have been a number of "copycat crimes." In Florida, in 1977, a teenaged boy killed an elderly woman. His defense? Insanity. His lawyer claimed that he had become "addicted" to TV violence—his favorite show: *Kojak*. TV, the lawyer claimed, had impaired his judgment. The adolescent was found guilty, but sued a TV network for damages in 1978.

And in 1974 a nine-year-old California girl was raped with a bottle by four other girls who admitted they had gotten the idea from a TV movie, *Born Innocent*. The victim's family sued the San Francisco TV station that showed the movie and the NBC network. The courts did not order the television officials to pay damages, noting that such an order might interfere with the right to free expression guaranteed by the First Amendment to the United States Constitution.

Does film and TV violence cause observers to be aggressive? A cause of behavior is an (a) necessary and (b) sufficient condition for that behavior. It may be that a particular film or TV show gives us the idea for behaving aggressively—those girls in San Francisco would have been unlikely to assault their victim if they had not seen *Born Innocent*. But many other watchers did *not* act aggressively as a result of the film, and thus it was not a sufficient condition for aggressive behavior.

Learning to Behave Aggressively. Perhaps we cannot say that the film *Born Innocent* caused four girls to assault another, but it is clear that we can learn to behave aggressively from observing others, and also from operant conditioning.

When we are frustrated, we may experience uncomfortable levels of arousal. These high levels of arousal motivate a variety of behaviors. If an aggressive response or operant serves to eliminate the source of frustration, the operant is reinforced. It becomes more likely to recur in a similar situation. If the aggressive operant is reinforced often, it may become a habit.

Aggressive operants may do more than eliminate sources of frustration. When we are uncomfortably aroused, aggressive behavior may lead to pleasant decreases in blood pressure (Geen et al. 1975; Kahn 1966), at least when we believe our aggression to be socially appropriate. Hokanson and his colleagues (Hokanson & Burgess 1962; Hokanson et al. 1963; Hokanson et al. 1968; Stone & Hokanson 1969) have found that aggressive behavior does not reduce ele-

Girls, like boys, learn from watching the behavior of others. But little girls usually do not expect that they will be rewarded for displaying aggressive behavior, in contrast to the girl in this picture.

vated blood pressure in women, nor in men when they act aggressively toward another male with higher status, such as a college professor.

The Hokanson findings highlight the relationship between our feelings about our behavior and social expectations. As we saw in Chapter 3, aggression is seen by many as an essential ingredient of the male sex-role stereotype. But little girls are likely to be ignored or chided if they show "inappropriate" aggressive behavior, behavior that is inconsistent with the traditional female sex-role stereotype (Abramson 1973). Although a girl's nervous system works like a boy's, and she may learn that it sometimes feels good to act aggressively, she may be less likely to show aggressive behavior for fear of social disapproval.

We do also learn by observing the behavior of others. Albert Bandura of Stanford University and his colleagues (1963a) showed that children will imitate aggressive models on film as well as live models, whether the film models are cartoons or real people. The probability of aggression in observers is enhanced when models are similar to observers and are rewarded for aggression. Girls will learn to imitate aggressive models as well as boys, but they may require more convincing that the social climate will tolerate aggression from them before they act out.

The news from social learning theory is not all bad, however. If aggression can be learned, it can also be unlearned. Nathan Azrin's rats may have had an instinctive tendency to respond to a powerful stressor—in this case, electric shock—with aggression. But Azrin et al. (1965) went on to show that the same animals, when rewarded consistently for *not* behaving aggressively, would often set aside their violent ways.

Instinct is not everything with cats. Kittens raised with rats for companions show fondness for them. What do you think will happen next in this picture? Will the mouse be a playmate or an appetizer?

DO CROWDS BRING OUT THE BEAST IN US?

Gustave Le Bon (1960), the French social thinker, did not endear himself to feminists and liberals when he wrote that men in mobs show the gullibility and ferocity of "primitive beings," such as women, children, members of the lower classes, and savages. He branded crowds and mobs as irrational, like a "beast with many heads." Mob actions such as race riots and lynchings seem to operate on a psychology of their own. Do mobs elicit the beast in us? How is it that many of us who are mild-mannered as individuals will commit atrocities and mayhem as members of a crowd?

In a small volume published in 1941, psychologists Neal E. Miller and John Dollard described the events of a southern lynching as vividly as such accounts of mob behavior have ever been done. In brief, a black man, Arthur Stevens, was accused of the murder of a white woman with whom he had been having an affair. The story went that she had wanted to put an end to the relationship. Stevens, angered, had brutally murdered her. He was arrested, questioned, and he confessed to the crime. The sheriff feared violence and moved Stevens to a town two hundred miles away in the dead of night. But his location was somehow uncovered. The next day a mob of one hundred stormed his jail and returned Stevens to the scene of the crime.

Outrage and anger spread from person to person like a plague bacillus. It infected laborers, professionals, women, adolescents, and law-enforcement officers alike. Stevens was tortured and emasculated. After he was mercifully dead, his body was dragged through the streets. Then the mob went on a rampage in town, chasing and attacking other black people of all ages. The riot ended only when troops were sent in to restore law and order.

As individuals, fear of consequences often prevents us from acting antisocially. Our behavior would be singled out as deviant and punished. But we may be anonymous in a mob and experience a sense of deindividuation (Zimbardo 1970): we set aside our own moral standards and accept the norms and values of the crowd. Self-observation and self-evaluation are weakened by the high degree of autonomic arousal. Self-criticism is suspended.

Spotting police and community leaders will normally prod the conscience, or at least awareness of the chances of being discovered and caught. But in the Stevens lynching, town leaders and agents of social control were in the forefront of the violence. Participants were not only freed from fear of consequences at the hands of their leaders—they were also able to pattern their own behavior after the behavior of people they had been urged all their lives to imitate. We may go so far as to speculate that some townspeople had at first been reluctant to join the mob. But once they saw the topsy-turvy world of the crowd, they felt they might have more to fear from crowd disapproval, if they refrained from joining in, than they would from joining the assault on Stevens. Aggressive, not passive, responses were rewarded by the "beast with many heads."

On an individual level, perhaps we can immunize ourselves to the influence of the crowd by instructing ourselves to take a minute to stop and think whenever we feel ourselves becoming highly aroused —before intense emotion saps our capacities for self-evaluation and self-control. Early we can act firmly to dissociate from the crowd by leaving the scene.

With cats, too, instinct is not everything. The lion may yet lie down with the lamb. Kittens who have been raised to kill rats do so, but kittens raised with no experience with rats may grow up to ignore them. And kittens who are raised with rats for companions play with them and fondle them. They will not attack rats even if they observe other cats on a killing spree (Vernon 1969).

Humans, too, can learn not to aggress. Preschool children exposed to aggressive TV models show less tolerance of frustration and break rules more often. But viewing TV films of models behaving in a patient, helpful manner acts to increase children's tolerance of delays and to decrease their aggressiveness toward others (Friedrich & Stein 1973).

The Challenge
of Human Relationships

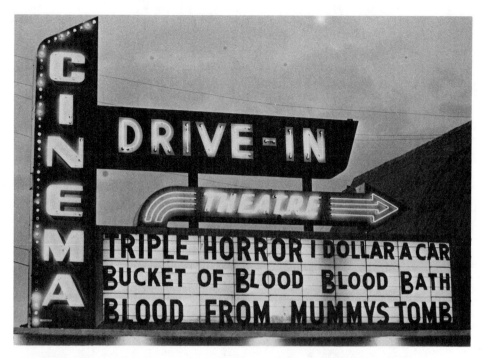

With violent films so common, it may be more difficult to explain why most people who watch them remain nonviolent than why a minority display aggressive behavior themselves.

Aggression and the Sense of Self

Why is it that some people are aggressive and others are not? Why do some of us imitate the aggressive behavior we witness on television and in the movies, while others do not?

We all have had the opportunity to observe aggressive behavior. Many of us may be as angered from time to time as the people we observe expressing anger. We may be as frustrated as the people we see ripping down and smashing the barriers that lie between their goals and themselves. We may very well know how to act aggressively. We may also feel that it is highly unlikely that we shall be punished for particular instances of aggressive behavior. So why is it that we cannot predict perfectly who will act out on anger and frustrations through aggressive behavior and who will not?

The sense of self, of personal identity, of who we are and how we feel we ought to behave may be the factor that separates those of us who are aggressive from those of us who are not. We may predict that a group of adolescents will act more aggressively after watching aggressive film models—as in the film *The Warriors*, which caused concern in 1979. But we must also recognize that many individuals are shocked and disgusted by viewing such films, rather than spurred to personal violence. For many of us, violence against our fellows is inconsistent with our beliefs concerning the ways in which we ought to behave. It is inconsistent with our values, our identities, our sense of self.

For the many of us who choose not to aggress, there may be prices to pay. Some of us who hold in our anger may be prone to higher blood pressure. We may be forgoing some of the rewards that are reaped by the more violent and aggressive among us. It may be, for example, that the difference between an excellent defensive football player and an adequate player is the desire to hurt the opponent. In extreme cases, choosing not to aggress, or not to retaliate, may mean that we do not survive.

Fortunately, behavioral scientists have been working to develop alternate ways of coping with intense emotional arousal and achieving personal and interpersonal rewards. These include the various forms of relaxation training that we discussed in Chapter 7, and the use of assertive responses in the place of aggressive responses to frustration or to a provocation.

EFFECTIVE COPING WITH ANGER

Since anger often stems from frustration, an effective method of coping with anger can be to remove sources of frustration. Sometimes this involves conscious examination of one's life goals, understanding the barriers that block attainment of the goals, and creating effective plans to surmount these obstacles. If the barriers cannot be removed, it may be possible to substitute more obtainable goals.

It can also be frustrating when our goals are uncertain. If earlier important goals have lost their meaning, we may become lost in an existential neurosis that leads to irritability as well as to feelings of depression. The college coun-

◢◣ **Mindflicks** ▭▭▭▭▭▭

RUNNING MOVIES AND MAINTAINING YOUR COOL

Close your eyes. Imagine that you are pushing a cart down the aisle of a supermarket. Someone pushes into you, so hard that it is doubtful that it was an accident, and then says, "What the hell's the matter with you? Why don't you watch where the hell you're going?"

This is a therapy method called running a movie. Researchers like Canadian psychologist Donald Meichenbaum (e.g., Meichenbaum & Turk 1976) ask clients to "run movies" or relive upsetting experiences to help them get in touch with the internal communications—which Meichenbaum refers to as self-statements—that intensify negative feelings and lead to ineffective behavior. If in your own movie you thought to yourself, "This so-and-so can't treat me this way; people can't act like that," you made the practical error of expecting other people to live up to your own high standards. This expectation can permit you to take other people's poor behavior personally and to become highly frustrated too early. As a doctoral student at Indiana University (1974), psychologist Ray Novaco of the University of California studied how control of internal communications and relaxation training could help thirty-four people

with chronic problems in dealing with frustrations and feelings of anger cope more effectively with just such provocations. The participants included eighteen men and sixteen women, ranging in age from seventeen to forty-two, whose difficulties with managing anger ran the gamut from picking fist fights in public places, to destruction of valuable possessions and property, to assaulting marital partners.

Novaco's treatment strategy included three phases: an educational phase, a planning phase, and an application-training phase. In phase one, participants were shown how a variety of attitudes and beliefs involved self-statements that intensified autonomic arousal. Inability to tolerate mistakes in others, unreasonably high expectations of other people, feeling no insult should be allowed to go unpunished, interpreting any provocation as a threat to one's own self-worth—all these cognitive stances intensified arousal and would likely lead to aggression. In phase two, participants were taught relaxation and deep breathing skills similar to those outlined in Chapter 7 and adjustive self-statements (statements incompatible with arousal) to use during four stages of a confrontation:

selor, the psychologist, professors, friends, family may all serve as resources to help clarify goals.

Prolonged, excessive anger may be coped with effectively by reducing overarousal and by changing the thoughts or "internal communications" that tend to magnify anger. Prolonged anger often stems from the irrational belief that because we have been insulted, injured, or frustrated, we must dwell on our provocation endlessly. Emotional arousal and thoughts interact with one another to create a vicious cycle that makes us increasingly angry. Now we shall discuss ways to break this vicious cycle through (a) relaxation, (b) coping with frustrating thoughts, and (c) acting assertively rather than aggressively.

Using Relaxation

If you have learned to relax by using one of the methods described in Chapter 7, you may use relaxation skills to counteract the arousal that accompanies strong feelings of anger directly.

Some individuals find that when they experience strong arousal it is useful to take a deep breath, tell themselves to relax, and exhale. Patricia Carrington (1977) describes using "mini-meditation" to cope with anger when she was extremely frustrated by the traffic backup at one of the tunnels from New Jersey

STAGE OF CONFRONTATION	ADJUSTIVE SELF-STATEMENTS
1. Preparing for a provocation	"If you get upset, you have plenty of coping strategies." "Take a moment out for a few deep breaths." "Remember: other people don't upset you: you aggravate yourself through what you say to yourself."
2. Confronting the provocation	"Don't take it personally." "Easy does it." "Don't get upset and you maintain control of the situation."
3. Coping with arousal and agitation	"No point to getting so upset." "Take a few deep breaths." "You can't expect other people to act the way you want them to."
4. Self-reward	"Congratulations! It worked! You avoided trouble. Pat yourself on the back."

In phase three, participants were asked to imagine common frustrating situations and to rehearse relaxing, breathing deeply and evenly, and using adjustive self-statements at each stage of the confrontation.

This combination of treatment strategies was highly effective in helping participants manage their anger as measured by responses to provocations in the laboratory and, later, outside. Thirty-four people with chronic problems in coping with anger responded to frustrations more effectively and also showed lower arousal during confrontations, as assessed by physiological measures.

The package of relaxation training combined with adjustive self-statements was superior to relaxation or self-statements used alone. When relaxation and self-statements were compared with each other, use of adjustive self-statements was largely superior to relaxation. At least in this one experiment, what individuals told themselves about their situations was more influential in reducing arousal than was an apparently more direct method: muscular relaxation and breathing exercises during periods of provocation.

Novaco's participants reported that perhaps the most effective aspect of therapy was the reconceptualization of a provocation as a problem demanding a solution rather than a threat demanding aggression.

This officer's "internal communications" seem to be aggravating his feelings of frustration, rather than cooling them.

to Manhattan. In effect, she allowed bodily sensations of relaxation to "flow in."

Coping with Frustrating Thoughts

Sometimes we magnify the impact of frustrating events through thoughts that increase rather than decrease arousal. Sometimes no injury has been done us at all. We may blow up when a parent asks us if we had a nice time on a date, or if a supervisor at work offers to give us a helping hand, and then we may wonder why. It may seem that we have become aroused for no reason at all. The parent was only interested in whether we had enjoyed ourselves, and the supervisor was trying to share our burdens. But we exploded. Why?

Ongoing conflicts and fears act as underlying sources of frustration and create hostility. Conflicts over independence, sexual behavior, and personal competence may be present constantly, yet the individual may not be aware of them. Psychiatrist Aaron Beck (1976) of the University of Pennsylvania suggests that conflicts and fears give rise to **internal communications**, things one says to oneself that create additional stress. But these internal communications may occur so fleetingly that they are not perceived unless the person works to tune in to them.

This is how it works. You carry your frustrations with you. A parent or supervisor makes an innocent remark. One or several internal communications that stem from your frustrations flash through your mind. You are angered and act aggressively. Since you were not fully aware of the internal communications, your behavior seems a mystery to you. It does not seem authentic and you disown it. Here are some examples of how sources of frustration can lead to internal communications that magnify anger and lead to behaving aggressively:

Possible Sources of Frustration	Situation	Internal Communications	Aggressive Response
Unresolved dependence-independence conflict	Your mother asks, "Did you see a nice movie?"	"Why does she always ask me that?"	"I don't want to talk about it!" You walk away angrily.
Need for privacy from parents		"That's my business!"	You make a noncommittal grunt and then walk away.
Concern about your worth as a person	You are caught in a traffic jam.	"Who the hell are they to hold me up?"	You lean on the horn. You weave in and out of traffic. You curse at drivers who respond to the jam nonchalantly.
Concern about competent behavior (work, date, athletics, etc.) at destination		"I'll never get there! It'll be a mess!"	
Frustration with sex-role expectations	Your husband says, "The baby's crying pretty hard this time."	"It's so unfair."	"So what do you want from me?"
Concern with your adequacy as a parent		"Are you blaming me?" "So do something!"	"Just leave me alone, will you?"

(continued)

Possible Sources of Frustration	Situation	Internal Communications	Aggressive Response
Concern with your adequacy as a student Competition with roommate (social, academic, etc.)	Your roommate asks, "How's that paper of yours coming?"	"He's got nothing to do, has he?" "Wouldn't he love it if I failed!"	"Why do you ask?" "I don't feel like talking about it, okay?"
Concern with your adequacy on the job Concern that your boss is acting like a parent —thwarting needs for independence and privacy	Your boss asks, "So, how did that conference turn out?"	"I can handle conferences by myself!" "Always checking up on me!"	You get flustered and feel your face reddening. You are so angry you can barely speak. You excuse yourself. When alone, you kick your desk.
Conflict over expression of sexual needs Concerns about sexual adequacy	Your fiancé asks, "Did you have a good time tonight?"	"He's always testing me!" "Didn't *he* have a good time?"	You feel your face redden. You scream, "Why do you always have to talk about it?"

Using Adjustive Alternatives. What we tell ourselves about other people's motives and about other frustrating situations can intensify arousal and prompt an aggressive response. This pattern can be broken by changing frustrating internal communications to adjustive alternatives.

Examples of adjustive alternatives to frustrating internal communications follow. In order to construct effective adjustive alternatives of your own:

1. Pay attention to your arousal.
2. When you feel overaroused, tell yourself to "Stop and think." Listen for the characteristic thought patterns that intensify anger. Or get in touch by "running a movie" (see pp. 276–77).
3. Pause and consider the evidence: Are you jumping to conclusions about the motives of others? Are you overreacting to frustration as in becoming highly aroused in a traffic jam?
4. Use more accurate, adjustive internal communications.

Internal communications. Aaron Beck's term for thoughts that may occur so fleetingly that we do not detect their presence. Yet they may interact with environmental stimulation to influence our behavior.

Situation	Internal Communications	Adjustive Alternatives
Your mother asks, "Did you see a nice movie?"	"Why does she always ask me that?" "That's my business!"	"She probably just wants to know if I had a good time." "She's not really prying. She just wants to share my pleasure."
You are caught in a traffic jam.	"Who the hell are they to hold me up?" "I'll never get there!" "It'll be a mess!"	"They're not doing it on purpose. They're probably no happier about it than I am." "So I'm late. It's not my fault. I'll survive. I'll just take the time I need when I get there."

(continued)

Violence in Contemporary Life

Situation	Internal Communications	Adjustive Alternatives
Your husband says, "The baby's crying pretty hard this time."	"It's so unfair."	"Make it fair. Ask him to help."
	"Are you blaming me?"	"Don't jump to conclusions. It's a statement of fact."
	"So do something!"	"Stop and think. Why not ask him to handle it this time?"
Your roommate asks, "How's that paper of yours coming?"	"He's got nothing to do, has he?"	"The paper is difficult, but that's not his fault."
	"Wouldn't he love it if I failed!"	"Stop and think. I won't assume I can read his mind. It could be a sincere question."
Your boss asks, "So, how did that conference turn out?"	"I can handle conferences by myself!"	"Cool it! Relax! Of course I can handle them. So why get bent out of shape?"
	"Always checking up on me!"	"Maybe she's just interested. She has to do some checking— it's her job—but maybe she's on my side, too."
Your fiancé asks, "Did you have a good time tonight?"	"He's always testing me!"	"Stop and think. Maybe it's an innocent question. And if he's checking, maybe it's because he cares for me."
	"Didn't *he* have a good time?"	"Stop reaching and digging. He only asked if I had a good time."

Note that adjustive alternatives have several purposes:

1. They help you focus on your reactions and weigh them.
2. They serve to help you control your level of arousal.
3. They help you avoid jumping to conclusions about the motives of other people. Some people may have ulterior motives in "innocent" remarks, but even so you need not become more aroused than you would like to be and do things you may regret later.
4. They help you focus on what is actually happening, rather than on a misinterpretation of events.

Sometimes you feel that an antagonist "deserves" an aggressive response, but it still may do you more harm than good to provide one. Aggression often provokes retaliation. Aggressive behavior may also be inconsistent with your personal system of values. You must deal with this question: Who is in charge of your feelings and your behavior—you or others?

Ray Novaco (1977) has successfully trained law-enforcement officers to use internal communications such as the following when they are provoked. Which would be effective for you?

"I can work out a plan to handle this. Easy does it."

"As long as I keep my cool, I'm in control of the situation."

"You don't need to prove yourself. Don't make more out of this than you have to."

"There is no point in getting mad. Think of what you have to do."

"Muscles are getting tight. Relax and slow things down."

"My anger is a signal of what I need to do. Time for problem solving."

"He probably wants me to get angry, but I'm going to deal with it constructively."

Self-Assertion—Not Explosion

We can use assertive behavior to express our authentic feelings, whether they are positive or negative. But with assertive behavior we do not threaten, insult, belittle, or attack.

We shall explore assertive behavior at length in Chapter 11, but here are some examples of assertive alternatives to the aggressive responses on pages 278 and 279. With assertive responses we may firmly request that other people change their behavior, but we do not threaten. Thus we tend to defuse the situation and to avoid behavior that is inconsistent with our values.

Situation	Assertive Response
You are caught in a traffic jam.	You tell yourself to relax, let tight muscles go, and slow down. You think, "It's annoying but *not* a tragedy. I'll survive. When I get there I'll still take things step by step. I will *not* be rushed." You survey the scenery.
Your roommate asks, "How's that paper of yours coming?"	"It's a pain! I absolutely hate it. I can't wait until I get the damned thing over with."

Here are some additional situations, with examples of aggressive responses and assertive alternatives. The assertive responses express feelings accurately, but they are not provocative:

Situation	Aggressive Response	Assertive Response
Your supervisor says, "I would have handled that differently."	"Well, that's the way I did it! If you don't like it, that's too damn bad about you."	"What is your concern?" If the supervisor becomes argumentative, you may say, "I handled it that way on purpose and believe I did it correctly. This is why. . . ." If you were incorrect, admit it.
A coworker says "You are a fool."	"Drop dead."	"That's an ugly thing to say. It hurts my feelings and I would like you to apologize."
A provocateur says, "So what are you going to do about it?"	You push or hit the provocateur.	"I think this is silly. Good-bye."
Your roommate has not cleaned the room.	"Damn it! You're a pig! Living with you is living in filth."	"It was your turn to clean the room. You agreed to clean it and I expect you to stick to it. Please clean it."

Violence in
Contemporary Life

Self-Reward

When you cope with frustrating interpersonal situations without losing control and behaving aggressively, pat yourself on the back. Tell yourself that you did a fine job without any false modesty. Ray Novaco (1977) suggests telling yourself things like:

"I handled that one pretty well. That's doing a good job."

"I could have gotten more upset than it was worth."

"My pride can get me into trouble, but I'm doing better at this all the time."

"I actually got through that without getting angry."

You can also say things to yourself like:

"This time I didn't do or say anything that I'll regret later."

"This time I caught myself and I'm proud of the way I handled things."

Note the difference in your state of arousal and your emotions when you have successfully resolved a conflict without aggression. Your muscles are probably more relaxed. Your heartbeat and respiration rate are probably lower. You are less likely to feel that the top of your head is coming off. These feelings can mean that you have channeled your arousal into appropriate expression of your feelings without provoking retaliation or feelings of guilt.

Feel proud that you controlled the situation, rather than allowing the situation to control you.

THE WAR AGAINST WOMEN

Certain types of aggressive behavior are particularly troublesome because they involve assault the physically stronger against the physically weaker, such as rape and wife beating.

Rape

Statutory rape (STAT-you-tore-ee). Sexual interaction with a willing person who is below the age of legal consent.
Forcible rape. An act in which a man (or woman) seeks sexual gratification with an unwilling woman through the use of violence or threats.

Rape has different meanings. **Statutory rape** is defined as a male having sexual relations with a female who is a minor, even if the female is willing or the initiator of the sexual activity. **Forcible rape** concerns us here—an act in which a man forces himself upon a woman sexually, through use of violence or threats. In some states, such as California, it is not necessary that the man actually enter the woman in order that his violation be classified as rape, but only that he attempt to achieve sexual gratification against the woman's will.

Assailant (ass-SAIL-ant). A person who engages in aggressive behavior.
Adultery (add-DULL-turr-ee). Sexual activity between a married individual and a person other than the spouse.

Throughout Western history, society's laws have been framed largely for the convenience and needs of men. For this reason rape was considered a crime against a man's property—his wife or his daughter—rather than a crime against a woman. In *Against Our Will*, Susan Brownmiller (1975) pointed out that women have long been considered responsible when they have been sexually assaulted, even if they attempted to fight off their **assailant**. In ancient Babylonia, a woman and her rapist might be tied and thrown into a river. The husband might save her, but also might choose to let her drown. After all, according to Babylonian custom she had committed **adultery**.

These may sound like curious notions, but many in our society still condemn the woman who has been raped. Many maintain the myth that no woman can be raped against her will. And recently a judge in the Midwest found a man to be innocent of rape because women dress in a provocative manner. He was not referring to the clothing worn by the particular woman assaulted, but to what he perceived as a general breakdown of moral standards in which women commonly attempt to make themselves alluring to men. This judge was removed from the bench soon afterward, but many people believe that a woman who is raped is usually getting what is coming to her.

The following quotation from *Our Bodies, Ourselves* (Boston Women's Health Book Collective 1976, p. 157) illustrates some of the problems women have experienced when they have brought rape to the attention of the authorities:

"Two patrolmen came and asked me to tell them what happened. I could tell they were skeptical because they remarked, 'Well, things certainly seem to be in order here now, what was the problem?' They treated me like a criminal; they kept asking me, 'What were you wearing, were your pants tight?' They were oblivious to how upset and scared I was. I had to cry before they took me seriously.

"Everyone seemed to believe that I was lying or exaggerating. I was beginning to realize that when you open your front door to a man, it is the same as inviting him to rape you in the eyes of the police and society."

Forcible rapes also occur within the institution of marriage, but, as women's groups complain, men have not been successfully prosecuted for raping their wives.

Patterns in Forcible Rape. Who is raped? When, where, and by whom? Any woman is a potential rape victim. In 1975 the FBI estimated that there were about 51 rapes reported for every 100,000 women in the United States—more than 56,000 in all! In a study of rape victims in the Denver area, the average age of an adult victim was 24, although rapes were reported with victims ranging in age from 3 to 74 (Hursch 1977). The typical rape victim is between 15 and 25, unmarried, and from the lower socioeconomic classes, although women from all age groups, races, and social classes have been victimized. Rape is so pervasive that the chances are about one in ten that a woman living in Los Angeles for thirty years will at some time encounter a rapist (Offir 1975).

The typical rapist is young, twenty to twenty-four, frequently married, and generally from lower income levels. A majority come from broken homes, and many are physically unattractive and emotionally immature (McCary 1978), yet rapists, as their victims, come from many different age groups and socioeconomic levels.

A study by Menachim Amir (1971) concerning cases of rape that occurred in Philadelphia, entitled *Patterns of Forcible Rape*, sheds some additional light on patterns of rape.

Amir wrote that it had been commonly believed that black men were more likely to attack white women than black women (p. 336), but he found that the great majority of rapes occurred within racial groups, so that black women were more likely to be the victims of black assailants. Rape, he found, occurs throughout the year. It is not a "hot-weather crime." Rape occurs more often on weekends than during weekdays, with Saturday the peak day. Almost half of all rapes occur within a six-hour period—between 8:00 P.M. and 2:00 A.M. Saturday night.

Most rapes do not occur between complete strangers. In a full 34 percent of the cases Amir studied, the rapist and his victim were known to each other as close acquaintances or neighbors. The rapes themselves often occurred nearby or within the home of the victim.

This magnificent statue, "The Rape of the Sabine Women" portrays a theme which has been darkly disturbing to women, and those who care for them, since the dawn of history.

Violence in Contemporary Life

Hursch (1977) found that among some three hundred rape attacks in Denver, 35 percent took place out of doors, in streets, alleyways, or parking lots usually near the victim's home; 59 percent occurred indoors, with 85 percent of these occurring in the victim's home; and only 5 percent took place in cars. Hursch, as Amir, found that rapes most often occurred in impoverished neighborhoods.

But rapes have also taken place with a date in a parked car or in the victim's parents' home. This so-called date rape (Kanin 1969) involves forcible intercourse, yet the rapist may not label his conduct as rape. Some men unfortunately believe that being on a date permits sexual advances, and that a woman's protests may be insincere.

In his studies of rape victims in the Denver area, Selkin (1975) describes a common pattern that characterizes the rape sequence by an unknown attacker. The rapist will often select a potential victim who appears to be most vulnerable: the woman alone in her apartment or walking along a deserted street, the older woman, the mentally retarded woman, or the sleeping or intoxicated woman. Following his selection of a target, the rapist begins to look for a relatively safe time and place to commit the rape—a deserted, run-down part of town, a darkened street, a second-floor apartment without appropriate window bars or locks. Selkin suggests that women who generally have helpful attitudes toward others and who are overtly friendly may be seen as vulnerable by a potential rapist. In fact, about one quarter of the rape victims studied in Denver between 1970 and 1972 were attacked after they responded positively to the rapist's request for help. When the target and the setting are chosen, the rapist frequently begins to test his victim to see if she can be frightened into submission. He may at first make some lewd or suggestive comment or taunt her, and if she acts terrified or immobilized, he may proceed to threaten her directly with such remarks as, "Take off your clothes or I'll kill you!" Selkin suggests that the woman's refusal to cooperate is the most effective means of preventing the rape. Among some three hundred women he studied who successfully resisted an attack, most succeeded by either running away, resisting physically, or screaming for help. In the Amir (1971) study in Philadelphia, 55 percent of women who encountered a rapist displayed submissive behavior, 27 percent screamed or tried to escape, and 18 percent fought back physically.

Amir makes the very controversial assertion that many of the cases of rape he studied—19 percent, in fact—were **victim-precipitated crimes,** or crimes in which the victim appeared to have been largely responsible for the crime. He lists, as victim-precipitated offenses, cases in which the woman at first agreed to have sexual relations with the offender but then changed her mind, or "did not resist strongly enough" (p. 346). He also characterized these situations as victim-precipitated: "cases in which the victim enters vulnerable situations charged with sexuality, especially when she uses what could be interpreted as indecent language and gestures or makes what could be taken as an invitation to sexual relations" (p. 346). Amir wrote that "one-fifth of the victims had a police record, especially for sexual misconduct. Another 20 percent had 'bad' reputations" (p. 336).

Amir's remarks concerning the incidence of victim-precipitated rape seem to emphasize the wrong end of the spectrum. Even if we were to allow that having a "bad" reputation can be measured accurately and is valid evidence of precipitation of sexual assault—which we shall not—Amir's own figures would suggest that a minimum of 60 percent of the victims he studied did not in any way precipitate the crime. Clearly, Amir does not make a convincing case that

Victim-precipitated crime (pree-SIP-it-tate-ed). A crime in which the victim plays a causal role, or encourages the crime directly or indirectly.

women deserve the offenses to which they fall prey. Even if a woman's sexual behavior has, in the past, gotten her into trouble with the authorities, she does not deserve to be forcibly raped.

Amir did find that for most rapists the case he studied was not isolated. Half the men had previous arrest records.

It does not seem that rape is a crime of passion, an explosive outburst of sexual desire. Amir found that 71 percent of his cases had been planned. Other researchers have also concluded that rape is a form of aggressive behavior in which sexual gratification is not the major motive (Brownmiller 1975; Gagnon 1977; Gebhard et al. 1965). Rape may more often be a way in which the offender expresses hostility toward women or other people in general. It may be that the rapist is expressing a need for power. Recent evidence (Abel et al. 1975) suggests that some rapists find sex with violence to be more sexually stimulating then sex between mutually agreeing and affectionate partners.

Rape Prevention.   Several useful suggestions for taking precautions against rape are presented in *Our Bodies, Ourselves* (p. 158):

- Establishing arrangements and signals with other women in an apartment building or neighborhood. Using whistles, calls for help, exchanging phone numbers, and walking in groups after dark.
- Listing only your first initials in the telephone directory or on the mailbox if you live by yourself, or adding the names of phony roommates (male).
- Using dead-bolt locks on doors and being certain you know exactly whom you are allowing in.
- Keeping windows locked and obtaining iron grids for first-floor windows.
- Keeping entrances and hallways brightly lit.
- Having keys ready to avoid dallying at the front door.

Here are some additional precautions women can take:

- Not walking alone in darkened parking lots or along city streets.
- Avoiding deserted areas.
- Never allowing a strange man into your apartment or home. Rapists frequently gain entrance by asking to make an emergency phone call or claiming they are repairmen. If a man claims he has been sent to repair or service the telephone, or to read the gas meter, ask him to slip his identification under the door and then telephone his dispatcher to verify the call. As an alternative, telephone the superintendent of your building.
- Driving with the car windows up and the doors locked at all times.
- Checking the rear seat of the car for intruders before entering.
- Avoiding living in an apartment building that is not safe from intruders.
- Not picking up male hitchhikers.
- Not talking to strange men on the street. Rapists often look for an "in." Don't give them one.

Adjustment of the Rape Victim.   The rape victim must adjust to the medical, legal, and emotional consequences of her experience.

A rape victim should consult a physician to determine the extent of the physical injury. She should be examined for **venereal disease,** and consult her physician concerning the possibilities of pregnancy.

Women who choose to have their assailant prosecuted must be prepared to face occasionally hostile or uninterested law enforcement officers and courts. As pointed out in *Our Bodies, Ourselves,* the defense may attempt to demonstrate that the victim has a bad reputation, or that she enticed the offender. It may be very difficult to convince a jury that the woman was totally innocent if she did, in fact, know the assailant prior to the crime. It is also necessary to relive the crime through testimony.

Masters and Johnson (1970) have pointed out that rape can be at the root of many sexual dysfunctions for women, that it may be difficult for a woman who has been raped to enter readily into a loving sexual relationship with a man. But women who have been raped must also sometimes face the harsh judgments of their husbands and their families, who may still harbor the notion that she is somehow guilty of the offense, or, just as serious, that she has somehow become "damaged goods."

It is also not unusual for a rape victim to undergo a serious period of self-questioning as to whether or not she did somehow precipitate the crime. She may wonder if "unconsciously" she emitted some sort of signal that she was interested in sexual activity. This may be especially true for women who have at one time or another engaged in sexual fantasies that involved themes of rape. And, as you will see in Chapter 13, such fantasies are not uncommon. But fantasies and actions are not the same thing, and an intermittent rape fantasy does not make a woman responsible for her own victimization—just as a rape fantasy in a man does not mean that he will actually go out and rape a woman.

Women who have been raped and are in need of help may contact expanding numbers of rape crisis centers in our cities. They may be located by telephoning the police (anonymously if desired) or the emergency room of a general hospital, or by contacting the Center for Women Policy Studies, 2000 P Street, N.W., Suite 508, Washington, D.C. 20036.

Wife Beating

"Wives and rugs should be beaten regularly." "Women should be struck regularly, like gongs." Only a few years ago, wife beating was joked about. There was laughter every time the subject was brought up. The humor involved several themes: It was necessary to beat women regularly, for their own good. Women, like furniture, were the property of the man of the house. There was something perverse about the nature of women that could goad even the most patient of men into beating them.

In her 1978 book *Conjugal Crime,* Terry Davidson, the daughter of a clergyman who had beaten her mother, sheds light on this open secret, drawing her information from interviews with mental-health professionals, a survey of the sparse research into wife beating, and from her own experiences. What surfaces is both ugly and surprising. Wife beating is not predominantly a problem of the working classes. It is also found at higher income levels—the wives of professors, physicians, and lawyers are not immune.

You might think that even people who privately beat their wives would denounce the practice in an interview. You might think that better-educated individuals would be less likely than their peers to approve of violence in the

If wife-beaters are clearly treated as criminals, they may be more likely to consider controlling their aggressive impulses.

home. Not so. According to one recent national survey, college-educated men were more likely than their less-well-educated peers to approve of slapping their mates—when "appropriate."

Just as nations are expected to avoid interfering in the "internal affairs" of other nations, police and courts have been reluctant to intervene in domestic conflicts. Some beaten women complain that they have been so desperately afraid that they have called in the police. But when the police come by, they take the husband out for a walk to "cool off" and come back laughing like "good drinking buddies." When confronted in social agencies, many men reverse the assaulter-victim roles: "I wouldn't hit her if she didn't push me into it." "If she'd shut up when I tell her to, that would be the end of it." "She knows damn well if she keeps on nagging me she's going to get it, so she must want it."

Terry Davidson described a typical scene from her own childhood. She and the other children were expected "to watch calmly, without reacting, without visibly flinching, whenever this self-righteous man punched my mother, pummeled her, kicked her. . . . At these times I was not allowed to leave the room, or hide, or even cover my face. If I cried out, he'd turn . . . on me. So I'd stuff my hand into my mouth and somehow stop time and feelings until he was finished."

More than hands and feet are used in aggression in the home. Davidson catalogues the findings of a study of middle-class men who beat their wives: "The weapons used, besides fists and feet, were guns, knives, a broom, a leather belt, a brush, a pillow (to smother), a hot iron, lighted cigarettes, and a piece of railroad track. . . . The assaults lasted anywhere from five to ten minutes to over an hour. The frequency range included a daily habit, once every two or three days, weekly, monthly, once every two months, four times a year." Davidson suggests that millions of men batter their wives on a regular basis, and quotes an estimate of the National Institute of Mental Health that perhaps half of American wives have been beaten by their husbands at least once.

What are wife beaters and their victims like? Are there any commonalities from case to case? There appears to be no universal pattern. Psychoanalytic, social learning, and cognitive views all seem to account effectively for some cases. Some men seem to assault their wives because of frustrations in their roles as breadwinners. Sometimes their wives earn more than they do, which, for them, lowers self-esteem. Some men appear to have doubts concerning their masculinity and resort to beating their wives as a method of asserting dominance. Some men have difficulty expressing anger verbally, so they act out aggressively. Some men uncritically follow in the footsteps of fathers who had beaten their mothers—wife beating, incredibly, seems to them to be a natural element of a marriage. Still other men view their wives as furniture, possessions, and find it no more deviant to kick a wife than to kick a chair.

Contrary to popular myth, the typical victim of beatings does not seek them out. She may know that complaining or "nagging" will instigate an onslaught, but she may also very well know that her husband will find excuses for beating her regardless of how perfect she tries to be. A handful of victims may be **masochistic,** but the great majority are simply dependent on their husbands and their marriages, and have conflicts and fears concerning taking the steps that would lead to separation. Some view their husband's violence as an illness, and harbor the hope that someday he will "get better"—especially if the wife can somehow get him to go for "treatment." Some victims do have low self-esteem and wonder if they deserve the beatings because they are rotten, unworthy people. We attempt to rationalize our suffering, and some women do assume they would not be beaten if they did not somehow deserve it. Women such as these often cling to their marriages regardless of the extent of the abuse. Some of them shrug their shoulders and explain, "No one else would want me."

Coping with wife beating requires hard decision making. Husband and wife must both take responsibility for their own behavior if the marriage is to be improved. Women may profit from forward movement in the working world to gain the self-confidence and independence that will prepare them for separation, if this is the only recourse. Many wife beaters are responding ineffectively to stress and frustration. Frustrations may be reduced through educational and vocational counseling and rehabilitation.

Wives need to communicate clearly that beatings are absolutely unacceptable—regardless of provocation, regardless of the husband's level of arousal. This position needs to be clearly echoed through social and legislative policy: wife beating must be clearly labeled as crime, wives must be clearly labeled as individuals and not as household property.

When all else fails. In recent years shelters for battered wives and their children have been established in many towns and cities. The addresses of these shelters and other community resources are available from counseling centers, hospitals, police, mental health clinics, and social welfare agencies.

Masochistic (mass-so-KISS-tick). Attaining pleasure or gratification through being mistreated, assaulted, or otherwise experiencing pain or humiliation.

Summary

- *On a commonly used psychological test, Nazi war criminals could not be distinguished from clergymen.* True. On a study with the Rorschach inkblots, war criminals and others had their strengths and their weaknesses.

- *When a pigeon's food supply is suddenly cut off, other pigeons would be well advised to leave town.* True. Some psychologists have felt that aggression stems from frustration; thus, if we removed sources of frustration such as social injustice, violence would vanish. However, frustration doesn't always lead to aggression, and people who are not frustrated can also be violent.

- *When you are angry, engaging in an aggressive response may lower your blood pressure.* Possibly. Many angry people report feeling better and show lower blood pressure when they have retaliated for some provocation. This has often been interpreted as a catharsis. But aggression sometimes stimulates further aggression in the aggressor. Clearly our feelings about our aggression are as significant in influencing our reactions to violence as is the aggression itself.

- *Raymond Dart uncovered a murder that had taken place more than half a million years ago and identified the blunt instrument that had done the deed.* The evidence is pretty powerful that this is the way it was, but the fact that forerunners of man had been violent does not mean that human violence is instinctive or inevitable. Our forefathers were capable of learning violence, as are we.

- *TV networks have been sued by persons claiming that TV violence causes murder and rape.* True enough, but the courts have held that TV is not responsible. There is no question that we can learn from observing others, but we do not automatically imitate others. It is true that we tend to imitate when those we observe are in situations similar to ours and are rewarded for their behavior. But our personal values tend to help us decide what we should and should not imitate.

- *Cats raised with rats develop emotional attachments for them and will not attack them even when they observe other cats on a killing spree.* Yes, cats raised to kill rats will do so, cats raised without experiences with rats may ignore them, and cats raised with rats consider them part of the family.

- *Some people are perfectly law abiding when they act on their own, yet will commit atrocities as members of crowds.* Unfortunately, true enough. Several crowd factors precipitate aggression: a vicious cycle of interstimulation, the disorganized thinking associated with high arousal, observing so many others (sometimes including law-enforcement officers) engaging in the mob action, a sense of anonymity. We may surrender our own norms and adopt the values of the crowd—this is deindividuation. We can best shelter ourselves from the influence of the mob by leaving crowds as soon as we detect heightening emotion and the emergence of norms contradictory to our own beliefs.

- *What we tell ourselves about an event can make us much angrier than the event itself.* True. Events have meanings—thoughts, feelings, memories they stir in us. We can misinterpret innocent statements and acts as provocations. We can build minor provocations into disasters. Events can control us, rather than our controlling them, if we are unaware of what we tell ourselves about them.

- *In ancient times, women who were raped were looked upon as being as guilty of the crime as their assailants.* Often true, among the ancient Babylonians, and, most unfortunately, among many men today. Some rapes may be victim-precipitated, but the great majority are not; yet too many women are viewed as having in some way allured their attackers.
- *Wives of professors, physicians, and lawyers are immune from being beaten by their husbands.* False. Wife beating is not limited by social class, education, or ethnic factors.

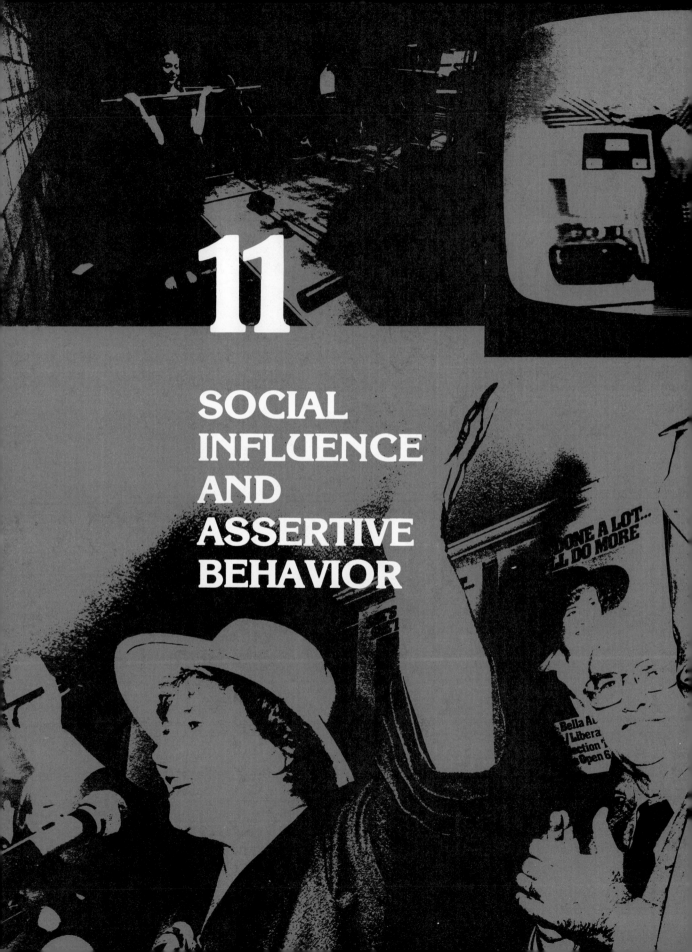

11

SOCIAL
INFLUENCE
AND
ASSERTIVE
BEHAVIOR

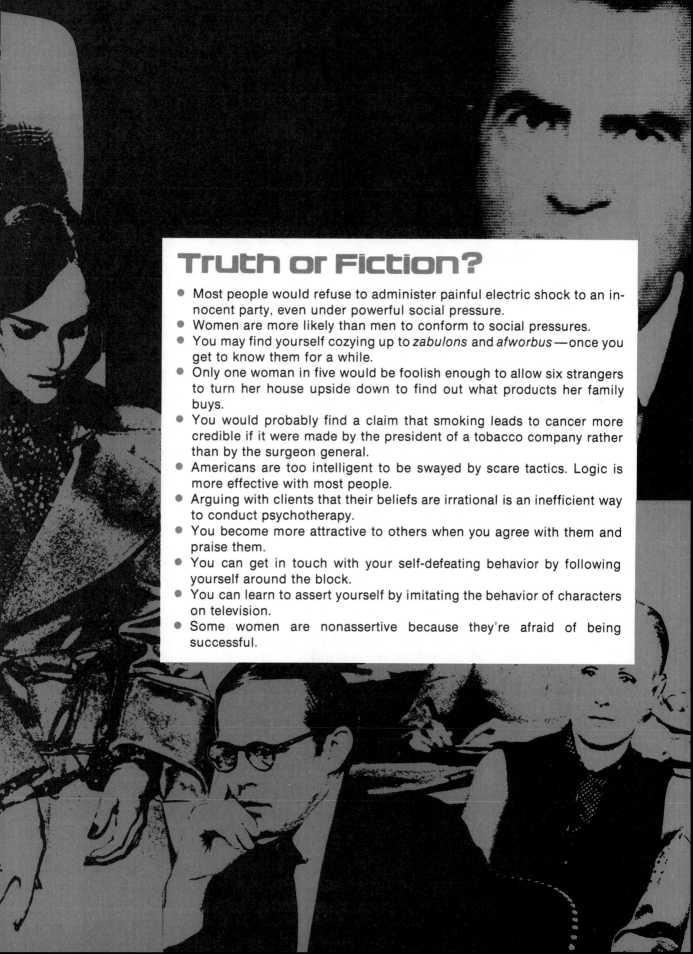

Truth or Fiction?

- Most people would refuse to administer painful electric shock to an innocent party, even under powerful social pressure.
- Women are more likely than men to conform to social pressures.
- You may find yourself cozying up to *zabulons* and *afworbus*—once you get to know them for a while.
- Only one woman in five would be foolish enough to allow six strangers to turn her house upside down to find out what products her family buys.
- You would probably find a claim that smoking leads to cancer more credible if it were made by the president of a tobacco company rather than by the surgeon general.
- Americans are too intelligent to be swayed by scare tactics. Logic is more effective with most people.
- Arguing with clients that their beliefs are irrational is an inefficient way to conduct psychotherapy.
- You become more attractive to others when you agree with them and praise them.
- You can get in touch with your self-defeating behavior by following yourself around the block.
- You can learn to assert yourself by imitating the behavior of characters on television.
- Some women are nonassertive because they're afraid of being successful.

Richard M. Nixon resigned the presidency of the United States in August of 1974. For two years the business of the nation had ground almost to a halt while Congress had investigated the burglary of an office in the Washington complex that was known as Watergate. This office was rented by the Democratic Party during the 1972 presidential campaign. The facts had come out that people very close to Nixon were involved in the burglary, and that Nixon himself might be part of what came to be known as the "cover-up"—efforts to keep the burglars quiet about the chain of command, and efforts to prevent the FBI from looking into the case too closely. For two years Nixon and his aides had been attacked by the press and the Congress. Now it was over. Some of the bad guys were thrown into jail, Nixon was exiled to the beaches of Southern California, and the nation got back to baseball, hot dogs, apple pie, and work. The new president, Gerald R. Ford, declared, "Our national nightmare is over."

But was it? Was it really over? Have we come to grips with the most important implications of the Watergate affair?

Compliance (come-PLY-ants). Giving in to the requests or demands of others.

The cover-up of the Watergate burglary, the My Lai massacre in Vietnam, the Nazi extermination of millions of Jews during World War II—according to Yale University psychologist Stanley Milgram, all these human disasters were made possible through the **compliance** of individuals who were more concerned with earning the approval of their supervisors than with asserting their own moral views (APA *Monitor*, January 1978). Otherwise, they would have refused to go along with these crimes.

People, of course, try to rationalize their misconduct. H. R. Haldeman was Nixon's right-hand man. During an interview with CBS newsperson Mike Wallace, he said he had prevented certain facts from coming to light during the investigation in order to protect the "presidency" of the United States. Some of the soldiers who had shot women and children to death at My Lai had heard that Vietnamese women and children had been involved in guerrilla attacks on their comrades. This killing, it seemed to them, was justified revenge. It might even encourage other Vietnamese civilians to refrain from future anti-American activity. Perhaps some Germans under Hitler's rule rationalized that there was nothing they could do. They were mere individuals and had to follow orders to protect themselves and their families.

Such rationalizations may not be fully effective. People who obey authority rather than assert their true feelings may experience the stress that derives from a severe avoidance-avoidance conflict—moral anxiety versus fear of the disapproval of an authority figure. For a long time, presidential aide John Dean was motivated to avoid Richard Nixon's disapproval. When he communicated requests for hush money to his supervisors, he rationalized that he was not personally doing the dirty work of the cover-up. He certainly was not the man issuing the orders at the top. He was only an agent, a middleman, an administrator. Later, during his testimony before the Senate committee, he would become famous for his "photographic memory." Yet he forgot such an important fact as the amounts of money requested by the burglars to maintain their silence. Why? Dean characterized his forgetting as "a great big repression" (APA *Monitor*, January 1978, p. 23).

John Dean also found another way to cope with his moral anxiety. He would "go home at night and jump into the Scotch bottle." When he eventually broke his own silence and told Congress everything he knew about the cover-up, he felt that he was finally "taking responsibility for myself" (APA *Monitor*, January 1978, p. 23).

Some of the major actors of the Watergate drama, as it unfolded on television screens across America. President Richard M. Nixon (above left), Robert Haldeman (above right), and White House attorney John W. Dean III (below right). Dean is pictured giving televised testimony before the Senate Watergate Committee, in a series of events that eventually led to Nixon's resignation.

SHOCKING STUFF AT YALE: THE MILGRAM STUDIES

Aren't these horrors from Vietnam, from Nazi Germany, and from the Nixon White House historical flukes? Wouldn't most of us place our own morality first and resist mass murder and cover-ups of crimes? Just how compelling is the need to obey authority figures at all costs?

Stanley Milgram also wondered how many of us would trust in the rightness of our own feelings and resist authority figures when necessary. To find out, he placed ads in newspapers in the New Haven area to enlist recruits for experiments on "learning and memory." In an early phase of his work, he recruited forty men ranging in age from twenty to fifty—teachers, engineers, laborers, salesmen, men who had not completed elementary school, men who had earned graduate university degrees. This was indeed a representative cross-section of the male population of this small Connecticut city on the north shore of Long Island Sound, some seventy-five miles to the northeast of New York City.

If you had answered the newspaper ad, you would have shown up at the university for a nominal fee of $4.50 and for the sake of science and your own curiosity. You probably would have been impressed. After all, Yale dominates the city, a venerable institution whose name is practically magical. You would not have been less impressed by the elegant laboratories where you would have met a distinguished behavioral scientist dressed in a white laboratory coat and, incidentally, another newspaper recruit—like you. The scientist would have explained to both of you that the specific purpose of the experiment was to study the *effects of punishment on learning*. The experiment would require a "teacher" and a "learner." By chance you would be appointed the role of teacher, and the other recruit the role of learner.

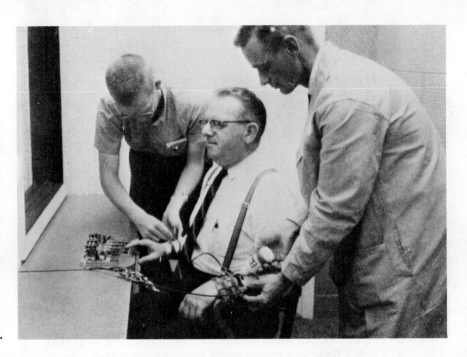

This man could be in for quite a shock. He is a "learner" in the Milgram studies of obedience carried out at Yale University.

You, the scientist, and the "learner" would go into a laboratory room with a chair that looked rather threatening: straps dangled from it. The scientist would secure the learner's cooperation and strap him into the chair. The learner would express some concern, but this was, after all, for the sake of science. And this was Yale University, was it not? What could happen to a person at Yale?

You would then be led into an adjacent room by the scientist, the room from which you would do your "teaching." This teaching promised to be extremely effective. The instrument you would use to punish the learner's errors was a fearsome-looking electrical control board with a series of levers marked from 15 to 450 volts. Written labels designated twenty-eight of thirty of them to run the gamut from "Slight Shock" to "Danger: Severe Shock." The last two levers were reminiscent of a film unfit for anyone under seventeen: they were simply rated "XXX." Just in case you had no concept of what electric shock felt like, the scientist gave you a sample 45-volt shock. You did not find it pleasant and pitied the fellow who might receive more.

Your learner was expected to learn word pairs. Pairs of words would be read from a list. After going through the list once, your learner would have to produce the word that was paired with a stimulus word. He would do this from his room by pressing a switch that would signify his choice from a list of four alternatives. His switch would light up one of four panels in your room. If it was the correct panel, you would simply proceed to the next stimulus word. If not, you would deliver an electric shock. If the learner continued to make errors, you would gradually increase the voltage of the shock, one step at a time.

You would probably have some misgivings about all this. Electrodes had been strapped to the learner's wrist, and the scientist had applied electrode paste to "avoid blisters and burns." When you were told that the shocks you were going to deliver might be extremely painful but would cause "no perma-

The experimental set-up in the Milgram study. When the "learner" makes an error, the experimenter prods the "teacher" to deliver a painful electric shock.

nent tissue damage," it would have been understandable if you had had your doubts. Still, the learner was going along, and, after all, this was Yale.

Now to begin. The learner answers a few items correctly and then makes some mistakes. With mild concern you press the levers up through 45 volts. You tolerated that much yourself. Then a couple of more mistakes are made. You press the 60-volt lever, then 75. Another mistake is made. You pause and look at the scientist. He is reassuring: "Although the shocks may be painful, there is no permanent tissue damage, so please go on." Further errors are made and you are quickly up to a shock of 300 volts. But now the learner is pounding on the wall of his room! Your chest tightens and you begin to perspire. Damn science and the $4.50, you think. You hesitate, and the scientist says, "The experiment requires that you continue." After the delivery of the next stimulus word, there is no answer at all. What do you do? "Wait for five to ten seconds," the scientist says, "and then treat no answer as a wrong answer." Yet after the delivery of that next shock, there is again the pounding on the wall! Now your heart is racing and you are convinced that you are causing extreme pain and discomfort. Is it possible that no lasting damage is being done? Is the experiment that important, after all? What to do? You hesitate again. The scientist says, "It is absolutely essential that you continue." His voice is very convincing. "You have no other choice," he says, "you *must* go on." You can barely think straight and for some unaccountable reason you feel laughter beginning in your throat. Your finger shakes above the lever. What do you do?

Social Influence and
Assertive Behavior

On Truth at Yale

Stanley Milgram (1963, 1974) found out what most people would do. Prior to the experiment, seniors at Yale had predicted that perhaps 3 percent of the population would administer shocks all the way through 450 volts, the maximum. Dr. Milgram's professional colleagues, psychologists and psychiatrists, had predicted that very few would go beyond 200 volts. But of the forty men in this phase of his research, only five refused to go beyond the 300-volt level, at which the learner had first pounded against the wall. Nine more teachers defied the scientist during the 300s. But twenty-six of the original forty participants complied with the experimenter throughout the entire series, believing that they were delivering 450 volts, triple-X-rated shocks.

Were these newspaper recruits simply emotionally blank and unconcerned? Not at all. Milgram was impressed by the signs of stress they showed. They trembled, they stuttered, they bit their lips. They groaned, they sweated, they dug their fingernails into their flesh. There were fits of laughter, though laughter was inappropriate. One forty-six-year-old salesman's laughter was so convulsive that he could not continue with the experiment. Such were these participant's payments for failure to assert their moral values.

Milgram wondered if college students, heralded for independent thinking, would show more defiance. But a replication of the study with Yale undergraduates yielded similar results. What of women, who are supposedly less aggressive than men? Women, too, shocked the learners. But surely this could happen only within the walls of Yale, where subjects would be overpowered by the prestige of the setting! Not so. Milgram found the same results in a dingy storefront rented in Bridgeport. All this in a nation that values independence and the free will of the individual. Our national nightmare may not be over at all.

On Deception at Yale

You are probably sufficiently skeptical to be wondering if the "teachers" in the Milgram study actually delivered electric shock to the "learners" as a result of pressing the levers on the control board. They didn't. The only shock actually delivered in this experiment was the 45-volt sample to the teacher, and the purpose of this shock was to lend credibility to the procedure.

The learners in the experiment were actually confederates of the experimenter. They had not answered the newspaper ads, but were in on the truth from the start. Teachers were the only real subjects in the experiment. Teachers were led to believe that they were randomly chosen for the teacher role, but it was rigged so that the newspaper recruits would always be placed in the teacher role.

Milgram had no interest in the influence of punishment on learning. He wished to determine how many people would *obey* the experimenter.

SOCIAL INFLUENCE

This tendency to obey authority figures blindly is a major problem in the psychology of **social influence**—an area of social psychology that examines how people exert pressure on other people to encourage them to behave in particular ways. Other important areas in the psychology of social influence include **conformity** and **persuasion**. Conformity is behavior similar to that of others—

Social influence. An area in psychology that studies the influence of people and groups on other people.
Conformity. Behavior that is in agreement with social customs, rules, laws, and morals, or that is similar to that of others.
Persuasion (purr-SWAY-shun). The act of influencing or changing another person's thoughts, feelings, or behavior; causing someone to do something by urging.

THE ASSERTIVENESS SCHEDULE

How assertive are you? Do you bow to social pressures and constantly do the bidding of others? Do you speak your mind and stick up for your rights? Or are you somewhere in between?

Find out how assertive you are by taking the following self-report test of assertive behavior. Then turn to the end of this chapter to find out how to determine your score, and to compare your results with the scores of 1400 students drawn from thirty-five college and university campuses across the United States.

Directions: Indicate how descriptive each item is of you by using this code:

> 3 very much like me
> 2 rather like me
> 1 slightly like me
> − 1 slightly unlike me
> − 2 rather unlike me
> − 3 very unlike me

_____ 1. Most people seem to be more aggressive and assertive than I am.*

_____ 2. I have hesitated to make or accept dates because of "shyness."*

_____ 3. When the food served at a restaurant is not done to my satisfaction, I complain about it to the waiter or waitress.

_____ 4. I am careful to avoid hurting other people's feelings, even when I feel that I have been injured.*

_____ 5. If a salesman has gone to considerable trouble to show me merchandise that is not quite suitable, I have a difficult time saying "No."*

_____ 6. When I am asked to do something, I insist upon knowing why.

_____ 7. There are times when I look for a good, vigorous argument.

_____ 8. I strive to get ahead as well as most people in my position.

_____ 9. To be honest, people often take advantage of me.*

_____ 10. I enjoy starting conversations with new acquaintances and strangers.

_____ 11. I often don't know what to say to attractive persons of the opposite sex.*

_____ 12. I will hesitate to make phone calls to business establishments and institutions.*

_____ 13. I would rather apply for a job or for admission to a college by writing letters than by going through with personal interviews.*

_____ 14. I find it embarrassing to return merchandise.*

_____ 15. If a close and respected relative were annoying me, I would smother my feelings rather than express my annoyance.*

_____ 16. I have avoided asking questions for fear of sounding stupid.*

_____ 17. During an argument I am sometimes afraid that I will get so upset that I will shake all over.*

_____ 18. If a famed and respected lecturer makes a comment that I think is incorrect, I will have the audience hear my point of view as well.

_____ 19. I avoid arguing over prices with clerks and salesmen.*

_____ 20. When I have done something important or worthwhile, I manage to let others know about it.

_____ 21. I am open and frank about my feelings.

_____ 22. If someone has been spreading false and bad stories about me, I see him (her) as soon as possible and "have a talk" about it.

_____ 23. I often have a hard time saying "No."*

_____ 24. I tend to bottle up my emotions rather than make a scene.*

_____ 25. I complain about poor service in a restaurant and elsewhere.

_____ 26. When I am given a compliment, I sometimes just don't know what to say.*

_____ 27. If a couple near me in a theater or at a lecture were conversing rather loudly, I would ask them to be quiet or to take their conversation elsewhere.

_____ 28. Anyone attempting to push ahead of me in a line is in for a good battle.

_____ 29. I am quick to express an opinion.

_____ 30. There are times when I just can't say anything.*

Source: **Rathus** (1973).

perhaps similarity in dress or similarity in the expression of opinions. Persuasion is the communication of messages that are designed to influence behavior. These messages include arguments, advice, and information. They may be communicated by political groups, health organizations, giant corporations, or your neighbor. After we take a look at each of these areas, we shall examine a type of behavior that could just put an end to our national nightmares of blind obedience, apelike conformity, and gullibility: assertive behavior.

CONFORMITY

In Chapter 1 you briefly met an eighteen-year-old college freshman named Jennifer. When she left home for the university, she knew that the majority of contemporary young women experienced premarital intercourse. It was impossible for her not to know. Sex was a constant topic on television talk shows, and the women's magazines seemed to sprout statistics like crabgrass. She had also attended "R" films and read stories and novels with explicit sexuality. So the statistics and the facts of life were not new to her at eighteen.

But social pressure toward sexual experimentation was. Back home she had moved with a clique of young women who had generally shared the view that intercourse was to be reserved for marriage. Back home, girls who had intercourse did not talk about it. Jennifer had engaged in some minor episodes of petting, but that was normal, she thought. Almost everyone had done that. But at the university her two roommates and the women who shared her floor talked openly about their sexual activities. It might have been easier to live with if it had been boastful talk or rebellious talk. Jennifer could then have thought that her friends were "trying too hard." But they seemed genuinely casual about their experiences. They seemed to have integrated mature sexuality as a regular part of their lives. Jennifer intellectually doubted it, but she caught herself thinking that she could be the only remaining virgin in the freshman class. This was distressful, causing her to challenge her personal values and to feel that she did not quite fit in with her classmates. After a while they stopped talking about sex with her, and she felt even more left out. Perhaps, she thought, she ought to get with it so that she would have something to share with the others. Let us have a look at an experiment that explores the influence of such social pressure.

Seven Line Judges Can't Be Wrong: The Asch Study

Do you believe what you see with your own eyes? Seeing is believing, is it not? Not if you had been recruited into an experiment run by social psychologist Solomon Asch in the early 1950s.

If you had become involved in this experiment, you would have entered a laboratory room along with seven other subjects in order to participate in an experiment on visual discrimination. If you had experience in psychology experiments, you might have been surprised: no rats and no electric shock apparatus anywhere in sight. Only a gentleman and some cards with lines on them in front of the room.

This gentleman would quickly seat the eight of you at a series of chairs. You would be assigned the seventh seat and not pay particular attention to this minor fact. He would then explain the task. On a card on your left was a single line. To the right was another card with three lines of different lengths. One

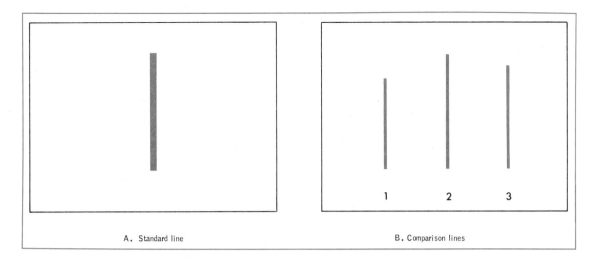

A. Standard line   B. Comparison lines

Cards used by Asch. Which is the same length as A? 1, 2 or 3? 2, right? But what if everyone else said 3?

line matched the line on the card to the left. All you and your fellow recruits had to do was call out, in order, which of the three lines was the same length as the one on the left, line A, B, or C. Simple.

You would try it out. Those to your right speak out one after the other: "C," "C," "C," "C," "C," "C." It is your turn. Line C is clearly the same length as the line on the first card, so you say "C." Then the fellow after you chimes in: "C." That's all there is to it. Then two other cards are placed in front of the room. This time line B is clearly the same length as the card on the left. "B," "B," "B," "B," "B," "B." Again it is your turn. "B," you say, and perhaps your mind begins to wander. Your stomach is gurgling a bit. Tonight you won't even mind dorm food particularly. "B," the last fellow says on your left.

Another pair of cards is held up. Line C is clearly the correct answer. The six people on your right speak in turn: "A," "A, . . ." Wait a second, you think. ". . . A," "A, . . ." You forget about dinner and study the three lines briefly. No, A is definitely too short, by about an inch and a half or so. ". . . A," "A," and it is your turn. Your hands have very quickly become sweaty and there is a lump in your throat. You want to say C, but is it right?

The Asch experiment in conformity. The experimenter is at the right and the unsuspecting subject is seated second from the right.

Social Influence and
Assertive Behavior

There is really no time, you have already paused just a bit. "A," you say. "A," the fellow on your left matter-of-factly confirms.

Now your attention is firmly riveted on the lines each time the cards are switched. Much of the time you agree with the other seven line judges, but occasionally you do not, and for some reason that is totally beyond your understanding, they are all in perfect agreement even when they are incorrect. It is a nightmare, and you begin to doubt your own judgment.

The nightmare in the Asch (1952) experiment was the pressure to conform. Actually, all of the other seven recruits were confederates of the experimenter. They agreed to give the incorrect response now and then, according to a prearranged schedule. The entire purpose of the experiment was to see whether you would go along with the erroneous responses because of the social influences acting upon you.

How many of Asch's subjects caved in? How many went along with the crowd rather than asserting what they believed to be the correct response? Seventy-five percent. *Three of four agreed with the majority on at least one occasion.*

What about you? Would you wear your blue jeans if everyone else was wearing slacks and skirts? What would you have done? Are you sure?

What factors lead to conformity, even at the price of failure to assert your true feelings? Certainly there are personal factors. For instance, Krech, Crutchfield, and Ballachey (1962) found that a strong tendency to conform is prevalent among people with feelings of personal inadequacy and of inferiority. But several social factors have also been looked into: the number of people who hold the majority opinion, your ability to find someone who shares your minority opinion, and your sex.

Numbers: Can 50 Million Frenchpersons Be Wrong? Let's put you back into the Asch study, with a difference. Rather than being tested along with seven other subjects, there is only one other person. When only one person disagrees with you, it is usually an easy matter to decide that this individual is rather foolish.

If Jennifer had felt pressured only by one roommate, or even by two roommates, she might not have felt so overwhelmed. But the appearance that perhaps all her classmates had been sexually intimate led her to perceive herself as deviant. Nor are advertising executives unaware of the pressures to conform. If they can give the impression that "everyone" is turning to their brand-new, improved, and superior laundry detergent or automobile, more as-of-yet underprivileged consumers are likely to experiment with the product. Gerard, Wilhelmy, and Connolley (1968) found that the tendency to conform, even to incorrect judgments, increases rapidly with group size up to five members, and then increases at a somewhat slower pace up to eight members.

Support: Am I Really the Only One? Jennifer was so concerned about her felt uniqueness that she visited her university counseling center. Her counselor passed no judgments on her behavior or the behavior of her friends, but did point out that she was not as alone as she thought. It was probably accurate that the majority of her women classmates had experienced sexual intimacy, but on her huge campus there would be many hundreds of women who preferred to wait until forming a lasting union, as did Jennifer. It might be that these women would be somewhat less vocal about sexual behavior, but Jennifer would find friends among these women if she wished to look.

In a variation of the Asch experiment, Allen and Levine (1971) provided recruits with just one confederate who would agree with them, and the other confederates, as in the Asch study, stuck to their erroneous ways. Now, this one confederate was not exactly the greatest gift to the visual discrimination study. In fact, this person had a vision impairment and wore glasses that were as thick and chunky as peanut butter. Yet even the support of this confederate was sufficient to encourage the actual recruits to stick to their guns and respond according to their genuine judgments more often.

Sex: Are Women Easier to Push Around than Men? Do women conform more readily than men? Does our society train men to become rugged individuals and women to accept authority?

As we saw in Chapter 3, parents are often more protective of girls, and possibly less likely to encourage them to show signs of independence than boys. But does this mean that women will cave in to group pressure more rapidly than men? In the early work on conformity, experimenters such as Asch did find women to conform to incorrect group judgments more often than men. But did Asch's findings mean that women conformed more readily or that women were less familiar with estimating the lengths of lines than men?

Sistrunk and McDavid (1971) studied the tendency for men and women to conform to group pressure on three types of items: items (1) more familiar to men, (2) more familiar to women, and (3) equally familiar to men and women. They found that women did conform more readily on items familiar to men. But they also found that men conformed more readily on items familiar to women. There were no sex differences on items equally familiar to both sexes. Sistrunk and McDavid's findings suggest that we all tend to conform more in situations in which we feel less personally competent, regardless of our sex.

But don't gamble all your savings on Sistrunk and McDavid, for their experiment is not the end of the story. Sandra Bem (1975) reasoned that since resistance to pressures to conform is usually considered a masculine trait, it would not be surprising if chesty men were more resistant than fluffy women. But **androgynous** individuals ought to be able to show traditionally masculine or feminine traits, depending on the requirements of the situation. Thus there ought to be no differences in resistance between androgynous men and women. Androgynous men and women should resist as well as the chestiest, masculine men, and these three groups would probably all show greater resistance than fluffy, feminine females.

Androgynous (ann-DRODGE-in-us). Possessing traits that are considered characteristic of both traditionally masculine and traditionally feminine sex roles.

Bem used her sex role inventory to define groups of masculine men, feminine women, and androgynous men and women, and then asked all her subjects to participate in rating a series of ninety-two cartoons for funniness. Each participant was placed in a separate room, but could hear the ratings of others through an earphone and microphone setup. They were called on in various sequences, sometimes first, sometimes last.

What Bem's subjects did not know is that the ratings they heard on their earphones were all phony tapes. The taped ratings were commonly in obvious error, categorizing the uproarious as dull and the dull as a million laughs. When these errors were made, the subject would be in the last position. Would the subject then respond on the basis of the content of the cartoons, or would the subject conform to the absurd ratings heard over the earphones?

Bem's predictions were borne out. Masculine men and androgynous men and women showed rather consistent tendencies to remain true to themselves and respond on the basis of the cartoons. Feminine women more often conformed to the ratings of others. We cannot ignore the powerful social expectation that feminine women are not to make waves after all.

PERSUASION

In 1741, a Puritan minister by the name of Jonathan Edwards delivered a sermon, "Sinners in the Hands of an Angry God," to his Connecticut congregation. As you can see from the following excerpt, he wanted his audience to shape up:

> The God that holds you over the pit of hell, much as one holds a spider or some loathsome insect over the fire, abhors you and is dreadfully provoked. He looks upon you as worthy of nothing else but to be cast into the fire. He is of purer eyes than to bear to have you in his sight. You are ten thousand times so abominable in his eyes as the most hateful venomous serpent is in ours. You have offended him infinitely more than ever a stubborn rebel did his prince, and yet 'tis nothing but his hand that holds you from falling into the fire every moment.
>
> Oh, sinner! Consider the fateful danger you are in. 'Tis a great furnace of wrath, a wide and bottomless pit full of the fire of wrath that you are held over in the hand of that God whose wrath is provoked and incensed as much against you as against many of the damned in Hell. You hang by a slender thread, with the flames of divine wrath flashing about it, and ready every moment to singe it and burn it asunder.

We think you have the message, so we'll cut the sermon short. Frankly, it's becoming a little warm around here. Edwards' sermon is one example of an attempt to persuade. His congregation no longer clung to the orthodoxy of the

Baseball great Joe DiMaggio sells coffee-makers in a television commercial. Why does a manufacturer gamble millions in a bet that an athlete can sell a coffee-maker?

generation that had settled Massachusetts, and he was hoping he could convince them to return to basics through his highly emotional appeals. If they could not be logically encouraged to rededicate themselves to the church, perhaps they could be frightened into it.

But Jonathan Edwards was too late. His flock was no longer of a mind to respond to fire and brimstone. His views were too far apart from those of his congregation. His sermons did not frighten this younger generation of New England churchgoers into changing what he thought were their sinful ways. His sermons **boomeranged**—they caused the congregation to reject him because they were so far out. By 1750 Jonathan Edwards was a preacher without a pulpit.

The emotional appeal is just one aspect of the social psychology of persuasion. Every time you watch television you are bombarded by commercial after commercial. Don't you get tired of all the repetition? At some point don't you decide you will never buy a product because you are sick of all those commercials? Probably not, as we shall see.

Several factors appear to determine the effectiveness of persuasive messages. They involve (1) the communicator or person who delivers the message, (2) the message itself, (3) the audience, and (4) the context in which the message is delivered.

Boomerang (BOOM-er-rang). A flat, curved stick that tends to return to the thrower when it is cast. Used by Australian aborigines as a weapon. A boomerang effect is the tendency of some efforts at persuasion to have the opposite of the intended effect.

The Persuasive Communicator: Whom Do You Trust?

Would you attend weight-control classes that were run by a 350-pound leader? Would you buy an automobile from an evasive salesperson who had been recently convicted for larceny? Would you leaf through fashion magazines if the models were unappealing? Your enthusiasm for these endeavors might understandably wane. For common sense as well as psychological evidence suggests that people who are effective and persuasive communicators tend to show (1) expertise or competence in their fields, (2) trustworthiness or sincerity, and (3) physical attractiveness and similarity to their audiences.

Health professionals enjoy high status in our society, so it is not surprising that several brands of toothpaste boast that their products have been found to be effective at preventing cavities by the American Dental Association. Health professionals are thought to be experts, and Mills and Harvey (1972), among others, have found that expertise makes messages more appealing. Why has Sanka coffee enlisted Robert Young for its commercials? In these commercials someone typically becomes quite upset over nothing and becomes ill-tempered. Perhaps next year they will detonate a homemade atom bomb. Robert Young then suggests Sanka brand coffee, which does not contain the stimulant caffeine. In the next scene our once-irritable caffeine victim is now as gentle as a puppy dog.

Robert Young, you may recall, played the character of Dr. Marcus Welby for a number of years—one of those rare father figures who almost always had the answer, knew where to get it if he didn't, and, on one of those rare occasions when even he was stymied, at least his personal warmth would make the pain portrayed on the video screen bearable. So it is the image of the physician that Sanka is betting will sell its product. But Sanka would not wish to be accused of false advertising when Robert Young endorses their product, so in one commercial he confesses that he is not, after all, a physician. True confessions.

Trustworthiness also seems to sell (Walster et al. 1966). Sam Ervin, the

CBS reporter Walter Cronkite may have more "credibility" than any other public figure in the United States. How much do you think corporations would pay him to endorse deodorants, toothpaste, or paper towels on television?

PATTY HEARST AND COGNITIVE DISSONANCE

In February of 1974, newspaper heiress Patty Hearst was abducted by a revolutionary group known as the Symbionese Liberation Army (SLA) while she was an undergraduate at University of California at Berkeley. The first communications from the SLA declared that the Hearst family must distribute millions of dollars' worth of food to the poor if they ever wished to see their daughter again. There was no suggestion that Patty was a willing prisoner.

But after several weeks, communications issued by the SLA contained statements by Patty that she had joined them. She expressed contempt for her family's capitalist values and declared that her new name was "Tania." A photograph of Tania was also issued, showing her holding a machine gun and wearing a guerrilla outfit. At this time she referred to her parents as "pigs." But her family still did not believe that Patty had actually changed her attitudes. After

Patty Hearst as the "urban guerrilla" Tania, and in manacles on her way to testify in court. After her kidnapping by the Symbionese Liberation Army, Patty was "brainwashed" into committing armed robbery and other acts that were inconsistent with her own sense of self. After a while, she came to view herself as a revolutionary. How can any of us tell where our "real selves" leave off and the influences of others begin?

former senator from North Carolina, was a prominent figure on the Senate committee that investigated the Watergate affair. Through televised sessions he became known to the nation as "a simple country lawyer" who was honest and clever. The American Express Company has enlisted Sam Ervin to sell its credit cards on television. In his commercials he must remind the viewing public that he is no longer a senator, just a "simple country lawyer."

Why does the brilliant and sophisticated Sam Ervin present himself as just a "country lawyer"? Why do politicians demonstrate their affinities for fried chicken, blintzes, tacos, pasta, baak choy, corned beef and cabbage, or bakall, she had been influenced by their values for twenty years, and she had been exposed to the SLA for only two months. It was an easy matter to explain her behavior as an effort to earn the goodwill of her captors and avoid mistreatment at their hands.

In April of 1974, the nation began to wonder about Patty. She and other SLA members robbed a San Francisco bank, and there were videotaped pictures of Patty holding a rifle. It was also reported that she had threatened a guard. But, the Hearst family maintained, perhaps the rifle had not been loaded and Patty had still been acting under fear of losing her life or other punishment. Yet Patty was soon thereafter involved in another incident, in which she covered the escape of SLA members William and Emily Harris from a store they had robbed with bursts of fire from an automatic rifle. She seemed clearly under her own influence at the time.

Patty and the Harrises were captured in San Francisco late in 1975. At first Patty was defiant, giving a revolutionary salute and identifying herself as the guerrilla fighter Tania. But once in prison, her attitudes appeared to undergo another transformation. She asked to be called Patty. At her trial she appeared quite remorseful, and the defense claimed that had it not been for the social influence of the SLA, Patty would never have engaged in criminal behavior or adopted revolutionary values. When President Jimmy Carter signed the order for Patty's early release from prison in 1979, he was operating under an admission from Patty's original prosecutors—that she, indeed, would not have engaged in criminal behavior if it had not been for her abduction by the SLA and the dread that she experienced in the days following her kidnapping.

How is it that a college undergraduate with typical American values came to experience attitudes that were so opposed to her own ideals?

At first, Patty's captors used methods that have been labeled brainwashing (Lifton 1963; Schein 1961). They first demonstrated that her world had turned upside down: They, the SLA, now had the power of life and death over her and controlled all the rewards and punishments in Patty's life; her parents—indeed, the United States—were powerless to help her. Patty was placed under prolonged stress in a cramped closet, exhausting her resistance to persuasion. She was continually assailed as being part of the capitalist establishment that the SLA portrayed as creating the class structure that led to deprivation for the common people. Only when Patty was thoroughly exhausted did they show a more supporting, gentle side, encouraging Patty to be reborn with a new identity—Tania.

According to social psychologist Leon Festinger (Festinger 1957; Festinger & Carlsmith 1959), such conversions in identity can be explained through the concept of cognitive dissonance. Cognitive dissonance theory suggests that when people hold conflicting thoughts, perceptions, or cognitions, they are motivated to reduce this conflict. For instance, if you have engaged in sexual experimentation but believe sex without marriage to be sinful, you may be motivated to change your belief to bring it into line with your behavior. Or if you do something you do not particularly enjoy for money, and the money is not sufficient to justify your behavior, you may develop more positive attitudes toward the activity. In other words, you are generally motivated to justify your behavior to yourself. The recognition that your cognitions are in conflict will supply the motivation to do so.

If we try to imagine the influences acting on Patty shortly after her capture, we find that she had to agree with the SLA, make love with SLA members, and learn their ways. At the time she was frightened and exhausted, yet she found herself doing many things that she could not justify so long as she firmly clung to her self-identity as Patty. But by adopting the new identity suggested by her captors, that of Tania, and allowing herself to experience Tania's attitudes, she could view herself as "liberated" rather than captured, and justify the behavior that was otherwise so disturbing.

lava—depending on the neighborhood in which they happen to be campaigning? Why does James Earl Carter prefer to be known as "Jimmy"? Psychological evidence suggests that communicators are more persuasive when they are felt to be just Plains folks (Byrne 1971; Berscheid & Walster 1974).

We also pay more attention to people who are attractive. You might not like to believe that that is so in our egalitarian society, but corporations do not gamble their millions on the physically unappealing to sell their products. Some advertisers look for the perfect combination of attractiveness and plain, simple folks: Ivory Soap commercials sport "real" people with even features

Social Influence and Assertive Behavior

who seem freshly scrubbed, scrubbed, and more scrubbed. You can practically smell the aroma of Ivory Soap in their hair through the TV set.

The Persuasive Message: Say What? Say How? Say How Often?

Young women at a private New England school for girls are continually exposed to Vivaldi and Mozart at lunchtime. Will bombarding them with classical music whet their appetites or turn them off? Does being exposed to the same television commercial repeatedly make us more or less likely to run to the store or reach for our checkbook? Is it foolishness or cleverness to expose us to the views of the opposition? What happens if arguments are too far out? Do scare tactics work, or are we all too smart for that? You won't be in suspense for long. Psychological research has much to say about the persuasiveness of repeating messages, presenting the other person's point of view, using messages that are too discrepant with preconceived notions, and using the emotional appeal.

How Much Is Too Much? Does Familiarity Breed Contentment? How do you feel about zabulons and afworbus? We would understand if you were not overly crazy about them, at least at first. But social psychologist Robert Zajonc (1968) found that people began to react more favorably toward these supposedly Turkish words (which were actually constructed especially for the experiment) just on the basis of repeated exposure to them.

What about abstract art and classical music? Studies by Heingartner and Hall (1974) and Smith and Dorfman (1975) suggest that it just might be possible to influence such tastes through repetition. Love for classical art and music may begin in the nursery environment—not with the conscious preferences of late childhood and adulthood.

Will prolonged exposure to classical music turn people on or drive them away to pop and rock?

And what of racial prejudice? Research by Hamm, Baum, and Nikels (1975) showed that white subjects responded more favorably to photographs of blacks merely as a function of having seen them ten times! Blacks in television commercials may do more than sell the product—they may lower negative racial feelings among whites.

Is there some upper limit? If you are more likely to try a product after seeing it advertised ten times, does your appetite increase further as a result of seeing it a thousand times? Perhaps not. We sometimes tend to tire of even our favorite foods and television shows—after the hundredth or five hundredth repetition. Some research suggests that our liking may continue to grow for relatively complex stimuli upon the umpteenth presentation, but decrease for simpler stimuli (Saegert & Jellison 1970; Smith & Dorfman 1975). This could explain why some of us never tire of *Hamlet*, or classical music, or dishes with the most subtle flavors. But a situation comedy, even well-written, may die in a decade, and a pop tune tends to pall within a few months.

Listen to the Other Side, Too—Well, Sort Of. Theologians and politicians know the value of exposing their followers to the arguments of their opposition. By raising issues the opposition will use, and then refuting them point by point, one can develop a sort of psychological immunity to those arguments among one's followers. Research by Hass and Linder (1972) suggests that it is especially effective for you to present a two-sided argument when the recipients are at first uncertain about their position. Perhaps it shows that you are fair enough to show both sides. On the other hand, there is always the risk that the people you are trying to persuade may develop the notion that maybe the other guy isn't so far out after all.

Assertiveness training is a recently developed group of psychological techniques designed to help clients become more effective, persuasive, and self-expressive. One commonly used assertiveness-training technique is **fogging.** In using fogging, you show that you understand the other person's point of view by paraphrasing that position. *But* (there's always a "but" after you have agreed with a social antagonist) then you go on to emphasize the correctness of your own position.

What if newspaper recruits in the Milgram study on obedience to authority had used fogging to resist the persuasive communications of the experimenter? Perhaps a recruit would have paused at the 300-volt shock level, and the experimenter would have said: "You must go on. The experiment requires that you continue." Our fogging recruit might have answered,

"I understand how important this experiment is to you. I know that it is all for the sake of science and that he is not supposed to suffer any permanent tissue damage. I can even see that we have already come a long way and that it would be a pity to stop now—*but* I am very concerned about the pain I am causing him, and I am trying to sort out my feelings and values. Surely you can understand that I wouldn't want to do something I might believe is morally wrong, can't you? I need some time to think it over."

When you use fogging and then disagree, you cannot be accused of failing to listen to or understand the other person's point of view. You can also put your opposition to sleep by running off endlessly at the mouth.

Discrepancy: When Far Out Is Out. Jonathan Edwards gave some very fine sermons. His language was colorful and his phrasing was tight and sure. But his audience wasn't having any. The days of the New England orthodoxy had gone

Assertiveness training (ass-SURT-tiv-ness). A method for helping individuals become more self-expressive that uses techniques such as role playing, coaching, and modeling.
Fogging. An effective method of showing disagreement in which one first shows that the other person's point of view is understood and appreciated.

YOU WOULDN'T MIND IF WE RANSACKED YOUR HOME, WOULD YOU?

How would you react if a man from some consumer group phoned you and asked if he and a six-man crew might stop by your house for only a few hours to inventory every product you had stuck away in your kitchen, bathroom, bedrooms, closets, attic, and basement? In an experiment by Freedman and Fraser (1966), only 22.2 percent of women phoned acceded to this rather troublesome request. But another group of women was more willing. In fact, 52.8 percent of them agreed to a visit from this wrecking crew. Why? Because they had been called a few days earlier, at which time they had agreed to answer a few simple questions about the types of soaps used in their homes. When the second call came, these women had already been primed for the larger request. The caller had gotten his foot in the door.

The foot-in-the-door technique has also been found effective at persuading people to make charitable contributions (Pliner et al. 1974) and to sign petitions (Baron 1973). This technique is also well known to the military. If your first command to a recruit was that he should jump out into enemy fire, you might expect that he would balk. But if he has first learned to obey commands concerning his dress, his walk, and other ways of behaving, the command to behave later on is more likely to be obeyed automatically.

Credibility (kred-uh-BILL-it-tee). Believability, reliability.
Discrepancy. Lack of agreement, inconsistency, difference.

the way of the Salem witch hunts. They were out of style. So instead of swaying his congregation, Jonathan Edwards destroyed his own **credibility** when his efforts at persuasion were too **discrepant** from their views. He was too far out, and soon he was out. He had to find work in New Jersey. When the gap between the message and the audience widens too far, the speech can boomerang (Eagly 1974). A boomerang in the stomach is not a pleasant experience for a communicator.

On the other hand, some communicators can maintain high degrees of credibility when they espouse positions that are apparently contradictory to their own points of view. If the owner of a whaling fleet were suddenly to come out and try to raise American consciousness about the fact that several species of these great mammals are in danger of becoming extinct, we would pay more attention than we would to a conservationist group. The whaler must be sincere—there is something for him to lose by embracing this view.

"You're in Big Trouble, but Maybe There's a Way Out": The Emotional Appeal. As mature and intelligent adults, we naturally consider all persuasive communications carefully and weigh them purely on the basis of the evidence for their positions. Don't we? Perhaps not. Grisly films of diseased, cancerous lungs and of operations to remove them are more effective at inducing attitude changes toward smoking than are calm verbal presentations based largely on statistics (Leventhal et al. 1967). Films of purpled, bloodied gums and blackened, decayed teeth are more likely to cause you to reach for a toothbrush than are logical discussions (Evans et al. 1970).

In the early 1960s, Senator Barry Goldwater of Arizona had earned a national reputation for being tough on communism. Lyndon Johnson carried the 1964 presidential election against Goldwater by a landslide. One of Johnson's television commercials showed a hydrogen bomb exploding. The commercial suggested that we could not trust the allegedly belligerent Goldwater to hold

SMOKING
CAN EAT YOUR LUNGS ALIVE!

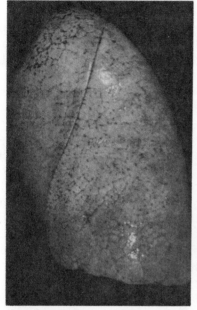 

This is a normal lung, with its characteristically healthy pink coloring.

This is a cancerous lung. The white growth at the top of the lung is the cancer.

ACCORDING TO THE AMERICAN LUNG ASSOCIATION, IF YOU SMOKE YOUR CHANCES OF DYING FROM LUNG CANCER ARE 700 TIMES THOSE OF NON-SMOKERS. IF YOU SMOKE, THIS COULD BE YOUR LUNG. THINK ABOUT IT THE NEXT TIME YOU LIGHT A CIGARETTE...IF THERE IS A NEXT TIME.

Which is more effective at inducing people to quit smoking? Fear campaigns with photos of blackened lungs, or calm and reasoned verbal appeals to the intellect?

the fate of our children in his hands. The emotional appeal is most effective when it is coupled with concrete recommendations for a way out—stopping smoking, brushing more often, and depressing the lever in the voting booth for Lyndon Johnson (Leventhal 1970). And the appeal must be credible—if not, it may boomerang. If voters had not at all believed the Johnson campaign rhetoric, Goldwater might have received a strong "sympathy vote."

The **emotional appeal** can create *fear*. The concrete recommendations are then effective because they offer a way out, a way to reduce this unpleasant arousal. And when arousal is very high you may jump at almost any opportunity to lower it, since high arousal sometimes leads to the presence of a number of competing thoughts—confusion.

But the emotional appeal is not confined to fear reactions. Numerous investigators (e.g., Freedman et al. 1967; Regan et al. 1972; Wallington 1973) have found that inducing *guilt* also leads people to be more easily persuaded. In these studies, people who believed that they had ruined an experiment or damaged or destroyed the property of others yielded to requests more readily.

Emotional appeal. The technique of persuasion that relies on arousing feelings of guilt or fear that a person will be motivated to avoid by following the advice of the communicator.

Social Influence and Assertive Behavior

Think for a moment of the Milgram study: How many recruits yielded to the experimenter's demands because they would otherwise have been guilty of destroying a study?

Characteristics of the Audience: Are You a Person Who "Can't Say No"?

Why do some people have "sales resistance" while others buy magazines from every bogus college student who rings the doorbell? There are probably a number of reasons. We have already seen that people with feelings of inadequacy are probably more dependent on the judgments of the crowd. But psychologists Robert Schwartz of Indiana University and John Gottman of the University of Illinois have found that people who have a difficult time refusing unreasonable requests (a) perceive themselves to be more tense than people who did refuse the requests, and (b) experience thoughts that prevent them from behaving assertively (1976).

People who did manage to refuse the unreasonable request more often reported, "I was thinking that it doesn't matter what the person thinks of me," "I was thinking that I am perfectly free to say no," or "I was thinking that this request is an unreasonable one." People who complied with the unreasonable request were more likely to report that "I was worried about what the other person would think about me if I refused," "I was thinking that it is better to help others than to be self-centered," or "I was thinking that the other person might be hurt or insulted if I refused" (p. 913).

Interestingly, subjects in this study who complied with the unreasonable request perceived themselves to be more tense, but did *not* actually experience higher heart rates (one sign of anxiety) than subjects who acted assertively. Subjects who complied were also just as knowledgeable about things that they *could* say to the person making the request. Their compliance was associated with their greater perceived self-tension and their attitudes. In short, compliance was consistent with their self-concepts. They saw themselves as the type of people who yield to the demands of others rather than disappoint them.

Social psychologists write about a phenomenon they call **psychological reactance**—the emotional stress you experience when you confront or are confronted by individuals who wish to control your behavior (Brehm 1972). There have probably been times in your life when you took positions you did not believe in just to irk someone who had picked an argument; or there have been times you did not comply with a request just because you did not like the attitude of the individual making the request. You may have laughed at Jonathan Edwards' sermon. But if his language had been more modern and he had actually been your pastor, you might have experienced psychological reactance. And we have all probably at one time or another vowed never to buy a product advertised on television because the commercial was so obnoxious or demeaning.

The Schwartz and Gottman study suggests that we may all tend to experience arousal and tension when we are faced with demands that we find to be inappropriate or unreasonable. We all probably know how to say no as well—or even how to say, "No, I believe that I would rather not," or "I need a few minutes to make up my mind." But our self-identities as people who stick up for our rights or who put the needs of other people before our own will lead some of us to act assertively when we experience psychological reactance and others of us to swallow our arousal and comply.

Psychological reactance (ree-ACT-ents). Emotional stress experienced when faced with people who are attempting to control behavior by exerting social influence.

YOU ARE WHAT YOU BELIEVE

Psychologist Albert Ellis began his professional life as a psychoanalyst. He listened passively as his clients free associated and recounted their dreams. Occasionally he offered an insight. Before long he found himself becoming increasingly dissatisfied with the slow progress of this form of therapy, and, on occasion, with its failure to encourage people to actively challenge irrational beliefs that prevented them from expressing their true feelings and changing futile life patterns.

Over the years Ellis developed a form of therapy that involved active disagreement with the false assumptions of his clients: rational-emotive therapy.

The premise of rational-emotive therapy is that your feelings (the emotive element) are based on your thoughts and attitudes (the rational element). He felt that your thoughts and attitudes were more important determinants of feelings and behavior than childhood experiences and unconscious processes. So this former psychoanalyst began to emotionally confront clients concerning their self-defeating outlooks.

Ellis has found that people hold many irrational beliefs in common. Here are some (1977) that might prevent you from behaving assertively, and some possible adjustive alternatives:

IRRATIONAL BELIEFS

1. I must always have the approval of people who are important to me.
   The danger: You may avoid doing anything that could lead to the disapproval of others, even when you believe you are right.
2. The views of respected authorities or of society must be right.
   The danger: You may follow authority figures even against your own better judgment—as in the Milgram study.
3. I must be completely competent in everything I do.
   The danger: You may avoid acting assertively for fear that your voice may tremble or you might jumble a word or two.
4. I am a product of my childhood experiences—of my heredity and environment.
   The danger: Your defeatism may prevent you from making any efforts to change.
5. If it is too difficult to change, I may just as well save the energy and the pain of trying and settle for what I can get now.
   The danger: You may settle for less than you are entitled to.

ADJUSTIVE ALTERNATIVES

It is nice when people I care for approve of me, but if I can't be myself and earn their approval at the same time, there will be times when I have to live with their condemnation.

It is difficult to challenge traditional and respected ways of viewing and doing things. But if I sincerely hold a discrepant view, I should be true to myself.

It's nice to do everything competently, but nobody's perfect and you've got to start somewhere.

I am strongly influenced by my past—true. But I can still change my behavior.

Change takes time and persistence. It can be frustrating. But at least I will have the satisfaction of attempting to express my true feelings.

"Get 'Em in a Good Mood": The Context of the Message

Of course you are all too clever and insightful to allow someone to persuade you by buttering you up, aren't you? And you all have the common sense not to ask someone in a rotten mood for a favor. We know that *you* do, but we suspect that someone out there might be influenced by a little bit of wine, a piece of cheese, and a good compliment.

Social Influence and Assertive Behavior

Dim lights, candles, soft music, and a little wine work wonders—sometimes. Why may wine fire the passion of love? Because alcohol stimulates sexual arousal, or because a person who accepts an invitation for a drink may see himself or herself as participating in a seduction? Check the effects of alcohol in Chapter 15 and you may believe, with the authors, that the foot-in-the-door technique is often the answer.

Similarly, attempts at seduction usually come at the tail end of a date—after the dinner, the film, the party, the wine, and all that marvelously with-it conversation about the energy crisis, contemporary mores, and the horrible state of our _____ (you fill it in—almost anything will do). An "assault" at the onset of a date might be viewed as a . . . well, as an assault. In the same vein, the food is often plentiful and delicious at charitable dinners—not only putting you in a good mood, but also playing on your feelings of guilt (you do at least have to cover the cost of the food a few times, don't you?). Food and pleasant music have been found to increase the acceptance of persuasive messages in psychological experiments (Janis et al. 1965; Galizio & Hendrick 1972).

It would also be somewhat counterproductive to call your date a jerk when he or she expresses some political belief—even though it is bound to be foolish if it doesn't agree with your own. Agreement and praise or compliments are highly effective ways of influencing others to accept your points of view (Baron 1971; Byrne 1971). You must, of course, appear sincere, or else your agreement will seem shallow and your compliments manipulative.

Shakespeare was a humanistic psychologist, noting, through Polonius' advice to his son, Laertes: "This above all: To thine own self be true, and it must follow, as the night the day, thou canst not then be false to any man" (*Hamlet*, Act I, scene 3). Or to any woman.

At some point, some people decide they must begin to stick up for their rights.

MEETING THE CHALLENGE OF SOCIAL INFLUENCE THROUGH ASSERTIVE BEHAVIOR

Assertive behavior involves the expression of your genuine feelings, standing up for your legitimate rights, and refusing the unreasonable requests of others. It also involves withstanding undue social influences, such as pressures to conform and to obey authority figures.

Assertive individuals may also make efforts to influence others to join them in social activities and political actions that they believe to be worthwhile. This may mean becoming involved in political campaigns, consumer groups, conservationist organizations, and a variety of situations that will advance causes they believe in.

Alternatives to assertive behavior include **nonassertive** (submissive) **behavior** and aggressive behavior. When we are submissive, our self-esteem plummets. Sometimes failure to express our feelings can lead to smoldering resentments which may eventually catch fire and lead to inappropriate, short-lived outbursts. Self-condemnation resulting from outbursts then further lowers our self-esteem. Aggressive behavior includes physical and verbal assaults, threats, insults, and belittling. We sometimes get our way by inducing fear when we act aggressively, but too often we foster the justified condemnation of others. And most of us know when we have been bullies: we are then disapproving of our own behavior, also contributing to lowered self-esteem.

Assertive behavior. Behavior that involves expressing genuine feelings and sticking up for one's rights. What is the difference between assertive and aggressive behavior?

Nonassertive behavior. Submissive, compliant behavior.

Becoming More Assertive

Perhaps you can't become assertive overnight, but you can certainly decide that you have been nonassertive long enough and construct a personal plan to remake your behavior so that it is more consistent with your genuine feelings. Personal growth takes time and effort.

You might as well face it at once: there may be times when you want to quit and revert to your nonassertive ways. Expressing individual values and

Social Influence and Assertive Behavior

personal beliefs may result in conflict—otherwise, we would do it all the time and never have to stand back, take a look at ourselves, and think about it. Often the people we must confront are those who are closest and most meaningful to us: parents, spouses, supervisors at work, close friends.

You can use the following four methods to act more assertively: (1) self-monitoring, (2) coping with irrational beliefs, (3) modeling, and (4) behavior rehearsal to put your knowledge and your convictions into action.

Self-Monitoring: Following Yourself Around the Block

Very often we are troubled about our relationships. We have vague feelings that something is wrong, but we cannot always put our finger on the problem. You can usually find the source of your problems by following yourself around for a while. You may recall from Chapter 7 that observing the context of our feelings is called a *functional analysis*. Monitoring your social interactions will help you pinpoint your problem areas, and may also help motivate you to take charge of your own relationships.

Self-monitoring. Keeping track of one's own behavior.

Self-monitoring is straightforward. Keep a notebook for a week or so and jot down brief descriptions of your social encounters, especially encounters that led to feelings such as anxiety, depression, and anger. For each encounter, note:

- the situation you were in.
- what you felt and said or did.
- what happened as a result of your behavior.
- how you felt as a result of the social interaction.

Below are some examples of self-monitoring taken from Rathus and Nevid (1977). All three people—an office worker, a teacher, and a medical student—were in their twenties:

Jane: Monday, April 6

9:00 A.M.   I passed Artie in the hall. I ignored him. He didn't say anything to me. I felt disgusted with myself.
Noon   Pat and Kathy asked me to join them for lunch. I felt shaky inside and told them I still had work to do. They said all right, but I think they were fed up with me. I felt miserable, very tight in my stomach.
7:30 P.M.   Kathy called and asked me to go clothes shopping with her. I was feeling down, and I said I was busy. She said she was sorry. I don't believe she was sorry—I think she knows I was lying. I hate myself, I feel awful.

Jane's record reveals a pattern of fear that she will not be competent in social interactions and consequent defensive avoidance. But her avoidance has short-lived benefits because of her loneliness, depression, and feelings of self-disgust.

Michael: Wednesday, December 17

8:30 A.M.   The kids were noisy in homeroom. I got very angry and screamed my head off at them. They quieted down, but looked at each other as if I were crazy. My face felt red and hot, and my stomach was in a knot. I found myself wondering what I was doing.

4:00 P.M. I was driving home from school. Some guy cut me off. I followed him closely for two blocks, leaning on my horn but praying he wouldn't stop and get out of his car. He didn't. I felt shaky as hell and thought someday I was going to get myself killed. I had to pull over and wait for the shakes to pass before I could drive again.

8:00 P.M. I was writing lesson plans for tomorrow. Mom came into the room and started crying—Dad was out drinking again. I yelled it was her problem. If she didn't like his drinking, she should divorce him. She cried harder and ran out. I felt pain through my chest. I felt drained and hopeless.

Michael was behaving aggressively, not assertively. Pinpointing the behavior that led to higher blood pressure and many painful bodily sensations helped him realize how he was living with many ongoing frustrations rather than making decisions and acting assertively.

Leslie was a third-year medical student whose husband was a professor of art and archaeology:

Leslie: Tuesday, October 5

10:00 A.M. I was discussing specialization interests with classmates. I mentioned my interest in surgery. Paul smirked and said, "Shouldn't you be going into pediatrics or family practice?" I said nothing, playing the game of ignoring him, but I felt sick and weak inside. I was wondering if I'd ever get through a residency in surgery if every doctor I worked with thought I should be in a less pressured or more "feminine" branch of medicine.

Thursday, October 7

7:30 P.M. I had studying to do but was washing the dinner dishes, as per usual. Tom was reading the paper. I wanted to scream there was no reason I should be doing the dishes just because I was the woman. I'd worked harder that day than Tom, my career was just as important as his, and I had homework to do. But I said nothing. I felt symptoms of anxiety or anger, I don't know which. My face was hot and flushed. My heart rate was rapid. I was sweating.

Leslie's case was typical. Men did not consider her accomplishments to be as significant as their own, even though she was competing successfully in medical school. It never occurred to Tom that he could help her with the dishes, or that they could rotate responsibility for such household tasks. Leslie resolved she must learn to speak out—to prevent male students from taunting her and to enlist Tom's cooperation around the house.

Coping with Irrational Beliefs: "That Can't Be *My* Attitude"

When you are following yourself around, try your best to listen to your conversations with yourself. Ferret out the attitudes and beliefs that lie between the social situations you find yourself in and your responses to them. Our attitudes and beliefs can become so ingrained that we no longer pay attention to them. By not paying attention, we lose the opportunity to reevaluate or update our beliefs about ourselves and our relationships with other people.

Jane was avoiding other people because of anxiety concerning her ability to relate to them successfully. She held several irrational beliefs that heightened this anxiety: She believed that she must be perfectly competent in her social interactions, or else she should avoid them. She believed that she was naturally shy, that her heredity and her childhood experiences had forged an unchangeable adult personality. She believed that it would be so difficult for her to act more assertively that she should settle for whatever pleasures she could obtain from life without exposing herself to social stresses.

Many of Michael's frustrations stemmed from a belief that life was somehow unfair to him. He behaved as though he felt people were being purposefully obstinate. People, perhaps, ought to anticipate his needs and try to fulfill them. He should not really have to find it necessary to take charge of his own feelings and his own relationships.

Leslie was quiet about her feelings because of her own failure to tell herself, loudly and clearly, that it was perfectly all right for her to pursue a career that had been traditionally reserved for men, and that it was also all right to expect her husband to assume some of the chores that had been traditionally reserved for women. She had been attempting just to slide by quietly, without making a fuss. Why? Perhaps she had been overly concerned that she might earn the disapproval of others. Perhaps she felt she could not live with such disapproval. Nonassertive people are typically more concerned than assertive people that others will disapprove of them if they express their true feelings (Schwartz & Gottman 1976).

Try to ferret out your own attitudes and beliefs by becoming more aware of your thought processes as you reflect upon your diary. Check the thoughts of Jane, Michael, and Leslie. Could any of them also belong to you?

Once you have outlined the beliefs that may be preventing you from expressing your true feelings, the procedure is very simple. Challenge them. Ask yourself if you are utterly overwhelmed by the power of their logic. Will the roof really cave in if someone disapproves of you? Will the Ice Age be upon us next week if you attempt to speak up and flub it once or twice? Will the gods really flit down from Mt. Olympus and strike you down with lightning if you should happen to question an authority figure who makes an unreasonable demand?

Modeling: Creating the New (Well, *Almost* New) You

Back in the 1950s a new hero came to the silver screen: James Dean. The movie was *Rebel Without a Cause*. Its hero, James Dean, captured the imagination of a generation of adolescents through his calmness in the face of social pressures from other high-school students. James Dean had "cool." As one fourteen- or fifteen-year-old said, after seeing the film, "Hey, man, he's really cool. He just don't care about nothin'." (Sorry, we are forever honorbound to protect the identity of this impressionable teenager.)

So James Dean didn't care about nothin'. He also wore his collar up. A generation of adolescent males, with the exception of a few of those college types (you know, the "colleeeges"), began to act as if they didn't care about nothin', and, yes, they wore their collars up. They had modeled their behavior after the behavior of James Dean.

Much of our behavior is modeled after that of people whom we respect and admire, people who appear capable of coping with problems and situations that pose some difficulty for us. James Dean was the perfect model of social success—if you happened to be chasing some girl with a pony tail who you believed (or wished) looked like Natalie Wood, the girl whom James Dean won

in the film. Here and there we adopt a characteristic, a gesture, a phrase, a tone of voice, a leer, or a sneer.

Therapists who train clients to behave more assertively use extensive modeling. They "model" or provide an example of a way to say something, a way to hold your head or to look the other fellow in the eye as you speak. Then you try it out. The therapist then gives you **feedback**—tells you how well you did.

Modeling is very useful when you are not certain how to go about acting assertively. Simply watch characters on television and in films or books with an awareness of the ways in which they take charge of their own relationships. What gestures do they employ? What words? Do any of them sound right or appropriate for you? Could they perhaps be made to fit if you just trimmed them a bit here and there so that they fit in better with your own individual style? If so, try that behavior pattern on for size. If you wear it for a while and it fits you well, you may swear that you were born with it.

Feedback. Information about one's own behavior.

Behavior Rehearsal: Practice Makes Much Better

After you have decided on making changes, and even given the new you a few lines to say, try them out a few times in a nonthreatening situation rather than immediately confronting others. This is behavior rehearsal. It will help you get used to the sounds of your assertive talk as they come from your own throat. You won't find them shocking and new in the real-life situation.

Assertiveness trainers well know the value of behavior rehearsal. In individual and group sessions, they encourage clients to try out assertive behavior. The trainers may also use **role playing:** they may act the parts of social antagonists, or they may encourage you and other group members to act out the roles of the important people in your lives. They alert you to your bodily posture, your tone of voice, and your possible problems in maintaining eye contact as well as to the actual content of what you are saying.

The following is a case taken from Rathus and Nevid (1977). Joan was a recently divorced secretary in her twenties. She returned home to live with her parents for financial reasons and emotional support. Six months later, her father died. Her mother, in her fifties, underwent a normal period of grief and mourning. Joan offered all the support she could. But as time passed—three, four, six months—Joan came to believe that her mother was now overly dependent on her. She would not go anywhere by herself, not even drive to the market for food. Joan had come to feel that she must somehow persuade her mother to begin to rely on herself again.

Role playing. A method of learning new behavior in which one practices a cluster or grouping of desired behavior patterns. In a group, one will then receive feedback on the adequacy of one's performance.

Social Influence and Assertive Behavior

Joan explained her situation in an assertiveness-training group. The therapist asked a group member to play the role of Joan's mother, and Joan rehearsed responding to many possible requests her mother might make. The goal was to refuse to help her mother in such a manner that the mother would eventually see that Joan was interested in her welfare. Joan used the techniques of fogging and the **broken record.** She showed that she understood her mother's feelings, but continued to repeat her basic position. Here is a sample dialogue that occurred in behavior rehearsal:

Broken record. An assertiveness-training technique in which one persuades through repetition of the same position.

MOTHER ROLE: Dear, would you take me over to the market?

JOAN: Sorry, Mom, it's been a long day. Why don't you drive yourself?

MOTHER ROLE: You know I haven't been able to get behind the wheel of that car since Dad passed away.

JOAN: I know it's been hard for you to get going again [fogging], but it's been a long day [broken record] and you've got to get started doing these things sometime.

MOTHER ROLE: You know that if I could do this for myself, I would.

JOAN: I know you believe that [fogging], but I'm not doing you any favor by constantly driving you around. You've got to get started sometime [broken record].

MOTHER ROLE: I don't think you understand how I feel. [At this point the group member playing the mother role has been instructed to begin to cry.]

JOAN: You can say that, but I think I really do understand how awful you feel [fogging]. But I'm thinking of your welfare more than my own, and I'm simply not doing you a favor by driving you everywhere [broken record].

MOTHER ROLE: But we need a few things.

JOAN: No, Mother, I won't be doing you any favor by taking you [broken record].

MOTHER ROLE: Does that mean you've decided not to help?

JOAN: It means that I'm thinking of your welfare as well as my own, and I'm not doing you any favor by taking you everywhere. You have to start sometime [broken record].

Joan's task was not easy, but eventually she and her mother reached a workable compromise. Joan agreed to accompany her mother for a while as the older woman drove. Then her mother would have to begin to drive herself.

It is sometimes possible to enlist the aid of trusted relatives and friends in role playing when you decide to become more assertive. They can give you valuable information, or feedback, concerning the effectiveness of your words as well as your style of delivery. It is also important to overcome perfectionistic self-demands. You will probably make some errors. Accept this. We often learn from our errors as well as from our successes. And at least you will have the comfort of knowing you are striving positively to grow and to take charge of your own relationships.

WOMEN AND ASSERTIVE BEHAVIOR

Women and men have many of the same types of concerns about their social behavior, but some areas are of particular importance to the contemporary woman: conflicts over writing checks and handling large sums of money, establishing credit, acquiring jobs despite their mate's concerns that they may be

New York politician Bella Abzug for many typifies the new assertive woman.

making more money than the man or that they are opening themselves up to the flirtations of other men, and negotiating the sharing of housecleaning and child-rearing chores.

There are also many double standards concerning dating and sexual behavior. Women will often sit home bored if they are not asked out for the evening. Too often they tend to view their power as limited to a "filtering" function: they have the right to say yes or no to the proposals of men, but they do not have the right to be socially assertive and ask men out (Rathus 1978). Researchers Noel Carlson and Diane Johnson of the University of Minnesota have run workshops that help women learn to become more sexually assertive (1975). Their agendas include challenging traditional beliefs that women are to be guided by men in order to achieve their own sexual satisfaction, that only men should initiate sexual activity, that sexually assertive women are sluttish or castrating, and that women should use artificial means such as makeup and scented sprays to make themselves more sexually appealing to men.

Women and Fear of Success

We are going to give you two glimpses into the lives of a few people. Take a careful look at each, then construct a brief story about it. In your story, indicate how you believe the people involved feel, how others will respond to them, and what the events described will mean for their futures.

Capsule 1: After first-term finals, Tom finds himself at the top of his medical school class.

Capsule 2: Ron is with his girl friend, Betty, when they find out that he has been admitted to graduate school.

Social Influence and
Assertive Behavior

USING ASSERTIVE BEHAVIOR TO GET A JOB

One of the more critical situations in which you may find it helpful to assert yourself is the job interview. If this prospect is distressing, you can build up to it step by step, through a hierarchy of experiences that involves gradual approach and behavior rehearsal. Early successes have a way of making later goals appear less frightening.

You can break down job-seeking skills into an easy practice level, a medium practice level, and the target behavior level or actual interview:

Easy Practice Level

Read through the advertisements in newspapers. Select several positions in which you have *no* interest. Call the prospective employer, introduce yourself by name, indicate how you learned of the opening, request a fuller job description than the one offered in the paper, and ask for a fuller description of the qualifications desired in applicants. Thank the employer for his time, and indicate that you will get in touch if you wish to pursue application. You may also wish to ask why the position has become available—through expansion, reshuffling of personnel, or employee resignation—and for information about the criteria used to determine raises and promotions.

Contact a number of friends and ask them if they are aware of any openings in your field.

Make a list of the assets and liabilities *you* would bring to a new job. List reliability and concern that a job gets done properly among your assets. Nonassertive people commonly have a blind spot for the value of these qualities in themselves.

Answer a newspaper advertisement for a job in which you might be interested by letter (unless telephoning is required).

Medium Practice Level

Go to your state employment office or list yourself with personnel agencies. Inform these agencies of your assets and of your preferred working conditions.

Use *behavior rehearsal* to practice an interview with a prospective employer. Write down a list of questions that you are likely to be asked. Include challenging questions such as why you are contemplating leaving your present position or why you are out of work. Expect to be asked what special talents or qualifications you can bring to the job. Look in the mirror and answer these questions. Maintain direct eye contact with yourself. Rehearse several statements that you will probably be able to use intact, at-

Now we are going to ask you to go through the procedure again. But we shall make a few minor changes:

Modified Capsule 1: After first-term finals, Ann finds herself at the top of her medical school class.

Modified Capsule 2: Betty is with her boy friend, Ron, when they find out that she has been admitted to graduate school.

What differences did these minor modifications make in the stories you constructed? We would not be at all surprised if the first time around you predicted happiness and success for everyone involved. Nor would we be surprised if some of your predictions changed to gloom the second time around.

These brief glimpses of life are the types of cues researchers (e.g., Horner 1972; Puryear & Mednick 1974; Mednick & Puryear 1976) have used to discover whether we have different expectations for the futures of successful men and successful women. In the Horner study, most college women responding to the capsule about Ann wrote stories in which she experienced social problems or had received high grades for illegitimate reasons. Ann might lose friends, remain single, and become progressively more socially isolated. Perhaps her grades resulted from computer error or the generosity of a powerful male professor with whom she was having an affair. But a male student's success was usually linked to wealth, social adjustment, and personal happiness—regardless of whether the storytellers were men or women.

The Challenge
of Human Relationships

tending to your tone of voice and bodily posture. Have a family member or confidant provide you with social feedback. Use someone who can be constructively critical, not someone who thinks that all your behavior is either perfect or beyond salvation.

Go to local businesses in person, ask for application forms, fill them out, and return them.

Write or, if possible, phone employers advertising openings in which you do have interest. Request a fuller job description by saying something like, "I wonder if you can tell me more about the opening." Indicate that you will send a résumé, as required, and that you look forward to the prospect of an interview.

Target Behavior Level

After you have sent in a résumé in response to an advertisement and waited for a reasonable period of time, phone the prospective employer and say, "I wonder if there is anything you can share with me about the recruitment process."

During interviews, be certain that you have had an opportunity to point out your assets for the position. Maintain direct eye contact with the interviewer. Admit freely and openly to liabilities that would become evident with the passage of time—such as lack of administrative experience in a given area. But also emphasize your capacity and interest in learning about new phases of your work. Point out your desire to "grow."

During interviews, be certain to ask what would be expected of you on a day-to-day basis. Inquire about the firm's policies for advancement and raises. Do not be afraid to inquire about the fiscal solvency of the firm. Have a few specific questions prepared that will show that you have knowledge of your field and are aware enough to wish to alert yourself to potential pitfalls in the new position. You must ask why the position has become open. If someone was unhappy with the job, you must inquire why. This inquiry need not be negativistic in tone, but failure to ask will make you appear very "hungry" for the position.

At the conclusion of an interview, thank the interviewer for his time. You may write a one- or two-line note of thanks. Indicate that you look forward to hearing from the firm. Keep it brief so that you will not appear overly anxious.

During interviews it is normal to be nervous. If your voice cracks at some point, or if your thoughts get momentarily jumbled, say straightforwardly that you are "somewhat nervous." This *is* assertive behavior. You are expressing an honest feeling.

Source: Rathus & Nevid (1977).

These researchers assumed that negative stories about Ann or about Betty reflected female storytellers' own **fear of success.** Any of the following would earn these storytellers "points" toward a high fear-of-success score: (a) an unhappy outcome for Ann or Betty in the present or the future, (b) negative feelings in Ann or Betty as a consequence of success, (c) activity ascribed to Ann or Betty in a direction away from continued success, or (d) having Ann or Betty express conflict about their success. It was assumed that in these unfortunate outcomes, women storytellers were expressing their own fear of success.

Fortunately, Mednick and Puryear (1976) report that female samples appear to be expressing less fear of success in more recent years. Women are becoming increasingly aware of this problem, but fear of the imagined ill consequences of becoming successful in the business world or in professional life may still prevent some women from asserting themselves in the marketplace and aspiring to nontraditional vocational roles.

Fear of success. Avoidance of success because of fear of consequences of success. In our culture, it is hypothesized that some women fear success because success is discrepant with the female sex-role stereotype.

Women and Irrational Beliefs: Is Consciousness Raising Enough?

Psychologists Janet Wolfe and Iris Fodor (1977) observed that contemporary women have been attending a number of consciousness-raising groups in re-

Social Influence and Assertive Behavior

Consciousness raising. A group process in which feelings are shared and early influences on behavior are discussed. An outgrowth of the women's movement.

cent years and wondered whether consciousness raising would be sufficient to alter both self-defeating attitudes and interpersonal behavior. They compared treatment approaches which included various combinations of modeling and behavior rehearsal (two assertiveness-training methods), rational-emotive psychotherapy, and **consciousness raising.** Consciousness raising is a group process that has grown out of the women's movement (Kirsch 1974) in which women share their problems with one another and learn about the influence of their past experiences and early sex-role conditioning.

Wolfe and Fodor found that treatments including (1) modeling and behavior rehearsal and (2) modeling and behavior rehearsal plus rational-emotive therapy were effective in increasing assertive behavior. Although women in a group that received consciousness raising believed that they had experienced some growth as a result of their group process, their actual behavior did not change. Finally, only women in the second group—modeling, behavior rehearsal, and rational-emotive therapy—showed lowered social anxiety. Perhaps this was due to the rational-emotive premise that our feelings are intrinsically related to our attitudes and beliefs. Women in the second group had challenged their beliefs that they must avoid social disapproval and that they must be perfect in their early attempts at assertive behavior.

Drs. Wolfe and Fodor (1975) have also pointed out that women receive early socialization messages that underlie many of the irrational beliefs they may show in adulthood. One common early message is "I need to rely on someone stronger than myself—a man." Many women are raised to believe that they cannot protect themselves, will not be good at mechanical tasks such

◢ Stand Up! ◢

THE CONTEMPORARY WOMAN'S BILL OF RIGHTS

The women's movement has made us more aware that women have as much right as men to behave assertively. A Bill of Rights for the contemporary woman:

1. The right to express your genuine needs and feelings
2. The right to assert yourself in the business world
3. The right to handle money
4. The right to complain if others are being insensitive to your needs
5. The right to negotiate household chores
6. The right to negotiate child-rearing chores
7. The right to ask for more information to make decisions
8. The right to ask for more time to make decisions
9. The right to say no
10. The right to say yes

as repairing automobiles and appliances, and will be unlikely to excel in subjects like math and science. Wolfe and Fodor suggest an adjustive alternative: "It would be nice to be able to lean on someone, but I am capable of learning to solve problems for myself."

Women are also often more anxious than men about hurting the feelings of others, even when they have been abused or mistreated and are considering sticking up for their legitimate rights. Wolfe and Fodor note that the damaging social influence in this reluctancy is the early socialization message that women are expected to assume a nurturant, mothering social role in which they place the needs and feelings of others before their own. Wolfe and Fodor suggest that women challenge the feeling that they will be "bad" or that they will seriously hurt others if they give equal weight to their own needs and feelings.

If we are to come to express ourselves truly as individuals, we must become aware of the social influences that act upon us to lead us to obey, to conform, and to act in manners that are inconsistent with our own values. When we allow ourselves to be swayed by the desires of others, our personal growth is blunted. Becoming assertive and resisting unreasonable demands is difficult at first, but it is also immensely satisfying. As Carl Rogers notes, "In the overwhelming majority of individuals, the forward direction of growth is more powerful than the satisfactions of remaining infantile. The child will actualize himself in spite of the painful experiences in so doing. In the same way, he will become independent, responsible, self-governing, socialized, in spite of the pain which is often involved in these steps" (1951, p. 490).

Summary

- *Most people would refuse to administer painful electric shock to an innocent party, even under powerful social pressure.* It would be wonderful if this were true, but Stanley Milgram's experiments on obedience showed that the majority of us would throw levers marked "Danger: Severe Shock" in a bogus experiment on the effects of punishment on learning.
- *Women are more likely than men to conform to social pressures.* Possibly—all the evidence isn't in yet. Solomon Asch found this to be the case in his experiments on judging line lengths. But more recent experiments have suggested that both men and women are less likely to conform in situations with which they are familiar, and that androgynous men and women are less likely to conform than are "fluffy" women.
- *You may find yourself cozying up to* zabulons *and* afworbus—*once you get to know them for a while.* True. Familiarity seems to breed content, as Robert Zajonc demonstrated by familiarizing subjects with these phony "Turkish" words. This is especially so with complex stimuli, such as classical music pieces. With simpler stimuli, such as pop tunes, excessive familiarity may lead to boredom.
- *Only one woman in five would be foolish enough to allow six strangers to turn her house upside down to find out what products her family buys.* Close enough. But if you first get your "foot in the door" by having these women answer some telephone questions a few days earlier, about half of them will then accede to such a request.

Social Influence and
Assertive Behavior

- *You would probably find a claim that smoking leads to cancer more credible if it were made by the president of a tobacco company rather than by the surgeon general.* True. By espousing a cause that is in opposition to their own apparent self-interests, communicators increase their credibility. Perhaps this is why some extremely wealthy politicians impress impoverished people as being sincere in their concern for them. Presenting both sides of an argument may also give more credibility, especially if the audience is somewhat ambivalent to begin with concerning the speaker's point of view.
- *Americans are too intelligent to be swayed by scare tactics. Logic is more effective with most people.* Not so—an emotional appeal that is highly arousing and also coupled with concrete recommendations for avoiding the threatened disaster is a highly persuasive message. People also become more compliant when they feel guilty about something.
- *Arguing with clients that their beliefs are irrational is an inefficient way to conduct psychotherapy.* Not necessarily. Albert Ellis tired of the traditional passive psychoanalytic techniques and then found it highly effective to use more active, persuasive techniques with many clients. His technique of rational-emotive therapy assumes that our feelings result largely from irrational beliefs, such as exaggerated fear of social disapproval and perfectionism.
- *You become more attractive to others when you agree with them and praise them.* True, unless you are seen through and found to be phony. Then there may be a boomerang effect. You are also more persuasive when you have wined and dined the recipient of your persuasive messages, or otherwise created a "good mood."
- *You can get in touch with your self-defeating behavior by following yourself around the block.* Accurate enough. Jotting down your behavior, the situation you are in, and the results of your behavior is known as self-monitoring. Through self-monitoring you can come to pinpoint problem areas in your social interactions.
- *You can learn to assert yourself by imitating the behavior of characters on television.* Yes, and in films and books as well. We model much of our behavior after that of those who seem more competent at attaining the rewards of life. Once we have decided to "try on" certain types of behavior, we can smooth over the rough edges through extensive behavior rehearsal. Behavior rehearsal may include role playing and the acquiring of feedback from others.
- *Some women are nonassertive because they're afraid of being successful.* True. Some women ascribe loneliness and misery to the woman who advances through the professional ranks. Sadly, assertiveness in the marketplace appears inappropriate for many traditionally minded women.

SCORING THE ASSERTIVENESS SCHEDULE (p. 299)

Tabulate your score as follows: Change the signs of all items followed by an asterisk (*). Then add the thirty item scores. For example, if the response to an asterisked item was 2, place a minus (−) sign before the 2. If the response to an asterisked item was − 3, change the minus sign to a plus sign (+) by adding a vertical stroke.

Scores on this test can vary from $+90$ to -90. The table below will show you how your score compared with those of 764 college women and 637 college men from 35 campuses all across the United States. For example, if you are a woman and your score was 26, it exceeded that of 80 percent of the women in the sample. A score of 15 for a male exceeds that of 55–60 percent of the men in the sample.

Women's Scores	Percentile	Men's Scores
55	99	65
48	97	54
45	95	48
37	90	40
31	85	33
26	80	30
23	75	26
19	70	24
17	65	19
14	60	17
11	55	14
8	50	11
6	45	8
2	40	6
−1	35	3
−4	30	1
−8	25	−3
−13	20	−7
−17	15	−11
−24	10	−15
−34	5	−24
−39	3	−30
−48	1	−41

Source: Nevid & Rathus (1978).

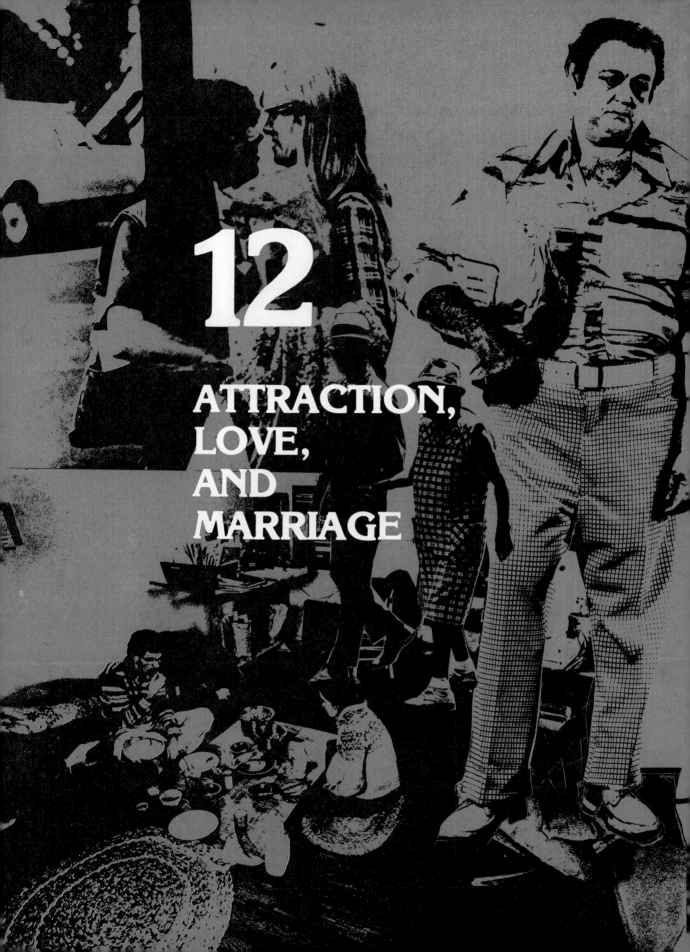

12

ATTRACTION, LOVE, AND MARRIAGE

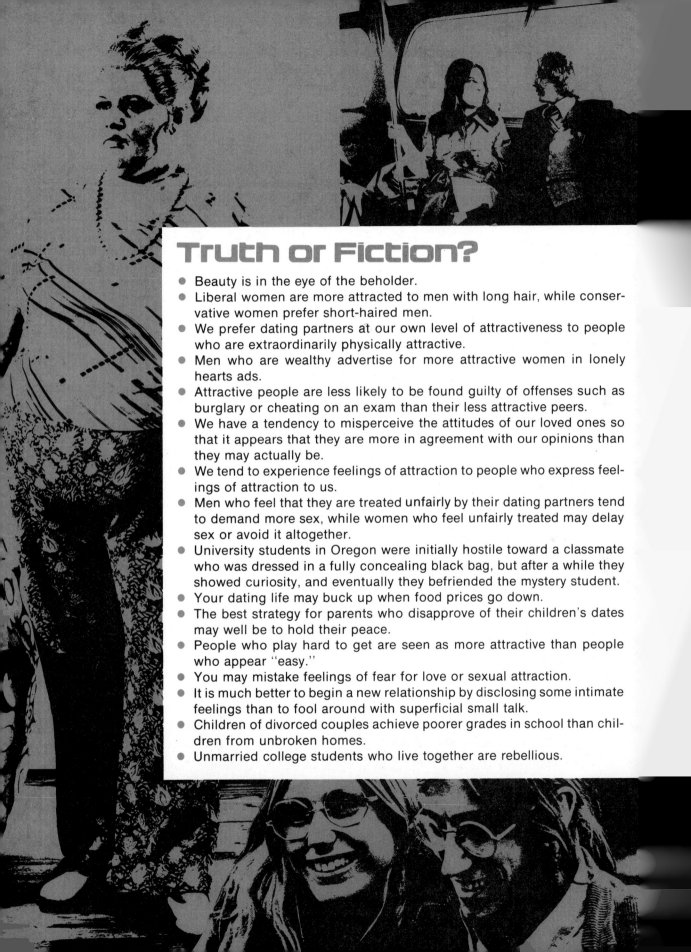

Truth or Fiction?

- Beauty is in the eye of the beholder.
- Liberal women are more attracted to men with long hair, while conservative women prefer short-haired men.
- We prefer dating partners at our own level of attractiveness to people who are extraordinarily physically attractive.
- Men who are wealthy advertise for more attractive women in lonely hearts ads.
- Attractive people are less likely to be found guilty of offenses such as burglary or cheating on an exam than their less attractive peers.
- We have a tendency to misperceive the attitudes of our loved ones so that it appears that they are more in agreement with our opinions than they may actually be.
- We tend to experience feelings of attraction to people who express feelings of attraction to us.
- Men who feel that they are treated unfairly by their dating partners tend to demand more sex, while women who feel unfairly treated may delay sex or avoid it altogether.
- University students in Oregon were initially hostile toward a classmate who was dressed in a fully concealing black bag, but after a while they showed curiosity, and eventually they befriended the mystery student.
- Your dating life may buck up when food prices go down.
- The best strategy for parents who disapprove of their children's dates may well be to hold their peace.
- People who play hard to get are seen as more attractive than people who appear "easy."
- You may mistake feelings of fear for love or sexual attraction.
- It is much better to begin a new relationship by disclosing some intimate feelings than to fool around with superficial small talk.
- Children of divorced couples achieve poorer grades in school than children from unbroken homes.
- Unmarried college students who live together are rebellious.

Candy and Stretch. A new technique for controlling weight gains? No—these are the names California psychologists George Bach and Ronald Deutsch (1970) give two people who have just met at a camera club that doubles as a meeting place for singles.

Candy and Stretch stand above the crowd—literally. Candy is almost six feet tall, an attractive woman in her early thirties. Stretch is plain-looking, but still wholesome, in his late thirties, and six feet five inches tall.

Stretch has been in the group for some time, and Candy is a new member. Let's follow them as they meet during a coffee break. As you will see, there are some differences between what they say to each other and what they are really thinking:

THEY SAY	THEY THINK
HE: Well, you're certainly a welcome addition to our group.	*Can't I ever say something clever?*
SHE: Thank you. It certainly is friendly and interesting.	*He's cute.*
HE: My friends call me Stretch. It's left over from my basketball days. Silly, but I'm used to it.	*It's safer than saying my name is David Stein.*
SHE: My name is Candy.	*At least my nickname is. He doesn't have to hear Hortense O'Brien.*
STRETCH: What kind of camera is that?	*Why couldn't a girl named Candy be Jewish? It's only a nickname, isn't it?*
CANDY: Just this old German one of my uncle's. I borrowed it from the office.	*He could be Irish. And that camera looks expensive.*
STRETCH: May I? [He takes her camera, brushing her hand and then tingling with the touch.] Fine lens. You work for your uncle?	*Now I've done it. Brought up work.*
CANDY: Ever since college. It's more than being just a secretary. I get into sales, too.	*So okay, what if I only went for a year? If he asks what I sell, I'll tell him anything except underwear.*
STRETCH: Sales? That's funny. I'm in sales, too, but mainly as an executive. I run our department.	*Is there a nice way to say used cars? I'd better change the subject.*
I started using cameras on trips. Last time it was in the Bahamas. I took—	*Great legs! And the way her hips move . . .*
CANDY: Oh! Do you go to the Bahamas, too? I love those islands.	*So I went just once, and it was for the brassiere manufacturer's convention. At least we're off the subject of jobs.*
STRETCH:	*She's probably been around. Well, at least we're off the subject of jobs.*
I did a little underwater work there last summer. Fantastic colors. So rich in life.	
CANDY:	*And lonelier than hell.* *Look at that build. He must swim like a fish. I should learn.*
I wish I'd had time when I was there. I love the water.	*Well, I do. At the beach, anyway, where I can wade in and not go too deep.*

On the basis of an initial physical attraction—and personal loneliness—Candy and Stretch have allowed their social selves to start to get to know one another. As Bach and Deutsch point out in this brief conversation (1970, pp. 83–85), their social selves are very different from their personal selves. Their personal selves have not met at all.

After they meet, Candy and Stretch have a drink, and then they talk, talk, talk—doing what Bach and Deutsch call "matching." They began their relationship by being tall together and sharing their separateness from the crowd. But now their conversation turns to likes and dislikes: clothing, cars, homes, politics, you name it. And they continue to match each other, expressing similar attitudes despite what they may really think. The attraction is very strong, and neither one is willing to risk turning the other one off by disagreeing.

Their matching leads them to Stretch's apartment, where they spend the weekend together and feel that they have fallen very much in love. There is one topic that they carefully avoid: religion. Their different backgrounds became apparent once they had exchanged last names. But that does not mean that they had to talk about it. Not then, anyhow.

They also put off introducing each other to their parents. The O'Briens and the Steins are narrow-minded concerning religion. If the truth be known, so are Candy and Stretch. Candy makes the mistake of telling Stretch, "You're not like other Jews I know" (p. 87). Stretch also fails to hide his feelings perfectly. After Candy has nursed him through a cold, he tells her, "You know, you're very Jewish" (p. 87). But Candy and Stretch manage to continue to cooperate in playing the games necessary to maintain the relationship. They both tell themselves that the remarks were mistakes—and, after all, anyone can make a mistake. In fact, the remarks were meant as compliments, weren't they? Certainly. Yet each is beginning to feel isolated from family and friends—narrowing their relationships to avoid tensions with each other.

One of the topics they failed to discuss was birth control. As a Catholic, Candy did not take oral contraceptives. Stretch later claimed that he had assumed that she had. Candy became pregnant. The couple chose to marry. But they had to begin to learn to know each other only after the marriage, with professional help. Their sexual relationship and their matching did not mean **intimacy**—they had not begun the process of disclosing their genuine feelings to one another.

Intimacy (in-tim-uh-see). The sharing of inmost thoughts and feelings.

In this chapter we have a look at some of the work social psychologists have been doing in the areas of attraction, love, and intimacy. We try to determine why people are attracted to one another, how attraction sometimes develops into feelings of love, and how relationships travel the road from superficial to intimate. We explore the institution of marriage and the phenomenon of divorce. We certainly do not ignore the opportunity to give you some hints on how to travel the road from establishing superficial acquaintances to forming intimate relationships, and how to go about resolving some of the conflicts that may occur in intimate relationships.

Attraction (at-TRACK-shun). The force which draws together or repels particles of matter or people, causing them to approach one another or move apart.

ATTRACTION

Whether you are talking about a pair of magnetic toys or two people in a singles bar, **attraction** is a force that draws bodies together. In the science of physics,

attraction is defined as that binding force. In the science of psychology, attraction is also thought of as a force that draws bodies together, and minds. Attraction can be **positive** or **negative,** as with liking or disliking. Those "kissing" magnetic toy dogs are usually built so that the heads attract one another, but unlike real dogs, a head and a tail will repel one another. As we shall see, people also tend to behave so that when there is a matching of the "heads"— that is, a meeting of the minds—we experience a positive attraction for one another. And, also like those toy dogs, when we consider the opinions of another person to be . . . well, asinine—we tend to be repelled.

You can see that attraction is based on our evaluation of another person. When we evaluate that person positively, we are drawn; when we evaluate that person negatively, we are repelled. Attraction has also been defined as an **attitude** toward other people (Berscheid 1976): attitudes include thoughts (positive or negative evaluations), feelings (good or bad "vibes"), and behavioral tendencies (to approach or to avoid).

Many factors are involved in the attraction we feel toward other people. These include physical attractiveness, similarity in attitudes, complementarity, reciprocity, propinquity, our emotions, and whether or not the other person is "hard to get."

Physical Attractiveness: How Important Is Looking Good?

You might like to think that we are all so intelligent and sophisticated that we consider a person's appearance to be rather low on a list of important personal qualities. You might like to think that we place more value on factors such as sensitivity, warmth, and knowledge. Some of us may do just that, of course, but it is possible that we may never have the opportunity to get to know other people's feelings and interests if they do not meet our minimal standards for physical attractiveness. After all, when you spot someone across a crowded room on some enchanted evening (to twist the song around just a bit), you are immediately attracted by physical appearance, not by attitudes toward a Marcel Proust novel or a political candidate.

Is Beauty in the Eye of the Beholder? Stretch and Candy were easy to spot across a crowded room: he was six feet five inches tall, and she was almost six feet. But would this height have turned on other people in the room, or was attractiveness purely in the eyes of the beholders? You may know that many women of Candy's height consider their tallness to be a problem. Many will tell you that they fear their height discourages shorter men from asking them out. They will often tell you that at some time in their lives they walked with a slight "hunch," sort of trying to minimize their height.

Both sexes in our culture tend to be more attracted to people who are slender (Lerner & Gellert 1969). Obesity is generally out of style, although there have been cultures in human history in which a woman's attractiveness was seen as a direct consequence of her weight—the more there was to love, the more love there was. Tallness is considered to be an attractive feature among men (Berkowitz et al. 1971), although, as we noted earlier, tallness in women is not viewed as positively. Women appear to prefer men who are not only tall, but who also have a "V-taper," men whose shoulders and backs are medium-wide, but whose waists, buttocks, and legs taper from medium-thin to thin (Lavrakas 1975).

It may be that a flat-chested look among women was a hallmark of the attractive profile during the 1920s "flapper" era, but ample busts seem to be desired by the average male today. It seems that women with larger than average breasts, yet medium-sized legs and small to medium buttocks are viewed most positively (Wiggins et al. 1968).

What of hair color? Do gentlemen (and gentlewomen) prefer blonds? Psychologist E. D. Lawson (1971) of State University College at Fredonia in upstate New York had male and female students rate blond, dark-haired, and redheaded men and women on several dimensions, including ugly-beautiful, intelligent-dumb, interesting-boring, and sincere-insincere. Since photographs were rated, there was no chance that these individuals were being rated on the basis of their actual behavior. In most "head-to-head" comparisons along these dimensions, male and female raters evaluated dark-haired men and women of both sexes more positively than blonds and redheads. When raters were sorted on the basis of their own hair color, dark-haired men rated dark-haired women more positively, but the ratings of blond men were split between blonds and brunettes. Women gave dark-haired men more positive ratings despite their own hair color, with one exception: women with dyed blond hair split their ratings between dark- and light-haired men.

Dark hair is "in," at least in upstate New York, although there is some tendency for blond men also to rate blond women more positively. We have not yet heard from California, of course. Perhaps we tend to rate others according to how they reflect our own best images of ourselves. Could this be why women who "aspire" to blondness are more likely to evaluate blond men positively?

Physical Attractiveness, Dating, and Marriage: Who Is "Right" for You?
Have you ever felt like approaching an extremely beautiful or handsome person for a date, but held back for fear of rejection? Do you feel more comfortable at the prospect of asking someone out who is just a bit less attractive? If so, you are not alone, but make no mistake: physical attractiveness may be the most central factor that motivates us to pursue relationships with people of the opposite sex, at least during the early stages of a relationship.

Psychologist Donn Byrne of Purdue University and his colleagues (1970) brought couples together for a brief "Coke date." Each individual was rated for physical attractiveness before the experiment. After a date of thirty minutes, each person was to judge the desirability of the date as a future date, a sex

HAIR, THERE, AND EVERYWHERE?

Long hair was a powerful influence in the life of Samson, according to the Old Testament. With it he could battle lions. Without it, he . . . wasn't with it.

Long hair was a common feature of men throughout history. But in the United States, shorter hair—even crew cuts—has often been associated with masculinity and been attractive to women. During the 1960s, long hair for men became associated with social rebelliousness, the drug culture, and alternate life-styles. But the "rebelliousness" of long hair did not start with the Beatles or in the 1960s. During the 1600s, the Puritans of Massachusetts spoke out against young folk who were wearing their hair longer—claiming that the Old Testament gave proof that long hair was a glory to woman, but hateful in the eyes of God.

Let us not speak for the eyes of God, but an experiment by Peterson and Curran (1976) speaks for the eyes of some contemporary women. Men these days are wearing their hair in an assortment of styles, from short to longer-than-shoulder length, and these researchers sought to find out if there were relationships between women's preferences for male hair styles and their own backgrounds and personalities.

Peterson and Curran simply had women rate videotapes of males with short, medium length, and long wigs according to how much they liked the people taped. Thus the researchers could rule out the possibility that long-haired subjects accidentally were also most attractive, or vice versa. Of course, they also had to arrange the tapes so that each woman saw the same male with only one hair style.

It turned out that some women preferred men with short hair, and others preferred men with long hair. These preferences were dramatically linked to personal characteristics of the raters. For instance, women raters who preferred long-haired men were more likely to have experimented with drugs, had dated more men and were more sexually experienced, attended church less frequently, and were more self-assertive. Women who preferred men with shorter hair were more conservative: they attended church more regularly, had not typically experimented with drugs, had had fewer sexual experiences, and appeared to endorse the more traditional feminine sex role.

Hair, at least with men, may be more than a matter of fashion. It may be an expression of a liberal or conservative political orientation, and women's preferences may be based on approval or disapproval of a prospective date's politics. But for women considering a change in style, hair may be neither hair nor there.

partner, and a potential spouse. Judgments were strongly related to physical attractiveness.

In another experiment, social psychologist Elaine Walster of the University of Wisconsin and her colleagues (1966b) arranged computer dates for a dance for university male and female freshmen. All participating students were rated for physical attractiveness at the time they bought tickets. Halfway through the dance, students filled out questionnaires indicating how well they liked their dates and whether they saw them as good prospects for future dates. Physical attractiveness was again the central factor in liking and desire for future contact. Academic achievement, intelligence, and personality variables had no bearing on interpersonal attraction at this dance.

But do not despair if you consider yourself to be less than extremely beautiful or handsome—along with the rest of us mere mortals. It may be quite right that we tend to rate the most attractive people as most desirable for dates, sex, and marriage. But that does not mean that the rest of us do not stand a chance. According to University of Minnesota psychologist Ellen Berscheid and her colleagues (1971), you and I will be saved from forever blending in with the wallpaper by something called the **matching hypothesis**—the idea that

Matching hypothesis. The view that men and women of approximately equal physical attractiveness will choose one another as dating and marital partners.

The Challenge of Human Relationships

As we see with the young couple on the left and the Duane Hanson statues on the right, people tend to select dates and mates who are more or less equal in attractiveness to themselves.

people tend to ask out people who are similar to themselves in physical attractiveness. If you think about it, this makes a good deal of sense, and not because life is fair. It is probably because we feel we are less likely to be rejected when we approach people who are not much more physically attractive than ourselves. We may all have ideals that are induced by our culture, but when it comes to real life and day-to-day living, it seems that we may tend to settle for those imperfect others who are similar to ourselves. So it is that Ellen Berscheid (Berscheid et al. 1971) found that when students matched by computer were considered potential rather than actual dates, they tended to follow through only with individuals who were similar in physical attractiveness to themselves.

This is not only true for selecting dates, but also for selecting mates. People also tend to select mates who are more or less equal in attractiveness to themselves (Murstein 1972). But do not think that this settling process is as dull as it sounds. Murstein also found that most people, male and female, tend to rate their marital partners as slightly more attractive than themselves. In other words, they may each commonly feel that they have gotten the better of the deal. This is not surprising either. We may be very aware of the steps we go through to present the most attractive appearance we can to the world, but when it comes to our mates, we will probably be highly motivated to focus on their most positive features and attributes. After all, that way we will feel happier about our marriages. The matching hypothesis has also been found to hold true for middle-aged, middle-class couples (Murstein & Christy 1976).

Of course there are exceptions. Have you ever seen an incredibly beautiful woman married to a plain-looking or even ugly man? What did you make of the relationship—how did you explain it? What would she see in him? According to one experiment (Bar-Tal & Saxe 1976), we might assume that such men make a great deal of money (as with the match between Jacqueline Kennedy and Aristotle Onassis), are highly intelligent, or highly successful in their jobs. We look for some unseen factor that will maintain the sense of balance. It does not appear to strike us as reasonable that highly attractive people will settle for plain-looking mates unless there are compensations. We may not be a very romantic lot, after all.

Attraction, Love, and Marriage

ARE GOOD LOOKS UP FOR SALE?

All the lonely people—where will you find them? You'll find some of them in the back pages of weekly newspapers, in personal advertisements. Some samples:

- Born-again Christian woman, 33, 4'9", queen-size, loves children, quiet home life, sunsets. Seeks marriage-minded man, 33 or over. Children, handicap, any height or weight welcome.
- Horseman, handsome, wealthy, 48, 5'10", 180 lbs., likes dancing, traveling. Seeking beautiful, slender girl, under 35, sweet, honest, neat, without dependents. Send full-length photo, details.
- Single, 28, 5'7", 128 lbs., with strawberry-blond hair, blue eyes. Wants to meet secure, sincere gentleman, 32–48, who loves the outdoors and dancing. Preferably Taurus. No heavy drinker need reply. Send photo first letter.
- Tall male, 40, slim, divorced, nice-looking, hardworking nondrinker, owns home and business. Seeks attractive, plump gal, 25–35, not extremely heavy, but plump, kind, sweet, for a lasting relationship. Photo, phone.

University of California at Davis psychologist Albert Harrison and Laila Saeed (1977) examined eight hundred lonely hearts advertisements like those above in terms of the matching hypothesis. They scored each advertisement for the suggested attractiveness of the advertiser, and the desired attractiveness of the respondent. In general, more attractive advertisers were seeking more attractive respondents. But women were more likely to advertise physical attractiveness than men, and men were more likely to advertise financial security as a selling point. Attractive women were more likely than their plainer peers to request financial security, and wealthy men advertised for more attractive women. Age was also important, with women seeking older men and men looking for younger women. You may be surprised to learn that men more often than women expressed an interest in marriage. But this may only mean that men believed willingness to marry could be a strong selling point, and that women wished to avoid frightening some men off.

The matching hypothesis survives. Like seeks like. And when someone advertises for a partner who is more attractive, the wallet is often right up front.

Do Good Things Come in Pretty Packages? Join us in a brief experiment. Take a look at the four people pictured below—persons A, B, C, and D—and

A

B

C

D

then rate them according to the scales underneath. For instance, if you find person A to be extremely poised, place the letter A in the space next to "poised." If you find person A to be extremely awkward, place the A next to "awkward." If A impresses you as being equally poised or awkward, or if you are unsure, place the A in the center space. Once you have rated person A on the fourteen scales, repeat the process for persons B, C, and D. It is perfectly per-

The Challenge
of Human Relationships

missible to place more than one letter in the same space. This will simply mean that you gave two or more people similar ratings on the scales.

poised	___ : ___ : ___ : ___ : ___ : ___ : ___						awkward
modest	___ : ___ : ___ : ___ : ___ : ___ : ___						vain
strong	___ : ___ : ___ : ___ : ___ : ___ : ___						weak
interesting	___ : ___ : ___ : ___ : ___ : ___ : ___						boring
self-assertive	___ : ___ : ___ : ___ : ___ : ___ : ___						submissive
sociable	___ : ___ : ___ : ___ : ___ : ___ : ___						unsociable
independent	___ : ___ : ___ : ___ : ___ : ___ : ___						dependent
warm	___ : ___ : ___ : ___ : ___ : ___ : ___						cold
genuine	___ : ___ : ___ : ___ : ___ : ___ : ___						artificial
kind	___ : ___ : ___ : ___ : ___ : ___ : ___						cruel
exciting	___ : ___ : ___ : ___ : ___ : ___ : ___						dull
sexually warm	___ : ___ : ___ : ___ : ___ : ___ : ___						sexually cold
sincere	___ : ___ : ___ : ___ : ___ : ___ : ___						insincere
sensitive	___ : ___ : ___ : ___ : ___ : ___ : ___						insensitive

Done? All right, now answer a few questions. Which man (A or D) and which woman (B or C) will be:

- More likely to hold a prestigious job?   A or D? B or C?
- More likely to be divorced?   A or D? B or C?
- More likely to be a good parent?   A or D? B or C?
- More likely to experience deep personal fulfillment? A or D? B or C?

Can you find any pattern to the responses given by yourself and by your classmates? If your responses were similar to those of sixty students at the University of Minnesota, you probably rated the more physically attractive member of the male and female pairs more favorably on most of the scales. Nor would we be surprised if you felt that the more attractive individual would be more likely to hold a prestigious job and be a better parent, more likely to feel fulfilled, and less likely to be divorced. For as social psychologists Karen Dion, Ellen Berscheid, and Elaine Walster (1972) found, there is a tendency in our culture to rate what is beautiful as good.

Beauty is not only good—beauty in our culture may also be rated as "talented." In another study, researchers at the University of Rochester (Landy & Sigall 1974) asked male students to judge the quality of a pair of essays on the effects of television on violence in children. Each of the essays had a photo attached, presumably of the author. One photo was of a young woman another group of students had rated as physically attractive. The other photo was of a young woman rated as unattractive. One of the essays was well-written— clearly organized, grammatically accurate, and clear. The other would have caused Shakespeare to turn over in his grave.

Actually, neither woman had actually written the attached essays. They were constructed by the experimenters, and the photos were attached on a random basis. In general, the superior essay was rated as better. But there was a relationship between the ratings of the essays and the photo attached. Essays assumed to be written by the more attractive female were rated as better than when they were assumed to be written by the unattractive female. The same essay was judged differently when it was attributed to a different author.

The attractiveness of the author was more influential with the poorly written essay. This suggests that some attractive individuals may learn they can

Farrah Fawcett sets the standard for beauty for many women in our culture. Are attractive people more successful and happy? More intelligent? More trustworthy? What do you think?

get by with producing a little less. (We never told you life is fair. It is up to you to make it fair.) But it also suggests that if you turn out a quality product, your appearance should not be so important when others judge your work.

Beauty may be good and talented, but is beauty also innocent? What about all those cartoons in which the pretty defendant crosses her legs and smiles at the judge and jury? In this nation we place more value on the weight of the evidence than on a smile, don't we? Possibly. Possibly not. It has been found that a physically attractive person who is accused of burglary or of cheating on a test is liked better by an experimental jury, more likely to be found innocent, and, when found guilty, often given a less severe punishment (Efran 1974). There are exceptions. If the accused have used their attractiveness to take advantage of others, as would be the case in "the confidence game" or swindling, they may be given harsher punishments by juror subjects than their less attractive peers (Sigall & Ostrove 1975).

In a summary of many studies relating physical attractiveness to other traits and personal success, Ellen Berscheid and Elaine Walster (1974b) find that attractive individuals will usually be found to possess more socially desirable traits: personality, popularity, sexuality, social influence and persuasiveness, occupational and interpersonal success, and, commonly, personal happiness. Judgments based on attractiveness begin early in life, so it is also not surprising that attractive people tend to be higher in self-esteem than their less attractive peers (Maruyama & Miller 1975).

Yet Berscheid and Walster did not find that attractive people are consistently rated to be more intelligent or trustworthy. And couples who are unattractive have actually been judged to be more happily married than attractive couples. Attractive people have also been found to be more vain and self-centered and judged more likely to engage in extramarital intercourse (Dermer & Thiel 1975). More attractive people are apparently expected to have more sexual opportunities—thus, while they may be more sexually active, they may be seen as being poorer risks for marriage.

Attraction and Attitudinal Similarity: If You Agree with Me, You Must Be Wonderful

In this land of free speech, we certainly respect the right of others to disagree with us, don't we? Perhaps we do, but we are not likely to be attracted to people who disagree with us very strongly. Candy and Stretch spent their early time together doing what Bach and Deutsch (1970) referred to as "matching"—they were physically attracted to one another and thus motivated to show that they were in agreement on a variety of preferences, tastes, and opinions. What of their difference in religious background? Sensing that they could run into trouble if they opened the topic of religion, they entered an unspoken agreement not to bring it up.

Birds of a feather flock together—especially when they are good-looking birds. You may not be surprised to learn that Donn Byrne and his colleagues (1970) found that college students were most attracted to computer match-ups who were both physically attractive *and* held similar attitudes. A date who was both unattractive and who held conflicting attitudes was, as you can imagine, extremely undesirable. But when it came to judging the relative merits of physically attractive dates who held similar attitudes, or physically unattractive dates with similar attitudes, it was a toss-up: physical attraction alone was favored about equally with similar attitudes.

But all attitudes are not equal. Some are more influential in determining whether others will be attracted to us than others. In a study at the University of Nevada at Reno (Touhey 1972), students were computer matched on the basis of similar or dissimilar attitudes about religion and sex. After the couples had become acquainted, they were asked how well they had liked their dates. For men, liking was influenced more by similarity in sexual than in religious attitudes. But women were more attracted to men whose religious views coincided with their own.

Why is it important to have people share one's attitudes? Why may it be upsetting to you to find out that your parents do not approve of your dating choices? Why may it be unsettling to discover, after several pleasant dates, that your dating partner holds political views that are strongly opposed to yours?

Social psychologist Theodore Newcomb (1971) of the University of Michigan explains our desire to associate with people who share our attitudes in terms of **balance theory.** According to balance theory, people have a psychological need to organize their perceptions, opinions, and beliefs in a manner that is "balanced"—symmetrical or harmonious. Put briefly, when people we like share similar attitudes, our perceptions of them and the objects of the attitudes are in balance. If we dislike other people, we are likely to be indifferent to their attitudes. This is called a state of **nonbalance.** But nonbalance is not distressing, since we are indifferent to the other person.

But what happens when a person whom you like a great deal suddenly expresses an attitude that shocks you? The relationship will probably survive if you prefer chocolate and your date prefers vanilla. But what if you are a committed liberal and you just discover that your date believes our first great mistake was rebelling against the British and that it has been all downhill since? Now you are in a state of **imbalance.** You and someone you like, someone to whom you have been attracted, find that you have dissimilar attitudes on an important subject. This imbalance is quite distressing—so distressing that you will probably be motivated to do something to remove it.

Candy and Stretch used one common method to maintain balance in their budding relationship. They both misperceived each other's religious preferences. They told themselves that the other might share their own preference, and then they purposefully suppressed the issue. In order to maintain the attraction, they also each purposefully misrepresented their own background and views on many issues. We could argue that misrepresentation is immoral for its own sake, but we do not want to sound like moralists. So let us note that by misrepresenting, by keeping certain issues below the surface, Candy and Stretch paid the price of having a narrowed relationship, one in which they could not share their genuine feelings with one another.

When we have entered a state of imbalance, there are several other ways in which we may attempt to restore balance. We may try to convince other people to change their attitudes. Candy and Stretch might each have tried to convince the other to convert to their own religion, but the relationship was rather young for such an issue to arise. We may also reevaluate our own attitudes to see whether it is possible to bring them in line with the other person's. Such reevaluation would also have been premature for Candy and Stretch.

We can also restore balance by changing our feelings toward the other person. But if we have been strongly attracted, even on a physical basis, this may

We tend to be attracted to people who hold attitudes similar to ours. Do you think these men have a basis for a friendship?

Balance theory. Theodore Newcomb's view that people have a need to organize their attitudes so that they are balanced or in agreement; the view that people seek psychological consistency.
Nonbalance. An indifferent psychological state in which two people who dislike one another are unconcerned about whether the other person shares their views.
Imbalance. An unpleasant psychological state in which two people who are attracted to each other are in disagreement about something.

Attraction, Love, and Marriage

be painful. Candy and Stretch were not willing to break up despite their religious differences.

Candy and Stretch were not willing to risk damaging their relationship at an early stage by openly expressing differing opinions. Thus, when we left them, they were trying to work out differences that many couples work through at an earlier stage. We all have to make our own decisions as to how much we are going to disclose during the formative stages of our relationships. Certainly it is foolish to express our most intimate feelings to strangers—they will probably feel that we do not understand unwritten social rules about when it is appropriate to disclose certain types of information. But holding back too much information because of fear of disapproval may lead us into relationships that are narrow, superficial, and continually stressful.

Complementarity: We May Be Different, But We Fit

Complementarity (kom-pluh-men-TARR-uh-tee). A situation in which differing traits or characteristics are seen as attractive because they somehow support or strengthen an individual.

While people who hold similar attitudes tend to be attracted to one another, opposites may also sometimes attract. In terms of traditional sex roles, the attraction between men and women was seen as a natural intermingling of the active and the passive, the dominant and the submissive. Now that traditional sex roles may be in the process of fading away, it is no longer possible to predict whether a person will be active or dominant on the basis of sex alone, but it may still be that a dominant individual will be attracted to someone who is submissive. This is **complementarity**—a situation in which opposing characteristics or traits tend to reinforce one another.

A relationship that has been based on complementarity runs into trouble when one party decides that it would be desirable to change the complementary role. Do you know of any marriages that are running into difficulties because the wife wants to undertake new, more assertive roles? The problem, of course, does not originate with the wife, but with the cultural expectations that women and men should adhere to traditional sex roles.

A One and a One?

BIRTH ORDER AND MARITAL CHOICE

Are ones attracted to ones and sixes attracted to sixes? If you are the oldest child in your family—number one in order of birth—are you more likely to be attracted to the eldest (or only) child in another family? If you are high in the order of birth, are you more likely to be turned on by number five or six in that family down the block? Could there be some sort of mysterious cosmic numbers game at work?

A survey of the marital choices of two hundred faculty members at the University of Maryland (Ward et al. 1974) shows a significant relationship between people's order of birth and the birth order of their mates. But this does not mean that mysteri-

ous forces are at work. Your order of birth in your family often gives you a certain role to play. First-borns, for instance, are often more responsible and "adultlike" than their siblings. They often achieve better in school. Later-borns, on the other hand, are often more socially outgoing, because the role of the academic achiever has already been taken. So they look for other means to earn social approval.

So if firstborns mesh with other firstborns, and later-borns fit in with other later-borns, it may be because they play similar social roles and hold similar attitudes. The game at work is a social game, not a cosmic numbers game.

EQUITY AND SEX: DO PEOPLE WHO GIVE MORE GET MORE?

All is fair in love and war, the saying goes. But Elaine Walster and her colleagues (1978) predicted that dating couples who felt that their relationships were unfair—that they were giving more to the relationship than they were receiving from it—would express their resentments through their sexual behavior.

Equity is fairness or fair treatment. According to equity theory, social psychologists predict that when you perceive your relationships to be unfair—with you stuck with the short end—you will be motivated somehow to restore equity. One possibility, of course, is to distort your perception of the relationship so that you can tell yourself it is fair, after all. This will eliminate the need to assert yourself or terminate the relationship—at least so long as you can continue to go through life with blinders on. Indirect methods for restoring balance in the relationship can be sought through appearance. If you feel you are getting the short end of the stick, you may begin to let your appearance go. After all, you may think, "Why should I be the one who always makes the effort?"

Concerning sex, Walster and her associates predicted that the traditional sexual double standard would lead men and women to behave differently when they saw themselves as the underprivileged member of their relationships. Men who felt that they had too little say about sex would probably demand sex more frequently. Women who were similarly troubled would probably attempt to delay sex as long as possible. But these predictions were not borne out in a survey of University of Wisconsin students. Rather, they found that students involved in relationships they perceived as inequitable or unfair had less sexual activity, from petting through intercourse, than students reporting equitable relationships.

Why would students involved in more equitable relationships have more sex? Sexual activity and sexual drive in the human being depend not only on physiological factors, but also on interpersonal attraction. When we feel that the efforts we put into a relationship are not fully reciprocated, we are resentful and attraction may decrease.

Reciprocity: If You Like Me, You Must Have Excellent Judgment

Has anyone ever told you that you are good-looking, brilliant, and mature? That your taste is refined? That you are truly a standout? If so, have you been impressed by such excellent judgment? Have you found yourself drawn to this admirable individual?

You may recall from Chapter 11 that when people praise us, we are more susceptible to whatever messages they are trying to deliver. When we are praised and admired, and believe the messages, we feel tempted to **reciprocate**—to feel the same way toward them. When people suddenly tell you that you are terrific, you may even begin to wonder why you did not pay much attention to them before.

Reciprocity (ress-sip-PROSS-sit-tee). An exchange between people in which we do unto them as they do unto us. For instance, if they like us, we are more likely to like them.

Propinquity: If You're Near Me, I Must Like You

Just why did Sarah Abrams walk down the aisle with Alvin Ackroyd and not Danny Schmidt? If they had gotten to know one another, Sarah and Danny would have found that they actually had more in common. But Sarah and Al sat next to one another in eleventh grade English. Why? The teacher used an alphabetical seating chart, and Sarah and Al sent subtle, smoldering glances

Attraction, Love, and Marriage

Attraction is more likely to develop between people who are placed in frequent contact with one another—people who share a classroom, an office, or, as with this couple, a commuter bus.

Propinquity (pro-PINK-quit-tee). Nearness or closeness.

toward one another for nine months that fateful year—because they simply happened to be sitting next to one another. Meanwhile, Danny sat diagonally across the room, near the back of the class, with no inkling that Sarah was really anything more than a name he heard called out when the teacher took attendance.

Attraction is more likely to develop between people who get to know one another—people who by chance are placed in frequent contact with one another. This is the effect of **propinquity,** or nearness.

In classroom settings, two students are more likely to develop relationships if they sit next to one another (Byrne & Buehler 1955). So it is not surprising that among a group of trainees in the Maryland State Police, almost half of the friendships developed between individuals who were back to back in alphabetical order (Segal 1974).

As you walk out of your suburban home each weekday morning, you are more likely to develop a friendship with your next-door neighbor than with someone down the block—especially if your driveways are adjacent to one another (Whyte 1956). If apartment living is your style, you will be more likely to make new friends among people who live nearby on the same floor than among people who live on other floors (Caplow & Forman 1950; Nahemow & Lawton 1975).

The effects of propinquity are so powerful that you may eventually find yourself attracted to people who make an effort to keep themselves "under wraps." Witness this news report of February 27, 1967, from Corvallis, Oregon (reported in Zajonc 1968):

"A mysterious student has been attending a class at Oregon State University for the past two months enveloped in a big black bag. Only his bare feet show. Each Monday, Wednesday, and Friday at 11:00 A.M. the Black Bag sits on a small table near the back of the classroom. The class is Speech 113—Basic Persuasion . . . Charles Goetzinger, professor of the class, knows the identity of the person inside, none of the students in the class do. Goetzinger said the students' attitude changed from hostility toward the Black Bag to curiosity and finally to friendship" (p. 1).

So, if you wish to make yourself more acceptable to attractive individuals who are almost complete strangers at work or at school, it may be worth your while to begin by sitting at a nearby table in the lunchroom. Being close, repeatedly, may remove a good deal of the worry of being close. When you finally "move in" to begin a verbal relationship, it may help you to know that males usually prefer to sit across from people they like, and females usually prefer to sit next to people they like (Byrne et al. 1971). By placing yourself in the favored position, you might just further increase your potential attractiveness.

Emotions and Attraction: When Bad News Is . . . Bad News

It is a good thing that we have an abundance of preposterous stories about the "old days"—whenever and wherever they were. You would never believe them if they were supposed to be about modern times.

Anyhow, in the "old days," if a messenger brought a king bad news, the messenger might be executed. As you can imagine, this would have been a very inefficient method for accurately communicating messages. Messengers would make a living—literally—by distorting the news in a positive direction.

Yet this story makes a point. It suggests that we can react to other people on the basis of other things that are happening at the time, even though they are not logically related to the traits or characteristics of those individuals. If we feel good, we are also likely to feel good about the people we are with. If we are miserable, we are unlikely to experience strong interpersonal liking.

Bad news was not only bad news for messengers in the "old days"—bad news may also be bad news for modern-day relationships. Veitch and Griffitt (1976) brought subjects to an office for an experiment on interpersonal attraction and attitudinal similarity. Subjects waited for the experimenter while a "radio" delivered a newscast in the background. Some subjects were exposed to a series of upbeat stories: A breakthrough had been found in treatment of cancer! Food prices were, unbelievably, on their way down! Students could now use faculty parking lots! Their long treks were over! Other subjects heard bleaker stories: An encouraging breakthrough in the treatment of cancer had been found to be painful and dangerous. Food prices, as usual, were soaring. New student parking lots were being built in Outer Mongolia.

These news stories, of course, were phony audiotapes. But they set the stage for another phase of the experiment in which subjects exposed to good or bad news then rated other subjects who were shown to possess similar or dissimilar attitudes. As you might expect, people with similar attitudes were liked more than people with dissimilar attitudes. But there was also an effect of the news stories: people who heard good news rated other people more positively than people who heard bad news—whether attitudes were similar or dissimilar. Don't expect much from your dates on days when they have flunked big tests and their car batteries have punked out.

Also be careful about the movie you go to. Gouauz (1971) found that women undergraduate students who have seen a slapstick comedy are more attracted to new acquaintances than women who have just seen a depressing documentary—in this case, a film about the career and assassination of John F. Kennedy.

Playing "Hard to Get": Is Hard to Get Hard to Forget?

We have a tendency to feel attracted to people who demonstrate that they are attracted to us. But what if their attraction to us is not a sign of their exquisitely exceptional taste? What if they are attracted to everyone, or easy to get? Are we more likely to be attracted to people who are hard to get—or who play hard to get—or to people who are easy to get?

Elaine Walster and her colleagues (1973) recruited male subjects for an experiment in computer matching, in which they were given the initial reactions of several women to them and to other men in the study. One woman was generally hard to get, reacting to all men in the study with indifference. A second woman was considered easy to get; that is, she responded favorably to all male participants. A third woman, however, showed the fine judgment of being attracted to just the one male subject. As you might expect, male subjects were overwhelmingly more attracted to the women who had eyes for them only, and selected them for dates a full 80 percent of the time.

We do not yet have the results for a comparable study with female re-

THE "ROMEO AND JULIET EFFECT"

What do you do when you bring your date home and afterwards your parents say, "What are you doing with this shlemiel? Is this what we brought you up for? Don't you know that _____ people just don't get along with our kind? This is bound to end in tears. But don't worry about our reactions to it—we won't be alive when you finally realize what you're doing. We're committing suicide."

Do you believe that parental opposition would destroy the relationship, or that you and your date might actually fight to maintain the relationship? That external pressures would make the two of you grow closer together rather than farther apart? In the Shakespeare play, of course, the two young lovers, Romeo and Juliet, grew closer together against the backdrop of the violent feud between their two families. But that is literature. What about real life?

Psychologists Richard Driscoll, Keith Davis, and Milton Lipetz (1972) sought to find the answer through a survey of dating and married couples at the University of Colorado. Students filled out two ques-tionnaires. The first allowed them to rate the degree of parental interference in the relationship: whether the parents had attempted to harm the relationship, whether they accepted their child's dating choice, whether they spoke against the choice, and so on. The second scale measured the intensity of feeling in the relationship.

The researchers found that parental opposition was associated with intensified feelings of love between nonmarried couples during a six- to ten-month period. But for married couples, changes in parental opposition were not associated with changes in intensity of feeling between the members of the couple.

It seems that for couples in the early stages of a relationship, parental opposition often has a boomer-ang effect: it leads to a greater commitment between the members of the pair. But for couples who have al-ready made a significant commitment to one another, as through marriage, it may be that parental opposi-tion tends to become irrelevant.

cruits, but common sense would have it that women are also more interested in men who look upon them as individuals. In the film *Play It Again, Sam*, Woody Allen (upon the advice of the imaginary Humphrey Bogart) tells Diane Keaton, "I have met a lot of dames in my life, but you are really something special." She is delighted.

Of course, when you tell your partners that they are really something spe-cial, it would be helpful if you have gotten to know them a bit first. Otherwise, your message may lack credibility, and you may wind up with that old boomer-ang in the stomach.

LOVE

Love. An intense emotional state involving sexual at-traction for and caring about another person.

Love—one of the most deeply stirring of human emotions, the emotion for which we will make great personal sacrifices, the emotion that launched a thousand ships in the ancient epic of *The Iliad*. What is it?

For thousands of years the great poets have sought to put love into words. One poet wrote that his love was as "a red, red rose." In the novel *Elmer Gan-try*, love is "the morning and the evening star." Love is beautiful, it is elusive, it is shining and brilliant and heavenly. It is also sexy and earthy—at least what we think of as romantic or passionate love is also sexy and earthy. In addition to an idealization of the one you love, and an utter absorption in the one you love, there is a solid dose of sexual longing and hunger.

Despite the obvious influence of romantic love in our lives, psychologist Zick Rubin (1970) of Brandeis University noted that behavioral scientists have

The Challenge of
Human Relationships

not paid love very much attention. But anthropologists, who study human behavior in different cultures, have noted that romantic or passionate love is not a universal phenomenon. In order to experience passionate love—as opposed to experiencing attachment (as between a parent and a child) or simply experiencing sexual arousal—it seems that you must grow up in a culture that has and idealizes the concept of romantic love.

In our own culture, passionate, romantic love is believed in very strongly. It is generally seen as the ideal relationship for which we should all strive, perhaps beginning with adolescence. During adolescence, we commonly label strong sexual arousal along with the constant fantasized image of the object of our desires as love. Perhaps one reason for this is the social acceptability of love and the somewhat negative view of sexual lust—especially when it comes to adolescents whose parents fear the possibility of unwanted pregnancies. It is more acceptable to speak of being in love with someone, or having a crush on someone, than to explain to the world that you want to bed someone. For many young people, the concept of being in love makes physical attraction and sexual arousal acceptable. We still have something of a double standard concerning sexuality, and young women often justify sexual experiences as having been with someone that they love. Young men usually need no justification for desiring sexual activity, so it is not surprising that many young men may consider love to be a "mushy" concept.

According to Ellen Berscheid and Elaine Walster (1974b), love, as other emotions, involves a combination of bodily arousal and some cultural or

Attraction, Love, and Marriage

345

learned reason for labeling that arousal *love*. They point out that the ideal combination of circumstances for arriving at the conclusion that you feel passionate or romantic love is powerful interpersonal attraction plus sexual attraction or arousal. As you will see in Chapter 13, that "warm, tingling gush" of love has a great deal to do with the flow of blood in your genital organs. But since love is a personally arrived at conclusion, based in part on bodily arousal, we can sometimes feel as though we are in love when the origins of our arousal are rather different.

Love and Arousal: If My Heart Is Pounding, I Must Love You

Ovid was a Roman poet who was ahead of his times. For instance, he advised young men who were suffering the pangs of unrequited or undesired passionate love that they might be able to overcome their passions by focusing on the negative qualities of their loved ones. Back then we were not all protected with underarm deodorants, and Ovid suggested that an unwilling lover could focus on the details of the undesirable odors of his partner. Or on undesirable bodily features, like warts.

Ovid also suggested that young men (his interests were quite sexist) might find their way into young ladies' hearts by taking them to stirring, arousing events—such as the bloody and lethal gladiator contests. The woman could easily attribute her arousal to the presence of her date and conclude that she was falling in love. Do you think that Ovid's advice might have inspired the inventors of the roller coaster? If Ovid were alive today, he would no doubt be lining up for tickets to the Superbowl as well as frequenting amusement parks.

You might almost think that Ovid had some part in the designing of a recent psychological experiment. Psychologist Stuart Valins (1966) of the State University of New York at Stony Brook asked male subjects to rate the physical attractiveness of a series of slides of partially dressed women. Each rater was wired so that he could constantly perceive his own heartbeat through a microphone and earphone set. During the experiment, subjects noted that their heartbeats speeded up when they viewed certain slides and slowed down when they looked at others. It turned out that their judgments of the physical attractiveness of the women in the slides were related to the heart rate feedback: in general, the faster the perceived heartbeat, the more attractive the rating of the photograph.

There was one catch. Valins had doctored his equipment so that the subjects in the study perceived heartbeats that were not their own. Rather, subjects were listening to heart rates that had been accelerated or slowed down at random. They were totally unrelated to the content of the slides. These young men interpreted what they assumed to be their own rapid heart rates as signs that they were sexually aroused. They *attributed* a perceived difference in heart rate to the women in the slides.

And these first impressions of being turned on were rather lasting. Four weeks later Valins showed the slides again, this time without the heart rate feedback, and the ratings of attractiveness held.

Rapid heartbeat is not only a sign of sexual attraction or love. It is also a sign of fear. Do you think it is possible that university students could mistake fear for sexual attraction or love? Impossible, you say? Not according to an experiment run in Vancouver, Canada (Dutton & Aron 1974).

This particular experiment got a rise out of the subjects. A rise of 230 feet, to be exact. Some subjects were interviewed by a woman on a spindly bridge that swayed menacingly high above a rocky canyon. In this unlikely setting, they were asked questions and wrote stories based on pictures of people in unclear situations. They were also given the phone number of the interviewer in case they wanted to learn more about the experiment. Other subjects were interviewed by the same woman on a lower and apparently much safer bridge. Subjects who had gotten high—230 feet high, that is—wrote stories about the pictures that contained more sexual content. They also phoned the woman more frequently afterward.

But wait, you say? The sexual content and the phone calls might have resulted from the height of the bridge alone? It might have had nothing to do with the interviewer? The investigators expected such an argument. So they also arranged for other groups of male subjects to be interviewed on these bridges by men. Subjects interviewed by men did not write stories containing sexual themes. They also made fewer phone calls afterward. We think you will have to admit that the high bridge and the sex of the interviewer both had something to do with the stimulation of sexual storytelling and phone calls. If your dates too often come to dull conclusions, you can always decide to take the high road in these matters.

No wonder tunnels of love have goblins hopping out from the dark!

Are these people in love? Psychologists and poets alike have found it difficult to measure romantic love.

The Measurement of Romantic Love

Zick Rubin (1970) tackled the question of how to measure romantic love for his doctoral research at the University of Michigan. First, he surveyed the psychological literature and poetry to develop a list of concepts of romantic love. There were many: desire to help the one you love, the wish to confide in him or her, idealization (believing that your love has few if any faults), possessiveness, the need to be with your love and share experiences, concern for your love's welfare, sexual attraction, and the feeling that you must have your love in order to feel content and whole.

Rubin's love scale consists of thirteen items, like the following:

- I feel that I can confide in _____ about virtually everything.
- If I could never be with _____, I would feel miserable.
- I feel very possessive toward _____.

Rubin found that love-scale scores were related to his subjects' statements that they believed themselves to be in love, to the probability that they would eventually marry, and to the amount of time they spent gazing in each other's eyes. Lovers, it seems, become absorbed in one another and largely indifferent to the passing world. Rubin finds some lines from a popular song appropriately describe lovers: "Millions of people go by, but they all disappear from view—'cause I only have eyes for you" (p. 272).

FROM ZERO CONTACT TO SELF-DISCLOSURE: DEVELOPING INTIMACY

"One, two, one, two." Great opening line? In *Play It Again, Sam*, Woody Allen plays the role of Allan Felix, a social klutz who has just been divorced.

Diane Keaton plays his good platonic friend Linda. At a bar one evening with Linda and her husband, Allan Felix spots a young woman dancing who is so physically attractive that he says he wants to have her children.

The thing to do, Linda prompts Allan, is to begin dancing and then dance over to the woman and say something to her. With a bit of prodding, Linda starts Allan dancing. It's so simple, she shows him. He need only keep time. "One, two, one, two," she says.

'One, two," Allan repeats. Linda now shoves him off to his dream girl to say something.

Hesitantly, Allan dances up to her. "One, two," he says. "One, two, one, two." He is ignored and finds his way back to Linda.

"Allan, try something more meaningful," Linda implores.

Once again, Allan dances up to his dream girl. He says "Three, four, three, four."

"Speak to her, Allan," Linda insists when he has made his way back.

Once again Allan tries. "You interested in dancing at all?" he manages.

"Get lost, creep," the young woman replies.

"What'd she say?" Linda asks.

"She'd rather not."

So much for "one, two, one, two," and "three, four, three, four" for that matter. Stretch's opener was a bit more positive: "Well, you're certainly a welcome addition to our group," he told Candy. This was obviously a complimentary response to her physical appearance. Candy accepted the compliment with a simple "Thank you," and the relationship had begun.

According to social psychologist George Levinger (1974) of the University of Massachusetts, relationships undergo a series of developmental stages. They may begin with **zero contact,** in which the parties are totally unaware of each other's existence. The first level of acquaintance is then an **awareness** stage, in which they gain some knowledge that the other exists, but they have not yet begun to relate to one another. People may spot someone who attracts them across a lunchroom. A new individual may enter the class or obtain a job nearby. Someone may move into the apartment across the hall, or you may bump into someone new in the elevator. Your impressions of the person at this stage are largely visual, although it is possible that your attraction may increase through overhearing the person converse with someone else. It is possible that you may also meet someone through a blind date or a computer match-up, but we usually get to meet others by accident. And the greatest single promoter of such accidents is propinquity, or physical nearness.

Not-So-Small Talk. If you have become aware of someone and would like to begin a relationship, you will probably want to say something other than "one, two." Mark Knapp (1978) of Purdue University notes that greetings are usually preceded by eye contact, and that you will gain an impression of the willingness of the other person to begin talking by whether or not eye contact is reciprocated. Try a smile and some eye contact. If the eye contact is reciprocated, choose an opener.

Knapp notes a variety of greetings (1978, pp. 108–109). Here are some of them:

- Verbal salutes, like "Good morning."
- Questions of personal inquiry, like "How're ya doin'?"

Zero contact. George Levinger's term for the situation in which two people are unaware of each other. *Awareness.* George Levinger's term for the situation in which one person is aware of the existence of the other, but they have not yet begun to interact with one another.

- Compliments, like "You're extremely attractive."
- References to your mutual surroundings, like "What do you think of that painting?" or "This is a nice place to live, isn't it?"
- References to people or things outside the immediate setting, like "How do you like this weather we've been having?"
- References to the other person's behavior, like "I couldn't help noticing you were sitting all alone over there."
- References to your own behavior, or yourself, like "Hi, my name is Allan Felix."

The simple verbal salute, "Hi!" or "Hello," is very useful. A friendly glance followed by a cheerful "Hello" ought to give you some idea as to whether the attraction you feel is reciprocated. If the "Hello" is returned with a friendly smile and inviting eye contact, follow it up with another greeting, such as a reference to your surroundings (Stretch referred to Candy's camera), your name, or, perhaps, a sincere compliment.

As Berger and Calabrese (1975) note, the initial communications between two parties are likely to include name, occupation, marital status, and hometown. Each person is seeking a sociological profile of the other in the hope that some common ground will be discovered that will serve as a logical basis for pursuing the conversation (Knapp 1978, p. 114). An unspoken rule seems to be at work: "If I provide you with some information about myself, you will reciprocate by giving me an equal amount of information about yourself. Or . . . 'I'll tell you my hometown if you tell me yours'" (Knapp 1978, p. 114). If the other party does not follow this unspoken rule, he or she may simply not be interested and you may be well-advised to try someone else. But it could also mean that you are being klutzy, perhaps disclosing too much information at once in your anxiety, and turning the other person off. You can gain some skill with opening conversations through behavior rehearsal and feedback with a trusted friend.

These initial verbal interactions are called **small talk**—a superficial sort of conversation that may provide for an exchange of some information, but which stresses a breadth of topics rather than in-depth pursuit of any particular subject. We may react negatively to the concept of small talk, equating it with superficiality or phoniness, but prematurely rapid self-disclosure may repel the other person (Wortman et al. 1976). We would not advise telling a brand-new acquaintance that your hemorrhoids have been acting up—not even after you say "Hi, how are you? My name is Pain." Be patient.

Small talk is important. We use it to make **surface contact** with another person. During surface contact we decide whether the relationship is going to be pursued on the basis of finding common ground and experiencing continued attraction. Knapp (1978, p. 112) describes small talk as an "audition for friendship." When small talk is successful, a couple may decide it will be worthwhile to begin to swim beneath the surface.

Mutuality: When the "We," Not the "I's," Have It. If surface contact has been mutually rewarding, a couple may proceed to the point of friendship and, perhaps, love. Once common ground has been established and strong interpersonal attraction remains, the members of the pair may begin to think of themselves as "we," no longer two "I's" touching just at the surface. This intersection of the selves, this "we," is what Levinger (1974) refers to as **mutuality**.

Small talk. A surface type of conversation that allows people to determine whether they wish to get to know one another better.

Surface contact. George Levinger's term for the situation in which two people have begun to interact with one another. If attraction is felt and commonalities are found, the relationship may deepen.

Mutuality (myoo-chew-AL-uh-tee). George Levinger's term for the situation in which two people have discovered common ground for the development of a relationship and attraction continues. The "I's" become a "we."

Attraction, Love, and Marriage

349

YOU TELL ME AND I'LL TELL YOU . . .
VERY CAREFULLY

When you meet someone new, how much is it safe to tell them? If you hold back completely, will you seem uninterested and self-protective? If you let too much light shine suddenly on your personal affairs, will you be seen as opening up too much too fast? Opening up, or self-disclosure, is a central factor in the formation of intimate relationships. Intimacy means, in fact, a sharing of your inmost thoughts and feelings. But psychological evidence suggests that we should show some caution in determining how rapidly we disclose information.

Confederates of the experimenters (Wortman et al. 1976) engaged in ten-minute conversations with recruited subjects. Some of the confederates were "early disclosers": they shared quite intimate information early in the conversations. Others were "late disclosers," sharing intimate information toward the end of the conversation. The experimental subjects then rated the confederates on several scales. Early disclosers were rated as significantly less mature, more phony, less secure, and less well-adjusted than the late disclosers. Subjects also indicated that they would prefer to continue relationships with the late disclosers rather than the early disclosers.

In a review of the literature on self-disclosure, Paul Cozby (1973) notes some sex differences in self-disclosure. Women tend to disclose more intimate information than men do—especially to other women. This is not too surprising, given the traditional stereotype of the strong but silent male that still governs the behavior of many individuals in our culture.

Cozby also notes that individuals labeled mentally healthy or well-adjusted do disclose a good deal of information about themselves to others, yet they tend to keep certain types of information that might be self-damaging or prematurely revealing hidden.

It is difficult to list the types of information it is "safe" to disclose early or better to save until you have gotten to know someone rather well. But an experiment in Chicago by Berger and his associates (1976) may provide some clues. They showed a list of one hundred fifty statements to two hundred adults in a suburb of the city, and asked them to pretend that they were deciding whether or not to disclose them in a two-hour conversation with a stranger. They sorted these statements into nine groupings. First were eight fifteen-minute segments, showing when they might bring up the topic during the conversation. Then came the ninth category: statements that would not be revealed at all during a conversation with a stranger—even toward the end of the two-hour period.

Some of these statements are given below. You will note that the general consensus was that only superficial information should be disclosed during the first fifteen minutes. Expression of preferences does not begin until the second fifteen-minute segment. What sort of topics are not revealed at all?

Segment 1: 0–15 minutes

1. I'm a volunteer at a local hospital.
2. I'm from New York.
3. My son is a freshman at Penn State.
4. I have a dog, three cats, and a parakeet.

Segment 2: 15–30 minutes

5. I've been skiing only once.
6. I like hunting for antiques.

Within our culture, most people still believe that the ideal climaxing of this felt mutuality is through the institution of marriage (Shope 1975). Marriage is more than a legal state. It is a public announcement of the commitment that two people have made to play a major role in each other's lives. It is experienced as a continuing commitment to help one another, to share intimate feelings and experiences, and to regard each other as occupying a special place in each's life.

Married couples are more likely to disclose their experiences and their feelings to one another than are people who have not established a sense of mutuality (Morton 1978). The question "How did it go today?" may lead to the

The Challenge of
Human Relationships

7. The Chicago Bears are a lousy football team.
8. My favorite movie of all time is *M.A.S.H.*

Segment 3: 30–45 minutes

9. I wish I knew more about politics.
10. The sight of blood makes me sick.
11. I am a Republican.
12. I read my horoscope every day and follow it faithfully.
13. I don't like men with long hair.

Segment 4: 45–60 minutes

14. I think singles bars are a disgrace.
15. I'll go out of my way to avoid hurting someone.
16. The trouble with America is that the average guy gets ripped off by the big corporation.
17. I think a woman has the right to decide whether or not she wants to have children.
18. I don't believe in capital punishment.
19. The United States should pull out of the United Nations.
20. I have trouble falling asleep.

Segment 5: 60–75 minutes

21. The only way to handle radicals is with force.
22. I'm a very emotional person.
23. Most men are insecure—at least the ones that I've dated.
24. I don't believe in evolution.

Segment 6: 75–90 minutes

25. I don't make friends easily.
26. I think I'm losing my hair.
27. I don't believe that there is an afterlife, but I'm not really sure.

28. I hate lying in bed at night, listening to the clock tick.
29. I'm forty-five pounds overweight.
30. My mother-in-law really dislikes me.
31. I have an ugly nose.

Segment 7: 90–105 minutes

32. I have a violent temper.
33. My wife makes too many demands upon me.
34. People always make fun of how fat I am.
35. I dress to please men and excite them.
36. I wish I were single again.

Segment 8: 105–120 minutes

37. Sometimes I'm afraid I won't be able to control myself.
38. Sometimes I think I hate myself.
39. I wonder why people stare at me wherever I go.
40. I think sex is dirty.
41. My husband and I stay together for the sake of the children.

Statements Not Disclosed at All During the Two-Hour Conversation

42. I had my first sexual experience when I was twenty-one.
43. My wife is having an affair with my best friend.
44. I make $13,000 a year.
45. My son was arrested last night for possession of marijuana.
46. I think my teenage daughter is pregnant.
47. We got married earlier than we'd planned because I was pregnant.

Source: Berger et al. (1976, pp. 34–39).

bursting of a dam of emotions in married couples, whereas superficial acquaintances may just respond, "Fine." Men in a marital relationship are likely to disclose things that have happened to them, and women are also likely to disclose feelings and personal opinions—but this is a sex difference, not necessarily a sign that the sexes view an intimate relationship differently.

During the early stages of a love relationship, couples may be overwhelmed by their feelings of passion toward one another, whereas later on, factors related to liking—such as mutual respect and trust—may become the more permanent cement of the relationship (Rubin 1974). As the sexual attraction loses some of its binding force, it is important that genuine liking plus the

Attraction, Love, and Marriage

commitment to help one another and share in each other's lives are present. Otherwise, the relationship may dissolve.

Stretch and Candy ran into problems because they had maintained their relationship at a level of surface contact even though they had had sexual intercourse. If they are to remain together and work through their problems, it will be because they are able to develop intimacy in rooms other than the bedroom.

MARRIAGE

The institution of marriage has a long and varied history. Among the ancient Hebrews, men dominated the important aspects of life. This system was known as a **patriarchy.** The man of the house had the right to choose wives for his sons and could take concubines or additional wives. He alone could institute divorce. While he could dally, his wife had to retain her virtue scrupulously. Failure to bear children was one ground for divorce.

In ancient Greece women were similarly viewed as the property of men. Their central purposes were to bear children and keep the household. In the city of Sparta, it is said, there was a time when marriage was not very formal. The man simply dragged his "bride" to his house and locked her in.

The Romans also had a powerful patriarchy in which the oldest man directed family life and could, if he wished, sell his children into slavery and arrange their marriages—or divorces. Women were given by their fathers to their husbands, as the men saw fit. At one point in Roman history, when military demands called for a population increase and women had obtained some freedom of choice in marrying, the Emperor Augustus decreed that women who remained childless or unmarried by the age of twenty could be fined.

In all three cultures, the patriarchies weakened with time, and women came to be viewed as worthy companions to men rather than mere property. They were gradually given more household responsibilities and recognized as fully capable of profiting from education. Yet the notion that a married woman might rightfully seek personal growth through a career unrelated to her husband's needs is a recent development.

Throughout the course of Western history, marriages have occurred as institutions for maintaining a home life, raising children, having sexual relations, and transferring money from one family to another. Notions like love, equality, and the very radical concept that men as well as women would do well to aspire to the ideal of faithfulness are relatively recent ingredients of the marital state.

Today our parents usually no longer arrange for our marriages—even though they may still hope that we will date the son or daughter of that marvelous couple from the church group. As a nation we tend to marry the people to whom we are attracted. And, most often, we are attracted to people who are similar to us in physical attractiveness, who hold reasonably similar attitudes, and who seem likely to be capable of fulfilling our material, sexual, and psychological needs. Interracial marriages may make headlines here and there, but they are relatively rare, accounting for about one marriage in a thousand. We also rarely marry outside our own socioeconomic class. Men, on an average, are two to three years older than their wives. By and large, we seem to be at-

At some point in a relationship two "I"s become a "we." This is known as mutuality.

Patriarchy (PAY-tree-ark-key). A social structure in which men have domineering, governing roles.

The Challenge of
Human Relationships

352

tracted to and marry the boy or girl almost next door in a dreadfully predictable and boring manner. Marriages seem to be made in "the neighborhood"—not in heaven.

We shall now turn our attention to marital conflicts and divorce.

Marital Conflict

As the glow of the honeymoon fades into the proverbial sunset of the Poconos or the Caribbean island paradise, we confront the challenge of attempting to adjust to the state of matrimony. There are some important early decisions to be made: How are the household chores to be divided? How is the daily menu to be planned? Who will decide how money is to be budgeted? Who will decide when, where, and how to have sexual relations?

In some marriages, responsibilities are delegated according to sex-role stereotypes. The wife cooks, cleans, and diapers. The husband earns a living and repairs the automobile. But in other marriages, one partner may rebel against this traditional approach. Or it may be that he would like to watch television, but she would like to go to a film or a concert, that she desires sexual

Attraction, Love, and Marriage

relations more frequently than he, or that he prefers Colonial furniture while she fancies a platform bed with electronic headboard controls.

When conflicts arise, some of the following strategies may be helpful in resolving them:

Negotiating Differences. It is possible to negotiate differences when both partners have an attitude of give-and-take and do not believe that the assigning of any particular chore has been dictated by the very structure of the universe. One strategy is to list day-to-day responsibilities and then have each spouse scale them according to their desirability. This is how Sarah and Ken ranked some chores:

5 = most desirable
4 = desirable
3 = not sure, mixed feelings
2 = undesirable
1 = Are you kidding? Get lost!

Task	Sarah's Ranking	Ken's Ranking
Washing dishes	3	1
Cooking	1	4
Vacuuming	2	3
Cleaning the bathroom	1	3
Maintaining the automobile	3	5
Paying the bills	5	3

Sarah wound up washing the dishes and paying the bills. Ken did the cooking and toyed with the car, a hobby of his. They agreed to alternate vacuuming and cleaning the bathroom. Both had careers, so the "breadwinning" responsibility was divided equally.

In modern marriages, chores are more likely to be negotiated. The woman doesn't automatically get stuck with the laundry.

Exchange Contracting. With exchange contracting (Knox 1971), the partners identify specific behavior patterns they would like their mates to change, and offer to modify their own disturbing behavior in exchange. Be specific about disturbing behavior. It is useless to say, "I'd like you to be nicer to me." Instead, say, "I don't want you to sneer every time I talk about my mother or about my homework." Be specific about the distressing behavior so that behavioral change is possible.

A sample contract:

> SHE: I agree to talk to you at the dinner table rather than watch the news on TV, if you, in return, help me type my business reports one evening a week.
>
> HE: I agree never to insult your mother, if you, in return, absolutely refuse to discuss our sexual behavior with her.

Showing Approval. It is more constructive to try to increase desirable behavior in a marriage than to focus on decreasing undesirable behavior (Stuart 1969). When your spouse does you a favor or pleases you, show approval: smile, say "Thank you," or show affection. Reinforcing behavior makes it more likely to recur, and will also communicate effectively what you find pleasing.

Too often in marriages we take the positive for granted and focus on condemning the negative. But remember that punishment may create angry feelings and that punishment, alone, does not provide useful information about the sort of behavior that you will find more pleasing.

Expressing Dissatisfaction. When you must express dissatisfaction, be as specific as possible, so that your spouse will understand precisely what behavior was disturbing. Keep your complaint to the present: becoming involved in arguing who did what to whom last summer muddies the issue and just increases feelings of hostility.

Avoid hurling insults; make complaints about *behavior*. As Rogers (1972) points out, it is more effective to express dissatisfaction in terms of your own feelings than through attacking the other person. It is more effective to say, "You know, it upsets me that you don't seem to be paying attention to what I'm saying," than to say, "You're always off in your own damn world. You don't give a damn about anybody else, and I don't think you ever will."

Express your dissatisfactions privately—not in front of the neighbors, the in-laws, or the children. When people are taken to task in front of others, they are more likely to feel the need to defend themselves because of social embarrassment.

When Marriage Fails: The Challenge of Divorce

Marriage is our most common life-style. In 1974, for example, about 63 percent of the adult males and 57 percent of the adult females in this country were married and living together with their spouses. Only 3 percent of the men and 4 percent of the women were divorced, and about 28 percent of the men and 22 percent of the women were single (Bernard 1975). The popularity of marriage is also shown by the fact that some 97 percent of all men and 96 percent of all women eventually marry (Bernard 1973), and that about four out of five divorced people remarry (Glick 1975).

Yet when marital conflicts cannot be resolved, divorce often becomes the

final alternative. About one in three marriages ends in divorce, and the numbers of divorces per year have been rising steadily—from 377,000 in 1955, to 915,000 in 1973, and more than a million in 1976 (Plateris 1978).

Divorce commonly involves financial and emotional difficulties. When a household splits into two, the resources often do not extend far enough to maintain the earlier standard of living for the partners. The divorced woman who had not pursued a career of her own may find herself suddenly struggling to compete with younger and more experienced people in the marketplace. The divorced man may find it prohibitively difficult to assume the costs of alimony and child support while attempting to establish a new home of his own.

In Chapter 9, we saw that divorce may lead to feelings of grief over the loss of the marriage, and prompt significant depression. A sense of personal failure as a spouse and parent, loneliness, and uncertainty about the future may further contribute to the emotional difficulties following a divorce. There may also be bitter fights over custody of the children, the division of property, and support payments.

Bohannan (1970) suggests that the most difficult adjustment to a divorce can be the process of psychologically separating from "the personality and the influence of the ex-spouse—to wash that man right out of your hair" (p. 53). Breaking the connections with the past relationship and becoming a whole, autonomous person once more—or, perhaps, for the first time—can be the most severe challenge as well as the most constructive aspect of one's adustment to divorce. This separation can, again, be especially difficult for the woman who has always viewed her role in life as supportive of her husband.

The Children of Divorce.   We hear many couples talk of staying together "for the sake of the children," despite the severity of their conflicts. Are children better off in an unbroken yet unhappy home?

It is estimated (Bane 1976) that 20–30 percent of the children growing up during the 1970s will experience the divorce of their parents before their eighteenth birthday, and some 12–20 percent more will experience a family disruption for some other reason, such as the death or separation of their parents. Although the research concerning the psychological impact of divorce on children is limited, it suggests that these children may not particularly differ from children raised in intact homes in terms of social adjustment, school achievement, and susceptibility to delinquency (Bane 1976). Although children at first may harbor feelings of guilt for the divorce, or not be able to imagine their lives under the new circumstances, they seem to bounce back from the stresses of divorce reasonably well, and Bane suggests that it may in fact be less damaging for a child to grow up in a broken home than in an unbroken but conflict-ridden home.

Getting Help.   Where do divorced people turn for help in dealing with their adjustment problems? Fortunately, in many communities there are groups such as Parents without Partners or divorce-adjustment seminars which help divorced people cope with the legal, financial, and emotional problems of divorce. People in such groups share their feelings and frustrations, socialize, and find valuable information concerning child rearing and employment and training opportunities.

Many divorced people enter psychotherapy to help them deal with their feelings and personal problems, while others rely on friends, family, and their own resources to adjust once more to life as a single person.

COHABITATION IN CONTEMPORARY AMERICA

Cohabitation, or living together outside of wedlock, has become an increasingly popular living arrangement for emotionally committed couples. Cornell University psychologist Eleanor Macklin (1972) reported that surveys had found that 25 percent of students at California State University at Northridge, 36 percent at the University of Texas, 20 percent at the City College of New York, 33 percent at Pennsylvania State University, 23 percent at Arizona State University, and 31 percent at Cornell admitted to engaging in a "live-in" relationship at some point during their college years. In another survey of 1,191 students in fourteen state universities across the country, about 25 percent reported that they had cohabited at some point, with most cohabitors believing that their parents probably didn't know about it and would certainly disapprove if they found out (Bower & Christopherson 1977).

Macklin compared cohabitors and noncohabitors at Cornell on several factors and dispelled some myths. For instance, there were no differences in grade-point averages between students who had cohabited and those who had not. Nor were students who had cohabited the products of emotional instabilities or the harborers of rebellion. They were not more likely to emanate from broken homes or to reject the institution of marriage as a future alternative. In the Bower and Christopherson nationwide study, 96 percent of the cohabitors and 99 percent of the noncohabiting students hoped to get married someday, although the cohabitors more frequently desired to delay marriage: 79 percent of the noncohabitors compared with 64 percent of the cohabitors wished to marry by the age of 25, for example. Nor was co-habitation frowned upon by students who had not personally shared each other's company and food bills: only 7 percent of those in Macklin's study who had personally avoided cohabitation believed that it was morally wrong. Fully half the noncohabiting students reported their reason for abstaining as either that they lived too far from their boyfriend or girl friend to cohabit, or they had not yet found the right person.

Most cohabiting couples in the Macklin study had tried to conceal their living arrangements from their parents, and they reported some common problems; 57 percent experienced jealousy concerning their partner's involvements with other people or in other activities; 62 percent were concerned that they had become overinvolved with their partners, and cut off from other friends and activities; 49 percent felt trapped at times; 62 percent had experienced fear of pregnancy; 71 percent had encountered a differing interest in frequency of sexual activity; and 62 percent of the women had intermittent difficulty achieving orgasm. The problem list appears to typify some early adjustment problems in marriage as well as in living together.

All in all, 96 percent of the cohabiting couples in the Cornell study rated their relationship as sexually satisfying, and 90 percent rated their living arrangement as a successful, pleasurable, and maturing experience. All but one couple would recommend the experience to others. Many, if not most, college students view the cohabiting life-style as a normal, acceptable, contemporary pattern of living or stage of courtship that evolves from an emotionally committed relationship.

Cohabitation has become an increasingly popular living arrangement for couples who are emotionally committed to one another.

Divorce as an Opportunity for Growth. While we have focused on some of the potentially negative aspects of divorce, we should point out that for many individuals divorce can be a constructive alternative to continuing in a marriage that is unsatisfying and destructive.

In *Creative Divorce*, Krantzler (1973) suggests that a divorce can be an enriching, creative experience when people use it as a "new start in life" to form meaningful relationships and change the old, destructive behavior patterns that led to the demise of the marriage. When people are open to learning new patterns of relating to others, of communicating and sharing, and of working through problems, divorce can lead to personal growth.

Of course, we must also pay attention to the meaning of divorce in terms of each individual's value system. In those instances in which divorce is perceived as sinful, it may be that it will lead more to feelings of guilt and self-recrimination than to an opportunity for growth. These are matters that must be decided by the individual. When the individual experiences conflict so severe that it is no longer possible to weigh the consequences of possible courses of action logically and make a logical decision, it may be time to seek psychotherapy.

In our contemporary lives, relationships begin with attraction, rather than with parental arrangements. By sharing our thoughts and our feelings with others, we have the opportunity to develop intimate relationships and interpersonal commitments. For most Americans, the logical outcome of the ideal relationship remains marriage. Yet marriage is not without its problems.

While relationships may carry their fair share of stresses, they also provide the frameworks in which couples can "pool their resources" and grow together. But in order for both members to grow, each must respect the other as a unique individual and be as proud of the partner's accomplishments and growth as of his or her own.

Summary

- *Beauty is in the eye of the beholder.* Not completely. Although we may have individual preferences, there tend to be common standards for beauty within any culture. In ours, fat is out and tall men are in. Both men and women tend to prefer slender to medium legs and slender to medium buttocks. Women like a "V-taper," and men prefer larger than average breasts. In a study in upstate New York, dark hair was preferred over blond and red hair.
- *Liberal women are more attracted to men with long hair, while conservative women prefer short-haired men.* True, some fashions can telegraph social and political attitudes. Women who prefer long-haired men are more likely to have experimented with drugs, to be sexually experienced, and to be self-assertive, but not to attend church frequently.
- *We prefer dating partners at our own level of attractiveness to people who are extraordinarily physically attractive.* False. We prefer highly attractive people but are less likely to approach them sexually for fear of rejection. Yet most couples tend to feel that their partners are slightly more attractive than they are. The tendency to date at our own level of attractiveness is known as the matching hypothesis.

- *Men who are wealthy advertise for more attractive women in lonely hearts ads.* True, attractive people usually request attractive partners, and wealthy men's ads suggest they feel they can exchange financial security for looks and youth.

- *Attractive people are less likely to be found guilty of offenses such as burglary or cheating on an exam than their less attractive peers.* True, experiments show that mock juries are softer on people they like, and they like people who look good. There is an exception: people who use their looks in their crimes, such as swindlers, are judged more harshly. Good-looking people are also generally assumed to be more sociable, more competent, more interesting, more talented. It is assumed that they will be better parents and mates, and more fulfilled. But they are not necessarily seen as more trustworthy or modest.

- *We have a tendency to misperceive the attitudes of our loved ones so that it appears that they are more in agreement with our opinions than they may actually be.* True. When our loved ones share our attitudes, our thoughts and perceptions about them and the rest of the world are in balance.

- *We tend to experience feelings of attraction to people who express feelings of attraction to us.* True. This is reciprocity. After all, what extraordinarily fine judgment they are displaying!

- *Men who feel that they are treated unfairly by their dating partners tend to demand more sex, while women who feel unfairly treated may delay sex or avoid it altogether.* False. The available evidence simply shows that individuals who feel unfairly treated have less sex than those who feel fairly treated, regadless of sex.

- *University students in Oregon were initially hostile toward a classmate who was dressed in a fully concealing black bag, but after a while they showed curiosity, and eventually they befriended the mystery student.* True. Familiarity bred contentment and not contempt. Propinquity, or nearness, may be responsible for the burgeoning of most relationships.

- *Your dating life may buck up when food prices go down.* True. People in good moods are more ready to experience attraction to others than people in depressed moods—which is why it can be bad news if your date listens to bad news before you get together.

- *The best strategy for parents who disapprove of their children's dates may well be to hold their peace.* True, for psychological evidence suggests that young lovers who experience parental opposition may develop a greater commitment to one another.

- *People who play hard to get are seen as more attractive than people who seem "easy."* Not necessarily, but people who are hard to get by everybody except you are likely to be seen as attractive.

- *You may mistake feelings of fear for love or sexual attraction.* True enough. Male subjects interviewed by a woman on a frighteningly high and unsteady suspension bridge experienced more sexual attraction to their interviewer than men interviewed by her on a lower, more secure structure. And men who experience strong (though phony) heartbeats may interpret their supposed bodily reactions as attraction. Love seems to require bodily arousal plus some socially appropriate cue—like the presence of a physically attractive person—for labeling this arousal love.

- *It is much better to begin a new relationship by disclosing some intimate feelings than to fool around with superficial small talk.* False. Premature self-disclosure may be seen as a sign of maladjustment, and small talk allows two people to determine whether they can find some common ground for the establishment of friendship or an intimate relationship. Relationships move from zero contact to awareness, surface contact, and mutuality—a stage in which two "I's" become a "we"—through gradual self-disclosure and sharing.
- *Children of divorced couples achieve poorer grades in school than children from unbroken homes.* False. Children of divorced couples show temporary signs of stress, but they do not appear to suffer impaired social adjustment, poor grades, or other significant problems in the long run.
- *Unmarried college students who live together are rebellious.* False. They are similar to other students in terms of grades, political views, stability of the home of origin, and future hopes for marriage.

Morton Hunt

AN ANALYSIS OF HUMAN SEXUAL
EDITED BY RUTH AND EDWARD BRECHER

13

SEXUAL
BEHAVIOR

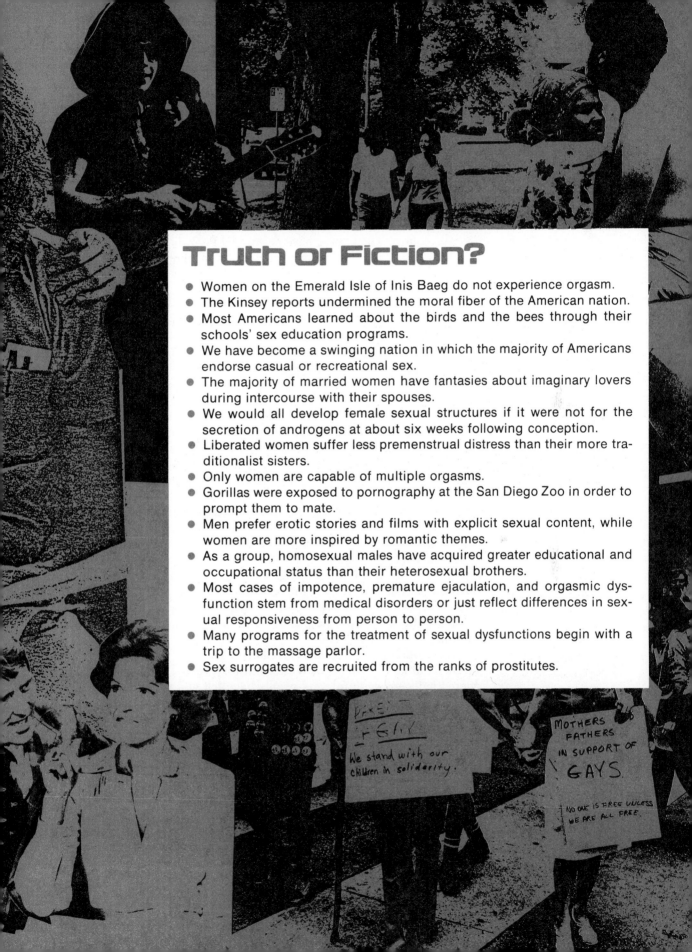

Truth or Fiction?

- Women on the Emerald Isle of Inis Baeg do not experience orgasm.
- The Kinsey reports undermined the moral fiber of the American nation.
- Most Americans learned about the birds and the bees through their schools' sex education programs.
- We have become a swinging nation in which the majority of Americans endorse casual or recreational sex.
- The majority of married women have fantasies about imaginary lovers during intercourse with their spouses.
- We would all develop female sexual structures if it were not for the secretion of androgens at about six weeks following conception.
- Liberated women suffer less premenstrual distress than their more traditionalist sisters.
- Only women are capable of multiple orgasms.
- Gorillas were exposed to pornography at the San Diego Zoo in order to prompt them to mate.
- Men prefer erotic stories and films with explicit sexual content, while women are more inspired by romantic themes.
- As a group, homosexual males have acquired greater educational and occupational status than their heterosexual brothers.
- Most cases of impotence, premature ejaculation, and orgasmic dysfunction stem from medical disorders or just reflect differences in sexual responsiveness from person to person.
- Many programs for the treatment of sexual dysfunctions begin with a trip to the massage parlor.
- Sex surrogates are recruited from the ranks of prostitutes.

Offshore from the misty coasts of Ireland is the small island of Inis Baeg. From the air it looks like a green jewel, fertile and inviting. From ground level it is not quite so warm.

The residents of Inis Baeg do not believe that women experience orgasm. A woman who chances to find pleasure in sex, especially the intense waves of pleasure that can accompany **orgasm,** is likely to be considered deviant (Messenger 1971). Premarital sex is practically unknown. During marriage the wife engages in sex to appease her husband's cravings. But she need not be too concerned about frequent performances since the men of Inis Baeg believe, erroneously, that sex will drain their strength. Sex in Inis Baeg is practiced in the dark, with the nightclothes on. The man is always on top, in the so-called missionary position. The man **ejaculates** as rapidly as he can, and then rolls over and falls asleep. The couple have performed their duty.

If Inis Baeg is not your bag (or Baeg), you may find the atmosphere of Mangaia more congenial. Mangaia is a Polynesian pearl of an island halfway around the world in the blue waters of the Pacific.

From an early age, Mangaian children, both boys and girls, are encouraged to get in touch with their own sexuality by **masturbating,** or stimulating their own genitals (Marshall 1971). Mangaian adolescents are expected to engage in sexual intercourse or **coitus,** and they may be found practicing techniques learned from the village elders on secluded beaches or beneath the fronds of palms. When are Mangaian children old enough? When they are old enough.

Thirteen-year-old Mangaian girls are introduced to coitus with their male peers, but soon graduate to older boys, who are more experienced and presumed to be capable of enhancing their sexual pleasure. Women are expected to climax, or experience orgasm, several times before their partners attain orgasm, and young men value their partner's orgasms and compete to see who will be more effective at providing young women with multiple orgasms.

The people of Inis Baeg and Mangaia have vastly different attitudes toward sex, and these attitudes influence both sexual behavior and the pleasure that people attain from sexual behavior. As William Masters and Virginia Johnson (1966) wrote in *Human Sexual Response*, no natural function has found as much variation with human beings as the sexual function. No other natural function has been so strongly influenced by religious and moral attitudes and societal beliefs. It is remarkable that social attitudes can make an act that is capable of bringing extreme pleasure into an act that is unfeeling or highly painful.

No other natural function has been associated with so much anxiety. Throughout large portions of Western history, sexual behavior has been considered indecent or sinful, and people have felt guilty about sexual behavior and sexual pleasure as a result. Today there can still be as much anxiety associated with sexual behavior. Some still feel that sex is evil at worst, and barely permissible at best. But others, who consider themselves to be the children of "the sexual revolution," can experience just as much anxiety that they are not free *enough* in their sexual behavior. Liberated women and liberated men may be anxious that they do not have as many sex partners as they feel they should, or they may worry if they are satisfied with just one orgasm.

In this chapter we first explore American sexual behavior, focusing, in particular, on the incidence and nature of masturbation, petting, premarital coitus, sexual behavior in marriage, and extramarital sex during the past several decades. We shall see that there has, indeed, been a sexual revolution. Then

A visit to most bookstores will immediately reveal the great interest the public has in human sexual behavior.

we look at human sexual equipment and the sexual response cycle that leads to orgasm. We shall see that men and women are more alike in both their anatomy and their sexual responsiveness than you may have imagined. We discuss some varieties of sexual experience, such as pornography and homosexuality, and we try to separate myths from realities. Finally, we discuss some common sexual dysfunctions, or problems, and describe the techniques that today's scientists have developed to help us adjust to these dysfunctions. You will see that these techniques may also be used to enhance and broaden our sexual experiencing.

AMERICAN SEXUAL BEHAVIOR IN PERSPECTIVE: A TALE OF TWO GENERATIONS

In the late 1940s and the early 1950s, the American public was shocked by the appearance of a couple of scientific surveys that resulted from the work of an Indiana University professor by the name of Alfred Kinsey. Two volumes— *Sexual Behavior in the Human Male* (Kinsey et al. 1948) and *Sexual Behavior in the Human Female* (Kinsey et al. 1953)—quickly became dubbed "the Kinsey Reports." These surveys of the sexual behavior of 5,300 men and 5,940 women contained to foul language and no suggestive phrasing; yet they created such a stir in a nation that had not yet learned how to discuss sex openly that a congressional committee charged that the Kinsey reports had undermined the moral fiber of our country and increased our susceptibility to a Communist takeover (Gebhard 1976).

In more recent years, numerous sex surveys have been conducted with little public concern, including one of 100,000 female readers of *Redbook* magazine (Levin & Levin 1975). The most frequently cited study of contemporary sexual practices and attitudes was based on interviews of 982 men and 1,044 women in the early 1970s, and reported by Morton Hunt in *Sexual Behavior in the 1970s* (1974).

Any comparison of sexual behavior in the 1940s and the 1970s must rely heavily on the data reported by Kinsey and Hunt, yet these studies have their faults. Both have been criticized on the basis that their samples do not adequately represent the general population of the United States (Cochran et al. 1954; Delora & Warren 1977). Kinsey's subjects included no blacks, for example. Kinsey's sample was also underrepresentative of the elderly, poorly educated people, southerners, and westerners. Hunt's sample was drawn randomly from phonebook listings in communities carefully selected to represent the diversity of the American population, but only about 20 percent of those contacted agreed to participate in the study. The Hunt sample thus represents only people who were willing to respond to interview questions about their sex lives. They may be more liberal about sex than the general population.

Despite their limitations, these studies, and others, have provided insight into the practices of masturbation, petting, premarital coitus, sexual behavior in marriage, and extramarital sex.

Today's coed campus dormitories would have been unthinkable a generation ago. Here, a bathroom in the Alice Lloyd dormitory at the University of Michigan provides one more site for social gatherings.

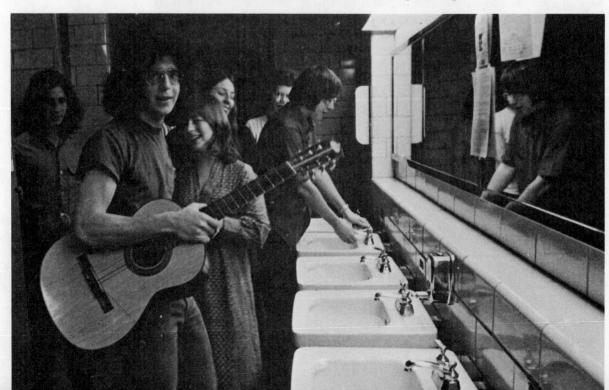

Masturbation

> In solitude he pollutes himself, and with his own hand blights all his prospects for both this world and the next. Even after being solemnly warned, he will often continue this worse than beastly practice, deliberately forfeiting his right to health and happiness for a moment's mad sensuality.
>
> J. W. Kellogg, M.D.
> *Plain Facts for Old and Young* (1882)

This description of the masturbator by one of the fathers of American breakfast cereals was typical of its day. Masturbation has been condemned for leading to diseases such as epilepsy, cancer, and heart attacks. It has been accused of leading to insanity, sterility, itching, and warts. All without a shred of evidence —an incredible example of how personal moral beliefs and personal prejudices can color the judgment of even highly educated individuals.

Kellogg, you might expect, believed that diet might influence sexual stimulation. Coffee and alcohol, he wrote, were particularly alarming in their ability to arouse sexually. He recommended "unstimulating" foods such as grains. The breakfast of champions may have been originally intended as the breakfast of abstainers.

Despite the prevalence of such frightening misinformation about masturbation, sexual self-stimulation is so common that almost all adult males and nearly two-thirds of adult females surveyed have reported masturbating to orgasm at some point during their lives (Kinsey et al. 1948, 1953; Hunt 1974). Although masturbation has been considered sinful, and labeled the "sin of Onan"—a biblical character who was punished for "spilling his seed upon the ground"—Hunt found that even among regular churchgoers, 92 percent of the males and 51 percent of the females have masturbated.

Masturbation is not reserved only for occasions when a sex partner is unavailable. Of the married men and women in the Kinsey studies, 40 percent of the men and 33 percent of the women in their twenties and thirties masturbated, with an average frequency of six and ten times a year, respectively. Hunt's data suggest an increase in recent years, with 62 percent of young husbands and 68 percent of young wives masturbating, with an average frequency of twenty-four and ten times a year, respectively. Many adults report masturbation to provide a change of pace, an additional path to sexual pleasure.

Americans no longer believe all the dire consequences of masturbation predicted by Kellogg and others, but Masters and Johnson (1966) found that every man interviewed, among a sample of 312, believed that "excessive" masturbation could cause mental disorders. What is "excessive" masturbation? Ironically, each of the 312 believed that his own level of masturbation did not exceed the critical limit. One man who masturbated once a month saw masturbation twice weekly as the danger point. Another, who masturbated two to three times daily, saw yet more frequent masturbation as dangerous. Could Sigmund Freud have found more solid evidence that we tend to look at the world in ways that help us reduce our own anxiety?

Despite the prevalence of misinformation about masturbation, including the belief that "excessive" masturbation can be harmful, Americans in general no longer consider masturbation to be wrong. Among the eighteen- to twenty-four-year-olds in the Hunt (1974) sample, only 15 percent of the males and 14

percent of the females agreed that masturbation is wrong. This figure rose with the age of the subjects, but among those fifty-five and older, only 29 percent of the men and 36 percent of the women agreed that masturbation is wrong.

As you can see in Table 13.1, men and women both report using fantasies when they masturbate.

Contemporary scholars of sexual behavior agree that masturbation is a physically harmless and pleasurable experience—when it fits with your personal values. If you are opposed to masturbation for religious or personal philosophical reasons, the moral anxiety you may experience can drain the pleasure and create the feeling that your behavior is not authentic. Those who do not object to masturbation for such reasons may agree with Woody Allen's thought that he could not knock masturbation since it meant having sex with someone he loved.

Petting

Petting. Sexual interaction that does not include coitus.

Foreplay. Sexual contact used to heighten sexual arousal or excitement in preparation for coitus.

Petting is sexual contact between two people that does not include the act of intercourse or coitus. The term "light petting" usually implies kissing and touching of areas other than the genitals, and "heavy petting" tends to imply massage of the genitals or oral contact with the genitals. Petting is practiced as a prelude to intercourse, in which case it is termed **foreplay,** and is used to heighten sexual arousal as well as provide pleasure for its own sake. But petting is also commonly used as a halfway measure between sexual abstinence and intercourse among the unmarried. It allows people to express affection, to heighten sexual arousal, and to find sexual release through orgasm, while permitting them to avoid the possibility of pregnancy and to maintain virginity.

Table 13.1 Masturbation Fantasies

	Percentage of Sample Reporting Fantasy	
Fantasy	*Men*	*Women*
Intercourse with a loved person	75	80
Intercourse with strangers	47	21
Sex with more than one person of the opposite sex at the same time	33	18
Doing sexual things you would never do in reality	19	28
Being forced to have sex	10	19
Forcing someone to have sex	13	3
Having sex with someone of the same sex	7	11

Source: Hunt (1974), pp. 91–93.

The Challenge of Human Relationships

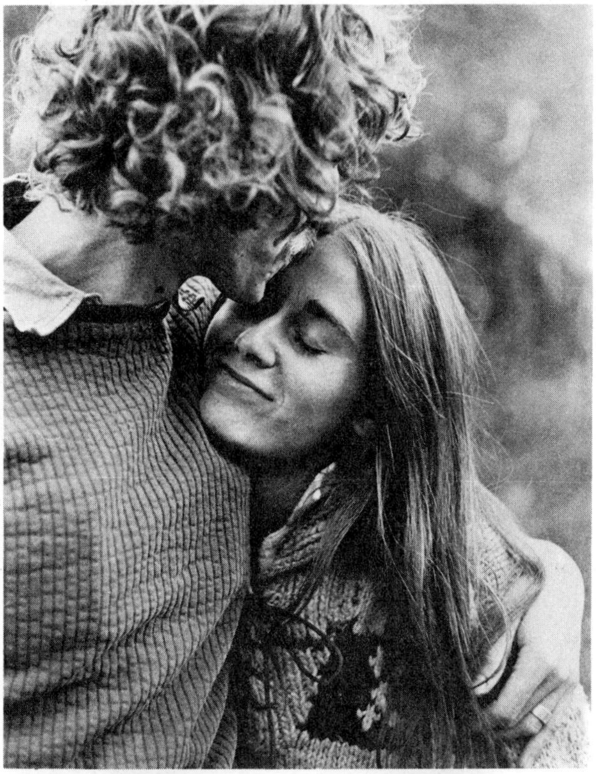

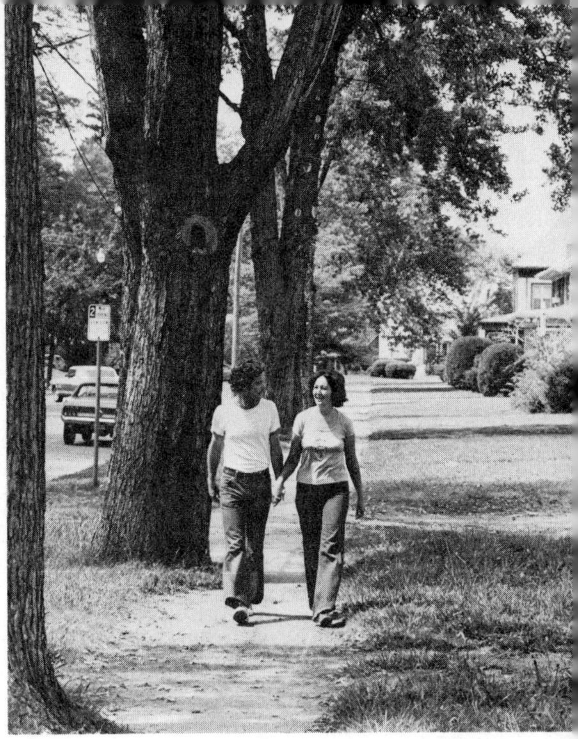

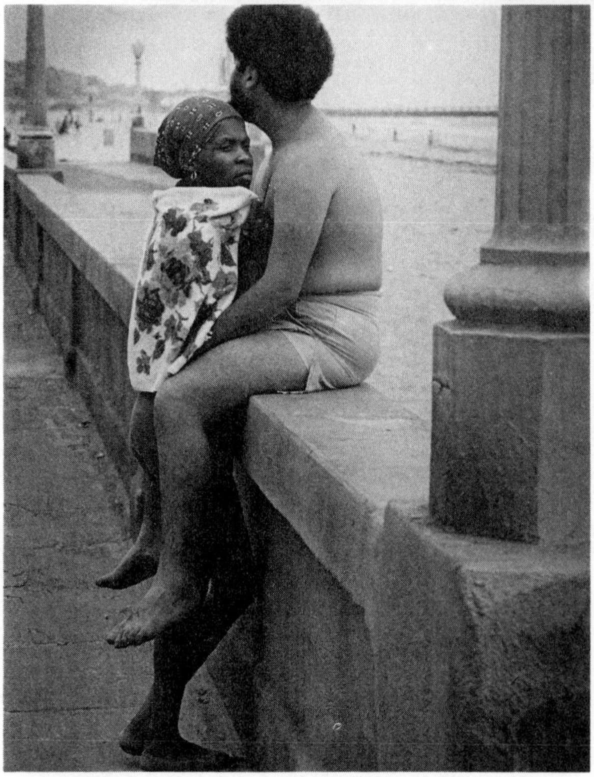

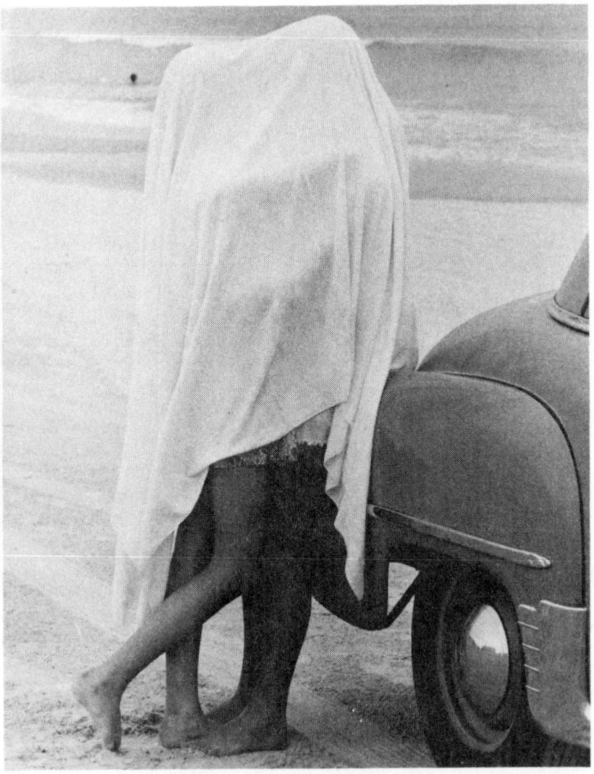

For many, it provides an adjustment to the pressures of adolescence, when sexual desire is high but sexual outlets are commonly restricted.

Kinsey and his colleagues (1948) found that premarital petting was practically a universal experience for men, and that for men who finished high school and attended college, thus delaying marriage, petting became a form of sexual adjustment for several years. Petting was also common among women (Kinsey et al. 1953). A full 94 percent of women who were unmarried at twenty had engaged in petting. Petting was also more frequent among women who delayed marrying.

Hunt (1974) found that young people in the 1970s had also almost universally practiced petting, but since the trend has been for higher percentages of young people to engage in premarital intercourse, and to engage in coitus at younger ages, the petting stage of adolescent courtship may be briefer today than in past years. Hunt's sample began petting at an earlier age than Kinsey's, and more frequently experienced orgasm through petting—with about two-thirds of the boys and half the girls petting to orgasm at some time or another.

For the girl, it seems that achieving orgasm prior to marriage—through masturbation, petting, or intercourse—is related to achieving orgasm early in marriage. Kinsey found premarital orgasm to predict orgasm in marriage more accurately than any other single factor in the girl's experience. While 44 percent of women without experience in orgasm failed to achieve orgasm during the first year of marriage, only 19 percent of those who had experienced orgasm earlier failed to attain orgasm during the first wedded year. And while 46 percent of the women who had earlier attained orgasm experienced orgasm always or nearly always during the first year of marriage, only 25 percent of those who had not experienced orgasm attained it regularly in marriage.

It must be understood that these data show a relationship, but not necessarily cause and effect. It may simply be that women who had experienced orgasm as girls are more receptive to their sexuality, a factor that would predict sexual pleasure at different ages and states of wedlock.

Premarital Coitus

In Kinsey's day, it seems that the double standard by which premarital coitus was acceptable for men but not for women was somewhat more in force than it

Table 13.2 How Boys and Girls Learn About the Facts of Life

	Percentages Reporting Source	
Main Source of Sexual Information	Males	Females
Friends	59	46
Reading	20	22
Mother	3	16
Father	6	1
School program	3	5
Adults outside home	6	4
Brothers, sisters	4	6
Other, and no answer	7	7

How did you learn about the birds and the bees? For the Hunt sample in the early 1970s, most learned about sex from friends and reading. Parents and school programs apparently imparted relatively little information. It is not surprising that there is so much misinformation about sex.
Source: Hunt (1974), p. 122.

Table 13.3 Some Birth Control Methods

Method	Procedure	Possible Complications
METHODS OF CONTRACEPTION (PREVENTING PREGNANCY FROM OCCURRING)		
Condom	The condom or "rubber" is a thin, tight sheath worn by the male. It serves as a mechanical barrier to sperm.	Condom may slip or tear, resulting in pregnancy, if caution is not used. Application may interfere with romantic mood.
Diaphragm	A flexible disk that is inserted into the vagina to act as a barrier to sperm. More effective if combined with a spermicide—a foam or jelly that kills sperm.	Must be individually fitted. Once in place it should not be felt. It may be inserted several hours before intercourse.
Intrauterine devices (IUDs)	"T" or coil-shaped devices inserted in the uterus by a physician and left to remain in place. Exact mechanisms for effectiveness are unknown— may prevent implantation of fertilized egg cells.	IUDs may not remain in place and can cause discomfort or bleeding in some women. There are fewer problems with women who have been pregnant.
Oral contraceptives ("The Pill")	Pills prescribed by a physician that are taken daily for a certain number of days throughout the menstrual cycle. Hormones inhibit ovulation by simulating a pregnant condition.	Side effects may include nausea, weight gain, and breakthrough bleeding, but usually subside with continued use. May be dangerous for women who smoke, and older women.
Withdrawal (Coitis Interruptus)	Removal of the penis from the vagina prior to ejaculation.	Highly unreliable, especially since fluids emitted by the male prior to ejaculation may contain sperm.
Rhythm method	Avoiding intercourse during the time of month when the woman is fertile (from a few days prior to a few days after ovulation). Body temperature rises about a degree just prior to this period, and a thermometer can be of help.	Ovulation can occur somewhat irregularly, especially under stress, so miscalculations can be frequent.
METHODS OF STERILIZATION (PREVENTING IMPREGNATION)		
Tubal ligation (Female)	A surgical procedure that involves tying off or cutting the tubes through which female egg cells travel. Menstrual and sexual functioning is not obstructed.	At this point in time, the tubal ligation should be considered permanent or irreversible. Otherwise, tubal ligations are generally safe.
Vasectomy (Male)	A surgical procedure that involves tying off or cutting the tubes (vas deferens) through which sperm travel from the testicles into the penis. Sexual functioning is not obstructed.	Vasectomies are most often permanent or irreversible. The operations are safe and rapid.
METHODS OF ABORTION (TERMINATING PREGNANCY)		
Vacuum aspiration	A plastic tube is inserted into the uterus and the contents are removed by suction. Used during first twelve weeks of pregnancy.	Repeated aspirations may be harmful.
Dilation and curettage (D & C)	A scooplike instrument (curette) is inserted into the uterus and scrapes out the contents. Used during first twelve weeks of pregnancy.	The D & C has more adverse effects than vacuum aspiration, but is considered more reliable.
Intraamniotic infusion	A salt solution or hormone injected into the uterine cavity induces labor (miscarriage) within eight hours to three days. This method is used if the woman has carried the fetus for more than twelve weeks, but not prior to the sixteenth week.	Intraamniotic infusion has more adverse effects than aspiration or D & C. It will not be used unless the woman has carried the fetus beyond the twelve-week limit.

Table 13.4 Percentage of Men and Women Who Report Having Premarital Coitus

	18–24	25–34	35–44	45–54	55 and over
Men	95	92	86	89	84
Women	81	65	41	36	31

Source: Hunt (1974), p. 150.

is today. He found that by the age of twenty, 77 percent of the single men but only 20 percent of the single women reported premarital coitus. Of those still single by the age of twenty-five, the figures rose to 83 percent for men but only 33 percent for women. The discrepancy between the figures for men and women is partially explained by the fact that men frequently visited prostitutes during the 1940s.

As you can see in Table 13.4, the incidence of premarital coitus appears to have exploded for both the young men and young women in the Hunt sample of the early 1970s.

Other surveys also suggest relatively high frequencies of premarital coitus for women today. The *Redbook* survey of 100,000 married readers, taken in the early 1970s, reported that 91 percent of the women who were single at twenty-five had experienced premarital coitus. A study of *Psychology Today* readers (Athanasiou et al. 1970) in 1969 reported 70 percent of the male and 76 percent of the female respondents had experienced premarital coitus at least once. But we must recall that the readers of these magazines do not represent the general American population. There is no way of even knowing how well respondents to these surveys represent all the *readers* of the magazines. But it appears that women have undergone a sexually liberating process during the past several decades, even if we cannot show precise figures.

Table 13.5 Percentages of Men and Women Who Report Premarital Sex to Be Acceptable from Several Studies

Acceptable Behavior	University of North Carolina Sample (1972)[1]		Hunt Sample (1974)[2]		Northeastern University Sample (1979)	
	Men	Women	Men	Women	Men	Women
FOR MALES						
Petting when in love	100	97	—	—	98	97
Petting with strong affection	100	95	—	—	94	91
Coitus when in love	92	92	82	68	92	97
Coitus with strong affection	87	75	75	55	89	82
Coitus without strong affection	55	32	60	37	49	24
FOR FEMALES						
Petting when in love	100	96	—	—	98	97
Petting with strong affection	100	92	—	—	91	91
Coitus when in love	100	100	77	61	92	91
Coitus with strong affection	89	72	66	41	78	79
Coitus without strong affection	62	26	44	20	32	24
Number of cases	107	68	982	1,044	192	170

Sources: [1]Bauman and Wilson (1976); [2]Hunt (1974).

Table 13.6 Reported Reasons for Not Having Premarital Coitus: Percentages

Reason	Men Under 35	Men 35+	Women Under 35	Women 35+
Religious or moral reasons	69	80	92	91
Fear of what others would think	—	27	52	53
Fear of being caught	—	27	33	26
Fear of effect on future marriage	15	31	34	28
Fear of pregnancy	23	55	59	52
Fear of disease	15	44	24	28
Never met anyone desired it with	15	13	21	23
Desired partners weren't willing	39	29	3	4

Source: Hunt (1974), p. 139.

Although there is an increased frequency of premarital coitus today, it would be wrong to assume that Americans in large numbers have come to believe in the acceptability of recreational sex. For instance, 54 percent of the women in the Hunt study who had premarital coitus had it with only one partner, often with the man they wished or planned to marry.

Table 13.5 suggests that we have come to find premarital sex with love or with strong affection to be acceptable for men and for women to a large degree. For all groups, women are less approving of premarital coitus without affection —that is, recreational sex—than men. And only one-fifth to one-fourth of all women sampled approve of recreational sex for women.

But we must keep in mind that Table 13.5 reveals only some group opinions and trends. We must all attempt to make individual decisions as to what is right or wrong for us, despite group pressures and "liberation." As you can see from Table 13.6, most individuals who have not had premarital coitus have abstained for religious or moral reasons.

Sexual Behavior in Marriage

Since Kinsey's day, the marital bed has become a stage with more varied parts for the players. Kinsey's sample was generally restricted to the male-superior or male-on-top position of coitus. Only a third of Kinsey's married couples also used the female-superior (woman-on-top) position for variety, but two-thirds of Hunt's sample had used the female-superior position. One-fourth of Kinsey's couples had used the lateral-entry (side-by-side) position, but with Hunt's sample the figure had more than doubled. In general, younger couples are more likely to experiment with different positions for coitus. Today the rear-entry, sitting, and more exotic positions observed in books such as *The Joy of Sex* have become spices commonly added to the usual sexual diet.

Oral sex has also become more popular. **Fellatio** is oral contact with the male genitals, and **cunnilingus** is oral contact with the female genitals. As you can see in Table 13.7, Hunt's sample used fellatio and cunnilingus more frequently than Kinsey's, and these practices have also been more popular with the more highly educated. Oral sex is more popular with the young: Hunt found that a full 90 percent of his married couples under twenty-five, across all educational levels, had used both fellatio and cunnilingus.

In Kinsey's day, anal sex was considered so infrequent that Kinsey and his colleagues collected no statistics on its prevalence. But Hunt estimated that

Fellatio (fell-LAY-shee-oh). Oral stimulation of the male genitals.
Cunnilingus (cun-knee-LING-gus). Oral stimulation of the female genitals.

Sexual Behavior

373

Table 13.7 Oral Sex in Marriage by Level of Education in the Kinsey and Hunt Samples

	Percentage of Marriages Using Fellatio		Percentage of Marriages Using Cunnilingus	
	Kinsey (1938–46)	Hunt (1972)	Kinsey (1938–46)	Hunt (1972)
High school males	15	54	15	56
College males	43	61	45	66
	Kinsey (1938–49)	Hunt (1972)	Kinsey (1938–49)	Hunt (1972)
High school females	46	52	50	58
College females	52	72	58	72

Source: Hunt (1974), p. 198.

more than half of his married couples under thirty-five experimented with manual stimulation of the anus, and about one-fourth had tried oral-anal sex.

It is very common for men and women to use sexual fantasies during foreplay and coitus, although many express concern that by doing so they are being "disloyal" to their mates. However, there is no evidence that such fantasizing leads to unfaithfulness or to loss of interest in one's mate. Table 13.8 shows the intercourse fantasies reported by a sample of married women from an affluent New York suburb, including PTA members and regular churchgoers. In total, 65 percent of these women reported using fantasies during coitus.

In the past, it was often erroneously assumed that the virile man ejaculated early during intercourse. Kinsey found that most men in his sample reached orgasm within two minutes of coitus, many within ten to twenty sec-

Table 13.8 Fantasies Used by Married Women During Intercourse

	Percentage of Women Reporting Fantasy
Thoughts of an imaginary romantic lover enter my mind	56
I relive a previous sexual experience	52
I enjoy pretending that I am doing something forbidden	50
I imagine that I am being overpowered or forced to surrender	49
I am in a different place, like a car, motel, beach, woods, etc.	47
I imagine myself delighting many men	43
I pretend that I struggle and resist before being aroused to surrender	40
I imagine that I am observing myself or others having sex	38
I pretend that I am another irresistibly sexy female	38
I daydream that I am being made love to by more than one man at a time	36
My thoughts center about feelings of weakness or helplessness	33
I see myself as a striptease dancer, harem girl, or other performer	28
I pretend that I am a whore or a prostitute	25
I imagine that I am forced to expose my body to a seducer	19
My fantasies center around urination or defecation	2

Source: Hariton and Singer (1974).

**Table 13.9 Estimates of the Frequency of Marital Intercourse:
Number of Times per Week**

The Kinsey Samples		The Hunt Sample	
Age Group	Median Estimate	Age Group	Median Estimate
16–25	2.45	18–24	3.25
26–35	1.95	25–34	2.55
36–45	1.40	35–44	2.00
46–55	.85	45–54	1.00
56–60	.50	55+	1.00

Source: Hunt (1974), p. 191.

onds. Women usually require more time to achieve orgasm, and this message may have been successfully communicated in recent years because Hunt found that the average length of coitus had increased to about ten minutes, and longer among younger couples.

The frequency of coitus decreases with age, but, as you can see from Table 13.9, Hunt's sample from the 1970s reported more frequent coitus than the Kinsey samples. How much is enough? This is a decison for you and your partner. Desire can be allowed to serve as the guide. Soreness or fatigue may suggest a change in technique, use of more foreplay, or a brief layoff.

Extramarital Sex

The Kinsey samples and the Hunt sample suggest that there has not been any great increase in the prevalence of extramarital sex—that is, sexual activity between married people and partners other than their mates—through the past several decades. For each group, about half the married men and 20 percent of the married women aged twenty-five and above reported having experienced extramarital sex. The only significant increase from Kinsey's day to Hunt's was among married women under twenty-five. Eight percent of this age group reported extramarital sex in Kinsey's sample, but 24 percent, or three times as many, within this same group reported extramarital sex in Hunt's sample. It may be that women's liberation has led some young women to believe that what is sauce for the gander is also sauce for the goose.

One type of extramarital sexual activity that has received considerable public attention today is **swinging,** or **comarital sex,** in which the husband and wife participate openly and jointly in extramarital encounters. A couple may swing with one other couple, or attend swinging parties in which several couples participate. Despite the publicity swinging receives, Hunt estimates that only 2 percent of the couples in his sample report swinging, and that most of the women involved report but one incident.

According to one study (Gilmartin 1975), swingers tend to be relatively affluent and well-educated and express the desire for sexual novelty as their major motive. Another investigator (Bartell 1970) reports that many swingers preserve marital stability through a strict prohibition against becoming emotionally involved with their swinging partners.

Swinging. Switching of sex partners.
Comarital sex. Swinging done together by married couples.

Sexual Behavior

Despite the publicity "swinging" receives these days, comarital sex is actually rather rare, and wives, more often than husbands, report being prodded into this activity by their mates.

The Challenge of
Human Relationships

THE PHYSIOLOGICAL BASIS OF SEX

Did you know that if it were not for the male sexual hormones, called **androgens,** we would all develop female sexual structures? All human embryos would develop the female genital anatomy if androgens were not secreted six weeks following fertilization, while we are still in the beginning stages of development within our mothers (Money 1974).

The male and female sex organs may actually be thought of as being more similar than different. The **penis** and the **clitoris** are comparable structures, and both are capable of arousal, although the smaller size of the clitoris may permit ignorance of arousal. The male's **testes** are also comparable to the female's **ovaries,** although the ovaries are deep within the woman's body and the testes normally descend into a sack called the **scrotum.** The testes produce sperm and the ovaries produce egg cells (ova).

For many animals, sexual arousal is largely under the control of hormones. Many mammals, like rodents and dogs and cats, will mate only when the female is "in heat," or, more technically, during **estrus.** This is the time during which egg cells are capable of being fertilized. Female sexual hormones, principally **estrogen,** are more plentiful in the bloodstream, and these females become receptive to the sexual advances of the male. Human females, of course, may become sexually aroused at any time, even during menstruation. Psychological factors are at least as influential as physiological factors in the stimulation of human sexual arousal: an enjoyable date and romantic love are more powerful than estrogen in the blood. Fantasy, a photo, catching a glimpse of a loved one may cause both men and women to become sexually aroused.

Among mice and monkeys, males are generally sexually aroused by the odor of **pheromones,** which are substances secreted in the **vagina** of the female. Male mice attempt to mate with other males when urine from the female is placed on their backs (Connor 1972). Vaginal secretions also excite male monkeys (Michael et al. 1971). We do not know whether human vaginal secretions sexually arouse males (Doty et al. 1975), but our culture usually teaches us to hide or to be repulsed by natural vaginal odors.

Female Sexual Anatomy

The visible female genital organs are called the **vulva,** from the Latin, for wrapping or covering. The vulva is also called the **pudendum,** from the Latin for "something to be ashamed of" (Delora & Warren 1977)—a clear reflection of some ancient sexism. The vulva has several parts: the mons veneris, the clitoris, the major and minor lips, and the vaginal opening.

Vulva (VUL-vah). The visible sex organs of the female.
Pudendum (poo-DEN-dum). Another term for vulva.

The **mons veneris** is the fatty cushion that lies over the pubic bone and is covered with short, curly hair called pubic hair. The mons veneris and pubic hair cushion the female during coitus. The woman's most sensitive sexual organ, the clitoris (from the Greek "a hill"), lies below the mons and above the urinary opening. The only known function of the clitoris is to receive and transmit pleasurable sensations.

Mons veneris (ven-NAIR-riss). The fatty cushion above the pubic bone in women which is covered with pubic hair.

During sexual arousal, the clitoris, like the penis, becomes engorged with blood and expands. The clitoris has two parts, a shaft and a tip, or **glans.** The glans is the more sensitive of the two parts and may become irritated if stimulated directly for any length of time. Women most commonly masturbate by stroking the clitoral shaft.

Glans. Tip or head.

The entrance to the vagina is lined by two layers of fatty tissue called the **major** or outer **lips,** and **minor** or inner **lips.** The outer lips are covered with hair and are not so sensitive to touch as the hairless, pinkish inner lips (Fisher 1973).

Major lips. Outer entrance to the vagina, covered with hair.
Minor lips. Pinkish, hairless, inner section of folded skin surrounding the entrance to the vagina.

The female's internal sexual and reproductive anatomy consists of the vagina, the cervix, the Fallopian tubes, and the ovaries. The vagina, from the Latin for "sheath," is a tubelike organ, surrounded by muscles, that contains the penis during coitus. When the female is unaroused, the walls of the vagina usually touch, and it may measure three to five inches in length. When aroused, the vagina may increase several inches in length and dilate to a diameter of two inches. Since the vagina expands as needed, it is a myth that a large penis is required to "fill" the vagina and provide sexual pleasure. The outer third of the vagina is highly sensitive to touch, but the inner two-thirds may be pleasurably sensitive to pressure, yet so insensitive to touch that minor surgery can actually be performed without an **anesthetic** (Barbach 1975).

When a woman is sexually aroused, a "sweating" action of the vaginal walls produces moisture that provides the lubrication necessary for coitus. Women who are not sufficiently aroused may find intercourse painful. In our society, arousal typically results from adequate foreplay, sexual attraction, fantasies, and positive emotions such as love. Anxiety over sexual behavior or concerning a particular sexual relationship may inhibit arousal.

Anesthetic (an-ess-THET-tick). A drug that reduces pain.
Cervix (SIR-vicks). A neck or passageway between the vagina and the uterus.
Uterus (YOU-turr-us). The pear-shaped organ in which human embryos and fetuses develop.
Fallopian tubes (fal-LOPE-ee-an). The narrow canals through which the ova pass on their way to the uterus, and in which conception usually takes place.

At the upper end of the vagina is an opening or "neck" that is called the **cervix.** Menstrual blood passes downward through the cervix, babies are delivered from the **uterus** through the cervix and vagina, and sperm swim upward through the cervix to the uterus and Fallopian tube. The cervix provides the passageway between the vagina and the uterus, in which the human fetus develops.

Through the slender, strawlike **Fallopian tubes,** the uterus is connected to a pair of ovaries, which produce egg cells and the female sex hormones es-

Figure 13.1 Female Sexual Anatomy

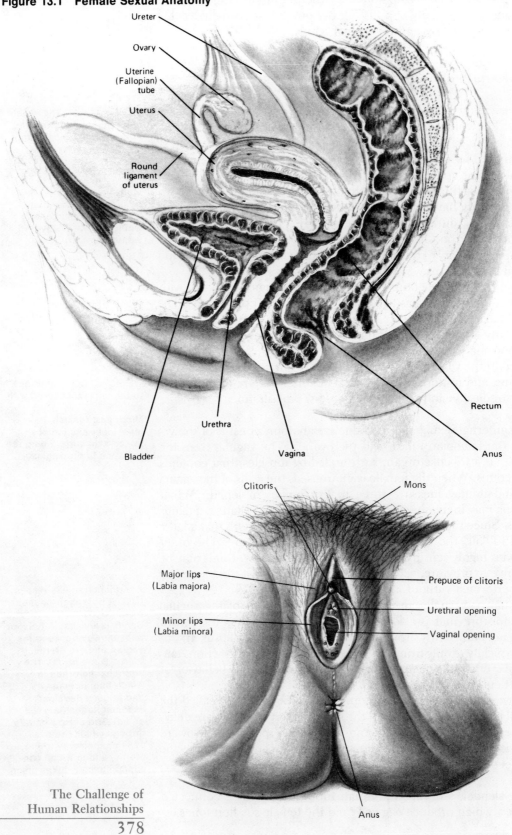

Ureter

Ovary

Uterine
(Fallopian)
tube

Uterus

Round
ligament
of uterus

Bladder

Urethra

Vagina

Rectum

Anus

Clitoris

Mons

Major lips
(Labia majora)

Minor lips
(Labia minora)

Prepuce of clitoris

Urethral opening

Vaginal opening

Anus

The Challenge of
Human Relationships

378

ON MENSTRUAL DISTRESS

In Peru, they speak of a "visit from Uncle Pepe," while in American Samoa they say "the boogie man is coming." The color red is a frequent reference to it as in the use of the word "cherry" in Samoa, "strawberry jam" in Japan, and "Little Red Riding Hood" in Colombia. In such countries as Brazil, France, Italy, Mexico, and Spain, it's often called "the rule"; in Vietnam, "the month"; while in Burma, Japan, Switzerland, Venezuela, and the United States, it's termed a "period." In Italy and Iran it's "the cycle," while for the Indonesians, "the moon comes." Hostilities between countries also come into play, as the French use the expression "the English are coming," while for the Iranians "the Indians have attacked" (Logan 1978). What is it? Menstruation, of course, and these are varieties of menstrual euphemisms used in various countries.

The New Testament and the Koran teach that menstruation is a time of pollution during which the woman is unclean and should be separated from others. In many primitive societies, the menstruating woman is dispatched to a separate hut, since it is believed that coming into contact with menstrual blood is dangerous. Men literally keep their distance, fearing for their lives, and sexual activity is strictly prohibited. American women are not sent off to special huts, but common knowledge and research evidence (Bardwick 1971; Ivey & Bardwick 1968) suggest that anxiety, hostility, and depression are highest just before or during menstruation. Other research (Dalton 1964) suggests that women are more likely to take part in crimes or to commit suicide about the time of menstruation.

Are mood changes that occur with menstruation due to the influence of changing hormonal levels—the so-called raging hormones theory—or are the "menstrual blues" the result of psychological factors? From a series of research studies by psychologist Karen Paige (1973) of the University of California at Davis, the answer appears to be that both physical and psychological factors are important. Evidence for the role of hormones comes from her finding that among women who use a type of birth-control pill that maintains a constant level of sex hormones throughout the cycle, there are no changes in a psychological test of mood changes in the levels of anxiety and hostility over the course of the cycle. Among non-pill users, whose hormone levels do fluctuate over the cycle, anxiety and hostility levels do increase at about the time of menstruation. Thus, when hormonal levels are steady, mood is steady; when hormonal levels fluctuate, so apparently does mood.

Yet hormonal fluctuations do not tell the whole story. Paige (1971) found that birth-control pill users who experienced a lessened flow while taking the pill showed less menstrual anxiety and hostility than women for whom the pill did not lessen normal flow. Paige reasons that in large measure the woman's menstrual distress is due to her apprehensiveness about menstrual bleeding. This point is further strengthened by the finding that 65 percent of the women who had reduced flows engaged in sex during menstruation, as compared with only 38 percent of those with normal flows. Paige also found that Catholic and Jewish women, apparently under the influence of religious taboos, were less likely to have sex during menstruation than Protestant women, although women of all religions have the same hormones. It should be pointed out that there are no medical reasons for avoiding sexual intercourse during menstruation.

Paige also found that women most bothered by menstrual cramps and other complaints held the traditional view that women belong in the home and not on the job, and restricted work and sexual activity during menstruation. The women who believed "menstrual blues" to be an inescapable part of the female life-style experienced more discomfort than the career-minded feminist.

It is also commonly believed that women fall off in their intellectual performance when they experience premenstrual tensions, but research with college coeds (Sommer 1972, 1973) found no relationship between intellectual functioning and phase of the menstrual cycle. Premenstrual tensions have been believed to be highest among women in their thirties and forties. Psychologist Sharon Golub (1976) did find that anxiety and depression were somewhat higher in these age groups just before menstruation, but these mood changes were moderate ones, and did not interfere with intellectual performance.

It seems clear that whatever discomfort menstruation may bring can be compounded by misinformation, cultural beliefs, fear, and attitudes toward sex roles. Women who correct misinformation and challenge their views of sex roles may experience less discomfort than their misinformed peers.

trogen and progesterone. It is usually in the Fallopian tubes that sperm and egg meet and conception takes place, beginning the drama of the unfolding of a human life.

Male Sexual Anatomy

The major male sex organs consist of the penis, the testes or testicles, the scrotum, and the series of ducts, canals, and glands that store and transport sperm and provide **semen,** the fluid that carries the sperm during ejaculation.

Semen (SEE-men). The fluid that contains sperm.

While the female pudendum has been historically viewed as "something to be ashamed of," the male sexual organs were highly prized in the classical civilizations of Greece and Rome. Greeks and Romans wore phallic-shaped amulets around their necks and adorned their doorways with phallic figures. The Greeks held their testicles when giving testimony, as we might be asked to swear on a Bible. The words "testimony" and "testicle" come from the same Greek root, meaning "to bear witness."

The two testes or testicles manufacture sperm and the male sex hormone, **testosterone.** The testes are housed in the scrotum, a sack that hangs away from the body since a lower-than-body temperature is optimal for sperm production. From the testes, the sperm are transported through a series of ducts and canals where they combine with nutrients and semen produced by various glands, particularly the prostate. Semen carries sperm and chemically activates it to increase its ability to swim and to fertilize the egg cell.

Testosterone (tess-TOSS-turr-own). A male sex hormone produced by the testes.

Figure 13.2   Male Sexual Anatomy

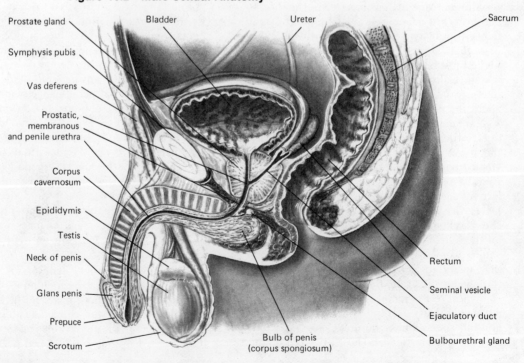

Prostate gland — Bladder — Ureter — Sacrum
Symphysis pubis
Vas deferens
Prostatic, membranous and penile urethra
Corpus cavernosum
Epididymis
Testis
Neck of penis
Glans penis
Prepuce
Scrotum
Bulb of penis (corpus spongiosum)
Rectum
Seminal vesicle
Ejaculatory duct
Bulbourethral gland

Contrary to one sex myth, there is no evidence that ejaculation drains a man's physical strength or "weakens the legs" so that sex on the evening before an athletic contest should be avoided. As the late baseball manager Casey Stengel remarked, it was not sex on the evening before a big game that tired his athletes, but rather the loss of sleep from hunting for a sex partner!

The ejaculate is discharged through the **urethra** in the penis—the passageway that also transports urine. But the bladder is closed off when the male is sexually aroused, so that the urine and sperm do not mix—a remarkable bit of biological engineering!

The penis consists of loose tissue which allows for erection in response to sexual arousal. The penis, like the clitoris, has a shaft and a tip or glans. The glans is most sensitive to sexual stimulation, particularly on the underside. Within three to eight seconds following sexual stimulation, blood will reflexively rush into the loose tissue of the penis, expanding these tissues and resulting in erection (Reckless & Geiger 1978).

Erections have been observed in newborn infants and ninety-year-old men. Males usually achieve erections every ninety to a hundred minutes while they are asleep. They may last for thirty to forty minutes, and, contrary to another myth, do not reflect the need to urinate (Karacan 1978). Nighttime erections are more likely to occur during rapid eye movement or REM sleep, which is associated with dreaming, as we shall see in Chapter 14. Almost all males and many females have experienced orgasm during dreams (Kinsey et al. 1948, 1953).

The Sexual Response Cycle

William Masters and Virginia Johnson of the Masters and Johnson Institute in St. Louis became renowned during the 1960s for their laboratory studies of human sexual response and sexual dysfunction. In contrast to the questionnaire or survey method, Masters and Johnson arranged for volunteers actually to perform sexual activities from masturbation to coitus while their physiological responses were being carefully monitored by elaborate recording equipment. Observations of hundreds of men and women led Masters and Johnson (1966) to outline a four-phase process that describes the sexual response cycle in both men and women. These four phases are the excitement, plateau, orgasm, and resolution phases.

The Excitement Phase. The **excitement phase** describes the initial physiological response to sexual stimulation. For both sexes, the heart rate, blood pressure, and rate of breathing increase. In the male, blood rushes to the penis and erection is achieved. In the female, the nipples become erect and swell in size, blood engorges the genital region and the clitoris expands, the inner vagina lengthens and dilates, and, within ten seconds to half a minute, vaginal lubrication appears.

The Plateau Phase. The **plateau phase** describes a heightening of sexual arousal that prepares the body for orgasm. The heart rate, blood pressure, and breathing rate continue to rise. In the man, the ridge of the penile glans becomes futher engorged and may turn a deep purplish color, while the testes increase in size and elevate in order to allow a full ejaculation. In the woman, the outer vagina becomes so engorged that its diameter is reduced by about one-third, and a "sex flush" or mottling of the skin becomes pronounced.

Urethra (you-REETH-rah). The passageway or canal in the penis through which semen is ejaculated and urine is discharged.

Excitement phase. The first stage in the sexual response cycle, during which sexual arousal begins.
Plateau phase (plat-TOW faze). The second stage of the sexual response cycle, during which sexual arousal is heightened.

Sex researchers William H. Masters and Virginia E. Johnson of the Masters and Johnson Institute in St. Louis.

The Orgasm Phase. During the **orgasm phase,** breathing, blood pressure, and heart rate reach a peak, and there are involuntary muscle contractions throughout the body. In the man, the muscles at the base of the penis contract and semen is expelled through the penis. In the woman, the muscles surrounding the outer third of the vagina contract rhythmically. For both sexes, the

Figure 13.3 The Male and Female Sexual Response Cycles

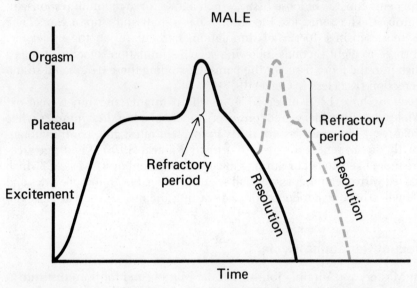

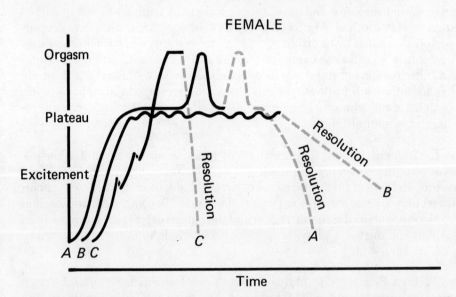

Solid lines show response cycles with one orgasm, and dotted lines show possible variations. For men, there is a refractory period following an orgasm. During this refractory period, it is generally not possible to become aroused to further orgasms, although men may sometimes experience two ejaculations before the refractory period when they are young. Pattern B with women demonstrates a plateau phase that is not followed by orgasm, and Pattern C demonstrates the possibility or orgasm without a preceding plateau phase. The dotted lines in Pattern A suggest the possibility of multiple orgasms. *Source:* Masters and Johnson (1966), p. 5.

initial contractions are most intense, and are spaced at 0.8-second intervals (five contractions every four seconds). The contractions then diminish in intensity and are spaced farther apart.

Psychologically, the experience of orgasm provides intense sexual pleasure and release of sexual tension for those who are receptive to sexual pleasure and who receive sufficient sexual stimulation. Yet it is possible for those who have been misinformed about sex, or for people who are strongly opposed to sexual pleasure for religious or philosophical reasons, to experience these contractions as pain. If such individuals are not successful at resolving their sexual conflicts through challenging their negative attitudes, and if they wish to experience pleasurable sex, they would be well advised to seek the assistance of a helping professional.

The Resolution Phase.   After orgasm, a **resolution phase** occurs in which the body gradually returns to its resting state. The heart rate, blood pressure, and breathing all return to normal levels, and the blood that had engorged the genitals is dispelled from the genital region.

In the case of a lengthy plateau phase that is not followed by orgasm, the genital engorgement may take longer to dissipate, and pelvic tension or discomfort may be experienced. In men, this discomfort has been labeled "blue balls." But, contrary to myth, women can experience this pelvic discomfort also (Barbach 1975).

Resolution phase (ress-so-LOO-shun). The fourth stage of the sexual response cycle, during which the body returns to a resting state.

Multiple Orgasms.   Women can often experience numerous or **multiple orgasms,** one quickly following another. Women may be satisfied with just one orgasm, but Masters and Johnson (1966) found that some women experienced as many as fifty orgasms during a single masturbation session with the aid of a vibrator! This potential has given some women the feeling that they ought not be satisfied with just one, the flip side of the old myth that a woman was not meant to enjoy sex. In sex, as in other areas of life, our "oughts" and "shoulds" are too often based on arbitrary standards and can serve to make us feel inadequate.

James McCary (1978) estimated that from 6 to 8 percent of males could also experience more than one orgasm in a single session. This capability becomes very infrequent after age thirty (Masters & Johnson 1966), and appears to be seldom missed.

Multiple orgasms (MULT-tip-pull). The experiencing of orgasms in succession, without return to a resting state between orgasms.

Sexual Response and Aging

"Just because there's snow on the roof doesn't mean there's no fire in the furnace"—so goes the saying. Quite accurate, according to Kinsey and Masters and Johnson. Kinsey found that three-fourths of the men in his sample aged seventy and half the men aged seventy-five achieved erections regularly (Kinsey et al. 1948). Masters and Johnson (1966) found women at these ages to be capable of multiple orgasms.

Some changes do occur with advancing age. Men may require increased sexual stimulation to achieve erection and may not be able to reachieve erection for eight to twenty-four hours following ejaculation by age fifty or so (Kaplan & Sager 1971). But from the woman's perspective, her mate may become the perfect lover: it may take older men longer to achieve ejaculation and the couple may be able to extend intercourse for protracted periods.

Many men continue to have intercourse into their eighties, but others experience a **climacteric**—an inability to reproduce brought about by a dropoff in testosterone production.

Following the female climacteric, or **menopause,** women may experience vaginal dryness or irritation as a result of decreased estrogen production. This condition may be corrected through use of artificial lubrication or estrogen treatment—although recent evidence suggests that excessive use of estrogen therapy may increase the risk of cancer. Menopause may signal the end of a woman's reproductive capacity, but certainly not of her sexual capacity. Women of eighty maintain the capacity to achieve orgasm.

VARIETIES OF SEXUAL EXPERIENCE

We may all possess the same equipment—or practically the same equipment —as the other members of our sex, but our individual sexual appetites and preferences may vary greatly on the basis of our own unique experiences and ways of looking at the world. In other words, we can learn to be aroused by sexual stimuli that could be meaningless to other people, and we may seek release of our sexual tensions through techniques or with people that others might find foolish, or even disgusting.

In this section we shall explore some of the varieties of sexual experience that may be sought out by our neighbors or ourselves, including pornography, homosexuality, bisexuality, and then some of the psychosexual disorders listed in the Diagnostic and Statistical Manual (DSM) of the American Psychiatric Association.

Pornography

Pornography (por-NOG-graf-fee). Explicit, uncensored portrayals of sexual activity that are designed to stimulate sexually. Also called erotica.
Erotic (air-ROT-tick). Sexually stimulating.

Every few months, and especially during election years, we hear of some mayor or of some city council becoming highly indignant and rushing out to seize some new **pornographic** film or try to shut down some "adult" bookstores. Since the Supreme Court rulings of the 1960s that **erotic** materials are generally protected by the First Amendment to the Constitution, which guarantees freedom of expression, there is no question that sections of American cities—like Times Square in New York and the Combat Zone in Boston— have openly and blaringly displayed the explicit nature of their films and other offerings. Some feel that this has led to a breakdown of moral standards, but in every generation people have believed that there has been a new "breakdown" of moral standards. Therefore, we have to address a couple of specific and very important questions: Do erotic materials inspire people to violent and deviant sexual acts, as some have feared? What do we know about the effects of erotica?

Does Erotica Inspire Sexual Violence? The United States Commission on Obscenity and Pornography (1970) reviewed numerous surveys and experiments with hundreds of subjects and concluded that exposure to pornography had not been shown to lead to any documented instances of rape, child molestation, exhibitionism, or other socially disruptive acts. The Commission found that 84 percent of the mental health professionals surveyed—including psychologists, psychiatrists, and social workers—believed that exposure to por-

Since the Supreme Court rulings of the 1960s that erotic materials are protected by the First Amendment to the Constitution, sections of many American cities openly display the explicit nature of their films and other offerings.

nography did not lead to either juvenile delinquency or adult antisocial behavior.

It may even be the case that antisocial and sexually aggressive individuals have had less exposure to erotic materials than their law-abiding peers. Some studies have shown that convicted rapists and child molesters had significantly less exposure to pornography during adolescence than the general public, and that they were highly unlikely to have been influenced by exposure to pornography just prior to their crimes (Eysenck 1972; Goldstein et al. 1971).

In Denmark, where erotic materials have been legal since 1969 and there have been "sex fairs" similar to American carnivals but with erotic materials, sex crimes were found to decrease following removal of restrictions, although cause and effect cannot be assumed.

What Are the Effects of Pornography on Normal Individuals? What about pornography and the normal gorilla? Gorillas may be large and burly, but they are not often sexually aroused—a fact that may lead to their eventual extinction in the wilds of Africa as well as in zoos. In a recent experiment in the San Diego zoo, gorillas were shown films of other primates in explicit sexual activity. Gorillas do like films and television—and, as reported by newscasts in 1979, they particularly seem to enjoy football games. But, sad to say, the gorilla "skin flicks" were a flop. They did not inspire their viewers to sexual monkey business.

ON WOMEN'S LIBERATION AND GRAFFITI

The most widely practiced "art" form is not pop art, op art, or even realism. It is graffiti. Gaffiti is found everywhere, from park benches, to bathrooms, to subway cars. Some consider graffiti vandalism, some the expression of the struggling self in a computerized society. In any event, graffiti has not been ignored by social scientists.

In his studies on sexual behavior in the 1940s, Kinsey and his colleagues noted that men produced more graffiti on bathroom walls than women. Female graffiti, where it existed, more often represented romantic content (such as "Mary loves John") than explicit sexual content.

But in a more recent study of the walls of bath-rooms in four Midwestern high schools, Wales and Brewer (1976) found that female graffiti outnumbered male graffiti by a ratio of 7–2! Overall, girls' graffiti was still more romantic and less sexually explicit than boys', but this finding largely resulted from the artwork of students from the lower socio-economic class. In more affluent schools, girls produced about as much sexually explicit material as romantic material.

Bathroom graffiti may provide a measure of women's liberation. It suggests that at least the more socially advantaged girl may be becoming more sexually expressive, and forgoing the traditional sex-role stereotype of sexual passivity.

Humans, male and female, do find erotic materials to be sexually stimulating. Erotic stories, slides, and films have all been found to inspire men and women to become sexually aroused and to have a greater number of orgasms during the twenty-four hours following exposure than do subjects who have been exposed to nonsexual stimulation—such as slides of geometric forms, and stories and films similarly devoid of sexual content (Hatfield et al. 1978; Herrell 1975; Schmidt et al. 1973; & Schmidt 1975). The increased frequency

Table 13.10   Photographic Slides Rated Most and Least Sexually Arousing

Most Arousing Themes	*Least Arousing Themes*
RATINGS BY MEN	
Sexual intercourse in various positions	Female physically hurting male
Genital petting	Male masturbating
Female engaging in oral sex with male: fellatio	Two males engaged in anal intercourse
Male engaging in oral sex with female: cunnilingus	Nude male
Female masturbating	Male in undershorts
Group oral sex	Male engaging in oral sex with male: homosexual fellatio
Male caressing female's breast	
RATINGS BY WOMEN	
Male engaging in oral sex with female: cunnilingus	Male physically hurting female
Sexual intercourse in various positions	Male in undershorts
Genital petting	Female physically hurting male
Male caressing female's breast	Two males engaged in anal intercourse
	Clothed female
	Male engaging in oral sex with male: homosexual fellatio
	Nude female
	Nude male

Source: Baron and Byrne (1977), p. 477.

of orgasm was through normal means—masturbation, coitus with spouses, or with usual boyfriends and girl friends.

There is something of a myth in our culture that men are more turned on by explicit sexual materials but that women are more aroused by romance. Psychologist Julia Heiman (1975) of the State University of New York at Stony Brook played a number of tape recordings to male and female students while their level of sexual response was being monitored by recording devices that were worn unobtrusively beneath their clothes. Increased blood flow to the genitals was measured by erection in the males and vaginal blood pressure in the females. Taped stories contained romantic content only, explicit sexual content only, explicit sex associated with a romantic story, or a control tape with just general conversation. For both sexes, the explicit sexual content—with or without romantic trappings—was most sexually arousing. But don't get the idea that romance serves no function. Both men and women report *preferring* stories that combine sex with romance (Schmidt et al. 1973).

There are also some interesting similarities between men and women in terms of the explicit themes that are most and least arousing. Baron and Byrne (1977) combined the results of several studies in which men and women were given the opportunity to rate photographic slides as highly arousing through unarousing. As you can see in Table 13.10, men and women were both highly aroused by heavy petting, caressing of the breasts, cunnilingus, and coitus itself. Neither men nor women reported being turned on by sexual sadism or homosexual themes in these studies.

What, you may wonder, will happen as our society becomes more and more saturated with erotica? Perhaps an answer was suggested in a study by Howard et al. (1973). They exposed male students to pornography for ninety minutes a day over a fifteen-day period. The students were not driven to sexual abandon. Their interest in these materials simply gradually waned. Too much of an arousing thing can apparently become a crashing bore.

What of those who remain staunchly opposed to erotic materials? People who disapprove strongly of erotic films have been called **eroticaphobes.** In a survey of the sexual attitudes, family background, and sexual behavior of eroticaphobes, Fisher and Byrne (1976) found eroticaphobes to be conservative, attend church regularly, rate themselves as having inadequate sexual knowledge, oppose premarital sex and recreational sex, disapprove of abortion and making birth control devices readily available, and to desire legal regulation of sexual

Eroticaphobes (air-ROT-tick-ah-fobes). Individuals who experience intense emotional discomfort in the presence of pornography, and who are morally opposed to pornography.

Playboy-itis?

ON CENTERFOLDS AND ACADEMIC AVERAGES

Who puts his *Playboy* centerfold on the wall, and who keeps it in the magazine or leaves it at the newsstand? At Weber State College in Utah, psychologists Richard Miller and Gary Carson (1975) peeked into the rooms of 169 male dormitory residents, checking whether *Playboy*-like photos adorned the walls.

They found that students with high grade-point averages were less likely to decorate the walls than students with an average of C or less, and that members of varsity teams were more likely to decorate than the less athletically inclined. Does magazine "modern art" distract college men from the academic life, or do the more intellectually oriented have less interest in these photos? We would bet that the "A" student is more likely to keep his fantasies in his mind than on his walls.

behavior. Yet erotica increases sexual arousal in eroticaphobes as well as others (Fisher 1976).

Homosexuality

Homosexuality is defined as a sexual preference for members of one's own sex. Homosexuality has apparently been a part of the human sexual experience since the dawn of recorded history, but public awareness of homosexuality has recently exploded with the **gay rights movements** in cities like San Francisco —which has been more receptive than most cities to people with differing sexual orientations—and the efforts of some individuals, like Anita Bryant, to deny equal rights to jobs and housing to the **gay** community.

Hunt estimated that as many as 2 percent of the male population and 1 percent of the female population were exclusively homosexual, although the rates are certainly higher in communities like San Francisco and New York's Greenwich Village.

Many continue to think of homosexuals as limp-wristed, twangy-voiced males and tough, "butch" women, but only a small percentage of homosexuals resemble these stereotypical pictures at all (Pomeroy 1966). It has recently been revealed, for example, that a number of football players are homosexual. Homosexuals are found in all walks of life, and they possess as wide a variety of personalities as do "straights." Rather than commonly being on the fringes of society, homosexual men, as a group, have achieved educational, occupational, and social statuses equal to those of married men and higher than those of single heterosexual males (Saghir & Robbins, 1973).

It is commonly assumed that within each homosexual couple one person assumes a traditional male, aggressive sexual role, and the other member assumes a female, passive sexual role. It is assumed that the "male" member does the acting, and that the "female" member is acted upon. The truth of the matter is that most homosexuals resent being characterized according to stereotypical masculine and feminine roles, and assert that they are neither—they are themselves, and roles are frequently alternated.

Brief homosexual encounters are actually quite common, particularly during childhood and adolescence. Hunt found that 20–25 percent of the men sampled and 10–20 percent of the women had engaged in a homosexual experience at some point in their lives. For most, these were isolated or brief affairs —the term homosexual is defined as preference for members of one's own sex.

The origins of homosexuality are a controversial topic, with some investigators suggesting that biological factors are central in importance, and others pointing to social learning factors. The behavioral view simply suggests that we may learn to wish to reduce sexual tensions in many different ways as a result of different reinforcement histories. If we find pleasure with persons of the opposite sex at a young age, it is logical to develop a preference for them. The psychoanalytic view suggests that homosexuals have resolved their Oedipal and Electra complexes in a fashion different from the majority, largely as a result of poor father-son relationships in the case of males (Siegelman 1974; Ibrahim 1976).

All these views must be looked at critically. There is no reliable evidence that imbalances in sex hormones (Rose 1975) or genetic factors (Brodie et al. 1974) play the critical role. We must also note that many homosexuals have had close relationships with their parents (Siegelman 1974).

Anita Bryant and her husband (above right) savor victory after their "Save Our Children" crusade led to the repeal of a law guaranteeing equal opportunity for homosexuals in Dade County, Florida. However, homosexuality remains widespread, and many (above left) support the gay rights movement.

Other Varieties of Sexual Experience

Bisexual (by-SEX-you-ul). Having sexual desire for members of both sexes.

Bisexuality. **Bisexuals** are men or women who engage in sexual relations with members of both sexes. Some bisexuals have a bisexual self-identity, and others view themselves as being basically heterosexual or homosexual, and merely seeking variety.

Some maintain that all bisexuals are basically homosexual, but that societal pressures to conform have prevented them from accepting their homosexual identities. Interestingly, in ancient Greece there was a distinction between "domestic love" and "romantic love." Domestic love was shared by men with their wives, and was the force that pulled Odysseus back to his Penelope after the twenty long years of *The Odyssey*. But romantic love was shared between men, and was the force that drove Achilles into battle after the slaying of his beloved Patroclus in *The Iliad*.

Transsexual (trans-SEX-you-ul). Feeling trapped in the body of a person of the opposite sex, and desiring to change sex through surgery.

Transsexualism. **Transsexuals** feel trapped in the body of the opposite sex. In contrast to homosexuals, transsexuals do not view their interest in members of their own sex as homosexual, since they believe they really belong to the opposite sex. Men who wish to be women usually assume a traditional female role in their sexual relations with men, and women who wish to be men assume traditional male roles with their women lovers (Langevin et al. 1977; Pauly 1974).

Transsexuals are usually repelled by their genitals and breasts and seek sex-reassignment surgery to help adopt the appearance of the opposite sex. Some three to four thousand American transsexuals have had such operations (McCary 1978), as with tennis player Dr. Renée Richards.

Transvestitism (frans-VEST-tie-tism). Attaining sexual gratification through wearing the clothing of members of the opposite sex. Also: transvestism.

Transvestitism. **Transvestitism** is the gaining of sexual pleasure through wearing the clothing of the opposite sex, and is more common among men than women. Some male transvestites derive sexual pleasure from wearing particular feminine articles, such as bras and panties. Others adopt full female dress.

Most transvestites are heterosexual and married. In fact, they are generally well adjusted in their married lives (McCary 1978). Homosexual males who dress as women may be referred to as "drag queens."

Fetishism (FETT-ish-ism). Attaining sexual gratification through contact with an object that is sexually arousing to the individual even though it may have no apparent sexual meaning to others.

Fetishism. **A fetish** is a sexual attraction for some object, such as an article of clothing, that has a particular sexual meaning for the individual. Gratification is typically achieved through masturbating in the presence of the object, or fantasies that involve the object. In our society, fetishes for undergarments, leather jackets, and leather boots are not uncommon.

Pedophilia (pedd-oh-FEEL-ee-uh). Sexual interaction between an adult and a child.

Pedophilia. **Pedophilia** is a social problem in which an adult engages in or desires sexual activity with a child. The child may be of the same or opposite sex. Only a small minority of cases actually involve coitus (Jaffe 1976), and violence is quite rare (McCary 1971).

Pedophilia may occur more often in individuals who experience difficulty in adult relationships. Behavior therapists have dealt with pedophilia by (a) teaching the individual social skills that will foster adjustment in adult rela-

The Challenge of Human Relationships

tionships, and (b) using electric shock paired with photographic slides of children (aversion therapy) to decrease the attraction toward youngsters.

Exhibitionism. **Exhibitionism** is the repeated urge to expose one's genitals in public, and is usually considered a problem limited to men, although some would say that female exotic dancers could be considered exhibitionists. Yet these dancers are paid for their nudity, and the male exhibitionist seeks to shock his victims more than to arouse them sexually.

Freudians suggest that exhibitionism represents the man's way of coping with castration anxiety—a fear of losing the penis that stems from the phallic stage of development. The act of exposure may represent the exhibitionist's assertion that he does possess a penis, and shock on the victim's face may be interpreted as recognition of this fact and be reassuring. Behaviorists again suggest that the act of exposure may have been accidentally associated with sexual excitement in the past—as in the case where a boy may be discovered urinating by a woman.

Exhibitionism (eggs-hibb-BISH-shun-ism). Attaining sexual gratification by exposing one's genitals in social situations in which such behavior is considered inappropriate.

Voyeurism. **Voyeurism** is a form of sexual variance in which the individual attains sexual gratification through watching other people who are nude or engaged in sexual activity. Voyeurs are also called "Peeping Toms," and, as this nickname suggests, voyeurism is usually found among males. Sexual excitement is often greatest when the voyeur is able to observe others secretly.

Naturally, it is exciting to watch your lover in the nude, but this is not considered voyeurism. The voyeur commonly prefers secretly to watch others engaged in sex, rather than have sexual activity. Voyeurs as a group are found not to be violent, and are usually treated as a nuisance by authorities.

Voyeurism (VOY-your-ism). Attaining sexual gratification through observing other people who are undressed or engaged in sexual activity. Also called Peeping Tomism.

Sexual Sadism. In **sexual sadism,** an individual attains sexual gratification through inflicting pain on sex partners. Sadism may be expressed through physical acts such as whipping, slapping, or biting, or verbally through teasing and sarcasm. It should not be confused with acts like little love bites, which can increase one's overall level of stimulation.

The Freudian view is that sadism may allow men to experience power over partners, thus unconsciously reassuring them that they are maintaining their sex organs, as with exhibitionism and voyeurism. It may also be that some individuals believe that sex is basically a filthy act and that their partners are deserving of punishment for allowing themselves to become involved in sexual relations.

Sexual sadism (SAD-ism). Attaining sexual gratification through inflicting pain on one's sex partner.

Sexual Masochism. Masochism and sadism are different sides of the same coin. In **sexual masochism,** an individual receives sexual gratification through receiving pain from sex partners. Masochists seek out not only physical punishment, but also verbal assaults for being naughty.

Masochists, as sadists, typically believe that sex is dirty, and it may be that the punishment they seek permits them to cope with their guilt. They "pay" for their sins, often in elaborate scripts in which they may be tied (this tying is called **bondage**), accused of wrongdoing, and then physically punished. People who join in at both ends of these scripts are "into **S/M**"—**sadomasochism.** The sadist gives and the masochist receives. Hunt (1974) found almost twice as many women as men to have received masochistic pleasure, and the incidence was five times as high among single as married women.

Sexual masochism (MASS-so-kism). Attaining sexual gratification through being hurt or humiliated by one's sexual partner.
Bondage. Attaining sexual gratification through tying one's sex partner or through being tied so that movement, or opposition to sexual assault, is not possible.
S/M. Abbreviation for sadomasochism.
Sadomasochism (SAD-oh-MASS-so-kism). A relationship in which one party plays a sadistic role and the other party plays a masochistic role.

Sexual Behavior

SEXUAL DYSFUNCTIONS

William Masters and Virginia Johnson (1970) estimate that as many as 50 percent of American marriages are troubled by some form of **sexual dysfunction,** or difficulty in achieving sexual arousal or attaining sexual gratification through orgasm. These sexual dysfunctions range from difficulty in becoming sexually aroused to difficulty in achieving orgasm.

Male sexual dysfunctions include **impotence** (inability to achieve or sustain erection long enough to have coitus), **premature ejaculation** (ejaculating prior to plan or the wishes of the couple), and **retarded ejaculation** (difficulty in reaching orgasm). In women these problems include **orgasmic dysfunction** (difficulty in reaching orgasm—comparable to retarded ejaculation in the male), **vaginismus** (involuntary muscle contractions in the vagina that prevent insertion of the penis), and **dyspareunia** (painful coitus).

In this section we explore the origins of these dysfunctions and the current methods of helping that were pioneered by researchers such as Masters and Johnson (1970), and developed and expanded by many others.

Psychoanalytic Factors

According to psychoanalytic theory, sexual dysfunctions reflect unconscious conflicts. Impotence in the male, or difficulty in achieving erection, may reflect castration anxiety (Fenichel 1945). In the male's fantasies, insertion of the penis into the vagina may be dangerous if the Oedipus complex has not been adequately resolved. Similarly, ejaculation may come early, to satisfy the unconscious wish to withdraw promptly to safety. This would explain premature ejaculation.

Inability to achieve orgasm in the woman may reflect unconscious failure to accept the female sex role and seek genital satisfaction. Vaginismus and dyspareunia may reflect attempts to express resentment toward the male who possesses the organ that the woman cannot have.

We should note that these views have not been borne out by research, and that psychoanalysis, as a therapeutic technique for treating sexual dysfunctions, has not produced reliable success.

Physical Factors

Most of the time, sexual dysfunctions result from psychological problems, but now and then physical factors play a role. For instance, it is known that the effects of aging may impede erection and retard ejaculation in the male. Alcohol and fatigue similarly may cause impotence and premature ejaculation in the male and orgasmic dysfunction in the female.

Vaginismus usually results from anxiety concerning coitus, but dyspareunia may result from infections or lack of sufficient lubrication as well as anxiety or lack of interest in coitus.

Because of the possible relationships between physical and psychological problems in creating sexual dysfunctions, it is wise to see a physician to determine that the sexual apparatus is in good physical working order when dysfunctions do not rapidly discontinue.

Marital Factors

It is possible to experience sexual dysfunctions because a marriage or other relationship is not working. Strong resentments and anxieties concerning relationships can inhibit sexual arousal and sexual gratification in both sexes. Men and women may both "withhold" orgasm, for example, as a way of making their partner feel inadequate and guilty when they cannot express their resentments verbally, or when the partner seems unresponsive to requests to change behavior.

When couples have significant problems in communicating, or when they are reluctant to change, it would be wise to consult a psychologist or other helping professional. A good relationship is not a guarantee of a gratifying sexual experience, but sex often suffers when the relationship is troubled.

Lack of Sexual Skills

To a large degree, sexual behavior results from operant conditioning. Through exploring our own bodies and the bodies of our sex partners, we come to learn what makes us feel good and what makes our partners feel good. Our own pleasurable sensations reinforce our successful acts, and we become likely to repeat them. The movements and verbal responses of our partners indicate when we have aroused and gratified them, and gradually we acquire the skills to do so more efficiently. We also learn to generalize our skills from one person to another, in those cases when we have more than one sex partner, and we can learn quickly to make discriminations when one partner does not enjoy what turned someone else on.

Yet some of us may not acquire adequate sexual skills because of personal beliefs, anxiety, or lack of opportunity. For instance, children who have been brought up to believe that sex is filthy or evil may experience strong anxiety at the prospect of caressing their own genitals or experimenting with playmates and young suitors. Even if some experimenting takes place, anxiety is likely to inhibit sexual arousal and minimize the chances for pleasure. In such instances, the learning processes may have to be begun in adulthood if such skills are to be acquired. But by then it is possible that we may have come to assume that we are somehow incapable of enjoying sexual activities, and lack the motivation to try new things.

Performance Anxiety

Masters and Johnson (1970) have shown us that one of the greatest impediments to sexual gratification is **performance anxiety.** This form of anxiety has many meanings and may stem from many sources.

A man may fail to attain erection because of a few alcoholic beverages, and worry that his problem will be repeated at his next opportunity. This worrying makes it more difficult to achieve erection, and if he fails again, he may begin to wonder if he is doomed to eternal failure. He may propel himself into a vicious cycle in which failure leads to personal doubts and anxiety, and these lead, in turn, to continued failure. He may then focus more on his own performance than his partner's attractiveness, or, as Masters and Johnson phrase it, become a spectator to his own sexual performance.

Performance anxiety.
Concern about one's ability to engage in successful sexual relations.

Sexual Behavior

Primary orgasmic dysfunction. Difficulty achieving orgasm in a woman who has never experienced orgasm.
Situational or secondary orgasmic dysfunction. Difficulty in achieving orgasm in a woman that is related to the circumstances in which she is attempting to achieve orgasm.

Ironically, the same anxiety that makes it difficult to attain erection can hurry ejaculation, so that a man ejaculates prematurely once he has managed to attain erection. Impotence and premature ejaculation are often found to trouble the same man.

Anxiety and lack of skills are likely to interact strongly in the case of the woman experiencing orgasmic dysfunction. If her problem is **primary orgasmic dysfunction,** or failure to have achieved orgasm at any point in her life, it may be that fear of self-exploration has prevented her from acquiring sexual skills, or even knowledge of what can feel good. *Situational* or *secondary orgasmic dysfunction* describes women who have had at least some past experience in achieving orgasm, but who presently may either be unable to achieve orgasm at all, or can achieve orgasm in some situations, such as masturbation, but not others, such as sex with their partners. If her problem is the result of a particular situation, such as her relationship with her lover, it may be that, because of anxiety, she is reluctant to guide her lover to teach the skills that will heighten her arousal and gratify her.

Women, too, become involved in vicious cycles. Failure to achieve orgasm, especially after lengthy stimulation during the plateau stage of the response cycle, can lead to frustration, discomfort, and expectations of future failure. They may look upon their next encounters with increased anxiety, which, in turn, further decreases the probability of finding release in orgasm. They, too, may become spectators to their sexual performance rather than willing participants.

Men and women may also make the error of attempting to *will* an erection, or will an orgasm. Erection and orgasm are both reflexes or involuntary responses. They cannot be forced. We can only set the stage for them by attaining sexual stimulation and focusing on the pleasure we are giving and receiving. Then we must *allow* them to happen. Trying to will them only increases performance anxiety and cannot possibly succeed.

Treatment of the Sexual Dysfunctions

Sex therapy. Methods for treating sexual dysfunctions that tend to emphasize the reduction of performance anxiety and the learning of sexual skills.

The most effective treatments for the sexual dysfunctions are brief programs that have been collectively labeled **sex therapy.** They are based on the behavioral model, and assume that sexual dysfunctions can be treated by directly changing the problem behavior that occurs in the bedroom. Treatment of most dysfunctions is enhanced by the cooperation of an understanding and patient sex partner, so it may be necessary to do some work on the couple's relationship before sex therapy itself will be effective.

Sex therapy focuses on the reduction of performance anxiety, the modification of self-defeating expectations, and the learning of sexual skills. Insofar as possible, both sex partners are involved in therapy. The sex therapists, often a male and female sex-therapy team, guide the couple through a program of homework assignments and meet with them regularly to discuss progress, trouble points, and strategies for the next homework assignment.

We shall have a look at some of the techniques that have been successful in treating impotence and premature ejaculation in the male, and primary and situational orgasmic dysfunction in the female.

Impotence. Masters and Johnson (1970) have found that successful treatment of impotence requires reducing the man's performance anxiety, teaching him to focus on erotic sensations rather than on his own performance, and reducing his partner's fears that he will not attain erection.

For several days, the couple "pleasure" each other through **sensate focus exercises** in which they massage each other without stroking the genitals or breasts. These exercises do not demand a result of erection, and the partners can learn to relax in each other's presence—a technique that can be practiced by all couples with similar relaxing results. As a second step, the couple take turns massaging each other's genitals and breasts. Each partner specifically guides the other through the use of hands and verbal directions to maximize the pleasurable sensations. In this manner, the couple learn what turns each other on. Erection is usually attained in this step, but coitus is forbidden, so that the man will not fear he must "perform" if he has an erection.

Then the woman repeatedly "teases" her partner's genitals to erection, allows the erection to go away, and teases again. In this way, both lose fear that erection is fleeting and will probably not be regained. After a few more days, the couple may practice coitus in the female-superior position. This allows the woman to straddle her partner and insert his penis when he attains erection. But once the penis is inserted, she does not move demandingly to achieve orgasm. Rather she contains the penis and rocks gently back and forth, allowing both to enjoy and focus on the pleasures of containment. If the erection goes away, teasing is resumed, and the penis inserted again when erection is regained. As confidence is regained, the couple tend to find their way to using additional positions and to achieve orgasm without further instruction.

Masters and Johnson reported these techniques to be successful with approximately 72 percent of the couples treated during two-week programs. While these techniques were developed to help people adjust to sexual dysfunctions, you may note that the methods of sensate focus, directed genital massage, and "teasing" will enhance the sexual experiencing of any couple. They provide an opportunity to communicate openly about what they find most sexually arousing, and encourage them to relax more in each other's company.

Premature Ejaculation. Masters and Johnson (1970) also use mutual pleasuring through sensate focus exercises as the first step in treating premature ejaculation. It allows the couple to learn that they can relax and enjoy each other's presence, rather than look forward to every encounter with fear that any interaction will lead to failure.

Then the woman and man adopt a position in which he lies on his back and the woman sits between his legs, facing him. In this position—which Masters and Johnson dub the training position—the woman stimulates the penis almost to ejaculation, and then squeezes the point where the shaft and glans meet with the thumb on the underside of the penis and the first and second fingers at the top. Masters and Johnson have found that this **squeeze technique** prevents ejaculation, although it is not quite known how, and they emphasize that the correct method for squeezing can be learned only through professional, personal guidance.

Stimulation and squeezing are repeated several times in the training position. Then the woman straddles the man and inserts the penis. She remains still at first, allowing her partner to become accustomed to vaginal sensations. If he signals he is about to ejaculate, she lifts off and squeezes, then repeats the process. Gradually the couple can shift to lateral-entry and the male-superior

Couples must learn to communicate in the bedroom in order to overcome sexual dysfunctions.

Sensate focus exercises. **Sexual interactions in which sex partners learn how to give and receive pleasure through massage of other-than-genital areas. Also called pleasuring.**

Squeeze technique. **A method of delaying ejaculation by pressing the penis at the point where the shaft meets the glans.**

PROSTITUTES OR THERAPISTS?

Something of a minor scandal erupted when it came out that Masters and Johnson had used surrogate partners in the treatment of many individuals with sexual dysfunctions whose spouses were uncooperative, or who did not have regular partners of their own. As you can imagine, treatment of problems like impotence and premature ejaculation require partners with a good deal of patience. Soon the use of surrogate partners in the place of spouses became common in sex therapy clinics from Berkeley, California, to New York.

But what, the public wanted to know, was the difference between surrogate partners and prostitutes? After all, these surrogate partners were having sex with clinic clients barely after they were introduced.

One major difference is that the surrogate partners do not consider themselves prostitutes and

have never practiced prostitution. Masters and Johnson specifically refused to use prostitutes as surrogate partners. Of thirteen women who served in this role over an eleven-year period, many had college degrees, were occupied in full-time careers, and some had participated in the studies on sexual response. Of course we cannot report on the backgrounds of all surrogate partners at all clinics, but reputable clinics report women with similar backgrounds. What motivates these women? Perhaps a combination of adventure and a desire to help.

The use of surrogate partners has not been without its problems, however. There are cases on record of wives suing their husbands for divorce, and even suing the sex clinics, when they learned of the use of surrogate partners. For this reason some clinics, including the Masters and Johnson Institute, no longer use surrogate partners.

Stop-and-go technique. A method of delaying ejaculation through discontinuing sexual stimulation until the "threat" of ejaculation passes.

positions, which are more stimulating to the penis. Masters and Johnson (1970) found the squeeze technique successful with 182 of 186 men treated!

Urologist James Semans (1956) developed a method called the **stop-and-go technique,** in which the man simply stops his partner's manual or oral stimulation, or coitus when he feels that he is about to ejaculate. After the "threat" of ejaculation passes, the couple resume their activity. The man's tolerance for sexual stimulation can gradually build in this manner without inducing ejaculation. The stop-and-go technique can obviously be used to prolong the pleasures of coitus even in cases in which the couple do not feel that the man has an ejaculatory problem.

Primary Orgasmic Dysfunction. Women who have never experienced orgasm usually harbor beliefs that sex is dirty and have been taught never to touch themselves. Thus they are at once anxious about their sexuality and have not had the opportunity to learn, through trial and error, what sorts of sexual stimulation will arouse them and bring them to climax.

Although Masters and Johnson (1970) have treated primary orgasmic dysfunction by working with the couple involved, it may well be that other sex therapists are correct in suggesting that it is more efficient for women first to learn how to attain orgasm through masturbation (Barbach 1975; Heiman et al. 1976; LoPiccolo & Lobitz 1972). These professionals generally argue that a woman can profit from learning what makes her feel good before she attempts to communicate her preferences to a sex partner, and that women without sex partners need not be denied the pleasure they can experience from stimulating themselves.

These programs all have several elements in common. They begin by instructing the woman about her own sexual anatomy, since women have too

The Challenge of
Human Relationships

often been culturally conditioned to feel ashamed of their genitals. Women examine themselves through the use of a mirror and their hands, and gradually learn what kinds of self-caresses heighten their arousal and can lead to orgasm. They are encouraged to focus on erotic fantasies and their own pleasurable sensations, and to allow anxiety to become extinguished. Anxiety is minimized by having the woman progress at her own pace.

Situational or Secondary Orgasmic Dysfunction.   In situational or secondary orgasmic dysfunction, the woman's difficulty in reaching orgasm may stem from problems in her relationship with her partner. It may be that she does not particularly like him, that he is unclean and she is afraid to tell him, that he is insensitive to her needs and she is reluctant to guide him, or any number of similar reasons. Masters and Johnson (1970) have found that in a relationship that remains generally functional, situational orgasmic problems may be dealt with effectively by treating the sexually dysfunctional couple. Situational orgasmic dysfunction is *their* problem, not *her* problem. Since different couples have different situations, each treatment program must be individually tailored to some degree, yet many programs share common elements.

As with impotence and premature ejaculation, the couple begin with sensate focus exercises in an effort to learn to relax in each other's company and to bring each other pleasure without demanding orgasm. After a few sessions, they move on to genital massage, during which the woman guides her partner's hands to show him what movements are sexually exciting to her. Masters and Johnson suggest a position in which the women sits between her partner's legs with her back to him. This allows them freedom in hand movements while she is firmly supported by leaning against him. The man is instructed not to stimulate the clitoral glans continually, since it may quickly become too sensitive to direct stroking, but perhaps to massage the shaft or other regions shown to him by his partner. The couple are instructed not to try to force orgasm, but to enjoy the massage for its own sake and allow orgasm to happen naturally.

Later, coitus is accomplished with the woman in the superior position, which allows her greater freedom of movement. The man is instructed not to ejaculate as his partner experiments to heighten her genital sensations, but to use the squeeze or stop-and-go method if necessary. Once orgasm is attained in the female-superior position, the couple experiment with additional positions.

As with other methods for overcoming sexual dysfunctions, these training sessions will help any woman teach her partner how to heighten her sexual arousal and enhance the couple's sexual experiencing.

Of 183 women treated for situational orgasmic dysfunction, Masters and Johnson reported helping 81 percent overcome their problem.

Summary

- *Women on the Emerald Isle of Inis Baeg do not experience orgasm.* False, some do; but it is considered a deviant response. No other natural human function has been so influenced by social custom and moral and philosophical beliefs as the sexual function.
- *The Kinsey reports undermined the moral fiber of the American nation.* False, of course, but many voiced this opinion in the public media at the time, the late 1940s and early 1950s. The Kinsey reports were the first

national surveys to show that acts like masturbation and premarital and extramarital sex were rather common and, at least from that perspective, normal. Masturbation was practically universal among males, and petting was common for both sexes, especially when marriage was delayed.

- *Most Americans learned about the birds and the bees through their schools' sex education programs.* False. The single most frequent source of information is friends, and next comes unguided reading.
- *We have become a swinging nation in which the majority of Americans endorse casual or recreational sex.* False. While higher percentages of respondents in the more recent Hunt survey were engaging in premarital coitus, especially among women, Hunt's sample and university surveys have shown that the majority of those polled disapprove of premarital coitus when it is not a reflection of love, or, at least, strong affection.
- *The majority of married women have fantasies about imaginary lovers during intercourse with their spouses.* True, at one time or another, according to present research.
- *We would all develop female sexual structures if it were not for the secretion of androgens at about six weeks following conception.* True. Androgens or male hormones spur development of the male genital system. However, sexual anatomy of men and women is more similar than dissimilar, with the penis and clitoris being comparable sex organs, as are the testicles and ovaries.
- *Liberated women suffer less premenstrual distress than their more traditionalist sisters.* True. Apparently women who view menstruation as an inescapable burden that is part of the traditional female life-style have more problems than career-minded women.
- *Only women are capable of multiple orgasms.* False, although only younger men are generally capable of two orgasms.
- *Gorillas were exposed to pornography at the San Diego Zoo in order to prompt them to mate.* True. While the sexual response of most mammals is controlled by the female's menstrual cycle and the male's perception of pheromones, humans respond to visual stimuli, fantasies, and other stimuli they have associated with sexual arousal and sexual gratification in the past. Since gorillas are like humans in many of their learning capacities, it was felt that these usually uninterested mammals might respond to visual stimuli also. But the venture was a flop—"skin flicks," or in this case hair flicks, were a big bore to the great apes.
- *Men prefer erotic stories and films with explicit sexual content, while women are more inspired by romantic themes.* False—another sex myth. Today, men and women are equally sexually aroused by explicit sexual content, especially content depicting coitus, petting, and cunnilingus, whether or not it involves a romantic theme. However, men and women report preferring romance to be involved as well.
- *As a group, homosexual males have acquired greater educational and occupational status than their heterosexual brothers.* True. Many beliefs about homosexuals have been found inaccurate. They do not typically play male or female roles, for example, and do not show more emotional disturbance than "straights."
- *Most cases of impotence, premature ejaculation, and orgasmic dysfunction stem from medical disorders or just reflect differences in sex-*

The Challenge of
Human Relationships

398

ual responsiveness from person to person. False. Sex researchers and therapists have shown that most cases of sexual dysfunction reflect misinformation, problematic attitudes, problem relationships, anxiety—including performance anxiety—and lack of sexual skills.

- *Many programs for the treatment of sexual dysfunctions begin with a trip to the massage parlor.* Not exactly, but most sex therapists begin by asking couples to massage each other in nongenital areas so that they can break down patterns of approaching each other with anxiety and expectations of failure. Only gradually are sexual organs brought into play.
- *Sex surrogates are recruited from the ranks of prostitutes.* This is certainly false, at least in the history of the clinic managed by Masters and Johnson. Surrogate partners have come from many walks of life, but are generally well educated and employed gainfully.

IV

THE
CHALLENGE
OF
SELF-CONTROL

14

SELF-DIRECTED BEHAVIOR

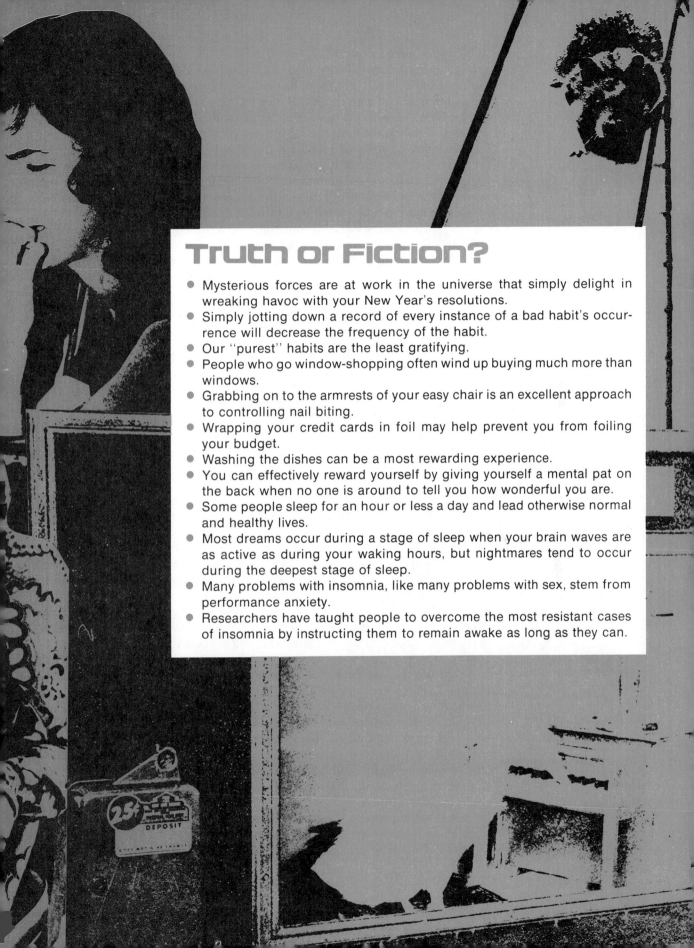

Truth or Fiction?

- Mysterious forces are at work in the universe that simply delight in wreaking havoc with your New Year's resolutions.
- Simply jotting down a record of every instance of a bad habit's occurrence will decrease the frequency of the habit.
- Our "purest" habits are the least gratifying.
- People who go window-shopping often wind up buying much more than windows.
- Grabbing on to the armrests of your easy chair is an excellent approach to controlling nail biting.
- Wrapping your credit cards in foil may help prevent you from foiling your budget.
- Washing the dishes can be a most rewarding experience.
- You can effectively reward yourself by giving yourself a mental pat on the back when no one is around to tell you how wonderful you are.
- Some people sleep for an hour or less a day and lead otherwise normal and healthy lives.
- Most dreams occur during a stage of sleep when your brain waves are as active as during your waking hours, but nightmares tend to occur during the deepest stage of sleep.
- Many problems with insomnia, like many problems with sex, stem from performance anxiety.
- Researchers have taught people to overcome the most resistant cases of insomnia by instructing them to remain awake as long as they can.

Did it ever seem to you that mysterious forces are at work in the universe that simply delight in wreaking havoc with your New Year's resolutions and your other resolves to take charge of bad habits? We have heard these "forces" jokingly referred to as a group called "they." "They" seem to have two major functions. First, "they" say things, as in "*They* say that falling in love is wonderful," or as in, "You know what *they* say, don't you?"

Second, they provoke you with almost unbelievable temptations, all at the most inopportune times. If you have just succeeded in talking yourself into getting down to some good studying this evening, it is "they" who arrange for your favorite television show to come on the air. If you have just resolved to control your impulsive eating and suffered through a watercress sandwich for lunch, it is "they" who are responsible for all those marvelous odors emanating from the bakery and the pizzeria at the shopping mall.

Perhaps there is no such group as "they." But we certainly seem to find no scarcity of temptations when we decide to exercise more self-control in our lives. The whole environment can seem to be engineered to lead to the downfall of our determination.

This and the following chapter show you how behavioral scientists have recently developed a variety of methods that you can use to redesign your own environment to help you resist the temptations that "they" seem to put in your path. In this chapter we shall learn how to view behavior in terms of its environmental context. We call this the ABC's of behavior. We shall see what leads to what, or what is a "function" of what—this is **functional analysis.** In this chapter we apply our knowledge to behavioral problems such as nail biting, incessant scratching, overspending, building study habits, and insomnia. In Chapter 15 we have a look at three consuming problem areas: the challenges of weight control, smoking, and drug use and abuse.

THE ABC'S OF BEHAVIOR: FUNCTIONAL ANALYSIS

Psychologists (e.g., Watson & Tharp 1972; Thoresen & Mahoney 1974) believe that we can do a great deal to change our own problem habits. Certainly we all know a great deal about behavior. You might be tempted to stroke the fur of a well-fed, sleepy lion, but you would steer clear of a hungry lion with a thorn in its paw. You probably very well know that you will accomplish more by studying five evenings for two hours at a time than during one ten-hour cram session, yet how often do you put things off until you are faced with a big test or the due date of a term paper?

During the past couple of decades, psychologists have begun to put the things we do know, along with some things that we may not have known, into problem-solving packages that help us exercise self-control. These packages emphasize the relationships between our environment and our problem habits: a functional analysis. They help us to manipulate the events that lead up to or antecede our problem behavior, to become more aware of the details of the problem behavior itself, and to manipulate the consequences or payoffs for our behavior. In short, they deal with the **ABC's of behavior:**

The A's of behavior are the *antecedents* of behavior.
The B's of behavior are the *behaviors* themselves.
The C's of behavior are the *consequences* of behavior.

Functional analysis. A systematic investigation of the stimuli that precede and follow our behavior, in an effort to determine the influences on our behavior.

ABC's of behavior. The antecedents of behavior, the behavior itself, and the consequences of behavior, as determined through a functional analysis.

The Challenge of Self-Control

Some of the "triggers" for overeating.

The Antecedents of Behavior: Getting Your Finger on the Triggers

We live in an environment filled with sights and sounds, external and internal sources of stimulation. A traffic light turning red may cause us to slow down, or, if we are impulsive or pressed for time, to speed up. The aroma of cooking food may trigger salivation, as may "pangs" in the midsection. An itch may cause us to scratch. Here the **antecedents of behavior** are logical. We can readily understand the relationship between these environmental events and our behavior.

Sometimes the connections between environment and behavior are not so logical. Our experiences may lead to new environment-behavior relationships. A conversation with a new acquaintance at a party may trigger reaching for a drink. Finishing a meal or an act of love may serve as a signal for us to light up a cigarette. We may find ourselves reaching for something to eat when we are bored or somewhat depressed. We may bite our nails when we sit in the classroom.

Some of these environment-behavior relationships are quite useful. Slowing down at red lights is a reasonably good habit to develop. In fact, we concentrate on other things once the mechanics of driving become automatic. This can be helpful—allowing us to solve problems and make plans while we go from place to place. It can also be frightening: many of us have had the experience of suddenly wondering how we arrived someplace, and of being quite happy to have made it. Habits can govern a good deal of our behavior.

Other environment-behavior relationships are maladaptive or harmful. It is not desirable to scratch an itchy patch of skin that is red and inflamed. Overeating is an unhealthy way to respond to boredom or depression. Smoking may be an unfortunate way to cope with the social pressure of making acquaintances. Such habitual ways of responding to the environment may become so ingrained that they appear to be automatic. That is, we do not have to think about them at all. We may be daydreaming and then suddenly "find ourselves" reaching for a snack or with a cigarette dangling from our lips. In such cases, *becoming more aware of the antecedents of our unwanted behavior is an aid in the development of self-control*.

Behavior: From Blinks to Chains

Blow in someone's eye. The person will blink. Other things may also happen, but we can be sure of the blink. Now that you are warmed up, chew a piece of bread or a bite of a roll. Don't swallow, just chew and chew. What happened? Where did the bread go? Did you swallow it without trying?

Blinking is a natural response to an airpuff. Swallowing is a natural response to an accumulation of food in the back of your mouth. These responses are reflexes.

Nail biting, scratching, smoking, overeating—these kinds of behavior may also seem involuntary, but they are actually fully under your muscular control. It may be fiendishly difficult for you to fight impulses and to exercise this control, but these acts are complex, voluntary, and learned. Yes, you can even engage in these activities without thinking about them. They can become habitual—you scratch your cheek and the next thing you know, your juicy fin-

Antecedents of behavior (ann-tee-SEED-dents). Those stimuli that regularly precede behavior and thus which often acquire the capacity to trigger the behavior itself.

Sometimes we may feel we are about to lose control of our impulses and are about to slide downhill.

gernail is between your upper and lower incisors, about to be convincingly chomped.

In this and the following chapter we shall see how we can develop self-control over unwanted behavior by such methods as response prevention and the use of competing responses. You will also learn how you can take advantage of the very complexity of unwanted behavior by unchaining the behavioral links one by one. Why end just one bad habit when, with a little imagination, you can give yourself the credit for terminating dozens of (smaller) habits?

The Consequences of Behavior: The "Now" Generation

We don't get too much for free on this planet, and perhaps we don't do too much without some payoff either. As we saw in Chapter 5, psychologists label these payoffs or **consequences of behavior** reinforcements. Reinforcements can vary from something as basic as food or proper room temperature to such complex and specifically human states as feeling that we have accomplished something important or done what is morally right.

As a rule of thumb, we tend to seek rewards and to avoid punishments. Behavior that repeatedly brings us rewards or repeatedly permits us to escape punishments tends to become increasingly habitual.

Psychologists have recently run numbers of experiments that have borne out what philosophers have taught about rewards and punishments for centuries. For instance, in a political tract written in 1822, Jeremy Bentham, the British philosopher, wrote that "Nature has placed mankind under the governance of two sovereign masters, pain and pleasure" (p. 33). The effectiveness of pain and pleasure in influencing our behavior would depend on their (1) intensity, (2) duration, (3) certainty or uncertainty, and (4) immediacy or remoteness (1822, p. 64). In short, punishments that are intense, lasting, certain, and immediate will be most effective.

Puzzle it out for yourself, then. Why may we scratch a sore though we may ultimately increase its inflammation and suffer more? Why may we buy a new outfit although we may run short of cash at the end of the month? Why may we run out to a movie rather than study? Overeat though we will gain weight? Smoke though we have heard the statistics about cancer and emphysema?

Very simply, we too often choose immediate gratification at the expense of long-range gratification and self-respect. Scratching the sore decreases the itch *now*. We can have the new outfit *now*. We can enjoy the film and forget about the test *now*. We can enjoy our food and our puff of cigarette smoke *now*. Perhaps the sore will not become inflamed. Perhaps we shall win the lottery. Perhaps the test will be postponed or the questions will be easy. We can start dieting tomorrow or next week. And what about cancer? Some get it, some don't. It's not all that *certain*, is it? In any event, it's many years in the future—the gratification of smoking is *now*.

Self-control involves **delay of gratification,** placing more value on long-term benefits than immediate rewards. Many of the self-control strategies we shall learn involve tipping our personal balance in favor of the delayed sources of gratification. We shall learn how to reward ourselves now for desired behavior, and how to bring home the consequences of our unwanted behavior now —not at some uncertain, distant point in the future.

Consequences of behavior.
Reinforcements.
Events that follow behavior, such as rewards and punishments

Delay of gratification (grat-tuh-fick-KAY-shun). The ability to put off reinforcements, or to behave with long-term consequences rather than immediate consequences in mind.

Self-Directed
Behavior

Self-Monitoring

How well do you understand the ABC's of your own problem behavior? You can undertake your own functional analysis by keeping a notebook. You can record each incident of engaging in the problem behavior—each time you bite your nails, scratch that itchy elbow, smoke a cigarette, or spend time studying. Note that you would probably want to cut down on nail biting, scratching, and smoking, but build up study time. Either way, record each incident of the problem behavior.

For each incident, jot down the following:

- Time of day
- Location
- Your activity, including your thoughts and feelings
- Reactions to the problem behavior (yours and others)

Self-monitoring has a variety of purposes. First, it will make you more aware of your problem behavior. You will learn where and when you are likely to practice the habit. You will gain insight into the triggers of your problem behavior. These insights can then be used in self-control strategies aimed at the *antecedents* of behavior. You will also gain insight into the thoughts and feelings that may serve as payoffs or reinforcements of the problem behavior. These insights can be used with self-control strategies that are aimed at the *consequences* of behavior.

Second, your heightened self-awareness may build your motivation to take charge of your own behavior. We have many defensive ways of minimizing the consequences of our problem behavior in our own minds. Coming face to face with our problem behavior and our ways of denying that we have problems can spur our making decisions that *now* is the time to do something.

Third, for individuals who are already motivated to do something about their problem behavior, self-monitoring alone may significantly influence the frequency of its occurrence. For instance, Johnson and White (1971) found that self-monitoring alone increases the amount of time spent studying. Komaki and Dore-Boyce (1978) showed that self-monitoring increases the percentage of time that highly motivated individuals will spend talking as members of a group. Lipinski and his colleagues (1975) found that self-monitoring reduced cigarette consumption for motivated individuals.

Table 14.1 shows how self-monitoring helped Brian, a twenty-four-year-old administrative assistant, discover that boredom and humdrum activities were implicated as antecedents of his nail biting. He did not note any pleasure in the activity. All his reactions were negative, yet boredom seemed to faithfully trigger his biting. After a few days of self-monitoring, the incidence of his nail biting seemed to decrease. But he still "found himself" biting his nails from time to time and took measures to make himself even more aware of his habit, as we shall see below.

Baseline Recording: Where Are You Now? We often fool ourselves about our habits. We may tell ourselves we smoke a pack of cigarettes a day when we smoke a pack and a half, that we study "a bit almost every night" when we study two to three times a week.

Self-monitoring can be used before you actually undertake the effort of changing problem behavior in order to establish an accurate **baseline.** The

Keeping a written record of your nailbiting may make for a less than exciting diary, but it will make you more aware of the when, where, and why of your unfortunate habit.

Self-monitoring. Tracking or recording our own behavior in an effort to heighten awareness of the behavior, and also of the antecedents and consequences of our behavior.

Baseline. The rate at which behavior occurs before we make an effort to change it.

Table 14.1 Excerpts from Brian's Nail-Biting Record

Incident	Time	Location	Activity (Thoughts and Feelings)	Reactions
April 14				
#1	7:45 A.M.	Freeway	Driving to work, bored, not thinking	Finger bleeds, pain
#2	10:30 A.M.	Office	Writing report	Self-disgust
#3	2:25 P.M.	Conference room	Listening to dull report	Embarrassment
#4	6:40 P.M.	Living room	Watching evening news	Self-disgust

baseline is the usual frequency of the problem behavior. Since behavior can vary from day to day, it is common practice to engage in baseline recording for a week or two, then to use the average daily performance as your baseline figure.

Once you have established your baseline, you will have a way to determine whether you are gaining self-control over problem behavior. By the end of the baseline recording period, your motivation to change will probably have grown dramatically.

CHANGING THE ABC'S OF YOUR BEHAVIOR

You can complain that it is impossible for you to study while the television is on, or you can turn the set off. You can complain that it is too easy to go over your budget when you have credit cards in your wallet, or you can leave them at home. Or fold, spindle, and mutilate them. You can complain that the consequences of smoking are too far off into the future to influence your behavior now, or you can sit down and think about them for a while.

You can systematically decrease the frequency of unwanted behavior or increase the frequency of desirable behavior by changing the antecedents of behavior, the behavior itself, or the consequences of behavior.

Changing the Antecedents of Your Behavior

Self-control strategies that involve changing the antecedents of your behavior include restricting the stimulus field, steering clear of powerful triggers for unwanted behavior, and stimulus control.

Restricting the Stimulus Field: Creating "Pure" Experiences. You can completely devour a handful of newly grown fingernails while you are fighting your way through one rush hour or worrying over the phrasing of one report. You can chugalug three cans of beer (well, some of you can) watching the first quarter of the football game. As your habits become frequently paired with events like driving, report writing, and football watching, these events can become powerful triggers for the unwanted behavior.

It is possible to begin to break down the connection between these triggers or antecedents and the problem behavior by making the problem behavior a "pure experience." Remove or **restrict the stimulus field**—practice the problem behavior as far outside the environment in which it usually occurs as you

Restricting the stimulus field. Practicing behavior only in an area that is relatively free of the usual antecedents of that behavior.

Self-Directed Behavior

409

can. When you feel the urge to bite your nails, to tug at your hair, or to scratch your elbow, get yourself to a boring, dull, practically "stimulus-free" area so that you can practice your unwanted habit with your attention devoted to it fully.

At home you may choose some dull corner of the basement, attic, or bathroom. At work, you may find a bathroom or locker room, or janitor's closet. If you must remain in your office, first clear your desk; put everything away, remove or cover all distractions.

Now that you have made your environment as dull and blank as possible, you are ready. Examine your nails carefully and bite them slowly. Listen for the crunch. Note the flavors. Check the progress as you whittle away at your fingers. Hair pulling? Study the resistance to each tug. Count the hairs that come out with each pull. Scratching? Watch the mottled colors of your elbow change with each scratch. Think about nothing but performance of the problem habit. Study, memorize every detail.

Remember: each time you feel the impulse, get to your preplanned, stimulus-deprived area. But wait, you say? Would you rather not allow your unwanted habits to occupy such a significant amount of your attention? Would you find your trips to the attic or the locker room annoying? We certainly hope so. If restricting the stimulus field is effective for you, it will probably be because it makes you more aware of your habits, and because you make the firm decision that you do not, after all, have room for this unwanted behavior in your life.

Avoiding Powerful Triggers: Leave the Windows at the Stores. People who go window shopping often wind up buying much more than windows. If you are attempting to remain within a strict budget, which is not uncommon for students, simply avoid some obvious sources of temptation.

If the sight of other people smoking tempts you to smoke, sit in non-smokers' cars of trains and sections of restaurants. If eating at Pizza Charlie's tempts you to forget about your diet, eat at home or at the Celery Stalk instead.

With a little bit of foresight, we can usually find ways to avoid many of the antecedents that our self-monitoring records suggest trigger problem behavior. If sitting down by the television set will interfere with your studying, plunk yourself down in the library instead. And don't pick the lounge, where all those hunks and foxes constantly parade by. Find yourself a comfortable but businesslike carrel, or a table among some remote stacks.

Stimulus Control: On Rats, Neighbors, and a Hot Meal. Perhaps you have not recently considered all the ways in which you could increase the alcohol consumption of laboratory rats. Such lapses are understandable, of course. Yet you may recall that one interesting and somewhat indirect method would be to inject their neighbors with 6-hydroxydopamine. In Chapter 9 we saw that this chemical causes rats to behave as if they are depressed, and somehow triggers greater drinking among their neighbors. Another method? Let rats live with an alcohol solution for a while. Then shock them as they are approaching their food trays. They will return to the alcohol to bolster their courage. Then— back to the food.

So depressed neighbors or supper spiced with shock will stimulate rats to give up their drinking. These methods give you **stimulus control** over the rats' drinking.

Similarly, people do not usually force themselves directly to sleep. In fact,

Stimulus control. Attempting to foster desired behavior by presenting the antecedents for that behavior.

Did you ever notice how everything goes on sale precisely at the moment you decided you are going to save money?

trying to force sleep can be an excellent method for remaining awake. Rather, people tend to lie down in bed or on a couch when they are tired, or at a certain time of day. Bed, for many, triggers sleep. Among other things.

In general, we can increase the frequency of desired behavior by placing ourselves in settings in which that behavior is more likely to occur. Perhaps you have been intending to jog more often, but your determination sits home in the easy chair. Why not put on some track shoes and sit out at the track instead for a while? See how long you can just sit.

Self-Directed
Behavior

There are a number of self-control methods that involve directly manipulating your own behavior—preventing or interfering with problem behavior, or gradually building up desirable behavior. These are response prevention, using competing responses, breaking down behavioral chains, and building desired responses through successive approximations.

Response prevention. Making it impossible or extremely difficult for unwanted behavior to occur.
Competing responses. Two or more types of behavior that prevent the other from occurring. Behavior that is mutually exclusive, such as sitting still and running around the block.
Chain breaking. Dividing an act into a series of smaller acts such that prevention of any of the smaller acts delayed the larger act from being completed.

Response Prevention: On Mittens in Hot Times. Infants sometimes have mittens placed on their hands when the weather is hot and sticky. Mittens effectively prevent them from responding to an itch by scratching and harming themselves. This is an example of **response prevention**—doing some environmental engineering that makes an unwanted type of behavior or response difficult or impossible.

Response prevention is applicable to many kinds of problem behavior. It is difficult to engage in impulse buying when you leave your checkbook and your credit cards at home. You can't just reach for the potato chips or for the strawberry cream cheese pie if you have left it at the supermarket.

Using Competing Responses: "Now, Scratch and Point." A brief experiment: Gently scratch the tip of your nose with the forefinger of your right hand. Now straighten your right arm at the elbow. And now, for the grand finale, do both at the same time: scratch with your right hand as your right arm is extended. Unless your name is Cyrano, you probably flubbed this last scene. Put simply, bending your arm at the elbow (which allows you to scratch your nose) and straightening your arm are incompatible or **competing responses**. You cannot do both at the same time.

This simple principle has been helpful in a variety of self-control problems. If you are attempting to control your weight, it is possible to reach for a stalk of celery or glass of water rather than cake or ice cream. The celery or water may also take the place of a cigarette.

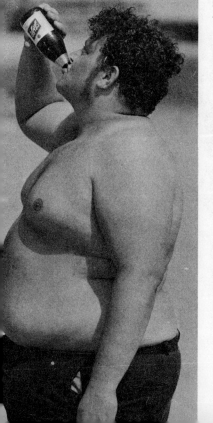

Put your beer down and pause between sips if you want to cut down on your drinking. "Sip, klunk, pause" is less filling than "Glugaglug."

Grasping something firmly is an excellent competing response for problems such as nail biting and hair pulling. Hold on to something or clench your fists so that you can feel pressure against your fingertips while you are thinking about engaging in the problem behavior. This will help you "connect" your impulses with engaging in the competing response and not the unwanted behavior. As Nathan Azrin (on p. 413) points out, it is helpful if you select and rehearse competing responses that you can practice without drawing attention to yourself in public.

Chain Breaking: Sip, Clunk, Pause—Not Glugaglug. The fast guns of the Old West were not particularly more rapid than many of us when we see something we simply must have at a clothing store. Out comes that checkbook or credit card as if it had grown from our fingertips. You can use response prevention and leave the checkbook and credit cards at home, or else you can take actions to slow down the behavioral chain of reaching for the card and handing it to the salesclerk. This is **chain breaking**. Consider wrapping these items in foil. Before you can use them, they must be unwrapped. Since you would probably feel foolish unwrapping them at the sales counter, you would seek some privacy. Feelings of foolishness, seeking privacy, unwrapping—all these steps would give you time to ask yourself, "Do I really need this? Is it worth it?"

USE OF COMPETING RESPONSES

"Hold the pen firmly while pressing the fingers of your other hand against the paper." "Place both hands on the wheel and hold it firmly." "Grab the armrests of your chair." "Grasp your clothing firmly." And, if there is nothing else to grab, "Clench your fists firmly so that your thumb and all fingers press against your palms." What have we here? Isometric exercises for politicians, preparing them to get out and press the flesh?

Actually these are all examples of competing responses recommended by psychologist Nathan Azrin (Azrin & Nunn 1977) for people who have problems with nail biting or hair pulling. All these responses make it impossible for you to bite your nails or to pull your hair. They can all be maintained for several minutes without appearing strange to anyone who happens to be watching you or accompanying you. You can select among them so that they do not interfere with your normal, ongoing activities—writing, driving, watching television, or standing and talking. They also increase your awareness that you are doing something else in the presence of the impulse to practice your unwanted habit.

Azrin suggests that you use the competing response as soon as you feel the urge to practice the habit, or, if you missed this first impulse and began to bite your nails or pull your hair, as soon as you become aware of your behavior. He then suggests that you continue the competing response for three full minutes. You may time yourself once or twice for practice, but then you need only approximate the time. He even suggests that you practice the competing response while you look in the mirror, making certain that there is nothing so noticeable about your technique that it will draw the attention of others. Watch out for stiffness, awkwardness, and signs of strain.

Now, if you have missed the first impulse and bitten a nail or pulled your hair, you have probably left yourself a tempting target once you have engaged in the competing response for three minutes. A half-bitten nail or loose strand of hair is just begging for a good chomp or yank. So Azrin suggests carrying a nail file or brush and comb. Slip away from the crowd when convenient and repair the damage. A neat nail, even short, is not nearly so tempting as all those luscious crags.

Perhaps you will decide to pass up this particular bargain once you are slowed down a bit.

For beer drinkers, one rapid glug has a way of leading to another. It is possible to quench your thirst and at the same time limit your beer intake by taking a sip rather than a glug, and then putting your beer down. Pause for a moment. If you want another sip, pick up the beer, sip, and put it down again. Each time you put the beer down, ask yourself if you want another sip. Perhaps you won't. Sip, clunk, pause, sip, clunk, pause is less filling than glugaglug. It may even be less filling than Lite beer.

Building Desired Habits Through Successive Approximations. Read the rest of this textbook without putting it down. Wait—where are you going? Too much, you say? It's not surprising, because making changes in your habits at too great a pace can be self-punishing. Through **successive approximations,** we gradually approach target behavior.

If you study in fits and starts, it may be unrealistic to set an immediate behavioral goal of studying four hours in the evening. It may be more rewarding for you to establish your baseline studying rate for a week, and then make a contract with yourself to increase your studying by something like 10 percent a day. For instance, if your baseline is about thirty minutes an evening, you may increase your study time by about three minutes an evening

Successive approximations (suck-SESS-siv ap-prock-see-MAY-shuns). A method for building desired behavior patterns which focuses on rewarding steps that come closer and closer to the target behavior, or goal.

Self-Directed Behavior

413

until you are up to fifty minutes or an hour. At that point you may increase by five or six minutes an evening. It will take you only a few weeks to triple or quadruple your study time, and you will not experience undue pressure at any step along the way.

By setting yourself realistic behavioral goals, you are more likely to experience success in changing your behavior. The experience of success will help motivate you to continue your behavioral program. Congratulate yourself for going from thirty to thirty-three minutes, and from thirty-three to thirty-six. After all, you are fully meeting your daily goals.

Some smokers find it less difficult to cut down their cigarette consumption gradually than to go "cold turkey." The body can become gradually accustomed to lower levels of nicotine, and it may be possible to cut down bit by bit without experiencing feelings of deprivation. Similarly, it is possible gradually to decrease the quantity of sugar used to sweeten coffee or tea at such a pace that you will never notice a difference in the amount of sweetness from day to day. You can go from three teaspoonfuls per cup to no sugar at all in a few months and find your beverage just as palatable at the conclusion of the procedure as at the outset.

Changing the Consequences of Your Behavior

There are several self-control strategies that involve manipulating the consequences or payoffs of your behavior. These include making rewards contingent upon desired behavior, response cost, the Premack Principle, covert reinforcement, and covert sensitization.

Making Rewards Contingent upon Desired Behavior: Don't Give Yourself Anything for Nothing. Behavior that is rewarded is more likely to be repeated. If you are told that you look wonderful every time you wear a particular outfit, the fabric of that outfit is likely to get worn out a bit more quickly than the material of your other clothing, and you may shop for other outfits that seem to you to be similar.

You can use the rewards in your own life to help fashion behavior that will be of use to you—perhaps building up more study time, perhaps trying to live within your budget. Have a look at the list of pleasant events in Chapter 9. What activities do you find rewarding? Perhaps you can make a list of pleasant events you involve yourself in each day—perhaps television watching, going for a walk on the beach, or reading a new novel. Then make some of these activities **contingent** upon meeting some behavioral goal for that day: Don't watch television until you have studied for forty-five minutes, or put off reading the novel until you have written five pages of the term paper due next week.

Manipulate only the rewards that you can do without if you must. Don't starve yourself unless you study! And remember to make your daily goals realistic. It is possible to build gradually toward your ultimate behavioral goals.

Response Cost: Contributing to Your Least Favorite Cause. Think of an organized group you detest. It is probably some sort of political group that holds public rallies, shouts slogans you find obscene, and promotes a point of view that you believe will wreck the country. Now imagine something just slightly more obscene—you put a quarter into a stamped envelope that is addressed to this group, seal the envelope, and drop it into the nearest mailbox,

Contingent (kon-TIN-jent). Dependent. A contingency is a reward or a punishment, some event that occurs when some behavior is performed.

PIANO PLAYING DUCK

We can eventually learn to do surprising things if we go about building good habits step by step through successive approximations.

even if you must ease yourself out of your reclining chair and drive half a mile.

Gruesome, isn't it? Can you imagine really going through with any such nonsense? If not, it may be just the sort of consequence for engaging in an unwanted response—scratching that sore elbow, eating a second dessert, buying that shirt or blouse that you didn't really need—that will be effective in helping you control your own behavior. This is **response cost**: doing something that makes your unwanted response costly. Punishing yourself, in short. And, as Jeremy Bentham pointed out, punishments are most effective when they are swift and certain.

If you decide to use the cash-in-the-envelope technique, you need a stamped, preaddressed envelope, and a quarter (or some amount of money that will be distressing yet not impossible for you to send off perhaps several times a week) immediately available. For the rule is, as soon as you engage in the unwanted response you follow through at the mailbox. Not an hour later— right then.

You can also use a point system. Perhaps you contract with yourself that you must earn 100 points studying during a week in order to go to *Jaws* VII that weekend. Six minutes of uninterrupted studying is a point, and for each unplanned episode of people watching or daydreaming, you dock yourself a point. This is also response cost.

John Nurnberger and Joseph Zimmerman of the School of Medicine at Indiana University (1970) used response cost to help motivate a thirty-one-year-old language professor to write his doctoral thesis. For two years his research had lain fallow as he found excuse after excuse to avoid the formidable writing task. When all else failed, he wrote out checks to several organizations, including the KKK and the American Nazi Party, that he found offensive.

Response cost. A method for decreasing unwanted behavior by making its occurrence punishing or costly.

Self-Directed
Behavior

The thought of sending hard-earned cash out to one's most hated cause is enough to encourage many of us to practice greater self-control.

Premack Principle (PREE-mack). Increasing the frequency of desired behavior by making frequently occurring behavior contingent upon the performance of the desired behavior.
Covert reinforcement (KO-vert). A pleasant mental event, such as imagining a pleasant scene or telling yourself how wonderful you are, that is used when you have done something you wish to do or stopped yourself from doing something you do not wish to do.

They would be mailed if he did not meet reasonable weekly writing goals. These organizations are not any richer today, and our professor has finally earned his Ph.D.

The Premack Principle: "Oh, Wow—Now I Can Brush My Hair!" If you were to make a list of the rewards of life, you would probably not include reading a newspaper or magazine, combing your hair, sitting down in the living room, or leaving the house. These things all have quite a mundane ring to them. Yet University of Pennsylvania psychologist David Premack (1965) has pointed out that routine but not aversive activities such as these can be quite effective rewards for desired behavior.

The **Premack Principle** states: you can increase the frequency of a desired behavior by making an already frequently occurring behavior contingent upon it. Do you brush your hair in the evening? Excellent. Don't brush unless you have studied for thirty-five or forty minutes. Do you frequently take coffee breaks while studying? Fine. Make your coffee breaks contingent upon reviewing the questions and answers in the study notes you took one week ago. Do you leave home each morning at 8:15? Good, but don't leave the house unless you have brushed your teeth.

Covert Reinforcement: When the Environment Is Stingy . . . This world can sometimes be unfair. Perhaps you have just shown unbelievable self-control. You just experienced an impulse to throw your textbooks into the incinerator and to switch on the fourteenth television rerun of *Son of Godzilla Applies to Stanford*, but you resisted the impulse and kept on studying. But nobody read your mind. Nobody is telling you that you are a wonderful person. Nobody is giving you a round of applause. Nobody is even looking in your direction. In short, nobody except you appreciates your monumental self-control. Yet you are just starving for a reinforcer. What to do? What to do?

According to psychologist Joseph Cautela (1970) of Boston College, this is a prime opportunity to use **covert reinforcement**. *Covert* means covered, hidden, or private. Covert reinforcements are mental reinforcements—pleasant thoughts, phrases, and images that you can use as self-rewards when the environment is being particularly stingy. Covert reinforcement can be logically related to resisting an impulse, as in telling yourself you are wonderful and deserving of praise for showing such self-control. But a covert reinforcement could also be a beautiful line from a favorite poem, a brief sexual fantasy, or focusing on an enjoyable memory.

You may find it useful to have some pleasant phrases or images prepared to use when you resist impulses or engage in other productive behavior, such as acting assertively when the recipient of your assertive behavior is unlikely to applaud you. If you have just told your mechanic, "The car is still hesitating, so I must ask you to check your work," you cannot expect your mechanic to say: "Yes, you are precisely correct, and the way you express yourself is wonderful."

You can also use covert reinforcements in elaborate fantasies, such as imagining that you are asking an attractive person out on a date. Your smile is charming, your voice is fluid, and you are successful. You imagine that your friends and relatives rally round you and pat you on the back. Psychologist Alan Kazdin (1975) of Pennsylvania State University reports that imagining engaging in assertive behavior that is rewarded may lead to more *overt* or observable assertive behavior later on.

Eat The Checkbook?

HOW TO LIVE WITHIN YOUR BUDGET

You are walking back to the office after lunch and spot a beautiful sweater on sale in a store window. You find one in your size for $17.50 and attempt to pay the cashier. You reach for your credit cards, but then recall that you have cut them into a hundred plastic slivers. Then you reach for your checkbook. No good—you left it locked in a box in your desk drawer at home. So you pull out your wallet. All singles—twenty of them. The clerk peers at you impatiently as you put one single on the counter, pause to ask yourself if you really need the sweater, put another single on the counter, pause again, and then put a third single on the counter. At this point you decide you don't really need the sweater after all, pick up the three bills and leave while the clerk shakes his head. You have just successfully used chain breaking to help you live within your budget.

Karen Paulsen and her colleagues at Southern Illinois University (1977) ran an experiment on the usefulness of self-control methods for putting an end to impulsive spending. They recruited twenty students from an undergraduate course in introductory psychology who considered themselves to be overspenders.

All students engaged in baseline recording for two weeks—obtaining daily totals for money spent on food, transportation, personal items, clothing, recreation, and medical care. They also recorded their monthly housing expenses, their incomes, and the balances of their savings, checking, and charge accounts. Thus their awareness of their financial conditions was heightened.

Students in the self-control treatment groups were given an explanation of the ABC's of behavior. They were taught to *break behavioral chains* to control spending. *If you carry only singles in your wallet and insist on taking them out one by one, you give yourself time to reconsider before throwing ten or fifteen dollars away.* It was suggested that they could destroy their credit cards also, or carry them and checkbooks only to make specific, preplanned purchases. They were also encouraged to make budgets, carry only small amounts of cash, shop from lists only, carry only enough cash to purchase items on the list, keep money in sealed envelopes for designated purposes, avoid borrowing, and set up a list of priorities for which they might want to save money, such as traveling or clothing.

Students in the self-control groups and in the psychoanalytic interpretation groups turned in weekly reports to account for all their spending. All students were mailed an additional weekly spending form twelve weeks after treatment as a follow-up measure.

During the two-week baseline recording period, students in the self-control groups spent an average of $30.11 per week, and students in the psychoanalytic interpretation groups spent an average of $34.23—a chance difference. By the end of treatment, students learning self-control methods reduced their weekly spending dramatically to a mean of $13.47 a week, whereas the mean weekly spending of the other students rose to $40.17. The drop in spending for self-control subjects was statistically significant.

All students used self-monitoring during treatment, so self-monitoring alone was not sufficient to encourage students in the psychoanalytic interpretation treatment to reduce their spending. But self-monitoring plus use of a variety of self-control strategies based on an understanding of the ABC's of behavior helped students cut their weekly spending in half.

Covert Sensitization: Creating Imaginary Horror Stories. If biting your nails *this time* would lead to a serious infection, or scratching yourself *this time* would draw blood, or failing to study *this evening* would destroy your chances of graduating from college, or eating *this* piece of pie would win you first prize in the bowling ball look-alike contest, you would probably control yourself quite well. But the negative consequences of much of our impulsive behavior tend to be delayed. So how can you bridge this gap and bring the consequences of your unwanted behavior forward in time?

Self-Directed
Behavior

417

Joseph Cautela (1967) suggests that you may be able to use the flip side of covert reinforcement—**covert sensitization.** Through the use of thoughts, phrases, mental images, and fantasies, you may be able to give your unwanted behavior such a distasteful quality that your motivation to take charge of your behavior will increase, and the relief you will experience upon *not* acting impulsively will be highly reinforcing.

As with covert reinforcement, the imagined consequences of behaving impulsively may be logically connected to the impulse or may simply be linked to the impulse through repetition. For nail biting, you may sit down, close your eyes, and run a mental movie in which you go out on a date with an attractive person. All evening long you do everything you can to hide your nails, using your pockets, making loose fists, trying to keep in the dark. Toward the end of the evening, during an affectionate moment, you inadvertently scratch your date with a craggy nail. The mood is shattered. You can see the distaste on your date's face. It is the end of the relationship.

Wagner and Bragg (1970) report that imagining smoking a cigarette made of vomit can be effective in reducing smoking frequency. In this sort of approach, you would be urged to paint rather gruesomely all the ugly odors and tastes in your fantasy—to go farther and imagine contracting cancer or other dreaded diseases, and what it would be like to be suffering from them *now*. Since smoking is potentially life threatening, the use of such extreme imagery may well be justified. But we would not recommend imagining death as the consequence for scratching your elbow or buying a pair of socks that you did not need.

SLEEP AND DREAMING

Sleep has always been a fascinating topic. After all, human beings spend approximately one-third of their adult lives sleeping. For most animals, sleep means collapsing and muscular relaxation, but birds and horses sleep upright, with their antigravity muscles in operation all night long. Most of us complain when we have not gotten enough sleep, but some people sleep an hour or less a day and lead otherwise normal and healthy lives. A common view of the purpose of sleep is that it allows us to recuperate from the effort involved in remaining awake and functioning throughout the day. Yet this explanation can be at best only partly correct, because brain cells are as active during much of the time we are asleep as during waking hours.

Dreams are a perplexing topic. Most of us dream several times during the night, while we are in a stage of sleep that is sometimes called **rapid-eye-movement** or **REM** sleep. Eye movement can be detected under our closed lids, and, if we are awakened during REM sleep, we usually report we have been dreaming. The brain is highly active during REM sleep, so much so that our brain waves resemble those of a waking state. For this reason, REM sleep has also been called **paradoxical sleep.**

The psychoanalytic view of dreams has been that they provide an outlet for the expression of impulses and fantasies that we would find unacceptable and repress during our waking hours. Sigmund Freud believed that an accurate analysis of dreams would provide an understanding of our unconscious conflicts. Others have suggested that dreams may be a method for reviewing the previous day's activities in order to help make their memory lasting. We do often tend to dream about images, thoughts, and fantasies we are harboring

Covert sensitization. An unpleasant mental event, such as imagining cancer, that might be used to help you avoid doing something you would rather not do.

Rapid-eye-movement Sleep (REM-Sleep). The stage of sleep during which we tend to dream.

Paradoxical sleep (pair-uh-DOCK-sick-ul). Rapid-eye-movement sleep, called paradoxical because brain waves are similar to those of a waking state.

prior to falling asleep, but this may mean no more than that mental activity set in motion prior to sleep may have some tendency to persist.

Nightmares seem to call for a category all their own (Broughton 1968). It is possible that we should not think of them as dreams at all since they seem not to occur during REM sleep. Like other nocturnal problems—bed-wetting and walking or talking while we are asleep—nightmares usually occur during the deepest stage of sleep, when brain waves are slowest. They may also occur if we are suddenly aroused from deep sleep. Drugs that decrease the amount of time spent in the deepest level of sleep seem to result in fewer nightmares.

The Challenge of Insomnia

Insomnia usually refers to three types of sleeping problems: difficulty in falling asleep (otherwise known as **sleep-onset insomnia**), difficulty in remaining asleep through the night, and awakening prematurely in the morning (Marks & Monroe 1976). Perhaps 10–30 percent of the population complain of insomnia, with women reporting a higher incidence of sleep disturbances than men (Raybin & Detre 1969). Perhaps 20 million Americans use sleeping pills (Luce & Segal 1969).

Insomnia (in-SOM-knee-uh). Difficulty sleeping.

People who complain of insomnia, as a group, show higher levels of bodily arousal as they attempt to get to sleep and as they sleep (Johns et al. 1971; Monroe 1967). Psychologist Stephen Haynes of Southern Illinois University and his colleagues (1974) found that people with sleep-onset insomnia obtain higher scores on anxiety questionnaires and show more muscular tension in the forehead than people without this problem. These findings have been confirmed in recent studies with adolescent poor sleepers who have taken the Minnesota Multiphasic Personality Inventory (MMPI), a psychological test that measures several psychological traits (Marks & Monroe 1976; Monroe & Marks 1977). Poor sleepers tend to worry more about possible bodily ailments, to be more depressed, to react to stress through developing physical symptoms, to be anxious, tense, and ruminative, and to be somewhat shy and retiring in social encounters. Thus it should not be surprising that insomnia can come and go with many individuals, becoming more pronounced during periods of greater anxiety and tension.

Insomnia is also one instance in which heightened awareness of a problem can compound the problem. Once you decide that you have insomnia, you may become obsessed by the need to fight it somehow each evening. Your concern may heighten rather than lower your arousal. Falling asleep also seems to require a certain degree of distraction. You cannot will or force yourself to fall asleep. You can only lie down or otherwise relax when tired, and allow sleep to occur. If you focus your attention on it too closely, it will elude you. Yet millions go to bed dreading the possibility of **sleep-onset insomnia**. Naturally they encounter the sort of performance anxiety that inhibits sexual performance: rather than focusing on pleasant thoughts and sensations, they become spectators to their own nightly confrontations with insomnia.

Sleep-onset insomnia. Difficulty in getting to sleep.

Meeting the Challenge of Insomnia

There is no question about it: the most common method in the United States for attempting to meet the challenge of insomnia is popping pills. And pill pop-

Self-Directed
Behavior

ping is often effective—for a while. Sleeping preparations generally work through reducing arousal, and at first the novelty of experiencing your arousal being lowered can also distract you from your usual nightly battle. This combination of lowered arousal, expectation of success, and distraction is very effective.

But there are problems in accomplishing your ends with sleeping pills. First of all, as with tranquilizing preparations, you attribute your success to the pill and not to yourself. This creates feelings of dependency on the medication rather than self-reliance. Second, sleeping preparations lose their effectiveness as our **tolerance** for their chemical compositions increases: over time we must use stronger doses of a chemical to achieve the same effects. These dosage levels can be dangerous, especially if we should happen to mix our sleeping preparations with a couple of alcoholic beverages before bedtime.

Recently many people have learned to apply various psychological procedures to the problems of insomnia. These procedures include behavioral methods for lowering arousal, and procedures involving our attitudes toward sleep, and our fantasies. By adopting more rational attitudes toward sleep, we reduce our performance anxiety farther. Fantasy allows us to distract ourselves, permitting us to fall asleep rather than attempting to will ourselves to sleep. Psychological methods also heavily rely on stimulus control—on manipulation of the antecedents of sleeping so that we convert our beds from enemies into friends.

Lowering Arousal: Turning Down Your Own Alarm to Fall Asleep. Focusing on letting go of tensions in the muscles is an effective procedure for many for variables such as **sleep-onset latency** (that is, amount of time required to fall asleep), number of times waking during the night, total hours of sleep, and experienced restfulness upon waking in the morning (e.g., Haynes et al. 1977; Lick & Heffler 1977; Haynes 1974; Nicassio & Bootzin 1974; Weil & Goldfried 1973). Progressive relaxation and other psychological methods for reducing arousal turn down the bodily reactions that serve as an alarm in the face of stress. Of course, if this arousal were justified, you would do well to stay awake and survey the environment for sources of threat. But in the case of people with insomnia, the alarm is usually a false alarm.

In a typical experiment, psychologists John Lick and David Heffler (1977) of the State University of New York at Buffalo enlisted adult insomniacs for free treatment through newspaper ads. Only individuals requiring an average sleep-onset latency of at least fifty minutes during a twenty-day pretreatment period of baseline recording participated in the research. The psychologists' final sample included fourteen men and sixteen women, ranging in age from twenty-nine to seventy-two.

Participants were assigned to one of four conditions: (a) progressive relaxation, (b) progressive relaxation plus taped relaxation instructions, (c) a placebo (phony treatment) group, and (d) a no-treatment control group. Subjects in the progressive relaxation group received individual relaxation-training sessions once weekly for six weeks. The relaxation instructions were similar to those on pages 188–90, focusing on sixteen muscle groups.

Participants who received progressive relaxation training alone decreased their sleep-onset latency by more than thirty-two minutes and increased their number of hours of sleeping by more than an hour during a twenty-day period following treatment. Subjects receiving the relaxation instructions and the tape recordings of their therapist's voice reduced their time required to fall

Tolerance (TOL-er-ants). The condition of becoming "used" to a substance so that we must increase its dosage to continue to achieve the same effects.

Sleep-onset latency (LATE-ten-see). The amount of time required to fall asleep.

asleep by more than twenty-three minutes and increased the number of hours slept by three-quarters of an hour. The placebo treatment and no-treatment control groups showed very small pre- and posttreatment differences.

In many procedures, individuals are told to use relaxation instructions that involve letting go of muscle tensions only when they have reliably learned to achieve relaxation through alternate tensing and relaxing. Haynes et al. (1977) found that biofeedback training involving relaxing of the muscles of the forehead was as effective as progressive-relaxation training for a sample composed of both university students and people responding to newspaper ads. Nicassio and Bootzin (1974) found that **autogenic training** can also help people significantly decrease their sleeping problems. Autogenic training is a method for lowering bodily arousal which employs a standardized series of suggestions that your limbs are becoming warmer and heavier, and that your breathing is becoming more regular.

Autogenic training (aw-toe-JEN-nick). A method for achieving relaxation and combating stress that uses phrases suggesting feelings of warmth and heaviness.

All these methods turn down your alarm system before you fall asleep. Perhaps just as important, they provide you with something to focus upon other than concern about whether you will remain awake.

Coping with Irrational Beliefs.   You need not be an expert on sleep to understand that convincing yourself that the following day will be ruined unless you can get to sleep *right now* is likely to increase rather than decrease bodily arousal. This belief will create performance anxiety, which is increased by lack of accurate information about the actual importance of getting "a good night's sleep."

Below are some irrational beliefs about sleeping that might create performance anxiety and some suggested adjustive alternatives.

Irrational Belief	Adjustive Alternative
If I don't get to sleep, I'll feel wrecked tomorrow.	Not necessarily. Some do well with less sleep than I get, and if I'm tired I can just take it easy.
It's unhealthy for me not to get more sleep.	Not necessarily. Some people get less than an hour's sleep and lead normal and healthy lives. Nobody has proved I need eight hours.
I'll wreck my schedule for sleeping for the whole week if I can't get to sleep soon.	Not at all. If I'm tired, I'll go to sleep earlier. All I have to do is get up at the designated time.
If I don't get to sleep, I won't be able to concentrate on that test or conference tomorrow.	Possibly, but perhaps my fears are exaggerated. I may as well just relax or get up and do something enjoyable.

The Use of Fantasy: Nightly Mind-Trips.   Mind-trips have some advantages over actual trips: They are less expensive, you are less likely to run into discourteous bellhops, and you can conserve fuel. Mind-trips in bed at night will also distract you from what you may unfortunately see as your nightly "task"—the felt need to confront insomnia and somehow get to sleep.

You may be able to ease yourself into sleep by focusing on pleasant images, such as lying on a sun-drenched beach and listening to waves lapping on the shore, or walking through a summer meadow among the hills. With a little imagination you can construct a few scenes like this and paint their details rather finely. As psychologist Jerome Singer (1975) of Yale University points out, fantasies or "daydreams" are an almost universal occurrence, and they tend to occur quite naturally in bed prior to falling asleep. It may be that you need only allow yourself to "go with them," rather than shut them off or focus instead on the problems you encountered during the day or the demands you will meet tomorrow.

Singer is quite a busy man with his responsibilities as a university professor, a psychotherapist, and a family man. His involvements could easily lead to obsessive thoughts at bedtime and increased bodily arousal. But he has been able to use a continuing or serial fantasy to help ease himself into sleep. He has constructed an imaginary football team and a legendary superstar, Poppy Ott:

"Now as I compose myself for slumber I begin the sequence of one of the famous games in which Poppy Ott starred. I start running through the sequence of plays, and within a short time I awaken in the morning to realize that I left Poppy Ott and his teammates with third down and five to go on the opposition's ten-yard line. This use of fantasy as a means of getting to sleep is now so effective . . . that once I start the sequence I rarely get more than a few plays run before I fall asleep" (1975, pp. 21–22).

What will happen to Poppy Ott and his teammates at third and five? Singer waits until the next night to continue the serial.

◣ Keep Those Eyes Open! ▮

HOW TO GO TO SLEEP? JUST STAY AWAKE AS LONG AS YOU CAN.

What if you had tried everything to help you get to sleep at night, from counting sheep and ducks, drinking a glass of warm milk, and taking sleeping pills to ten sessions of training in progressive relaxation at the Temple University Behavior Therapy Unit in Philadephia—and nothing helped? What would you think if your therapist then told you that you were going about it backwards? That you should actually be trying to remain awake as long as you possibly could? Would you feel that the wrong individual was in treatment, or would you try this suggestion?

These were the instructions actually given five patients at the Temple Behavior Therapy Unit by L. Michael Ascher (Ascher & Efran 1978) when all else failed. For the five patients, sleep-onset latency ranged from a mean of twenty-nine to ninety minutes during a two-week baseline recording period. But when the five patients made every effort to remain awake to follow the therapist's instructions, sleep-onset latencies fell dramatically, to means ranging from six to fourteen and one half minutes.

Why were instructions to remain awake helpful with these five patients? Do we chalk it up to the general perversity of the human species? This is not necessary. Each of these individuals had been trapped in a vicious cycle in which anxiety over ability to fall asleep led to heightened arousal, and the heightened arousal then confirmed the expectation of inability to fall asleep. Ascher and Efran note that instructions to stay awake removed their patients "from this system," from this vicious cycle of focusing attention on falling asleep and heightened arousal.

This approach is not unique to sleep-onset problems. Existential psychiatrist Viktor Frankl (1975) has long used this method with many problems related to anxiety. It is called paradoxical intention. Sometimes people are more effective at accomplishing their ends when they try not to achieve them. But one should be careful with carrying this method beyond its limits—after all, you are not likely to do well in a course if you purposefully miss all classes and tests and never crack the textbooks.

Stimulus Control: Making Your Bed a Friendlier Place. What does your bed mean to you? A place where you can relax and escape from the tensions of the day? Or the arena for a nightly contest between you and the performance anxiety that may interfere with falling asleep?

One way to make your bed into a friendlier place is to do your ruminating or thinking about the responsibilities of tomorrow elsewhere. When you lie down in preparation for falling asleep, you may allow yourself a few minutes to organize your thoughts about the day's events and the future, but then allow yourself to relax and perhaps to engage in fantasy. If an important thought or plan comes to you, don't fight it—note it down on a pad nearby so that you are not in danger of losing it. If thoughts or ruminations persist, get up and go elsewhere. Let bed be the place you collect yourself and sleep—not your study. Even a waterbed is not a think tank.

Similarly, you may want to avoid studying or snacking lying in bed throughout the day. A bit of subtle conditioning could take place, and lying down could lead you to think about studying or eating.

Bed can also take on more of the meaning of sleep to you if you establish a regular routine, at least during the working-week nights. Simply set your alarm for the same time each morning and then get up, regardless of how much sleep you have had the night before, regardless of how well rested you feel. It may be that by allowing yourself to oversleep in the morning to compensate for a long sleep-onset latency, you are subtly encouraging yourself to remain awake for an hour or so before falling asleep.

Summary

- *Mysterious forces are at work in the universe that simply delight in wreaking havoc with your New Year's resolutions.* It sometimes seems so, but these "mysterious forces" are simply the environmental contexts of our behavior. We can pinpoint the influences on our behavior through a functional analysis.
- *Simply jotting down a record of every instance of a bad habit's occurrence will decrease the frequency of the habit.* Perhaps, especially when you are motivated to change your behavior. Studies have shown that a combination of high motivation and self-monitoring can decrease smoking and increase participation in a group discussion.
- *Our "purest" habits are the least gratifying.* True—making habits a "pure" experience by isolating them from the usual antecedents heightens our awareness of them and may, consequently, increase our motivation to show self-control. This approach is also called restriction of the stimulus field.
- *People who go window-shopping often wind up buying much more than windows.* True. It can be foolhardy to expose ourselves to excessive temptation when we are attempting to control our behavior. Overspenders are well advised to avoid shopping centers, and overeaters do well to avoid pizza parlors.
- *Grabbing on to the armrests of your easy chair is an excellent approach to controlling nail biting.* Yes. You can't occupy both hands and bite your nails at the same time.
- *Wrapping your credit cards in foil may help prevent you from foiling your budget.* True, the need to unwrap them in order to make a pur-

chase will give you an opportunity to reconsider the necessity of the purchase. It breaks the behavioral chain of reaching for the credit card and making the purchase.

- *Washing the dishes can be a most rewarding experience.* True, according to psychologist David Premack. The "Premack Principle" states that you can increase the frequency of a desirable behavior (such as tooth brushing) by making an already frequently occurring type of behavior (such as dishwashing or leaving the house) contingent on the desirable behavior.

- *You can effectively reward yourself by giving yourself a mental pat on the back when no one is around to tell you how wonderful you are.* True. Psychologist Joseph Cautela refers to mental rewards as covert reinforcements. They include pleasant thoughts, phrases, images, and fantasies. Cautela also suggests the use of fantasy as a punishment to deter unwanted behavior: covert sensitization.

- *Some people sleep for an hour or less a day and lead otherwise normal and healthy lives.* True. The exact functions of sleep remain unknown, as do the minimum amounts of sleep individuals may require.

- *Most dreams occur during a stage of sleep when your brain waves are as active as during your waking hours, but nightmares tend to occur during the deepest stage of sleep.* True, most dreams occur during REM or rapid-eye-movement sleep, a period of light sleep that recurs in cycles through the night, and whose brain waves are similar to those of the waking state.

- *Many problems with insomnia, like many problems with sex, stem from performance anxiety.* True, sleep-onset insomnia, especially, appears to result from high levels of bodily arousal and from fear that sleep will elude us.

- *Researchers have taught people to overcome the most resistant cases of insomnia by instructing them to remain awake as long as they can.* True. In a study at Temple University, five people for whom relaxation training and distraction methods were not sufficient were instructed to remain awake as long as they could—either to note their anxiety-inducing thoughts or to practice prolonged relaxation instructions. They "failed"—that is, they all fell asleep too quickly to carry out these instructions. Apparently the "stay awake" suggestion removed them from the vicious cycle of performance anxiety and heightened bodily arousal.

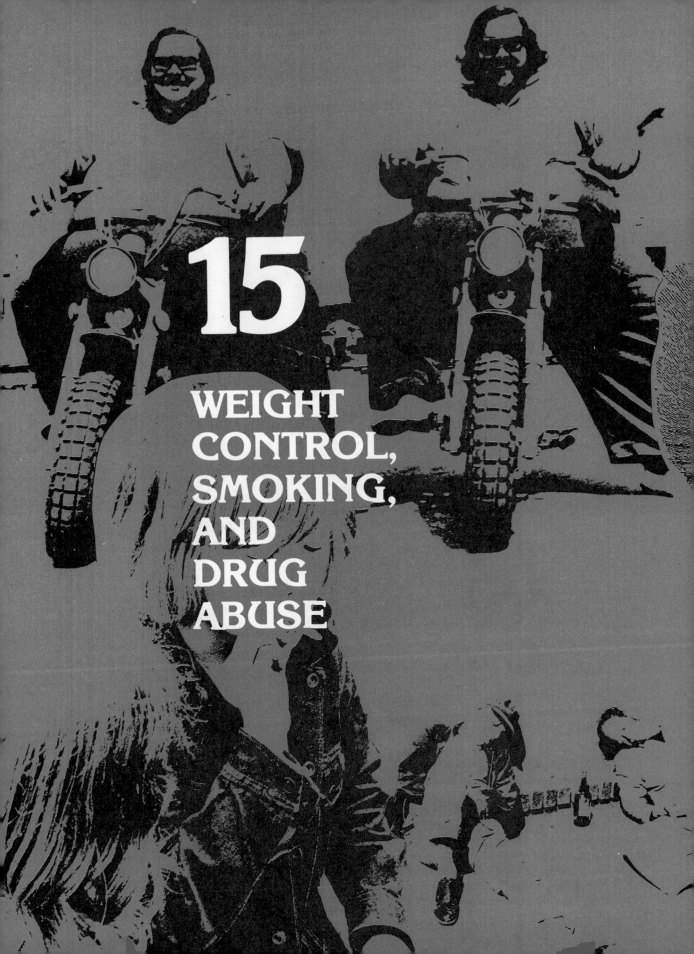

15

WEIGHT CONTROL, SMOKING, AND DRUG ABUSE

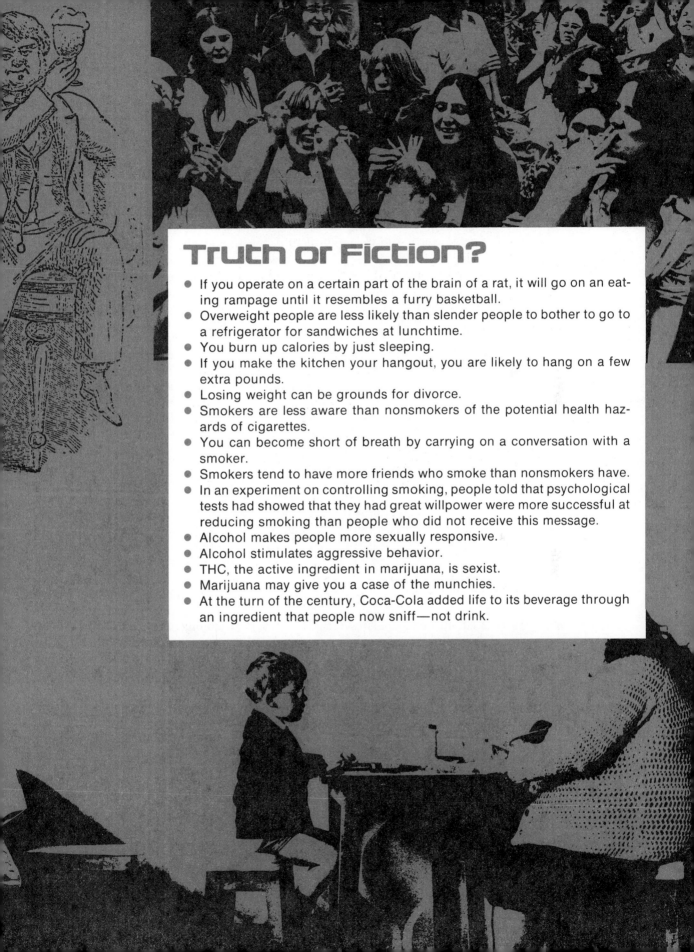

Truth or Fiction?

- If you operate on a certain part of the brain of a rat, it will go on an eating rampage until it resembles a furry basketball.
- Overweight people are less likely than slender people to bother to go to a refrigerator for sandwiches at lunchtime.
- You burn up calories by just sleeping.
- If you make the kitchen your hangout, you are likely to hang on a few extra pounds.
- Losing weight can be grounds for divorce.
- Smokers are less aware than nonsmokers of the potential health hazards of cigarettes.
- You can become short of breath by carrying on a conversation with a smoker.
- Smokers tend to have more friends who smoke than nonsmokers have.
- In an experiment on controlling smoking, people told that psychological tests had showed that they had great willpower were more successful at reducing smoking than people who did not receive this message.
- Alcohol makes people more sexually responsive.
- Alcohol stimulates aggressive behavior.
- THC, the active ingredient in marijuana, is sexist.
- Marijuana may give you a case of the munchies.
- At the turn of the century, Coca-Cola added life to its beverage through an ingredient that people now sniff—not drink.

Have you ever wondered why some people rarely think of food and others seem always to be hungry? Why so many people continue to smoke despite warnings that cigarettes can cause cancer and other dreaded diseases? Whether alcohol aids your cause on dates or just puts your date to sleep? The world is a super-market of substances. What are they really like? What factors lead us to use them wisely, to abuse them, or to choose to avoid them altogether?

THE SUBSTANCE AND THE CHALLENGE

Food is more than a means of survival for most of us. It is a symbol of family togetherness and caring. We associate food with the closeness of parent-child relationships, with the family coming together at Thanksgiving time and other holidays. Friends offer food when we come into their homes: acceptance is a symbol of renewal of the relationship, and rejection of food may be interpreted as maintaining an interpersonal distance. Bacon and eggs for breakfast, coffee with cream and sugar, meat and potatoes mashed in butter can be a part of being American, a part of feeling that you have a share in American culture and American abundance.

Yet 40 to 80 million Americans are paying one price of abundance, according to the U. S. Public Health Service—obesity. With few exceptions, the heroes and heroines of television and film dramas, successful public figures, fashion models, and sex symbols are slender. So, for many of the Americans who more than measure up to these popular images, food may have replaced sex as a major source of guilt. Many of us experience guilt from overeating, then we repent our sins and resolve to lose weight through diets. Perhaps we stick to starvation diets for a while and lose a few pounds. But then we often return to our wicked, fattening ways and feel guilty once again.

If food has been a symbol of closeness and of caring, cigarettes have been used by adolescents as signs of independence and doing one's own thing. No one questions the virility of the Marlboro man, and women, who have for years been urged that it is "unladylike" to smoke in public, are now repeatedly exposed to advertisements that show young, contemporary women smoking and proclaim, "You've come a long way, baby."

While the surgeon general has claimed that smoking cigarettes is danger-ous to your health and the numbers of adults smoking may, in fact, have dwindled, cigarette smoking remains very popular among adolescents—who then, of course, grow up to be our next generation of smoking adults. Interestingly, many adolescents rationalize that the harsh claims against cigarette smoking are likely to be exaggerated—pointing to the copious horror stories about mari-juana that they have often found to be exaggerated.

Quitting smoking for some is easy, for others very difficult. Mark Twain, the great American humorist, felt that it was easy—after all, he said, he had done it a dozen times. As Mark Twain subtly pointed out, the majority of people who quit smoking return to the habit within a year.

America is also flooded with hundreds of chemicals that alter conscious-ness and change mood—chemicals that take you up, let you down, and move you across town. Some use drugs because their friends do or because their parents don't want them to. Some are seeking pleasure, some are seeking inner truth. We go off on our own trips, and, many times, drugs provide the vehicle and the fuel.

Alcohol has reasserted its dominance among the drugs used on the college campuses, following some dropoff in popularity during the 1960s. College students who have not tried marijuana are in the minority, and perhaps one in five students smokes marijuana on a regular basis. America takes pills to go to sleep at night and to get up in the morning. Valium, a minor tranquilizer used predominantly for relief of anxiety and tension, is the most widely prescribed drug in the Western world. While heroin may be literally the opium of the lower classes, cocaine is the toy of the well-to-do. Despite laws, moral pronouncements, medical warnings, and even despite exaggerated horror stories, drugs are with us and likely to stay for a while, if not forever.

Food, cigarettes, alcohol and other chemicals—they are all available. The world is a supermarket of substances that we can use or abuse or choose to avoid. In this chapter we first look at some of the antecedents of overeating and at ways in which we can learn to control our food intake without feeling overly deprived or jeopardizing our health. Then we look at cigarettes, at the triggers of smoking in our culture and in ourselves, and at ways to cut down and to quit altogether. Finally, we look at alcohol and other drugs: exploring the antecedents and self-control of problem drinking, and the effects of a wide variety of other chemicals that are likely at some time or another to intersect the paths of our lives.

WEIGHT CONTROL: PROBLEMS AND STRATEGIES FOR ADJUSTMENT

Obese individuals are often motivated to lose weight for more than social reasons. Overweight people experience more than their fair share of medical illnesses—heart disease, **arteriosclerosis, diabetes, gout,** and a variety of other disorders.

When we were children, we had overweight friends who found a one-word alibi for their weight problems: "glands." It is true that endocrine disorders may interfere with the rate at which the human body metabolizes food and cause some individuals to be obese. But for more than 95 percent of obese people the cause is much simpler: eating more food than is necessary to maintain bodily functions.

Some breakfast cereals and other foods are advertised as being high in "food energy." This makes them sound like quite a bargain. But "food energy" is not equivalent to protein or to vitamins or to any particular sort of substance that is essential to your health. Food energy, pure and simple, means **calories.** And the more calories you eat, the more weight you will gain.

If you eat 3,500 more calories than your body burns up, you will gain roughly one pound. If you eat 3,500 fewer calories than you burn up, you will lose a pound. How many calories do you burn up in one day? As you can see from Table 15.1, your calorie expenditure is largely a function of your activity level and your weight. Sex and age also figure in, but not as significantly. You will notice that a 200-pound individual burns up 185 calories more an hour by running than a 150-pound person. (But we do not recommend putting on an extra fifty pounds so that you will then lose weight faster.) You also burn up more calories from the activity of eating than from sitting quietly. Unfortunately, if you eat a bit longer than you should, you will more than make up for this difference in calories consumed.

Marijuana has become extremely popular among the young. Perhaps one in five college students smokes marijuana on a regular basis, and many start smoking at a younger age.

Arteriosclerosis (ar-tair-ee-oh-skluh-ROW-sis). Thickening of the walls of the arteries.
Diabetes (die-uh-BEE-teas). A disease characterized by excesses of sugar in the blood and the urine.
Gout. A disease characterized by swelling and pain, especially in the big toe.
Calories (KAL-or-rees). Food energy, scientifically expressed in ability to raise temperature or give off heat. One pound of body weight is the equivalent of 3,500 calories.

Weight Control, Smoking, and Drug Abuse

Table 15.1 Calories Expended in One Hour of Activity

	Body Weight				
Activity	100 lbs.	125 lbs.	150 lbs.	175 lbs.	200 lbs.
Sleeping	40	50	60	70	80
Sitting quietly	60	75	90	105	120
Standing quietly	70	88	105	123	140
Eating	80	100	120	140	160
Driving, light housework	95	119	143	166	190
Desk work	100	125	150	175	200
Walking slowly	133	167	200	233	267
Walking rapidly	200	250	300	350	400
Swimming	320	400	480	560	640
Running	400	500	600	700	800

Fuel for the Fire: How Many Calories Do You Burn?

What about you? How many calories do you burn up during a day? You can use the approximations in Table 15.1 to make an estimate. Let's follow Paul, a rather sedentary office worker, through his day. He takes out his pocket calculator after dinner and jots down his weight: 150 pounds. First he notes that he sleeps about eight hours a night. As we see in Table 15.2, 8 × 60 (the approximate number of calories a 150-pound person burns up by sleeping for an hour) = 480. Then he notes that he spends about six hours a day doing desk work. He eats for about an hour, plus or minus; probably minus, but this is only an estimate. Oh yes, he drives for perhaps an hour a day. That adds up to sixteen hours.

Well, he admits to himself, *if the truth be known I sit quietly for about five hours a day, watching television or reading*. Then for another couple of hours he works on his stamp or coin collection or his other hobbies—that, too, is desk work. But recently he has begun to walk for an hour a day. Now, he believes, he walks rather rapidly. So walking rounds out a typical twenty-four-hour day, for a total of approximately 2,768 calories burned up in a day.

Overfilling the Fuel Tank

When you overfill your gasoline tank, you may spill fuel on the ground and pollute the environment. But your car does not gain weight. Not so with us—it

Table 15.2 Approximate Number of Calories Burned Up by Paul in One Day

Activity	Hours/Day		Calories/Hour		Subtotal
Sleeping	8	×	60	=	480
Desk work	6	×	150	=	900
Driving	1	×	143	=	143
Eating	1	×	120	=	120
Sitting quietly	5	×	105	=	525
Hobbies	2	×	150	=	300
Walking rapidly	1	×	300	=	300
TOTALS	24				2,768

may go directly to the spare tire around the waist, then spread to the rest of the body.

Why do some of us constantly overfill our bodily fuel tanks while others seem to know just when to stop in order to maintain an appropriate body weight? Early inquiries into this question suggested that most of us were largely dependent on contractions in the stomach to signal hunger. These contractions do have some influence on our behavior, but more recent investigations (e.g., Keesey & Boyle 1973; Nisbett 1972; Powley & Keesey 1970; Teitelbaum et al. 1969) suggest that centers in the brain and fat cells may also play a significant role in the stimulation of hunger.

On Fat Rats and Obese People. The **hypothalamus** is a small structure in the middle of your brain which is about the size of a pea. For a tiny thing, it appears to have a great deal to do with your emotions, your sexual response, the control of your body temperature—and hunger. It's something like a thermostat. It integrates messages from various systems in the body and then sends out signals of its own in order to maintain certain bodily balances. Some of these messages are messages to eat. And, when you have eaten enough, to stop eating.

If you were given a surgical operation, food would probably be the last thing on your mind after you awoke from the anesthesia. But if you operate on rats to destroy a particular portion of the hypothalamus, they somehow fight for the strength to struggle over to their food supplies as soon as they awaken. They then proceed to consume massive quantities of Purina Rat Chow or whatever other goodies you have given them. Their eating will level off when they resemble furry basketballs. However, if you destroy a different section of the hypothalamus, hunger drops off.

Psychologist Stanley Schachter of Columbia University noted some extraordinary similarities between overweight rats and some overweight people

Hypothalamus (high-po-THALL-uh-muss). A structure in the brain that is involved in hunger, sex, and other drives.

Faulty hypothalamus or simple overeating? Whatever the triggers of their overeating, these minibikers weigh in at 700 pounds each.

which led him to wonder if some cases of obesity involve problems with the hypothalamus (Schachter 1971; Schachter & Rodin 1974). Heavy people, like heavy rats, are more sensitive than normal-weight individuals to the taste of food. They eat relatively larger quantities of tasty food, such as vanilla milkshakes, and lower quantities of bitter foods. They also eat larger meals than normal-weight individuals and consume them more rapidly.

Behavioral researchers in the United States and Canada have recently invaded cafeterias and the homes of the Whoppers in order to confirm Schachter's conclusions about the eating habits of overweight people (LeBow et al. 1977; Marston et al. 1977). Michael LeBow and his colleagues descended on a hamburger chain in Manitoba and inconspicuously tapped or scratched the face of a hidden microphone when normal-weight and obese subjects they were observing took bites of their hamburger or bites of French fries. Overweight people took less time to finish their meals, took fewer bites, and chewed less frequently than normal-weight individuals. Albert Marston of the University of Southern California and his associates found that overweight individuals observed in a cafeteria took larger mouthfuls of food and cleaned their plates more often than normal-weight eaters. Obese eaters were also more "businesslike," toying with their food and hesitating between bites less frequently than the normal-weight subjects. Do obese eaters merely tend to have eating habits that differ from normal-weight individuals, or may there be, at least in some cases, a problem with the hypothalamus? We simply do not know.

On Fat Cells and Obese People. Are obese people who manage to diet down to their desired weight doomed to feel deprived of food for the rest of their lives? This is a reasonable question to consider since many formerly obese individuals complain that they always feel hungry, and many people with this complaint constantly go up and down in their body weights, but rarely maintain their desired weight over a prolonged period of time.

Psychologist Richard Nisbett (1972) of the University of Michigan has theorized that many unfortunate people may be sabotaged in their efforts to maintain a slender profile by microscopic units of life within the body: **fat cells.** Fat cells are not overweight cells—they are cells that store the body's fat. We all inherit different numbers of fat cells, and it appears that many obese people have greater numbers of fat cells than normal-weight individuals.

Nisbett further assumes that our desire to eat will be related to the amount of fat stored in fat cells. An individual with a greater amount of fat cells may feel hungry when slender, and thus be motivated to eat more.

But it also seems that the number of fat cells can be influenced by dietary habits early in life. Obese children appear to develop a greater number of fat cells. This suggests that obesity in childhood may lead to constant feelings of deprivation among adults who wish to be slender. But, as we shall see in the following section, there is a great deal of evidence that suggests that obese individuals may be less influenced by internal sensations of hunger than they are by the sight and aroma of food. We should be rather cautious before leaping to the support of the fat cell hypothesis: it may be eventually found that it does little more than supply overeaters with another rationalization for their dietary habits.

External and Internal Eaters: Out of Sight, Out of Mouth? As anyone who has seen all those enticing food commercials on television will readily understand, internal sensations are not the only triggers of the desire to eat.

Fat cells. Cells that store fat in the body.

Does this woman have a larger number of fat cells than her normal-weight peers? What do you think her dinner companion is learning from eating with her?

Yet there is a growing body of evidence that overweight people tend to be more responsive than normal-weight individuals to external or environmental stimulation to eat.

When you are hungry, especially in the morning, you are likely to look for things to swallow other than balloons. But psychiatrist Albert Stunkard (1959) of the University of Pennsylvania recruited obese and normal-weight subjects into an experiment in which they swallowed balloons following an all-night fast. Stomach balloons, filled slightly with water, provide a way to measure stomach contractions. Each fifteen minutes subjects were asked whether they were experiencing hunger. Normal-weight individuals were more likely to report hunger than obese individuals when their stomachs contracted—they were more likely to respond to internal cues.

Stanley Schachter and a colleague (Schachter & Gross 1968) involved some students in paper-and-pencil tasks for fifty minutes prior to dinnertime, when their stomachs might have begun to do some grumbling. At the end of this period they left a box of Wheat Thins with each student and gave them some additional tasks. The students did not know that Schachter was only interested in measuring the number of Wheat Thins they would eat during this second time period. He used a doctored clock during the first 50 minutes, such that some subjects believed only 25 minutes had passed and others believed that an hour and 40 minutes had gone by and that it was very near dinnertime.

Obese students who believed it was dinnertime ate twice as many Wheat Thins as obese students who believed it was earlier in the afternoon. These differences were not found among normal-weight students.

Richard Nisbett (1968) asked underweight, normal-weight, and overweight students to carry out some paper-and-pencil tasks near the lunch hour. He generously provided them with roast beef sandwiches and informed them that additional sandwiches were available in a refrigerator. Obese students tended to eat whatever was left in sight and were unlikely to use the refrigerator. Underweight and normal-weight individuals tended to use the refrigerated supply when only one sandwich was left with them and to leave some roast beef uneaten when three sandwiches were left with them. Obese students ate more than their fellow students when three sandwiches were left with them, but significantly *less* when only one was in sight. For the obese it may well be that out of sight means out of mouth.

Hunger, for the overweight, is more likely to be triggered by the clock, by the sights and smells of food, and by watching other people eating. When the overweight thus go on diets, it is more likely that they will be tempted to lose self-control by expectations that they will be hungry (because dinnertime is nearing), or by eating with other people who are consuming large quantities of fattening foods, than they will by actually experiencing stomach contractions or other internal cues for hunger. Dieting will thus be facilitated by a bit of environmental engineering to overcome the tyranny of the clock and the visual stimulation of fattening foods.

You and Your Ideal: Are You Satisfied with Your Own Weight?

You will probably never pay much attention to your weight unless you are somewhat dissatisfied with your appearance. Perhaps you find yourself a bit too bony, or perhaps you are beginning to hang over a bit at the waist.

Michael and Karen Mahoney (1976) provide formulae for figuring out what they consider to be your ideal weight. All you need is a pencil, some paper, knowledge of your height, and, possibly, to take a deep breath and relax. Adult women of average frame multiply their height, in inches, by 3.5, and then subtract 110. A woman who is five feet three inches tall would multiply 63 by 3.5 (product = 220.5), and then subtract 110, for an ideal weight of 110½ pounds.

Adult men of average frame multiply their height in inches by four, and then subtract 130. A man of five feet eleven would thus calculate his ideal weight to be 154 pounds.

The Mahoney formulae are a bit strict. It may be more palatable if men add an inch to their height and women add two inches—keeping their shoes on, so to speak. People with large frames can then still add another 10 to 20 pounds. But do not fool yourself: we determine frame measurements from bone widths, not waist measurements.

You will also weigh more than the Mahoney ideals if you are quite muscular. If a six feet two inch linebacker weighed 166, the Mahoney ideal, he would be blown off the football field. (But also remember that the mortality rate among retired football players who do not exercise and lose weight is extremely high!)

Burning Up More Than You Consume: Less Fuel for a Bigger Fire

Use Table 15.1 to estimate the number of calories you burn up each day. If you want to lose weight, you will have to take in fewer calories, burn up more calories, or do both. Do not underestimate the importance of exercise. Not only does it burn up calories, it helps metabolize fat, may decrease the appetite, promotes the conditioning of your heart and lungs, and may lead to a sense of psychological well-being (Horton 1974; Stalonas et al. 1978).

One pound of body weight equals 3,500 calories. If you burn up 2,700 calories a day but eat 3,200, you have a daily surplus of 500. This means you will gain about a pound a week—or some 50 pounds in a single year! But if you eat only 2,200 calories a day, you will have put yourself on an effective, restricted-calorie diet in which you will lose about a pound a week.

Taking in fewer calories doesn't mean only eating less. It may also mean switching to lower-calorie foods: relying more on fresh, unsweetened fruits and vegetables, lean meats, fish and poultry, and skim milk and cheese products. It may mean cutting down or eliminating foods like butter, oil, and sugar.

To get started in all this, you need a book that lists the calories in various food products and a physician. The book will suggest the foods to avoid or go easy on. The physician will tell you how far you may safely cut down your calorie intake or how rapidly you may safely increase your daily exercising. Calorie-counting books may be found in bookstores, and at the checkout counters of supermarkets and drugstores. Physicians may be found in these places too, but would probably prefer being consulted in their offices.

Developing a Specific Plan

Efforts to control weight are facilitated by the development of specific plans (Stuart 1978). These plans should include (1) a clear statement of your goals, (2) knowledge of where you stand at the beginning and at each step along the way, and (3) a list of the steps that you can use to accomplish your goals.

After you have spoken with your physician, you will probably have determined a target weight that you both consider healthful, and a safe rate for taking off pounds. If you have been told that it is safe for you to take off a pound a week, this translates into eating 3,500 fewer calories than you burn up each week, for a calorie deficit of 500 a day. If you plan to lose 20 pounds, this will take you twenty weeks. If you cannot bring yourself to reduce your daily intake by 500 calories all at once, you can start by reducing your daily intake by 100 calories for a few days, then by 200 calories, and so on. It will take you a few weeks longer to achieve your target weight, but you will get there. The way to eat an elephant is one bite at a time. The way to remove a mini-elephant from your mid-region can be to have just a few bites less at a sitting.

Psychologist Raymond Romanczyk and his colleagues (1973) found that keeping daily records of weight loss is ineffective as a *sole* method for losing weight, but counting calories often leads to reliable reductions. Daily weight records are often frustrating, involving temporary factors such as water weight.

Use a couple of weeks of baseline recording to determine how many calories you usually take in each day and the sorts of daily encounters that make it difficult for you to exercise self-control. Keep a notebook in which you record:

- What you have eaten
- Estimated number of calories (from the calorie book)
- Time of day, location, your activity, and your reactions to eating

Your record may suggest foods you will want to eat less of or cut out altogether, places you should try to avoid (like that new French restaurant with those superb Burritos Parisiens), or times of day when you are particularly vulnerable to snacking, such as midafternoon or late evening. Planning small, low-calorie snacks for these periods will prevent you from feeling deprived and from inhaling two shelves of your refrigerator.

Once you have used baseline recording to analyze the ABC's of your eating habits, maintain a daily record of calories consumed throughout the weight-loss program. It is in your calorie record that you want consistency. It is fine for you also to keep a daily record of your weight, so long as you do not become discouraged by temporary bodily resistances to weight loss—such as water weight—and you also keep your daily calorie record.

Use some of the following methods to help you keep down the number of calories you eat. Pick ones that feel right for you. If they work, continue to use them. If they don't, try some of the others.

Restricting the Stimulus Field

- Break the habit of eating while watching television or while studying by eating in one place only at home and at work or school.

Avoiding Powerful Triggers for Eating

- Avoid places and situations your baseline record suggests are powerful influences. Shop at the mall with the Alfalfa Sprout, not the Gushy Gloppy Shoppe.
- Use smaller plates, and remove or throw out leftovers and uneaten food quickly. We have it from reliable sources that people in China are no longer starving, so leave food uneaten without guilt.
- Do not starve yourself—binge eating can result from deprivation.
- Order by plan in a restaurant—not from that appetizing menu with the full-color photos.
- Pay attention to your own plate, not to that sumptuous dish at the next table.
- Shop from a list, walk briskly through the market, preferably after dinner, when you are no longer hungry. Don't browse in the supermarket or those colorful, fattening packages may get you.
- Keep out of the kitchen. Study, watch television, write letters, make love elsewhere.

Response Prevention

- Keep fattening foods out of the house.
- Prepare only enough food to fit the restrictions of your diet.

BEHAVIORAL WEIGHT CONTROL: THE WOLLER-SHEIM STUDY

If you were told of a group of people who wore little turtle tags, red pig-shaped tags, or yellow stars depending on whether they had been good or bad, you would probably think that we were referring to children in nursery school or kindergarten. But these symbols were actually worn by university students in a "social-pressure group" in an experiment comparing various weight-control procedures run by psychologist Janet Wollersheim (1970).

Wollersheim recruited seventy-nine female students weighing in at an average of 157 pounds for an experiment on the effectiveness of an approach to weight-control based on the ABC's of behavior—behavior therapy. All students had unsuccessfully attempted to lose weight before. Students were assigned at random to one of four groups: a social-pressure group, a nonspecific treatment group, a behavior therapy group, and a no-treatment control group whose participants were simply placed on a waiting list throughout the course of the experiment.

Women in the social-pressure group made a public commitment to lose weight and were weighed in at weekly meetings for twelve weeks. Weight loss was rewarded with verbal reinforcement and the yellow star. Weight gainers wore the pig tags, and women who neither gained nor lost wore the turtles. Group discussion focused on factual information concerning pounds and calories, health, and general nutrition. Women in the nonspecific treatment group discussed possible underlying causes of their weight problems and held psychoanalytically oriented therapy groups during the twelve-week period.

Women in the behavior therapy group self-monitored their eating and did a functional analysis to discover the antecedents and the consequences of overeating. They learned a variety of self-control techniques, including avoiding triggers for eating, chain breaking, use of competing responses, response cost, covert reinforcement, and covert sensitization. They were also encouraged to find areas of life that could provide them the enjoyment they had obtained from food and to make these substitutions.

All three treatment groups showed significant weight losses at the end of twelve weeks, while the control group gained an average of two pounds. The behavior therapy group was superior to the other methods.

We should point out that the Wollersheim study does not do a very adequate job of demonstrating the superiority of behavior therapy to psychoanalysis. Psychoanalysis does not easily translate into a twelve-week procedure, and the therapists were not fully trained psychoanalysts. Thus it is more accurate to consider the nonspecific treatment group to be another control group which, as Wollersheim pointed out, controls for the factors of therapist-client contact and participants' expectation of benefit and behavioral change. Nonetheless, the Wollersheim study did demonstrate the usefulness of behavioral strategies for achieving weight loss following the twelve-week treatment period and another eight-week follow-up period.

Using Competing Responses

- Stuff your mouth with celery rather than ice cream or candy.
- Eat premade, low-calorie snacks rather than losing control and swallowing a jarful of peanuts.
- Try jogging for half an hour rather than eating an unplanned snack.
- Reach for your mate, the expression goes—not your plate.

Chain Breaking—Making Emily Post Happy

- Make a place setting before any snack.
- Take small bites, chew slowly and thoroughly.

Weight Control, Smoking, and Drug Abuse

- Put down your utensils between bites.
- Take a five-minute break sometime during the meal to allow your body to begin to signal you that you are no longer famished. Ask yourself if you really need to eat the whole thing when you return.

Building Desired Habits Through Successive Approximations

- Increase your daily calorie deficit by 100 calories or so on a weekly basis to avoid feeling overly deprived.
- At first schedule frequent, low-calorie snacks. Gradually space them out.
- Build your daily exercise time by a few minutes each week.
- Cut out favorite but fattening foods from your diet one by one on a gradual basis to avoid feeling deprived.

Making Rewards Contingent upon Desired Behavior

- Do not eat dinner until you have exercised.
- Do not go to *Flash Gordon's Trip to Bermuda* unless you have met a weekly calorie-reduction goal.
- Put money in the bank toward that new camera or that vacation every time you meet your weekly calorie-intake goals.

Response Cost

- Keep a quarter in a stamped envelope addressed to your most hated cause. If the cheesecake wins, mail it immediately.
- Dock yourself a dollar toward the new camera every time the cheesecake wins.

Covert Reinforcement

- Imagine reaching for something fattening, stop yourself, and congratulate yourself. Imagine your pride, all your friends congratulating you.
- Imagine how wonderful you are going to look when you can wear a new swimsuit on the beach next summer.
- Mentally rehearse your next visit to your parents, in-laws, or other relatives—the ones who always try to stuff you like a pincushion—and imagine how you will politely but firmly refuse seconds. Think of how proud of yourself you will be.

Covert Sensitization

- When you are tempted by a fattening dish, imagine that it is really rotten, that you would feel nauseous from it later on and have a sick taste in your mouth for the rest of the day.
- When you feel tempted, strip in front of the mirror or handle a fatty area of your body. Ask yourself if you really want to put on more weight, or would prefer to take it off.
- When tempted, imagine all the extra work your heart must do for every pound of extra weight, imagine your arteries clogging up with dreaded substances.

The Premack Principle

- Keep six to ten business-sized cards in your wallet. On half, print proreducing statements ("I'll be able to fit in that new swimsuit," "I'll get rid of this roll of fat," "I'll be sexually appealing," etc.), and print antiovereating statements on the others ("Think of the way you look in a mirror," etc.). Shuffle these cards and read them each time you are about to leave home or engage in another common activity. Gradually replace them with newer messages. Thoughts of the benefits of losing weight and the miseries of remaining obese will tend to remain in the mind.

How to Put Weight *On*

If you are too slender, you can put weight on by reversing many of the strategies we have discussed. But do not do yourself the disservice of avoiding exercise: it is beneficial for the thin as well as the overweight. You should also discuss your plans with a physician to be certain that a weight-gain program will be healthful for you.

◢ Fear of Being Thin

ARE THE LOSERS WINNERS OR LOSERS?

If you were 100 pounds overweight, you might expect that you would go to bed each night praying to wake up slender. If you were to lose this weight, you would expect that your life would be a (scrawny) bowl of cherries.

Do not underestimate the distinctly human capacity to snatch confusion from the jaws of certainty. Psychologist Sandra Haber of New York interviewed four men and eight women who had all lost at least 100 pounds (Haber & Shapiro 1978). Were they unequivocally blissful about their new selves? Haber found that strong ambivalences clouded feelings of happiness and self-pride. New selves found it necessary to establish new relationships and new roles—both of which involve departures from known paths.

You would expect that your friends would applaud the emerging new you—find every opportunity to tell you how wonderfully you are progressing. But friends of these magnificent losers wondered if they were feeling well. After all, they had lost those plump, rosy cheeks. Some friends are apparently in competition with us and resent our successes.

Friends of the formerly plump can no longer entertain feelings of superiority.

Since slenderness is the cultural ideal, the newly slender are usually provided with more sexual opportunities than their former selves. One single male weight loser was finding himself a social winner, but pointed out that relationships, especially frequently forming relationships, can create anxiety. When he had been obese he had been unhappy, to be sure. But at least there was a certain sense of comfort and security in his very predictable unhappiness.

The four married people who were interviewed all noted that the new slenderness had placed certain strains on their marriages. A husband was afraid that he would be tempted to have affairs, which could be emotionally and financially costly. A wife refused to make a corporate move with her husband, preferring to remain in her own town. She reported that she no longer fit the victim role—she felt she must act on her own initiative.

Healthful weight loss requires adjustments, as do all changes. The loser who does not adjust may well be a . . . well, loser.

Some strategies that you may find particularly useful include:

- Browsing leisurely in the supermarket, buying attractive foods on impulse.
- Substituting high-calorie foods for low-calorie foods when possible.
- Being certain that food is always on hand so that you can snack on something that you enjoy at a moment's notice.
- Hanging around the kitchen and checking out the refrigerator and cupboards every so often.

But enough! For the larger number of readers who are overweight, this section is a torture chamber.

SMOKING

It is no secret that smoking is harmful. It has been related to perhaps two to three hundred thousand early deaths each year in this country alone (Mausner & Platt 1971). A recent study reported by the American Cancer Society (1972) followed over 400,000 men for a period of three years. Subjects were matched by height, race, occupation, educational level, alcohol consumption, and several other variables, and it was found that:

- 110 cigarette smokers died from lung cancer, while only 12 nonsmokers died from this disease.
- 654 of the smokers died from heart disease, while this disease killed only 314 nonsmokers.
- Overall, 1,385 of the smokers died, as compared to 662 of the nonsmokers.
- Smokers showed an overall increased likelihood of contracting diseases from **emphysema,** a respiratory illness, to cancers of the mouth and bladder.

With findings such as these replicated throughout the years, the Public Health Cigarette Smoking Act has required cigarette packs to carry this warning since 1970: "Cigarette Smoking Is Dangerous to Your Health." Since 1971 cigarette advertising has been banned on television. Smoking has been banished increasingly in public places. Many restaurants now have sections reserved for nonsmokers, and legislation has appeared here and there to ban smoking in all public places.

Millions of American adults have quit smoking, yet smoking may be becoming increasingly popular among adolescents and preadolescents. As Lawrence Pervin and Raymond Yatko (1965) discovered in a study at Princeton, smokers and nonsmokers alike shared knowledge of the links between smoking and cancer. Yet the smokers tended to delude themselves about personal invulnerability. Smokers were more likely to express the beliefs that a cure would be found for cancer before they were personally afflicted, or that their own smoking was within a safe range. A very common rationalization for smoking is the claim: "Look, I've tried, but I just can't quit. So that's that." Unfortunately, people who believe they cannot quit usually find it more difficult to quit.

Emphysema (em-fizz-SEEM-muh). A disease in which breathing is impaired.

For some adolescents, smoking is a symbol of having come of age, of being daring, rugged, and adventurous.

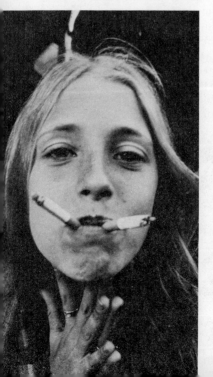

Components of Tobacco Smoke: Where There's Smoke There's Chemicals

Tobacco smoke contains **carbon monoxide, hydrocarbons** (known as **tars**), and **nicotine.**

Carbon monoxide is an odorless, colorless gas that combines with **hemoglobin** in the blood. Hemoglobin transports oxygen. Carbon monoxide is a selfish passenger and interferes with the hemoglobin's ability to supply the body with oxygen. One result: shortness of breath.

Some hydrocarbons or tars have been shown to cause cancer in laboratory animals. Nicotine is a **stimulant** that causes cold, clammy skin, faintness and dizziness, occasional nausea and vomiting, and diarrhea. These account for the sometimes dire experiences of the novice smoker. But nicotine also leads to a discharge of the hormone **epinephrine** into the bloodstream. Epinephrine, similar to norepinephrine, creates a burst of autonomic activity: rapid pulse, release of sugar into the blood, a sort of mental "kick." Nicotine, in short, is responsible for the stimulating property of cigarette smoke, but its effects are short-lived. In the long run it can contribute to fatigue.

Nor do these chemicals afflict only smokers. People trapped in closed spaces with smokers show rapid increases of carbon monoxide in the bloodstream. The quantities can be sufficient to trigger asthma attacks and cause severe distress to individuals suffering from heart disease (Doyle 1974).

Carbon monoxide (mo-KNOCKS-side). A colorless, odorless gas. Chemical formula: CO.
Hydrocarbons (HIGH-dro-CAR-buns). Substances containing carbon and water.
Tars. A term for hydrocarbons.
Nicotine (NICK-oh-teen). A stimulant found in tobacco.
Hemoglobin (HE-mo-GLOW-bin). The reddish substance in the blood that carries oxygen.
Stimulant. A substance that leads to increased activity in the nervous system.
Epinephrine (epp-pee-NEFF-rin). A hormone that increases autonomic activity. Also called adrenaline.

Why People Smoke

If smoking is dangerous and most smokers are aware of this, what attracts them to cigarettes?

For the young, smoking may be seen as a way of asserting maturity and individuality. In one study (Weir 1967), male college students were asked to rate photographs of men with and without cigarettes according to a list of adjectives. Men smoking were rated as rugged, daring, adventurous, and individualistic. Nonsmokers were rated as more timid, shy, and awkward.

Bernard Mausner (1966) of Beaver College wrote an article reporting the almost total failure of an antismoking clinic to induce college women to give up cigarettes. He noted that many of the clinic discussions centered on cigarette smoking as a vehicle through which the women developed and refined a self-image of being bright, sophisticated, and career oriented. Since smoking was so intertwined with these desirable traits, many women equated smoking cessation with the undermining of a liberated self-image.

Smoker See, Smoker Do? There is also a **social-facilitation** factor in cigarette smoking. If our friends and associates smoke, we are more likely to smoke.

In an American Cancer Society survey (Lieberman Research, Inc. 1967), 19 percent of nonsmokers reported that most of their friends smoked. For smokers this figure was a whopping 56 percent. In a study comparing men who successfully quit smoking with men who did not (Schwartz & Dubitsky 1968), it was found that the successful quitters were less likely to have wives who smoked, and less likely to smoke with someone whom they loved. Smoking couples may consider trying to quit together.

Social facilitation (fuh-sill-uh-TAY-shun). The increased likelihood of engaging in an activity because people nearby are engaged in that activity.

Weight Control, Smoking, and Drug Abuse

Table 15.3 Percentages of Male and Female Smokers Reporting Symptoms During Withdrawal

	Percentage Reporting Symptom	
Withdrawal Symptom	Females	Males
Nervousness	77	65
Drowsiness	61	59
Anxiety	58	53
Energy loss	52	39
Headaches	47	41
Fatigue	42	38
Constipation or diarrhea	38	27
Lightheadedness	32	44
Insomnia	32	29
Dizziness	25	26
Cramps	23	16
Palpitations	21	12
Tremors	15	15
Sweating	10	18

Source: Guilford et al. (1966).

Addiction (add-DICK-shun). Physiological dependence on a substance, which is known by the presence of an abstinence syndrome upon discontinuation or sudden drop in level of usage of the substance. *Abstinence syndrome* (AB-stin-ents). A cluster or grouping of symptoms that occurs upon doing without a substance.

Addiction: An Exercise in Escape Learning. **Addiction** to any substance is known by the presence of an **abstinence syndrome** upon doing without the substance. Abstinence means doing without, and a syndrome is a group of symptoms. Joan Guilford and her colleagues at the American Institutes of Research found that a large percentage of male and female habitual smokers who go without cigarettes report many symptoms (1966, pp. 114–117):

It is no surprise that the addicted smoker finds it difficult to do without cigarettes. Smokers may be struck by the urge to smoke anywhere from ten to sixty times a day. If the urge is prolonged, discomfort increases. Discomfort can be escaped or avoided by smoking—escape learning. Smoking can thus be *negatively reinforcing*: it allows addicted smokers to escape the discomforts of abstinence.

Of course, the smoker who would prefer to quit is placed in conflict. Quitting means experiencing the abstinence syndrome *now*. Continuing to smoke means facing the prospect of lung disease, cancer, and heart problems *later*. Rationalization and suppression can help tip the balance in favor of avoiding the abstinence syndrome now: "I'll quit some day—I don't have to think about it right now."

Kicks. Some do find pleasure in the act of smoking, of course. Some enjoy the taste of cigarettes, handling them ("It gives me something to do with my hands"), that surge of stimulation.

Some even use cigarettes as a form of anxiety relief. Smoking can, of course, relieve the anxiety that may attend not smoking. For some this form of anxiety relief seems to generalize. They claim that smoking helps them cope with the anxiety produced by exams and other forms of stress.

Cutting Down and Quitting

Sometimes we hear that the best way to cut down or quit smoking is simply to do it—to marshal your willpower (or, in this case, your won't-power) and decide that you are going to cut down or stop as of a certain date. Isn't this all nonsense? Doesn't effective smoking control begin with use of experimentally validated behavioral techniques?

Perhaps not—perhaps won't-power *is* the major factor. Michael Perri and his colleagues (1977) at the University of Missouri interviewed twenty-four successful and twenty-four unsuccessful smoking reducers to try to isolate the factors that led to effective self-control. In their study, "successful" reducers were defined as people who had decreased their daily number of cigarettes smoked by at least 50 percent from their baseline estimates, maintained this lower rate of smoking for at least four months, and felt happier with the new smoking rate. Successful reducers did use a variety of self-control techniques, including self-reinforcement, more frequently and consistently than the unsuccessful reducers. But successful reducers also rated themselves as significantly more highly motivated and committed to reducing smoking.

In a recent Israeli experiment, researchers from Bar-Ilan University and the University of Haifa (Blittner et al. 1978) worked with fifty-four smokers from kibbutzim who were an average of thirty-eight years old and had smoked an average of twenty-eight cigarettes a day for sixteen years. Smokers in two treatment groups used behavioral self-control methods, but subjects in one of these groups also received a "cognitive self-control treatment **set**" or expectation. They were told that psychological tests had "showed that they had strong willpower and great potential to control and conquer their desires and behavior. Thus it was quite certain that during the course of treatment they would completely stop smoking" (p. 555). Throughout a two-month treatment process, this message was reinforced. Both treatment groups reduced their smoking significantly more than control subjects at the end of treatment and during several months of follow-ups, and the smokers who were given the expectation that they had superior willpower smoked consistently fewer cigarettes than smokers who had used behavioral methods alone.

Set. A way of looking at things; a group of expectations.

David Premack (1970) suggests that **humiliation** is a prime factor for the millions who have quit smoking spontaneously—without training in self-control, without professional intervention of any kind. That is, at some point we become disgusted with our own inability to take charge of our own behavior and quit this revolting habit—perhaps we see our children beginning to fiddle with our cigarettes, perhaps we burn a hole in our furniture or clothing. Recognition that we are defiling our bodies, that we have surrendered our roles as masters of our fates creates "humiliation shock." When we feel humiliation, our self-identities as smokers can suffer a death blow, and, as Theodore Sarbin and Larry Nucci (1973) of the University of California at Santa Cruz put it, we may seek a rebirth or purification as nonsmokers.

Humiliation. An intense emotional state of displeasure characterized by feelings of self-disgust.

Does all this suggest that self-control methods are useless in helping us reduce or quit smoking? Not at all. They were useful even in the Perri and Blittner studies. However, strong motivation to quit—fueled by negative consequences of smoking and humiliation that we have not been able to take charge of our own behavior—appears to make self-control more likely to succeed.

Quitting Cold Turkey vs. Cutting Down Gradually. Is cutting down smoking gradually just an extended period of torture, or does it allow you to become gradually accustomed to lower quantities of nicotine and make quitting less painful? If you are going to quit, period, should you do it now or plan a target date, say, a couple of weeks in the future?

Weight Control, Smoking, and Drug Abuse

443

ON WIVES, CIGARETTES, CHAIRS, AND BASEMENTS

Youngsters may sneak a cigarette behind the garage or in the cellar, but it sounds unlikely that the wife of a sophisticated psychologist would have to smoke in the basement. Or does it?

The wife of J. Dennis Nolan, a psychologist at Ohio State University, had tried to quit smoking unsuccessfully many times (Nolan 1968). Mr. and Mrs. Nolan applied restriction of the stimulus field to the wife's problem by designating a smoking chair—the one place Mrs. Nolan could smoke. She could smoke as frequently as she wished so long as she did so in this chair. But *all* she could do in this chair was smoke. She could not watch television, or read, or talk to anyone. Thus, smoking became disconnected from its usual triggers, and Mrs. Nolan became acutely more aware of her habit. This method reduced her smoking from twenty-four to twelve cigarettes a day. Then the chair was removed to a remote section of the basement, where the level dropped off to seven a day. After some weeks, Mrs. Nolan became disgusted with her trips to the basement and her inability to cut out smoking altogether. So she quit—the role of humiliation.

But do not think that only basements work these wonders. Psychologist Alan Roberts (1969) of the University of Minnesota used his bathroom to tackle his twenty-three-year-old pack-a-day habit. Within several weeks his smoking was decreased by 75 percent. Then he developed a cold and quit altogether.

Many studies have yielded confusing results, but an experiment by Judith Flaxman of the University of North Carolina provides some useful information. Flaxman (1978) recruited participants from her community through public service announcements. They had smoked an average of twenty-six cigarettes a day for twenty years, and many had tried to quit smoking in the past unsuccessfully. In fact, some reported dozens of attempts. Flaxman compared several treatment approaches: immediate quitting ("cold turkey"), a delayed quitting date, cutting down gradually, a partially gradual condition in which smoking was terminated abruptly when daily rates fell to 50 percent of baseline, and **aversion therapy**. All participants were taught self-control techniques, including making a public commitment to friends and other acquaintances that they were going to quit, using competing responses, covert reinforcement, and covert sensitization. Subjects in the gradual condition then restricted their smoking to fewer environments every three days. Partial-gradual subjects stopped altogether when smoking was reduced to half the baseline rate. Target-date subjects chose a date to quit approximately two weeks distant. "Immediate" subjects quit after a single one-and-a-half-hour session. Some subjects from these four treatment methods received aversion therapy as a follow-up treatment, while others met with their therapists to discuss their progress.

The participants' progress was followed for two months through weekly postcards that showed daily cigarette counts, and then through follow-up phone calls six months later. Use of a target date resulted in lower smoking frequencies than the gradual and the partial-gradual conditions, but delaying the quitting date was more effective for women participants, while men fared better quitting immediately. Aversion therapy was helpful at reducing rates only for men in the partial-gradual condition. Subjects in almost all treatments showed increased smoking at the six-month follow-up, when compared with rates during the first eight weeks.

Aversion therapy (uh-VURR-shun). A method of decreasing unwanted behavior by associating an unpleasant stimulus with that behavior. Also called aversive conditioning.

The Challenge of Self-Control

Thus using an immediate or delayed target date for quitting may be more effective than gradually cutting down. Perhaps the limited goals of gradually cutting down tend to interfere with motivation to quit; perhaps the lingering quality of the struggle stretches the patience. The fact that immediate quitting was more effective for men than women may be consistent with the cultural stereotype of the aggressive, curt male: perhaps men feel that they ought to take charge of their own behavior *now* more than do women in our culture.

Quitting Cold Turkey. Perhaps you always preferred your turkey with hot giblet gravy anyway, but if you decide that quitting **cold turkey** is the way for you to stop smoking there are a number of suggestions that you can follow:

Cold turkey. Discontinuing use of a substance abruptly.

- Tell your family and friends that you are quitting—make a public commitment.
- Plan ahead things you can tell yourself when fighting the urge to smoke —how you will be stronger, free of fear of illness, and so on.
- Remind yourself as needed that the first few days are most difficult— after that, withdrawal symptoms wane and many of the old triggers for smoking have lost their effectiveness.
- When you see other smokers, tell yourself how superior you are. (After all, they're unlikely to run over and pat you on the back.)
- Start in the morning, when you have already gone eight hours or so without nicotine.
- Avoid triggers for smoking by trying to initiate quitting when you move or go on a vacation. (Take a purposeful smoke-ending vacation.)
- Throw out ashtrays. Rid your home of all smoking paraphernalia. Do not invite smoking friends over for several weeks.
- Do not carry matches. Do not light others' cigarettes.
- Sit in nonsmoking cars of trains, nonsmoking sections of restaurants.
- Fill your days with novel activities—new hobbies, novels, people, and places.
- Keep sugar-free mints, candies, and gum available as competing responses. Use Chap Stick repeatedly (but wash it off before your mouth becomes mistaken for a wax candle).
- Fantasize that you are a spy withholding essential information from the enemy. They are trying to break you by withholding cigarettes, but if you can last for just a few days, you'll have them licked!
- Put all the money you're saving by not buying cigarettes into a special reward fund, and watch it mount. Treat yourself to some things you have been hesitant to buy.

Cutting Down Gradually. If you decide that you would rather reduce your smoking bit by bit, adopt some of these self-control measures:

- Use self-monitoring to establish your baseline and do a functional analysis of the triggers of your smoking. Gradually restrict the number of environments in which you smoke. Have a smoking chair handy? If so, make it a bit less handy: basement time!
- Involve yourself in activities and in places where smoking is not allowed.
- Switch to a brand you do not like, and hold your cigarettes with your other hand only.

Weight Control, Smoking, and Drug Abuse

- Keep only enough cigarettes in the house to meet (reduced) daily goals. Never buy more than one pack at a time.
- Use sugar-free candies, gum, or Chap Stick instead of smoking to fiddle with something that can provide oral gratification.
- Jog rather than smoke. Or swim, or walk, or make love.
- Wrap your cigarette pack in foil and keep it on the top shelf in a closet. Get only one cigarette at a time, and replace the pack—wrapping and all—before you begin to smoke.
- Pause before lighting up, put your cigarette down in an ashtray between puffs. Ask yourself, each time, if you really want the cigarette, or to continue the cigarette. If not, stop.
- Put the cigarette out before you have eaten the filter. (We have it from a reliable source that people in China are not having nicotine fits. Thus, you need not feel guilty when you waste tobacco.)
- Gradually space out the amount of time between cigarettes.
- Buy yourself little rewards with the cash saved from not smoking.
- Get that quarter into that envelope—all ready to be shipped to that hated cause if you do not meet a daily or weekly goal.
- Imagine living a prolonged, noncoughing life. Ah, freedom!
- Picture blackened lungs, coughing fits, and the possibility of cancer and heart disease while you smoke—the emotional appeal.
- Read an assortment of antismoking and proquitting cards each time before you engage in a high-frequency behavior, such as turning on the television set or leaving the house. Cards with statements such as, "I feel sick when I think that I can't control myself," "My mate will be so proud when I quit," "I'm just getting closer to cancer every day," "If I quit I'll live long enough to find a mate," etc. This will help change your attitudes. And make David Premack very happy.

The Cure

SOME NOTES ON THAT FABULOUS NEW VACCINE FOR SMOKING

What if there were a vaccine for smoking? What if it were absolutely guaranteed to break your addiction to cigarettes by getting you through the withdrawal period—with just one hitch?

The hitch? Some side effects. For two to three days following taking the vaccine, many people complain of intermittent nervousness and drowsiness. Some people experience headaches and constipation or diarrhea. Tremors and sweating are less common, but are experienced by perhaps fifteen people in a hundred. However, your physician would assure you, all these side effects are harmless and quite temporary. They fade rapidly after just a few days and, most likely, are completely gone in a week. Considering the alternatives—fear of cancer, other diseases, the price of cigarettes, and your own humiliation at not being able to kick the habit—would you be tempted to take this vaccine?

If you would, this "vaccine" exists and is readily available. It's known as *stopping smoking*—we have merely described some symptoms of the abstinence syndrome. As Sarbin and Nucci (1973) point out, you need not *interpret* these symptoms as discomforting signs of withdrawal. You can think of them as fully voluntary—signposts that your body is adjusting to lack of nicotine and other poisons, signposts that you will probably improve your health.

This is also true in weight control. Dieters need not interpret hunger as torturous signals that they are starving themselves. They can look upon hunger as a sign that they are *winning*. After all, you do not feel hunger when you continually stuff yourself.

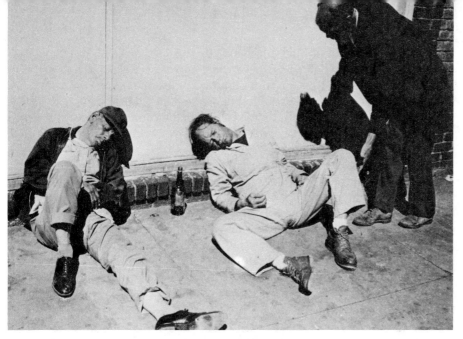

Two views of drinking, one negative, the other positive.

ALCOHOL

No substance has meant so much to so many people in our culture as alcohol. It is our dinnertime tranquilizer, our bedtime sedative, our cocktail party social facilitator. We use alcohol to applaud each other's accomplishments and to express our wishes for a fruitful and joyous future. We use alcohol to celebrate religious holy days. The young use alcohol to assert their maturity. The elderly use alcohol to stimulate circulation of the blood into peripheral areas of the body. We use alcohol to kill germs on surface wounds and to quench our thirsts. Some pediatricians even suggest swabbing the painful gums of teething babies with alcohol.

Perhaps no substance in the history of our culture has been so abused as alcohol. According to the National Council on Alcoholism (1973), 100 million Americans use alcohol. Of these, perhaps 5 to 10 million are considered **alcoholics,** or have problems controlling their use of alcohol. Compare this to perhaps 200,000 who use heroin regularly, or 300,000 to half a million who abuse sedatives. Most alcoholics do not reside on Skid Row. The highest proportion of heavy drinkers in this country is found among men aged 30 to 34 and 45 to 49, and among women aged 21 to 24 and 45 to 49. So alcohol is the companion of men in the Catch Thirties and women in the Trying Twenties, and both men and women in the Fearsome Forties (Cahalan et al. 1969). And despite widespread marijuana use, alcohol is the drug of choice among adolescents.

Effects of Alcohol

Why is alcohol so popular? Why has it been used in both the West and the East for thousands of years? Alcohol, put simply, is the magical tranquilizer you can buy without a doctor's prescription. It is the relief from anxiety that you can swallow in public without being criticized or stigmatized. You are just considered social. Chemically, alcohol is a **depressant:** it slows the activity of the central nervous system. It deadens minor aches and pains, relaxes, and may serve

Alcoholic (al-ko-HOLL-lick). An individual who has difficulty controlling use of alcohol, or whose social, vocational, or personal functioning is impaired as a result of drinking.

Depressant (dee-PRESS-ant). A substance that slows down the activity of the body.

Weight Control, Smoking, and Drug Abuse

to release people from normal inhibitions by reducing fear of consequences—especially if this is what you expect will happen. Self-doubts and criticism may be washed away by feelings of elation.

But increased quantities of this depressant fog the senses, jumble the speech, and foul up motor coordination. Sufficient alcohol in one sitting would kill us, but, fortunately, most of us will have passed out long before we have reached this **toxic** level.

Alcohol is fattening, but chronic drinkers may be malnourished. Though alcohol is high in calories, it does not contain nutrients, such as protein and vitamins, that are necessary for good health. Insufficient protein can lead to **cirrhosis of the liver,** a disease in which connective fibers replace active liver cells and thus impede circulation of the blood. Rupture of small blood vessels, especially in the nose, can lead to swelling and redness. (So now you have the scoop on Rudolph the red-nosed reindeer.) Chronic alcohol use has also been linked to heart disease, high blood pressure, and brain damage. As we saw in

Toxic (TOCKS-sick). Poisonous.

Cirrhosis of the liver (si-ROW-sis). A disease of the liver that has been linked with alcohol.

◤ Watch Out! ◢

DOES ALCOHOL MAKE YOU SEXY AND AGGRESSIVE?

It is a well-known fact of life that alcohol lowers the inhibitions of the sexually reluctant and makes our lives more amorous. Why else do we spend a fortune attempting to influence each other with wine and liquor in expensive restaurants? Good question.

G. Terence Wilson and David Lawson (1978) explored the effects of alcohol on forty university women volunteers at Rutgers University. They reasoned that if alcohol increases sexual responsiveness, women drinking vodka ought to show increased sexual arousal to erotic stimuli—in this case, pornographic films. But they also reasoned that if drinking women were more sexually responsive, it might only be because they expected that alcohol would increase their responsiveness. Thus women believing they had drunk vodka might show more arousal than women who did not believe they had drunk vodka—regardless of whether they had actually drunk vodka or only tonic water.

Fortunately, the taste of vodka with tonic water cannot be distinguished from tonic water alone. Wilson and Lawson created four experimental conditions: women who drank vodka and believed they drank vodka, women who drank vodka but believed they had drunk only tonic water, women who drank tonic water and believed they drank tonic water, and women who drank tonic water but believed it had contained vodka.

The measure of sexual arousal was vaginal blood pressure: aroused women experience heightened blood flow to the genitals. Blood pressure was measured by a plethysmograph, a small instrument that is inserted into the vagina. Then the women were shown the erotic films. The volunteers inserted the plethysmographs and watched the films in a private room, while the readings from the plethysmographs could be monitored from an adjoining room.

It turned out that both speculations were incorrect. Women who drank vodka actually showed less sexual response than women who had drunk tonic water only, regardless of their knowledge of what they had drunk. Alcohol, which is a depressant, may have depressed their sexual responsiveness. Similarly, in an earlier experiment with male college students, Wilson and another colleague (Briddell & Wilson 1976) found that the male's sexual response to erotic films, as measured by penile erection, decreased with increasing amounts of alcohol.

Are we to conclude that alcohol clearly reduces sexual responsiveness, in both men and women? Perhaps. And perhaps not. While these experiments were conducted very carefully, we must remember that erotic films are only one kind of sexual stimulation. Actual exposure to an attractive, warm, and familiar person might yield rather different results. We should also consider that the sample was limited to volunteering university students. Volunteers for such an experiment are likely to be rather sexually liberated and may not truly represent all students.

Chapter 3, even moderate drinking by a pregnant woman can be damaging to the fetus.

Use, Abuse, Tolerance, Dependence, Addiction

Where does alcohol use leave off and **abuse,** or **alcoholism,** begin? We cannot simply talk about certain amounts of alcohol as being crucial, because we rapidly develop a tolerance for alcohol; that is, we require larger amounts of alcohol to achieve similar relaxing or sedative effects once we have become used to the drug. Heavy drinking may be considered appropriate at parties, and especially on New Year's Eve, but is usually condemned as abuse in the morning.

Workable definitions of abuse or alcoholism tend to recognize that we need a *problem* associated with drinking. For instance, the American Psychiatric Association (1968) defines alcoholism as drinking that repeatedly inter-

Abuse. **Use of a substance that is considered harmful, or that interferes with functioning.**
Alcoholism. **Problem drinking. Drinking occurring at a level such that it interferes with one's functioning or impairs one's health.**

Nor do students necessarily represent the population at large.

Perhaps the effects of alcohol on sexual arousal remain unclear, but alcohol stimulates us to act aggressively, doesn't it? Why else would we hear about the fabled barroom brawl?

Psychologist Alan Lang and his colleagues at the University of Wisconsin (1975) investigated the relationship between alcohol and aggression by setting up a minor electrical brawl in a psychological laboratory. Like Wilson and his colleagues, the Lang group created four conditions with undergraduate male social drinkers: students who drank vodka and students who drank tonic water only; students who were given accurate information about what they had drunk and students who were deceived. Then they borrowed the "teacher-learner" technique from Stanley Milgram (Chapter 11), and the phony electric-shock machine.

Lang's subjects were told they were in an experiment to study effects of alcohol on learning and personality. In Phase 1, subjects traced geometric figures after drinking, seated next to other subjects. The other subjects made neutral remarks or else insulted their tracing ability. Insulted subjects were considered *provoked* by the experimenters.

In Phase 2, subjects were put in teacher roles with the other subjects. When "learners" made errors in a learning task, a red light would be shown on a panel. Then the teachers could press a lever to deliver an electric shock as a punishment. They could choose the voltage level by themselves and maintain the shock as long as they wished.

By now, of course, you are skeptical enough to

realize that the "learners" were actually confederates of the experimenter. They had insulted the real subjects in the experiment as an experimental method of inducing retaliation with the electric-shock machines.

In this experiment, provoked subjects delivered shocks of greater intensity and duration than nonprovoked subjects. The subjects who thought they had drunk alcohol delivered shocks of greater intensity and duration than subjects who believed they had drunk tonic water only—regardless of whether or not they had actually drunk alcohol. So, expectations about the presence of alcohol led to aggression, not alcohol itself.

But wait—is it possible that these subjects had simply not drunk enough alcohol to have an effect? No, their blood alcohol levels were at the level legally defined as intoxicated—enough to land you in jail if you are found driving at the time. Subjects who had drunk alcohol also took longer to react to the red light, a sign that their central nervous systems were, in fact, somewhat depressed.

In the Lang study, alcohol did not directly stimulate or energize aggression. Nor did it encourage aggression through diminishing fear of consequences of using high shock levels. It seems that it is more likely that alcohol encourages us to play more aggressive social roles because of our expectations about the drug. And perhaps some of us seize the opportunity to be aggressive when we believe we can attribute our aggressive behavior to the alcohol and not ourselves. For many people who are aggressive when they drink, it may just be that there is more gusto in their expectations than in their bloodstreams.

feres with your physical, personal, or social well-being. If you are missing work because you are drunk or because you are "sleeping it off," you fit the definition.

Psychological dependence on alcohol is repeated use of alcohol to deal with stress—whether the stress is related to the job, relationships with others, or personal conflict. **Physiological dependence** or addiction to alcohol can also develop from chronic use. Addiction is determined by the presence of an abstinence syndrome upon withdrawal: anxiety, tremors, restlessness, weakness, sweating, rapid pulse, and high blood pressure. Some chronic alcoholics experience **delirium tremens (DT's)** upon abrupt withdrawal: terrifying hallucinations—often of creepy, crawling animals—heavy sweating, restlessness, and general confusion. Severe withdrawal symptoms and DT's are best handled as medical problems. A physician should be consulted as soon as possible.

Is Alcohol a Problem for You?

The Boston Marathon is a twenty-six-mile race, which takes the fastest runners two and a quarter hours. A special group of racers is given a head start of one half hour. The runners pass this group only at about the twenty-one-mile marker. What is special about this head-start group? They have lost the use of their legs and race in wheel chairs, propelling themselves by huge arm and shoulder muscles and finishing the race in under three hours. Is their "handicap" a problem for them? When you huff and puff just watching them roll by, you realize that problems are relative.

Similarly, you must determine for yourself whether alcohol is a problem for you. If it interferes with your personal or social functioning, or with your physical health, it fits the American Psychiatric Association definition of alcoholism. But there is a subjective quality to "interference" with one's life. Here are some early signs that alcohol may be becoming a problem:

- Reaching for a drink when you experience stress—anxiety, tension, frustration, conflict, and so on.
- Drinking more than other members of your group. Drinking in situations and at times of the day when you did not usually drink.
- Drinking more rapidly than other members of your group.
- Drinking by yourself. Sneaking drinks.
- Being sure to keep your liquor supply up so that there is no danger you will be caught short.
- Drinking to deaden the pain from a hangover.
- Planning your days around your drinking. Allowing time for drinking between meetings and appointments. Considering how to carry or buy alcohol on trips and vacations.
- Experiencing "blackouts"—being unable to remember drinking episodes.

Nobody is motivated to control drinking unless convinced that drinking has become a severe problem. There are many resources available for people who have come to feel this way, including **AA (Alcoholics Anonymous)** and self-control methods.

Psychological dependence. Repeated use of a substance in a wide variety of circumstances, evidenced by psychological concern over discontinuation of that substance.

Physiological dependence (fizz-ee-oh-LODGE-uh-kul). Addiction, known by presence of an abstinence syndrome upon discontinuation of a substance.

Delirium tremens (dee-LIRR-ree-um TRE-mens). A problem sometimes brought about by sudden discontinuation of large dosages of alcohol that is characterized by sweating, agitation, hallucinations, and panic.

DT's. Abbreviation for delirium tremens.

Blackout. Amnesia for events that occurred while one was intoxicated.

AA. Abbreviation for Alcoholics Anonymous.

Alcoholics Anonymous. An organization that helps individuals who have drinking problems.

Two A's and Four Con's: Identity Conversion at AA

To the folks at AA, meeting the challenge of alcoholism is similar to a religious conversion or rebirth. You experience the social influence of a *con*gregation of fellow sinners, many of whom already belong to the ranks of the reborn. You publicly *con*fess your sins—how you have allowed evil (alcohol) to wreck your life. You make a public commitment to change your ways, and your identity is *con*verted to that of **reformed alcoholic**—a person who has sinned, but sworn never to touch another drop. Your new identity becomes *con*firmed each day you do not drink and encourage others to join you to swear off evil.

AA shows some impressive conversion rates, but statistics are problematic because AA does not count people who attend one meeting and drop out as treatment failures. AA also teaches that reformed alcoholics must abstain permanently, because a reformed alcoholic can never exercise reliable self-control. This is a controversial stand. Recent experiments (Sobell & Sobell 1973; Sobell et al. 1972) suggest that many people who have alcohol problems can restrict themselves to acceptable levels of social drinking through self-control methods.

Reformed alcoholic. An individual who has stopped drinking, according to AA.

Controlled Social Drinking

It is possible to cut down alcohol use by analyzing the ABC's of your own drinking and then using self-control strategies, including self-monitoring, to limit your alcohol intake.

If stress triggers drinking, change your life to eliminate sources of stress, or else learn to meet the challenge of stress through techniques such as progressive relaxation or meditation. If drinking buddies serve as triggers, spend more time with coffee buddies or milk buddies. Switching from hard liquor to wine or beer will dilute the alcohol content of your beverages. Or you can substitute soda at parties. Pause between sips and ask yourself whether you really need to finish this drink. Think about the problems that your drinking holds for you. Think about the relief that cutting down will provide.

And, if you experience withdrawal symptoms when you control your drinking, it is time to consult a physician.

MARIJUANA

One person's weed is another person's garden treasure. The **cannabis** plant is a weed found in many parts of the world. This would arouse little interest, except for the fact that **marijuana** is produced from cannabis. And marijuana is of interest because it contains an ingredient that can relax you, elate you, and sometimes produce mild hallucinations. The ingredient is far from secret. It is **delta-9-trans-tetrahydrocannabinol,** which, in a moment of mercy, researchers decided we could safely abbreviate as **THC.** You may as well know that THC is sexist: it prefers female cannabis plants, being most abundant in female seeds and flowers.

In the last century, marijuana was smoked almost as frequently as aspirin is swallowed today—for headaches and minor aches and pains. You could buy it in any drugstore—no prescription needed. There is still discussion of medi-

Cannabis (KAN-ah-biss). The name of the plant from which marijuana is extracted, or the name for the flowering tops of the plant. Also called hemp. *Marijuana* (mar-ee-WAHN-uh or mar-ee-HWAHN-uh). The substance in the cannabis plant that relaxes and intoxicates.
Delta-9-trans-tetrahydrocannabinol (TET-trah-HIGH-dro-kan-NAB-uh-noll). The active, intoxicating ingredient in marijuana.
THC. Abbreviation for delta-9-trans-tetrahydrocannabinol.

Weight Control, Smoking, and Drug Abuse

451

Marijuana is smoked openly on many college campuses, even in states in which possession of marijuana is a criminal offense.

Glaucoma (glaw-ко-muh). A disorder of the eye that can lead to blindness.

cal usage. Marijuana decreases nausea and vomiting in cancer patients receiving chemotherapy. It reduces pressure in the eye for **glaucoma** patients. It may even offer some relief from asthma. But there are side effects. Marijuana can increase the heart rate, and there is some discussion that marijuana smoke may be as much a cause of cancer as tobacco smoke.

Bacon, Eggs, and the Munchies

Marijuana is condemned by many Americans because it was strongly associated with the rebellious 1960s. Films of students boycotting classes at the end of that decade also show marijuana. So when some Americans think of marijuana, they also think of demonstrations, free love, leftist politics, hippies, and anarchy.

Yet marijuana knows no politics and is smoked by people at all socioeconomic levels, conservatives and liberals alike. Perhaps this is because of its "high"—a positive shift in mood. Marijuana also seems to slow the passage of time and increase your absorption in whatever you are doing. It is not surprising that marijuana and sex have been thought to go together like bacon and eggs. Marijuana also increases the pleasure of eating (Tart 1971), and may, as smokers say, give you a case of the "munchies."

Marijuana and Amotivational Syndrome

Studies in Costa Rica (Coggins, 1979) and an earlier study in Jamaica (Rubin & Comitas 1975) address other concerns about marijuana use. It had been sus-

SOME INTERESTING FACTS ABOUT AN OLD BEVERAGE

Have you heard those commercials about Coke adding life? This is truth in advertising. Given its caffeine and sugar content, Coke should give you quite a lift. But it hasn't been the real thing since 1906. Between 1896, when Coca-Cola was first marketed, and 1906, the manufacturers used coca leaves, which contained cocaine—a stimulant that induces a powerful high called a state of euphoria. It also deadens pain, increases self-confidence, and stirs the sexual appetite. Since 1906 the Coca-Cola company has used leaves from which the cocaine has already been extracted.

Cocaine—also known as coke and snow—was used since the early 1800s as a local anesthetic. It came to the attention of one Viennese neurologist in 1884—a young chap by the name of Sigmund Freud, who used it to fight depression and published an early one-sided paper on the drug, "Song of Praise."

You can brew coca leaves, or snort (i.e., breathe in) or inject cocaine extract. People do not become physically addicted to cocaine, but can grow psychologically dependent. Overdoses can lead to extreme restlessness, tremors, hallucinations and delusions, nausea, and even convulsions. Cocaine has been illegal since the Harrison Narcotic Act of 1914.

pected that marijuana use could lead to **amotivational syndrome,** a lack of interest in taking charge of your own life—a sort of generalized melting away of ambition. These fears had been fueled by some correlational evidence that regular and heavy marijuana smokers in the college ranks did not strive to succeed as much as their nonsmoking or infrequently smoking peers. But we cannot confuse correlational relationships with cause and effect, and other studies have suggested that students choosing to smoke marijuana heavily may already be somewhat less highly motivated to achieve than other students.

Amotivational syndrome (ay-mo-tiv-VAY-shun-ul). Loss of ambition, lack of interest in achievement.

Weight Control, Smoking, and Drug Abuse

Table 15.4 A Personal Guide to Selected Substances in the World Supermarket

Substance	Type of Substance	Method of Use	Medical Uses	Potential for Dependency	Potential Results of Abuse
Alcohol	Depressant	Oral	To relieve pain, insomnia, circulatory problems in the aged	Tolerance, psychological and physical dependence	Drowsiness, nausea, loss of appetite, impaired judgment and coordination, slurred speech
Amphetamines: Benzedrine (Bennies), Dexedrine (Dexies), Methedrine (speed, crystal Meth)	Stimulants	Oral or by injection	To relieve fatigue, reduce appetite for dieters (rarely used today)	Tolerance, psychological dependence, no physical dependence	Restlessness, tremors, hallucinations and paranoid delusions, insomnia, loss of appetite, irritability
Barbiturates: amobarbital, Nembutal, phenobarbital, pentobarbital, secobarbital	Depressants	Oral	To relieve anxiety and tension, insomnia, epilepsy, high blood pressure; quick-acting anesthetic	Tolerance, psychological and physical dependence	Drowsiness, motor impairment, slurred speech, irritability, poor judgment. Convulsions possible upon withdrawal
Cocaine (coke, snow)	Stimulant	Snorted or by injection	Local anesthetic (no longer used)	No tolerance, psychological dependence, no physical dependence	Restlessness, tremors, hallucinations, paranoid delusions, insomnia, loss of appetite, nausea, convulsions
LSD (lysergic acid)	Hallucinogen	Oral	Experimental use in alcoholism	Tolerance, psychological dependence, no physical dependence	Visual and auditory hallucinations, anxiety, panic, poor motor coordination
Marijuana (pot, joint, reefer, tea, weed, hash, Mary Jane)	Hallucinogen	Smoked	To relieve pain (no longer used); research in glaucoma, control of nausea in chemotherapy patients	No tolerance, psychological dependence, no physical dependence	Drowsiness or restlessness, laughter, increased appetite, impaired judgment and coordination, panic
Mescaline (peyote)	Hallucinogen	Oral	Research only	Tolerance, psychological dependence, no physical dependence	Excitement, hallucinations, rambling speech
Methadone	Depressant	Oral or by injection	"Maintenance" of narcotics addicts; to relieve pain	Tolerance, psychological dependence, physical dependence	Drowsiness, stupor, panic, altered time perception, impaired judgment and coordination; euphoria possible
Minor tranquilizers, e.g., Atarax, Librium, Serax, Valium	Depressants	Oral or by injection	To relieve anxiety and tension, high blood pressure, muscle spasms	Tolerance, psychological dependence, possible physical dependence	Drowsiness, impaired coordination
Opiates, e.g., codeine, heroin, meperidine (Demerol), morphine, opium	Depressants	Oral or by injection; opium can be smoked	To relieve pain; codeine relieves coughing; meperidine is used as a preoperative relaxant	Tolerance, psychological dependence, physical dependence	Drowsiness, stupor, panic, altered time perception, impaired judgment and coordination; euphoria possible

Table 15.4   (continued)

Phencyclidine (PCP, angel dust)	Tranquilizer-anesthetic; hallucinogen	Oral, often sprinkled on marijuana or tobacco and smoked	To relieve pain (a veterinary anesthetic)	Tolerance, psychological dependence, no physical dependence	Drowsiness, stupor, altered perceptions, impaired judgment and coordination, nausea and vomiting; euphoria, depression, paranoia possible

The Jamaican and Costa Rican studies seem to have confirmed the weakness of any cause-and-effect relationship between amotivational syndrome and marijuana smoking. Heavy smokers in Jamaica and Costa Rica had no difficulty attaining or holding jobs. None of the subjects showed genetic damage or abnormal brain-wave recordings. An interesting finding of both studies was that marijuana users weighed an average of seven pounds less than nonsmokers, but the subjects were in as good health as the nonsmokers. Perhaps it is difficult to fit food and a marijuana cigarette into your mouth at the same time. Jamaican smokers showed no withdrawal symptoms when they abstained for a period of six days, despite heavy usage over many years.

Marijuana and the Law

You have heard the lament, "Why is everything I like immoral, illegal, or fattening?" Marijuana has been illegal in the United States since the 1930s. There is only slight reason to believe that this situation will change in the near future, despite a 1973 report by the Presidential Commission on Marijuana and Drug Abuse that use of cannabis may be considered a minor problem when compared with abuse of alcohol and other drugs in our society.

Supporters of marijuana note that attempts to prove that the drug is harmful have largely been inconclusive, and that while no one can claim that highly potent marijuana smoked in large quantities would have *no* long-range detrimental effects, the evidence that alcohol is more of a problem is quite concrete. Yet alcohol is not prohibited. Opponents of marijuana, who are also cognizant of these findings, note that the alcohol analogy is not an adequate reason for turning loose another potentially harmful drug.

Summary

- *If you operate on a certain part of the brain of a rat, it will go on an eating rampage until it resembles a furry basketball.* True. Destroying a part of the hypothalamus results in obesity in the rat, while destroying another section of the hypothalamus results in loss of appetite. Stanley Schacter noted that the behavior of obese people often resembles that of these fat rats: greater sensitivity to taste, eating larger meals, eating more rapidly.
- *Overweight people are less likely than slender people to bother to go to a refrigerator for sandwiches at lunchtime.* True. Obese people respond more to external stimulation (sight and odor of food) than slender

Weight Control, Smoking, and Drug Abuse

people, but less to internal sensations of hunger. Slender people are more responsive to stomach contractions and less responsive to the clock.

- *You burn up calories by just sleeping.* True, although you burn more when you are awake, and still more by exercising. A comprehensive weight-loss program will ideally include exercise as well as calorie restriction. A calorie is a unit of food energy; 3,500 calories are equal to one pound of body weight.

- *If you make the kitchen your hangout, you are likely to hang on a few extra pounds.* True enough. The sights and odors of the kitchen may be powerful triggers for eating. You can use the ABC's of behavior to devise a variety of strategies to help you control your weight.

- *Losing weight can be grounds for divorce.* Not directly, but Sandra Haber discovered that weight losses of 100 pounds or more, while desirable, may tax our adjustive capacities and pose new problems for us. Now that people are more attractive, they may be exposed to more sexual temptations. One newly slender housewife felt she ought to stop playing a victim role and began to assert herself in her marriage.

- *Smokers are less aware than nonsmokers of the potential health hazards of cigarettes.* False, Princeton researchers found that smokers are just as aware, but they tend to rationalize their inability to stop smoking. Cigarette smoke contains carbon monoxide, which reduces the blood's ability to carry oxygen by combining with hemoglobin; hydrocarbons (tars), which cause cancer in laboratory animals; and nicotine, a stimulant.

- *You can become short of breath by carrying on a conversation with a smoker.* True. Blood samples from people trapped with smokers in small spaces show elevations in carbon monoxide levels, which can be sufficient to trigger asthma attacks or distress in people suffering from heart disease.

- *Smokers tend to have more friends who smoke than nonsmokers have.* True. Many people smoke as a result of social influences, and it is often helpful for a married couple to try to quit smoking together. Other reasons for smoking include pleasure, stimulation, anxiety relief, physical addiction, the opportunity to do something with your hands, and just plain habit.

- *In an experiment on controlling smoking, people told that psychological tests had showed that they had great willpower were more successful at reducing smoking than people who did not receive this message.* True. Cognitive factors such as commitment to quit and humiliation at past failures to take charge of your own behavior can be powerful influences in quitting smoking. Once you have come to see yourself as a nonsmoker, self-control strategies based on the ABC's of your own behavior can help you cut down gradually or quit cold turkey. Quitting cold turkey may be somewhat more effective than cutting down with eventual hopes of quitting entirely, and it is unclear whether quitting immediately or setting a date a couple of weeks off is a superior strategy.

- *Alcohol makes people more sexually responsive.* Not in experiments at Rutgers University, in which male and female university students who drank vodka showed decreased sexual responsiveness to erotic films. Nor did belief that they had drunk alcohol lead to increased arousal.

- *Alcohol stimulates aggressive behavior.* False, but believing that you have drunk alcohol seems to lead to increased aggression. Perhaps this is because alcohol gives people aggressive roles to play in our culture. After all, you can always blame it on the liquor.
- *THC, the active ingredient in marijuana, is sexist.* Well, in a manner of speaking. THC is most abundant in the flowers and the seeds of female cannabis plants, from which marijuana is produced. Marijuana was used frequently in the last century to relieve minor aches and pains. It is currently being tested for possible medical use in treatment of glaucoma, treatment of nausea in patients receiving chemotherapy for cancer, and other medical disorders.
- *Marijuana may give you a case of the munchies.* True, marijuana stimulates the appetite and also seems to increase the pleasure of sexual activity for some individuals. On the other hand, evidence that marijuana may cause amotivational syndrome, or genetic damage, is sparse and contradictory.
- *At the turn of the century, Coca-Cola added life to its beverage through an ingredient that people now sniff—not drink.* True. This ingredient was cocaine, a substance used as a local anesthetic during the 1800s, and used by Sigmund Freud to combat his own depression. Now Coca-Cola uses coca leaves from which the cocaine has already been extracted.

V

PERSONAL GROWTH AND THE QUALITY OF LIFE

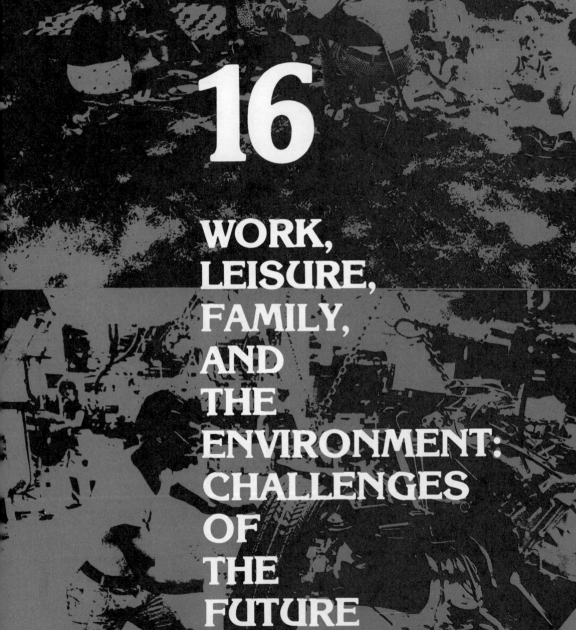

16

WORK, LEISURE, FAMILY, AND THE ENVIRONMENT: CHALLENGES OF THE FUTURE

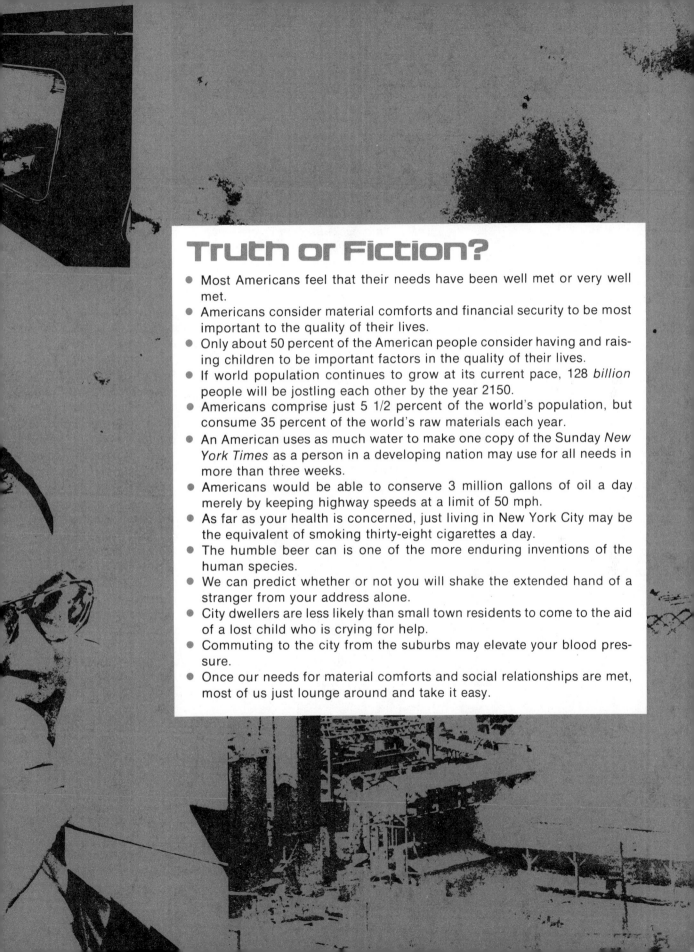

Truth or Fiction?

- Most Americans feel that their needs have been well met or very well met.
- Americans consider material comforts and financial security to be most important to the quality of their lives.
- Only about 50 percent of the American people consider having and raising children to be important factors in the quality of their lives.
- If world population continues to grow at its current pace, 128 *billion* people will be jostling each other by the year 2150.
- Americans comprise just 5 1/2 percent of the world's population, but consume 35 percent of the world's raw materials each year.
- An American uses as much water to make one copy of the Sunday *New York Times* as a person in a developing nation may use for all needs in more than three weeks.
- Americans would be able to conserve 3 million gallons of oil a day merely by keeping highway speeds at a limit of 50 mph.
- As far as your health is concerned, just living in New York City may be the equivalent of smoking thirty-eight cigarettes a day.
- The humble beer can is one of the more enduring inventions of the human species.
- We can predict whether or not you will shake the extended hand of a stranger from your address alone.
- City dwellers are less likely than small town residents to come to the aid of a lost child who is crying for help.
- Commuting to the city from the suburbs may elevate your blood pressure.
- Once our needs for material comforts and social relationships are met, most of us just lounge around and take it easy.

Mara is 30, married, with four children. Her husband is out of work. They barely subsist, even with government aid. They may have to move into a less expensive apartment in a less desirable neighborhood. She has a husband, children, relatives, friends, and responsibilities. She needs material comforts and financial security to enrich the quality of her own life.

Flo is 28, single, depressed. She has a good job and is in good physical health, but she is very lonely. She is afraid of men and does not make friends easily. Recently she has stopped thinking that she was just born shy and fearful. She is becoming desensitized to her fears and has joined an assertiveness-training group for women in order to develop social skills. She believes that she will enrich the quality of her own life if she can begin to develop relationships.

Gil is 50, married, with three children and a fine home on the South Shore, a suburb of Boston. He used to drive back and forth to work each day along the Southeast Expressway. It took an hour and a quarter back and forth into the city. He had begun to cough extensively and his blood pressure was elevated. His physician informed him that the emissions from the rush hour traffic were like smoking a pack of cigarettes a day and that fighting the traffic was more than enough stress to send his blood pressure crashing through the roof of the car. Now he commutes by mass transit boat to Boston from the South Shore, and uses the time to watch the gulls and the sun on the water and to meditate. His health has improved. He has also become involved—joining conservation groups to confront pollution and preserve the environment.

Lilia has it all—money, a fine home in Marin County to the north of San Francisco, two young children, a solid marital relationship, and her health. It took her a while to figure out just why she was so miserable. The one thing her life was lacking was meaning. She spoke to her neighbors, and now she has taken up meditation, running, and she has joined a group for personal growth and self-actualization. She still doesn't have the answers, but she has enriched the quality of her own life by beginning to look for them.

Lilia, Flo, Gil, Mara—you and me, all of us are distinct individuals, with different wants and needs, different ideas about what it would mean for our needs to be met. What are your needs? How well met are they?

In this chapter, we first have a look at how well Americans are doing. We find out what ingredients enter into the quality of our lives and how Americans rate the quality of their lives. We learn what needs Americans have and how well these needs have been met, especially in three important areas: work, leisure, and the family. Then we explore some contemporary challenges to the quality of life: the problems of overpopulation, dwindling resources, pollution, and city life. Finally we examine a "movement" that is not really a movement at all. Rather, it is what many Americans, as individuals, in small groups and occasionally in larger groups, are doing to make their own lives more meaningful. It is called the Human Potential Movement, for lack of a better name.

When you turn on the news in the evening, you hear about one problem after another—economic difficulties, social upheavals, international tensions. The list is endless. So it may be something of a surprise to you to learn that Americans feel that they are doing well. But we shall also see that doing well is not enough for Americans. No, as a nation we do not rest our hands on our bellies and begin to snooze once we have begun to do well. Rather we seem to focus our attention on striving to become everything we are capable of being. We redirect our attention to personal growth.

Critical incidents. Life experiences that have an impact on the course of future events.

THE QUALITY OF LIFE

"Think of the last time you did something very important to you or had an experience that was especially satisfying to you. What did you do or what happened that was so satisfying to you? Why did this experience seem so important or satisfying?"

What has been "a continuing source of pleasure to you"? Of trouble? What experiences have had a strong emotional impact on you?

With questions such as these, John Flanagan (1978) and his colleagues at the American Institutes for Research in Palo Alto, California, interviewed three thousand people from differing backgrounds in all regions of the United States. They were searching for **critical incidents**—important life experiences that had an impact on the quality of people's lives. No important American group was omitted. They talked to people from black Harlem and Spanish Harlem in New York City. They interviewed people in the rural areas of the South and the Midwest. They talked with senior citizens in Phoenix, Arizona, and people of Oriental extraction who lived in San Francisco's Chinatown. Suburbanites were also sampled. It was not important that the number of people interviewed in each group correspond to the size of that group among the general population. What was important was that critical incidents be sampled from every type of experiential background.

Components of the Quality of Life

From thousands of critical incidents from all over the United States, a gradual sorting and refining process was undertaken. Finally, these incidents led to the establishment of fifteen categories that Flanagan listed under five headings:

Physical and Material Well-Being

A. *Material well-being and financial security.* Having a good, secure home, good food, decent possessions, material comforts, and expectations about the future. Money is central to this need. Most people expect to meet this need through their own work or the work of their spouse.

B. *Health and personal safety.* Freedom from illness, physical and emotional fitness, freedom from accidents and hazards. This category also includes concerns about alcohol and drugs, aging and death.

Work, Leisure, Family, and the Environment

Relations with Other People

C. *Relations with parents, siblings, or other relatives.* Sharing experiences and feelings with parents and other relatives. Enjoying being with them, feelings of belonging and having people to discuss one's life with.

D. *Having and raising children.* Becoming a parent, watching one's children grow, influencing their development, and enjoying being with them.

E. *Relations with spouse (girl friend or boyfriend).* Marriage, a girl friend or boyfriend. Significant factors include sexual satisfaction, companionship, love, understanding, contentment.

F. *Relations with friends.* Being able to share activities and feelings with close friends. Being accepted by them, being valued, being able to visit and socialize with them.

Social, Community, and Civic Activities

G. *Activities related to helping or encouraging other people.* Helping children and adults as an individual or as a member of a group or organization. Participating in a volunteer group such as a church or a hospital.

H. *Activities related to local and national governments.* Keeping aware of current events, voting, influencing government regulations and laws through political and social activities.

Personal Development and Fulfillment

I. *Intellectual development.* Understanding and appreciating an intellectual subject or area. Attending school, acquiring knowledge, graduating, being able to solve intellectual problems.

J. *Personal understanding and planning.* Gaining a sense of purpose and guiding principles for life. Values. The experience of personal growth, of ability to influence the course of one's own life. Making decisions, planning. Religious or spiritual activities. Gaining personal insight and self-acceptance.

K. *Occupational role (job).* Having work that is stimulating, challenging, and rewarding. Doing well, using one's abilities, obtaining recognition, achieving.

L. *Creativity and personal expression.* Artistic creation and self-expression. Art, music, writing, photography, crafts. Hobbies.

Recreation

M. *Socializing.* Visiting friends, giving parties, attending social gatherings, making new acquaintances, interacting with people. Joining clubs, organizations.

N. *Passive and observational recreational activities.* Watching television, going to the movies, the theater, museums, spectator sports, reading.

O. *Active and participatory recreational activities.* Sports, boating, camping, fishing, hiking, running, jogging, traveling, and sightseeing. Dancing, acting, singing, playing an instrument. Games.

Different areas may mean different things to different people. As a line in a song about living in apartments goes, one person's ceiling may be another person's floor. To one person, health may mean survival. To another, it may mean being able to run ten miles in under an hour. Intellectual development may mean learning to read and write for some, and graduate university degrees to others. To you, personal expression may mean art, photography, speech, hobbies. To us, one important form of self-expression is writing.

The Quality of Life in Contemporary America: A Survey

What about the quality of life in contemporary America? Do we all have hot dogs and hamburgers in the backyard? Do we all drive to Disneyworld or fly to warmer climes during winter vacations? Are we happy with our work? Are we out there in force during pleasant weather—burning the rubber off sneakers and bicycle tires, and turning flab into muscle? Do we find our lives meaningful?

Again, we must remember that we are all individuals and that the United States is a country that houses peoples from all over the world. Some prefer tacos and burritos to hamburgers and hot dogs. (The authors freely admit their addiction to all four.) Some prefer to ski rather than seek palm trees when the thermometer dips. Still others are perfectly content watching the annual gridiron struggles on their television set.

John Flanagan (1978) and his colleagues conducted a national survey to determine how important the fifteen components of the quality of life were to 30-, 50-, and 70-year-olds, and how well needs and wants in these fifteen areas were being met. Their sample was representative of the differing population groups within the United States and involved 2,200 people: 1,000 30-year-olds, 600 50-year-olds, and 600 70-year-olds. During three-hour interviews, subjects rated the importance of each area of life (very important, important, moderately important, only slightly important, not at all important) and how well their needs and wants in each area were being met (very well, well, moderately well, only slightly well, or not at all well).

Results of this survey are shown in Table 16.1. It is clear that most Americans find their needs in these fifteen areas to be well met or very well met—especially in areas that are considered most important to the quality of life, such as health and personal safety, having a close relationship with someone of the opposite sex, having and raising children, and work. The findings are very much alike for men and for women, and even generally similar among the three age groups.

Work

In Table 16.1, we note that from 85 to 91 percent of the men and women aged 30 and 50 consider work to be important or very important. But work is markedly less important to men and women in the 70 age group. Most individuals are retired at this age, of course, and many have been forced to retire. Thus it is adjustive that work is considered less important at this time.

But notice that there is more agreement among the age groups about the degree of satisfaction experienced in the area of work. From 68 to 79 percent of the people in all age groups of both sexes report that their work needs have been well met or very well met, and the elderly (aged 70) are not more dissatisfied than the 30- and 50-year-olds.

Work, of course, means different things to different people. If we follow a hierarchy of needs similar to that of Abraham Maslow (see Chapter 4), we note

Table 16.1 Percentages of a Sample of 1,000 30-year-olds, 600 50-year-olds, and 600 70-year-olds Reporting Each of the 15 Components as Important or Very Important to Their Quality of Life[a] and Percentages (in parentheses) of the Same Sample Reporting Their Needs as Well Met or Very Well Met for Each Component[b]

Component	Male			Female		
	30 years	50 years	70 years	30 years	50 years	70 years
Physical and material well-being						
A. *Material comforts*—things like a desirable home, good food, possessions, conveniences, an increasing income, and security for the future	80 (74)	85 (73)	87 (75)	75 (76)	86 (69)	87 (74)
B. *Health and personal safety*—to be physically fit and vigorous, to be free from anxiety and distress, and to avoid bodily harm	98 (86)	96 (84)	95 (85)	98 (86)	98 (81)	96 (80)
Relations with other people						
C. *Relationships with your parents, brothers, sisters, and other relatives*—things like communicating, visiting, understanding, doing things, and helping and being helped by them	68 (81)	63 (72)	60 (74)	83 (81)	76 (72)	78 (70)
D. *Having and raising children*—this involves being a parent and helping, teaching, and caring for your children	84 (80)	85 (86)	83 (80)	93 (83)	92 (86)	88 (84)
E. *Close relationship with a husband/wife/a person of the opposite sex*	90 (84)	88 (80)	85 (88)	94 (81)	83 (71)	46 (70)
F. *Close friends*—sharing activities, interests, and views; being accepted, visiting, giving and receiving help, love, trust, support, guidance	71 (81)	76 (82)	70 (78)	79 (82)	80 (78)	87 (77)
Social, community, and civic activities						
G. *Helping and encouraging others*—this includes adults or children other than relatives or close friends. These can be your own efforts or efforts as a member of some church, club, or volunteer group.	60 (61)	71 (72)	64 (71)	71 (62)	74 (73)	78 (75)
H. *Participation in activities relating to local and national government and public affairs*	47 (54)	62 (63)	64 (63)	42 (54)	58 (64)	58 (62)
Personal development and fulfillment						
I. *Learning*—attending school, improving your understanding, or getting additional knowledge	87 (58)	68 (66)	50 (75)	81 (50)	67 (57)	60 (64)
J. *Understanding yourself* and knowing your assets and limitations, knowing what life is all about and making decisions on major life activities. For some people, this includes religious or spiritual experiences. For others, it is an attitude toward life or a philosophy.	84 (74)	84 (77)	80 (75)	92 (71)	90 (77)	88 (81)
K. *Work* in a job or at home that is interesting, rewarding, worthwhile	91 (79)	90 (77)	55 (75)	89 (79)	85 (68)	59 (79)
L. *Expressing yourself* in a creative manner in music, art, writing, photography, practical activities, or in leisuretime activities	48 (60)	39 (69)	36 (73)	53 (57)	54 (69)	58 (72)

Table 16.1 *(Continued)*

Recreation

M. *Socializing*—meeting other people, doing things with them, and giving or attending parties	48 (73)	47 (73)	49 (72)	53 (74)	49 (69)	60 (73)
N. *Reading, listening to music, or observing sporting events or entertainment*	56 (71)	45 (73)	52 (81)	53 (70)	56 (75)	63 (80)
O. *Participation in active recreation*—such as sports, traveling and sightseeing, playing games or cards, singing, dancing, playing an instrument, acting, and other such activities	59 (64)	48 (59)	47 (63)	50 (63)	52 (62)	52 (67)

[a] "At this time in your life, how important to you is _____?"

[b] For 50- and 70-year-olds, the question read, "How well are your needs and wants being met in this regard?" For the 30-year-olds, the question read, "How satisfied are you with your status in this respect?"

Source: American Psychologist, February 1978, p. 141.

first of all that work is a means to meeting basic physiological needs, such as earning the money to buy food, clothing, and shelter. There are many purposes to work. Work can provide for some or all of the following:

Physiological needs. Through working we earn money, which we exchange for food, clothing, shelter, and so forth. In Table 16.1, we note that from 75 to 87 percent of Americans considered material comforts to be important to them, and that from 69 to 76 percent of those surveyed reported their needs in this area to be well met or very well met.

Health and safety needs. Work also provides the means to medical care and to a secure home for most of us. These needs were most important to the group sampled, and from 80 to 86 percent of the respondents indicated that their health and safety needs were well met.

A sense of order. Work can be one method for organizing our lives. It gives us something to do and some place to go each working day. Of course, for those who might prefer to organize their lives around other pursuits, work may be viewed as an interference.

A sense of forward movement. For many of us, advancement on the job provides us with the feeling that we are achieving and continuing to grow through the years. Levinson and his colleagues (1978) pointed out that during the thirties, especially, workers may see themselves as striving to move upward on a job ladder within their chosen fields.

A sense of belongingness. For many Americans, work provides friends and an organization to belong to. Company outings provide opportunities for socialization. When family pressures build, or a spouse dies, work can provide the continuing, supporting environment that we need to help us adjust.

A sense of competence. Doing well on the job, no matter what it is, can provide the sense that we are capable of mastering that segment of the technology of our times with which we have become involved. Of course, some today are finding that they must seek jobs at levels that they may believe are beneath them. Sometimes persons with B.A.'s and B.S.'s compete for positions that require only a high-school diploma. Still, we can focus on doing a job well and reap satisfaction from that.

A sense of identity. Many identify with their work. A person does not just install wiring, but is an electrician. One does not just get a job in nursing—one becomes a nurse. Similarly, people may become plumbers, writers, physicians, lawyers, managers. It's not just what you do—it can also be what you are.

The great majority (85 to 91 percent) of men and women aged 30 and 50 in the Flanagan study considered work to be important or very important to their quality of life, and most reported that their work needs had been well met.

A sense of aesthetics. For some—conductors, writers, artists, copy writers, photographers, and others—work may also satisfy aesthetic needs. Doing things neatly, even typing a handsome letter or fact sheet, can satisfy some aesthetic needs.

Self-exploration. Some can define their jobs in ways that permit them to explore their own potentials. Professors may fully activate their imaginations in research, an administrator can develop novel and more efficient methods. We note in Table 16.1 that expressing oneself is less important to most people than are other areas of life, but many for whom it is extremely important manage to find some opportunities for self-expression in their work. Work for some can provide the pathway to self-actualization, while for others it is but an effort to adjust to basic challenges of life such as physiological, health, and safety needs.

Leisure

Americans seem to be rather oriented toward work, material comforts, health and safety, and the family. We note in Table 16.1 that they place less value on socializing, passive and active recreation, community and civic affairs, and self-expression.

Yet it appears that Americans do experience needs in this area. For instance, only 59 to 67 percent of Americans feel that their needs for active recreation have been well met. Only 54 to 64 percent feel that their needs to participate in government and public affairs have been well met. It may be that some Americans have difficulty meeting their needs in these areas because of new challenges to American life, such as the nature of city or suburban life, and, perhaps, the quality of the environment. For some Americans overcrowding may also interfere with opportunities to make the most of their leisure time, although America currently has less of a population crunch than do many other nations. We shall explore these issues further in the following pages.

FEELING GOOD ABOUT YOURSELF IN YOUR WORK

No longer is the scramble for the almighty dollar the major motive for America's young adults. In a recent study of 23,000 *Psychology Today* readers, money and job security were rated as less important than the "intangibles" by people making career decisions (Renwick & Lawler 1978). The opportunity to do things that make you feel good about yourself, the chance to accomplish something worthwhile, the opportunity to learn new things, the chance to develop skills and abilities—all these were ranked higher than money to today's workers.

What makes you feel good depends on your interests and your psychological needs. Psychologists have developed tests that can help us pinpoint these interests and needs when we are in doubt—tests like the Strong/Campbell Interest Inventory (SCII)

and the Edwards Personal Preference Schedule (EPPS).

The SCII can tell us how our interests compare to those of people in various lines of work. Eighteen-year follow-up studies with Stanford University students (Strong 1955) show considerable evidence that individuals tend to remain in occupational fields in which they share recreational, artistic, social, and other interests with others. Other tests, like the EPPS, help us to understand which of our psychological needs take precedence over others. Below are the fifteen psychological needs assessed by the EPPS, and a few occupations that are consistent with some of them. Can you think of occupations that might be appropriate for people who have strong psychological needs in some of the other areas?

Table 16.2 Psychological Needs and Conistent Occupations

Need	Sample Occupations
Achievement—to accomplish important goals, overcome obstacles, excel, master, surpass	
Deference—to yield to opinions of others, admire and support superiors, conform	
Order—to organize, to balance; to be neat, tidy, and precise	Accountant
Exhibition—to attain attention; to shock, amaze, excite, and entertain	Acting, modeling
Autonomy—to do things independently; to be free, defy convention, shake off restraints	
Affiliation—to join groups, be a member, belong; to be loyal, to cooperate	
Intraception—to attain insight into human feelings and motives	Psychologist
Succorance—to seek support; to be nursed, protected, guided, consoled, gratified by others	
Dominance—to wield power, to influence, direct, command, prohibit	
Abasement—to humble oneself before others; to submit, accept blame; to admit error	
Nurturance—to support, protect, guide, gratify, console	Nursing, teaching
Change—to have novel stimulation, variety, sensation	
Endurance—to persevere, to continue despite discomfort and hardship	
Heterosexuality—to be attractive, to be aroused, to form erotic relationships	
Aggression—to show strength and power; to attack, fight, take revenge	Contact sports

Family

For most Americans, having a close relationship with a husband or wife, a person of the opposite sex, is very important. Only women aged seventy seemed to report that this aspect of life has lost some of its importance, and many at this age are, of course, widowed. Still, 70 percent of the women at this age reported that this need was well met. In general, we note that men are more likely (80 to 88 percent) to report that this need has been well met than women (70 to 81 percent). As we saw in Chapter 12, more women than men are likely to remain single.

Having and raising children are important to the people sampled by Flanagan and his colleagues. From 83 to 93 percent of the individuals sampled reported that children were important, and from 80 to 86 percent reported their needs in this area to be well met. Women at the various age levels reported children to be more important than did men, although the overwhelming majority of the men also considered them important.

Many Americans in their twenties and thirties are now delaying having children, or deciding not to have children at all. They consider themselves to be childfree rather than childless. Children in our culture generally no longer make a financial contribution to their parents, as they might have when they were once needed to help on the farm and help push back the frontiers. Nor, with Social Security, are they viewed as necessary for our support in our old age.

"Mr. Thompson, I'd like a short sabbatical to find myself—
within the corporation, of course."

Americans who choose to have families these days usually do so because they wish to experience certain qualities of family life—as opposed to the life of a single person or of a childfree couple. Perhaps some also see in their children a way to seek immortality. But children are expensive. It may cost about $100,000 for a middle-class couple to raise a child. And many Americans seem to be quite ambivalent about their children. There are about one million cases of child beating reported to the authorities each year. It is estimated that for each serious abuse reported, there is at least one that escapes report, with parents successfully claiming injury was due to an accident or avoiding medical consultation altogether.

Americans are rethinking children, although there is some tendency for those who decide against children in their twenties to change their minds in their thirties or in their forties. One thing is clear: the things we once took for granted, including family structures, are now viewed as options by America's young people. More and more, we are *choosing* to adopt certain life-styles, even traditional life-styles. We are no longer just falling into them.

CONTEMPORARY CHALLENGES TO THE QUALITY OF LIFE

We all have our private and individual concerns, yet we are all also inhabitants of Spaceship Earth—our own chunk of rock warmed by a sun 93 million miles away, with a thin layer of breathable atmosphere, on some inconceivable journey through the black reaches of space.

Spaceship Earth is not the same as it used to be. To be sure, Earth has been constantly changing and evolving. Once its surface was riddled with fiery volcanoes, once the land and water were barren of life, once the continents were not shaped as they now look to us, once much of the planet was in the grips of a shroud of ice that was more than a mile deep. These things took place long ago.

But Spaceship Earth is also vastly different from what it was one hundred years ago, or even a generation ago. Earth has had its impact on us, and we have had to adjust. But we have also had our impact on the Earth, and we do not yet know if Earth will be able to adjust to us. For we have been using up the planet on which we live at a faster rate than ever before. And there are more of us than ever before.

Today our biggest challenge is ourselves—our ability to maintain and enrich the quality of our lives in the faces of overpopulation, dwindling resources, pollution, and the character of urban life.

The Challenge of Population Growth

Ramdas is more fortunate than other men in his village. At the age of thirty-five he is only beginning to look middle-aged. He owns a farm that produces more than enough food for his family, and in good years there is much left over to sell in the city. And he has six sons and two daughters.

Government officials visited the village to talk of the dangers of too many people, and women from the city spoke to his wife about **birth control**. Ramdas is tolerant of crazy people, but he knows that he has done well. He has sons to help him in the fields, sons to care for him in his old age, sons to go to the cities

Birth control. Methods to limit population growth by restricting the number of births.

Americans report that leisure activities are less important to the quality of their lives than are work, material comforts, health and safety, and the family. Yet the majority of Americans feel that their recreational needs have been well met.

when they are ready to find good jobs and send money home, and sons to conduct the last rites when he dies, so that he can be assured his soul will find peace.

Ramdas is a typical villager in the country of India, whose population exceeds that of the continents of North America and South America combined. His country's population stands at about 650 million, with 22 million Indians being born each year. But each year only 9 million Indians die. So there is a **population growth** of 13 million people each year. (Population growth = **birth rate − death rate**.) At this rate of growth, the population of his country will *double* within the next twenty-five years.

Yet India must now import food from countries such as the United States, Canada, and Australia to support its millions. Most of the Indian population live in poverty, with inadequate medical care. Almost 500,000 new people attempt to enter the job market each *month*, and the jobs are simply not there. Ramdas may understandably fear having a small family from his narrow perspective. Yet from a national or world perspective, India is in great jeopardy if its people do not adopt effective birth control measures. For food supplies and other resources will effectively limit population growth in India and elsewhere. What is not accomplished through birth control will later, unfortunately, be accomplished through **death control.**

The Population Explosion. The population of Spaceship Earth is now a bit over 4 billion. It took us thousands of years to get here. Ten thousand years ago only 3 million or so walked the entire planet—equivalent to the entire population of the infant United States during the Revolutionary War. It then took 1,000 to 2,000 years for the population to double because of factors such as **infant mortality,** disease, and population loss to predators such as the leopard. At that time we had a toehold on our planet. Our survival was far from guaranteed.

At the time Columbus walked the shores of the New World the world population had grown to almost half a billion. The reliable food supply afforded by agriculture was responsible for most of this increase. Our toehold had become a solid foothold. This was 1492.

By 1950, only 250 years later, our population had grown sixfold, to 3 billion. Medical advances had reduced the death rate, and agricultural advances had increased the food supply. Our foothold had become an armlock. But Spaceship Earth did not yet cringe.

But today we have more than 4 billion, with the world population threatening to double to 8 billion by the year 2010, or in thirty short years. We now have a crushing stranglehold on the planet. We may outrun our abilities to provide adequate nourishment, despite agricultural advances. We may deplete natural resources such as petroleum and iron ore within the next century. We may even choke on our own waste products. Our land, our air, our water are filled with the end products of attempting to supply our billions with the nourishment needed to survive. In our own country, with a relatively well-housed 220,000,000, we struggle to provide the good life. The struggle is no longer easy. We used to be self-contained, quite proud of being self-sufficient. But recently we have found it necessary to import an increasingly high percentage of the oil that America burns to provide the good life.

Sitting on Top of the Explosion. Sitting on top of an explosion is not easy, especially a population explosion. Not only are there issues involved in how you try to educate billions of people concerning methods of birth control (70 percent of the people in Ramdas' country cannot read or write), but you must also cope with attitudes that oppose the goals of birth control.

Ramdas is opposed to birth control for a number of practical and religious reasons. For him to become interested in birth control, it would be necessary

Family life does not seem in jeopardy in contemporary America. The great majority of the Flanagan sample reported a close relationship with someone of the opposite sex, and having and raising children, were very important to the quality of life.

Figure 16.1. The Curve of Human Population Growth

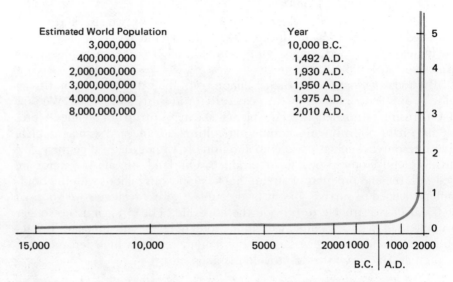

Estimated World Population	Year
3,000,000	10,000 B.C.
400,000,000	1,492 A.D.
2,000,000,000	1,930 A.D.
3,000,000,000	1,950 A.D.
4,000,000,000	1,975 A.D.
8,000,000,000	2,010 A.D.

The world population doubled between 1930 and 1975, and may double again, to 8 billion, by year 2010. If this rate of population growth were to continue, 128 billion people would be walking Spaceship Earth by the year 2150. That would mean rubbing a lot of elbows.

Zero population growth. The situation in which the birth rate balances the death rate.
Virility (vir-RILL-uh-tee). Characteristics thought to be possessed by an adult male.

for his society to be structured so that fewer children would be a material advantage rather than a threat to his standard of living and his old age. At the very least, this would require increased mechanization on the farm and government guarantees of social security. In Western societies with advanced technologies, we are now heading toward **zero population growth**—or a balancing of the birth rates and the death rates. In fact, in some Western nations, the population has experienced small decreases during the past decade.

In some cultures, the number of children is interpreted as a sign of the father's **virility**—a concept involving general "masculine strength," not just

A view of Spaceship Earth, constantly changing, still filled with magnificent beauty. Today our biggest challenge may be to maintain the Earth and the quality of our own lives in the face of overpopulation, dwindling resources, pollution, and the character of urban life.

the physical ability to father children. As the Reverend Jesse Jackson has maintained in several speeches, we will enrich the quality of our lives, and of our children's lives, when we think of parenting as the tedious, day-to-day process of responsibly raising our children—not simply conceiving them.

Religious values may also come into play in influencing attitudes toward birth control. Some religions oppose particular methods of birth control, whereas others oppose any method of birth control. When individuals hold such religious views and also place their religious values ahead of other considerations, they cannot be expected to value zero population growth. In fact, it may be that they must oppose any measures to limit the numbers of humans that come into the world. As individuals we must all make our own decisions. For some of us life will have no quality at all if we must break away from traditional religious beliefs.

The Challenge of Dwindling Resources

Have you ever noticed the way automobiles begin to fall apart after their warranties have run out? Or have you noticed how Detroit manages to come out with a brand-new series of automobiles every three years or so, just when you have managed to pay off your car, and how these new automobiles seem designed to make you absolutely miserable with your free-and-clear jalopy?

Back in the 1950s, every year the new automobiles were advertised as longer, lower, wider, and more powerful. They were packing so much horsepower into the engines that a hundred hooves were sticking out from every vent. Nowadays, of course, the swing has been to advertise the new automobiles as more efficient—more conserving of gasoline and your dollar. But every three years or so we are still exposed to a "brand-new," "more energy-efficient" line of supercars. And we may still wind up just as dissatisfied with our older gas guzzlers.

This has been called **planned obsolescence.** There are automobile executives and advertising executives who make a living at making you dissatisfied with your older, dingy, less efficient products. This is as true of television sets, appliances, and new energy-efficient homes. The reason is very simple: when you are stimulated to buy new products, people are put to work at making them. Then still other people make a profit from each product.

Planned obsolescence (ob-so-LESS-ents). The manufacture of products with a limited span of usefulness.

This is the American way of doing business. While the profit motive has worked very well to provide us with one of the highest standards of living in the world, it has also contributed to what we can call *the throwaway society*. When you are done with your car, you throw it out. When a building loses its attractiveness, the bulldozer plows it under. When you are done with your soda bottle or your beer can, most often directly into the garbage it goes. The old typewriter and stove often suffer the same fate.

In short, we are using up our national and international resources at a furious pace. And all too often it is for the construction of products that we have been conditioned to want, but may not necessarily need.

Nor can we blame just the profit motive. It is not that simple. When we consume products, other people are put to work to make more. We don't just swell the bank accounts of the few who are rich. There are more jobs for all of us.

American science and technology is the largest consumer of resources in the history of our planet. Think of the world as consisting of 1,000 people; only

55 of them are Americans, but we use as many of the world's raw materials each year as if we were 350 people (Miller 1975). We drive half of the world's automobiles, which consume more than half the world's gasoline production.

We understand that there is a **finite** or limited quantity of fossil fuels, such as petroleum and coal. But American water consumption is also extremely high, and given the effects of pollution, we could experience shortages in the near future. According to Miller (1975), the average individual in a developing nation in South America, Africa, or Asia uses about 12 gallons of water a day. Americans use 5 gallons a minute when they shower, 80 gallons when they water their lawns, 25 gallons to do a wash, 280 gallons to produce one copy of the Sunday *New York Times*, and 2,500 gallons to produce one pound of hamburger meat. An astonishing 1,800 gallons of water are used each day for each American. This is nearly 150 times as much as for the inhabitant of the developing nation. We lose 200 million gallons of water every day through leaky faucets and toilets in New York City. That's just about one gallon for every man, woman, and child in the nation.

At current rates of usage, we may be out of aluminum, copper, lead, tin, and zinc by the end of this century, give or take a year or two (Meadows et al. 1972). We should run out of iron ore in one hundred years.

What can we do about all this? Is there any hope that we can take charge of our behavior on a national scale so that we will use the resources of Spaceship Earth more wisely?

Learning to Live with Less. Sandra was only in her twenties, but she did not like the looks of her legs. They were flabby. She struggled to take off a few pounds, but this did nothing for the condition of her legs. Then she bought a bicycle. Strange things happened. In a few months, she found that she was on talking terms with her legs again. And she fell in love with her bicycle. In fact, she was now commuting the twelve miles to work by bicycle.

Strange things happened. Not only did Sandra's legs tighten up, but she no longer needed to diet to remain at her desired body weight. And when she went skiing that winter and swimming that summer, she no longer had to huff and puff herself into shape. In fact, she took staircases two and three steps at a time. She also discovered that she spent less money for gasoline, and less for wear-and-tear on her old klunker. In moments of "raised social consciousness," as she phrased it, she also delighted to recognize that she was **conserving** gasoline and contributing less to air pollution. All because she had traded in four wheels for two. She had learned to live with less and had enriched the quality of her own life by doing so.

By riding her bicycle back and forth to work, Sandra also helps conserve all the materials it requires to make a new automobile, since the life of her klunker has been extended. We are not talking only about metals and plastics. It also takes about 100,000 gallons of water to create an automobile (Miller 1975).

There are many measures that we can all take as individuals to help conserve energy. Table 16.3 lists some of them.

Will we take such measures in order to conserve energy? Several studies (e.g., Lingwood 1971; Winston 1974) have found that there is little relationship between personal awareness of environmental problems such as dwindling resources and actual personal commitment to change our behavior. Perhaps this is understandable: if we reduce our highway speeds, we may save gas in the long run, but it takes us longer to reach our destinations *now*. If we set our

Finite (FY-nite). Limited.

Conservation (kon-sir-VAY-shun). Preserving of resources through curtailing usage.

Table 16.3 Some Energy Conservation Measures

Behavioral Change	Savings on National Level
Reducing driving speeds to a limit of 50 mph	3 million gallons of oil a day
Shutting off furnace pilot lights in summer	2½ million gallons of oil a day
Washing in cold water	½ million gallons of oil a day
Resetting thermostats to 3 degrees warmer in the summer and 3 degrees cooler in the winter	½ million gallons of oil a day

Source: Bell et al. (1978), p. 355.

thermostats up in summer and down in winter, we may save fuel in the long run, but we may be just a bit uncomfortable *now*. Delayed reinforcements are less effective than immediate reinforcements. Reluctance to change our behavior now will cause our grandchildren to live on a vastly depleted Spaceship Earth.

Recycling: The New Mines. Consider stumbling across the find of the century! A vast system of conveniently located surface mines containing metals, paper, every conceivable sort of material wealth we could ever hope to use. Laid out before your vision is steel, aluminum, glass, nickel, copper, chromium, and wood.

Turn around. You will probably see the skyline of your city or the familiar buildings of your town, because you are standing by one of your city dumps.

Reusing, or **recycling**, formerly used materials is another way of conserving resources. We have neglected to do this in the throwaway society because, in most instances, the price of fresh materials has been cheaper than that of used materials. Used materials must be collected from spread-out sources and then sorted from unwanted materials.

Yet as new sources of materials become more difficult to find and more expensive, it is beginning to pay to recycle many materials. And when free economics do not make recycling pay, laws can. Laws in states like Oregon and Vermont require that expensive deposits be paid for bottled goods. Most people in these states can simply no longer afford to litter the countryside with beer bottles.

If we also paid deposits on our automobiles, used cars would no longer litter the countryside. It would become more worthwhile for manufacturers to exhaust all previously used materials before paying for new ones. Making Sunday editions from recycled paper would save thousands of acres of timber every week.

New Sources of Energy: Riding the Fires of the Sun. **Solar energy** is nothing new. Our oil and coal deposits represent the **fossils** of millions of generations of plants that lived and died before anyone was around to notice. The sun provided the energy that enabled these plants to combine air and water into food, and give birth to new generations.

We are now seeking new ways to harness the energy of the sun, to store this energy, and to convert it into heat in winter and coolness in summer. For the time being, solar energy is expensive. The average family would have to have the costs of solar heating added to their mortgage on a new home. But the

Recycling (ree-SIGH-kling). Reusing, processing so as to make usable again, rather than throwing away.

Solar energy (SO-lurr). Power derived from the sun.
Fossil. Remains or traces of prehistoric plant or animal life.

Work, Leisure, Family, and the Environment

A rather strange-looking building powered by solar energy. Solar technology is still in its infancy, yet it holds the promise of a practically infinite and pollution-free source of energy.

technology is advancing, and we do not have to be concerned about running out of sunlight. At least for a few billion years.

We have more than enough coal for the next century or so, and we can also expand our reliance on nuclear energy. But these sources of energy have strong negative environmental impacts: fumes from burning of coal contribute to air pollution, and nuclear waste products are highly poisonous. These forms of energy have thus been labeled **dirty**.

Dirty. **Polluting.**

In the future we may also be able to harness the winds through "windmills" that will dwarf their ancestors of the countryside. We may harness the oceans' tides, we may harness the heat within the Earth itself. For the time being, our best bets may be a combination of conservation and development of solar energy.

The Challenge of Pollution

Spaceship Earth is vast. At the rate of five hundred miles an hour, it take six hours to fly from New York to Los Angeles. Yet this is less than one-eighth the distance around the Earth. Suspended in time and space between these two points on the Earth, you are overwhelmed by peace and beauty. You seem disconnected from everyday cares and from people on the surface below, who are too small to be seen.

Yet the works of people are quite visible. In some places, geometric shapes of farms stretch from horizon to horizon. Over the rivers, you see different-colored patches in the water—greens and blues where chemical plants have emptied their waste products into the water. You see highways snaking up and down the sides of the Rockies, among the evergreens and the snow. When you reach the West Coast, you may not see Los Angeles at all. It may be lost in a hazy, off-white blur we call **smog**—a lethal combination of smoke and fog.

No, as individuals, you cannot see us from an airplane winging across the country at a height of six or seven miles. But you can see our handiwork. And all too often, our handiwork leaves ugliness, desolation, and poison behind.

Air Pollution: Is Breathing Good for You? The smog over Los Angeles is one example of **air pollution**—air with concentrations of toxic substances high enough to damage living beings. The most common source of air pollution is the carbon monoxide from cars and trucks. Carbon monoxide decreases our ability to carry oxygen in our blood, and may lead to headaches, cramps, nausea, and vision problems. Other emissions from cars and trucks compound the problem.

Emissions from cars and trucks may also turn brownish when exposed to the sun, and stink. **Industrial smog** is gray and sooty, a side product of the burning of coal and oil.

In Los Angeles, people are advised to remain indoors on especially smoggy days, and to avoid activities that could lead to deeper breathing, such as jogging. But do not think that we are singling out Los Angeles. Living in New York City may be the equivalent of smoking thirty-eight cigarettes a day (Rotton 1979). But do not think that we are singling out the United States. Industrial smog killed four thousand people in London during the air pollution disaster of 1952.

Women in St. Louis may go through several pairs of stockings in one week. This has nothing to do with leg watchers burning holes. Industrial smog can combine with moisture in the air to dissolve the fabric. Industrial smog also causes serious crop damage in the industrial Northeast and in Southern California. When industrial smog can eat away at the mortar in brick buildings, it is not surprising that it is a factor in bronchitis and emphysema.

Water Pollution: Silent Streams and Dead Oceans. When you fly from New York to London, or from Los Angeles to Hawaii, it seems incredible that anyone is concerned about water shortages or about **water pollution**. Spaceship Earth's water supply seems endless.

Yet all that water in the oceans is too salty for human use, except at vast expense. While the average American uses 1,800 gallons of water a day, most people on the planet do not have enough water for their day-to-day purposes—or their supplies are becoming increasingly contaminated. Water pollution is making water unfit for use through some kind of contamination.

Off the coast of New York City, to the southeast, there is a vast dead territory on the ocean floor. A diver swimming in this forbidding region would find no fish. The water would be brown and cloudy—sunlight from above trapped out. The diver would swim across an underwater landscape of cans and rotting peels, bottles and unknown chemicals. For this is one dumping ground for the garbage of New York City.

Waterways all across the country have become dumping grounds for the throwaway society. Industrial plants dump their chemical wastes into rivers and streams. Cities flush their human excrement into the same bodies of water. Thus these bodies of water become unfit to drink, or even to swim in.

Industrial emissions foul the air in this picture of a Pittsburgh steel mill in the 1880s. Industrial pollution may no longer be so murderous, but it is still estimated that just living in New York City may be as harmful as smoking 38 cigarettes a day.

Smog. A mixture of smoke and fog.
Air pollution. Air with concentrations of harmful substances that are sufficient to damage living beings.
Industrial smog. A particularly dirty sort of smog which contains high concentrations of sulphur.
Water pollution. Concentrations of harmful substances in water that are sufficient to damage living beings.

Work, Leisure, Family, and the Environment

The waterways even suffer from runoffs of the **pesticides** (such as **DDT**) and fertilizers that we use to grow our crops.

Land Pollution: Beer Cans and Sandboxes.   A beer can is an incredible invention. It is easy to hold, it prevents spoilage and evaporation, and if made of aluminum, it lasts just about forever. The summer afternoons of the Arizona deserts, the wintry nights of Minnesota and Montana would take their toll on us—but they have no effect on this incredible invention: the beer can. So beer cans and other inventions like it not only litter our landscape—they will not rot away in a dozen lifetimes. They are not **biodegradable**—they will not be broken down by the microscopic life of Spaceship Earth.

But littering is one small factor in land pollution, the process of altering the land so that it cannot be used for a given purpose. If your flight across the United States takes you over the hills of western Pennsylvania, you will notice great gouges in the land. You might think of them as sandboxes in which some gigantic children had scooped out every tree and blade of grass with mile-wide shovels. But these are no sandboxes. Here and in other states millions of acres have been overturned through the process of **strip mining.** Here and there it is economical to mine coal by simply ripping back the growing earth, rather than digging down into it.

If your flight should happen to bring you into Los Angeles on a clear day, you may see roads and highways that seem to go on forever. An increasing proportion of the land we inhabit is being devoted to the concrete and asphalt of our roadways.

Meeting the Challenge of Pollution: A Question of Values.   It may be difficult to believe, but we have already won most of the conceptual or intellectual battles concerning ways to reduce or eliminate pollution. Put simply, we know how to do a great deal more than we are now doing. The reason that we do not put everything we know into use is simple: money.

We can cut down on air pollution by creating vast and efficient mass transit systems—systems so comfortable and convenient that people would want to use them. But we don't because of money. We can cut down on industrial smog through trapping the substances that do the damage, or recycling them and burning them. But we don't do this often enough, or convert our industrial plants rapidly enough, because of money.

Human waste products and the chemical waste products from industrial plants can be treated before they are released into waterways. But this is expensive. Similarly, we have the technology and even the political structures that would permit us to end the use of products that are not biodegradable. We can outlaw strip mining if we are willing to pay more for ore. With more mass transportation and more use of our legs, through walking or bicycling, the problem of the concrete and asphalt landscape would take care of itself.

The problem is a policy gap—a gap between the technology we have available, and the money and the willpower to use it. Why this reluctance? Values.

What will enrich the quality of your life? Are vast quantities of material comforts of greatest importance to you, or would you be willing to pay a bit more for products so that they could be produced in ways that would not pollute the environment, in ways that recycled materials wherever possible?

What will motivate you to do with fewer material comforts? Take a walk outside and sniff the air. Is it clean, or do you sometimes wonder if you are damaging your lungs with every breath? Carefully observe the next sunrise or sunset. Is it a glorious interplay of bright colors that make their way up and down the spectrum, or is it a weak growing or dimming of sickly oranges, browns, and grays? Look all around you. Do you see blues and greens, or do you see grays and dingy browns?

By cutting back just a bit in material comforts, you may be enriching the quality of your life in many other areas, starting with personal health and passive and active recreation. By working with others to bring about change, you may also begin to meet your needs to have your say in governmental and public affairs. These choices are your own. It is up to you to determine what will enrich the quality of your own life.

The Challenge of City Life

What would you do if a perfect stranger approached you on the street with hand extended? Would you take the hand and shake it? Or would you rebuff this stranger? What if we were to tell you that we would be very happy to make bets on what you would do? All we would have to know is if you were in a large city or a small town. Knowing that one bit of information, we would be quite convinced that we could make a living at predicting the outcome.

The fact of the matter is that city dwellers react or adjust to strangers differently than do people who live in small towns. In one experiment, Stanley Milgram (1977) had undergraduates approach strangers, with their hands extended in a friendly manner. In a small town, 66 percent of those approached accepted the hand and shook it. But only 38.5 percent of the city dwellers would take the handshake. If your friends will accept even bets, and you predict yes for small towns and no for cities, you will become rich very quickly.

For most of us, city life is a central factor in the quality of our lives. In 1800 only 6 percent of all Americans lived in metropolitan areas, but today more than 70 percent of the population resides in or adjacent to the city (Gottmann 1966).

Where Do You Stand?

A SURVEY OF ATTITUDES TOWARD AND KNOWLEDGE ABOUT THE ENVIRONMENT

Where do you stand? Do you think that we are in serious jeopardy of destroying the quality of our lives through our mistreatment of the environment, or do you believe that all this talk is nonsense? Do you talk a good game of being devoted to measures such as conservation and recycling, but then keep your thermostat high in winter and low in summer? How much do you know about the problems facing the environment—and all of us?

Answer the following true-false and multiple choice items. Then check the scoring key at the end of the chapter to compare your answers to those of members of the Sierra Club—a conservationist group—college students, and individuals not in college.

1. I'd be willing to ride a bicycle or take the bus to work in order to reduce air pollution.   T   F
2. I guess I've never actually bought a product because it had a lower polluting effect.   T   F
3. I feel people worry too much about pesticides on food products.   T   F
4. I would probably never join a group or club that is concerned solely with ecological issues.   T   F
5. I keep track of my congressman's and senators' voting records on environmental issues.   T   F
6. It frightens me to think that much of the food I eat is contaminated with pesticides.   T   F
7. I would be willing to use a rapid transit system to help reduce air pollution.   T   F
8. I have never written a congressman concerning pollution problems.   T   F
9. It genuinely infuriates me to think that the government doesn't do more to help control pollution of the environment.   T   F
10. I'm not willing to give up driving on a weekend due to a smog alert.   T   F
11. I have contacted a community agency to find out what I can do about pollution.   T   F
12. I feel fairly indifferent to the statement, "The world will be dead in forty years if we don't remake the environment."   T   F
13. I'm not really willing to go out of my way to do much about ecology since that's the government's job.   T   F
14. I don't make a special effort to buy products in recyclable containers.   T   F
15. I become incensed when I think about the harm being done to plant and animal life by pollution.   T   F
16. I would donate a day's pay to a foundation to help improve the environment.   T   F
17. I have attended a meeting of an organization specifically concerned with bettering the environment.   T   F
18. I'm usually not bothered by so-called noise pollution.   T   F
19. I would be willing to stop buying products from companies guilty of polluting the environment, even though it might be inconvenient.   T   F
20. I have switched products for ecological reasons.   T   F
21. I get depressed on smoggy days.   T   F
22. I'd be willing to write my congressman weekly concerning ecological problems.   T   F

23. I have never joined a cleanup drive.   T   F

24. When I think of the ways industries are polluting, I get frustrated and angry.   T   F

25. I probably wouldn't go from house to house to distribute literature on the environment.   T   F

26. I have never attended a meeting related to ecology.   T   F

27. The whole pollution issue has never upset me too much since I feel it's somewhat overrated.   T   F

28. I would not be willing to pay a pollution tax even if it would considerably decrease the smog problem.   T   F

29. I subscribe to ecological publications.   T   F

30. I rarely ever worry about the effects of smog on myself and family.   T   F

31. Soil pollution is generally due to: (A) sparse rains, (B) improper farming methods, (C) poisonous metals, (D) overfertilization, (E) poor crop rotation.

32. Most smog in our big cities comes from: (A) automobiles, (B) supersonic jets, (C) industrial plants, (D) large trucks, (E) refuse disposal.

33. High concentrates of chlorinated hydrocarbon residues: (A) cause sheep to die, (B) are found in large amounts in our atmosphere, (C) accumulate in flesh-eating birds and upset breeding behavior, (D) are no longer legal in pesticides, (E) are readily biodegradable.

34. Mercury has been found at unacceptable levels in: (A) fruit, (B) vegetables, (C) seafood, (D) beer, (E) soft drinks.

35. Which of the following does not appreciably reduce pollution by automobiles? (A) properly tuned engine, (B) high octane gas, (C) low lead gas, (D) smog control devices, (E) propane engines.

36. The most common pollutants of water are: (A) arsenic, silver nitrates, (B) hydrocarbons, (C) carbon monoxide, (D) sulfur, calcium, (E) nitrates, phosphates.

37. Ecology is best described as the study of: (A) the relationship between man and the environment, (B) the relationship between organisms and the environment, (C) pollution and its control, (D) the environment, (E) recycling of products.

38. Which of the following materials usually takes longest to decompose? (A) tin, (B) iron, (C) copper, (D) aluminum, (E) steel.

39. Birds and fish are being poisoned by: (A) iron, (B) mercury, (C) silver, (D) lead, (E) magnesium.

40. All but one of the following decompose in ocean water: (A) sewage, (B) garbage, (C) tin cans, (D) plastic bags, (E) chemical fertilizer.

41. What is the harmful effect of phosphates on marine life? They (A) cause cancer, (B) render fish sterile, (C) induce nervous reactions in fish, (D) make H_2O cloudy, (E) feed algae, thereby suffocating fish.

42. Which of the following well-known groups is primarily interested in conservation issues? (A) Boy Scouts of America, (B) The Sierra Club, (C) Kiwanis, (D) 4-H Club, (E) The Ecology Association.

43. Practically all the lead in our atmosphere is caused by: (A) cars, (B) industrial plants, (C) airplanes, (D) burning refuse, (E) cigarettes.

44. How long does DDT take to deteriorate into harmless chemicals? (A) it never does, (B) 10 to 20 months, depending on the weather, (C) about 200 years, (D) about 400 years, (E) anywhere from several days to several years.

45. Ecology assumes that man is a(n) —————— part of nature. (A) differential, (B) integral, (C) inconsequential, (D) superior, (E) original.

Source: Test from Maloney, M. P., Ward, M. O., & Braucht, C. N. A revised scale for the measurement of ecological attitudes and knowledge. *American Psychologist*, 1975, 30, 787–790. Copyright 1975 by the American Psychological Association. Reprinted by permission.

As shown in these views of Florence (above right), Amsterdam (left), and New York (above left), cities tend to have their own special character.

The Character of the City. If you had to describe the place in which you live in just a few words, what would you say? Stanley Milgram (1970) found that the cities of New York, London, and Paris all had rather distinct characters. New York tends to be distinguished from other cities by its physical properties, especially the "skyscraper," its hectic pace, and its stress. Paris is impressive because of both its physical majesty and the qualities of the people.

Cities may have their distinctive characters, but most cities tend to have certain features in common that set them apart from small town or rural life. Cities are the business centers of the world, where large corporations build, sell, and promote their products. They have museums of art and natural history, theaters, symphonies, and professional sports. They are transportation centers—if you want to travel from a small town in the United States to a small town in another country, you will probably have to find your way through airports in at least two major cities.

Cities also have crowding, pollution, crime, and social tensions. Admission to these world centers is not free.

The Effects of City Life. What happens when you walk down the busiest, noisiest block in your city during rush hour? Are you jostled by other people as they rush by? Are you assaulted by cigar and cigarette smoke, by exhaust from cars and buses? Are your ears pounded by horns, sirens, and the grinding gears of buses? Is there a rumble of subway cars beneath your feet? Do you find yourself clutching your purse or pocketbook just a bit more strongly, or do you find yourself checking to see that your wallet is still in your pocket? Is there some sort of psychological pushing and pulling on you that seems to come from all the people who are milling around you?

Some psychologists (e.g., Glass & Singer 1972) suggest that city life can be harmful because it exposes us to many sources of stress—noise, crowding, fear of crime, Type A behavior, polluted air. The negative elements of city life give rise to bodily responses to stress—continued overarousal. Overarousal may lead to defensive coping reactions, such as defensive avoidance or aggression.

Other psychologists (such as Milgram 1970) point to the sum total of stimulation that acts on city dwellers, and maintain that we can tolerate just so much stimulation, even positive. City dwellers may suffer harmful effects from stimulus overload. There are just too many things happening all at once, too many environmental changes, and too much of even a good thing can make us ill. Overload theorists predict that we will act to try to reduce the overwhelming amount of stimulation the city affords.

Adjustment to City Life. You may have heard that people who live in cities are not as friendly as people who live in small towns. We have seen that city dwellers are less likely to shake the hands of strangers than people in small towns. What about eye contact? What do you do when a stranger just looks at you? Do you look back, or do you avoid the glance?

In one study (Newman & McCauley 1977) confederates of the experimenters simply sought out eye contact with strangers passing by in center-city Philadelphia, Bryn Mawr (a Philadelphia suburb), and Parkesburg, a rural

Large cities can so overload us with stimulation that we may not even notice this gentleman strolling leisurely across New York's Fifth Avenue.

Table 16.4 Percentage of Passersby Making Eye Contact with Experimenters at Post Office and Stoire in Parkesburg, Bryn Mawr, and Philadelphia

Sex of Experimenter	Parkesburg		Bryn Mawr		Philadelphia	
	Post Office	Store	Post Office	Store	Post Office	Store
Female	80	82	45	50	15	18
Male	75	73	40	45	12	10

Source: Newman and McCauley (1977).

town in Pennsylvania. The results are shown in Table 16.4. You will note that eye contact was accepted more often in Bryn Mawr than Philadelphia, and still more often in the small town. Passersby also seem to have been willing to make somewhat more eye contact with females than with males at each location. Can it be that we are less likely to expect violence when we encourage social interaction with female strangers?

But here we are talking about contact with adults. Surely, city dwellers would open their hearts to children's needs as readily as residents of small towns, wouldn't they? Perhaps not. Milgram (1977) found that when children pretended to be lost, strangers in small towns were more likely to offer them a helping hand than strangers in cities. We are unlikely to fear small children, so perhaps city dwellers are more concerned with reducing the sum total of the stimulation to which they have to respond, or figure that some municipal authority will attend to the child's needs.

We should also keep in mind that city dwellers may perceive themselves as being more anonymous than small town residents. Thus they may feel that their lack of social behavior or helping behavior is unlikely to be found out by individuals whose judgments they value. If you ignore a crying child in the street in midtown Manhattan, your spouse is not likely to condemn you for it that evening.

In a study of people who have moved into the city from rural areas (Franck et al. 1974), it was found that newcomers become more deliberate in their daily activities. They use more planning ahead to take safety precautions, and they increase their vigilance.

The Flight to the Suburbs. Since the end of World War II, Americans have made an enormous effort to have the best of both worlds—the stimulation and financial opportunities of the city combined with the peace and safety of the country. More people now live in American suburbs than within city limits.

Mowing lawns, picking weeds, driving the kids to the movies, barbecuing in the backyard, interchanging storm windows and screens, paying for the second car, chatting across the back fence—these have become elements in the lives of millions of Americans.

For many it is the best of all possible worlds. The cultural events of the city are available, and the serenity of being separated from neighbors by patches of lawn is also a fact of life. Vast shopping malls and industrial complexes have followed the population out to the suburbs, so that, for many, all visits into the city have become voluntary and infrequent. Life often means traveling from one suburb to another.

For others, the dark side of suburban life remains the daily necessity of trudging into the city to work. Some people spend one of every eight waking hours fighting traffic on freeways. For them, suburban life may be taking its

toll. Greater commuting times and distances are associated with elevated blood pressure (Stokols et al.1977).

Yet for those who have adequate mass transportation, commuting time can be an opportunity for meditating, writing reports, reading the newspaper, or just sitting back and thinking. For a few others who commute by boat from Marin County to San Francisco, or from the South Shore into Boston, commuting is considered a religious experience.

The American suburbs— heaven or hell? Whether suburbs represent the height of the good life or a cultural wasteland, the majority of Americans now live in them.

THE HUMAN POTENTIAL MOVEMENT

Brad is having an uplifting experience—literally. Six people whom he has not met until today have cradled him gently in their arms and raised him from the floor. His eyes are closed. They hold him in midair, rock him gently back and forth, and walk with him about the room. Brad is no paralyzed patient in a hospital. He has just become a member of an encounter group—a personal growth group in which he hopes he will be able to learn to trust other people and relate to them as individual human beings, not blurs passing him on the sidewalk. To develop his potential, he wants to break down some of the defensive barriers instilled in him by his parents and by city life.

Joy moves an orange about in the palms of her hands, focusing on the rough texture of the rind. Now she rolls it slowly across her face and experiences its temperature against her skin. Then she peels it, studying the squirting juice, the harsh crackling of the rind. She smells the orange luxuriously, breaks it into sections, and eats it—one section at a time. Joy is in a **sensory awareness group,** attempting to become more sensitive to the sights, sounds, smells, tastes, and feel of a world that she feels she has too long taken for granted.

Brad and Joy are both participating in what psychologists have come in recent years to term the **Human Potential Movement.** This is no organized movement—there is no central governing group that provides leadership and

Sensory awareness group. A group in which members learn to become more sensitive to the sights, odors, touch, and other characteristics of objects in the environment and of each other.
Human Potential Movement (po-TEN-shul). The activity of many individuals who are attempting to actualize themselves, to become whatever they are capable of being.

Work, Leisure, Family, and the Environment

487

For some, commuting to work from the suburbs is a lonely, dulling daily trek . . .

. . . while for others, commuting almost takes on the character of a religious experience.

organizing principles. Rather, this is the term given to a number of groups, activities, and individual efforts that seem to have sprung up in contemporary America to give us all added dimensions to our lives.

Social critics noted as early as during the 1960s that Americans had been generally successful at achieving material comforts. While large pockets of poverty still existed, and certainly are with us today, many Americans had earned suburban homes with television antennae stretched across the suburban treescapes. Two and even three cars reflected the sun in the driveways, and power lawn mowers buzzed across green lawns like a plague of angry electric insects. But material comforts had too often been achieved at the expense of an emotional or personal emptiness—a loss of values and meaning in life.

For too many of us, the hectic pace of contemporary life may have caused us to lose touch with the beauty of the world, and with our personal quests for meaningfulness and understanding. In order to meet financial needs and social demands, too many of us may have had to scurry along with blinders on. Once, perhaps, we availed ourselves of the museums and theaters of the city. But now many of us catch the last train in and the first train out, or fight the infinite freeways, and then run along the streets. Culture may require special weekend treks, when we are exhausted already from the enterprises of the week. To meet our financial needs and still survive, many of us have constructed habitual, brusque, unfeeling ways of dealing with many people and many events. These habitual reactions are often efficient, at least for our pocketbooks, but they are also narrow and rigid. Our encounters with others become restricted; for many of us, even our mates and children have become strangers.

In order to meet the challenges of contemporary life and restore meaning and purpose to life, many Americans have bought self-help books or joined groups to enhance the quality of their lives through improving their relationships or their self-knowledge. Others are attempting to develop their creative potentials more fully. Couples attend weekend **marriage encounter groups** in an effort to restore intimacy in their relationships, or go for transactional analysis (TA) to discover if they are relating to one another as adults, parents, or children. Insight-oriented therapies, like psychoanalysis or nondirective therapy, in the past were usually sought by individuals with pressing personal problems and inner conflicts. Now they are also undertaken by people who wish to undertake personal trips to discover the far reaches of their own minds, or the personal meanings of childhood experiences.

Marriage encounter group. Guided experiences in which married couples become increasingly sensitive to the needs of their partners.

Beyond the Challenges of Contemporary Life

The Human Potential Movement has not only helped us to meet the challenges of contemporary life. It has also stressed personal growth—movement beyond meeting the challenges of life in very personal, individualized directions. The reason for this is simple: many people who have been highly successful at coping with stress, many people who are financially secure and happy with their interpersonal relationships, are still not content. They want more. Much more. Not necessarily more money, not necessarily more relationships. Part of the motivation is the pleasure of the process of attempting to discover what will further satisfy and enhance the self.

Beyond the meeting of the basic challenges of life lies self-actualization. Abraham Maslow predicted that once our basic survival needs were met, we would turn to higher level pursuits—social recognition, love, even a purely personal endeavor to make of ourselves whatever we are capable of becoming. We would attempt to actualize ourselves fully.

But what will we become when we are self-actualized? What potentials lie deep within each of us, waiting to be released and enhanced in the summers of our being? The answer, of course, is an individual answer. For Shakespeare it

This encounter group member is having an uplifting experience.

was poetry. For Mozart and Beethoven it was music. For Picasso it was art. For others, self-expression and creativity may take a social form—the building of a hospital, volunteer work, organization of a social group. Some may be more oriented toward the out-of-doors: mountain climbing, skiing, swimming across the sands of the ocean floor. What is right for us may also change and grow. Next year's daily activity may be this year's wildest fantasy. We are all distinct individuals. What will enrich the quality of your life may have little meaning for your neighbor.

Millions of Americans have now joined this Human Potential Movement. Some have done so quite consciously, such as those who have joined encounter or sensory awareness groups. Many more have turned to meditation, yoga, vegetarianism, adult education in their own school districts. It seems that despite the challenges of changing times, of stress, of emotions, of relationships, and of self-control, despite the challenges of the environment and of urban life, more Americans are involved in the quest for the self than ever before.

Perhaps as a nation we are beginning to realize that we have a right, even a need, to be selfish in the best sense of the word—that is, to try to learn to understand and enhance our selves. Once we assert that we are ourselves, the centers of our own worlds, we begin the search to find out just who and what we are. Perhaps as a nation, we are beginning to say, "I am myself, the center of my world. But who am I?"

Summary

- *Most Americans feel that their needs have been well met or very well met.* True. A study by the American Institutes for Research isolated fifteen factors most important in the consideration of the quality of our lives. Then samples of 1,000 30-year-olds, 600 50-year-olds, and 600 70-year-olds indicated that their needs in the areas they personally considered to be important revealed that the majority of their needs and wants had been met.

- *Americans consider material comforts and financial security to be most important to the quality of their lives.* False. Personal health and safety are most important. While material comforts are listed as important. having a close relationship with someone of the opposite sex, having and raising children, and work are all considered more essential.

- *Only about 50 percent of the American people consider having and raising children to be important factors in the quality of their lives.* False. Among the groups sampled, from 83 to 93 percent of the respondents rated having and raising children as important or very important. Less important areas included governmental activities and public affairs, self-expression, socializing, and passive and active recreation.

- *If world population continues to grow at its current pace, 128 billion people will be jostling each other by the year 2150.* True. World population is now doubling every thirty-five years. Begin with a figure of 4 billion for the year 1975, and figure it out for yourself. Population growth equals the birth rate minus the death rate. Modern medicine and modern agriculture have decreased the death rate, and the birth rate remains high in many areas of the world, especially in underdeveloped, largely agricultural nations.

- *Americans comprise just 5 1/2 percent of the world's population, but consume 35 percent of the world's raw materials each year.* True. We belong to a throwaway society in which planned obsolescence seems to keep the economy at a high level. We drive half the world's automobiles and use more than half the world's oil supply.

- *An American uses as much water to make one copy of the Sunday* New York Times *as a person in a developing nation may use for all needs in more than three weeks.* True. It takes 280 gallons of water to produce one copy of the Sunday edition of a newspaper, whereas an individual in a developing nation may use a total of 12 gallons of water a day for all purposes. Although the water supply seems renewable, more streams and rivers become polluted each day because of human and industrial wastes and runoffs of materials like pesticides and fertilizers.

- *Americans would be able to conserve 3 million gallons of oil a day merely by keeping highway speeds at a limit of 50 mph.* True, but most Americans are unwilling to make material sacrifices because the sacrifices must be made now, and the consequences of failing to make sacrifices may be experienced by our children or our grandchildren. In addition to conserving fuel, we shall make more of an effort to switch to truly endless energy sources, such as solar energy, in the future. But for the time being, solar energy is not as economical as oil or nuclear power.

- *As far as your health is concerned, just living in New York City may be the equivalent of smoking thirty-eight cigarettes a day.* True, according to one study. Air is polluted by emissions from cars and trucks, industrial plants, and other sources. Smog is not only harmful to human lungs, it also destroys crops and even eats away at the mortar in brick buildings.

- *The humble beer can is one of the more enduring inventions of the human species.* True, an aluminum beer can can last a thousand years. The countryside is becoming polluted with beer cans and other materials that are not biodegradable. In order to put an end to such pollution, we may need to change materials and also to make it financially unwise to throw away items like cans and bottles.

- *We can predict whether or not you will shake the extended hand of a stranger from your address alone.* To some degree, true. City dwellers will rebuff the handshake two of three times, but small town residents will accept the hand in the majority of instances. It may be that adjusting to life in the city requires measures such as being more vigilant of strangers and cutting down on the total quantity of stimulation we allow ourselves to react to.

- *City dwellers are less likely than small town residents to come to the aid of a lost child who is crying for help.* True. City dwellers are also less likely to engage in eye contact with strangers in public places like post offices and stores.

- *Commuting to the city from the suburbs may elevate your blood pressure.* True. People moved to the suburbs to combine the financial and cultural advantages of city life with the peace and safety of country life. But those who must do combat with rush hour traffic twice a day may pay a dear price. In the future, these problems may be ameliorated by movement of more business and industry to the suburbs, and development of more efficient and comfortable mass transit systems.

Work, Leisure, Family, and the Environment

- *Once our needs for material comforts and social relationships are met, most of us just lounge around and take it easy.* False. Self-expression and personal understanding were rated as important by most Americans. It seems that when many of us have satisfied our needs for health, safety, material goods, financial security, and close relationships, we then go on to attempt to enhance ourselves by expanding our awareness and exploring the meaning of life. This factor has given rise to what is called the Human Potential Movement.

KEY FOR "WHERE DO YOU STAND?" TEST

This test consists of four subscales: (1) your *Emotional Response* to environmental problems, (2) your *Verbal Commitment* to making changes that will be helpful for the environment, (3) your actual or *Behavioral Commitment,* which may differ from your verbal commitment, and (4) your *Knowledge* about environmental issues.

Give yourself one point for each of the answers below. Score each subscale separately. Then compare your scores to those of other college students, members of the Sierra Club (a group concerned with environmental issues), and noncollege individuals.

Emotional Response: 3-F, 6-T, 9-T, 12-F, 15-T, 18-F, 21-T, 24-T, 27-F, 30-F
Verbal Commitment: 1-T, 4-F, 7-T, 10-F, 13-F, 16-T, 19-T, 22-T, 25-F, 28-F
Behavioral Commitment: 2-F, 5-T, 8-F, 11-T, 14-F, 17-T, 20-T, 23-F, 26-F, 29-T
Knowledge: 31-C, 32-A, 33-C, 34-C, 35-B, 36-E, 37-B, 38-D, 39-B, 40-D, 41-E, 42-B, 43-A, 44-C, 45-B

Mean Scores for Three Groups

	Emotional Response	Verbal Commitment	Behavioral Commitment	Knowledge
Sierra Club	9.00	8.68	8.61	11.35
College students	7.77	6.37	3.61	8.64
Noncollege	6.12	5.02	1.97	6.75

Note that for Sierra Club members, the behavioral or actual commitment to environmental issues is compatible with the verbal or expressed commitment, but that college students and noncollege persons show a greater discrepancy between verbal and behavioral commitments. In other words, their words speak louder than their actions.
Source: Maloney et al., 1975.

References

ABEL, G. G., BARLOW, D. H., BLANCHARD, E. B., & GUILD, D. The components of rapists' sexual arousal. Paper presented to the American Psychiatric Association, Anaheim, Calif., May 1975.

ABRAMSON, L. Y., SELIGMAN, M. E. P., & TEASDALE, J. D. Learned helplessness in humans: Critique and reformulation. *Journal of Abnormal Psychology*, 1978, 87, 49–74.

ABRAMSON, P. R. Familial variables related to the expression of violent aggression in preschool-age children. *Journal of Genetic Psychology*, 1973, 122, 345–346.

ADORNO, T. W., FRENKEL-BRUNSWICK, E., LEVINSON, D. J., & SANFORD, R. N. *The authoritarian personality*. New York: Harper, 1950.

AGRAS, S., SYLVESTER, D., & OLIVEAU, D. The epidemiology of common fears and phobias. Unpublished manuscript, 1969. (Cited in G. C. Davison & J. M. Neale, *Abnormal psychology*, 2d ed. New York: John Wiley, 1978, p. 135.)

AKISKAL, H. S., & McKINNEY, W. T., JR. Overview of recent research in depression: Integration of ten conceptual models into a comprehensive clinical frame. *Archives of General Psychiatry*, 1975, 32, 285–305.

ALLEN, V. L., & LEVINE, J. M. Social support and conformity: The role of independent assessment of reality. *Journal of Experimental Social Psychology*, 1971, 7, 48–58.

American Cancer Society. *The dangers of smoking, the benefits of quitting*. New York: Author, 1972.

American Psychiatric Association. *Diagnostic and statistical manual of the mental disorders (DSM-II)*, 2d ed. Washington, D.C.: Author, 1968.

American Psychiatric Association. *Diagnostic and statistical manual—III* (draft). Washington, D.C.: Author, 1977.

AMIR, M. *Patterns in forcible rape*. Chicago: University of Chicago Press, 1971.

APA Monitor, January 1978, 9, 5 & 23.

APA Monitor, February 1978, 9, 4.

ARDREY, R. *African genesis*. New York: Dell, 1961.

ARDREY, R. *The territorial imperative*. New York: Dell, 1966.

ASCH, S. E. *Social psychology*. New York: Prentice-Hall, 1952.

ASCHER, L. M., & EFRAN, J. S. Use of paradoxical intention in a behavioral program for sleep onset insomnia. *Journal of Consulting and Clinical Psychology*, 1978, 46, 547–550.

ATHANASIOU, R., SHAVER, P., & TAVRIS, C. Sex. *Psychology Today*, 1970, 4, 39–52.

AZRIN, N. H., HUTCHINSON, R. R., & McLAUGHLIN, R. The opportunity for aggression as an operant behavior during aversive stimulation. *Journal of Experimental Analysis of Behavior*, 1965, 7, 223–227.

AZRIN, N. H., & NUNN, R. G. *Habit control in a day*. New York: Simon and Schuster, 1977.

BACH, G. R., & DEUTSCH, R. M. *Pairing*. New York: Peter H. Wyden, Inc., 1970.

BACKMAN, E. L. *Religious dances in the Christian church and in popular medicine*. London: Allen & Unwin, 1952.

BAKER, B. L., COHEN, D. C., & SAUNDERS, J. T. Self-directed desensitization for acrophobia. *Behaviour Research and Therapy*, 1973, 11, 79–83.

BALLENTINE, R. M. *The science of breath*. Glenview, Ill: Himalayan Institute, 1976.

BANDURA, A. *Social learning theory*. Englewood Cliffs, N. J.: Prentice-Hall, 1977.

BANDURA, A., BLANCHARD, E. B., & RITTER, B. The relative efficacy of desensitization and modeling approaches for inducing behavioral, affective, and cognitive changes. *Journal of Personality and Social Psychology*, 1969, 13, 173–199.

BANDURA, A., & ROSENTHAL, T. L. Vicarious classical conditioning as a function of arousal level. *Journal of Personality and Social Psychology*, 1966, 3, 54–62.

BANDURA, A., ROSS, S. A., & ROSS, D. Imitation of film-mediated aggressive models. *Journal of Abnormal and Social Psychology*, 1963a, 66, 3–11.

BANDURA, A., ROSS, D., & ROSS, S. A. A comparative test of the status envy, social power, and the secondary reinforcement theories of identificatory learning. *Journal of Abnormal and Social Psychology*, 1963b, 67, 527–534.

BANE, M. J. Marital disruption and the lives of children. *Journal of Social Issues*, 1976, 32, 103–117.

BARBACH, L. G. *For yourself: The fulfillment of female sexuality*. New York: Doubleday, 1975.

BARDWICK, J. M. *Psychology of women: A study of biocultural conflicts*. New York: Harper & Row, 1971.

BARON, R. A. Behavioral effects of interpersonal attraction: Compliance with requests from liked and disliked others. *Psychonomic Science*, 1971, 25, 325–326.

BARON, R. A. The "foot-in-the-door" phenomenon: Mediating effects of size of first request and sex of requester. *Bulletin of the Psychonomic Society*, 1973, 2, 113–114.

BARON, R. A., & BELL, P. A. Aggression and heat: The influence of ambient temperature, negative affect, and a cooling drink on physical aggression. *Journal of Personality and Social Psychology*, 1976, 33, 245–255.

BARON, R. A., & BYRNE, D. *Social psychology: Understanding human interaction*. Boston: Allyn & Bacon, 1977.

BARON, R. A., & LAWTON, S. F. Environmental influences on aggression: The facilitation of modeling effects by high ambient temperatures. *Psychonomic Science*, 1972, 26, 80–83.

BARON, R. A., MANDEL, D. R., ADAMS, C. A., & GRIFFEN, L. M. Effects of social density in university residential environments. *Journal of Personality and Social Psychology*, 1976, 34, 434–446.

BARON, R. A., & RANSBERGER, V. M. Ambient temperature and the occurrence of collective violence: The "long hot summer" revisited. *Journal of Personality and Social Psychology*, in press.

BARRACLOUGH, B. M. Differences between national suicide rates. *British Journal of Psychiatry*, 1973, 122, 95–96.

BARRACLOUGH, B. M., NELSON, B., BUNCH, J., & SAINSBURY, P. The diagnostic classification and psychiatric treatment of 100 suicides. Proceedings of the 5th International Conference for Suicide Prevention, London, 1969.

BAR-TAL, D., & SAXE, L. Perceptions of similarly and dissimilarly physically attractive couples and individuals. *Journal of Personality and Social Psychology*, 1976, 33, 772–781.

BARTELL, G. D. Group sex among the mid-Americans. *Journal of Sex Research*, 1970, 6, 113–130.

BASS, B. M. Confessions of a former male chauvinist. *American Psychologist*, 1979, 34, 194–195.

BAUMAN, K. E., & WILSON, R. R. Premarital sexual attitudes of unmarried university students. *Archives of Sexual Behavior*, 1976, 5, 29–37.

BECK, A. T. *Cognitive therapy and the emotional disorders*. New York: International Universities Press, 1976.

BECK, A. T., WARD, C. H., MENDELSON, M., MOCK, J. E., & ERBAUGH, J. K. Reliability of psychiatric diagnoses II: A study of consistency of clinical judgments and ratings. *American Journal of Psychiatry*, 1962, 119, 351–357.

BECKER, J. *Depression: Theory and research*. New York: Halstead Press, 1974.

BEERS, T. M., & KAROLY, P. Cognitive strategies, expectancy, and coping style in the control of pain. *Journal of Consulting and Clinical Psychology*, 1979, 47, 179–180.

BELL, P. A., & BARON, R. A. Aggression and heat: The mediating role of negative affect. *Journal of Applied Social Psychology*, 1976, 6, 18–30.

BELL, P. A., FISHER, J. D., & LOOMIS, R. J. *Environmental psychology*. Philadelphia: W. B. Saunders, 1978.

BELLOW, S. *Herzog*. New York: Viking, 1961.

BEM, S. L. The measurement of psychological androgyny. *Journal of Consulting and Clinical Psychology*, 1974, 42, 115–162.

BEM, S. L. Sex role adaptability: One consequence of psychological androgyny. *Journal of Personality and Social Psychology*, 1975, 31, 634–643.

BEM, S. L., & BEM, D. J. Training the woman to know her place: The power of a nonconscious ideology. In L. S. Wrightsman & J. C. Brigham (eds.), *Contemporary issues in social psychology*, 2d ed. Monterey, Calif.: Brooks/Cole, 1973.

BEM, S. L., & LENNEY, E. Sex typing and the avoidance of cross-sexed behaviors. *Journal of Personality and Social Psychology*, 1976, 33, 48–54.

BENECKE, W. M., & HARRIS, M. B. Teaching self-control of study behavior. *Behaviour Research and Therapy*, 1972, 10, 35–41.

BENSON, H. *The relaxation response*. New York: William Morrow, 1975.

BENSON, H., MANZETTA, B. R., & ROSNER, B. A. Decreased systolic blood pressure in hypertensive subjects who practiced meditation. *Journal of Clinical Investigation*, 1973, 52, 8(a).

BENTHAM, J. (1822). Introduction to the principles of morals and legislation. In M. Warnock (ed.), *John Stuart Mill: Utilitarianism, On Liberty, Essay on Bentham*. Cleveland: Meridian Books, 1962.

BERGER, C. R., & CALABRESE, R. J. Some explorations in initial interaction and beyond: Toward a developmental theory of interpersonal communication. *Human Communication Research*, 1975, 1, 99–112.

BERGER, C. R., GARDNER, R. R., CLATTERBUCK, G. W., & SCHULMAN, L. S. Perceptions of information sequencing in relationship development. *Human Communication Research*, 1976, 3, 29–46.

BERKOWITZ, W. R., NEBEL, J. C., & REITMAN, J. W. Height and interpersonal attraction: The 1960 mayoral election in New York City. Paper presented at the annual convention of the American Psychological Association, Washington, D. C., September 1971.

BERNARD, J. *The future of marriage*. New York: Bantam, 1973.

BERNARD, J. Notes on changing lifestyles, 1970–1974. *Journal of Marriage and the Family*, 1975, 37, 582–593.

BERNE, E. *Games people play*. New York: Ballantine, 1976a.

BERNE, E. *Beyond games and scripts*. New York: Grove Press, 1976b.

BERNHEIM, H. *Hypnosis and suggestion*. New Hyde Park, N. Y.: University Books, 1964.

BERSCHEID, E. Theories of interpersonal attraction. In B. B. Wolman & L. R. Pomeroy (eds.), *International encyclopedia of neurology, psychiatry, psychoanalysis, and psychology*. New York: Springer, 1976.

BERSCHEID, E., DION, K., WALSTER, E., & WALSTER, G. W. Physical attractiveness and dating choice: A test of the matching hypothesis. *Journal of Experimental Social Psychology*, 1971, 7, 173–189.

BERSCHEID, E., & WALSTER, E. A little bit about love. In T. L. Huston (ed.), *Foundations of interpersonal attraction*. New York: Academic Press, 1974a.

BERSCHEID, E., & WALSTER, E. H. Physical attractiveness. In L. Berkowitz (ed.), *Advances in Experimental social psychology*, vol. 7 New York: Academic Press, 1974b, pp. 158–215.

BERSCHEID, E., WALSTER, E., & BOHRNSTEDT, G. Body image, the happy American body: A survey report. *Psychology Today*, 1973, 7(6), 119–123, 126–131.

BERZINS, J. I., WELLING, M. A., & WETTER, R. E. The PRF ANDRO scale: User's manual. Unpublished manuscript, University of Kentucky, 1977.

BLITTNER, M., GOLDBERG, J., & MERBAUM, M. Cognitive self-control factors in the reduction of smoking behavior. *Behavior Therapy*, 1978, 9, 553–561.

BOHANNAN, P. The six stations of divorce. In P. Bohannan (ed.), *Divorce and after*. Garden City, N. Y.: Doubleday, 1970.

BOSHIER, R. Name style and conservatism. *Journal of Psychology*, 1973, 84, 45–53.

Boston Women's Health Book Collective. *Our bodies, ourselves*. New York: Simon and Schuster, 1976.

BOWER, D. W., & CHRISTOPHERSON, V. A. University student cohabitation: A regional comparison of selected attitudes and behavior. *Journal of Marriage and the Family*, 1977, 39, 447–452.

BRAUN, P. Personal communication. 1978.

BRAUN, P. R., & REYNOLDS, D. J. A factor analysis of a 100-item fear survey inventory. *Behaviour Research and Therapy*, 1969, 7, 399–402.

BREHM, J. W. Responses to loss of freedom: A theory of psychological reactance. Morristown, N. J.: General Learning Press, 1972.

BRENA, S. F. *Yoga and medicine*. New York: Julian Press, 1971.

BRIDDELL, D. W., & WILSON, G. T. Effects of alcohol and expectancy set on male sexual arousal. *Journal of Abnormal Psychology*, 1976, 85, 225–234.

BRISCOE, C. W., & SMITH, J. B. Depression in bereavement and divorce:

Relationship to primary depressive illness, A study of 128 subjects. *Archives of General Psychiatry*, 1975, 32, 439–443.

BRODIE, H. K. H., GARTRELL, N., DOERING, C., & RHUE, T. Plasma testosterone levels in heterosexual and homosexual men. *American Journal of Psychiatry*, 1974, 138, 82–83.

BRONFENBRENNER, U. Freudian theories of identification and their derivatives. *Child Development*, 1960, 31, 15–40.

BROUGHTON, R. J. Sleep disorders. Disorders of arousal? *Science*, 1968, 159, 1070–1078.

BROVERMAN, F. K., BROVERMAN, O. M., CLARKSON, F. E., ROSENKRANTZ, P. J., & VOGEL, S. R. Sex-role stereotypes and clinical judgments of mental health. *Journal of Consulting and Clinical Psychology*, 1970, 34, 1–7.

BROWN, B. *Stress and the art of biofeedback*. New York: Harper & Row, 1977.

BROWN, M., & RATHUS, S. A. Loss of love ceremonies: Death vs. divorce. Unpublished paper, Northeastern University, 1980.

BROWNMILLER, S. *Against our will: Men, women and rape*. New York: Simon and Schuster, 1975.

BYRNE, D. *The attraction paradigm*. New York: Academic Press, 1971.

BYRNE, D., BASKETT, G. D., & HODGES, L. Behavioral indicators of interpersonal attraction. *Journal of Applied Social Psychology*, 1971, 1, 137–149.

BYRNE, D., & BUEHLER, J. A. A note on the influence of propinquity upon acquaintanceships. *Journal of Abnormal and Social Psychology*, 1955, 51, 147–148.

BYRNE, D., ERVIN, C. R., & LAMBERTH, J. Continuity between the experimental study of attraction and real-life computer dating. *Journal of Personality and Social Psychology*, 1970, 16, 157–165.

CAHALAN, D., CISIN, I. H., & CROSSLEY, H. M. *American drinking practices: A national study of drinking behavior and attitudes*. Monograph No. 6. New Brunswick, N. J.: Rutgers Center of Alcohol Studies, 1969.

CALHOUN, J. B. Population density and social pathology. *Science*, 1962, 206, 139–148.

CAMPBELL, A. The American way of mating: marriage sí, children only maybe. *Psychology Today*, 1975, 8(12), 37–43.

CANNON, W. B. *Bodily changes in pain, hunger, fear, and rage*, 2d ed. New York: Appleton, 1929.

CANNON, W. B. Voodoo death. *Psychosomatic medicine*, 1957, 19, 182–190.

CANTOR, P. C. Personality characteristics found among youthful female suicide attempters. *Journal of Abnormal Psychology*, 1976, 85, 324–329.

CAPLOW, T., & FORMAN, R. Neighborhood interaction in a homogeneous community. *American Sociological Review*, 1950, 15, 357–366.

CARLSON, N. R., & JOHNSON, D. A. Sexuality assertiveness training. *The Counseling Psychologist*, 1975, 5(4), 53–59.

CARRINGTON, P. *Freedom in meditation*. New York: Anchor Press/Doubleday, 1977.

CAUTELA, J. R. Covert sensitization. *Psychological Reports*, 1967, 74, 459–468.

CAUTELA, J. R. Covert reinforcement. *Behavior Therapy*, 1970, 1, 33–50.

CHESLER, P. *Women and madness*. New York: Doubleday, 1972.

CIALDINI, R. B., BORDEN, R. J., THORNE, A., WALKER, M. R., FREEMAN, S., & SLOAN, L. R. Basking in reflected glory: Three (football) field studies. *Journal of Personality and Social Psychology*, 1976, 34, 366–375.

CLORE, G. L., WIGGINS, N. H., & ITKIN, S. Judging attraction from nonverbal behavior: The gain phenomenon. *Journal of Consulting and Clinical Psychology*, 1975, 43, 491–497.

COCHRAN, W. G., MOSTELLER, F., & TUKEY, J. *Statistical problems of the Kinsey report on sexual report in the human male*. Washington, D. C.: The American Statistical Association, 1954.

COGGINS, W. J. The general health status of chronic cannabis smokers in Costa Rica. In S. Szara & M. Braude (eds.), *Pharmacology of marihuana*. New York: Raven Press, in press.

COHEN, E. J., MOTTO, A., & SEIDEN, R. H. An instrument for evaluating suicide potential: A preliminary study. *American Journal of Psychiatry*, 1966, 122, 886–891.

COHEN, R. Answers to hard questions. *New York*, May 15, 1978.

COMFORT, A. (ed.). *The joy of sex*. New York: Crown, 1972.

Commission on Obscenity and Pornography. *The report of the Commission on Obscenity and Pornography*. New York: Bantam, 1970.

CONNOR, J. Olfactory control of aggressive and sexual behavior in the mouse. *Psychonomic Science*, 1972, 27, 1–3.

COOPER, A. J. Treatment of male potency disorders: The present status. *Psychosomatics*, 1971, 12, 235–244.

COOPERSMITH, S. *Antecedents of self-esteem*. San Francisco: Freeman, 1967.

COYNE, J. C. Depression and the response of others. *Journal of Abnormal Psychology*, 1976, 85, 186–193.

COZBY, P. C. Self-disclosure: A literature review. *Psychological Bulletin*, 1973, 79, 73–91.

CRUMBAUGH, J. Cross-validation of purpose-in-life test based on Frankl's concepts. *Journal of Individual Psychology*, 1968, 24, 74–81.

DALTON, K. *The premenstrual syndrome*. Springfield, Ill.: Charles C. Thomas, 1964.

DARWIN, C. *The expression of emotion in man and animals*. New York: Philosophical Library, 1955. (Originally published 1873.)

DAVIDSON, T. *Conjugal crime*. New York: Hawthorn Books, 1978.

DAVIS, E. G. *The first sex*. New York: G. P. Putnam's Sons, 1971.

DAVISON, G. C. The elimination of a sadistic fantasy by a client-controlled conditioning technique: A case study. *Journal of Abnormal Psychology*, 1968, 73, 84–90.

DAWLEY, H. H., GUIDRY, L. S., & CURTIS, E. Self-administered desensitization on a psychiatric ward. *Journal of Behavior Therapy and Experimental Psychiatry*, 1973, 4, 301–303.

DELAHUNT, J., & CURRAN, J. P. Effectiveness of negative practice and self-control techniques in the reduction of smoking behavior. *Journal of Consulting and Clinical Psychology*, 1976, 44, 1002–1007.

DELORA, J. S., & WARREN, C. A. B. *Understanding sexual interaction*. Boston: Houghton Mifflin, 1977.

DERMER, M., & THIEL, D. L. When beauty may fail. *Journal of Personality and Social Psychology*, 1975, 31, 1168–1176.

DERNER, G. Biofeedback Workshop, Adelphi University, Garden City, N. Y., May 7, 1977.

DIMSDALE, J. E. The coping behavior of Nazi concentration camp survivors. *American Journal of Psychiatry*, 1974, 131, 792–797.

DION, K. K., BERSCHEID, E., & WALSTER, E. What is beautiful is good.

Journal of Personality and Social Psychology, 1972, 24, 285–290.

DOERR, H. O., & HOKANSON, J. E. A relation between heart rate and performance in children. *Journal of Personality and Social Psychology*, 1965, 2, 70–76.

DOOB, A. N., & WOOD, L. Catharsis and aggression: The effects of annoyance and retaliation on aggressive behavior. *Journal of Personality and Social Psychology*, 1972, 22, 236–245.

DOTY, R. L., FORD, M., PRETI, G., & HUGGINS, G. R. Changes in the intensity and pleasantness of human vaginal odors during the menstrual cycle. *Science*, 1975, 190, 1316–1318.

DOYLE, N. C. The facts about second-hand cigarette smoke. *American Lung Association Bulletin*, 1974, 60, 13–15.

DRISCOLL, R., DAVIS, K. E., & LIPETZ, M. E. Parental interference and romantic love: The Romeo and Juliet effect. *Journal of Personality and Social Psychology*, 1972, 24, 1–10.

DUTTON, D. G., & ARON, A. P. Some evidence for heightened sexual attraction under conditions of high anxiety. *Journal of Personality and Social Psychology*, 1974, 30, 510–517.

EAGLY, A. H. Comprehensibility of persuasive arguments as a determinant of opinion change. *Journal of Personality and Social Psychology*, 1974, 29, 758–773.

EFRAN, M. G. The effect of physical appearance on the judgment of guilt, interpersonal attraction, and severity of recommended punishment in a simulated jury task. *Journal of Research in Personality*, 1974, 8, 45–54.

ELLIS, A. *Reason and emotion in psychotherapy*. New York: Lyle Stuart, 1962.

ELLIS, A. The basic clinical theory of rational-emotive therapy. In A. Ellis & R. Grieger (eds.), *Handbook of rational-emotive therapy*. New York: Springer, 1977.

ELLISON, G. D. Animal models of psychopathology: The low-norepinephrine and low-serotonin rat. *American Psychologist*, 1977, 32, 1036–1045.

ENGLISH, H. B. Three cases of the "conditioned fear response." *Journal of Abnormal and Social Psychology*, 1929, 34, 221–225.

ERIKSON, E. H. *Childhood and society*, 2d ed. New York: W. W. Norton, 1963.

ERIKSON, E. H. *Life history and the historical moment*. New York: W. W. Norton, 1975.

EVANS, R. B. Sixteen personality factor questionnaire scores of homosexual men. *Journal of Consulting and Clinical Psychology*, 1970, 34, 212–215.

EVANS, R. I., ROZELLE, R. M., LASATER, T. M., DEMBROSKI, T. M., & ALLEN, B. P. Fear arousal, persuasion, and actual versus implied behavioral change: New perspective utilizing a real-life dental hygiene program. *Journal of Personality and Social Psychology*, 1970, 16, 220–227.

EYSENCK, H. J. Obscenity—officially speaking. *Penthouse*, 1972, 3(11), 95–102.

FAST, J. *Body language*. New York: Pocket Books, 1970.

Federal Bureau of Investigation. *Uniform crime report*. Washington, D. C.: U. S. Government Printing Office, 1975.

FENICHEL, O. *The psychoanalytic theory of the neuroses*. New York: W. W. Norton, 1945.

FERSTER, C. B. A functional analysis of depression. *American Psychologist*, 1973, 28, 857–870.

FESTINGER, L. *A theory of cognitive dissonance*. Evanston, Ill.: Row, Peterson, 1957.

FESTINGER, L., & CARLSMITH, J. M. Cognitive consequences of forced compliance. *Journal of Abnormal and Social Psychology*, 1959, 58, 203–210.

FIBEL, B., & HALE, W. D. The generalized expectancy for success scale—A new measure. *Journal of Consulting and Clinical Psychology*, 1978, 46, 924–931.

FISHER, J. D. Situation-specific variables as determinants of perceived environmental aesthetic quality and perceived crowdedness. *Journal of Research in Personality*, 1974, 8, 177–188.

FISHER, S. *Female orgasm: Psychology, physiology, fantasy*. New York: Basic Books, 1973.

FISHER, W. A. Individual differences in behavioral responsiveness to erotica: Cognitive labeling, transfer of arousal, and disinhibition considerations. Master's thesis, Purdue University, 1976.

FISHER, W. A., & BYRNE, D. Individual differences in socialization to sex as mediators of responses to an erotic film. Paper presented at the Midwestern Psychological Association, Chicago, May 1976.

FITCH, G. Effects of self-esteem, perceived performance, and choice on causal attribution. *Journal of Personality and Social Psychology*, 1970, 16, 311–315.

FLANAGAN, J. C. A research approach to improving our quality of life. *American Psychologist*, 1978, 33, 138–147.

FLAXMAN, J. Quitting smoking now or later: Gradual, abrupt, immediate, and delayed quitting. *Behavior Therapy*, 1978, 9, 260–270.

FLIPPO, J. R., & LEWINSOHN, P. M. Effects of failure on the self-esteem of depressed and nondepressed subjects. *Journal of Consulting and Clinical Psychology*, 1971, 36, 151.

FLORA, C. B. The passive female: Her comparative image by class and culture in women's magazine fiction. *Journal of Marriage and the Family*, 1971, 33, 435–444.

FRANCK, K. D., UNSELD, C. T., & WENTWORTH, W. E. Adaptation of the newcomer: A process of construction. Unpublished manuscript, City University of New York, 1974.

FRANKL, V. E. *Man's search for meaning*. New York: Washington Square Press, 1963.

FRANKL, V. E. Paradoxical intention and dereflection. *Psychotherapy: Theory, Research and Practice*, 1975, 12, 226–236.

FREEDMAN, A. M., KAPLAN, H. I., & SADOCK, B. J. *Comprehensive textbook of psychiatry*, 2d ed. Baltimore: Williams & Wilkins, 1975.

FREEDMAN, J. L., & FRASER, S. C. Compliance without pressure: The foot-in-the-door technique. *Journal of Personality and Social Psychology*, 1966, 4, 195–202.

FREEDMAN, J. L., WALLINGTON, S. A., & BLESS, E. Compliance without pressure: The effect of guilt. *Journal of Personality and Social Psychology*, 1967, 7, 117–124.

FREUD, S. (1909). Analysis of a phobia in a five-year-old boy. In *Collected papers*, vol. III. (Translated by Alix & James Strachey.) New York: Basic Books, 1959, pp. 149–287.

FREUD, S. (1922). Postscript (to "Analysis of a phobia in a five-year-old boy"). In *Collected papers*, vol. III. New York: Basic Books, 1959, pp. 288–289.

FREUD, S. *Civilization and its discontents*. (Translated by James Strachey. First German edition, 1930.) New York: W. W. Norton, 1961.

FREUD, S. (1933). New introductory lectures. In Vol. XXII of *The standard edition of the complete works of Sigmund Freud*. London: Hogarth Press, 1964.

FRIEDMAN, M., & ROSENMAN, R. H. *Type A behavior and your heart*. New York: Alfred A. Knopf, 1974.

FRIEDRICH, L. K., & STEIN, A. H. Aggression and prosocial television programs and the natural behavior of preschool children. *Monographs of the Society for Research in Child Development*, 1973, Serial No. 151, 38(4), 1–64.

GAGNON, J. H. *Human sexualities*. Chicago: Scott, Foresman, 1977.

GALDSTON, I. *Beyond the germ theory*. New York: Health Education Council, 1954.

GALIZIO, M., & HENDRICK, C. Effect of musical accompaniment on attitude: The guitar as a prop for persuasion. *Journal of Applied Social Psychology*, 1972, 2, 350–359.

GATCHEL, R. J., & PROCTOR, J. D. Effectiveness of voluntary heart rate control in reducing speech anxiety. *Journal of Consulting and Clinical Psychology*, 1976, 44, 381–389.

GEBHARD, P. H. The institute. In M. S. Weinberg (ed.), *Sex research: Studies from the Kinsey Institute*. New York: Oxford University Press, 1976.

GEBHARD, P. H., GAGNON, J. H., POMEROY, W. B., & CHRISTENSON, C. V. *Sex offenders*. New York: Harper & Row, 1965.

GEEN, R. G., STONNER, D., & SHOPE, G. L. The facilitation of aggression by aggression: Evidence against the catharsis hypothesis. *Journal of Personality and Social Psychology*, 1975, 31, 721–726.

GERARD, H. B., WILHELMY, R. A., & CONOLLEY, E. S. Conformity and group size. *Journal of Personality and Social Psychology*, 1968, 8, 79–82.

GILMARTIN, B. G. That swinging couple down the block. *Psychology Today*, 1975, 8(9), 54.

GINZBERG, E. *The development of human resources*. New York: McGraw-Hill, 1966.

GLASS, D. C. *Stress and coronary prone behavior*. Hillsdale, N.J.: Lawrence Erlbaum Associates, 1977.

GLASS, D. C., & SINGER, J. E. *Urban stress*. New York: Academic Press, 1972.

GLICK, P. C. A demographer looks at American families. *Journal of Marriage and the Family*, 1975, 37, 15–26.

GOLDBERG, S., & LEWIS, M. Play behavior in the year-old infant: early sexual differences. In U. Bronfenbrenner (ed.), *Influences on human development*. Hinsdale, Ill: Dryden Press, 1969.

GOLDFRIED, M. R., & DAVISON, G. C. *Clinical behavior therapy*. New York: Holt, Rinehart and Winston, 1976.

GOLDFRIED, M. R., LINEHAN, M. M., & SMITH, J. L. Reduction of test anxiety through cognitive restructuring. *Journal of Consulting and Clinical Psychology*, 1978, 46, 32–39.

GOLDSTEIN, A. J. Separate effects of extinction, counterconditioning, and progressive approach in overcoming fear. *Behaviour Research and Therapy*, 1969, 7, 47–56.

GOLDSTEIN, M., KANT, H., JUDD, L., RICE, C., & GREEN, R. Experience with pornography: Rapists, pedophiles, homosexuals, transsexuals, and controls. *Archives of Sexual Behavior*, 1971, 1, 1–15.

GOLEMAN, D. J., & SCHWARTZ, G. E. Meditation as an intervention in stress reactivity. *Journal of Consulting and Clinical Psychology*, 1976, 44, 456–466.

GOLUB, S. The effect of premenstrual anxiety and depression on cognitive function. *Journal of Personality and Social Psychology*, 1976, 34, 99–104.

GOTTMAN, J. The growing city as a social and political process. *Transactions of the Bartlett Society*, 1966, 5, 9–46.

GOUAUX, C. Induced affective states and interpersonal attraction. *Journal of Personality and Social Psychology*, 1971, 20, 37–43.

GOULD, R. Adult life stages: Growth toward self-tolerance. *Psychology Today*, 1975, 8, 74–81.

GREEN, R. Homosexuality as mental illness. *International Journal of Psychiatry*, 1972, 10, 77–98.

GREEN, R. Adults who want to change sex; adolescents who cross-dress; and children called "sissy" and "tomboy." In R. Green (ed.), *Human sexuality: A health practitioner's text*. Baltimore: Williams & Wilkins, 1975.

GRIFFEN, J. H. *Black like me*. Boston: Houghton Mifflin, 1960.

GUILFORD, J. S., et al. *Factors related to successful abstinence from smoking:*

Final report. Pittsburgh: American Institutes, 1966. (Table abstracted from Table XXIX, pp. 114–115 & Table XXX, pp. 116–117.)

HABER, S., & SHAPIRO, H. Fear of thinness: An alternative approach to the treatment of obesity. Paper presented at the American Psychological Association, Toronto, Canada, August 1978.

HALPERIN, K. M., & SNYDER, C. R. Effects of enhanced psychological test feedback on treatment outcome: Therapeutic implications of the Barnum effect. *Journal of Consulting and Clinical Psychology*, 1979, 47, 140–146.

HAMM, N. H., BAUM, M. R., & NIKELS, K. W. Effects of race and exposure on judgments of interpersonal favorability. *Journal of Experimental Social Psychology*, 1975, 11, 14–24.

HARBURG, E., ERFURT, J. C., HAUENSTEIN, L. S., CHAPE, C., SCHULL, W. J., & SCHORK, M. A. Socioecological stress, suppressed hostility, skin color, and black-white male blood pressure: Detroit. *Psychosomatic Medicine*, 1973, 35, 276–296.

HARITON, E. B., & SINGER, J. L. Women's fantasies during sexual intercourse: Normative and theoretical implications. *Journal of Consulting and Clinical Psychology*, 1974, 42, 313–322.

HARRIS, T. A. *I'm OK—You're OK*. New York: Harper & Row, 1967.

HARRISON, A. A., & SAEED, L. Let's make a deal: An analysis of revelations and stipulations in lonely hearts advertisements. *Journal of Personality and Social Psychology*, 1977, 35, 257–264.

HARROWER, M. Were Hitler's henchmen mad? *Psychology Today*, 1976 (July), 10, 76–80.

HARTMAN, W. E., & FITHIAN, M. A. *Treatment of sexual dysfunction: A bio-psychosocial approach*. Long Beach, Calif. Center for Marital and Sexual Studies, 1972.

HARVEY, J. R. Diaphragmatic breathing: A practical technique for breath control. *The Behavior Therapist*, 1978, 1(2), 13–14.

HASS, R. G., & LINDER, D. E. Counterargument availability and the effects of message structure on persuasion. *Journal of Personality and Social Psychology*, 1972, 23, 219–233.

HATFIELD, E., SPRECHER, S., & TRAUPMAN, J. Men's and women's reaction to sexually explicit films: A serendipitous finding. *Archives of Sexual Behavior*, 1978, 6, 583–592.

HAWLEY, P. What women think men think. Does it affect their career choice? *Journal of Counseling Psychology*, 1971, 18, 193–199.

HAYNES, S. N., FOLLINGSTAD, D. R., & McGOWAN, W. T. Insomnia: Sleep patterns and anxiety level. *Journal of Psychosomatic Research*, 1974, 18, 69–74.

HAYNES, S. N., SIDES, H., & LOCKWOOD, G. Relaxation instructions and frontalis electromyographic feedback intervention with sleep-onset insomnia. *Behavior Therapy*, 1977, 8, 644–652.

HAYNES, S. N., WOODWARD, S., MORAN, R., & ALEXANDER, D. Relaxation treatment of insomnia. *Behavior Therapy*, 1974, 5, 555–558.

HEIMAN, J. R. The physiology of erotica: Women's sexual arousal. *Psychology Today*, 1975, 8, 90–94.

HEIMAN, J., LoPICCOLO, L., & LoPICCOLO, J. *Becoming orgasmic: A sexual growth program for women*. Englewood Cliffs, N.J.: Prentice-Hall, 1976.

HEINGARTNER, A., & HALL, J. V. Affective consequences in adults and children of repeated exposure to auditory stimuli. *Journal of Personality and Social Psychology*, 1974, 29, 719–723.

HERRELL, J. M. Sex differences in emotional responses to "erotic literature." *Journal of Consulting and Clinical Psychology*, 1975, 43, 921.

HIRAI, T. *Zen meditation therapy*. Tokyo: Komiyama, 1975.

HIRSCH, J., & KENISTON, K. Psychological issues in talented college dropouts. *Psychiatry*, 1970, 33, 1–20.

HOKANSON, J. E., & BURGESS, M. The effects of three types of aggression on vascular processes. *Journal of Abnormal and Social Psychology*, 1962, 64, 446–449.

HOKANSON, J. E., BURGESS, M., & COHEN, M. F. Effects of displaced aggression on systolic blood pressure. *Journal of Abnormal and Social Psychology*, 1963, 67, 214–218.

HOKANSON, J. E., WILLERS, K. R., & KOROPSAK, E. Modification of autonomic responses during aggressive interchange. *Journal of Personality*, 1968, 36, 386–404.

HOLMES, T. H., & RAHE, R. H. The social readjustment rating scale. *Journal of Psychosomatic Research*, 1967, 11, 213–218.

HOLROYD, K. A., WESTBROOK, T., WOLF, M., & BADHORN, E. Performance, cognition, and physiological responding in test anxiety. *Journal of Abnormal Psychology*, 1978, 87, 442–451.

HOOKER, E. The adjustment of the male overt homosexual. *Journal of Projective Techniques and Personality Adjustment*, 1957, 21, 18–23.

HORN, D. (Developer). *Smokers self-testing kit, I & II*. Washington, D.C.: Public Health Service, Center for Disease Control, U. S. Department of Health, Education, and Welfare, DHEW (#CDC) 75-8716, December 1973.

HORNER, M. Toward an understanding of achievement-related conflicts in women. *Journal of Social Issues*, 1972, 28, 157–175.

HORNEY, K. *Feminine psychology*. Harold Kelman, ed. New York: W. W. Norton, 1967.

HORTON, E. S. The role of exercise in the prevention and treatment of obesity. In G. A. Bray (ed.), *Obesity in Perspective*. Washington, D.C.: U. S. Government Printing Office, 1974.

HOWARD, J. L., LIPTZIN, M. B., & REIFLER, C. B. Is pornography a problem? *Journal of Social Issues*, 1973, 29, 133–145.

HUNT, M. *Sexual behavior in the 1970s*. Chicago: Playboy Press, 1974.

HURSCH, C. J. *The trouble with rape*. Chicago: Nelson-Hall, 1977.

HUXLEY, A. *Brave new world*. New York: Harper & Row, 1939.

HYDE, J. S. *Understanding human sexuality*. New York: McGraw-Hill, 1979.

IBRAHIM, A. The home situation and the homosexual. *Journal of Sex Research*, 1976, 12, 263–282.

ILLINGWORTH, D. J., & SYME, G. J. Birthdate and femininity. *Journal of Social Psychology*, 1977, 103, 153–154.

IVEY, M. E., & BARDWICK, J. M. Patterns of affective fluctuation in the menstrual cycle. *Psychosomatic Medicine*, 1968, 30, 336–345.

JACOBSON, E. *Progressive relaxation*. Chicago: University of Chicago Press, 1938.

JAFFE, A. C. Child molestation. *Medical Aspects of Human Sexuality*, April 1976, pp. 73, 96.

JANIS, I. L., KAYE, D., & KIRSCHNER, P. Facilitating effects of "eating while reading" on responsiveness to persuasive communications. *Journal of Personality and Social Psychology*, 1965, 1, 181–186.

JANIS, I., & MANN, L. *Decision-making*. New York: Free Press, 1977.

JANIS, I., & WHEELER, D. Thinking clearly about career choices. *Psychology Today*, May 1978, 11(12), 66–76, 121–122.

JOFFEE, C. Sex-role socialization and the nursery school: As the twig is bent. *Journal of Marriage and the Family*, 1971, 33, 467–475.

JOHNS, M. W., MASTERSON, J. P., & BRUCE, D. W. Relationship between sleep habits, adrenocortical activity and personality. *Psychosomatic Medicine*, 1971, 33, 499–507.

JOHNSON, P. B. Women and power: Towards a theory of effectiveness. *Journal of Social Issues*, 1976, 32(3), 99–110.

JOHNSON, S. M., & WHITE, G. Self-observation as an agent of behavior change. *Behavior Therapy*, 1971, 2, 488–497.

JONES, E. *The life and work of Sigmund Freud*. New York: Basic Books, 1961.

JONES, H. E., & JONES, M. C. Fear. *Childhood Education*, 1928, 5, 136–143.

JONES, M. Community care for chronic mental patients: The need for a reassessment. *Hospital and Community Psychiatry*, 1975, 26, 94–98.

JONES, M. C. Elimination of children's fears. *Journal of Experimental Psychology*, 1924, 7, 381–390.

JONG, E. *How to save your own life*. New York: Holt, Rinehart and Winston, 1977.

KAGAN, J. The concept of identification. *Psychological Review*, 1958, 65, 296–305.

KAHN, M. The physiology of catharsis. *Journal of Personality and Social Psychology*, 1966, 3, 278–286.

KANFER, F., & GOLDFOOT, D. Self-control and tolerance of noxious stimulation. *Psychological Reports*, 1966, 18, 79–85.

KANIN, E. J. Selected dyadic aspects of male sex aggression. *Journal of Sex Research*, 1969, 5.

KAPLAN, H. S. *The new sex therapy: Active treatment of sexual dysfunctions*. New York: Brunner/Mazel, 1974.

KAPLAN, H. S., & SAGER, C. J. Sexual patterns at different ages. *Medical Aspects of Human Sexuality*, 1971, 5(6), 10–23.

KARACAN, I. Advances in the psychophysiological evaluation of male erectile impotence. In J. LoPiccolo & L. LoPiccolo (eds.), *Handbook of sex therapy*. New York: Plenum, 1978.

KARLIN, R. A., MCFARLAND, D., AIELLO, J. R., & EPSTEIN, Y. M. Normative mediation of reactions to crowding. *Environmental Psychology and Non-Verbal Behavior*, 1976, 1, 30–40.

KAZDIN, A. E. Covert modeling, imagery assessment, and assertive behavior. *Journal of Consulting and Clinical Psychology*, 1975, 43, 716–724.

KEESEY, R. E., & BOYLE, P. C. Effects of quinine adulteration upon body weight of LH-lesioned and intact male rats. *Journal of Comparative and Physiological Psychology*, 1973, 84, 38–46.

KELLOGG, J. H. *Plain facts for old and young*. Burlington, Iowa: I. F. Segner, 1882. (Republished: Buffalo: Heritage Press, 1974.).

KESEY, K. *One flew over the cuckoo's nest*. New York: Viking, 1962.

KIMBLE, G. A., & KENDALL, J. W. A comparison of two methods of producing experimental extinction. *Journal of Experimental Psychology*, 1953, 45, 87–90.

KINSEY, A. C., POMEROY, W. B., & MARTIN, C. E. *Sexual behavior in the human male*. Philadelphia: W. B. Saunders, 1948.

KINSEY, A. C., POMEROY, W. B., MARTIN, C. E., & GEBHARD, P. H. *Sexual behavior in the human female*. Philadelphia: W. B. Saunders, 1953.

KIRSCH, B. Consciousness-raising groups as therapy for women. In V. Franks and V. Burtle (eds.), *Women in therapy*. New York: Brunner/Mazel, 1974.

KNAPP, M. L. *Social intercourse: From greeting to goodbye*. Boston: Allyn & Bacon, 1978.

KNOX, D. *Marriage happiness: A behavioral approach to counseling*. Champaign, Ill.: Research Press, 1971.

KNOX, V. Cognitive strategies for coping with pain: Ignoring versus acknowledging. Doctoral dissertation, University of Waterloo, 1972.

KOHEN, W., & PAUL, G. L. Current trends and recommended changes in extended care placement of mental patients: The Illinois system as a case

in point. *Schizophrenia Bulletin*, 1976, 2(4), 575–594.

KOHLBERG, L. Moral development and identification. In National Society for the Study of Education, 62d Yearbook, *Child Psychology*. Chicago: University of Chicago Press, 1963.

KOLB, L. C. *Modern clinical psychiatry*. Philadelphia: W. B. Saunders, 1977.

KOMAKI, J., & DORE-BOYCE, K. Self-recording: Its effects on individuals high and low in motivation. *Behavior Therapy*, 1978, 9, 65–72.

KONEČNI, V. J. Annoyance, type and duration of postannoyance activity, and aggression: The "cathartic" effect. *Journal of Experimental Psychology: General*, 1975, 104, 76–102.

KOOCHER, G. P. Swimming, competence, and personality change. *Journal of Personality and Social Psychology*, 1971, 18, 275–278.

KRANTZLER, M. *Creative divorce: A new opportunity for personal growth*. New York: M. Evans, 1973.

KRAPFL, J. E. Differential ordering of stimulus presentation and semi-automated versus live treatment in the systematic desensitization of snake phobia. Doctoral dissertation, University of Missouri, 1967.

KRECH, D., CRUTCHFIELD, R. S., & BALLACHEY, E. L. *Individual in society*. New York: McGraw-Hill, 1962.

KÜBLER-ROSS, E. *On death and dying*. New York: Macmillan, 1969.

KUTNER, N. G., & LEVINSON, R. M. The toy salesperson: A voice for change in sex role stereotyping. *Sex Roles* (February 1978), 4(1), 1–8.

LANDY, D., & SIGALL, H. Beauty is talent: Task evaluation as a function of the performer's physical attractiveness. *Journal of Personality and Social Psychology*, 1974, 30, 299–304.

LANG, A. R., GOECKNER, D. J., ADESSO, V. J., & MARLATT, G. A. Effects of alcohol on aggression in male social drinkers. *Journal of Abnormal Psychology*, 1975, 84, 508–518.

LANGEVIN, R., PAITICH, D., & STEINER, B. The clinical profile of male transsexuals living as females vs. those living as males. *Archives of Sexual Behavior*, 1977, 6, 143–154.

LAVRAKAS, P. J. Female preferences for male physiques. Paper presented to the Midwestern Psychological Association, Chicago, May 1975.

LAWSON, E. D. Hair color, personality,

and the observer. *Psychological Reports*, 1971, 28, 311–322.

LAYNE, C. The Barnum effect: rationality versus gullibility? *Journal of Consulting and Clinical Psychology*, 1979, 47, 219–221.

LE BON, G. *The crowd* (1st ed.: *La foule*, 1895). New York: Viking, 1960.

LEBOW, M. D., GOLDBERG, P. S., & COLLINS, A. Eating behavior of overweight and nonoverweight persons in the natural environment. *Journal of Consulting and Clinical Psychology*, 1977, 45, 1204–1205.

LEONARD, C. V. Depression and suicidality. *Journal of Consulting and Clinical Psychology*, 1974, 42, 98–104.

LEONARD, C. V. The MMPI as a suicide predictor. *Journal of Consulting and Clinical Psychology*, 1977, 45, 367–377.

LERNER, R. M., & GELLERT, E. Body build identification, preference, and aversion in children. *Developmental Psychology*, 1969, 1, 456–462.

LEVENTHAL, H. Findings and theory in the study of fear communication. In L. Berkowitz (ed.), *Advances in experimental social psychology*, vol. 5. New York: Academic Press, 1970.

LEVENTHAL, H., & AVIS, N. Pleasure, addiction, and habit: Factors in verbal report or factors in smoking behavior? *Journal of Abnormal Psychology*, 1976, 85, 478–488.

LEVENTHAL, H., WATTS, J. C., & PAOGANO, F. Effects of fear and instructions on how to cope with danger. *Journal of Personality and Social Psychology*, 1967, 6, 313–321.

LEVIN, R. J., and LEVIN, A. The *Redbook* report on premarital and extramarital sex. *Redbook*, October 1975, 38.

LEVINGER, G. A three-level approach to attraction: Toward an understanding of pair relatedness. In T. L. Huston (ed.), *Foundations of interpersonal attraction*. New York: Academic Press, 1974.

LEVINSON, D. J., DARROW, C. N., KLEIN, E. B., LEVINSON, M. H., & MCKEE, B. *The seasons of a man's life*. New York: Alfred A. Knopf, 1978.

LEWINSOHN, P. M. The behavioral study and treatment of depression. In M. Hersen, R. M. Eisler, & P. M. Miller (eds.), *Progess in behavior modification*, vol. 1. New York: Academic Press, 1975.

LEWINSOHN, P. M., & AMENSON, C. S. Some relations between pleasant and unpleasant mood-related events and depression. *Journal of Abnormal Psychology*, 1978, 87, 644–654.

LEWINSOHN, P. M., & GRAF, M. Pleasant activities and depression. *Journal of Consulting and Clinical Psychology*, 1973, 41, 261–268.

LEWINSOHN, P. M., & LIBET, J. Pleasant events, activity schedules, and depression. *Journal of Abnormal Psychology*, 1972, 79, 291–295.

LICHTENSTEIN, E., & GLASGOW, R. E. Rapid smoking: Side effects and safeguards. *Journal of Consulting and Clinical Psychology*, 1977, 45, 815–821.

LICHTENSTEIN, E., HARRIS, D., BIRCHLER, G., WAHL, J., & SCHMAHL, D. Comparison of rapid smoking, warm, smoky air, and attention placebo in the modification of smoking behavior. *Journal of Consulting and Clinical Psychology*, 1973, 40, 92–98.

LICK, J. R., & HEFFLER, D. Relaxation training and attention placebo in the treatment of severe insomnia. *Journal of Consulting and Clinical Psychology*, 1977, 45, 153–161.

Lieberman Research, Inc. The teenager looks at cigarette smoking. Unpublished report of a study conducted for the American Cancer Society, November 1967.

LIFTON, R. J. *Thought reform and the psychology of totalism.* New York: W. W. Norton, 1963.

LINGWOOD, D. A. Environmental education through information-seeking: The case of an environmental teach-in. *Environment and Behavior*, 1971, 3, 220–262.

LIPINSKI, D. P., BLACK, J. L., NELSON, R. O., CIMINERO, A. R. Influence of motivational variables on the reactivity and reliability of self-recording. *Journal of Consulting and Clinical Psychology*, 1975, 43, 637–646.

LOGAN, D. D. Variations on "the curse": Menstrual euphemisms in other countries. Paper presented at the meeting of the American Psychological Association, Toronto, August 1978.

LoPICCOLO, J., & LOBITZ, C. The role of masturbation in the treatment of sexual dysfunction. *Archives of Sexual Behavior*, 1972, 2, 163–171.

LORENZ, K. *On aggression.* New York: Harcourt, Brace, and World, 1966.

LOWRY, T. P. *The clitoris.* St. Louis: W. C. Green, 1976.

LUCE, G. G., & SEGAL, J. *Sleep.* New York: Coward McCann, 1969.

McCAGHY, C. H. Child molesting. *Sexual Behavior*, August 1971, pp. 16–24.

McCARY, J. L. *McCary's human sexuality*, 3d ed. New York: D. Van Nostrand, 1978.

MACCOBY, E. E., & JACKLIN, C. N. *The psychology of sex differences.* Stanford: Stanford University Press, 1974.

McDAVID, W. J., & HARARI, H. Stereotyping of names and popularity on grade-school children. *Child Development*, 1966, 37, 453–459.

MACFARLANE, J. Perspectives on personality consistency and change from the guidance study. *Vita Humana*, 1964, 7(2).

MADDI, S. R. The existential neurosis. *Journal of Abnormal Psychology*, 1967, 72, 311–325.

MAHONEY, M. J. *Cognition and behavior modification.* Cambridge, Mass: Ballinger, 1974.

MAHONEY, M. J., & MAHONEY, K. Fight fat with behavior control. *Psychology Today*, 1976, 9(12), 39–43, 92–94.

MALONEY, M. P., WARD, M. O., & BRAUCHT, C. N. A revised scale for the measurement of ecological attitudes and knowledge. *American Psychologist*, 1975, 30, 787–790.

MARCUS, M. G. The power of a name. *Psychology Today*, 1976, 10(5), 75–76, 108.

MARKS, I., & GELDER, M. Transvetism and fetishism: Clinical and psychological changes during faradic aversion. *British Journal of Psychiatry*, 1967, 113, 711–729.

MARKS, P. A., & MONROE, L. J. Correlates of adolescent poor sleepers. *Journal of Abnormal Psychology*, 1976, 85, 243–246.

MARSHALL, D. S. Sexual behavior on Mangaia. In D. S. Marshall and R. C. Suggs (eds.), *Human sexual behavior: Variations in the ethnographic spectrum.* New York: Basic Books, 1971.

MARSTON, A. R., LONDON, P., COHEN, N., & COOPER, L. M. In vivo observation of the eating behavior of obese and nonobese subjects. *Journal of Consulting and Clinical Psychology*, 1977, 45, 335–336.

MARTIN, B. *Abnormal psychology: Clinical and scientific perspective.* New York: Holt, Rinehart and Winston, 1977.

MARUYAMA, G., & MILLER, N. Physical attractiveness and classroom acceptance. Social Science Research Institute Report 75-2. University of Southern California, Los Angeles, 1975.

MARX, M. B., GARRITY, T. F., & BOWERS, F. R. The influence of recent life experience on the health of college freshmen. *Journal of Psychosomatic Research*, 1975, 19, 87–98.

MASLOW, A. H. The need to know and the fear of knowing. *Journal of General Psychology*, 1963, 68, 111–124.

MASLOW, A. H. *Motivation and personality*, 2d ed. New York: Harper & Row. 1970.

MASLOW, A. H. *The farther reaches of human nature.* New York: Viking, 1971.

MASTERS, W. H., & JOHNSON, V. E. *Human sexual response.* Boston: Little, Brown, 1966.

MASTERS, W. H., & JOHNSON, V. E. *Human sexual inadequacy.* Boston: Little, Brown, 1970.

MAUSNER, B. Report on a smoking clinic. *American Psychologist*, 1966, 121, 251–255.

MAUSNER, B., & PLATT, E. S. *Smoking: A behavioral analysis.* New York: Pergamon Press, 1971.

MAY, R. What is our problem? In E. S. Morrison and V. Borosage (eds.), *Human sexuality: Contemporary perspectives*, 2d ed. Palo Alto, Calif.: Mayfield Publishing Company, 1977.

MEADOWS, D. H., MEADOWS, D. L., RANDERS, J., & BEHRENS, W. W. *The limits to growth.* New York: New American Library, 1972.

MEDNICK, M. T. S., & PURYEAR, G. R. Race and fear of success in college women: 1968 and 1971. *Journal of Consulting and Clinical Psychology*, 1976, 44, 787–789.

MEHRABIAN, A. Inference of attitudes for the posture, orientation, and distance of a communicator. *Journal of Consulting and Clinical Psychology*, 1968, 32, 296–318.

MEICHENBAUM, D. Toward a cognitive theory of self-control. In G. Schwartz & D. Shapiro (eds.), *Consciousness and self-regulation: Advances in research.* New York: Plenum Press, 1976.

MEICHENBAUM, D. *Cognitive behavior modification: An integrative approach.* New York: Plenum Press, 1977.

MEICHENBAUM, D., & TURK, D. The cognitive-behavioral management of anxiety, anger, and pain. In P. O. Davidson (ed.), *The behavioral management of anxiety, depression, and pain.* New York: Brunner/Mazel, 1976.

MESSENGER, J. C. Sex and repression in an Irish folk community. In D. S.

Marshall and R. C. Suggs (eds.), *Human sexual behavior: Variations in the ethnographic spectrum*. New York: Basic Books, 1971.

MICHAEL, R. P., KEVERNE, E. B., & BONSALL, R. W. Pheromones: Isolation of male sex attractants from a female primate. *Science*, 1971, *172*, 964–966.

MILGRAM, S. Behavioral study of obedience. *Journal of Abnormal and Social Psychology*, 1963, *67*, 371–378.

MILGRAM, S. The experience of living in cities. *Science*, 1970, *167*, 1461–1468.

MILGRAM, S. *Obedience to authority*. New York: Harper & Row, 1974.

MILGRAM, S. *The individual in a social world*. Reading, Mass.: Addison-Wesley, 1977.

MILLER, G. *Living in the environment: Concepts, problems, and alternatives*. Belmont, Calif.: Wadsworth, 1975.

MILLER, N. E. Learning of visceral and glandular responses. *Science*, 1969, *163*, 434–445.

MILLER, N. E., & DOLLARD, J. *Social learning and imitation*. New Haven: Yale University Press, 1941.

MILLER, R. L., & CARSON, G. L. Playboy stuff and other variables: Scholarship, athletics, and girl friends. *Journal of Social Psychology*, 1975, *95*, 143–144.

MILLER, W. R. Behavioral treatment of problem drinkers: A comparative outcome study of three controlled drinking therapies. *Journal of Consulting and Clinical Psychology*, 1978, *46*, 74–86.

MILLER, W. R., & CADDY, G. R. Abstinence and controlled drinking in the treatment of problem drinkers. *Journal of Studies on Alcohol*, 1977, *38*, 986–1003.

MILLS, J., & HARVEY, J. Opinion change as a function of when information about the communicator is received and whether he is attractive or expert. *Journal of Personality and Social Psychology*, 1972, *21*, 52–55.

MINTZ, R. S. Prevalence of persons in the city of Los Angeles who have attempted suicide. *Bulletin of Suicidology*, National Institute of Mental Health, 1970, No. 7.

MIRSKY, I. A. Physiologic, psychologic, and social determinants in the etiology of duodenal ulcer. *American Journal of Digestive Diseases*, 1958, *3*, 285–314.

MISCHEL, W. Toward a cognitive social learning reconceptualization of personality. *Psychological Review*, 1973, *80*, 252–283.

MONEY, J. Psychosexual differentiation. In J. Money (ed.), *Sex research, new developments*. New York: Holt, Rinehart and Winston, 1965.

MONEY, J. Prenatal hormones and postnatal socialization in gender identity differentiation. In J. K. Cole and R. Dienstbier (eds.), *Nebraska symposium on motivation*. Lincoln: University of Nebraska Press, 1974.

MONEY, J. Sex assignment in anatomically intersexed infants. In R. Green (ed.), *Human sexuality*. Baltimore: Williams & Wilkins, 1976.

MONEY, J., & EHRHARDT, A. *Man and woman, boy and girl*. Baltimore: Johns Hopkins University Press, 1972.

MONROE, L. J. Psychological and physiological differences between good and poor sleepers. *Journal of Abnormal Psychology*, 1967, *72*, 255–264.

MONROE, L. J., & MARKS, P. A. MMPI differences between adolescent poor and good sleepers. *Journal of Consulting and Clinical Psychology*, 1977, *45*, 151–152.

MORTON, T. L. Intimacy and reciprocity of exchanges: A comparison of spouses and strangers. *Journal of Personality and Social Psychology*, 1978, *36*, 72–81.

MOWRER, O. H. *Learning theory and behavior*. New York: John Wiley, 1960.

MURSTEIN, B. I. Physical attractiveness and marital choice. *Journal of Personality and Social Psychology*, 1972, *22*, 8–12.

MURSTEIN, B. I., & CHRISTY, P. Physical attractiveness and marriage adjustment in middle-aged couples. *Journal of Personality and Social Psychology*, 1976, *34*, 537–542.

NAFFZIGER, C. C., & NAFFZIGER, K. Development of sex role stereotypes. *The Family Coordinator*, 1974, *23*, 251–258.

NAHEMOW, L., & LAWTON, M. P. Similarity and propinquity in a friendship formation. *Journal of Personality and Social Psychology*, 1975, *32*, 205–213.

National Council on Alcoholism, Inc. *Facts on alcoholism*. New York: Author, 1973.

NEMY, E. Suicide now no. 2 cause of deaths among young. *New York Times*, April 16, 1973, p. 1.

NEVID, J. S., & RATHUS, S. A. Multivariate and normative data pertaining to the RAS with a college population. *Behavior Therapy*, 1978, *9*, 675.

NEWCOMB, T. M. Dyadic balance as a source of clues about interpersonal attraction. In B. I. Murstein (ed.), *Theories of attraction and love*. New York: Springer, 1971.

NEWMAN, J., & McCAULEY, C. Eye contact with strangers in city, suburb, and small town. *Environment and Behavior*, 1977, *9*, 547–558.

NICASSIO, P., & BOOTZIN, R. A comparison of progressive relaxation and autogenic training as treatments for insomnia. *Journal of Abnormal Psychology*, 1974, *83*, 253–260.

NISBETT, R. E. Taste, deprivation, and weight determinants of eating behavior. *Journal of Personality and Social Psychology*, 1968, *10*, 107–116.

NISBETT, R. E. Hunger, obesity, and the ventromedial hypothalamus. *Psychological Review*, 1972, *79*, 433–453.

NOLAN, J. D. Self-control procedures in the modification of smoking behavior. *Journal of Consulting and Clinical Psychology*, 1968, *32*, 92–93.

NOVACO, R. A treatment program for the management of anger through cognitive and relaxation controls. Doctoral dissertation, Indiana University, Bloomington, Indiana, 1974.

NOVACO, R. A stress inoculation approach to anger management in the training of law enforcement officers. *American Journal of Community Psychology*, 1977, *5*, 327–346.

NURNBERGER, J. I., & ZIMMERMAN, J. Applied analysis of human behavior: An alternative to conventional motivational inferences and unconscious determination on therapeutic programming. *Behavior Therapy*, 1970, *1*, 1–3.

OFFIR, C. W. Don't take it lying down. *Psychology Today*, 1975, *8*, 73.

ORNE-JOHNSON, D. Autonomic stability and transcendental meditation. *Psychosomatic Medicine*, 1973, *35*, 341–349.

ORNSTEIN, R. *The psychology of consciousness*. New York: Viking, 1972.

PAIGE, K. E. Effects of oral contraceptives on affective fluctuations associated with the menstrual cycle. *Psychosomatic Medicine*, 1971, *33*, 515–537.

PAIGE, K. E. Women learn to sing the menstrual blues. *Psychology Today*, 1973, *7*(4), 41.

PARKES, C. M. *Bereavement: Studies of grief in adult life*. New York: International Universities Press, 1972.

PAUL, G. L. Outcome of systematic desensitization II: Controlled investigations of individual treatment, technique variations, and current status. In C. M. Franks (ed.), *Behavior therapy: Appraisal and status*. New York: McGraw-Hill, 1969a.

PAUL, G. L. Physiological effects of relaxation training and hypnotic suggestion. *Journal of Abnormal Psychology*, 1969b, 74, 425–437.

PAULSEN, K., RIMM, D. C., WOODBURN, L. T., & RIMM, S. A. A self-control approach to inefficient spending. *Journal of Consulting and Clinical Psychology*, 1977, 45, 433–435.

PAULY, I. B. Female transsexualism: Part 1. *Archives of Sexual Behavior*, 1974, 3, 487–508.

PAVLOV, I. P. *Conditioned reflexes*. London: Oxford University Press, 1927.

PELLEGRINI, R. J. The astrological "theory" of personality: An unbiased test by a biased observer. *Journal of Psychology*, 1973, 85, 21–28.

PELLEGRINI, R. J. Birthdate psychology: A new look at some old data. *Journal of Psychology*, 1975, 89, 261–265.

PERLS, F. S. *Gestalt therapy verbatim*. New York: Bantam, 1971.

PERRI, M. G., RICHARDS, C. S., & SCHULTHEIS, K. R. Behavioral self-control and smoking reduction: A study of self-initiated attempts to reduce smoking. *Behavior Therapy*, 1977, 8, 360–365.

PERVIN, L. A., & LILLY, R. S. Social desirability and self-ideal self ratings on the semantic differential. *Educational and Psychological Measurement*, 1967, 27, 845–853.

PERVIN, L. A., & YATKO, R. J. Cigarette smoking and alternate methods of reducing dissonance. *Journal of Personality and Social Psychology*, 1965, 2, 30–36.

PETERSON, K., & CURRAN, J. P. Trait attribution as a function of hair length and correlates of subjects' preferences for hair style. *Journal of Psychology*, 1976, 93, 331–339.

PHILLIPS, R. E., JOHNSON, G. D., & GEYER, A. Self-administered systematic desensitization. *Behaviour Research and Therapy*, 1972, 10, 93–96.

PITTS, F. N., & McCLURE, J. N. Lactate metabolism in anxiety neurosis. *New England Journal of Medicine*, 1967, 277, 1329–1336.

PLATERIS, A. *Divorces and divorce rates, United States*. Vital and Health Statistics: Series 21, No. 29, National Center for Health Statistics. Washington, D.C.: U.S. Government Printing Office, 1978.

PLINER, P., HART, H., KOHL, J., & SAARI, D. Compliance without pressure: Some further data on the foot-in-the-door technique. *Journal of Experimental Social Psychology*, 1974, 10, 17–22.

POMEROY, W. B. Parents and homosexuality: I. *Sexology*, 1966, 32, 508–511.

POWLEY, T. L., & KEESEY, R. E. Relationship of body weight to the lateral hypothalamic feeding syndrome. *Journal of Comparative and Physiological Psychology*, 1970, 70, 25–36.

PREMACK, D. Reinforcement theory. In D. Levine (ed.), *Nebraska Symposium on Motivation*. Lincoln: University of Nebraska Press, 1965.

PREMACK, D. Mechanisms of self-control. In W. A. Hunt (ed.), *Learning mechanisms in smoking*. Chicago: Aldine, 1970.

PURYEAR, G. R., & MEDNICK, M. S. Black militancy, affective attachment, and the fear of success in black college women. *Journal of Consulting and Clinical Psychology*, 1974, 42, 263–266.

RAHE, R. H., & LIND, E. Psychosocial factors and sudden cardiac death: A pilot study. *Journal of Psychosomatic Research*, 1971, 15, 19–24.

RAND, A. *Anthem*. New York: Signet Books, 1946.

RASMUSSEN, K. J. V. The *Netsilik Eskimos: Social life and spiritual culture*. Copenhagen: Gylendal, 1931.

RATHUS, S. A. A 30-item schedule for assessing assertive behavior. *Behavior Therapy*, 1973, 4, 398–406.

RATHUS, S. A. Assertive training: Rationales, principles, and controversies. In J. M. Whiteley & J. V. Flowers (eds.), *Approaches to assertion training*. Monterey, Calif.: Brooks/Cole, 1978.

RATHUS, S. A., & NEVID, J. S. BT: *Behavior therapy*. Garden City, N.Y.: Doubleday, 1977.

RATHUS, S. A., & SIEGEL, L. Delinquent attitudes and self-esteem. *Adolescence*, 1973, 8, 265–276.

RAYBIN, J. B., & DETRE, T. P. Sleep disorder and symptomology among medical and nursing students. *Comprehensive Psychiatry*, 1969, 10, 452–462.

RECKLESS, J., & GEIGER, N. Impotence as a practical problem. In J. LoPiccolo and L. LoPiccolo (eds.), *Handbook of sex therapy*. New York: Plenum Press, 1978.

REES, L. The significance of parental attitudes in childhood asthma. *Journal of Psychosomatic Research*, 1964, 7, 253–262.

REES, W. D., & LUTKINS, S. G. Mortality of bereavement. *British Medical Journal*, 1967, 4, 13–16.

REGAN, D. T., WILLIAMS, M., & SPARLING, S. Voluntary expiation of guilt: A field experiment. *Journal of Personality and Social Psychology*, 1972, 24, 42–45.

REHM, L. P. Mood, pleasant events, and unpleasant events. *Journal of Consulting and Clinical Psychology*, 1978, 46, 854–859.

REID, E. C. Autopsychology of the manic-depressive. *Journal of Nervous and Mental Disease*, 1910, 37, 606–620.

REISS, I. L. *The social context of premarital sexual permissiveness*. New York: Holt, Rinehart and Winston, 1967.

RENWICK, P. A., & LAWLER, E. L. What you really want from your job. *Psychology Today*, May 1978, 11, 53–65, 118.

REYNOLDS, B. J. Psychological treatment models and outcome results for erectile dysfunction: A critical review. *Psychological Bulletin*, 1977, 84, 1218–1238.

RICHTER, C. P. On the phenomenon of sudden death in animals and man. *Psychosomatic Medicine*, 1957, 19, 191–198.

RIZLEY, R. Depression and distortion in the attribution of causality. *Journal of Abnormal Psychology*, 1978, 87, 32–48.

ROBERTS, A. H. Self-control procedures in the modification of smoking behavior: A replication. *Psychological Reports*, 1969, 24, 675–676.

ROBINS, E. J., GASSNER, J., KAYES, J., WILKINSON, R., & MURPHY, G. E. The communication of suicidal intent: A study of 134 successful (completed) suicides. *American Journal of Psychiatry*, 1959, 115, 724–733.

ROBINSON, F. P. *Effective study*, 4th ed. New York: Harper & Row, 1970.

ROGERS, C. R. *Client-centered therapy*. Boston: Houghton Mifflin, 1951.

ROGERS, C. R. Actualizing tendency in relation to motives and to consciousness. In M. R. Jones (ed.), *Nebraska Symposium on Motivation*. Lincoln: University of Nebraska Press, 1963.

ROGERS, C. R. *Becoming partners: Marriage and its alternatives*. New York: Delacorte Press, 1972.

ROMANCZYK, R. G., TRACEY, D. A., WILSON, G. T., & THORPE, G. L. Behavioral techniques in the treatment of obesity: A comparative analysis. *Behavior Research and Therapy*, 1973, 11, 629–640.

ROSE, R. M. Testosterone, aggression, and homosexuality: A review of the literature and implications for future research. In E. J. Sachar (ed.), *Topics in psychoendocrinology*. New York: Grune & Stratton, 1975.

ROSEN, G. M., GLASGOW, R. E., & BARRERA, M. A controlled study to assess the clinical efficacy of totally self-administered systematic desensitization. *Journal of Consulting and Clinical Psychology*, 1976, 44, 208–217.

ROSENHAN, D. L. On being sane in insane places. *Science*, 1973, 179, 250–258.

ROTTER, J. B. Generalized expectancies for internal versus external control of reinforcement. *Psychological Monographs*, 1966, 80, Whole No. 609.

ROTTER, J. B. External control and internal control. *Psychology Today*, 1971, 5, 37–42, 58–59.

ROTTER, J. B. Some problems and misconceptions related to the construct of internal versus external control of reinforcement. *Journal of Consulting and Clinical Psychology*, 1975, 43, 56–67.

ROTTON, J. Air pollution is no choke. *Psychology Today*, 1979, in press.

RUBIN, V., & COMITAS, L. *Ganja in Jamaica*. The Hague, Netherlands: Mouton, 1975.

RUBIN, Z. Measurement of romantic love. *Journal of Personality and Social Psychology*, 1970, 16, 265–273.

RUBIN, Z. From liking to loving: Patterns of attraction in dating relationships. In T. L. Huston (ed.), *Foundations of interpersonal attraction*. New York: Academic Press, 1974.

SAEGERT, S. C., & JELLISON, J. M. Effects of initial level of response competition and frequency of exposure to liking and exploratory behavior. *Journal of Personality and Social Psychology*, 1970, 16, 553–558.

SAGAN, C. *The dragons of Eden: Speculations on the evolution of human intelligence*. New York: Random House, 1977.

SAGHIR, M. T., & ROBINS, E. *Male and female homosexuality: A comprehensive investigation*. Baltimore: Williams & Wilkins, 1973.

SARASON, I. G. Experimental approaches to test anxiety: Attention and the uses of information. In C. D. Spielberger (ed.), *Anxiety and behavior*, vol. 2. New York: Academic Press, 1972.

SARASON, I. G. Test anxiety and cognitive modeling. *Journal of Personality and Social Psychology*, 1973, 28, 58–61.

SARASON, I. G. The test anxiety scale: Concept and research. In C. D. Spielberger & I. G. Sarason (eds.), *Stress and anxiety*, vol. 5. New York: Halsted-Wiley, 1978.

SARBIN, T. R., & NUCCI, L. P. Self-reconstitution processes: A proposal for reorganizing the conduct of confirmed smokers. *Journal of Abnormal Psychology*, 1973, 81, 182–195.

SAWREY, W. L., CONGER, J. J., & TURRELL, E. S. An experimental investigation of the role of psychological factors in the production of gastric ulcers in rats. *Journal of Comparative and Physiological Psychology*, 1956, 49, 457–461.

SAWREY, W. L., & WIESZ, J. D. An experimental method of producing gastric ulcers. *Journal of Comparative and Physiological Psychology*, 1956, 49, 269–270.

SCHAAR, K. On advertising by psychologists. *American Psychological Association Monitor*, November 1978, 9, 17.

SCHACHTER, S. Some extraordinary facts about obese humans and rats. *American Psychologist*, 1971, 26, 129–144.

SCHACHTER, S., & GROSS, L. P. Manipulated time and eating behavior. *Journal of Personality and Social Psychology*, 1968, 10, 98–106.

SCHACHTER, S., & RODIN, J. *Obese humans and rats*. Washington, D.C.: Erlbaum/Halsted, 1974.

SCHEIN, E. H. *Coercive persuasion: A socio-psychological analysis of the "brainwashing" of American civilian prisoners by the Chinese Communists*. New York: W. W. Norton, 1961.

SCHMIDT, G. Male-female differences in sexual arousal and behavior during and after exposure to sexually explicit stimuli. *Archives of Sexual Behavior*, 1975, 4, 353–364.

SCHMIDT, G., SIGUSCH, V., & SCHÄFER, S. Responses to reading erotic stories: Male-female differences. *Archives of Sexual Behavior*, 1973, 2, 181–199.

SCHMIDT, H. O., & FONDA, C. P. The reliability of psychiatric diagnosis: A new look. *Journal of Abnormal and Social Psychology*, 1956, 52, 262–267.

SCHWARTZ, J. L., & DUBITSKY, M. One year follow-up results of a smoking cessation program. *Canadian Journal of Mental Health*, 1968, 59, 161–165.

SCHWARTZ, M., & TANGRI, S. S. A note on self-concept as insulator against delinquency. *American Sociological Review*, 1965, 30, 922–926.

SCHWARTZ, R. M., & GOTTMAN, J. M. Toward a task analysis of assertive behavior. *Journal of Consulting and Clinical Psychology*, 1976, 44, 910–920.

SEGAL, M. W. Alphabet and attraction: An unobtrusive measure of the effect of propinquity in a field setting. *Journal of Personality and Social Psychology*, 1974, 30, 654–657.

SELIGMAN, M. E. P. Fall into helplessness. *Psychology Today*, June 1973, 7, 43–48.

SELIGMAN, M. E. P. *Helplessness*. San Francisco: Freeman, 1975.

SELIGMAN, M. E. P., ABRAMSON, L. Y., SEMMEL, A., & VON BAEYER, C. Depressive attributional style. *Journal of Abnormal Psychology*, 1979, 88, 242–247.

SELKIN, J. Rape. *Psychology Today*, 1975, 8, 71–72, 74–76.

SELYE, H. *The stress of life*. New York: McGraw-Hill, 1976.

SEMANS, J. Premature ejaculation: A new approach. *Southern Medical Journal*, 1956, 49, 353–358.

SENNA, J., RATHUS, S. A., SIEGEL, L. Delinquent behavior and academic investment among suburban youth. *Adolescence*, 1974, 9, 481–494.

SHEEHY, G. *Passages: Predictable crises of adult life*. New York: Dutton, 1976.

SHERMAN, A. R. Real-life exposure as a primary therapeutic factor in the desensitization treatment of fear. *Journal of Abnormal Psychology*, 1972, 79, 19–28.

SHERWOOD, J. J. Self-identity and referent others. *Sociometry*, 1965, 28, 66–81.

SHIPLEY, R. H., BUTT, J. H., HORWITZ, B., & FARBRY, J. E. Preparation for a stressful medical procedure: Effect of amount of stimulus preexposure and coping style. *Journal of Consulting and Clinical Psychology*, 1978, 46, 499–507.

SHNEIDMAN, E. S., & FARBEROW, N. L. *The psychology of suicide*. New York: Science House, 1970.

SHNEIDMAN, E. S., & MANDELKORN, P. How to prevent suicide. In E. S. Shneidman, N. L. Farberow, & R. E. Litman (eds.), *The psychology of suicide*. New York: Science House, 1970.

SHOCKET, B. R. Recognizing the suicidal patient. *Modern Medicine*, 1970, 38, 114–117, 123.

SHOPE, D. F. *Interpersonal sexuality*. Philadelphia: W. B. Saunders, 1975.

SIEGEL, L., RATHUS, S. A., & RUPPERT, C. Values and delinquent youth: An empirical reexamination of theories of delinquency. *British Journal of Criminology*, 1973, 13(3), 237–244.

SIEGELMAN, M. Adjustments of male homosexuals and heterosexuals. *Archives of Sexual Behavior*, 1972, 2, 9–25.

SIEGELMAN, M. Parental background of male homosexuals and heterosexuals. *Archives of Sexual Behvior*, 1974, 3, 3–18.

SIEGELMAN, M. Psychological adjustments of homosexual and heterosexual men: A cross-national replication. *Archives of Sexual Behavior*, 1978, 7, 1–11.

SIGALL, H., & OSTROVE, N. Beautiful but dangerous: Effects of offender attractiveness and nature of the crime on juridic judgment. *Journal of Personality and Social Psychology*, 1975, 31, 410–414.

SINGER, J. L. *The inner world of daydreaming*. New York: Harper & Row, 1975.

SIROTA, A. D., SCHWARTZ, G. E., & SHAPIRO, D. Voluntary control of human heart rate: Effect on reaction to aversive stimulation: A replication and extension. *Journal of Abnormal Psychology*, 1976, 85, 473–477.

SISTRUNK, F., & McDAVID, J. W. Sex variable in conforming behavior. *Journal of Personality and Social Psychology*, 1971, 17, 200–207.

SKINNER, B. F. *The behavior of organisms: An experimental analysis*. New York: Appleton-Century, 1938.

SKINNER, B. F. *Walden two*. New York: Macmillan, 1948.

SKINNER, B. F. *Beyond freedom and dignity*. New York: Alfred A. Knopf, 1972.

SMITH, G. F., & DORFMAN, D. The effect of stimulus uncertainty on the relationship between frequency of exposure and liking. *Journal of Personality and Social Psychology*, 1975, 31, 150–155.

SOBELL, L. C., SOBELL, M. B., & CHRISTELMAN, W. C. The myth of "one drink." *Behaviour Research and Therapy*, 1972, 10, 119–123.

SOBELL, M. B., & SOBELL, L. C. Individualized behavior therapy for alcoholics. *Behavior Therapy*, 1973, 4, 49–72.

SOMMER, B. Menstrual cycle changes and intellectual performance. *Psychosomatic Medicine*, 1972, 34, 263–269.

SOMMER, B. The effects of menstruation on cognitive and perceptual motor behavior: A review. *Psychosomatic Medicine*, 1973, 35, 515–534.

SOTILE, W. M., & KILMANN, P. R. Treatments of psychogenic female sexual dysfunction. *Psychological Bulletin*, 1977, 84, 619–633.

SPEER, D. C. An evaluation of a telephone crisis service. Paper presented at the Midwestern Psychological Association Meeting, Cleveland, 1972.

STALONAS, P. M., JOHNSON, W. G., & CHRIST, M. Behavior modification for obesity: The evaluation of exercise, contingency management, and program adherence. *Journal of Consulting and Clinical Psychology*, 1978, 46, 463–469.

STAUB, E., TURSKY, B., & SCHWARTZ, G. Self-control and predictability: Their effects on reactions to aversive stimulation. *Journal of Personality and Social Psychology*, 1971, 18, 157–162.

STENGEL, E. *Suicide and attempted suicide*. Baltimore: Penguin, 1964.

STOKOLS, D. The experience of crowding in primary and secondary environments. *Environment and Behavior*, 1976, 8, 49–86.

STOKOLS, D., NOVACO, R., STOKOLS, J., & CAMPBELL, J. Traffic congestion, Type A behavior, and stress. Paper presented at the meeting of the American Psychological Association, San Francisco, August 1977.

STONE, L. J., & HOKANSON, J. E. Arousal reduction via self-punitive behavior. *Journal of Personality and Social Psychology*, 1969, 12, 72–79.

STRONG, E. K., JR. *Vocational interests eighteen years after college*. Minneapolis: University of Minnesota Press, 1955.

STUART, R. B. Operant-interpersonal treatment for marital discord. *Journal of Consulting and Clinical Psychology*, 1969, 33, 675–682.

STUART, R. B. *Act thin, stay thin*. New York: W. W. Norton, 1978.

STUNKARD, A. J. Obesity and the denial of hunger. *Psychosomatic Medicine*, 1959, 1, 281–289.

SUINN, R. M. The STABS, a measure of test anxiety for behavior therapy: Normative data. *Behaviour Research and Therapy*, 1969, 7, 335–339.

SUINN, R. M. How to break the vicious cycle of stress. *Psychology Today*, December 1976, 10, 59–60.

SZASZ, T. J. The myth of mental illness. *American Psychologist*, 1960, 15, 113–118.

SZASZ, T. J. The myth of mental illness: Three addenda. *Journal of Humanistic Psychology*, 1974, 14, 11–19.

TART, C. *On being stoned*. Palo Alto, Calif.: Science and Behavior, 1971.

TASTO, D. L., & HINKLE, J. E. Muscle relaxation treatment for tension headaches. *Behaviour Research and Therapy*, 1973, 11, 347–350.

TAVRIS, C., & SADD, S. *The Redbook report on female sexuality*. New York: Delacorte Press, 1975, 1977.

TAYLOR, C. B., FARQUHAR, J. W., NELSON, E., & AGRAS, D. Relaxation therapy and high blood pressure. *Archives of General Psychiatry*, 1977, 34, 339–343.

TEITELBAUM, P., CHENG, M. F., & ROZIN, P. Stages of recovery and development of lateral hypothalamic control of food and water intake. *Annals of the New York Academy of Science*, 1969, 157, 848–860.

THORESEN, C. E., & MAHONEY, M. J. *Behavioral self-control*. New York: Holt, Rinehart and Winston, 1974.

TOUHEY, J. C. Comparison of two dimensions of attitude similarity on heterosexual attraction. *Journal of Personality and Social Psychology*, 1972, 23, 8–10.

TOUHEY, J. C. Effects of additional women professionals on ratings of occupational prestige and desirability. *Journal of Personality and Social Psychology*, 1974, 29, 86–89.

TURK, D. Cognitive control of pain: A skills training approach. Unpublished manuscript, University of Waterloo, Ontario, 1975.

TURNER, J. S., & HELMS, D. B. *Exploring child behavior*. Philadelphia: W. B. Saunders, 1981.

TWAIN, M. *The mysterious stranger and other stories*. New York: Harper and Brothers, 1916.

ULLMANN, L. P., & KRASNER, L. *A psychological approach to abnormal behavior*. Englewood Cliffs, N. J.: Prentice-Hall, 1975.

United States Riot Commission. *Report of the National Advisory Commission on Civil Disorders*. New York: Bantam, 1968.

VALINS, S. Cognitive effects of false heart-rate feedback. *Journal of Personality and Social Psychology*, 1966, 4, 400–408.

VEITCH, R., & GRIFFITT, W. Good news, bad news: Affective and interpersonal effects. *Journal of Applied Social Psychology*, 1976, 6, 69–75.

VERNON, W. M. Animal aggression: Review of research. *Genetic Psychology Monograph*, 1969, 80, 3–28.

WAGNER, M. K., & BRAGG, R. A. Comparing behavior modification approaches to habit decrement smoking. *Journal of Consulting and Clinical Psychology*, 1970, 34, 258–263.

WALES, E., & BREWER, B. Graffiti in the 1970's. *Journal of Social Psychology*, 1976, 99, 115–123.

WALLINGTON, S. A. Consequences of transgression: Self-punishment and depression. *Journal of Personality and Social Psychology*, 1973, 29, 1–7.

WALSTER, E., ARONSON, E., & ABRAHAMS, D. On increasing the persuasiveness of a low prestige communicator. *Journal of Experimental Social Psychology*, 1966a, 2, 325–342.

WALSTER, E., ARONSON, E., ABRAHAMS, D., & ROTTMAN, L. Importance of physical attractiveness in dating behavior. *Journal of Personality and Social Psychology*, 1966b, 4, 508–516.

WALSTER, E., WALSTER, G. W., PILIAVIN, J., & SCHMIDT, L. "Playing hard to get": Understanding an elusive phenomenon. *Journal of Personality and Social Psychology*, 1973, 26, 113–121.

WALSTER, E., WALSTER, G. W., & TRAUPMANN, Equity and premarital sex. *Journal of Personality and Social Psychology*, 1978, 36, 82–92.

WARD, C. D., CASTRO, M. A., & WIL-

COX, A. H. Birth-order effects in a survey of mate selection and parenthood. *Journal of Social Psychology*, 1974, 94, 57–64.

WATERMAN, A. S., GEARY, P. S., & WATERMAN, C. K. A longitudinal study of changes in ego identity status from the freshman to the senior year at college. *Developmental Psychology*, 1974, 10, 387–392.

WATERMAN, A. S., & WATERMAN, C. K. A longitudinal study of changes in ego identity status during the freshman year in college. *Developmental Psychology*, 1971, 5, 167–173.

WATERMAN, C. K., & NEVID, J. S. Sex differences in the resolution of the identity crisis. *Journal of Youth and Adolescence*, 1977, 6, 337–342.

WATERS, W. F., McDONALD, D. G., & KORESKO, R. L. Psychophysiological responses during analogue systematic desensitization and non-relaxation control procedures. *Behaviour Research and Therapy*, 1972, 10, 381–393.

WATSON, D. L., & THARP, R. G. *Self-directed behavior: Self-modification for personal adjustment*. Monterey, Calif.: Brooks/Cole, 1972.

WATSON, J. B. Psychology as the behaviorist views it. *Psychological Review*, 1913, 70, 158–177.

WATSON, J. B. *Behaviorism*. New York: W. W. Norton, 1924.

WATSON, J. B., & RAYNER, R. Conditioned emotional reactions. *Journal of Experimental Psychology*, 1920, 3, 1–14.

WEIL, G., & GOLDFRIED, M. R. Treatment of insomnia in an eleven-year-old child through self-relaxation. *Behavior Therapy*, 1973, 4, 282–294.

WEINER, H., THALER, M., REISER, M. F., & MIRSKY, I. A. Etiology of duodenal ulcer: I. Relation of specific psychological characteristics to rate of gastric secretion. *Psychosomatic Medicine*, 1957, 17, 1–10.

WEIR, J. M. Male student perceptions of smokers. In S. V. Zagona (ed.), *Studies and issues in smoking behavior*. Tucson: University of Arizona Press, 1967.

WEISS, J. M., GLAZER, H. I., & POHORECKY, L. A. Neurotransmitters and helplessness: A chemical bridge to depression. *Psychology Today*, 1974, 8, 58–65.

WERTS, C. E. Parental influence on career choice. *Journal of Counseling Psychology*, 1968, 15, 48–52.

WHYTE, W. W., JR. *The organization man*. New York: Simon and Schuster, 1956.

WIGGINS, J. S., WIGGINS, N., & CONGER, J. C. Correlates of heterosexual somatic preference. *Journal of Personality and Social Psychology*, 1968, 10, 82–90.

WILLIAMS, J. E., BENNETT, S. M., & BEST, D. L. Awareness and expression of sex stereotypes in young children. *Developmental Psychology*, 1975, 11, 635–642.

WILSON, G. T., & LAWSON, D. M. Expectancies, alcohol, and sexual arousal in women. *Journal of Abnormal Psychology*, 1978, 87, 358–367.

WINSTON, B. J. The relationship of awareness to concern for environmental quality among selected high school students. *Dissertation Abstracts International*, 1974, 35A, 3412.

WOLFE, J. L., & FODOR, I. G. A cognitive/behavioral approach to modifying assertive behavior in women. *The Counseling Psychologist*, 1975, 5(4), 45–52.

WOLFE, J. L., & FODOR, I. G. Modifying assertive behavior in women: A comparison of three approaches. *Behavior Therapy*, 1977, 8, 567–574.

WOLLERSHEIM, J. P. Effectiveness of group therapy based upon learning principles in the treatment of overweight women. *Journal of Abnormal Psychology*, 1970, 76, 462–474.

WOLPE, J. *Psychotherapy by reciprocal inhibition*. Stanford, Calif.: Stanford University Press, 1958.

WOLPE, J., & LAZARUS, A. A. *Behavior therapy techniques*. New York: Pergamon Press, 1966.

WOLPE, J., & RACHMAN, S. Psychoanalytic "evidence": A critique based on Freud's case of Little Hans. *Journal of Nervous and Mental Disease*, 1960, 131, 135–147.

WORTMAN, C. B., ADESMAN, P., HERMAN, E., & GREENBERG, P. Self-disclosure: An attributional perspective. *Journal of Personality and Social Psychology*, 1976, 33, 184–191.

YESSLER, P. G., GIBBS, J. J., & BECKER, H. A. On the communication of suicidal ideas. *Archives of General Psychiatry*, 1961, 5, 12–29.

ZAJONC, R. B. Attitudinal effects of mere exposure. *Journal of Personality and Social Psychology*, Monograph Supplement 2, 1968, 9, 1–27.

ZIMBARDO, P. G. The human choice: Individuation, reason, and order versus deindividuation, impulse, and chaos. *Nebraska Symposium on Motivation*, 1970, *18*, 237–307.

ZWEIGENHAFT, R. L. Signature size: A key to status awareness. *Journal of Social Psychology*, 1970, *81*, 49–54.

ZWEIGENHAFT, R. L. Name styles in America and name styles in New Zealand. *Journal of Social Psychology*, 1975, *97*, 289–290.

ZWEIGENHAFT, R. L. The other side of unusual names. *Journal of Social Psychology*, 1977, *103*, 291–302.

INDEX

The numbers of pages on which glossed terms appear are set in bold-face type.

A

ABC's of behavior, **404**–418
  and controlled social drinking, 451
  and quitting smoking, 445–446
  and weight control, 436–440
  see also functional analysis
abnormal behavior, 114–134
  affective disorders, 130–131
  anxiety disorders, 131
  conversion disorders, 131–132
  dissociative disorders, 132–134
  explanations of, 117–125
  medical model of, 121
  paranoia, 129
  personality disorders, 134
  schizophrenic disorders, 126, 128–129
  treatment of, 134–145
abortion, **371**, 387
abreaction, **139**
abstinence syndrome, **442**
  and alcohol, 450
  and smoking, 442
accepting responsibility, 178–181, 294
acrophobia, **211**, 221
adaptation stage, of general adaptation
    syndrome, 164
addiction, **442**
  alcohol, 449, 450
  cigarette, 442
  to drugs, 454–455
adjustive alternatives
  to catastrophizing thoughts, 184,
    226–227
  to depressing thoughts, 250
  to frustrating thoughts, 279–281
  to irrational beliefs, 313, 317–318, 325,
    421
adjustment, 8–11, **9**, 14–17, 23
  behaviorism and, 15
  humanistic psychology and, 15–17
  of Nazi concentration camp survivors,
    10–11
  problems, 114–134
  psychoanalysis and, 15
adolescence, 58, 60, 70–71, 94, 150
  exposure to pornography during, 385
  and frustration, 157
  and identity crisis, 30, 43
  and petting, 370
  rebelliousness, 268

adolescence *(cont.)*
  and sexual arousal, 345
  and sexual behavior, 364
  and smoking, 428, 440
adrenalin, **161**
adult development, 71–82
adult ego state, 144–145
adultery, **282**
advertising
  credibility of communicator in, 305–308,
    309–310
  emotional appeal in, 310–312
  and planned obsolescence, 475
  repetition in, 308–309
affective disorders, 130–131
African Genesis (Ardrey), 270
Against Our Will (Brownmiller), 282
aggression, 108, 167–**168**, 264–290
  and alcohol, 449
  vs. assertive behavior, 315
  and behavior theory, 272–274
  biological views of, 267
  and city life, 485
  and crowding, 154–155
  displaced, **168**
  and heredity, 56
  and humanistic-existential theory,
    275–276
  and obedience to authority, 294–298
  and occupational choice, 469
  and psychoanalytic theory, 267–271
  and sex roles, 66–68
  and temperature, 166–167
aging, 75–79
  and death and dying, 78–80
  and forced retirement, 76, 78
  and integrity, 75–76
  and life satisfaction, 76, 77
  and quality of life, 463
  and sexual response, 383–384
agoraphobia, **211**
alarm reaction, **163**–164, 165, 166, 167,
    185
  in fear response, 210, 215
  and insomnia, 420, 421
  and neurotransmitters, 236
alcohol, 410, 428, 429, 440, 455, 463
  abuse of, 449–450
  addiction, 450
  and aggression, 12, 448–449

alcohol *(cont.)*
  and controlled social drinking, 451
  effects of, 447–449
  and self-control, 412–413
  and sexual arousal, 314, **448**–449
  and sexual dysfunction, 392
  and sleeping pills, 420
  and stress, 152, 237, 294
  and suicide, 252
  use during pregnancy, 58, 449
  uses of, 447
Alcoholics Anonymous (AA), **450**–451
alcoholism, **449**
alienation, 107
  and suicide, 255
alpha waves and meditation, 202
American Psychiatric Association, 117,
    126–128, 384, 450
American Psychological Association, 138,
    157
amnesia, **132**, 217
  and alcohol, 450
amniotic fluid, **57**
amniotic sac, **57**
amotivational syndrome, 452 **453**, 455
amphetamines. 454
anal expulsive traits, **92**
anal retentive traits, **92**
anal stage, 91–**92**
androgens, **376**
androgyny, **68**–70, **303**
  see also sex roles; masculine and feminine
    behavior
angel dust, 455
anger, 100, 139, 156, 257, **266**
  and aggression, 266–267
  coping with, 276–282
  and frustration, 191
  and hypertension, 165
  and social interactions, 316
  as stage in dying, 79
anorexia nervosa, **169**
antecedents of behavior, 404, **406**, 409–411
  and alcohol, 429
  and insomnia, 420
  and overeating, 429
  and self-monitoring, 408
  and smoking, 429
  and weight control, 436
anti-depressant drugs, **131**, 135, 139

507

B

C

D

H

I

J

K